Human Rights Law

DIRECTIONS

4th Edition

DR HOWARD DAVIS

Reader in Public Law, Bournemouth University

Efallai nad yw'r wybodaeth
sydd yn y rhifyn hwn yn
adlewyrchu
DEDDFWRIAETH
BRESENNOL

Information contained within
this edition may not be
CURRENT LAW

OXFORD

UNIVERSITY PRESS

OXFORD
UNIVERSITY PRESS

Great Clarendon Street, Oxford, OX2 6DP,
United Kingdom

Oxford University Press is a department of the University of Oxford.
It furthers the University's objective of excellence in research, scholarship,
and education by publishing worldwide. Oxford is a registered trade mark of
Oxford University Press in the UK and in certain other countries

First edition 2007
Second edition 2009
Third edition 2013

Impression: 1

Published in the United States of America by Oxford University Press
198 Madison Avenue, New York, NY 10016, United States of America

British Library Cataloguing in Publication Data
Data available

Library of Congress Control Number: 2016942483

ISBN 978-0-19-876588-2

Printed in Great Britain by
Bell & Bain Ltd., Glasgow

To Stella, Lydia, and Edmund

Guide to the book

Human Rights Law Directions is enriched with a range of features designed to help support and reinforce your learning. This guided tour shows you how to fully utilise your textbook and get the most out of your study.

Learning objectives

Each chapter begins with a bulleted outline of the main concepts and ideas you will encounter. These serve as a helpful guide to what you can expect to learn.

 LEARNING OBJECTIVES

- The main provisions of the Human Rights Act 1998 (HRA), including:
  - interpretation of statutes (sections 3, 4, and 10);
  - the duty on public authorities and the definition of 'public authority' (section 6);
  - the role of the courts under the HRA;

Thinking points

Particular issues of legal difficulty or controversy are identified for you to consider, question, and pursue.

 THINKING POINT

Should the UK courts be prepared to provide more extensiv than at Strasbourg? Consider, for example, Lewis, J. 'The E Rights' [2007] Public Law 720.8

Discussion topic boxes

Broader themes and questions on areas of controversy are explored and discussed, encouraging you to develop a critical perspective and consider the wider issues in a methodical way.

 DISCUSSION TOPIC

The balance between courts and Parliament in the Human Rights Act

The HRA creates a particular constitutional balance between Parliament (dominate the government) and the courts. Has the right balance in terms of both effectiveness legitimacy been achieved? Does the Act create foundations for proper mutual res between Parliament and the courts? To consider this issue, it is necessary both to con

Case close-up boxes

Summaries of cases are highlighted for ease of reference.

 CASE-CLOSE UP

Aston Cantlow Parochial Church Council v Wallbank [2003] UKHL 37

Mr and Mrs Wallbank purchased a property that was subject to a traditional duty required them to pay for the upkeep and repair of the chancel of the local parish (the area of a church used by the clergy). This duty to repair was enforced by th Parochial Church Council (PCC) exercising statutory powers. Mr and Mrs Wallbank a

Bigger picture boxes

Valuable sources for critical evaluation and deeper research on particular topics of interest are identified. The author explains the significance of the source and what you should look out for in your further study, to give you the option of delving deeper into the subject in a focused way.

 BIGGER PICTURE

Arguments in academic writing by senior judges arguing for a greater recog common law include:

- Lord Judge, LCJ, 'The Judicial Studies Board Lecture 2010' 17 March judiciary.gov.uk/— Media > speeches > March 2010.)

Cross-references

The book is made easy to navigate through the use of clearly marked cross-references that pinpoint particular sections or pages of the book where related themes or cases are covered.

ions of incompatibility had been made since 2000, of which 20
2010 and 2015 only 3 were made. This indicates a 'significant
rights Joint Committee 2014–2015 Seventh Report, HL 130/HC

 CROSS REFERENCE
For further discussion of the desirability of declarations of incompatibility, see the Discussion Topic, at section 4.4.7.

ossible': interpretation not legislation

ossible' for the courts to do. Section 3 permits 'interpretation' not
the House of Lords said in *Re S* [2002] UKHL 10:

Chapter summaries

The central points and concepts covered in each chapter are distilled into summaries at the end of chapters. These provide a mechanism for you to reinforce your understanding and can be used as a revision tool.

 Summary

- The HRA creates the legal framework in terms of which the co freedoms in the ECHR are given further effect in UK law.
- There are two principal ways in which the Act does this: by impos to interpret legislation 'so far as it is possible to do so' for compa

End of chapter questions

Self-test questions and exam questions (problem and essay type) at the end of each chapter will help you to develop analysis and problem-solving skills. The Online Resource Centre that accompanies this book provides suggested approaches to answering these questions and will help you to develop your own successful approach to assessments and examinations.

? **Self-test questions**

1. What would you say was the principal reason for enacting the HRA?
2. What is the 'mirror' principle governing the relationship with Strasbourg u HRA and what are the major exceptions to it?
3. When should section 3 HRA be used rather than 'ordinary' canons of statut pretation when a court is applying a statute?

Further reading

Selected further reading is included at the end of each chapter to provide a springboard for further study. This will help you to take your learning further and guide you to some of the key academic literature in the field.

≡ **Further reading**

Amos, M. (see Preface) Parts 1–5

Bamforth, N. 'The Application of the Human Rights Act 1998 to Public A and Private Bodies' (1999) 58(1) *CLJ* (March) 159–170

Edwards, R. 'Judicial Deference under the Human Rights Act' (2002) 65 *MLR*

Gearty, C. *Principles of Human Rights Adjudication* (2004) Oxford: OUP

Guide to the
Online Resource Centre

The Online Resource Centre that accompanies this book provides students and lecturers with ready-to-use teaching and learning resources. They are free of charge and are designed to maximise the learning experience.

 www.oxfordtextbooks.co.uk/orc/davis_directions4e/

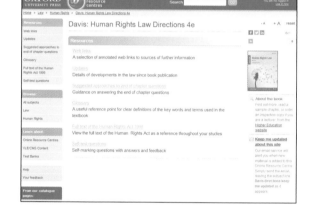

For students

Accessible to all, with no registration or password required, enabling you to get the most from your textbook.

Web links

A selection of annotated web links chosen by the author allow you to easily research those topics that are of particular interest to you. These links are checked regularly to ensure they remain up-to-date.

Liberty's Guide to the Human Rights Act
www.yourrights.org.uk/yourrights/the-human-rights-act/index.html

The Government's Guide to the Human Rights Act
www.dca.gov.uk/peoples-rights/human-rights/pdf/act-studyguide.pdf

The Home Page of the House of Lords House of Commons Joint Committee on Human Rights

Regular updates

An indispensable resource allowing you to access changes and developments in the law that have occurred since publication of the book. These are added to the website twice a year, with specific chapter references, to enable you to easily identify which material has been superseded or supplemented. Updates allow you to keep up-to-date with developments without buying a new book.

Davis: Human Rights Law Directions

Chapter 2

Significant reform of the Convention system is proposed by Protocol 14. Under it the individual cases.

Suggested approaches to end of chapter questions

Guidance is given on answering the end of chapter questions. These will help you to develop your skills in constructing a well-balanced argument.

> **Chapter 4**
>
> Question 1
>
> • Consider the meaning of "so far as it is possible to do so" (see section 4.5 especially 4.5.5 and 4.5.6. The best answer is (c).
>
> Question 2
>
> • Consider how "public authorities" are identified. (see section 4.5.5 and 4.5.6)

Flashcard glossary

A series of interactive flashcards containing key terms and concepts to test your understanding of human rights law.

> PREVIOUS   FLIP CARD   NEXT
>
> Companies (corporations) are, in law, independent legal persons. They exist legally separately from their owners (shareholders), managers and employees. They are said to have 'artificial' legal personality. No matter how vast and wealthy they may be, no matter how much

Human Rights Act 1998

The full text of the Human Rights Act 1998 to use as a reference throughout your human rights studies.

> 2   Interpretation of Convention rights.
>
> (1)   A court or tribunal determining a question which has arisen in connection with a Convention right must take into account any—
>
> (a)   judgment, decision, declaration or advisory opinion of the European Court of Human Rights,
>
> (b)   opinion of the Commission given in a report adopted under Article 31 of the Convention,

Multiple choice questions

A selection of multiple choice questions, arranged by chapter, allows you to quickly assess your knowledge of the various topics in human rights.

> Question 5
>
> Which **one** of the following statements best expresses the rule in Article 5(2) requiring a person to be informed of the reason they have been deprived of their liberty?
>
> ○ a) Anyone arrested on reasonable suspicion of having committed a criminal offence must be told, at the time of their arrest, precisely why they have been arrested.
>
> ○ b) Anyone deprived of their liberty for any of the reasons listed in Article 5(1) has a right to be informed promptly of the reason for their detention, in a way they can understand and with enough precision to enable them to challenge the basis of the detention.

New to this edition

This edition has been fully revised as of January 2016, and key updates include:

- Discussion, in so far as information allows, of the repeal of the Human Rights Act and its replacement with a British Bill of Rights (see Annex to Chapter 4 and the Online Resource Centre).
- A consideration of the significant ECtHR case law on unlawful rendition.
- The European Court of Human Rights approach to fact finding and proof.
- Developments concerning deportation in respect of both conditions in the 'receiving state' and in the UK.
- The impact of human rights on warfare and the condition of British troops abroad.
- Human rights and the cuts in legal aid.
- Human rights and the issue of retrospective punishments and Article 7.
- Recent cases on the impact of Article 8 on abortion and assisted suicide.
- A consideration of current concerns over surveillance and communications data.
- A discussion of how far human rights law has an impact on controversies over religious dress (such as the burqa ban in France).
- Counter-terrorism law, including Justice and Security Act.

Preface the basics

Two texts

This book is an introduction to human rights law in the United Kingdom. Primarily, it involves consideration of two texts: the European Convention on Human Rights (ECHR) and the Human Rights Act 1998 (HRA).

1. ECHR

- This contains a list of human rights and freedoms which are applied by the European Court of Human Rights (ECtHR).
- The Convention, being international law and neither an Act of Parliament nor rule of common law, is not part of UK law. Therefore the Convention cannot be directly enforced in UK courts.

2. HRA

- This is an Act of the UK Parliament and therefore part of the law of the UK, which creates legal rights and duties enforced in UK courts.
- The HRA gives effect to the rights and freedoms in the ECHR in UK law. It does this in specific ways.

Sources

ECHR

The text of the Convention is available on the Council of Europe website by following links to 'Human Rights' and then 'Basic Texts'. The Convention needs to be read with Protocol 1 and Protocol 13. The website is updated and contains changes to the Convention that result from the coming into effect of Protocol 14.

Strasbourg case law can be read, amongst other sources, in the European Human Rights Reports (EHRR); these are on Westlaw. Alternatively HUDOC is the Court of Human Rights' searchable database, to which there is free access.

Human Rights Act 1998

Googling 'the Human Rights Act 1998' leads to the original text, including the Schedules. The text has been subject to minor amendments, the most important of which are

- references in section 1(1)(c) to Protocol 6 are now to Protocol 13;
- derogations in Schedule 3 Part 1 have been withdrawn.

UK cases are reported through the standard law reports series. In this book the neutral citation is given to allow ease of internet use. The cases are available on BAILII, which gives free access.

Terminology

- 'Articles': the ECHR is divided into 'Articles'.
- 'Sections': the HRA is divided into 'sections'.
- 'Convention rights': the name given to the Articles from the ECHR which are given effect through the HRA.
- 'Schedule': a sort of appendix to an Act of Parliament. Schedule 1 HRA contains the 'Convention rights'.

Properly, the Articles in the ECHR given further effect in UK law by means of the HRA should be referred to as 'Article ? of Schedule 1 HRA'. For brevity reference in this book will just be to 'Article ?' whether under the ECHR or through the HRA.

United Kingdom

The HRA applies throughout the United Kingdom. The term 'UK law' is used in relation to general themes. Much of the book is on the application of Convention law to the law of England and Wales. This is made clear, as appropriate, in the text. There are three chapters looking in more detail at the application of human rights law to prisoners, to police powers, and to the media.

Further reading

There are a number of in-depth studies of the Act and the Convention. Two works are referred to, where appropriate, in the 'Further reading' section at the end of each chapter.

- Lester, A., Pannick, D., and Herberg, J. *Human Rights Law and Practice* 3rd edn (2009) London: Lexis Nexis (this gives a full, detailed examination of Convention and UK law. It is available online via LexisNexisButterworths (Athens)).
- Amos, M. *Human Rights Law* (2014) Oxford: Hart Publishing (focused on UK case law under the HRA).

Outline contents

Detailed contents

Table of cases

Page references in **bold** indicate 'Case Close-ups'

Table of legislation

Statutory instruments

Treaties and conventions

Directives

PART 1

HUMAN RIGHTS: THE EUROPEAN CONVENTION, THE HUMAN RIGHTS ACT, AND PERVASIVE PRINCIPLES

1 Human rights: the idea and the law

☐ LEARNING OBJECTIVES

- The idea of human rights.
- Issues relating to political, legal, and constitutional theory.
- What human rights do we have?
- The international context of law-based human rights protection.

Introduction

Terrorist suspects are subjected to treatment that causes them severe pain and psychological disturbance; there is no effective investigation when an Asian man is put in a cell with a white racist who murders him; two men are convicted of a vicious murder and given long sentences on the basis of evidence they did not know about and could not challenge; the law prevents a newspaper from publishing articles investigating the responsibility of a drug company for marketing a tranquilliser which, when used by pregnant women, caused serious birth defects.

These are all examples of human rights abuses. They all involve the United Kingdom and were chosen because this book is about the protection of human rights in the United Kingdom. In fact, as some of the cases considered in this book demonstrate, these examples are somewhat at the mild end of the full spectrum of human rights abuses found in other parts of Europe or, emphatically, in the rest of the world.

In this chapter the idea of human rights is introduced, as are a range of political and constitutional issues to which they give rise. There is also an introduction to the general history of the international protection of human rights from which the United Kingdom system is derived.

1.1 General idea of human rights

1.1.1 Human dignity

The general idea of human rights is to give practical effect to an intuition or a feeling which, it is believed, all reasonable human beings share and which marks out our common human-ity. This intuition or feeling is that in whatever we do, we need to accord proper respect to the dignity of all individual human beings. States and governments, in particular, must ensure that individual dignity is respected in their laws and practices. No matter how noble or popu-lar a cause, no matter how much a policy may contribute to the overall wealth, security or common good of society, it is necessary to limit our actions in such a way as to respect the human dignity of all the individuals affected. The need to respect human dignity applies when states and governments act for the general good; the need applies all the more strongly when government policies are oppressive, dictatorial, or simply negligent.

Dignity is hard to define but at its core are two ideas.

Autonomy

Autonomy describes the freedom to live according to one's own sense of values and not to be compelled to live under the domination of others; not to be merely an object serving the interests of others but a 'person' with interests and desires of his or her own and the ability to pursue them. Obligations requiring obedience to the will of others (such as under an employ-ment contract, for example) can be entered into but they must be voluntary, at least in the sense of not being compelled by the law. Put simply, autonomy is at the heart of what it means to be, and to be recognised as, an individual person.

Democracy

Dignity implies some idea of democracy and self-rule: the right to participate in the processes of government and the formation of the law and the choice of policies through which our common social interest is pursued. Such participation is mainly indirect (through voting for representatives), but there needs to be a place for more direct participation too (through other forms of political activity such as meetings, marches, and demonstrations).

1.1.2 Philosophical underpinnings

The philosophical justification for this idea of human rights is difficult to make. That there are basic entitlements on which personhood and individuality depend and which act to restrain the actions of others, including state officials, has proved hard to establish in a universally con-vincing way. Under a religious justification, for instance, the Ten Commandments, reinforced by Christ's injunction to 'love thy neighbour as thyself', can be restated as rights (the right to life, for instance, being a necessary consequence of the injunction 'thou shalt do no murder', and so on). Similar deductions can be derived from the texts and precepts of the other great religions. But for many, divine authority is too mysterious, or non-existent, to satisfy as an explanation for rights.

For natural lawyers (and American revolutionaries of the eighteenth century) rights are based on 'self-evident truths'. These are self-evident in the sense of being derived, using the 'reason' with which we are all endowed by nature, from simple reflection on the basic social conditions necessary for individual freedom (Finnis). Immanuel Kant (1724–1804) provides us with a philosophically sophisticated understanding of autonomy rooted in the possibilities of reason and expressing the values of the 'enlightenment'.

The horrors of the first half of the twentieth century, however, led many to reject the possibility of 'reason' as the ultimate guide. Today, perhaps, it is 'science' that has authority. If so, a better explanation for human rights may lie in evolution—an evolving tendency to compassion in human beings explains our current pursuit of human rights (Gearty). 'Postmodernists', on the other hand, deny the possibility of an *a priori* single principle that explains human rights.

It is clearly difficult to get agreement on the point of human rights if the aim is to describe some essential fact of human life from which human rights are derived. An alternative, 'political', approach is to ask whether there are social and political purposes for which human rights have a particular justificatory role. Thus it has been argued that human rights are defined and limited by being those values which are capable of justifying a just war; specifically, these days, military intervention in the affairs of a sovereign state (Rawls; Raz). Others have suggested a wider definition of human rights by which they are the discourse in terms of which progressive politics is now conducted (Gearty).

Lawyers (in their capacity as such) do not have to resolve these problems. They are concerned to identify and interpret the 'human rights' that have been agreed in the sense that they are found in international treaties or national legal systems etc. Philosophers (and lawyers too) then identify the values that best explain and justify the fact that we have those rights. The idea of individual 'autonomy', for example, emerges, *ex post*, as a presumed, underlying value which explains and justifies our having rights such as the right to life, not to be tortured, to freedom of expression, etc. (Griffin).

1.1.3 **Legal protection**

Human rights involve the idea that it is possible and desirable to identify the fundamental attributes of human dignity and to express these attributes as legal rules. The idea is that human rights are not just desirable but obligatory. They are part of the law, they should be enforced by courts and should be legally binding on states and their governments, and there should be procedures and remedies by which a person's rights can be upheld. Legal protection means that it is sovereign states, such as the United Kingdom, which, through their institutions (government, Parliament and courts) have the primary responsibility for securing human rights for their populations.

1.1.4 **Respecting difference**

Recognising human dignity implies the recognition of basic standards to be applied to all individuals, standards which reflect our common humanity. It also involves the recognition of difference. The point is that individuals hold different beliefs on religion and on politics, have different senses of right and wrong, different desires and interests, etc. The idea of human rights is that these differences are basic to what we are, both as private individuals and as citizens acting with others in society—in commerce, politics, religion, etc. Respecting common humanity implies allowing such differences to flourish.

1.1.5 The nice and the nasty

Most individuals, as persons, are 'alright', some are very nice, but some are peculiarly nasty. One of the things that is hardest to accept about human rights is that they are shared by the good and the bad alike. The most violent murderers or vicious racists are entitled to the protection of their human rights. Of course, these are not rights to enable them to murder or pursue racist activities. But even the worst of persons is entitled to proper treatment in prison, and to a fair trial and other basic rights.

1.1.6 Rights and freedom—absolute and qualified rights

At the heart of the theory of human rights is the recognition that individual lives are led in a social context and that it is entirely legitimate for states to place reasonable restraints on individuals in order to pursue the common good by advancing common interests and protecting general security. Thus identifying the rights individuals have will usually involve, first, recognising that individual freedom may be qualified by duties owed to others; second, that individual freedom must be qualified by recognising the rights of others; and, third, that identifying rights may require a 'balancing' or 'weighing' of individual interests or desires with the pursuit of legitimate social purposes. There are some exceptions: no one should be tortured, for example, or denied a fair trial just because there is a strong public interest that would be benefited. These are sometimes referred to as 'absolute' rights. But very often the language of human rights law is the language of the fair balance and a recognition that the particular content of an individual right can depend upon the socio-political context in which it is claimed. Often, but not exclusively, this relates to a claimed right to some freedom—to be private or to speak, for example. The importance of 'balance' and 'context' will become clear in the examination of the specific rights derived from the European Convention on Human Rights that forms much of the text of this book. It is found both in the text of the Convention and in the interpretation and application of the Convention by the European Court of Human Rights (ECtHR).

1.1.7 Universalism

One of the difficult questions about human rights is whether they are 'universal' and apply equally to all men and women throughout the world, or whether they are culturally specific. The latter can mean that, in some cultures, the concept of human rights simply makes no sense. Thus, it might be argued, in cultures which emphasise obedience and duty to God or to traditional structures of authority, the idea of basic individual entitlements which must be respected by such authority may make little sense.

The argument that human rights are culturally specific can also mean that the content of human rights—what particular rights we have—differs between cultures. Thus what counts as 'fair' in the context of a fair trial, or what particular limits to freedom of speech are 'necessary', may differ culture to culture. One argument, for instance, is that human rights embody so-called 'Western values'. They promote a particular form of individual freedom which is necessary for the consumer capitalism of the West but which is inappropriate for non-capitalist societies that have not fully embraced the capitalist way and are seeking other ways forward or simply to maintain pre-capitalist traditions. Other cultures may emphasise concepts of obedience and service over individualism. The African conception, for example, embodied in the African Charter, refers to the 'historical tradition and values of African civilization', stresses anti-colonialism, and gives significant emphasis to the rights of 'peoples' and to the importance of familial relationships. The point is that such concepts are, as much as individual freedom, attached to ideas of personhood and of human dignity and so are not simply contradictions of human rights. From such perspectives, the claims of human rights can seem to be a form of cultural imperialism.

The claim to cultural relativism in human rights often misses some of the main points of the universalist approach.

- Some rights, like the prohibition of torture, are hard to make culturally relative.
- A universalist has no difficulty in accepting that the content of other rights, like freedom of expression, is culturally specific. All a universalist insists on is to protect the core, the central, meaning of such a right. The suppression of political speech is likely to be inconsistent with a universalist conception of freedom of speech in a way that restricting pornography, for example, is not.
- Cultural relativism about human rights, particularly about the core of the freedom human rights should offer, can be simply a mask for dictatorship and tyranny. Likewise the opponents of such oppressive regimes may find themselves bereft of effective argument and intellectual resources for their campaigns.
- There can also be arguments about what rights we have that may appear to be relativist but which, in fact, are about what rights, universally, we ought to have. Thus feminists may take the view that mainstream human rights embody the values of a patriarchal society. If this is true it is an argument for expanding our understanding of rights to ensure they are genuinely universal; it does not reinforce the argument for cultural relativism.

1.2 Political, legal, and constitutional theory

To approach a theoretical understanding of human rights, it can be helpful to consider the matter at three different levels: political theory, legal theory, and constitutional theory. These can be very complex and abstract. The aim in what follows is no more than to introduce some general themes. There is no attempt at a systematic presentation or understanding of general theories or particular works.

1.2.1 Political theory

A political theory is a set of general ideas about how government and state power can best be understood and justified, and under what conditions it can be said that citizens have real obligations to obey the laws of the country they live in. Political theory is important because the fundamental point of human rights is that basic entitlements of the autonomous person are to be protected by the law and the state.

Liberalism, broadly defined

Human rights presuppose the truth of what might be called 'liberal' theories of politics, using the term 'liberal' in a very broad and inclusive way and certainly not with a 'large L' (ie not confined to Liberal political parties). Put in very general terms, human rights assume that, whatever else a political theory proposes, it must accept that the only thing with ultimate, non-instrumental, moral value is the human individual. The state, associations, groups, cultures, etc may be necessary for human flourishing and may make demands on the freedom of individuals, but they should not be ends in themselves and should not have ultimate moral significance into which the individual can be merged, subordinated, or sacrificed. Liberal theories require that the 'private', an individual's sovereignty over his or her own affairs, must be accepted to some extent (even though the precise place where private and public matters divide is endlessly controversial). Liberal theories also require that government should be ultimately based on the consent of the governed (even though the nature and form that consent takes may be equally controversial).

John Locke (whose *Second Treatise on Government* was published in 1690), writing in part to justify the Glorious Revolution,1688 (the assumption of the monarchy by William III and Mary II on the basis of some general conditions imposed by Parliament), has given the classic justification of a liberal form of government. Locke destroyed the idea that the authority of government was traditional and ultimately divine. Rather, he asserted that individual rights to 'life, liberty and estates (property)' were natural to mankind. Through reason mankind understands that these rights need protection. The authority of legitimate government stems, therefore, from the people consenting to law and government in so far as it protects these basic rights. Government failure in this regard might justify revolution.

In the second half of the twentieth century liberal ideas have been reformulated, especially by John Rawls, initially in *A Theory of Justice* (1972). The idea of natural rights is replaced by an attempt to work out what basic principles, to be reflected in constitutions and laws, would be chosen by people who have to choose without knowing whether they themselves would be winners or losers from the outcome. The argument is that reasonable people would choose, and give normal priority to, a system of equal basic rights and liberties. Such a system requires everyone's rights, including those of the least well off, to be recognised. (Rawls's work is complex and has been developed over the years.)

Non-liberal theories

Political theories which, for instance, depend upon enforcing the superiority of one race over another (Nazism), or which invest the state with a monopoly of moral or social truth to which the masses must subscribe (Stalinism), or which subordinate the law to the word of God as this is interpreted by an untouchable class of clerics, are theories which are unlikely to leave much room for recognising and supporting human rights.

Even non-authoritarian political theories, such as anarchism (not the bomb-throwing kind), may be hard to reconcile, theoretically, with human rights. Anarchism is a political theory that explores the possibility that individuals in their communities can conduct their affairs in the absence of states, laws, and rules. Freed from these restraints, communities will develop their own inclusive and informal ways of self-government. But human rights imply entitlements embodied in authoritative, binding rules, which we call law. It implies the separation of powers by which the rules are impartially enforced by officials who are institutionally separated from the procedures by which social goals are chosen. This commitment to 'law', central to human rights, is hard to reconcile with anarchist approaches to politics.

This is no more than a suggestion that some general political theories may be incompatible with human rights. Of course the real problem, from a human rights point of view, is less the ideas and more the practices of violence and oppression by which non-liberal states conduct their affairs (this should not be taken to imply that liberal states never use oppression and violence).

1.2.2 **Rights and utility**

Utilitarian approaches to government do not sit easily with human rights. Utilitarians take the view that the proper standard for evaluating government actions relates to its outcomes. A policy is to be evaluated by one standard only, which is whether it maximises the common good or the well-being of individuals. Human rights theory, on the other hand, argues that policies must respect human rights no matter how beneficial they might be. So, for example, crime would probably be reduced if the police were allowed very wide powers to arrest, detain, and administer summary punishments, and if the courts were allowed to convict on a balance of probabilities rather than beyond reasonable doubt. The reduction in crime would enormously improve the lives of vast numbers of people and, furthermore, it is likely that some seriously unpleasant criminals would be removed from circulation. Why, the utilitarian might argue, should such a policy not be pursued so long as the suffering of the small number of genuinely innocent people who are wrongly convicted was outweighed by the benefits? The argument for human rights is opposed to this in principle (ie not just because the number of wrongful convictions might be high and the suffering of those convicted very intense). Human rights is an argument about individuals' entitlements which should be upheld even if the interests of the majority or society as a whole are thereby less well served.

But even the most dogmatic utilitarian is likely to be committed to at least a 'procedural' account of human rights. Utilitarians need to have some way of calculating how to maximise individual happiness. In making this calculation the interests of every individual must be taken into account and given equal weighting. This creates individual entitlements to vote, for example, or to be able to express preferences in other ways such as by speech or association. These are human rights.

1.2.3 **Legal theory**

As noted at section 1.1.3, essential to the concept of human rights is the idea that they should be expressed as 'law', rules involving enforceable obligations which are binding on states. This takes us to the interface between the two dominant ways of thinking about the nature of law.

- 'Positivism' refers to a complex body of legal theory which identifies law as the willed actions of states. The law, in this sense, is identified in terms of legal sources such as legislation, case law, international treaties, etc. The law is known from these sources alone and, the point is, it can be identified without any need for an evaluation of whether it is good or bad, right or wrong, moral or immoral. Such questions (what common purposes should we follow by means of the law, what behaviour should the law prohibit, etc.) are essentially 'moral' or 'political' matters, distinguished from law.

- 'Natural law' identifies the law not in terms of the content of a range of sources, whatever that happens to be, but in terms of the real, the true, obligations that we have towards others and towards society. The task of the natural lawyer is to try and identify such true obligations on the basis, for example, of the will of God or the necessary inferences from the use of reason.

The point about human rights law is to get human rights values, expressed as enforceable rules, accepted as part of the 'positive law' of the countries of the world. But human rights law also seems to involve a 'natural law' claim that human rights values express a truth from which a series of genuine, objectively true obligations derive. These are obligations which exist whatever states choose to do. They are objective legal standards against which the positive law of states can be measured.

1.2.4 **Constitutional theory**

Human rights law, because it is pre-eminently aimed at states, raises a number of constitutional issues involving the general power of a state and the relations between its component parts.

Sovereignty

The world is made up of sovereign states claiming freedom to act as they see fit, particularly as regards their own population. Human rights law asserts that there are limits to the freedom of action of the governments of these states, particularly over their own people, and so it undermines the basic idea of sovereignty.

Majority rule

Human rights law claims that some form of democracy is the only acceptable form of government. However, it does not mean democracy as majority rule. Majorities can only rule subject to the rights of minorities and individuals: no matter how popular a cause, it cannot be supported by the law and the state if it violates individuals' rights.

The judiciary

Perhaps the most difficult constitutional issue arising from human rights law is the enhanced role within the constitution that it gives to judges. Human rights are to be enforced by the courts. On some view of human rights, judges should have the power to strike down legislation and declare it invalid (that it is not law at all). This power is not available in the United Kingdom nor in many other states. Even without this power, it remains the case that, in deciding human rights cases, judges may have to deny the view of the public interest and the common good chosen by government and Parliament. The constitutional problem, of course, is that judges are not elected nor are they accountable to elected representatives. Nevertheless, human rights are expressed in general 'open-textured' terms which require interpretation if they are to be applied to particular cases. This job of interpretation and application falls on the judges and will often involve 'political' judgments of, for example, what specific restraints on freedom of speech are needed for the proper workings of a democratic society.

Deference and the constitutional balance

In fact human rights law tends not to involve out and out assertions by judges that they know better than government or legislature how to square the pursuit of the common good with protecting human rights. Human rights law tends, instead, to involve what has been called a form of constitutional discourse, between the different branches of the state—the courts, Parliament, and the government. This is well illustrated under the Human Rights Act 1998 in the United Kingdom where, even if the courts adjudge legislation to be incompatible with human rights, they still cannot refuse to put it into effect. Rather, they may make a 'declaration of incompatibility'. The consequence is that the issue returns to government, which may propose alterations to the law which Parliament, subject to its normal pressures, accepts or rejects. Issues such as whether a policy has been approved by Parliament, or whether a policy has been decided by a public body expressly established to take decisions that impact on human rights (issues about privacy and the media, for example) are clearly significant in the way judges are likely to assess and understand their role. On some issues, like fair trials, judges may feel especially competent to make judgments, whilst on others, involving national security, for example, judges may be more willing to defer to the view of government. The point is that the role of the judges in human rights matters is complex, involving questions about the nature and importance of the right in question, the circumstances of the case and the proper role of Parliament and government. In the end, however, under human rights law, the proper understanding of the constitutional role of judges includes their responsibility for protecting individuals from serious human rights abuses.

Democratic politics

One important form of doubt and criticism about human rights is concerned that human rights law narrows the scope for a society to debate and decide issues in democratic and participative ways. Proponents of this view support the idea of human rights but doubt whether legal–judicial mechanisms are the best way forward. They tend to see human rights law as undermining other forms of political participation and democratic decision-taking. Important issues, like what can be published, where the border between the public and the private lies, what forms of sexual behaviour are acceptable, and so on, are removed from processes of democratic debate, persuasion, and choice. Instead, in human rights discourse, they become recast into arguments of abstract principle which are decided by judges or other bodies of the great and good. The objection is not to the idea of human rights as such, but to human rights in its judicialised, judge-based form. On this view there should be greater trust in the democratic, participative, institutions in which such issues can be decided through the arguments and debates of representatives.

1.3 What rights do we have?

1.3.1 Civil and political rights

Nothing has so far been said about the nature and content of the rights that human beings enjoy. It is reasonable to identify a core list of human rights whilst recognising that the exact expression of the items on the list depends upon the treaty or other legal instrument in which they are laid down. It is also important to remember that our conception of what is fundamental to the dignity of an individual and necessary for an effective democracy can, whilst building on some basics, develop with time and depend upon cultural factors.

A standard list, derived from the United Nations Declaration on Human Rights of 1948 (UNDHR) includes the following: whoever they are, a person has a right that their life should be protected; they should not be tortured or enslaved, nor be subject to arbitrary, lawless treatment by those in authority; they should be given fair trials; enjoy basic privacy and basic freedoms such as freedom of religion, speech, association and assembly, and the right to voluntary marriage, rights to vote and stand for election, and rights not to suffer discrimination on racial, sexual, and other grounds.

These rights are articulated and specified in a range of instruments built on the UNDHR, including the European Convention on Human Rights. They tend to be thought of as civil and political rights.

Civil rights

Civil rights aim at individual liberty and at securing (in the United States' phrase) 'equal protection of the laws'. All men and women are to have equal legal status and equal rights to pursue their own way of life in society free of state oppression. Such civil rights are 'private' in the sense that they protect the liberty of individuals in their personal, economic, familial, religious, and social lives. The list tends also to include rights to property. The latter can be controversial since large, commercial corporations have massive property interests which clearly involve the exercise of social power. The extent to which the exercise of such power needs protection through human rights law is controversial.

Political rights

'Political' rights are those which protect the freedoms necessary for a democracy in which there is participation in political processes: freedom of speech and association, the right to vote and stand in elections, and so on.

1.3.2 Social and 'third generation' rights

The conventional list of civil and political rights excludes 'social' rights. These are, for example, rights to housing, health, education, and welfare support. Without these, human beings are bound by the necessities of staying alive and are unable to exercise any of the freedoms human rights seek to protect, and which are essential to autonomy and flourishing. At issue is the question of what is so fundamental to being human that it needs the special protection offered by human rights. Obviously this changes over time. Although there is little express recognition of social rights in the UNDHR or the European Convention, they have been increasingly accepted at the international level during the second half of the twentieth century.

What entitlements are considered fundamental in the early years of the twenty-first century? So-called 'third generation' rights are being promoted and developed (civil and political rights are 'first generation', social rights are 'second generation' in this taxonomy). Third generation rights include issues such as rights to a safe and sustainable environment, rights of peoples to self-development and to the protection of their cultural heritage. Of these, it is probably environmental rights which are best developed in terms of 'hard law'—court-enforceable rules. Other aspects of third generation rights tend to be more 'soft law'—policy aspirations to which states agree but to which they are not firmly bound.

1.3.3 Discrimination

Human rights also include the need for laws outlawing 'discrimination'. A person should be protected from general disadvantage or from less favourable treatment based on irrelevant criteria such as skin colour, race, sex, religion, etc. The types of forbidden reason for treating someone less favourably than another change over time (it is now widely accepted, for example, that discrimination based on sexual orientation should be made unlawful). The second half of the twentieth century saw a widespread recognition at national and international levels that people have a right to legal protection from discrimination. This is embodied in particular treaties and is established as a general principle of interpretation of all legal instruments.

1.3.4 Negative and positive obligations

A distinction is made between negative and positive obligations. Negative obligations require a state, through the government, not to commit wrongs (e.g. not to torture its prisoners). Positive obligations require states, through their governments, to undertake actions, usually involving the expenditure of resources. These might be, for example, to provide a system of police and courts in order to deter crime and ensure fair trials. In fact, the positive/negative distinction is often not very illuminating since the securing of most rights involves states in a combination of doing and not doing which cannot be easily separated.

1.3.5 **Human rights and the distribution of wealth**

As mentioned in section 1.2.4, under 'Democratic politics', some critics of human rights law are concerned that it takes too much away from Parliament and the democratic forum and gives too much power to the judiciary.

Such a view has greatest force where human rights require states to make large expenditures from scarce resources. These matters involve choices between different desirable goals and should be taken democratically. For this reason, distributive justice, the question of 'who gets what, when and where', the question of how resources and wealth are to be distributed, tend, above a basic minimum, to be excluded from the domain of human rights law. Lord Hoffmann put the point in this way:

> Human rights are the rights essential to the life and dignity of the individual in a demo-cratic society. The exact limits of such rights are debatable and, although there is not much trace of economic rights in the 50-year-old Convention, I think it is well arguable that human rights include the right to a minimum standard of living, without which many of the other rights would be a mockery. But they certainly do not include the right to a fair distribution of resources or fair treatment in economic terms—in other words, dis-tributive justice. Of course distributive justice is a good thing. But it is not a fundamental human right.
>
> (*Matthews* v *Ministry of Defence* [2003] UKHL 4, para 26)

1.4 Human rights movement

1.4.1 **Some historical roots**

The core idea behind human rights, that government is limited by a need to respect minimum entitlements of individuals, has a long history. It can probably be traced back to aspects of classical political thought such as that of the Roman jurist Cicero (106–43BC). Modern mani-festations of the idea are found in the work of seventeenth-century political philosophers, particularly John Locke. At the level of practical politics, the revolutions in the American colo-nies and France, at the end of the eighteenth century, both resulted in new regimes founded on the basis of written constitutions which included statements of what are in effect (though not necessarily called as such) human rights. Of course, European history in the nineteenth century and the first half of the twentieth century is, to a great extent, a history of imperial autocracy giving way to dictatorship. Under neither did human rights flourish, and under both autocracy and dictatorship constitutionally based rights were set aside or ignored and the population oppressed.

In Britain, legal restraints on government can be traced back to Magna Carta (when, in 1215, King John accepted certain restraints imposed upon him by the feudal lords) and to the English idea of Kingship, which is that the King's authority is derived from the law so that he rules on the basis of law and not on the basis of his will alone (this idea is associated, in particular, with Henry Bracton, whose major work on legal theory was written, probably by a number of scholars, in the mid-thirteenth century). In the absence of a written constitution (except during the time of the Cromwellian Protectorate between 1653 and 1660), the common law developed on the basis of the idea that a person is free to do whatever is not forbidden by law (by statutes, rules of common law, and the decisions of juries).

The system in Britain has been complicated. The eighteenth century, through legal writers such as Blackstone, proclaimed the virtues of the common law as embodying liberty and basic rights, especially to property, which the law would protect. Bentham, at the end of the century, was, however, appalled at the arbitrary, cruel, and uncertain way in which the common law, so dependant on the will of judges, was applied. Equally, however, he rejected the grand statements of human rights associated with the French and American revolutions. Bentham regarded these lists of rights as being so general and abstract as to be meaningless 'nonsense on stilts'. His solution was for rational reforms, on utilitarian principles, to be achieved by statute.

The nineteenth century saw the common law continuing to give legal force and recognition to many of the freedoms that today are expressed as civil and political rights. Dicey's conception of the rule of law expresses the common law's presumption of liberty and the need for restrictions to be focused and specifically justified. Like Bentham, he thought the grand lists of rights found in continental constitutions problematic—they were not linked to remedies and were often suspended by autocratic governments. Where liberty derived from the constitution (rather than being a simple presumption of law) such suspensions left the population vulnerable. Dicey, of course, also recognised the supremacy of Parliament. The common law could not provide some important entitlements. A number of important basic rights, such as the right to vote, depended upon Parliament responding to popular political movements. Likewise it is only Parliament that could provide for education etc. and other social conditions under which basic rights can flourish.

Though Britain was not invaded and did not suffer dictatorship, the nineteenth century and the first half of the twentieth century saw times of intense political oppression and, in the context of class politics, the application of laws in a far from even-handed manner.

1.4.2 The development of international human rights law

This book is about the Human Rights Act and the European Convention on Human Rights to which the Act gives effect in United Kingdom law. The Convention (which is discussed in Chapter 2) is a part of the international human rights movement. This movement is itself part of a broader expansion of public international law which has origins in the Middle Ages and came to its current maturity through a range of international agreements entered into in the nineteenth and twentieth centuries. The central idea is that sovereign states have obligations, as states operating in the international community, not only to respect the sovereignty of other states (the traditional focus of international law), but also to act with proper restraint towards their own populations and others, including their enemies.

This context includes the following:

- Laws of war. International, legal restraints on the conduct of war go back at least to Pope Innocent II's ban on the use of crossbows against Christians in 1139. Hugo Grotius codified these laws in *De Juri Belli ac Pacis*, 1625. Binding international agreements came later. By the Hague Convention 1907, states agreed to instruct their armed forces to obey the restatement of the laws and customs of war annexed to the Convention. This restatement is still in force as the basis of the legal regulations of the conduct of war by states and their forces.

- Humanitarian law. The Geneva Conventions (the first dates from 1864) are international agreements dealing with the treatment of wounded members of the armed forces, prisoners, and civilians during wartime. Today there are four Conventions, which have been added to by three protocols. The Fourth Geneva Convention relates to the protection of civilians in time of war, and the first two Protocols thereto relate to the protection of the victims of international and non-international 'armed conflict' (e.g. conflicts involving non-state groups). These are of particular relevance to terrorist violence and states' responses to it in the twenty-first century.

- The League of Nations was established at the end of the First World War. Under its auspices, the laws of war and laws against slavery were enhanced and there was an attempt to give international protection to the rights of minorities. With the rise of European and Japanese fascism in the 1930s, the weakness of the League in the face of aggressive sovereign states was exposed.

The League ceased to exist at the end of the Second World War. It was replaced by the United Nations. It is under the auspices of the latter organisation that what we call the international human rights movement has developed and expanded.

1.4.3 United Nations

The founding document of the United Nations is its Charter. This expresses the chief aims of the organisation. These are to secure peace and security throughout the world and 'to reaffirm faith in fundamental human rights, in the dignity and worth of the human person, in the equal rights of men and women and of nations large and small'. Under the auspices of the UN a network of treaties, commissions, and monitoring committees has been established. In particular the Human Rights Council (which replaced the Human Rights Commission in 2011) has a major role in promoting human rights and reviewing their protection amongst member states. A range of other human rights focused organisations report to the Council.

THE BIGGER PICTURE

For the functions and organisation of the United Nations, in respect of human rights, see Smith, chapters 3–5.

1.4.4 The international bill of rights

At the heart of the United Nations' commitment to human rights is the 'International Bill of Rights'.

Universal Declaration of Human Rights

The Universal Declaration of Human Rights (UDHR) was adopted as an international standard by the General Assembly in 1948. It is the basic list of fundamental rights and freedoms, identified and accepted by the nations of the world. It is the inspiration and moral authority for the human rights movement. It does not, however, directly create legally binding duties and obligations on states. Nevertheless it is referred to in the constitutions of some states. There is also judicial opinion that the Declaration, or at least some of its most fundamental terms such as the bans on torture and slavery, can be considered to be part of customary international law (see section 1.4.5) and thus binding on states. In any event, like other UN Declarations, it has great persuasive and inspirational authority on national and regional courts. It stands behind a number of regional systems of human rights, including the European Convention on Human Rights.

International Covenant on Civil and Political Rights

Through the International Covenant on Civil and Political Rights (ICCPR) the rights and freedoms in Articles 1 to 21 of the UDHR are made into binding obligations on states. States agree to ensure that the rights and freedoms listed in the Covenant are effectively protected in their national laws (Article 2 ICCPR). Articles 1 to 21 contain the fundamental civil and political rights derived from the principle of autonomy (rights to life, not to be tortured, to physical liberty, to freedom of expression, etc.) mentioned in section 1.3.1.

The period after the Second World War was characterised by international tensions and fundamental ideological divisions. This meant that it was not until 1966 that a majority (but not all) UN states accepted such obligations and signed the Covenant; it then took a further ten years for the Covenant to be brought into effect. Most countries in the world are 'parties' to the Covenant and accept its obligations (167 in June 2012).

The main mechanism for enforcement is through five-yearly reports from the states on the measures they have taken to ensure compatibility with the Covenant. The reports are sent to the Human Rights Committee (established by the Covenant and to be distinguished from the Human Rights Council, mentioned in section 1.4.3), which is supervised by the Economic and Social Council of the UN and, ultimately, the UN's General Assembly. The reports from states can be commented upon by interested non-governmental organisations (NGOs) such as Amnesty. The Committee then makes its own comments on the state reports. Ultimate enforcement is through the publicity given to the Committee's comments through the annual report of the Committee to the General Assembly. The Committee also produces General Comments which involve a detailed examination on how particular articles of the Covenant should be implemented. There is a system allowing one state to bring a case before the Committee against another state, but this tends to be ineffective because it depends upon the agreement of both states involved and, for diplomatic reasons, states are reluctant to challenge each other.

The First Optional Protocol to the Covenant introduces a system for individuals to petition the Committee on violations of the Covenant of which they have been the victim and which have not been remedied by their national law. The Committee presents its 'views' on the case to the state involved and to the complainant, and summarises these individual cases in its annual report. Individual application is an important element in the enforcement of the Covenant. The First Protocol is, however, optional for states. In June 2012, of the 167 parties only 114 were parties to the First Protocol (the United Kingdom, like the United States, has not agreed to the Protocol).

International Covenant of Economic, Social and Cultural Rights

Signatory states to the International Covenant of Economic, Social and Cultural Rights (ICESCR) agree to the progressive realisation, relative to their resources, of a range of rights such as a right to work and earn a living, rights to health, education and welfare, and rights to a cultural life. The Covenant is based on Articles 22 to 29 of the UN Declaration. Enforcement is by reporting alone and, it is generally agreed, the Covenant is predominantly aspirational (identifying policy goals which it is the hope and intention of a state to achieve, rather than setting out specific legal obligations.) Such second-generation social rights are resource intensive and so it is hard to require states to accept full legal obligations in these areas.

There are many other instruments of international law, many based on the authority of the United Nations, which bear on human rights. Examples include

- International Convention on the Elimination of All Forms of Racial Discrimination (1966);
- Convention on the Elimination of All Forms of Discrimination against Women (1979);

- Convention against Torture and Other Cruel, Inhuman or Degrading Treatment or Punishment (1984);
- Convention on the Rights of the Child (1989);
- Convention against Transnational Organised Crime (2003) and its Protocol to Prevent, Suppress and Punish Trafficking of Persons, Especially Women and Children (2003).

Each Convention has its own methods of enforcement. It must be remembered that, at international law, a country is only bound by the treaties and obligations it has accepted. Some Conventions have additional protocols which can be important for making the protection effective (e.g. by allowing individuals to complain). But these may be voluntary and agreed to by a small number of states which may, in any case, be the states that have the least to fear.

International Criminal Court

The role of the International Criminal Court (ICC) is to prosecute individuals, including state officials, for the crimes (as defined in the statute) of genocide, crimes against humanity, and war crimes. Its authority is based on the Rome Statute. It is linked to but independent of the United Nations. In 2012 it delivered its first judgment in the case of *Lubanga* ICC-01/04-01/06-2842.

Individual actions

The UN, acting through its institutions such as the Security Council, can require states to act, including requiring steps to be taken against particular individuals. For example, the Security Council's Al-Qaida and Taliban Sanctions Committee can authorise the freezing of assets of named persons. Likewise actions taken (in Iraq for instance) based on UN authority, can involve the detention of individuals. These actions can raise difficult questions about whether the procedures are fair to the individuals and whether their other human rights, especially the right to liberty, are properly protected.

> **CROSS REFERENCE**
> See, for example,
> *R (Al-Jedda)* v *United Kingdom* (2011) 53 EHRR 23 considered in Chapter 2, section 2.4.5, Effective control over an area.

1.4.5 Customary international law and the common law

There are some rules and practices that are universally recognised by states as being part of their general legal obligations as states; not just things they do voluntarily and in their own interests, but things they do as requirements of their status as civilised states recognising the rule of law. These obligations apply generally and irrespective of any treaty obligations. Such obligations are part of the so-called compelling law of nations (*jus cogens*) and apply *erga omnes* (they are enforceable by all states against any one). As an overriding, non-voluntary obligation on states, it seems that an action based on a breach of the *jus cogens* can be heard in national courts, including those of the United Kingdom.

1.4.6 Regional

The United Nations has inspired a number of 'regional' developments. The Organization of American States, the African Union, and the League of Arab States are regional international organisations which have developed institutions for the securing of human rights in ways that those organisations consider reflect the societies and cultures of the region, the problems they have to deal with, and the power structures that apply. Thus there is the American Convention on Human Rights (1969), the African Charter on Human and People's Rights (1981), and the Arab Charter on Human Rights (2004). Linked to these Conventions and Charters are a range of other instruments and systems for enforcement.

The European Convention on Human Rights was created by the Council of Europe after the Second World War. In terms particularly of enforcement and authority it is probably the most effective of all the regional systems for protecting human rights. It is the substance of the rights and freedoms contained in this Convention that have been given further effect in the law of the United Kingdom by means of the Human Rights Act 1998 and which forms the subject matter of the rest of this book.

Summary

To make sense of the European Convention on Human Rights and the Human Rights Act 1998, it is helpful to

- understand some of the basic issues about human rights—what they are in philosophical and theoretical terms and what general issues of a political, legal, and constitutional kind the enforcement of human rights is likely to give rise to;
- know the traditional content of human rights, and the question of how, if at all, that content should develop to reflect a modern political agenda; and
- understand in basic outline the development of the international human rights movement of which the European Convention is a part.

On the basis of this understanding, it is possible to move on to consider the Act and the Convention in more detail. Many of the issues addressed in this chapter underlie legal problems about the interpretation and application of the Act that are developed later.

Self-test questions

1. What is the difference between civil rights, political rights, and 'third generation' rights?

2. What is the difference between 'absolute' rights and 'qualified' rights?

3. Given the UN Declaration of Human Rights, why was it necessary to get states to agree to the International Covenant on Civil and Political Rights?

 For suggested approaches, please visit the Online Resource Centre.

Exam questions

1. Critically assess the difference between, on the one hand, rights based and, on the other, utilitarian approaches to the limits of freedom of expression under the law. Your answer may include references to Article 10 case law but should focus on theory.

2. The government of Ruritania (a member of the UN and signatory to all UN human rights treaties) is considering how to give effect to human rights in its law. As a senior civil servant in the relevant ministry, write a position paper advising the government on the alternative approaches, in terms of the relationship of courts, legislature, the executive, and international law, that might be adopted.

 For suggested approaches, please visit the Online Resource Centre.

 # Further reading

Introductions to international human rights law

Smith, R. *Textbook on International Human Rights* 6th edn (2014) Oxford: OUP

On the concept of human rights

Dworkin, R. *Taking Rights Seriously* (1977) London: Duckworth, esp Chapter 4

Finnis, J. *Natural Law and Natural Rights* (1980) (2011) Oxford: Clarendon Press

Gearty, C. A. *Principles of Human Rights Adjudication* (2004) Oxford: OUP

Griffin, J. *On Human Rights* (2008) Oxford: OUP

Rawls, J. *The Law of Peoples* (1992) Cambridge, Mass.: Harvard UP

Raz, J. 'Human Rights without Foundations' (2007) Oxford Legal Studies Research Paper No 14/2007

Critical discussion on human rights can be found in

Campbell, T. et al (eds) *The Legal Protection of Human Rights Sceptical Essays* (2011) Oxford: OUP

Waldron, J. (ed) *Theories of Rights* (1984) Oxford: OUP

For discussion of different constitutional theories see

Allan, T. R. S. *Constitutional Justice* (2001) Oxford: OUP

Hickman, T. 'Constitutional Dialogue, Constitutional Theories and the Human Rights Act 1998' [2005] *Public Law* 306

Tomkins, A. *Our Republican Constitution* (2005) Oxford: Hart Publishing

Waldron, J. *Law and Disagreement* (1999) Oxford: OUP

2 The European Convention on Human Rights

Introduction

It is very important to distinguish the Human Rights Act 1998 (HRA) from the European Convention for the Protection of Human Rights and Fundamental Freedoms, usually known as the European Convention on Human Rights (ECHR). The Act is an ordinary Act of Parliament and is part of the law of the United Kingdom. The Convention is a legal instrument of the Council of Europe (the Council is identified and explained later in the chapter). The Convention is not, in itself, part of UK law. However, its content, the rights and freedoms contained in it, are given effect in the law of England and Wales, Scotland, and Northern Ireland by the Act. The Convention is interpreted and applied by the ECtHR. Its judgments are not directly binding as legal judgments in the United Kingdom; however, the principles developed by the ECtHR in interpreting the Convention must be taken into account (and are usually followed) by UK courts dealing with HRA cases.

2.1 The history and development of the Convention system

The term 'convention', in this context, simply means an international agreement between sovereign states by which they agree to be bound by the terms of the convention; it means broadly the same thing as a 'treaty'. The term 'convention' can also mean an unwritten rule based on practice, and this is the sense in which we talk of 'constitutional conventions' in Constitutional Law. It is important to distinguish between these two meanings.

As mentioned in Chapter 1, the general idea of legally protected human rights began to gather force at the end of the Second World War. The inspiration was the emergence of the United Nations, whose Charter came into force in October 1945 and which adopted the Universal Declaration on Human Rights in December 1948. The context was the appalling devastation, disruption, and state of turmoil of large parts of the world when hostilities ceased in 1945. Europe, at the end of the war, had to deal with massive social and economic problems and the legacies of the Holocaust, widespread atrocities, racism, and all the deadly corruption of public life associated with totalitarian dictatorships. The need after 1945 was not only to deal with these problems by reconstruction, but also to try to create institutions which would help to remove the causes of war for the future and provide protection from any threat that totalitarian government might revive. Two principal solutions were adopted: the European Union (as it has now become), and the Council of Europe. These need to be distinguished.

2.1.1 The European Union

The European Union, as it is now known, had its origins in the Treaty of Rome 1956. Its principal aim was to encourage European economic integration in order to eliminate the causes of war. Its aim now is to 'promote peace, its values and the well-being of its peoples', and its values include 'respect for human rights' (Articles 3 and 2 Treaty on European Union (TEU)). The original six members have now expanded to twenty-seven. The European Union has, of course, developed into one of the major economic and trading blocs in the world. Economic integration implies wider social and political linking, and the extent to which economic unity (through a free internal market) requires common laws and rules in other areas such as taxation, employment law, welfare policy, criminal law, health and safety, and even foreign policy is, of course, one of the most delicate and controversial matters of twenty-first century European politics.

The European Union has committed itself to the protection of human rights, and this is discussed in Chapter 3, section 3.4.

It is a common mistake is to believe that the Human Rights Act and the ECHR are linked directly to the European Union. This is wrong. The Convention comes from the Council of Europe, which is separate from the European Union and has a different history, aims, organisation, etc. Many countries are members of the Council of Europe without being members of the European Union. However, the Convention is part of the 'general principles of the Union's law' and, following the Lisbon Treaty, the EU is committed to acceding to the Convention (Article 6 TEU).

2.1.2 **The Council of Europe**

A second solution was the Council of Europe. Since the principal instrument by which the Council achieves its aims is the ECHR, the Council needs to be considered in some detail.

2.2 The Council of Europe

2.2.1 **Introduction**

The Council of Europe was established by the Treaty of London in 1949. There were originally ten members: Belgium, Denmark, France, Italy, Luxembourg, the Netherlands, Ireland, Norway, Sweden, and the United Kingdom. Where the European Union (as it now is) sought greater unity by predominantly economic means, the Council of Europe had and has a much wider aim, which embraces social, political, and cultural development, and the protection of human rights.

> **CROSS REFERENCE**
> The international context of the development of human rights is discussed in Chapter 1, sections 1.4.2 and 1.4.3.

The Council of Europe is perhaps the most successful of the regionally based international organisations that take their inspiration from the United Nations and its Declaration of Human Rights.

2.2.2 **Membership**

The 'Cold War' created a divided Europe and, until the early 1990s, membership of the Council of Europe increased but was confined to western European states. Such states enjoyed broadly common interests: they had capitalist or 'mixed' economies, were Christian in heritage (with the major exception of Turkey, which joined in 1950), and had liberal democratic political institutions based, for example, on elected governments and the rule of law. There were few big disagreements between the members (the main exception being the dispute between Turkey and Greece over Cyprus). This common culture made the creation and development of the Council of Europe easier than if it was trying to establish itself amongst nation states that were fundamentally hostile to each other. With the ending of the Cold War, east European countries, Russia and other nations created out of the Soviet Union have joined. Members must be European states that are pluralist democracies which respect both the rule of law and human rights. In June 2012 there were forty-seven full member states.

2.2.3 **Aims of the Council of Europe**

The Statute of the Council of Europe is its constitution. Article 1(a) defines its basic purposes:

> The aim of the Council of Europe is to achieve a greater unity between its members for the purpose of safeguarding and realising the ideals and principles which are their common heritage and facilitating their economic and social progress.

The principal means to achieve this is defined in Article 1(b):

> This aim shall be pursued through the organs of the Council by discussion of questions of common concern and by agreements and common action in economic, social, cultural, scientific, legal and administrative matters and in the maintenance and further realisation of human rights and fundamental freedoms.

The most important way of promoting these aims has been the production, in 1950, of the ECHR and the creation, in 1959, of the ECtHR to enforce the Convention. But the aims of the Council go beyond securing human rights. It has, for example, a significant role in promoting amongst member states high common standards in relation to social cohesion, education, sport, and culture; it also pursues 'integrated projects' on themes such as democracy or domestic violence. The Council has an important position in promoting and investigating human rights compliance by member states. It is also concerned in a huge variety of issues, not just human rights. These include (to name but a few): children's rights, migration in Europe, health care, media freedom and the internet, and violence in sport. It takes positions on international issues, such as (in 2012) the 'Arab Spring' and the violence in Syria.

The Council has also adopted many other conventions on human rights issues that go beyond the terms of the ECHR. These include

- the European Social Charter 1961, dealing with social and economic rights;
- the European Convention for the Prevention of Torture and Inhuman and Degrading Punishment 1987, which enhances state responsibilities on the treatment of prisoners and others;
- the European Convention on the Adoption of Children (revised) 2011, which updates principles dealing with adoption, for example requiring paternal consent.

2.2.4 Institutions of the Council of Europe

The principal institutions created by the statute

The Statute of the Council of Europe created two controlling 'organs':

The Committee of Ministers is the Council's decision-making body responsible for determining policy and putting the aims into effect. As a 'guardian of the Council's fundamental values', it also has the principal role in enforcing and monitoring the way in which member states comply with their Council of Europe obligations. This includes ensuring that states respond fully to adverse judgments by the ECtHR. The members of the Committee are the foreign ministers of the member states or their representatives. States may also appoint a Permanent Representative, usually a senior diplomat, who keeps continual contact between the state and the Council. The Committee represents the interests of the governments of the member states as they struggle both to protect their national interests but also to pursue the collective aims of the Council of Europe.

The Parliamentary Assembly (originally known as the Consultative Assembly) is the chief deliberative organ of the Council of Europe which debates issues and makes recommendations to the Committee of Ministers. It consists of delegations chosen from and by the national legislatures; the size of the delegation relates to the population of the country. The United Kingdom is allowed a delegation of eighteen, chosen from the House of Commons and House of Lords.

Institutions created by the Council of Europe

The Committee of Ministers, exercising its powers under the statute, and acting on recommendations from the Parliamentary Assembly, has created a number of 'institutions' and bodies such as:

- the ECtHR, which is described later in this chapter and whose judgments form an important part of this book;

- the Congress of Local and Regional Authorities, which provides a forum for the promotion and monitoring of democracy as embodied in the local and regional government in member states.

Of particular importance in the human rights context is the Human Rights Commissioner.

- The Office of the Human Rights Commissioner was established by the Council of Europe in 1999. The Commissioner's role is to promote education, awareness, and effective protection of human rights amongst the member states of the Council so that there is full enjoyment of these rights for all. Under Article 36(3) the Commissioner has standing to submit comments and take part in the hearings of cases before the Court.

- The Commissioner also identifies and comments on shortcomings of the law and practice of the member states in respect of human rights. To this end, the Commissioner visits member states and reports on the human rights protection in those states in general terms or in respect of particular issues (but not individual cases). During these visits he meets not only with government officials but also with non-government organisations (e.g. organisations promoting prison reform or the interests of asylum seekers) and others. These reports provide a very valuable means of measuring the success of member states in securing human rights for all persons in their territories; they also indicate the kinds of issues that are currently creating difficulties and problems for human rights protection. There have been general visits to all forty-seven countries. The current Commissioner (Nils Muiznieks) is now more concerned with focusing on particular issues.

THE BIGGER PICTURE

The Commissioner visited the United Kingdom in 2004 (which focused on anti-terrorism law, the detention of asylum seekers, and anti-social behaviour orders) and again in 2008 (which focused on child custody). His concerns in 2012 related to juvenile justice and travellers' rights. The reports are a valuable source for critical evaluation of the state of human rights in the United Kingdom. See the Council of Europe Portal http://www.coe. int, follow the links to 'Commissioner for Human Rights' then 'Activities' then 'Country Monitoring'. These can be searched by country or by year.

Secretariat

The statute also establishes a Secretariat, led by the Secretary General. The Secretariat provides administrative and secretarial services to the Committee of Ministers and to the Parliamentary Assembly and to the institutions they have created, including the ECtHR.

Council of Europe and European Union

It is easy to confuse some of the offices and institutions of the Council of Europe with similar-sounding institutions of the European Union. Thus:

- The Council of Europe must be distinguished from the 'European Council' (where the heads of government of the member states of the European Union meet to decide basic policy) and 'the Council' (which has important legislative and executive functions in the EU and consists of ministers from member states).

- The Parliamentary Assembly must be distinguished from the 'European Parliament' (which is the directly elected assembly with various advisory and law-making powers of the European Union).

- The ECtHR, which sits in Strasbourg, must be distinguished from the Court of Justice of the European Union (which sits in Luxembourg and is the court which interprets and applies the treaties of the European Union).

- The European Commission of Human Rights, which, until it was abolished in 1998, decided which cases could be heard by the ECtHR (a role now performed by the Court itself) must be distinguished from the 'European Commission' (which is the chief executive body of the European Union).

- The flags and anthems of the Council of Europe and of the European Union are the same: a blue flag with a circle of twelve yellow stars, and Beethoven's tune from his setting of Schiller's 'Ode to Joy' in the Ninth Symphony.

2.3 European Convention on Human Rights: the rights and freedoms

2.3.1 Introduction

In fulfilment of its aims, the Council of Europe sought to create an effective means, legally enforced, for the protection of the human rights of the people living in the member states. The essential features of the system are:

- a list of fundamental rights and freedoms;

- an obligation on member states to secure these rights and freedoms for all the people in their territory;

- a system for enforcement and remedies based on a court of human rights whose decisions should be accepted by member states: failure to accept the decision can lead to political or diplomatic pressure from the Committee of Ministers;

- a 'right of individual application' by which individuals can take their own governments before the ECtHR alleging they have been the victim of a violation of one or more of the rights or freedoms.

2.3.2 The drafting of the Convention

The Convention was adopted (signed and ratified by ten member states of the Council of Europe, the number needed to bring it into effect) in 1950 and came into force in 1953. In 1954 three rights (property, education, and elections), which were not agreed in time, were added by the First Protocol to the Convention. Since then, there have been fourteen Protocols, some adding to the list of rights and freedoms and others dealing with the structure of the Court and procedural matters. Protocol 14 introduced important procedural reforms and came into effect in June 2010. Protocols 15 and 16 are not yet in force.

A Protocol is a further agreement which develops, amends, or modifies the main Convention and has the same legal force as the main Convention. Some Protocols are voluntary and so states can have obligations under the main Convention without having to agree to the new Protocol (the United Kingdom, for example, has not agreed to Protocol 4 on freedom of movement and other matters). Other Protocols, such as Protocol 14, are compulsory in the sense that all signatories of the main Convention must agree to them.

2.3.3 Rights and freedoms (the 'substantive rights')

The rights guaranteed by the Convention are:

The original Convention (section 1 of the Convention)

▶ CROSS REFERENCE

See Chapter 5, section 5.1 for Article 13 and Chapter 7 for the other ancillary rights.

The right to life (Article 2); the right not to suffer torture or inhuman or degrading treatment or punishment (Article 3); the right not to suffer slavery or forced labour (Article 4); the right to liberty and security (Article 5); the right to a fair trial (Article 6); the right not to be punished other than on the basis of law (Article 7); the right to respect for private and family life, home, and correspondence (Article 8); the right to freedom of thought, conscience, and religion (Article 9); the right to freedom of expression (Article 10); the right to freedom of assembly and association (Article 11); the right to marry (Article 12).

Section 1 also includes ancillary rights, which qualify the way the other rights are secured: the right to a remedy (Article 13), the right not to suffer discrimination (Article 14, see section 2.3.3 and Chapter 7, section 7.1), the power of states to 'derogate' from (to suspend) parts of the Convention (Article 15), the power of states to restrict the political activities of aliens (Article 16), and the prohibition on the abuse of rights (Article 17).

The First Protocol

The right to the peaceful enjoyment of possessions (Article 1), the right to education (Article 2), the right to free elections (Article 3).

The Fourth Protocol

The right not to be imprisoned for debt (Article 1), the right to freedom of movement (Article 2), the right not to be expelled from the territory of one's nation state (Article 3), the right of aliens (foreigners) not to suffer collective expulsion (Article 4).

The Seventh Protocol

The right of an alien not to be arbitrarily expelled (Article 1), the right to an appeal in criminal cases (Article 2), the right to compensation for wrongful conviction of a crime (Article 3), the right not to be tried or punished twice (Article 4), the right of spouses to equality (Article 5).

The Thirteenth Protocol (replacing the Sixth Protocol)

The right not to suffer the death penalty even in time of war (Article 1).

Discrimination (Article 14 and the Twelfth Protocol)

Article 14 of the original Convention provides the right not to suffer discrimination, but it is confined to discrimination in the way the other rights in the Convention and Protocols are secured; Article 1 of the Twelfth Protocol creates a general right not to suffer discrimination which is not restricted to the context of a Convention right.

Section 2 of the original Convention and the other Protocols

These deal with the ECtHR and with procedural matters.

2.3.4 Types of rights

The Convention secures different freedoms in different ways:

- Absolute rights. The Convention aims to secure some freedoms by imposing duties on states that must be performed in all circumstances. In particular, the freedom must be secured even in times of national emergency and if there are strong public interests or rights of others that would be served or protected if the duty was not performed. The right not to be tortured, in Article 3, is the best example.

- Limited rights. Some Convention Articles seek to secure a particular freedom by asserting it in general terms and then identifying the only circumstances in which it can be limited. Thus Article 5 asserts the right to personal liberty and then goes on to itemise the only circumstances in which it is legitimate to limit it, for example by imprisonment after conviction for an offence.

- 'Qualified' or restrictable rights. Articles 8, 9, 10, and 11 provide rights to private life, freedom of belief, freedom of expression, and freedom of association and assembly. In all four instances, it is easy to think of examples in which, in order to protect the rights of others or to protect a public interest, it is perfectly proper and legitimate to use the law to restrict the exercise of these freedoms. This is recognised in the Convention. For example, there is no serious objection in principle to restricting freedom of speech (especially of the media) in order to protect the fairness of trials. There is, though, likely to be disagreement on precisely how extensive these restrictions should be. As we shall see, each of these Articles allows the freedom they deal with to be restricted if it is done lawfully, if the restriction serves a legitimate purpose, and if the restriction is necessary and is no more than a proportionate burden on the individual affected.

2.3.5 The Convention and the modern political agenda

As a reading of the list given at section 2.3.3 shows, the Convention expresses predominantly civil and political rights.

Some critics argue that, despite its capacity to evolve, the Convention fails to embody rights that reflect the political priorities and assumptions of the twenty-first century.

> **CROSS REFERENCE**
> Civil and political rights are defined in Chapter 1, section 1.3.1.

 DISCUSSION TOPIC

Has the 'human rights agenda' moved on and left the Convention looking rather old-fashioned and limited?

Consider:

(a) Whether the Convention really does establish basic rights protecting the most important interests of individuals. For example, it is not strong on social rights

(rights to health, education, housing, welfare, etc.) which, for most people, might be much more important than various civil and political rights that are never in issue for them.

(b) Whether there are 'new' interests and concerns that have come to the top of the political agenda in Europe and which ought to be considered for protection as human rights in the Convention. For example, the Convention gives no express protection to the environment (though some environmental rights are implied from Article 8); no special recognition of children's vulnerabilities and their need for rights protection; though committed to pluralism, there is little in the Convention that imposes duties on states to protect and empower women, ethnic or religious minorities, etc.; nothing in the Convention protects animals.

(c) Arguments against expanding Convention rights in this way might include considering

- whether widening the scope of court-enforceable human rights undermines democracy by taking too much away from political representatives and giving too much influence to judges;

- whether legal protection for welfare etc. is best achieved by particular, tailor-made conventions, rather than being grafted onto the European Convention. This, in fact, is what is happening with international conventions of an ever-widening range of matters, including the rights of children and the environment.

CROSS REFERENCE

Consider, on this point, the discussion in Chapter 1, section 1.2.4 (Democratic politics).

2.3.6 Comparisons with the International Covenant on Civil and Political Rights

Though the Convention was inspired by the United Nations, there are a number of rights in the International Covenant on Civil and Political Rights that are not in the Convention. The Fourth and Seventh Protocols of the Convention (see section 2.3.3) added rights from the Covenant that were left out of the original Convention.

In some areas the Covenant continues to give wider or more particular protection than the Convention appears to:

- The Covenant contains specific rights relating to the treatment of prisoners, such as the need to separate remand from convicted prisoners and to treat prisoners humanely.

- The Covenant expressly recognises, to some extent, the particular situation of children.

- The Covenant expressly gives a wider right to participate in public affairs than does the Convention.

CROSS REFERENCE

The International Covenant on Civil and Political Rights is discussed in Chapter 1, section 1.4.4.

- The Covenant gives a right not to suffer discrimination which is more extensive in its effects than the same right in the Convention.

- The Covenant expressly guarantees rights for minorities.

- The Covenant expressly outlaws propaganda for war.

2.4 The states' obligations and the impact of the Convention in domestic law

2.4.1 Sovereign states and international law

The Convention, produced by the Council of Europe, is part of the system of international law. International law operates on the basis of sovereign states that control their own affairs and should not interfere in the affairs of other states. There is no system of 'World government'; the authority of the United Nations comes solely from the agreement of sovereign states. It follows that the primary responsibility to protect individuals from human rights abuses lies with the states. The irony is obvious, since the states are also the perpetrators of human rights abuses. The Convention, therefore, is, ultimately, a voluntary system by which the member states agree to uphold human rights in their territories. To emphasise the 'voluntary' nature of the obligation is, however, slightly misleading. Of course European states can choose not to sign the Convention or to leave the Council of Europe. States are entitled to 'denounce' the Convention and no longer be bound by it, though Article 58 requires a minimum period of five years from signing before this can be done. But such steps are likely to be politically embarrassing and damaging, and considerable costs may flow from the loss of reputation that will follow.

2.4.2 The obligation of the states

Under the Convention and the Protocols, the 'High Contracting Parties' (the nation states that have signed and ratified the Convention) agree to the following:

- **Secure the rights for everyone.** By Article 1 the states agree 'to secure to everyone within their jurisdiction the rights and freedoms defined in section 1 of this Convention'. This is the basic, general obligation that the states enter into. It obliges states to alter and amend their laws if necessary and also the practices of their government, police, and other public authorities in order to ensure that the Convention rights and freedoms are secured. It may also impose 'positive duties' which require states to introduce new laws or new government practices, perhaps even to spend large sums of money on so doing. States must do what is required to secure human rights; though, in contexts where money may have to be spent, what is required may be no more than is reasonable in the circumstances.

  CROSS REFERENCE

  The 'positive duties' of states are discussed in Chapter 6, section 6.6.

  It is important to note that a state's duty under Article 1 is owed to 'everyone'. What this means is that the state must protect the human rights not only of 'citizens' but of all human beings, including, for example, foreigners or people who are in the country illegally. In particular, it means that states cannot do what, for example, the Nazis did in respect of Jews, and identify a group for discrimination and simply declare that they are not citizens.

- **Provide effective remedy in national courts.** By Article 13 the states agree to provide an effective remedy in their courts for violations of the Convention. This demonstrates that the first and primary responsibility for human rights protection, the

▶ **CROSS REFERENCE**
Article 13 is discussed in Chapter 5, section 5.1. Exhausting domestic remedies is discussed in detail later in this chapter (section 2.7.2).

first line of defence for victims, lies with the national courts, not the ECtHR. The latter should only be called upon following a failure or inability of the national courts to put the Convention properly into effect. It follows that applicants to the ECtHR must have 'exhausted their domestic (national) remedies' before their case can be 'admissible' and heard by the Court.

- **Allow access to the ECtHR.** States must ensure that a person who is unable to get satisfaction from the national courts is able to exercise their right under Article 34 of the Convention and go to the ECtHR in Strasbourg. Article 34 requires that states do not 'hinder in any way the exercise of that right'.

- **Accept judgments of the ECtHR.** Where a case goes to the ECtHR the signatory states, under Article 46, agree to 'abide by the final judgment of the Court in any case to which they are parties'. Thus, if the Court orders the payment of money as 'just satisfaction' for the violation, then the states agree to pay it.

2.4.3 'The state'

These obligations are on the state in all its forms: a 'government', which makes policy and puts it into effect using the resources of the state (in the United Kingdom: the Prime Minister, Cabinet, ministers, and civil service, etc.); a 'legislature' that make the laws for society, laws which apply to both the population and the government (in the United Kingdom: the House of Commons and the House of Lords); and the 'courts' or 'judiciary' who interpret and apply the laws in particular cases (in the United Kingdom: the courts and tribunals). Under the Convention the state as a whole (represented at Strasbourg by the government) has responsibility to ensure that all these bodies comply with the Convention. As can be seen in Chapter 4, however, the situation is different under UK law. In particular, Parliament, under the Human Rights Act, is not required only to legislate compatibly with the Convention, and the courts must apply national law even if it is incompatible.

A whole range of other public bodies also exercise state power in the sense that the state, through the government, is responsible for them to Strasbourg. These include regional and local government and the huge range of so-called 'non-departmental public bodies' or 'quangos' which characterise the 'multi-layered' character of modern administrative life. Indeed, the ECtHR has even insisted that, in some circumstances, 'the state' can be responsible for the activities of private companies or organisations (e.g. independent schools in respect of punishments which may violate Article 3).

2.4.4 Reservations

When signing the Convention and accepting its general obligations, states may, nevertheless, choose to exempt particular laws from the provisions of the Convention. This is called 'making a reservation'. A reservation can be made in respect of any provision in the Convention. Reservations are controversial and undesirable since they enable states to choose the Convention rights they will protect.

> **reservations and derogations** Making a reservation can be contrasted with the power to 'derogate' under Article 15. A derogation is a suspension of agreed Convention obligations. States can only derogate in times of war or national emergency and cannot derogate in respect of the most fundamental rights, such as the right not to be tortured. Derogation is discussed in Chapter 7, section 7.2.

Article 57 Reservations

1. Any state may, when signing this Convention or when depositing its instrument of ratification, make a reservation in respect of any particular provision of the Convention to the extent that any law then in force in its territory is not in conformity with the provision. Reservations of a general character shall not be permitted under this article.

2. Any reservation made under this article shall contain a brief statement of the law concerned.

The scope of this power was discussed by the ECtHR in *Belilos* v *Switzerland* (1988) 10 EHRR 466 (paras 52–59). Reservations must be interpreted restrictively. The ECtHR stressed that a reservation cannot be general in scope. It must identify, clearly and precisely, a specific legal provision or provisions to which it applies and the kinds of disputes and issues which are thereby likely to be exempted from Convention control. The brief statement of the law that is to be exempted, which is required by Article 57(2), is necessary for legal certainty and so its absence makes any purported reservation invalid. This provision must be fulfilled even if the nature of the legal system makes this difficult (as was the case in *Belilos* dealing with criminal procedure in a federal system). Reservations apply to the statutes etc. they specify. They do not automatically apply to similar laws enacted later (*Dacosta Silva* v *Spain* App 6996/01, judgment of 2 February 2007). Where, however, a reservation meets the requirements of Article 57, it will be given effect by the Court (see, for example, *Jecius* v *Lithuania* (2002) 35 EHRR 16).

The United Kingdom has a reservation in respect of Article 2 of the First Protocol, the right to education. It is maintained under the terms of the Human Rights Act 1998. The reservation, and possible problems with it, are discussed in Chapter 24, section 24.5.

2.4.5 **Extra-territorial application of the Convention**

There is an important question as to whether a state can have obligations under the Convention in respect of actions it undertakes outside its territory. In particular, the end of the Cold War has seen an increasing willingness of European powers (particularly the United Kingdom as an ally of the United States), and not always with the support of the international community, to take military action against states and governments that it believes threaten world peace. The bombing by NATO in Kosovo and Serbia (former Yugoslavia) and the wars in Afghanistan and Iraq are well-known examples. The approach of the ECtHR to applications brought against signatory states in respect of such 'extra-territorial' actions is a developing jurisprudence.

 CASE CLOSE-UP

Al-Skeini v *UK* (2011) 53 EHRR 18

The Grand Chamber considered whether the UK had a duty under Article 2 to investigate deaths of civilians caused by British troops on active service in Iraq. UK courts had held that Article 2 only applied to a detainee who died in a British army prison. Following *Bankovic* (discussed later in this section) it held that Article 1 'jurisdiction' was normally based on a state's territory. There were exceptions and these included where the state exercised effective, overall, administrative control over a state as a consequence of invasion, lawful or otherwise. Effective control was a matter of fact, though the strength of the military presence was a primary factor. On the facts, the UK had a duty, under Article 2, to fully investigate the deaths.

In this case the Grand Chamber has authoritatively summarised the general principles that apply (paras 130–42):

Jurisdiction—the internationally recognised territory

The starting point is that states are obliged to secure Convention rights to everyone within their 'jurisdiction' (Article 1 ECHR). Jurisdiction is defined, primarily, in terms of a state's internationally recognised national territory.

There are, however, significant exceptions to this principle.

European 'espace juridique'

If one Convention country invades another (as Turkey invaded Greece in 1974) then the invading power is, as a matter of principle, responsible for protecting the Convention rights of the invaded population. This is not just based on the fact that the invader exercises political and military control (see Effective control over an area, later in this section) but also on the principle that the Convention is a Europe-wide constitutional instrument and, within Europe, its requirements must be upheld (e.g. *Cyprus* v *Turkey* (2002) 35 EHRR 30; *Al-Skeini*, paras 141–142).

But exceptions to the territorial concept of jurisdiction can also be found in terms of the actions of a Convention state outside Europe.

Embassies and other diplomatic and consular buildings

Actions taken within overseas embassies etc. are considered to be within the jurisdiction of the state. This is consistent with international law, which the ECtHR has adopted.

Extra-territorial jurisdiction can also be found not, as above, on the basis of constitutional principle or international law but, rather, as a matter of fact in an individual case, that some form of control is being exercised.

Effective control: consent

Where a Convention state exercises 'effective control' over an area outside its territory and does so through the 'consent, invitation or acquiescence' of the other state it is likely to have responsibility for Convention breaches attributable to its agents.

Effective control over an area

Whether by consent or otherwise, if a state by lawful or unlawful acts of war obtains effective control over an area then it has the responsibility to secure the rights and freedoms of the population. This applies whether the occupying state governs directly or through its control of the local administration.

In *Al-Jedda* v *UK* (2011) 53 EHRR 23, a Grand Chamber held that the UK had responsibilities under Article 5 (the right to liberty) in respect of an individual detained by the British Army in Iraq. In *Al-Saadoon* v *UK* (2009) 49 EHRR SE11, the UK owed duties under Article 3 (the prohibition on torture) in respect of another Iraqi detainee. In both cases the UK's Convention liability was based on its effective control, based on military action, of parts of Iraq following the invasion in 2003. It was clear from an examination of the facts that *de facto* control was retained by the UK even after UN involvement.

The control must be effective. *Bankovic* v *Belgium* (2007) 44 EHRR SE5 involved alleged breaches of the Convention by NATO-member signatory states in respect of the bombing of a broadcasting station in Belgrade. The Grand Chamber held that bombing from the air did not have the degree of continuity necessary for effective control over former Yugoslavia.

Actions of soldiers and other agents

Even if there is no effective control (whether by consent or otherwise) a state may be responsible for the behaviour of its soldiers and other agents outside its borders. In particular this can apply where the forces of a Convention state have an individual in their custody. In *Issa* v *Turkey* (2005) 41 EHRR 27, the Court accepted that Turkey would have been liable for the actions of its soldiers had they been responsible for kidnapping and murdering Iraqi shepherds in Iraq. Whenever agents of a Convention state exercise *de facto* control over an individual, they are responsible for his or her Convention rights (*Al-Skeini*, 136 and 137).

Vessels and aircraft

Actions on board vessels or aircraft flying the flag of a signatory state or registered in the signatory state are taken to be within its jurisdiction in particular where control is exercised over individuals.

In *Hirsi Jamaa* v *Italy* App 27765/09, Grand Chamber judgment of 23 February 2012, would-be migrants were picked up on the high seas by Italian Navy ships and forcibly returned to Libya. These actions were within Italy's jurisdiction. Similarly, France was responsible for actions by its Navy in boarding an alleged drug-running ship on the high seas (*Medvedyev* v *France* App 3394/03, Grand Chamber judgment of 29 March 2010).

'Dividing and tailoring'

There are, therefore, a number of circumstances in which a signatory state acting outside its territory, in particular acting outside Europe, must adhere to the Convention. It may not be necessary for the Convention state to secure the full gamut of negative and positive obligations expressly found or implied in the Convention to individuals under its control. The ECtHR accepts that the state only has duties to secure those rights that are relevant to the situation of the applicant. Thus the Convention can be 'divided and tailored' in respect of its extra-territorial jurisdiction (*Al-Skeini*, para 137).

 BIGGER PICTURE

This case law is important in respect of the question whether the Human Rights Act applies to the actions of UK soldiers overseas, in Afghanistan, for instance. The issue is addressed in Chapter 4, section 4.11.3.

2.4.6 The Convention and UN measures

Article 103 of the UN Charter states that obligations deriving from a state's membership of the UN are to prevail over any other international obligations they may have entered into. As mentioned in Chapter 1, the UN can require states to take actions which directly affect the rights and freedoms of individuals, and Article 103 appears to remove from such individuals the protection of the ECHR. Thus *Al-Jedda* v *United Kingdom* (2011) 53 EHRR 23 involved an individual interned (detained indefinitely without a fair hearing) by British forces in Iraq. Internment is incompatible with the right to liberty in Article 5 ECHR. The question was whether this right was displaced by the UN Security Council Resolution under which British forces were acting.

Courts have adopted three kinds of answer to this problem.

One is to accept the priority of UNSC resolutions but to minimise the impact on human rights. Thus the UK House of Lords in *R (Al-Jedda)* v *SSD* [2007] UKHL 58 accepted that the applicant could be detained (in breach of Article 5(1)) but he retained rights under other features of Article 5 (such as, perhaps, access to a court under Article 5(4)).

A second approach is to apply human rights norms in disregard of Article 103. In *Kadi* v *Council of the European Union* [2009] 1 AC 1225, the European Court of Justice held that anti-terrorism measures, authorised by the UN, which froze Kadi's financial assets, were illegal under EU law. These orders were incompatible with the EU's commitment to the rule of law, which included respect for human rights as found in the ECHR. Kadi's rights to a fair hearing (Article 6 ECHR) and to the peaceful enjoyment of his possessions (Article 1 of the First Protocol) were violated. The trouble with this position is that it has the danger of placing the states and organisations which do this in what appears to be a deliberate disregard of their obligations under international law.

The third approach is for a national or international court to interpret UN measures in a way that avoids incompatibility with human rights. This was the approach of the Grand Chamber in *Al-Jedda* v *UK*. UNSC Resolutions and other instruments have to be read in the light of the purposes and principles of the UN. These include respect for human rights. It must be presumed, therefore, that UNSC Resolutions do not authorise actions which violate international human rights (such as in the ECHR) unless a clear contrary intention can be discerned. Ambiguities in the language must be resolved in a way that protects human rights (see *Al-Jedda*, paras 102–105). On the facts in *Al-Jedda* no such unambiguous contrary intention could be found and so Article 5 applied and the applicant's internment was found to be a violation. This interpretative approach, however, leaves unanswered the question of what to do if human rights are expressly excluded by the UN measure.

 THINKING POINT

Of these different arguments, which is the most convincing?

2.5 Enforcing the Convention

Rights without remedies and means of enforcement are pointless. Convention rights are enforced either:

- by a state bringing a case against another state (state action) or, more usually,
- by an individual bringing a case against his or her own state (the right of individual application).

2.5.1 State actions (Article 33)

Article 33 Inter-State cases

Any High Contracting Party may refer to the Court any alleged breach of the provisions of the Convention and the protocols thereto by another High Contracting Party.

By signing the Convention each state agrees to be part of a collective system of human rights protection. States are well resourced and able to bring actions, and human rights protection should not be left to the victims, who are the most vulnerable and perhaps least able to proceed. Article 33 does not require the state bringing the action to be acting on behalf of its own nationals. In reality the inter-state procedure has been little used (as of 1 January 2004 there had only been twenty cases and only two dealt with by the ECtHR).

BIGGER PICTURE

For fuller discussion of state actions, see Steiner, H. and Alston, P. *International Human Rights in Context* 3rd edn (2007) Oxford: OUP, Chapter 11B, section 5.

There have been two important inter-state cases dealt with by the ECtHR.

In a case brought by Ireland against the United Kingdom, the ECtHR held that various interrogation techniques used against suspected members of the IRA violated Article 3 (the case, *Ireland* v *United Kingdom* (1979–80) 2 EHRR 25, is discussed in Chapter 9, section 9.2).

The long-standing dispute between Cyprus and Turkey, over the invasion by Turkey in 1974 and the resulting division of the island, has come before the ECtHR. (The Commission had reported large-scale violations in three cases brought in the 1970s.) In *Cyprus* v *Turkey* (2002) 35 EHRR 30, the Court found that there were serious and continuing violations of the Convention in respect of missing and displaced persons.

2.5.2 The right of individual application (Article 34)

The vast majority of cases brought before the Strasbourg institutions are brought by individuals (people, companies, or non-governmental organisations) who allege that they have been the victims of a violation of one or more Convention rights and that the courts of their own country have, for whatever reason, been unable to recognise this and to provide an effective remedy. States are obliged to ensure that anyone in their population is allowed to make such applications and that there are no barriers or hindrances.

Individual application is unusual in international law, though, perhaps, becoming less so. Usually international law depends upon inter-state actions or goes little further than a reporting process by which an international body reports on the extent to which individual countries have fulfilled their obligations. Under the European system an individual, by his or her own motion, can bring their case to the ECtHR and, if the Court rules there has been a violation, obtain a ruling that the Convention has been violated. Consequently the state has an obligation to change the law or its practices for the future. In some cases the Court requires the states to pay financial compensation by way of 'just satisfaction'.

The question of who is able to bring a case under Article 34 is discussed further in section 2.7.1.

2.5.3 **Implementation**

The system of implementation

The strength of the Convention lies in the system of enforcement. Enforcement has two stages.

First, application must be made to the ECtHR (discussed in section 2.6), which decides whether or not there has been a violation of the Convention in particular cases. If there has been a violation, the Court declares this and may, if it thinks it appropriate, award just satisfaction (damages).

 CROSS REFERENCE

Admissibility is discussed at section 2.7.2.

Second, it is the obligation of the state against which the violation has been found to implement the ECtHR's judgment (Articles 1 and 45). The Committee of Ministers has the responsibility of ensuring that the judgments are put into effect both in terms of the individual applicant (the payment of just satisfaction, for example) and in terms of any changes to national law or administrative practice that should follow. The Committee can exert political and diplomatic pressure on states if they are reluctant to execute the judgment. The Committee's ultimate sanction is expulsion from the Council of Europe. Expulsion would have very serious consequences for the reputation of a state and might also have detrimental political, economic, and social effects. Furthermore, expulsion leaves the victim and future victims defenceless. States can also denounce the Convention (as Greece did in 1969).

Friendly settlements

Article 39 requires the ECtHR to 'place itself at the disposal of the parties' with a view to obtaining a 'friendly settlement'. If such a settlement is obtained, the case is then to be struck out of the list. The negotiations and terms of any settlement are secret. There is a danger that a friendly settlement could be a compromise or a pay-off by which a significant breach of human rights is, in secrecy, brushed under the carpet. The Court must be satisfied that any settlement is consistent with respect for human rights and a settlement can be refused if it means that an important issue remains unresolved.

Pilot judgment procedure

Since 2004 the ECtHR has developed a 'pilot' procedure. This is where the Court identifies a 'structural or systemic' problem, or 'similar dysfunction' in the law or practice of a state which causes a large number of similar cases to come before it. In a pilot judgment the Court can identify the problem, specify the remedial action that needs to be taken and the time scale. It can then adjourn any individual cases whilst the reforms are being made (these can be resumed if the state fails to act). The Committee of Ministers is informed and, retaining its Convention role of supervising implementation, can seek to ensure the remedial action is taken. The Committee can refer the state's proposals for change back to the Court for final evaluation.

🔍 CASE CLOSE-UP

Greens v United Kingdom [2011] 53 EHRR 21

The case illustrates the Court dealing with a continuing violation of a Convention right which gives rise to a large number of pending or potential applications—in this case the UK's refusal to give at least some serving prisoners the vote in breach of a clear ruling (for discussion of the substantive issue refer to Chapter 25, section 25.3.2.)

1. The Court reaffirmed that even in situations where states are refusing to remedy a situation, it will not award punitive damages (i.e. a financial penalty which aims at punishment and therefore goes beyond compensation for what has been lost or suffered).

2. The Court then adopted a pilot judgment procedure (see earlier in this section).

3. As part of the pilot judgment:

    (a) it imposed a timetable, six months, on the UK to come up with appropriate remedial measures;

    (b) struck out pending cases from individual prisoners and refused to accept any new ones but with the threat of resumption if the UK failed to adopt suitable measures;

    (c) urged the UK to adopt general measures but also to consider other solutions, such as friendly settlements, of the outstanding cases.

The case illustrates the increasing importance of the Court's role in implementation. This complements the political and diplomatic role of the Committee of Ministers and gives implementation a more judicial quality, which is easier to reconcile with the rule of law.

 BIGGER PICTURE

Pilot procedures are discussed in, for example, *Broniowski* v *Poland* (2006) 43 EHRR 1, paras 189–194, and formalised in Rule 61 of the Court's Rules.

2.6 The European Court of Human Rights (ECtHR)

2.6.1 History

The ECtHR sits in Strasbourg in France. It was established in 1959 and decided its first case (*Lawless* v *Ireland*) in 1960. It must, of course, be distinguished from the Court of Justice of the European Union, the highest court of the European Union, which sits in Luxembourg.

Under the original Convention (signed in 1950) the Court was envisaged as a part-time institution. Then, the assumption was that, since member states were democratic, pluralist, and committed to the rule of law, cases that needed to go to the Court would be few and far between. Originally, the Court was assisted by another part-time institution, the European Commission of Human Rights. The Commission had a principal role in deciding whether applications made to the Court were admissible (i.e. were the kind of case the Court was able to hear). Then, as now, the majority of applications were not: they were inadmissible. The Commission would then forward most admissible cases to the Court for a decision on the merits; it would make its own assessment of the merits which the Court would consider. The Commission also had a role in organising or undertaking fact-finding.

Protocol 11

The European Convention on Human Rights has been one of the most (if not the most) success-ful systems for the international protection of human rights. The success has been particularly based on the right of individual petition and the general willingness of signatory states to accept and respond to adverse decisions of the Court.

The enormous (and continuing) expansion in the number of cases could not be dealt with under the part-time two-tier system of Commission and Court. The system became chroni-cally overloaded, with resulting delays. The Council of Europe eventually responded with the Eleventh Protocol, which introduced major reforms in 1998. The most important of these was the abolition of the Commission and the old part-time court. A new full-time court was created in its place. The new court, assisted by the Registry and the Secretariat, took over admissibility decisions and other functions of the Commission. The Commission's reports on both admis-sibility and merits continue to be referred to by the ECtHR. They must also be 'taken into ac-count' by United Kingdom judges deciding cases under the Human Rights Act 1998, section 2.

Many other important changes to procedure and to the powers of the Court were made by Protocol 11. This led to considerable rewriting of Part 2 of the Convention (which deals with those matters). Provisions which were retained often needed to be renumbered. For example, the right of individual application, originally Article 25, was renumbered as Article 34.

Protocol 11 did not solve the problem of the backlog of cases, and further changes to the procedures and powers of the Court were made by Protocol 14, which came into force in June 2010.

2.6.2 **Functions**

The principal function of the Court is to declare whether or not, in particular cases, there has been a violation of the Convention. Virtually all the cases brought before it are from individuals bringing cases in their own interest against their own state.

- The Court receives an application from the person who alleges they are a victim of a violation or from the state that alleges a violation by another state.
- It considers whether or not the case is admissible (before 1998 this was done by the Commission), see section 2.7.2.
- If a case is admissible the Court can then seek further details and receive further submis-sions from the parties.
- The Court makes a judgment on whether there has been a violation of the Convention. If so, it rules on whether the finding of a violation is a sufficient remedy or whether dam-ages, just satisfaction, should be paid by the state involved and whether the state should also pay the applicant's costs.
- The Court submits its findings, on whether there has been a violation and what the remedy should be, to the Committee of Ministers, which has the responsibility to super-vise the judgment and ensure it is put into effect by the government of the state involved.
- Under Article 47 the Court can be asked by the Committee of Ministers to give an ad-visory opinion. These cannot concern any matter involving the content or scope of the substantive rights, otherwise the opinion might prejudge a later case to be decided by the Court. A request to advise on the compatibility of the Convention with a human rights instrument applying to post-Soviet Union states was rejected on this ground in 2004.

Issues about the election of judges to the Court were the subject of advisory opinions in 2008 and 2010.

If Protocol 16 is brought into effect, highest national courts will be able to seek non-binding advisory opinions on matters of principle relating to particular cases. Advisory opinions are given by the Grand Chamber (see section 2.6.4, The Grand Chamber).

2.6.3 **Publicity and openness**

The ECtHR does most of its work in private, on the basis of forms and other paperwork. The Court holds public hearings, under Article 40, when deciding the merits of a case, but many of its admissibility decisions, especially those taken by a Committee, are done in private and cannot be appealed. The Court must give reasons for its decisions. Reasoned dissenting judgments are permitted. Court documents should be public unless the Court decides otherwise. However, under the oath taken by the judges, the actual deliberations of the judges are secret.

2.6.4 **Organisation and procedure**

The organisation and procedure of the Court is based on Part 2 of the Convention (as amended by Protocols 11 and 14) and on the Rules of the Court. These Rules are made by the Court on the authority of the Convention. The current Rules were brought into effect on 1 January 2016. In all it does, the Court is assisted by a Registry and by legal secretaries.

 BIGGER PICTURE

The Rules of the Court can be found at the website of the ECtHR http://www.echr.coe.int/ECHR/, accessed via 'Basic Texts'.

Plenary Court, President and Vice-Presidents, Sections, Committees, and Chambers

- The full Court is the 'Plenary Court'. It has forty-seven positions, allowing for one judge from each country. In April 2016 there were forty-seven judges with no vacancies. The function of the Plenary Court, under Article 25, is to elect the President and Vice-Presidents and set up the Chambers. The Plenary Court adopts the Rules and elects the Registrar.

- There is a President of the Court and two Vice-Presidents.

- The Court is organised, for administrative purposes, into at least four (currently five) Sections presided over by a President (Rule 25). These Sections have a balance of male and female judges and reflect the geography of Europe. Importantly they also reflect the different legal systems in Europe (e.g. common law or civilian).

The Court can act in the following ways (Articles 26–29):

- Single judge formation. This was introduced under Protocol 14 to help deal with the backlog of cases. Straightforward admissibility decisions can be taken by a single judge appointed by the President. A single judge can declare an application inadmissible, or strike it out, and his or her decision is final—there is no procedure for appeal. If the application is not straightforwardly inadmissible, the single judge must forward it to a Committee or Chamber for further consideration of admissibility.

- Committee. Committees are set up within each section. They consist of three judges of the section and their tasks include decisions on the admissibility of cases brought by individuals (Article 28 and Rule 27). If the Committee disagrees on an admissibility issue, it is then decided by a Chamber. Importantly, a Committee also has jurisdiction to decide the merits of a case it finds admissible (i.e. it can decide whether there has been a violation or not). This is confined to cases which involve well-established principles of Convention law. These decisions, since they do not involve difficult issues of law, are final and not open to re-examination by a Chamber or Grand Chamber.

- Chambers. Chambers are made up of seven judges chosen from within a Section. They are judicial formations within each section. The Chambers decide the admissibility of cases which a Committee is unable to decide. Most importantly, it is the Chambers that decide the merits of the case—whether there has been a violation of a Convention right. The President of the Section sits in each Chamber. A Chamber deciding a case should have on it the judge elected from the state concerned. If not a member of the Section involved, then he or she is appointed ad hoc (for that case only) to the Chamber. The other members of the Chamber are appointed by rotation from the members of the Section (Article 29 and Rule 26).

The Grand Chamber

The Court can also sit as a Grand Chamber and is then at its most authoritative. A Grand Chamber consists of seventeen judges who represent the Court as a whole. Most of the judges who form a Grand Chamber are chosen by lot, but a Grand Chamber must include the President and Vice-Presidents of the Court and the Presidents of the Sections.

Article 30 allows a Chamber to 'relinquish' (hand over) a case to a Grand Chamber if the case raises serious issues about the interpretation of one or more Convention rights or if the case is one which might require an outcome which is inconsistent with a previously delivered judgment by the Court (the Court is not strictly bound by its own earlier decisions and allows the substance of Convention rights to evolve in line with developments in legal, political, and social opinion in Europe). The agreement of both parties is required (this will be dispensed with if Protocol 15 comes into force).

Under Article 43, a Grand Chamber can decide (on the basis of a recommendation by a panel of five of its members) to accept a case referred to it by either party. This is the nearest there is to an appeal under the Convention. To be heard, the panel must accept that the case is exceptional and that it raises a serious question about the interpretation or application of the Convention or a 'serious issue of general importance'. The Grand Chamber rehears the case as it was when declared admissible in the first instance (though it can examine aspects of the admissibility decision if it so wishes). It is concerned with the case as a whole, not just with the particular issues in dispute—see *Yumak and Sadak v Turkey* (2009) 48 EHRR 4, Grand Chamber, paras 71–72. It takes into account the decision of the Chamber but is not bound to agree with that decision. Article 43 allows this right to a rehearing not only to the applicant but also to the defendant state. Though some cases have been controversial (e.g. the decision by the Grand Chamber in *Hatton v United Kingdom* (2003) 37 EHRR 28, which reversed a Chamber's decision that night flying regulations for Heathrow Airport violated the rights of residents to respect for their private and family lives), there is no evidence that the Grand Chamber is any more 'state friendly' than a Chamber.

2.6.5 The judges

At full compliment there are as many judges as there are High Contracting Parties (signatories of the Convention)—forty-seven in 2016.

The judges are elected. They are chosen by the Parliamentary Assembly, which votes for one name out of a list of three provided by the government of each state. The judges do not need to be nationals of the state that puts their name forward (though they usually are) and it must be stressed that they do not sit as representatives of the states that nominate them. They sit in their individual capacity and are expected to be impartial and to display the judicial virtues.

Independence and impartiality

Judges of the ECtHR must be of 'high moral character' and must be qualified in their own country for high judicial office or similar (Article 21(1)). They are required to desist from activities which are incompatible with the demands of a full-time judicial role or with the requirements of independence or impartiality. Political activity, such as being a minister, a member of a legislature, or a prominent activist, is likely to be barred to them on these grounds (see Rule 4). They are elected for a period of nine years and may not be re-elected (Article 23). This was a change introduced under Protocol 14 in June 2010 to avoid the danger that seeking re-election might undermine independence and influence judgments. They cannot be dismissed unless two-thirds of the other judges, in a vote, so decide.

2.7 Taking a case to Europe

A person wishing to take a case to Strasbourg must make a written application to the Court on the form provided (the form is on the Court's website). Applicants need to state (sensibly, but not necessarily, with the help of a legal representative) the facts, the respondent state, the Convention Articles that are alleged to have been violated, the fulfilment of admissibility criteria, the remedy sought, and so on. It should be accompanied by any relevant documentation. The form is submitted to the Registry.

2.7.1 Standing: Article 34

Article 34 controls who can bring a case before the ECtHR (i.e. who has 'standing'). As we shall see in Chapter 5, section 5.4.4, the Article 34 approach is adopted under the HRA for the purpose of bringing human rights cases before the UK courts.

Article 34

The Court may receive applications from any person, non-governmental organisation or group of individuals claiming to be the victim of a violation by one of the High Contracting Parties of the rights set forth in the Convention or the protocols thereto. The High Contracting Parties undertake not to hinder in any way the effective exercise of this right.

The ECtHR is concerned with protecting the rights of individuals and is not a political forum for dealing with general disputes over the law. On the other hand it needs to ensure that real victims, who may be vulnerable and easily silenced, are able to bring cases.

Directly affected

Cases can only be brought by a 'victim', as this is defined by the ECtHR. A victim is a 'person directly affected by the act or omission which is in issue' (*Eckle* v *Germany* (1983) 5 EHRR 1, para 66). Thus a person can only bring a case if their rights have been directly affected by the alleged breach of the Convention.

Potentially, if not actually, affected

A person can be 'directly affected' and a victim even if they have not actually suffered from a breach of a Convention right but they are in a group or class who might potentially suffer. Article 34 does not require a victim to have suffered from a 'measure of implementation'. The ECtHR has said that a law can violate the Convention rights of a person who 'runs the risk of being directly affected by it'.

In *Open Door Counselling* v *Ireland* (1993) 15 EHRR 244, the issue was whether a ban on counselling on the availability of abortions in the United Kingdom, given the illegality of abortions in Ireland, violated Article 10 (right to freedom of expression). Some of the applicants were individual women, none of whom were pregnant but who were women of child-bearing age who could potentially be affected by the ban. The ECtHR held that they were victims (see paras 41–44).

Indirect victims

There are, however, situations in which the ECtHR allows a case to be brought by an 'indirect victim' such as a close relative of the direct victim. The overriding aim is to ensure the Convention remains effective as a system for the protection of human rights.

For instance, where the direct victim has died after lodging the claim, it may be continued by his or her heirs. They are acting on behalf of the direct victim.

The Court does not generally permit applications to be brought by heirs or close relatives when the direct victim died before lodging a claim. The Court is, generally, unwilling to allow the direct victim to be represented by another where that other is claiming to speak, as it were, for the direct victim. Representation of this kind is generally only permitted where the representative has been directly chosen and authorised by the direct victim (see Rules of Court 36 and 45(3)).

However the need to ensure effective protection of human rights has meant that there are important exceptions to the idea that a case can only be brought by a live, direct, victim. These apply particularly, though not exclusively, in the context of alleged violations of Articles 2, 3, and 8.

If the issue involves a serious human rights question and the applicant has sufficient interest (e.g. as a close relative of the direct victim) the Court may allow a case to be brought after the victim's death. This is particularly important in the context of cases alleging breaches of the Convention rights of victims who have died or disappeared when in the custody of the respondent state. Furthermore, it is even possible for someone who is not a relative but who has an interest in the case to bring an action on behalf of the direct victim. Thus in *SP* v *UK* (1996) 22 EHRR CD148, the solicitor who had represented young children in care proceedings was allowed to bring a case on the children's behalf alleging breaches of the Convention in those proceedings. In these situations the concern of the Court is that otherwise the direct victim will be deprived of effective protection of his or her rights, but it is also insistent that there must not be a conflict of interests between the victim and the applicant (see *Lambert*, later in this section, para 102).

Close relatives may even be able to bring cases based upon their own rights (rather than the rights of the deceased or disappeared person), as where their concerns for relatives who have disappeared are met with 'flagrant, continuous and callous disregard' by the authorities which causes suffering in breach of Article 3 (see *Varnava v Turkey* (2010) 50 EHRR 21, a case concerning Turkey's failure to investigate disappearances of members of the Cypriot armed forces during the active phase of the Turkish invasion of Cyprus in 1974.)

 CASE CLOSE-UP

Centre for Legal Resources on behalf of Campeanu v Romania **App 47848/08, Grand Chamber judgment of 17 July 2014**

The ECHR granted standing to an applicant organisation which alleged serious breaches of the Convention in respect of a patient, of Roma origin, who suffered from profound mental illness. He had no known next of kin and no guardian had been appointed by the state. Of particular importance for the Court was that without allowing the Centre to bring the case, serious allegations of neglect of the direct victim would not be heard. In the case the Grand Chamber summarised the rules on standing (see paras 96–103).

 CASE CLOSE-UP

Lambert v France **App 46043/14, Grand Chamber judgment of 25 June 2015**

The ECtHR refused to allow the parents and half-siblings of Vincent Lambert, a man in a 'persistent vegetative state', to challenge, as if they were his direct representatives, the decision to withdraw artificial nutrition and hydration from him, a decision which would lead to his death. In this case (unlike *Campeanu*, above) Vincent Lambert's situation could still be assessed by the Court since the applicants, though not to be treated as Vincent Lambert's representatives capable of expressing his will, were nevertheless close relatives who had standing as indirect victims. Indeed, the Court heard the case and found that there was no breach of Article 2. Secondly, however, the applicants could not be considered as Vincent Lambert's representatives because (unlike the solicitor in *SP v UK*, earlier in this section) there was an apparent conflict of interest between the applicants and Vincent Lambert's wife and also his wishes in so far as these could be known. In that situation the applicants could not be treated as embodying the wishes and interest of the direct victim.

Corporations (companies)

'Person' in Article 34 can include an artificial legal person. Thus commercial corporations, no matter how vast and powerful they may be, can have legally recognised human rights. Company rights are expressly recognised in the Convention in respect of the right to property in Article 1 of the First Protocol, but the Strasbourg institutions have accepted that companies also have other rights, such as the right to a fair trial (Article 6) or a right to freedom of expression (media companies, for instance, enjoy Article 10 rights).

Shareholders are not usually victims of an alleged violation affecting their company. They are not directly affected by a wrong done to the company. In *Agrotexim* v *Greece* (1996) 21 EHRR 250, shareholders in a brewery challenged a range of planning restrictions coupled with inaction by Athens council. The council's actions affected the ability of the brewery to develop its site and hence the value of the applicant's shares. The ECtHR held that it was the company, not the shareholders, which was directly affected. The company, as a legal entity, chose not to bring a case.

Political parties, trade unions, and other 'non-governmental' groups

Other organisations, such as political parties, trade unions, and pressure groups, can also have standing under Article 34 (and also, therefore, before UK courts under the HRA) but only in respect of wrongs done to them as organisations. Trade unions can bring cases in their own name when their complaint is a matter of trade union law, and political parties on issues which affect them organisationally. In *United Communist Party* v *Turkey* (1998) 26 EHRR 121, a political party had no difficulty in showing that they were directly affected by a banning order.

No 'actio popularis'

The ECtHR does not allow **actio popularis**. These are cases in which the allegation is simply that the laws or administrative practices of the state are in breach of the Convention. The person or group making the allegation have not been affected and their rights not interfered with. Most legal systems restrict such actions, since the courts do not like to resolve political disputes rather than to determine the rights of individuals. Standing before the ECtHR requires someone to have been a direct victim (see section 2.7.1) or, in respect of future events, demonstrate a 'reasonable and convincing evidence of the likelihood that a violation affecting him personally will occur' (*Campeanu*, para 101).

Thus associations, pressure groups, political parties, etc. can bring cases which affect them as associations; but they are normally not able to bring cases that simply allege there has been a breach of the Convention on behalf of the population generally, a section of the public, or their members. The issue can be complex: are political parties who put forward candidates at elections directly affected by the electoral system, or is it only the voters? In *Liberal Party* v *United Kingdom* (1982) 4 EHRR 106, for example, the Commission left open the question whether the Liberal Party was a victim of the first-past-the-post electoral system for parliamentary elections in Britain. There were other applicants who, as voters, were directly affected and, anyway, the case was lost on the merits.

In *Norris and the Gay Federation of Ireland* v *Ireland* (1986) 8 EHRR CD 75, the Commission (which in those days had primary responsibility for deciding admissibility), decided the admissibility of an allegation that Irish laws criminalising homosexual activity were in breach of Article 8. The application by N, a gay man, was admissible as he was a potential victim of the laws. The application by the Federation was not admissible since the laws in question could not be applied to them. They were a group campaigning for a change in the law.

Governmental bodies

Government bodies, however, do not have human rights. Under the Convention, it is the state and its agencies which have primary responsibility to protect human rights. Public bodies should not, therefore, be bearers of human rights themselves. Given that 'non-governmental' bodies can be victims, it follows that 'governmental' bodies cannot be. Governmental bodies are organisations which 'participate in the exercise of governmental powers or run a public service under government control' (*Radio France* v *France* App 53984/00, admissibility decision of 23 September 2003).

2.7.2 **Admissibility: Article 35**

Applications must be admissible—they must relate to issues which are within the jurisdiction of the Court to deal with and must disclose a possible violation. The overwhelming majority of applications are not admissible (about 90 per cent). As already mentioned, straightforward admissibility decisions (usually rejections) are taken by a single judge or a Committee and more complex decisions go to a Chamber. There is no direct appeal against a refusal to admit, though both the Chamber and Grand Chamber may deal with issues relating to admissibility if, for instance, these are interlinked with the merits (*Yumak*, para 72). The role of the Registry and the legal secretaries in preparing and advising the Committees on admissibility decisions is very important.

Article 35 lays down the basic admissibility criteria.

Exhaustion of domestic remedies, Article 35(1)

First responsibility for securing human rights lies with the states and they must be given the opportunity to discharge this obligation and remedy any defects in their national laws and practices. Therefore, as is normal in international law, a person who feels that he or she is a victim of a violation must first pursue their case in the national courts. The burden is on the applicant to show that he or she has pursued the issue to the highest level of national court capable of giving a definitive ruling on the national law. In the United Kingdom, for example, this will normally be the Supreme Court.

If the respondent state alleges that domestic remedies have not been exhausted, the burden is on it to show that such remedies exist.

The ECtHR accepts that the rules relating to exhaustion of remedies must be applied

> with some degree of flexibility and without excessive formalism [and] with regard to the object and purpose of those rules and of the Convention generally, which, as a treaty for the collective enforcement of human rights and fundamental freedoms, must be interpreted and applied so as to make its safeguards practical and effective.
>
> (*Ilhan* v *Turkey* (2002) 34 EHRR 36, para 51)

The available remedies must be effective and 'sufficient in theory and practice'. There may be special reasons which absolve the applicant of the need to exhaust domestic remedies. If, for example, going to the national courts would be futile because remedies are merely theoretical rather than real, or evidence suggests that the state and the courts seem incapable of action in the face of serious allegations of official misconduct, then the requirement may be waived.

In *Ocalan* v *Turkey* (2005) 41 EHRR 45, the applicant, a leader of the Turkish Kurds, was wanted on terrorism charges and he was effectively 'kidnapped' by Turkish security police whilst travelling abroad. He was held in detention. He had not sought judicial review of his detention. There was evidence indicating that applications to the Turkish courts in such situations was pointless. Detainees did not have a fair hearing and, even if the court found irregularities, release was never ordered. The ECtHR held that there were special reasons justifying Ocalan's failure to exhaust domestic remedies.

⟩ CROSS REFERENCE
See Chapter 4,
section 4.4.3 on
'declarations of
incompatibility'.

The exhaustion principle does not mean that an applicant must seek an ineffective remedy. In the United Kingdom, for instance, there is currently no need to take a case to the Supreme Court if the best that can be obtained is a 'declaration of incompatability' under section 4 HRA 1998.

However, if there is established a regular practice by which declarations of incompatibility regularly lead to appropriate changes in UK law or administrative practice, the situation may change: see *Burden v United Kingdom* (2008) 47 EHRR 38, Grand Chamber, paras 40–44.

The need to exhaust domestic remedies applies to both state and individual applications. The other admissibility rules, now discussed, only apply to individual applications submitted under Article 34.

Application within six months, Article 35(1)

Individual applications will be inadmissible if they are submitted to the Court later than six months from the date that the applicant was aware or should have been aware of the decision by which domestic remedies were exhausted. The initial application letter or form must be sent to the Secretariat by that time. Where the alleged violation is a continuing situation (e.g. a legal rule which violates a Convention right) and not a specific action taken against the applicant, the six-month rule is irrelevant. The time period will be reduced to four months when Protocol 15 is brought into effect.

Anonymous applications, Article 35(2)(a)

The Court cannot admit individual applications that are anonymous, though, under Rule 47(3), the President can, if requested, take steps to ensure anonymity, and it is clear from the number of cases where the applicant is designated by a letter (e.g. *X* v *a country*) that this is often done.

Substantial similarity, Article 35(2)(b)

The Court will not admit an individual application that is dealing with the same factual situation that it has already examined in an earlier Convention case nor one where the same issue has been submitted to some other form of international investigation (an application to the United Nations Human Rights Committee under the optional protocol to the ICCPR, for example).

Incompatible with the Convention or a Protocol, Article 35(3)(a)

The Court must reject an individual application if it relates to matters that are outside the scope of the Convention's protection. This can be for various reasons such as

- the Convention or Protocol relied on was not in force in the applicant's country at the time of the incident complained about ('*ratione temporis*' (for a reason relating to time)), or
- the applicant is complaining about an alleged wrong not dealt with by the Convention or Protocols ('*ratione materiae*' (for a reason relating to substance)), or
- the applicant was not a victim of the violation ('*ratione personae*' (for a reason relating to the legal person)).

Manifestly ill-founded, Article 35(3)(a)

The majority of individual applications are rejected because they do not disclose an arguable breach of the Convention. The Section Committee or Chamber may consider the merits of the case and report that, on examination, no likely breach is disclosed. The application is then rejected as inadmissible. Merits reviews in the context of admissibility proceedings are an important source of interpretation and understanding of the Convention.

Abuse of the right of application, Article 35(3)(a)

The Court will not admit an application that involves an abuse of the Convention system. The case law, summarised in *SAS* v *France* [2015] 60 EHRR 11 para 67, suggests that an abuse can arise from dishonest or misleading applications, vexatious or threatening language in the application, deliberate breaches of confidentiality in the application, or applications which are, subject to minor quibbles, repeats of earlier rejected ones.

Applicant has not suffered a significant disadvantage

Where an applicant's losses or sufferings are trivial, he or she may find their case is inadmissible. This provision, introduced by Protocol 14, reflects the fundamental nature of human rights. It also assists with reducing the backlog of cases. A case should attain a minimum level of severity, though this is relative. A court should consider both the importance of the matter for the applicant and what is objectively at stake in the case (see *Diaceno* v *Romania* App 124/04, judgment of 7 February 2012, para 41).

In *Ionescu* v *Romania* (2010) 51 EHRR SE7, the applicant had lost a breach of contract case worth €90. Since this was, for him, a small sum the Court found the application inadmissible.

However, a matter with trivial consequences may still be admissible if so required by proper respect for human rights. Likewise, an issue which has not been adjudicated by a national court cannot be rejected on the no significant disadvantage ground (this second proviso will not apply after Protocol 15 comes into effect).

2.7.3 Interim measures

Rule 39 of the Court's Rules permits the Court to take interim measures which it considers appropriate and which prevent a state from taking actions, such as deportation, whilst the full hearing and judgment by the Court is awaited. These are binding on the state concerned and are appropriate where the Court considers the applicant otherwise faces a 'real risk of serious, irreversible harm' (see the Practice Direction first issued in 2003). Such measures are particularly relevant to deportation and extradition cases.

The deportation of Omar Othman (Abu Qatada) from the United Kingdom was prevented for about three years until the Court's final decision (which, anyway, held that it would violate Article 6). In 2012 the issue returned to the domestic courts.

2.7.4 Fact-finding

When a case is declared admissible it is the duty of the Court (under Article 38) to continue to examine the case. This usually involves seeking further information from either party and seeking agreement as to the facts. The Court's resources are such that for most situations it must rely on the representations of the parties. However, Article 38 authorises the Court to 'undertake an investigation'. Under Rule A1 a Chamber may adopt 'any' investigative measures, and these can include appointing one or more of its members to conduct an on-site investigation. The respondent state, as well as the applicant, must assist the implementation of these measures.

2.7.5 Evidence and proof

The Court is aware of its role as a protector of the human rights of, often, very vulnerable people. As such there are no procedural barriers to evidence. 'The Court adopts the conclusions that are, in its view, supported by the free evaluation of all evidence, including such inferences as may flow from the facts and the parties' submissions' (*DH v Czech Republic* (2008) 47 EHRR 3). Likewise it does not always insist that the burden of proof must lie with the applicant.

2.8 Reform

The huge backlog of cases experienced by the Court in the early years of the twenty-first century is much reduced. This follows from reforms, discussed earlier, such as the single judge formation (dealing with the many inadmissible applications that are received, see section 2.6.4), the pilot judgment procedure (dealing with single issues which generate multiple applications, see section 2.5.3), toughening the admissibility criteria (the need for 'significant disadvantage', see section 2.72), and a system for identifying and dealing with priority cases, see section 2.6.4.

For the Conservative government in the UK there remains a wider problem. The Court, it is alleged, has allowed the Convention to evolve beyond anything that was anticipated in 1950. Under the spur of individual application, the Convention has developed into something approaching a European bill of rights, aiming to establish a common basis of human rights throughout Europe, irrespective of the existence of genuine threats of totalitarianism. Many of its cases are against countries and governments which have strong, democratic institutions, albeit imperfect ones, and a clear commitment to pluralism and the rule of law. Some countries feel that the independence and authority of their own courts, parliaments and governments are being challenged.

These points contribute to the critique of the Court which is part of the context of the Conservative government's reforms of human rights law in the UK in 2016.

Summary

- The Convention and the ECtHR are the creation of the Council of Europe (not the European Union) and grew out of the devastation of Europe at the end of the Second World War.
- Under the Convention, member states of the Council of Europe agree to secure for everyone in their territories the rights and freedoms listed in the Convention and agree to abide by the judgments of the ECtHR, a court created by the Council.
- The great strength of the Convention system lies in the right of individual application by which individual victims of a violation of Convention rights can take their own government to the Court.
- Court procedure and organisation is important. About 90 per cent of all applications to the Court are 'inadmissible' and do not go forward to judgment. The grounds of admissibility include the need to 'exhaust domestic remedies', which gives effect to the point that the primary duty to secure human rights for all lies with the nation states.

? Self-test questions

1. Distinguish the Council of Europe from the European Union.

2. What are the institutions established by the statute of the Council of Europe and what is their primary function?

3. What is the function of the Office of the Human Rights Commissioner of the Council of Europe?

4. What are the principal obligations of states under the ECHR?

5. What is the basic principle governing the extra-territorial application of the ECHR? Give two examples of where it has been applied.

6. In outline, what are the purposes of Protocols 11, 14, 15, and 16?

7. What is the function of the Grand Chamber?

8. How does someone become a judge of the European Court of Human Rights?

9. What is a 'pilot procedure'? Give an example of its use.

10. What is the right of individual application?

 For suggested approaches, please visit the Online Resource Centre.

? Exam questions

1. Critically discuss the view that the ECtHR has become a constitutional court for Europe rather than a final backstop aimed at preventing the rise of undemocratic and oppressive governments.

2. Josephine Bloggs, who lives in the UK, alleges that she has been a victim of a violation of her rights under the ECHR. Are her claims admissible (do not discuss their substance unless relevant to admissibility)?

   (a) She complains that her privacy has been invaded when she was photographed in the street, violating Article 8. The photographer immediately destroyed the film, but Josephine feels there is an important principle at stake.

   (b) She complains that, under a court order relating to anti-social behaviour, she is prevented from visiting the town where her friends live and this violates Article 2 of the Fourth Protocol.

   (c) Her lawyer advises her that taking her cases through the UK courts is pointless because of clear Court of Appeal decisions, so she goes straight to Strasbourg.

 For suggested approaches, please visit the Online Resource Centre.

Further reading

Specialist works on the convention include

Lester, A., Pannick, D., and Herberg, J. (see Preface) Chapter 1, D

Ovey, C. and White, R. *The European Convention on Human Rights (Jacobs and White)* 5th edn (2010) Oxford: OUP, Chapters 1 and 2

On the Grand Chamber

Mowbray, A. 'An Examination of the Work of the Grand Chamber of the Court of Human Rights' [2007] *Public Law* (Autumn) 507–528

On reform and remedies

Suchkova, M. 'An Analysis of the Institutional Arrangements within the Council of Europe and within Certain Member States for Securing the Enforcement of Judgments' [2011] 4 *EHRLR* 448–463

3 The European Convention and the law of the United Kingdom

LEARNING OBJECTIVES

- The Convention as an obligation in international law on the United Kingdom.
- The inability of individuals to enforce their Convention rights directly in UK courts.
- Changes to law and administrative practice following from adverse judgments by the ECtHR.
- The persuasive influence of the Convention on UK law.

Introduction

The European Convention on Human Rights (ECHR, discussed in Chapter 2) was never part of UK law (and still is not). Its provisions were not and are not applied directly by UK courts. The Convention was, and remains, part of international law and international law is not directly enforceable in UK courts. The Human Rights Act 1998 (HRA) brings the substance of the rights and freedoms in the ECHR into UK law in particular ways. These are discussed in Chapters 4 and 5. However, prior to the Act coming into force, the ECHR had a significant and increasing influence on UK law and it is this influence which is discussed in this chapter.

3.1 Putting the Article 1 obligation into effect

The UK signed the Convention in 1950. In doing so it accepted the obligation under Article 1 of the Convention to 'secure for everyone within [its] jurisdiction the rights and freedoms in Section 1 of this Convention' (and the Protocols signed up to). This means:

- ensuring that not only the laws, but also the policies and conduct of government and administration under the law, are compatible with the Convention;

CROSS REFERENCE

For further detail on state obligations under the Convention see Chapter 2, section 2.4.2.

- accepting and putting into effect adverse judgments of the European Court of Human Rights (ECtHR).

The right to individual application was granted in 1966. As a consequence, there was an increasing flow of cases taken to the ECtHR alleging breaches of the Convention and, in a significant number of cases, that Court found the United Kingdom to be in violation of the Convention.

CROSS REFERENCE

The right of individual application is explained in Chapter 2, section 2.5.2.

Nothing in the HRA prevents people from continuing to take their cases to Strasbourg. In 1999 (a year before the HRA came into effect) 1,054 applications were received by the Court, though only 32 were admissible. In 2014 the total number of applications was 1,243 (less than half of the 3,663 made in 2011). Of these only 27 resulted in a judgment (30 in 2011). The United Kingdom has one of the lowest application levels as a proportion of the population and the vast majority are inadmissible.

Generally the United Kingdom has fulfilled its obligations under the Convention and made changes to law or administrative practice where required. This has involved, in particular:

- creating a legal framework to regulate matters that relate to Convention rights and which were previously unregulated;
- amending Acts of Parliament;
- changing administrative practices.

Examples are given in what follows.

3.1.1 Matter previously unregulated by 'law'

The Convention is based on the rule of law. Any exercise of government power which affects a Convention right must be adequately regulated by law. In the United Kingdom, this will usually mean an Act of Parliament, but not always. Government authority can also be based on the Royal Prerogative (the residue of the traditional, absolute authority of the Crown that does not require the authority of an Act of Parliament); or on the common law assumption that something that is neither permitted nor forbidden by law is taken to be lawful. In both cases it can be hard to know what specific rules, if any, regulate the conduct in issue. Much is left to the discretion of officials, which can be difficult to challenge in the courts. As a result of the Convention, statutes have been enacted to regulate various government activities which, previously, were not effectively regulated on the basis of law.

- Telephone tapping. In *Malone* v *United Kingdom* (1985) 7 EHRR 14, the ECtHR held that the absence of effective legal regulation of telephone tapping was a violation of Article 8, the right to respect for private life. As a result, the Interception of Communications Act 1987 was enacted. This created an offence of telephone tapping but also introduced a system by which the authorities could obtain interception warrants. By the beginning of the century better control over new forms of surveillance allowed by new technology was necessary. With Article 8 very much in mind, the Regulation of Investigatory Powers Act 2000 was passed, which creates a complex structure of regulation over a number of forms of surveillance.
- The security and intelligence services. In 1989 (the Security Service Act) and 1994 (the Intelligence Services Act) the secret services were, for the first time, identified by Act of Parliament. They were given a legal identity, their functions were described (albeit in very

general terms), and, in particular, a legal structure was created to give some degree of control over their surveillance activities.

3.1.2 Amending or repealing Acts of Parliament

An adverse judgment may require the United Kingdom to change the terms of an Act of Parliament which is regulating some activity.

The law on sexual offences, such as buggery and indecency between males, was reformed by the Sexual Offences (Amendment) Act 2000 (now replaced by the Sexual Offences Act 2003). In part this was a response to the decision of the ECtHR in *ADT* v *United Kingdom* [2001] 31 EHRR 33, which held that the previous law, the Sexual Offences Act 1956, failed to secure the right to private life of homosexual men.

Such changes are not necessarily narrow, mechanistic responses to an adverse judgment. They may also be explained by a range of other political and social pressures. The Sexual Offences Act 2003, for example, was a wide-ranging, comprehensive reform of the law involving much more than putting Convention rights into effect.

3.1.3 Administrative policies

The state must ensure that not only the law but also the policies it pursues within the law and the activities of its agents (its civil servants, police, prison officers, and others) are compatible with the Convention. The Convention has had some of its most significant effects in this area. Examples include:

- The rights of prisoners. A large number of cases involving the United Kingdom have been to do with prisoners' rights. The Convention has been a significant influence for the reform not only of the law but also the practices of the Prison Service on issues like prisoners' rights to correspond with lawyers, to be subject to fair disciplinary procedures, and to have the length of their sentence determined by the judiciary rather than the executive. Prisoners' cases are found throughout this book, but are considered especially in Chapter 21.

- Homosexuals in the military. The general ban on gay men and lesbian women in the British armed forces was ended as a result of an adverse decision of the ECtHR (*Smith and Grady* v *United Kingdom* (2000) 29 EHRR 493).

3.2 The status of international law

3.2.1 The dual system: no direct enforceability

Changes like those just mentioned were derived from the UK's obligations under international law that flowed from its signature to the ECHR. What was not possible was for a person to take a case to a UK court and to have a right or freedom found in the Convention directly enforced as a matter of UK law: the point of the HRA is to make this possible. The rights and freedoms in the Convention, therefore, were not and are not part of UK law.

The Convention is an instance of treaty-based international law. It is one of the many international treaties the United Kingdom has entered into. Many such treaties deal with general issues, such as the environment, and do not aim to create rights for individuals. Others aim at creating international rights, in the sense of rights recognised and enforced at the international level (e.g. the Rome Statute which creates the International Criminal Court). But there are other treaties which oblige the states that agree to them to secure various rights and freedoms in their own national law. An example, mentioned in Chapter 1, is the International Covenant on Civil and Political Rights (ICCPR).

▶ **CROSS REFERENCE**

For the ICCPR, see Chapter 1, section 1.4.4 and Chapter 2, section 2.3.6.

Under the legal system in the United Kingdom the individual rights and freedoms in such treaties cannot be directly enforced in United Kingdom courts. The United Kingdom operates a 'dual' system, which distinguishes between international and national law, and it is national law that is enforced in the courts.

- International law, found in treaties and other sources, imposes obligations on the United Kingdom as a whole, as a state, and is enforced by whatever mechanisms the treaties, in their separate ways, make available (e.g. the reporting obligation in the ICCPR).
- National law, the law enforced by the courts, consists of Acts of Parliament, including subordinate legislation, and rules of common law.

The reason for 'dualism' is the separation of powers: treaties are made by the executive (though they may require 'ratification' by Parliament) and the executive should not make the law. Some judges, particularly Lord Kerr in the Supreme Court of the United Kingdom (UKSC), would like to see, specifically, human rights treaties made to apply directly in the UK. In his view human rights norms are internationally agreed as being for human good, therefore the separation of powers argument does not apply.

THINKING POINT

Consider Lord Kerr's argument (in *R (SG)* v *Secretary of State for Work and Pensions* [2015] UKSC 16, paras 235–257—do you agree?

It follows, therefore, that for individual rights in international treaties to be enforced there needs to be an Act of Parliament bringing them into effect.

BIGGER PICTURE

The European Union provides a good example.

- EU treaties provide for various individual rights, such as the rights of women to equal pay (Article 157 of the Treaty on the Functioning of the European Union (TFEU)).
- These rights can be directly enforced in UK courts. This is because of two necessary and complementary facts:
  - the United Kingdom is a signatory of the Treaty; *and*
  - the United Kingdom has enacted legislation (section 2 of the European Communities Act 1972) which requires that individual rights found in the EU treaties should be part of the law of the United Kingdom and enforced in the national courts.

It should be noted, though, that whilst treaty-based international law is not directly enforced in the United Kingdom, *jus cogens* (the compulsory, customary law of nations) is treated as an enforceable part of the common law of the United Kingdom.

In *A* v *Secretary of State for the Home Department* [2005] UKHL 71, the House of Lords recognised that the prohibition of torture was part of the *jus cogens* (see para 33). The case is discussed in Chapter 9, section 9.4.

CROSS REFERENCE

Jus cogens is defined in Chapter 9, section 9.4.1.

3.2.2 A 'persuasive and pervasive influence'

Even though they are not directly enforced, individual rights founded in international law, such as those in the ECHR, are not merely ignored. They cannot have priority over clear national law, but can be taken into account by the courts and can influence the decisions they make in various ways.

The point was made by Lord Bingham in *R* v *Lyons* [2002] UKHL 44, which was a case dealing with the impact of the ECHR prior to the HRA; but what his lordship says of the Convention applies to all other international treaties.

> rules of international law not incorporated into national law confer no rights on individuals directly enforceable in national courts. But although international and national law differ in their content and their fields of application they should be seen as complementary and not as alien or antagonistic systems. Even before the Human Rights Act 1998 the Convention exerted a persuasive and pervasive influence on judicial decision-making in this country, affecting the interpretation of ambiguous statutory provisions, guiding the exercise of discretions, bearing on the development of the common law. I would further accept . . . that the efficacy of the Convention depends on the loyal observance by member states of the obligations they have undertaken and on the readiness of all exercising authority (whether legislative, executive or judicial) within member states to seek to act consistently with the Convention so far as they are free to do so.
>
> (para 13, Lord Bingham)

Examples of the 'persuasive and pervasive' influence of the Convention, prior to the HRA, are given in what follows in this chapter.

3.3 The impact of the Convention on the development of the law

3.3.1 The interpretation of statutes

An important influence of the Convention prior to October 2000 was on the way 'ambiguous' statutory provisions were interpreted. The basic constitutional position is that Parliament is 'supreme' and free of constitutional restraint as to content. No court can invalidate an Act of Parliament on the grounds that it is unconstitutional or incompatible with human rights. Nevertheless, the words in an Act of Parliament need to be interpreted (made sense of) and applied to the facts of particular cases. This is the constitutional role of the courts.

The general rule of statutory interpretation is that the courts aim to give effect to the intention of Parliament and this intention is best found by a 'literal' reading of the words (using their ordinary, dictionary definitions). Where the meanings of the words are uncertain, where, for example, they may be ambiguous (capable of more than one meaning), or where they lead to an absurd result that Parliament would not have intended, the courts have to decide what the intention of Parliament was. In doing this they:

> have recourse to recognised principles of interpretation [such as the principle that Parliament intends to legislate compatibly with the UK's international obligations, mentioned immediately] and also a variety of aids, some internal, found within the statute itself [such as the 'long title' to the Act or section headings], some external, found outside the statute [such as Royal Commissions or other reports to which the Act is a response and which therefore indicate the problem (the 'mischief') the Act aims to resolve].
>
> *Wilson v First County Trust (No 2)* [2003] UKHL 40, para 56

Parliament intends to legislate compatibly with international law

One of the recognised principles of statutory interpretation is that the courts will apply unclear or ambiguous words (words capable of more than one meaning) in an Act of Parliament by using various assumptions. One of these is an assumption that Parliament intends to legislate in a manner that is compatible with the UK's international obligations (such as the ECHR).

In a case involving European Union law, the House of Lords said:

> the words of a statute passed after [a] Treaty has been signed and dealing with the subject-matter of the international obligations of the United Kingdom, are to be construed, if they are reasonably capable of bearing such a meaning, as intended to carry out the obligation and not to be inconsistent with it.
>
> (*Garland v British Rail Engineering* [1983] 2 AC 751, 771 (Lord Diplock))

If the legislation is clear, however, it needs to be given full effect by the courts even if to do so is to violate an international obligation of the United Kingdom. This point was clearly made in *R v Lyons* involving the Convention prior to the HRA.

 CASE CLOSE-UP

R v Lyons [2002] UKHL 44

Criminal defendants (who were company directors accused of fraud) alleged that their trial, which took place before the HRA came into effect, was in breach of Article 6 ECHR. They had been required to incriminate themselves because they were convicted on the basis of answers to questions that, under company law, they had been compelled to give. The House of Lords accepted the general principle that uncertainties in legislation (here companies legislation which made refusal to answer companies inspectors' questions an offence) should be resolved by reference to international law. On the facts, however, there was no such uncertainty. It was clearly Parliament's intention that the prosecution should be able to rely on the compelled evidence, and, under UK law, this intention should be followed.

General words in Acts of Parliament

Acts of Parliament often confer wide, general powers on ministers or others. Such general powers grant a wide discretion (area of judgment and choice) to a minister or other official to make decisions, enact rules, etc. as he or she thinks is appropriate. However, it is a general rule of administrative law in the United Kingdom that such discretion is never unlimited and must be properly exercised. Under the influence of international law, particularly human rights law, the courts have developed the principle that general words in an Act of Parliament cannot authorise actions that violate fundamental human rights. If Parliament does intend that such a discretion may be exercised in a way that violates human rights, then it must make this intention expressly clear and leave no room for judicial interpretation. This embodies the idea of 'legality' and depends on the common law's recognition of 'fundamental rights' which is discussed towards the end of this chapter (at 3.5.2). It is a principle that applies to the interpretation of statutes generally and is not just related to the HRA.

Secondary or subordinate legislation

The UK courts, again acting independently of the HRA, have developed the legal rule that subordinate legislation is void if it is incompatible with fundamental rights, such as those in the Convention.

> **secondary or subordinate legislation** These are regulations of various kinds which are enacted not by Parliament but by a minister, a department, a governmental body, etc. The authority to enact these rules is found in an Act of Parliament. The Act identifies the point and purposes of the regulations and any regulation that goes beyond that which the Act allows can be challenged in court and declared to be invalid (without legal effect). The courts say it has been enacted *ultra vires* (beyond the powers in the Act). (See also Chapter 4, for further discussion.)

The ultimate supremacy of Parliament is accepted since subordinate legislation which is required, by the clear words of its authorising Act, to disregard fundamental rights will be applied.

In *R* v *Secretary of State for Social Services ex parte Joint Council for the Welfare of Immigrants* [1996] 4 All ER 385, the government, on the basis of a general power to make social security regulations, introduced regulations that denied asylum seekers benefits unless they applied instantly on arrival in the United Kingdom. In the view of the Court of Appeal the regulations meant that genuine asylum seekers were placed in a dilemma between pursuing their fundamental right to seek asylum but starving whilst doing so, or giving up their claim and being deported but probably fed. The regulations were void: such a policy needed express, unambiguous primary legislation.

Why the Human Rights Act?

Given these existing influences on the way legislation is interpreted and applied by the courts, why was the HRA necessary? As can be seen in Chapter 4, nothing in the Act allows the courts to invalidate an Act of Parliament. But the Act does:

- place a legal (statutory) duty on the courts to continue what they were previously doing on a discretionary basis;
- allow them, as we shall see, much more scope to give effect to statutes in ways which are compatible with the Convention. The interpretative moves, illustrated earlier in this section, are confined to places where the meaning of an Act is uncertain or unclear. As we

shall see, the HRA allows the courts to give effect to legislation in Convention-compliant ways, even when the words of the Act are clearly not compliant, so long as this does not undermine the basic policies the Act is putting into effect. This goes much further than what was permissible prior to the Act.

3.3.2 Development of public law rights and judicial review

The law has recognised public law rights at least since the time of Queen Elizabeth I. Today these rights are normally asserted through a procedure called 'judicial review'. An individual, company, or organisation can challenge a decision or action of a public authority, including a minister, on the grounds that the decision or action was, in outline terms, unlawful (done outside the authority's powers), unreasonable, or unfair.

Judicial review and human rights

Judicial review involves the High Court reviewing the lawfulness of an official's decision, not retaking the decision in place of the official. The issue, prior to the HRA, was whether the court could require an official (including a minister) to take a person's human rights into account or even require the official to protect human rights as determined by the court. Perhaps the most important case is *Smith*, the 'gays in the military' case. An earlier case, involving the Northern Ireland broadcasting ban (*Brind* v *Secretary of State for the Home Department* [1991] 1 AC 696), is also relevant.

 CASE CLOSE-UP

R v *Ministry of Defence ex parte Smith* [1996] 1 All ER 257

A number of gay men and lesbian women were dismissed from the armed forces. This was done on the basis of a rule, made under the Royal prerogative, that homosexuals were to be administratively discharged from the armed forces irrespective of their service record or behaviour. The ban was based on the simple fact of a person's sexual orientation. The ban was challenged in the courts on the basis that it was an unreasonable exercise of power, by the Ministry of Defence, because it violated the right to respect for private life (Article 8 ECHR). The Court of Appeal upheld the ban.

- Under ordinary judicial review the issue was whether the ban was within the range of decisions and policies that were open to a reasonable decision-maker.

- Where human rights are involved, it is not necessary to prove bad faith or an abuse of power by the minister. It was accepted (by Lord Bingham) that 'the more substantial the interference with human rights, the more the court will require by way of justification before it is satisfied that the decision is reasonable [in the public law sense of the term]'.

- However, the Convention could not be directly enforced in the courts: it is no more than part of the 'background' to the case and (said Lord Bingham) 'The fact that a decision-maker failed to take account of Convention obligations when exercising an administrative discretion is not of itself a ground for impugning that exercise of discretion'.

- The primary decision-maker was the Ministry of Defence. The ministry had grounds for the ban (e.g. the efficiency of the armed forces), which, it judged, outweighed whatever rights the individuals might have.

- There were clearly issues relevant to the question whether the Convention had been complied with, but these were not for the Court of Appeal.

- Under ordinary principles of judicial review, there was no basis to set the decision aside as being unreasonable.

The principle in *Smith* requiring compelling justification for a decision that interferes with Convention rights was followed, and strengthened, in later cases (e.g. *R v Lord Saville of Newdigate ex parte A* [1999] 4 All ER 860).

In *Doherty v Birmingham CC* [2008] UKHL 57, the House of Lords dealt with an unqualified statutory power of a public authority landlord to evict. They thought that the 'reasonableness' of the eviction could be challenged, by the tenant, through ordinary judicial review proceedings. The similarity of judicial review grounds with those based on human rights was emphasised (see paras 108–109 and 135, in particular).

But the basic problem remained: under the principles of judicial review the particular balance that the public authority (minister or official) made, between a Convention right and the public interest, could not be set aside by a UK court so long as the authority had acted in good faith and had taken the Convention right fully into consideration. In other words, a court could not adjudicate directly on whether or not a Convention right had been violated but only on whether it had been properly taken into consideration.

The issue came to a head when the *Smith* case went to Strasbourg. In *Smith and Grady v United Kingdom* (2000) 29 EHRR 493, the ECtHR held that there had been a violation of Article 8 (the right to respect for private life) and (more importantly in the context of this chapter) of Article 13, the right to a remedy. Judicial review proceedings did not allow UK courts to give proper consideration to Convention rights. The ECtHR said:

> the threshold at which the High Court and the Court of Appeal could find the Ministry of Defence policy irrational was placed so high that it effectively excluded any consideration by the domestic courts of the question of whether the interference with the applicants' rights answered a pressing social need or was proportionate to the national security and public order aims pursued, principles which lie at the heart of the Court's analysis of complaints under Article 8 of the Convention.

(para 138)

Why the Human Rights Act?

The HRA places a clear duty on the UK's courts to ensure that, unless legislation requires otherwise, ministers, officials, and public authorities protect the Convention rights of the people they deal with when exercising their powers. The courts now have the job of deciding whether the Convention rights have been secured (this matter is explained in Chapter 4, particularly section 4.6.1). Previously this could not be done directly and the courts had to accept decisions that might not have been compatible with the Convention but which were within the range of 'reasonable' decisions the authorities could take. The situation remains that, in cases not involving the HRA, there was and is no enforceable legal duty on officials to exercise statutory discretions in line with the ECHR (confirmed by *R (Hurst) v London Northern District Coroner* [2007] UKHL 13, para 56).

3.3.3 Development of private law

The Convention, of course, is primarily to do with the relations between state and individual (though it sometimes requires the states to make changes to private law to ensure that the Convention rights and freedoms are properly secured). Nevertheless, even when developing private law principles, English courts have taken fundamental rights into account.

Defamation and political bodies

▶ CROSS REFERENCE

For freedom of expression see Chapter 17; the celebrity cases are discussed in Chapter 22.

The law of defamation allows a person to seek damages from another on the grounds that the other has published something that lowers his reputation. Commercial companies can protect their reputations in this way but the courts have held that political and public bodies, including local councils, cannot. The reason is to protect freedom of expression and to ensure that the right to criticise and oppose public bodies is not curtailed. In *Derbyshire County Council* v *Times Newspapers Ltd* [1993] AC 534, the House of Lords, disagreeing with the Court of Appeal, made it clear that this recognition of freedom of speech was based on fundamental principles in the common law and was not the direct enforcement of Convention rights.

Confidentiality and privacy

The common law and equity have long provided remedies to protect certain sorts of confidential information, such as medical records or matrimonial intimacies. Under the influence of the right to respect for private life in the Convention, the protection of 'confidentiality' has become the protection of 'privacy' (a wider notion altogether). The point is illustrated by a number of celebrity cases, such as litigation in which Michael Douglas and Catherine Zeta-Jones sued *Hello!* magazine for publishing unauthorised photographs of their wedding. What has happened is that a well-established legal principle allowing a person to protect matters which are 'confidential' (e.g. medical history, commercial secrets) has been developed to include matters which are merely 'private' (the Douglas–Zeta-Jones wedding, publicised and attended by many guests, could not be said to be 'confidential'; but it was intended to be private). The right to 'private life' in Article 8 of the Convention clearly influenced the way the courts approached the matter.

Why the Human Rights Act?

▶ CROSS REFERENCE

This so-called 'horizontal effect' of the Convention on private law is discussed in Chapter 4, section 4.7.

The HRA further strengthens this approach by the courts and makes a consideration of the Convention a duty, not just judicial discretion. The Act does not directly impose the Convention on private law; however, it does put a general duty on courts to act in line with the Convention, including when dealing with private law.

3.4 The European Union

European Union (EU) law recognises and gives effect to human rights. Since its early cases the European Court of Justice (ECJ) (now the Court of Justice of the European Union (CJEU)) insisted that EU law should uphold fundamental rights. These rights were found in the ECHR but also reflected the legal and constitutional traditions of member states. Member states wished to give this commitment to fundamental rights the authority of a treaty. To this end the EU's Charter of Fundamental Rights was proclaimed in 2000 and annexed to the Nice Treaty but it did not have direct legal force. It was not until the Lisbon Treaty (in force from 2009) that the Charter was given binding effect, and so equal to a treaty.

The Charter of Fundamental Rights codifies and makes more 'visible' the fundamental rights already recognised by the EU. By Article 6 of the Treaty on European Union (TEU), the EU 'recognises' the Charter—though it also continues to recognise fundamental rights in its general law.

The Charter has the same legal value as an EU Treaty. Its terms are binding on EU institutions (such as the EU Commission); but they are also binding on member states (acting through their parliaments, courts, executives, and administrative systems) when they are implementing EU law. For example, the Court of Appeal in *R (Sandiford)* v *Foreign and Commonwealth Office* [2013] EWCA Civ 581, held that a decision to refuse legal aid to a woman facing the death penalty in Indonesia was not a decision implementing EU law and therefore did not engage her Charter rights, including Article 47—the right to a fair trial, including the possibility of legal aid (the decision was upheld without reference to this argument by the Supreme Court).

The Charter lists individual rights and freedoms found in the ECHR (such as the right to liberty, Article 6), but also rights and freedoms from other sources (such as the right to asylum, Article 18, or access to documents, Article 42). It also contains a number of principles, which are not expressed as rights, but which must be given weight by courts applying the Charter (e.g. that the EU should respect the rights of the elderly, Article 25). It includes, therefore, but goes way beyond the civil and political rights in the ECHR. Title IV on 'solidarity', for instance, contains a number of employment, social, and environmental rights.

The rights, freedoms and principles are to be interpreted in line with general provisions in Title VII. Article 52 allows rights etc. to be limited in their application, but only so long as the 'essence' of the right is guaranteed and the limitations are lawful and subject to tests of proportionality and necessity. Where Charter rights correspond with ECHR rights, their meaning is the same as under the ECHR, although the EU can give 'more extensive' protection.

The point of the Charter is to codify and give formal expression to existing EU fundamental rights. Article 6(1) makes it clear that the Charter does not 'in any way' extend the competences (areas of activity) of the EU. An explanatory document sets out the sources of the rights (in treaties, ECJ/CJEU case law, etc.), and this document must be given 'due regard' in applying the Charter. These restraints are unlikely to undermine the evolutionary nature of rights, particularly those originating in the ECHR and subject to the jurisdiction of the ECtHR.

EU law, of course, applies in the UK by virtue of the European Communities Act 1972. Individual rights are directly enforced on the authority of section 2(1), and this will include the fundamental rights found in the 'general law' of the Union. Any conflicts with UK statutes are resolved in favour of EU law by virtue of section 2(4) and interpretation of EU law by the CJEU must be followed by UK courts (section 3). A good example is *R (Davis)* v *Secretary of State for the Home Department* [2015] EWHC 2092, where the High Court declared that the Data Retention and Investigatory Powers Act 2014 (DRIPA) (an Act of Parliament dealing with the retention and disclosure of communications data) was incompatible with Articles 7 and 8 of the Charter, as these provisions had been interpreted by the CJEU in *Digital Rights Ireland* v *Minister for Communications, Marine and Natural Resources* [2015] QB 127. The High Court disapplied the Act from 31 March 2016. Though Article 8(3) does not expressly say so, it was interpreted by the CJEU as mandating domestic law to require judges to participate in the issuing of warrants to compel ISPs to retain and disclose communications data. This was absent in DRIPA. This is an example of the CJEU giving 'more extensive protection' than the ECtHR has done in relation to Article 8 ECHR.

CROSS REFERENCE

For further discussion in the context of Article 8 ECHR – see Chapter 15, section 15.10.2.

By Protocol 30 TEU, however, the UK (along with Poland) seemed to opt out of the Charter. But the impact of the Protocol is not clear. It does not in any general way limit the impact of the Charter's civil and political rights in the UK. This is made clear by the CJEU in *NS* v *SSHD* C-411/10. The Protocol, perhaps, will have more of an opt-out effect in respect of the Charter's social, employment, and economic rights. But even this can be doubted, given that such rights may already be part of EU law, independent of the Charter, and hence already applying in the UK.

Article 6 TEU commits the EU to accede to the ECHR. When this happens, Union institutions will be subject to the jurisdiction of the ECtHR. In *Bosphorous v Ireland* (2006) 42 EHRR 1, the ECtHR accepted a rebuttable presumption that reasoned decisions of the CJEU, based on EU fundamental rights, were also compatible with the ECHR. Such a presumption is not given to the highest courts of the signatory states subject to the ECHR. After accession, the ECtHR may be less 'deferential' to EU institutions and member states implementing EU law. In Opinion 2/13 of 18 December 2014, the CJEU held that the draft agreement on accession was not compatible with Article 6(1) TEU. Fundamentally the relationship between the CJEU and the ECtHR was problematic. As it stood, the preeminent role of the ECtHR on the meaning of Convention rights would adversely affect the autonomy of EU law and compromise the CJEU's treaty-guaranteed position as the final authority on EU law.

3.5 'Human rights' protection in the United Kingdom before the Human Rights Act: a mixed story

Any idea that, prior to the HRA, the United Kingdom was a land in which civil and political rights were unrecognised, is false. It fails to take into account the recognition, development, and protection of such rights through the activities of both Parliament and the courts. It is, of course, a mixed story, but the UK's record on these matters was better than most European countries in the nineteenth and twentieth centuries.

3.5.1 **Parliament**

Some of the most important principles upon which human rights law is based are expressed, and thereby given legal recognition, in Acts of Parliament which remain on the statute book.

- Magna Carta ('the Great Charter of the Liberties of England') was first granted by King John to the nobles in 1215 but was renewed with the authority of a statute in 1297, of which Chapter 29 is still in force. From a human rights perspective, it represents one of the first attempts to express, in specific terms, a range of limits on the powers of the King. Though much of it is to do with the privileges of the landed nobility, the principle of the rule of law and opposition to arbitrary government are famously expressed and can still be cited in court today.

    Chapter 29. No freeman shall be taken or imprisoned, or be disseised of his freehold, or liberties, or free customs, or be outlawed, or exiled, or any other wise destroyed; nor will we not pass upon him, nor condemn him [deal with him] but by lawful judgment of his peers, or by the law of the land. We will sell to no man, we will not deny or defer to any man either justice or right.

- The Bill of Rights 1688. The great constitutional struggles of the seventeenth century ended with the forced abdication of James II (brother of the restored monarch Charles II) and the accession to the throne of William and Mary. From a human rights point of view, the importance of this is that the new monarchs reigned on terms established by Parliament. Under the Bill of Rights Parliament is strengthened and protected (e.g. by securing the right to 'freedom of speech and debates' in Parliament); also it is clearly made unlawful for the Crown to seek to set the laws aside. The Bill of Rights also contains the famous ban on 'cruel and unusual punishments'.

- Habeas Corpus Acts 1640, 1679, 1803, 1804, 1816, and 1862. The prerogative writ of habeas corpus enables a detained person to challenge the legality of his or her detention. It is still available today, though other procedures are often preferred. In the past it has been an important weapon to be used against the threat of arbitrary arrest and detention on the order of the King (as in the seventeenth century). The Acts regulate the procedure, usually, though not always, making the writ easier to obtain.

Some of the most important developments in the recognition and protection of human rights have involved Parliament and legislation. Through political activity, particularly in political parties, but also through pressure groups, protest, and demonstration, the great social and economic struggles of history have forced their attentions on Parliament, which has brought about major reforms bearing on human rights. For example:

- the expansion of the franchise (the right to vote) first for all adult men and then, later, for all adult women;
- the equal rights of women;
- the rights of workers to organise into trade unions.

In particular, of course, the HRA itself should be recognised as Parliament's insistence that the governance of the United Kingdom should be consistent with human rights.

Parliamentary history is, of course, a mixed story. Parliament tends to reflect the interests and concerns of the socially and economically dominant classes; it is also under the sway of the government, and it will react to the issues and threats of the day as these are perceived by its members and by government. Just as there is legislation, such as indicated in this chapter, which enhances human rights protection, so Parliament has enacted legislation which threatens and diminishes it. Particularly in times of war or national emergency, the government has had Parliament enact emergency powers which, for example, allow detention without trial, increase the powers of the police, and restrict speech. Statutes such as these were enacted at the end of the eighteenth century, when the government feared French revolutionary ideas would cross the channel; notoriously wide-ranging Defence of the Realm Acts were enacted during both the First and Second World Wars, and, since the Second World War, we have seen a succession of anti-terrorism statutes which have given wide, discretionary powers to police and government. These were first aimed at terrorism in the context of Northern Ireland; they are now aimed at international Islamist terrorism and may be thought to be as draconian as any emergency laws have ever been.

3.5.2 **The common law**

The history of the common law's protection of human rights is, likewise, a mixed story.

In *Entick v Carrington* (1765) 19 Howell's State Trials 1030, 95 ER 807, the judges upheld the rule of law by denying that the Crown, the government, could enter and search the premises of a political opponent on the basis of a general warrant for which there was no legal authority.

On the other hand, in *Duncan v Jones* [1936] 1 KB 218, the High Court accepted that police officers had acted within their duty when they arrested Mrs Duncan. She had refused to cooperate with police, who wanted to stop her making a speech in a public place. The police acted because they said they feared that the speech, though lawful in itself, might provoke others to violence. In upholding the police view, the High Court denied that Mrs Duncan had any 'right' to speak which should be weighed against the alleged threat to public order.

These are just two examples from a myriad of cases that indicate that the history of the common law in protecting what we now call human rights is complex.

In the last few decades judges have expressly recognised fundamental rights as inherent in the common law (e.g. *Morris* v *Beardmore* [1981] AC 446, especially p. 464, per Lord Scarman). This development (which may be no more than a continuation of the older commitments to 'liberty' by using new 'human rights' terminology) is partly inspired by the Convention, though it does not involve the direct application of Convention rights. Common law rights in this sense cover much the same content as Convention rights and, according to the judges, enjoy much the same flexibility. For some judges there is little, if anything, in the ECHR which does not enjoy equivalent protection through the common law. In particular, both common law and the Convention embody the need to seek a fair and proper balance between the rights and freedoms of individuals and the public interest whose proper protection may require some limits to individual liberty.

The weakness of the common law is, in particular, in its ultimate subordination to Parliament. But this is a changing matter. Constitutionally the law is moving away from a merely absolutist conception of parliamentary sovereignty. In particular the courts have developed the idea of 'legality'. Put simply, this is the idea that Parliament retains its sovereignty. However, if Parliament wishes to enact legislation which authorises officials to take actions which interfere with human rights or these fundamental rights recognised by the common law, then it must do so deliberately and expressly. In particular, general powers in a statute will not authorise such interferences.

 CASE CLOSE-UP

Ahmed v The Treasury [2010] UKSC 2

In the context of the 'war on terror', the UN Security Council (UNSC) required states to freeze the bank accounts of named terrorist suspects. The UK issued the Taliban and Al-Qaida Orders, in order to fulfil this obligation. These orders had a devastating effect on the private lives of the individuals concerned and could not be properly challenged in court. These measures were Orders in Council (a form of delegated legislation) issued with the authority of the United Nations Act 1948. The Act allowed any provision to be made by Order in Council which appeared to be 'necessary or expedient' for giving effect to UNSC measures.

The Supreme Court held that these general, vague, words, enacted decades previously, could not possibly be read as authorising these significant interferences with the fundamental and human rights of the applicants and they were invalidated as being *ultra vires*.

This is just one of a number of cases in which the UK courts have narrowed the scope of statutes or limited the powers of the executive in order to protect the fundamental rights of individuals as recognised by the common law. One of the major statements of this position was given by Lord Hoffmann in *R* v *Secretary of State for the Home Department, ex p Simms* [2000]

AC 115. His main point is not to deny Parliament the power to enact legislation which breaches fundamental rights, but to insist that, if it is to do so, it must be aware of what it is doing and face up to the political cost. Much of this is now superseded by the duty, in section 3 HRA, on the courts to interpret legislation 'so far as it is possible to do so' for compatibility with the Convention (see Chapter 4). But the common law has not lost its vitality. It has, for instance, been stressed as the proper starting point for analysis rather than Convention rights (*Osborn* v *Parole Board* [2013] UKSC 61, see para 57) or, by some judges, it is seen as providing a possibly more effective remedy (*Kennedy* v *Charity Commission* [2014] UKSC 20). There are well known obiter dicta (such as by Lords Steyn and Hope in *Jackson* v *Attorney General* [2005] UKHL 56 paras 102–105) which go so far as to raise the possibility of the courts even invalidating an Act of Parliament. In *Moohan* v *Lord Advocate* [2014] UKSC 67, the UKSC thought this a possibility if Parliament removed the right to vote in an abusive way (para 35). But the situation has not arisen and, for most judges, it is hoped that the interpretative inventiveness of the common law can prevent it from ever doing so.

Summary

- Prior to the coming into force of the HRA, the Convention was already having an impact on UK law: the UK government and Parliament were responding to adverse judgments from Strasbourg and the courts were influenced by the Convention in the way they developed the law.

- The recognition of what, today, are called 'human rights' is not something new in UK law. Important rights were already secured by Acts of Parliament and also by the common law. It is, however, a mixed story, with both Parliament and the courts capable of actions which are hardly compatible with human rights.

- Membership of the European Union is an increasingly important influence on UK law, which requires respect for human rights.

? Self-test questions

1. When did the population of the UK obtain the right of individual application to the ECHR and what was the consequence of that?

2. Explain the 'dualist' approach to international law and consider its implications for the role of the ECHR in the UK.

3. Give three examples of the impact of the ECHR on UK law and administrative practice prior to October 2000.

4. What is the principle of 'legality' and how does it relate to human rights law?

5. What is judicial review and, independently of the HRA, is it an entirely suitable procedure for dealing with human rights claims.

 For suggested approaches, please visit the Online Resource Centre.

? Exam questions

1. As a member of the House of Commons Library staff, write an outline briefing paper for MPs which explains the EU Charter of Fundamental Rights, what it does, how it relates to the ECHR, and how, if at all, it applies in the law of the UK.

2. Critically evaluate the extent to which English courts have been able to give effect to Convention rights (or at least the norms they express), independently of the HRA. Explain this process, consider its limits, and give examples.

 For suggested approaches, please visit the Online Resource Centre.

☰ Further reading

Lester, A., Pannick, D., and Herberg, J. (see Preface) Chapter 1F and 1G

Civil liberties books

Fenwick, H. *Civil Liberties and Human Rights* 4th edn (2007) Oxford: Routledge-Cavendish, Chapter 3

Historical perspective

Ewing, K. and Gearty, C. *The Struggle for Civil Liberties* (2000) Oxford: Clarendon Press

Standard works on judicial review are

Wade, Sir William and Forsyth, C. *Administrative Law* 10th edn (2009) Oxford: OUP

Craig, P. *Administrative Law* 6th edn (2008) London: Sweet & Maxwell

On European union law and human rights

Denman, D. 'The Charter of Fundamental Rights' [2010] 4 *EHRLR* 349–359

On fundamental rights at common law

Clayton, R. 'The empire strikes back: common law rights and the Human Rights Act' [2015] *Public Law* 3–13.

4

The Human Rights Act 1998 (1): rights and duties

LEARNING OBJECTIVES

- The main provisions of the Human Rights Act 1998 (HRA), including:
  - interpretation of statutes (sections 3, 4, and 10);
  - the duty on public authorities and the definition of 'public authority' (section 6);
  - the role of the courts under the HRA;
  - the role of ministers and Parliament.
- Bringing the HRA into effect.
- The territorial application of the HRA.

Introduction

The Human Rights Act 1998 (HRA) does not incorporate the European Convention on Human Rights (ECHR) into English law but gives 'further effect' in UK law to the content of the rights therein. The precise way it does this is the subject of the chapter.

Decisions under the Act have had a significant impact on people's lives. A right to private life has been developed, journalists have been protected, soldiers have basic rights even when on duty abroad, the rights of protestors have been secured, and so on—Part 2 of this book is full of examples.

But it is in the nature of human rights that unpleasant and unpopular people also, as humans, have rights. The Act has helped prisoners, deportees, those on the 'sex offenders register', and others. This has led to significant criticism and, as a consequence, in 2015, the Conservative government's intention is to repeal the Act and replace it with a 'British Bill of Rights'. By January 2016 it was still unclear what this might mean. The issues are discussed in the annex to this chapter. However, it would be extraordinary if the 'Bill of Rights' meant that the development and understanding of human rights based on the HRA over the last fifteen years was to count for nothing. Reform will not take us back to the situation in October 2000 when the Act came into force. The Act still needs to be known and understood. It retains its importance not just whilst it remains in force but also in the aftermath of its repeal.

 For updates on the topic of the Human Rights Act, please visit the Online Resource Centre www.oxfordtextbooks.co.uk/orc/davis_directions4e/.

> **'Articles' and 'sections'** The ECHR, which is an Act of the Council of Europe (see Chapter 2, section 2.2), is divided into 'Articles'. The HRA, which is an act of the UK Parliament, is divided into 'sections'. The HRA provides the legal means by which the rights in the ECHR can be enforced in UK courts. Schedule 1 HRA (a schedule is like an appendix) has the text of the ECHR rights.

4.1 Origins of the Human Rights Act

The United Kingdom was a signatory of the ECHR from the beginning in 1950 and it granted its population the right of individual petition in 1966. However, the ECHR is international law. As such it was not part of the law of the United Kingdom and could not be directly enforced before the UK's courts.

> **CROSS REFERENCE**
>
> The impact of the ECHR in the United Kingdom is the topic of Chapter 3.

Pressure for making Convention rights directly enforceable in the courts of the United Kingdom dates at least from lectures delivered by Sir Leslie Scarman, then Law Commissioner, later a Law Lord, in 1974. In the 1980s and 1990s, other senior judges followed suit in arguing for incorporation in one way or another (but it should not be thought that all members of the senior judiciary were in favour). There was also support from some parliamentarians, resulting in Private Members' Bills being introduced in both the Commons (1987) and the Lords (1994 and 1996), though without success. It was the adoption of the policy of incorporation of the European Convention by the Labour Party in 1996 that gave the required political impetus. After Labour's victory in 1997, a White Paper, *Rights Brought Home: the Human Rights Bill* Cm 3782, was produced and the Human Rights Act was enacted in 1998 and brought into effect in October 2000.

4.1.1 **Arguments for the Act**

The content of UK law

There was a growing sense that in certain areas UK law was failing to secure and keep pace with emerging international standards of human rights protection such as the ECHR or the International Covenant on Civil and Political Rights (ICCPR) (discussed in Chapter 1, section 1.4.4). The flexibility of the common law and its subordination to Parliament meant that, in times of political emergency (as in Northern Ireland in the 1970s), legislation could be passed which gave the security forces wide powers and the individuals affected little protection. Nor was it possible to argue in any direct way that human rights had been violated in areas such as the laws on political meetings, marches, and demonstrations. These, it was argued, authorised wide police discretion and the priority of maintaining public order rather than a recognition of political rights. Advocates of some form of incorporation hoped for significant changes in these and other areas.

Another group of reasons for introducing human rights protection related to the ability of UK law to control effectively the exercise of state power. In the 1980s, serious political disturbance (e.g. the miners' strike, the peace movement, race riots, and racial tension) was met by significant legislative responses, such as the Police and Criminal Evidence Act 1984, the Public Order Act 1986, the Official Secrets Act 1989, and the Criminal Justice and Public Order Act 1994. This created a significant body of opinion concerned that traditional civil liberties were under threat and that some form of legally enforceable protection for human rights was necessary.

CROSS REFERENCE

The effectiveness of the HRA in the context of anti-terrorism laws in the early twenty-first century remains a matter of debate—see Chapter 26.

 BIGGER PICTURE

For an examination of the extent to which UK law in the mid-1990s complied with the ICCPR, see Klug, F., Starmer, K., and Weir, S. *The Three Pillars of Liberty* (1996) London: Routledge.

It was not the case that all those concerned about political liberty in the 1980s thought that a bill of rights was the right answer—compare, for example, Dworkin, R. *A Bill of Rights for Britain* (1990) London: Chatto & Windus, with Ewing, K. and Gearty, C. *Freedom under Thatcher: Civil Liberties in Modern Britain* (1990) Oxford: Clarendon Press.

The unfairness of 'the road to Strasbourg'

The most widely accepted argument was procedural. The UK, by signing the ECHR, had an obligation under international law to secure the Convention rights and freedoms for all within its jurisdiction. Yet (as we saw in Chapter 3) it was unable to provide a remedy for violations of those rights in the courts. An aggrieved person had to take his or her case to Strasbourg and, in the mid-1990s, this could take about five years and cost about £30,000. For example, it was unjust for a person to be convicted for a criminal offence in a UK court fully aware that an adverse judgment from the European Court of Human Rights (ECtHR) was the likely result.

In *R v Morrisey* [1997] 2 Cr App Rep 426, the Court of Appeal upheld the conviction of a company director. His conviction was on the basis of evidence the admissibility of which was almost certainly a violation of Article 6 ECHR, but which was clearly lawful under UK statutes. The Court of Appeal accepted that the situation was 'very unsatisfactory' (pp 433–434; see also *R v Lyons* [2002] UKHL 44, Chapter 3, section 3.3.1).

In addition (as noted in the White Paper), some form of incorporation would enable human rights to be more 'subtly and powerfully woven into our law' and enable UK judges to make a distinct, British contribution to the developing standards of human rights protection. Direct enforcement of human rights would also enable closer and more effective scrutiny of government actions by the courts.

4.1.2 The form the 'Bill of Rights' should take

Once the principle of bringing human rights into the law of the United Kingdom was accepted, the next question was, what specific form should this take? The government rejected a strong form in which the courts would be able to invalidate (set aside) an Act of Parliament. Lord Scarman's proposal, made back in the 1970s, was for such a measure which would embody what was, for him, the basic point: that human rights are a form of higher law binding on states, including their legislatures. For the British government such a view was a step too far. It was incompatible with British traditions and, in particular, with the sovereignty of Parliament and the ultimate deference of the judiciary to Parliament.

The solution, as we shall see, was one in which the courts have a widely drawn obligation to interpret existing and future legislation for compatibility with the Convention, but, if that is impossible, the legislation remains valid, though the courts can make a 'declaration of incompatibility'. The Act also places a duty on public authorities to act compatibly with Convention rights and this is enforceable in the courts subject, again, to legislation which requires the public authority to act in the way it does. The Act does not otherwise impose duties on private individuals or companies, though, as we shall see, it is likely to have some impact of that kind.

4.2 Identification of Convention rights

⟩ **CROSS REFERENCE**
For discussion of this point, see Chapter 2, section 2.3.5.

The purpose of the Act is to give 'further effect' to the rights and freedoms in the ECHR. It makes no attempt to add to or modify the provisions of the Convention. Nothing in the Act, for example, strengthens what little human rights protection there is in the Convention for the environment or for basic social welfare. Nor is there a stronger anti-discrimination provision than in the Convention, nor unambiguous duties to take positive steps to advance the interests of under-represented groups defined by gender, ethnicity, etc. In other words, the rather traditional human rights protection of the Convention is adopted into UK law (albeit that the evolving nature of the Convention needs to be recognised).

4.2.1 The Convention rights and ancillary rights

Section 1 identifies the rights and freedoms in the ECHR whose content is to be given further effect by the Act. They are listed in Schedule 1 and are properly to be referred to as 'the Convention rights'. These are

- Articles 2–12 and Article 14 (i.e. not Article 1 or Article 13);
- Articles 1, 2, and 3 of the First Protocol;
- Article 1 of the Thirteenth Protocol (which requires the complete abolition of the death penalty in all circumstances).

These rights are to be 'read with' Articles 16 to 18 of the Convention. (Article 16 allows certain restrictions on the political activities of foreigners, Article 17 prohibits the use of Convention rights in order to abuse the rights of others, and Article 18 prohibits states from restricting a right or freedom other than on the grounds allowed for in the Convention.)

4.2.2 Rights not included in Schedule 1: Articles 1 and 13

Article 1 and Article 13 are not included in the Convention rights in Schedule 1. Article 1 is the general duty on states to secure human rights for 'everyone within their jurisdiction'. Article 13 is the duty on states to provide an effective remedy in national courts for breaches of the Convention. The government's position is that the HRA is itself giving effect to these Articles and so their inclusion would be pointless. We shall see that, under section 2 HRA,

UK courts are required to take the rulings of the ECtHR into account when interpreting Convention rights. These rulings do deal with Articles 1 and 13 and so may influence UK courts indirectly. For example, in *R (Al-Skeini)* v *Secretary of State for Defence* [2007] UKHL 26, the House of Lords, following section 2, took into account the ECtHR's understanding of the term 'jurisdiction' found in Article 1. They did this in order to determine whether the HRA applies to British troops operating in Iraq (see section 4.11.3).

4.2.3 Rights not included in Schedule 1: Protocols 4 and 7

Protocol 4 ECHR creates a qualified right to 'freedom of movement'. Protocol 7 creates a range of rights found in the ICCPR but not in the original Convention. Protocol 4 has been signed but not ratified by the UK; Protocol 7 has neither been signed nor ratified. Neither is, therefore, listed in Schedule 1. The absence of Protocol 4 has significance for anti-terrorism law in the United Kingdom (see Chapter 26).

> **CROSS REFERENCE**
> 'Protocols' are defined in Chapter 2, section 2.3.2.

4.2.4 Derogations and reservations: Article 15

Article 15 ECHR, which allows states to 'derogate' from the Convention (suspend their duties), is not in Schedule 1 HRA. Section 1(2) HRA, however, makes it clear that the Convention rights in Schedule 1 are to have effect subject to any derogations or reservations made by the United Kingdom. Section 14 HRA allows existing derogations to be continued and new derogations to be made. Under section 16, derogations need the approval of Parliament and they lapse after five years unless renewed for an extra five years.

Despite Article 15 not being in Schedule 1, the House of Lords held that an anti-terrorist derogation was not compatible with the requirements of Article 15 in *A (FC)* v *Secretary of State for the Home Department* [2004] UKHL 56.

Article 57 of the Convention allows states to make reservations—to choose, at the time of signature or ratification, not to be bound by specific provisions of the Convention. The United Kingdom made one reservation, in respect of parental choice in education (discussed in Chapter 24, section 24.5) and this is expressly referred to in section 15 of the Act. New reservations can be made (in respect of new Protocols, for example). Under section 17 of the Act the government must keep any reservations under review.

Derogations are discussed in more detail in Chapter 7, section 7.2. The derogation from Article 5, now lapsed, made in the context of anti-terrorism law, is mentioned in Chapter 26, section 26.3.2. Reservations are discussed in Chapter 2, section 2.4.4.

4.3 Section 2 HRA: the ECHR and 'Convention rights'

4.3.1 The importance of section 2

The Human Rights Act 1998 does not incorporate the ECHR into UK law in the sense of making the Convention directly part of UK law and the judgments of the Court of Human Rights directly enforceable in UK courts. This difference between the ECHR (international law) and the

'Convention rights' under Schedule 1 HRA (UK law) is insisted on by UK courts: see *R (Hurst)* v *London Northern District Coroner* [2007] UKHL 13.

What the HRA does is to make the content, the guarantees, of the rights and freedoms in the ECHR enforceable by UK courts applying those rights as UK law in so far as the HRA allows. However, because the aim behind the HRA is to give effect in UK law to the rights found in the Convention, the Convention itself remains of great importance. It is the basic source for UK courts to use when interpreting the rights listed in Schedule 1 HRA. Section 2 HRA requires that the interpretations of the Convention made by the Strasbourg institutions (the Court of Human Rights, the Commission of Human Rights (until 1998), and the Committee of Ministers) to be *'taken into account'* by any UK *'court or tribunal determining a question that has arisen in connection with a Convention right'*. Thus the case law developed by the Strasbourg institutions must be taken into account to assist UK courts when interpreting the Convention rights and freedoms in Schedule 1 HRA.

Section 2 does not, therefore, require the Strasbourg rulings to be always followed. In this sense it can be compared with section 3 of the European Communities Act 1972 which, in respect of EU law, requires UK courts to follow the rulings of the Court of Justice of the European Union. Unlike the European Union, the Convention is not designed to be the basis of a common, integrated legal system.

What section 2 requires, what 'taken into account' means, is a matter of UK law. It is for UK courts to decide what that phrase means for the purpose of developing human rights law in the United Kingdom.

4.3.2 'The mirror principle'

An early, seminal, case (usually the starting point for analysis) is *R (Ullah)* v *Special Adjudicator* [2004] UKHL 26. Here the House of Lords (UKHL) followed Strasbourg case law on the issue of whether Article 9 (freedom of belief) could be used to prevent a deportation from the UK. In Lord Bingham's words, under section 2 HRA, 'the duty on national courts is to keep pace with the Strasbourg jurisprudence as it evolves over time: no more but certainly no less' (para 20).

In *R (Gentle)* v *Prime Minister* [2008] UKHL 20, for example, Baroness Hale would have happily read into Article 2 (the right to life) a duty on states not to send troops to fight in unlawful wars. But that would have gone beyond what the ECtHR's jurisprudence on Article 2 had contemplated: 'We are not free to foist upon Parliament or upon public authorities an interpretation of a convention right which goes way beyond anything we can reasonably foresee that Strasbourg might do' (para 56). This view sees the parliamentary intention behind the HRA as being to mirror in the UK courts the rights available in Strasbourg.

4.3.3 Specific applications

This does not mean that UK courts are bound by specific applications of the Convention to UK institutions. In *Secretary of State for the Home Department* v *JJ* [2007] UKHL 45, Lord Bingham said that Strasbourg is 'laying down principles and not mandating solutions to particular cases' (para 13). Where, for example, the ECtHR has not been fully appraised of the factual context of a situation, its decisions, its applications of Convention rights in specific situations (as distinct from its enunciation of general principles) will not need to be followed. An example is *R (Brooke)* v *Parole Board* [2008] EWCA Civ 29, involving different views on the independence and impartiality of the Parole Board.

4.3.4 A more 'generous' position?

This idea that UK courts should not interpret Convention rights in more restrictive, less 'generous', more executive friendly ways than Strasbourg is not controversial. If UK courts began to diverge too far in this direction, disappointed applicants would still have recourse to the ECtHR, and the point of the HRA would be lost.

Concern arises, however, when the mirror principle appears to stand in the way of UK courts adopting more 'generous', more 'extensive' approaches to rights than are available at Strasbourg. As in *Gentle* (discussed in 4.3.2), the mirror principle is likely to prevent UK courts departing in a radically more generous direction when the Strasbourg case law is clear. This has been challenged by some judges. In *Moohan v Lord Advocate* [2014] UKSC 67, the UKSC upheld the well-established position of Strasbourg that the 'right to vote', found in Article 3 of the First Protocol, did not apply to voting in referendums, only general elections. The minority (Lords Kerr and Wilson) would have departed from this position predominantly on the ground that the Strasbourg approach was wrong. Indeed Lord Wilson's judgment has annexed to it a list of cases in which the mirror principle has come under critical scrutiny.

Some Supreme Court justices recognise the possibility of more generous outcomes in domestic law but, if they purport to be applications of Convention rights, they should not go beyond what is 'recognized by or reasonably envisaged within, existing Strasbourg jurisprudence'— *Rabone v Pennine Care NHS Foundation Trust* [2012] UKSC 12, per Lord Brown.

> **THINKING POINT**
>
> Should the UK courts be prepared to provide more extensive human rights protection than at Strasbourg? Consider, for example, Lewis, J. 'The European Ceiling on Human Rights' [2007] Public Law 720.8

4.3.5 New situations

New situations may arise in UK cases in which there is no clear and established Strasbourg jurisprudence to apply. Lord Brown, in *Rabone* (discussed in 4.3.4), summarised the position, again emphasising the need to keep with the grain of Strasbourg jurisprudence:

- If the domestic court is inclined to uphold a Convention challenge against a public authority in a new situation it should not refuse so to do merely because there is no Strasbourg decision on the point.
- However, the domestic court needs to be satisfied that what it is doing is applying Convention rights in a way that 'flow[s] naturally' from existing Strasbourg case law.

4.3.6 Important principles of UK law

But the mirror principle has never been seen as requiring UK courts to depart from important principles of UK law. The situation is expressed authoritatively in *Pinnock v Manchester CC* [2010] UKSC 45.

> Where ... there is a clear and consistent line of decisions whose effect is not inconsistent with some fundamental substance or procedural aspect of our law, and whose reasoning does not

appear to overlook or misunderstand some argument or point of principle, we consider that it would be wrong for this court not to follow that line.

(para 48)

Pinnock suggests, therefore, that even clear and consistently expressed statements of the scope and meaning of a Convention article need not always be followed if they challenge a well-established principle of UK law and procedure or are based on misunderstandings of facts, reasoning, or principle.

Famously in *R* v *Horncastle* [2009] UKSC 14, the UKSC refused to follow a principle that Strasbourg Chambers had consistently reiterated. This was that, under Article 6, a criminal conviction could not be 'solely or decisively' based on hearsay evidence. The UKSC carefully analysed this Strasbourg jurisprudence and held it to be not well grounded in principle or properly reasoned and it was not appropriate to common law systems. Later, a Grand Chamber, taking *Horncastle* into account, reformulated the Strasbourg principles to the effect that the 'solely or decisively' rule (in the criminal trial context) was not absolute and could be departed from if there were sufficient safeguards in the trial process (*Al-Khawaja* v *UK* (2012) 54 EHRR 23). These cases represent a good example of how section 2 HRA permits a form of 'dialogue' between the UKSC and Strasbourg over difficult questions of human rights law. Indeed the possibility of such 'dialogue' is the main reason why even clear and consistent Strasbourg principles need not always be followed (*Pinnock*, para 48).

▶ CROSS REFERENCE

The terrorism cases are discussed in the context of anti-terrorism law in Chapter 26, section 26.9.1.

Generally, however, the UKSC is likely to follow principles enunciated by the Grand Chamber of the ECtHR (i.e. the Court speaking with its fullest authority). In *A* v *UK* (2009) 49 EHRR 29, for example, the Grand Chamber expressed a principle concerning the fairness of procedures followed in the UK in respect of terrorist suspects. This principle was contrary to the somewhat more flexible approach of the UKHL enunciated in an earlier case on a related issue (*MB/AF* v *UK* [2007] UKHL 46).

In later proceedings the UKHL felt obliged to change its position and adopt the Strasbourg approach (*Secretary of State for the Home Department* v *AF* [2009] UKHL 28). Lord Rodger said: 'in reality, we have no choice: Argentoratum locutum, iudicium finitum—Strasbourg has spoken, the case is closed' (para 98).

The *Pinnock*, statement, at the beginning of this section, suggests it is not quite as final as that and that departing even from clear Grand Chamber principles remains open 'in theory'. In *Chester* v *Secretary of State for the Home Department* [2013] UKSC 63, the UKSC limited this to where a principle enunciated by a Grand Chamber was inconsistent with 'some truly fundamental principle of our law or [resulted from] some most egregious oversight or misunderstanding.' (Lord Mance, para 27).

It is now not exceptional to find UK courts declining to follow (albeit Chamber rather than Grand Chamber) judgments of the ECtHR.

- In *R (Kaiyam)* v *Secretary of State for Justice* [2014] UKSC 66, the Supreme Court did not follow a Chamber judgment on whether rehabilitation of prisoners was a direct requirement of Article 5 (see Chapter 21).

- In *R (Hicks)* v *Commissioner of Police for the Metropolis* [2014] EWCA Civ 3, the Court of Appeal did not follow a Chamber judgment on the nature of the police's intention when making an arrest (see Chapter 11).

4.3.7 **HRA and common law**

Cases such as the above indicate that UK judges do not slavishly follow the principles of interpretation laid down by the ECtHR. Indeed, an aspect of the discussion on section 2 HRA is a willingness of some Supreme Court justices to promote the claims of the common law and the fundamental rights it recognises as being equivalent to the Convention and, perhaps, providing a more 'generous' remedy.

Kennedy v *Charity Commission* [2014] UKSC 20 involved the question of whether the Charity Commission could be compelled to disclose certain information. The UKSC split on whether the common law principle of open justice could provide a more extensive remedy than Article 10 and the HRA. In *R (Osborn)* v *Parole Board* [2013] UKSC 61, the court agreed with Lord Reed that 'the importance of the [HRA] is unquestionable, it does not however supersede the protection of human rights under the common law or statute, or create a discrete body of law based upon the judgments of the European Court.'. The precise requirement inherent in section 2 is a matter on which judges disagree.

BIGGER PICTURE

Arguments in academic writing by senior judges arguing for a greater recognition of the common law include:

- Lord Judge, LCJ, 'The Judicial Studies Board Lecture 2010' 17 March 2010 (www.judiciary.gov.uk/—Media > speeches > March 2010.)
- Lord Justice Laws 'The Common Law and Europe' https://www.judiciary.gov.uk/wp-content/uploads/JCO/Documents/Speeches/laws-lj-speech-hamlyn-lecture-2013.pdf.

But this issue remains controversial. A firmer approach, based on legal certainty needing a hierarchy of courts, can be found in, for example:

- Sir Philip Sales 'Strasbourg Jurisprudence and the Human Rights Act: A Response to Lord Irvine' [2012] *Public Law* 253–267.
- Bratza, N. (President of the ECtHR) 'The Relationship between the UK Courts and Strasbourg' [2011] 5 *EHRLR* 505–512.

4.3.8 **Section 2 and precedent**

Nothing in the HRA undermines the basic structures of UK law; the domestic system of precedent should be upheld and followed. So section 2 HRA does not entitle the Court of Appeal to depart from a UKHL/UKSC precedent on the grounds that it is inconsistent with Convention law laid down by the Strasbourg court (e.g. where Convention law has evolved since the UKHL/UKSC ruling involved). The Court of Appeal should follow the UKHL/UKSC (other than in wholly exceptional circumstances). It is then up to the UKSC to reconsider its position in the light of the Strasbourg judgment (*Kay* v *Lambeth* [2006] UKHL 10, paras 40–45). Where, however, there is no ruling of the UKHL/UKSC to follow, the Court of Appeal (Civil Division) may, if it thinks appropriate, depart from its own earlier decision (Convention compatibility is, therefore, another exception to the general rule in *Young* v *Bristol Aeroplane* [1946] AC 163). These positions are confirmed in *R (RJM)* v *Secretary of State for Work and Pensions* [2008] UKHL 63.

4.4 Legislation and the Human Rights Act: sections 3, 4, 5, and 10

4.4.1 Introduction

Sections 3, 4, 5, and 10 HRA concern the first of the two principal ways in which the Act gives further effect to Convention rights in UK law. These sections deal with Acts of Parliament and the way they are to be interpreted and given effect by the courts. In summary:

- Acts of Parliament should be read and given effect, if they can be, in a way that is compatible with the Convention rights in Schedule 1.
- If this is not possible then the offending legislation remains valid but the courts may issue a 'declaration of incompatibility'.
- Although such a declaration does not affect the validity and effect of the law, a minister may choose to take 'remedial action' and change the law by an order made under the Act.

These points will now be looked at in more detail.

4.4.2 The duty to interpret legislation for compatibility with scheduled Convention rights (section 3 HRA)

3 Interpretation of legislation

(1) So far as it is possible to do so, primary legislation and subordinate legislation must be read and given effect in a way which is compatible with the Convention rights.

(2) This section—

    (a) applies to primary legislation and subordinate legislation whenever enacted;

    (b) does not affect the validity, continuing operation or enforcement of any incompatible primary legislation; and

    (c) does not affect the validity, continuing operation or enforcement of any incompatible subordinate legislation if (disregarding any possibility of revocation) primary legislation prevents removal of the incompatibility.

There are a number of important points to note.

An interpretative duty

Section 3 HRA imposes an interpretative duty on the courts. Acts of Parliament are to be interpreted ('read and given effect') so that the rights, duties, powers, and liberties that they establish can only be exercised in ways that are compatible with, and do not lead to breaches of, Convention rights.

No power to invalidate a statute

But the interpretative duty only applies 'so far as it is possible to do so'. Under section 3, no court, not even the Supreme Court, has the authority to invalidate an Act of Parliament. Section 3(2)(b) makes it clear that legislation which cannot be read or given effect in a way that is compatible with Convention rights remains valid and the courts are required to enforce it. Parliament retains its 'sovereignty' and remains free to enact legislation that clearly and intentionally permits or requires violations of Convention rights. This approach to human rights protection can be compared with, for example, the systems in the United States or in Germany. In those countries rights and freedoms are listed in a written constitution and a constitutional court (the US Supreme Court or the German Constitutional Court respectively) has the power to invalidate acts of the legislature on the grounds that they are unconstitutional.

Applies to legislation 'whenever enacted': enactments made before October 2000

Section 3(2)(a) means that in-force legislation that was enacted prior to October 2000 (when the HRA came into effect) is subject to the interpretative duty. In this way, the HRA empowers the courts to undertake a form of ad hoc law reform resolving incompatibilities between existing legislation and human rights on a case-by-case basis. This is, no doubt, a more efficient approach than trying to perform the same task by a massive Act which identifies and amends all such incompatible legislation in the abstract.

Applies to legislation 'whenever enacted': enactments made after October 2000

The interpretative duty applies to all legislation enacted after the HRA was brought into effect. It should be noted that post-October 2000 legislation which is apparently incompatible with Convention rights does not implicitly repeal the HRA. Rather, it is dealt with under that Act's terms: the new legislation is either capable of being read and given effect in a Convention-compatible manner or it is put into effect as legislation which is incompatible but still valid.

Subordinate legislation

'Subordinate legislation' (which can also be called 'secondary' or 'delegated' legislation) refers to rules which are enacted under the authority of an Act of Parliament (primary legislation). These rules have the full force of law. Typically, primary legislation empowers someone, such as a government minister, a government department, a 'quango' (e.g. the Health and Safety Executive), or a local council, to produce legally enforceable rules and regulations. The Act identifies the general purpose which the regulations etc. are to achieve, but the specific rules are left to the minister etc. Examples include 'Orders in Council' or regulations made by ministers under statute (these are likely to be 'statutory instruments') and by-laws made by local councils. There are many other forms.

The duty under section 3 HRA to read and give effect to legislation in a way that is compatible with Convention rights applies to subordinate legislation.

Unlike primary legislation, subordinate legislation which cannot be interpreted for compatibility with Convention rights is invalid and not to be applied by the courts. This is implied by section 3(2)(c) HRA. It is already a general principle of law, independent of the HRA, that subordinate legislation which is incompatible with 'fundamental rights', as recognised by the common law, is invalid. It is *ultra vires* (outside the powers), which means that it has been enacted in a way or for a purpose which was not authorised by the primary Act of Parliament. In the court's view Parliament cannot have intended to authorise ministers etc. to make subordinate legislation which violates fundamental rights. If Parliament does so intend, this intention must be clearly there in the text of the Act. Apparently unlimited power to make regulations does not mean any regulations made can violate fundamental or human rights (see *Ahmed* v *The Treasury* [2010] UKSC 2). Section 6 HRA, as we shall see, makes it unlawful for a minister etc., to make regulations which violate Convention rights.

> **CROSS REFERENCE**
>
> For examples of this see Chapter 3, section 3.3.1, secondary or subordinate legislation.

Suitable remedies for invalid subordinate legislation (such as a common law declaration of invalidity) are not always available. In *R (T) v Chief Constable of Greater Manchester* [2014] UKSC 35, for instance, the retrospective impact (e.g. on regulators of various kinds) of declaring invalid the Rehabilitation of Offenders Act 1974 (Exceptions) Order 1975 would have been so drastic that the UKSC declined to do it. The Order, in a blanket way, removed the protection of the Rehabilitation of Offenders Act 1974 from persons seeking employment with children and vulnerable adults and violated the claimant's Article 8 rights. Invalidity would have had a huge impact on, for example, various regulatory bodies which had been relying on the Order since it came into force.

Subordinate legislation which is incompatible with Convention rights remains valid if the primary legislation under which it is made prevents the removal of incompatibility (section 3(2)(c) HRA). If primary legislation gives a minister etc. broad, general powers to make subordinate legislation, the courts will be unlikely to read these powers as preventing the removal of incompatible regulations. It is more likely that the courts will 'read down' the scope of such a broad and general law-making power in the primary legislation so as to exclude incompatible regulations.

The subordinate legislation covered by section 3 is identified in section 21 HRA, the interpretation section. It includes

- Orders in Council if made on the authority of an Act of Parliament;
- any 'order, rules, regulations, scheme, warrant, byelaw or other instrument made under primary legislation';
- Acts of the Scottish Parliament, Acts of the Northern Ireland Assembly and Executive, and Measures and Acts of the National Assembly for Wales.

It expressly excludes Orders in Council made under the Royal Prerogative and some provisions relating to Northern Ireland, which are therefore treated as primary legislation

4.4.3   Declarations of incompatibility, section 4 HRA

4 Declaration of incompatibility

(1) Subsection (2) applies in any proceedings in which a court determines whether a provision of primary legislation is compatible with a Convention right.

(2) If the court is satisfied that the provision is incompatible with a Convention right, it may make a declaration of that incompatibility.

If a court finds that it is not possible to read and give effect to primary legislation in a manner that is compatible with the Convention, it has the discretion to make a 'declaration of incompatibility'. Such a declaration can also be made in respect of subordinate legislation whose repeal is prevented by its authorising primary legislation. A declaration of incompatibility is discretionary: a court is not bound to issue one. Such a declaration does not affect the validity of the legislation involved, which remains valid and enforceable. Nor does it affect the parties to the case in which it was made—their legal position is determined by the valid, enforceable, but incompatible law. Only the senior courts can make declarations of incompatibility. In England and Wales these are the High Court, Court of Appeal, and Supreme Court (see section 4(5) HRA for a complete list).

Though such declarations do not affect the validity or enforceability of legislation, they are made with the authority of the senior judiciary and are not to be lightly disregarded by government. Before a declaration of incompatibility can be made, the government must be given the chance to make representations to the court (see section 5 HRA).

Magistrates' or Crown Courts hearing criminal trials, or a county court dealing with a civil matter, or a tribunal are unable to make declarations of incompatibility. Under section 3 they are required to interpret the legislation they are dealing with, if possible, for compatibility. If a compatible interpretation is impossible then they must apply the incompatible law (e.g. convict a defendant even though the conviction may be a violation of his or her Convention rights). The defendant may then appeal to the High Court (usually the Divisional Court of the Queen's Bench) or the Court of Appeal (Criminal Division). These appellate courts would have to uphold the conviction if they agree with the lower court that a compatible interpretation of the legislation is not possible, but they are able to complement that with a declaration of incompatibility if it is appropriate.

Examples of declarations of incompatibility include:

- In *International Transport Roth GmbH* v *Secretary of State for the Home Department* [2002] EWCA Civ 158, the Court of Appeal (Laws LJ dissenting) made a declaration of incompatibility in respect of primary legislation which penalised international road hauliers for bringing people into the country illegally hidden in their lorries. The legislation placed the burden of proof on the companies to disprove their liability and was incompatible with Article 6; other elements of the scheme were disproportionate and incompatible with Article 1 of the First Protocol (the protection of property).

- In *R (H)* v *Mental Health Review Tribunal N&E London Region* [2001] EWCA Civ 415, the Court of Appeal made a declaration of incompatibility in respect of section 73 of the Mental Health Act 1983. This placed the burden of proving to a Mental Health Review Tribunal that the grounds for detaining a person for treatment in a mental hospital still existed, on the applicant rather than the hospital, and was incompatible with Article 5, the right to liberty and security.

> **CROSS REFERENCE**
> See section 4.4.4 for what happened next in these cases.

Declarations of incompatibility under section 4 HRA need to be distinguished from the ordinary 'declaratory' remedy.

4.4.4 Consequences of incompatibility: section 10, remedial action

If a UK court makes a declaration of incompatibility under section 4 HRA (or if the ECtHR in Strasbourg decides that the UK has violated the Convention) there are three courses open to the government.

1. Do nothing. Neither a declaration of incompatibility from a UK court nor an adverse finding from Strasbourg changes UK law. The government may decide to keep the incompatible law, or administrative practice it authorises, as it is. No court in the UK has the power to order a minister to introduce legislation to change the law (confirmed by section 6(6) HRA). If nothing is done, a person directly affected may still take their case to Strasbourg and the UK could be faced with an adverse judgment from the ECtHR. Nevertheless, the option of doing nothing is clearly one of the possibilities envisaged by the approach to human rights protection introduced by the Act. However, where a case is taken to Strasbourg following a declaration of incompatibility, the UK government is likely to seek a 'friendly settlement' (see Chapter 2, section 2.5.3); an example is *Kent* v

United Kingdom App 21843/04, decision of 30 August 2005, following the *International Transport Roth* case in section 4.4.3.

2. Change the law or administrative practice. The usual practice (and the practice adopted prior to the Act coming into force in respect of Strasbourg judgments) is to change the law or administrative practice purportedly authorised under it. The government may, for example, introduce new legislation to Parliament or withdraw and redraft subordinate legislation.

3. Remedial orders.

10 Power to take remedial action

(1) This section applies if—

(a) a provision of legislation has been declared under section 4 to be incompatible with a Convention right and [any appeal process has been completed] or

(b) it appears to a Minister of the Crown . . . that [after an adverse finding by the ECtHR] a provision of legislation is incompatible with an obligation of the United Kingdom arising from the Convention.

(2) If a Minister of the Crown considers that there are compelling reasons for proceeding under this section, he may by order make such amendments to the legislation as he considers necessary to remove the incompatibility.

Section 10 HRA introduces an important innovation. Following a declaration of incompatibility, an adverse judgment from Strasbourg or the quashing of incompatible subordinate legislation, a minister may introduce changes to Acts of Parliament or to subordinate legislation in order to remedy the incompatibility. The normal way to amend primary legislation is by a second, amending, Act of Parliament. Under section 10, however, repeal or amendment to legislation can be made simply by an order made by the minister: an Act of Parliament is not required. Since the section 10 power permits the executive to change primary legislation, it can only be exercised subject to the following safeguards.

- The minister must have 'compelling reasons' for introducing a remedial order. There is no indication in the Act of what these could be. The need to make amendments speedily is an obvious reason. The decision by a minister to proceed or not to proceed under section 10 cannot be challenged in the courts (see section 6(6)(b) HRA).

- Any order is limited by what the minister considers is necessary to remove the incompatibility.

- The legal process in the UK has been exhausted. Thus all rights of appeal have either been given up by the parties (who must signify this in writing) or have been unsuccessfully pursued in the courts.

- Parliamentary approval. This is the most important safeguard. Orders made under section 10 are subject to parliamentary approval. The detail of this is in Schedule 2 HRA. It should be remembered that Acts of Parliament, especially those concerned with emergencies and restricting human rights, have often had rather short and cursory examination in Parliament (especially by the House of Commons). It is possible that the kind of scrutiny remedial orders will get under Schedule 2 will be at least as careful, probably more careful, than the same terms would get in an Act of Parliament. During the approval process there are opportunities for representations to be made and for amendments to the draft order. Furthermore, since a remedial order is subordinate legislation, the Parliament Acts 1911 and 1949 do not apply. The Order may require the consent of the House of Lords.

The consequences of the declarations of incompatibility in the two cases mentioned previously were as follows:

Following *International Transport Roth GmbH* v *Secretary of State for the Home Department* [2002] EWCA Civ 158, the Immigration and Asylum Act 1999 Part II was amended by the Nationality, Immigration and Asylum Act 2002. Schedule 8 introduced a Code of Practice to deal with the issues on which the declaration of incompatibility was based.

Following *R (H)* v *Mental Health Review Tribunal N&E London Region* [2001] EWCA Civ 415, the Mental Health Act 1983 was amended by a remedial order by which the burden of proof on whether grounds for detaining a person in a mental hospital existed was now placed on the hospital. (See Mental Health Act 1983 (Remedial) Order 2001 (SI 2001/3712).) The need to allow the tribunals to continue functioning, not to detain people longer than was necessary, and to prevent a build-up of cases were 'compelling reasons' for such an order.

4.4.5 The meaning of 'so far as it is possible to do so': general principles

The House of Lords has decided a number of important cases on the meaning and impact of the courts' interpretative duty under section 3. In this section the general principles will be identified; in the next section some of the important, illustrative, cases will be discussed.

Three general techniques are open to the courts:

- 'reading down'—introducing limiting words or meanings to an Act of Parliament to ensure its possible effects are Convention compatible. Where, for example, an Act of Parliament seems to give a minister a widely drawn discretionary power, the scope of this power might be 'read down' by the courts inserting a provision restricting the discretion so it can only be exercised in a manner compatible with Convention rights.

- 'reading in'—introducing words or meanings into an Act of Parliament which create necessary safeguards to ensure that the Act is compatible with Convention rights.

- 'reading out'—in which courts remove or will not enforce provisions in an Act of Parliament which would otherwise make it incompatible with Convention rights.

What is unclear is when the use of such techniques is appropriate. Although some judges are unwilling to be too specific about what section 3 does or does not permit, certain broad principles concerning when it is appropriate to use such techniques can be identified.

Section 3 only applies when there is incompatibility under 'normal' canons of interpretation

Section 3 only applies when under 'normal' canons of statutory interpretation (i.e. the literal rule, the golden rule, the mischief rule, etc.) it is not possible to read the legislation as being compatible with Convention rights. This is confirmed by the UKSC in *S* v *L* [2012] UKSC 30, paras 15–17.

Thus the approach of a court should be, first, to decide what the legislation means by applying ordinary principles of statutory interpretation. The aim is to construct the intention of Parliament by giving the words of a statute their ordinary meaning (the 'literal rule'). If that meaning is ambiguous or unclear, the courts are allowed to use various principles of statutory interpretation and various internal and external aids to obtain what they take to be the intention of Parliament (the 'golden rule'); also to look at the general context of the legislation including the problem the Act aims to resolve; and interpret the Act to that effect (the

> **CROSS REFERENCE**
> See Chapter 3, section 3.3.1.

'mischief rule'). Of particular importance in this context is the presumption, which pre-dates the HRA, that Parliament does not intend to breach its international obligations (which, of course, include the ECHR).

So, it is only if the ordinary meaning of the legislation, the meaning required by ordinary statutory interpretation, is incompatible with Convention rights that meanings and interpretation that might be 'possible' under section 3 should be considered. Section 3, therefore, permits meanings to statutes that it would not be possible to come to under ordinary principles of statutory interpretation.

Section 3 overrides the literal rule

Under the literal rule the intention of Parliament is known through the ordinary meaning of the words used. Under section 3, however, the words of the statute are no longer ultimately decisive and so the intention of Parliament at the time is no longer followed. The House of Lords has said, for example:

> In accordance with the will of Parliament as reflected in section 3 it will sometimes be necessary to adopt an interpretation which linguistically may appear strained.

> (*R* v *A* [2001] UKHL 25, para 44)

> In the ordinary course the interpretation of legislation involves seeking the intention reasonably to be attributed to Parliament in using the language in question. Section 3 may require the court to depart from this legislative intention, that is, depart from the intention of the Parliament which enacted the legislation.

> (*Ghaidan* v *Godin-Mendoza* [2004] UKHL 30, para 30)

Ambiguity or uncertainty is not necessary

Thus, even when the words of an Act of Parliament are, on ordinary principles of statutory interpretation, clear, they can still be departed from, added to, or ignored under section 3 if it is necessary to do so in order to achieve compatibility with Convention rights.

> Section 3 is only invoked where, to achieve compliance with the convention, the court must depart from the unambiguous meaning the legislation would otherwise bear.

> (*R (Hurst)* v *Northern London District Coroner* [2007] UKHL 13, para 49, per Lord Brown)

Declarations of incompatibility: a last resort?

The implication of all this is that a court should try, first, to interpret the legislation so it is compatible with Convention rights. There is a consistent stream of judicial opinion that a declaration of incompatibility should be a 'last resort' (e.g. *R (L)* v *Commissioner of Police for the Metropolis* [2009] UKSC 3, para 74, per Lord Neuberger). Courts should do all they can to achieve compatibility. There is no point to section 3 if problems of compatibility with Convention rights are continually being put back to the government and Parliament. The purpose behind the HRA is to delegate to the courts the bulk of the work of creating Convention compatibility in the law. Parliament, of course, remains free to legislate again and restore the incompatibility (though this would reopen the possibility of a further challenge before the ECtHR). But judges do not take an absolute, mechanical approach. A declaration may be chosen because it is the most appropriate solution even if, in strict terms, a section 3 reading is possible (see the dissenting minority in *R (G)* v *Metropolitan Police Commissioner*, discussed in section 4.4.7). Some commentators see a virtue in the declaration precisely because it ensures parliamentary responsibilities for human rights (see the Discussion Topic, at section 4.4.7).

By March 2015, 29 declarations of incompatibility had been made since 2000, of which 20 survived appeal. Between 2010 and 2015 only 3 were made. This indicates a 'significant downward trend' (Human Rights Joint Committee 2014–2015 Seventh Report, HL 130/HC 1088, section 4).

▶ CROSS REFERENCE
For further discussion of the desirability of declarations of incompatibility,
see the Discussion Topic, at section 4.4.7.

4.4.6 What is not 'possible': interpretation not legislation

There are limits to what is 'possible' for the courts to do. Section 3 permits 'interpretation' not 'legislation' by the courts. As the House of Lords said in *Re S* [2002] UKHL 10:

> In applying section 3 the courts must be ever mindful of this limit [not to go beyond interpreting legislation]. The 1989 Act reserves the amendment of primary legislation to Parliament. By this means the 1998 Act seeks to preserve parliamentary sovereignty. The 1998 Act maintains the constitutional boundary. Interpretation of statutes is a matter for the courts; the enactment of statutes, and the amendment of statutes, are matters for Parliament.

> (para 39)

What is not 'possible': maintain consistency with fundamental features of the Act in question

Any reading in, reading out, or reading down must be consistent with the 'fundamental features' of the sections of the Act being interpreted. A section 3 interpretation is only possible if it goes 'with the grain' and is consistent with the 'underlying thrust' of the legislation (these terms are taken from *Ghaidan* v *Godin-Mendoza*, para 33). Behind the words lies the 'concept' of the statutory provisions in issue and any section 3 interpretation must not do violence to this concept.

What is not 'possible': maintain the proper balance between the courts and Parliament

Section 3 does not license the courts to rewrite legislation in a manner that usurps or undermines the relationship between the courts and Parliament. To some degree, section 3 has redefined this relationship in favour of the courts, but, even so, it does not make 'possible' a reading in, out, or down that (a) is incompatible with a fundamental feature of the legislation or with the broad policy the legislation is putting into effect, (b) undermines a provision in an Act that has been expressly endorsed by Parliament, or (c) involves the court in a complex policy judgment for which they are ill-equipped.

In this way the courts recognise and give effect to the primacy and proper role of Parliament. There are two intertwined reasons. The first is a constitutional reason. Under the constitution, the legitimacy and authority of the courts stems from their ultimate subordination to Parliament. The second is a practical reason. The courts are ill-equipped to alter the underlying policy an Act pursues; or to alter an Act in a way that has significant implications for the policy of the law. The courts decide disputes between individuals based on their assessment of the legal rights of those individuals. This is very different from policy-making, when a range of options should be considered in the light of all relevant issues and all foreseeable consequences. This is for administrators and politicians, not judges.

Clarity and certainty

The courts understand section 3 as allowing them to depart from the clear and unambiguous meaning of a statute. The difficulty is that this may have increased uncertainty. It is not at all clear that the 'grain' or 'concept' or 'fundamental feature' of a statute, supposedly implicit in the Act, will be clear. In both the cases from which these general principles have been derived (*Ghaidan* v *Godin-Mendoza* and *R* v *A*) there were important doubts expressed and dissension over the application of the principles. It remains to be seen whether the distinction between 'interpretation' and 'legislation' under section 3 is one that can be convincingly applied by the courts in the cases that come before them.

4.4.7 The meaning of 'so far as it is possible to do so': some leading cases

The principles discussed in previous sections have been identified and applied in a number of leading cases including these that follow.

Q | CASE CLOSE-UP

***Ghaidan* v *Godin-Mendoza* [2004] UKHL 30**

The legislation to be interpreted

Schedule 1 Rent Act 1977:

2(1) The surviving spouse (if any) of the original tenant, if residing in the dwelling-house immediately before the death of the original tenant, shall after the death be the statutory tenant if and so long as he or she occupies the dwelling-house as his or her residence.

(2) For the purposes of this paragraph, a person who was living with the original tenant as his or her wife or husband shall be treated as the spouse of the original tenant.

Paragraph 3(1) of the Schedule went on to say that if paragraph 2 did not apply but the claimant was living as a 'family member', then they could continue to live in the dwelling house but only as an 'assured tenant', which gave them fewer rights and greater vulnerability to rent rises and changes in terms.

The issue: whether the surviving member of a same-sex relationship could succeed to a statutory tenancy despite words in the legislation ('spouse', 'wife', and 'husband'), which, if read literally, suggested that only those in heterosexual relations could benefit.

The Convention question: whether such a statutory provision discriminated against same-sex couples in violation of Article 14, the right not to suffer discrimination with respect to Convention rights, when read with Article 8, the right to private life.

The House of Lords held that it was 'possible' to read the schedule in a way that included same-sex couples. A declaration of incompatibility was not necessary.

The case illustrates a reading of a legislative provision which, though probably at odds with the unambiguous literal meaning of the words (which imply relationships only between men and women), is 'possible' in the sense that it 'goes with the grain', the 'underlying thrust', of the legislation. Paragraph 2(2) of the Schedule indicates an intention by Parliament to provide rights to unmarried persons and the social policy which explained that would also justify extending the right to same-sex couples. Otherwise the Act would discriminate against same-sex couples. Discrimination against same-sex couples was not required by the Act and, without such a requirement, could not be justified.

A word of caution must be noted, however. Lord Millett dissented in *Ghaidan*. He accepted the general approach adopted towards section 3, but felt that the underlying thrust of the statute, especially its extension under paragraph 2(2), was confined to heterosexual relations and that extending them to same-sex relations was to legislate, not interpret. Perhaps this is an illustration of uncertainties that may arise when judges depart from the words and claim to know the 'concept' or 'thrust' of the legislation they are dealing with.

On the basis of the approach summarised in *Ghaidan*, the courts have sometimes used section 3 for radical interventions. This is especially so in the context of protecting rights to a fair hearing (Article 6), which the courts see as their preserve.

- In *R v A* [2001] UKHL 25, an early decision under the HRA, the court restored the discretion of a judge in a rape trial to allow cross-examination of the victim about her sexual history. Parliament, in legislation, had quite deliberately sought to narrow this discretion as part of a policy of encouraging victims to go to court. Some of the judges used section 3 HRA to read in the need to protect the defendant's Article 6 rights.

- *R (Hammond) v Secretary of State for the Home Department* [2005] UKHL 69 involved legislation which allowed life-sentence prisoners to apply to a judge for a reassessment of the minimum time they had to spend in jail. The legislation expressly said that the judge should decide the matter 'without an oral hearing'. The right to an oral hearing was, nevertheless, read into the legislation if necessary to protect prisoners' Article 6 rights.

The next case is an example of the courts accepting that the will of Parliament was clear and that to read a Convention-compliant meaning would be, in effect, to legislate.

 CASE CLOSE-UP

R (Anderson) v Secretary of State for the Home Department [2002] UKHL 46

The legislation to be interpreted

Section 29 Crime Sentences Act 1997 (now repealed):

(1) If recommended to do so by the Parole Board, the Secretary of State may, after consultation with the Lord Chief Justice together with the trial judge if available, release on licence a life prisoner who is not [a discretionary life prisoner].

(2) The Parole Board shall not make a recommendation under subsection (1) above unless the Secretary of State has referred the particular case, or the class of case to which that case belongs, to the Board for its advice.

The issue: judges have no discretion over the punishment of murderers. They must pass a life sentence. Most life sentences do not result in imprisonment for life. The words in the Act gave the Home Secretary the power to release those serving such a 'mandatory' life sentence on licence if recommended to do so by the Parole Board. The Parole Board could only make a recommendation if the Home Secretary chose to refer the matter to them. The Home Secretary had a well-established policy. Before a prisoner could be referred to the Parole Board he would have to serve what was then called the 'tariff', the period to be served for the purposes of punishment. After the 'tariff' had been served, the Parole Board could be asked to consider release on the basis of whether the prisoner was still dangerous. The Home Secretary set the tariff after consultation with the trial judge and the Lord Chief Justice. In Anderson's case the trial judge and Lord Chief Justice had recommended 15 years but the Home Secretary had set it at 20 years.

The Convention question: whether the setting of the tariff by the Home Secretary was in essence a sentencing exercise, which, under Article 6 of the Convention (the right to a fair trial), should be done by an 'independent and impartial tribunal', meeting a range of fair trial requirements. The Home Secretary was not such a tribunal.

The House of Lords held that the Home Secretary's powers were incompatible with Article 6 but it was not 'possible' to read section 29 compatibly with Article 6: a declaration of incompatibility was issued.

This case illustrates the limits to section 3. To have read into section 29 provisions establishing compatibility with Article 6 would have been to go against the clear and express policy of Parliament. It was clearly the intention of Parliament that the Home Secretary should have the final say in respect of the punishment of mandatory life sentence prisoners.

The declaration of incompatibility meant that the statute remained valid and in force. Following this case and a further adverse judgment in Strasbourg, the law has now been changed giving the Parole Board a greater role.

Q | CASE CLOSE-UP

Bellinger v Bellinger [2003] UKHL 21

The legislation to be interpreted

Section 11 Matrimonial Causes Act 1973:

A marriage ... shall be void on the following grounds ...

(c) That the parties are not respectively male and female.

The issue: a woman had been born a man but had gone through a process of gender reassignment and, physically and emotionally, she was a woman. She had gone through a ceremony of marriage with a man. She sought a declaration that her marriage was valid. The problem was that, in various ways, she remained a man in the eyes of the law; in particular, her birth certificate could not be changed.

The Convention question: whether section 11 of the Matrimonial Causes Act was compatible with Mrs Bellinger's rights under Article 8 (private life) and Article 12 (the right to marry).

The House of Lords held that her Convention rights had not been secured, however, it was not 'possible' to read section 11 in a compatible manner and so a declaration of incompatibility was issued.

This case illustrates the point that major policy changes ought not to be brought in under section 3. To have redefined 'male and female' in order to accommodate transsexual persons would involve a major change in the law which would have far-reaching ramifications. There would be significant issues of 'social policy and administrative feasibility' to be dealt with; perhaps there should be public consultation. These are matters for Parliament, both because that is the constitutionally proper place for changes of such significance to be made, but also because the courts are simply not equipped to deal with the full range of factors involved.

Q CASE CLOSE-UP

The DNA database cases

The cases here (*Marper* in the House of Lords under the HRA, *Marper* at Strasbourg under the ECHR, and *R(G)*, where the issue is returned to under the HRA) illustrate the working of the Act.

The underlying facts were that section 64 Police and Criminal Evidence Act 1984 (PACE) gave the police powers to retain DNA from suspects even if not convicted. DNA profiles, from the samples, were held on the national DNA database and regulated on the basis of Guidelines issued by the police. The police's refusal, following the Guidelines, to remove the applicants' profiles was challenged under the HRA as being incompatible with Article 8 (the right to private life).

1. *R (Marper)* v *Chief Constable of South Yorkshire* [2004] UKHL 39

The UK case under the HRA

The House of Lords held that retaining samples and profiles on the database did not breach Article 8.

2. *Marper* v *UK* (2009) 48 EHRR 50

The Strasbourg case

Marper then applied to the ECtHR, which disagreed with the UKHL and held that the database did violate Marper's Article 8 rights.

▶ CROSS REFERENCE

The issues in the cases are discussed in Chapter 20, section 20.6.2.

3. *R (G)* v *Metropolitan Police Commissioner* [2011] UKSC 21

G brought a case in the UK courts after, and based on, the principles as laid down by the ECtHR in *Marper* v *UK*.

(a) Section 2 HRA means that UK courts must take into account the principles in *Marper* v *UK* and (given the way UK courts have interpreted this provision) should follow these principles unless there are exceptional reasons not to (see section 4.3).

(b) There were no exceptional reasons, so the principles in the UK case had to be replaced by those in the Strasbourg case. Therefore section 64 PACE and the Guidelines had to be interpreted with reference to those Strasbourg principles.

(c) The Supreme Court had two options:

   (i) To accept that it was not 'possible' to read section 64 PACE so that it only authorised actions (such as producing Guidelines) which were compatible with Article 8 (as interpreted in *Marper* v *UK*). Taking this option would mean that a declaration of incompatibility, under section 4 HRA, could be issued. Any further action designed to ensure compatibility with Article 8 would then be for the executive and Parliament.

   (ii) To use section 3 HRA and 'read down' section 64 PACE so that, as a matter of law, it could only authorise actions compatible with Article 8. In that case the Guidelines would be unlawful because they would have been made without statutory authority.

(d) The majority of the Supreme Court chose option (ii). In enacting the legislation, Parliament did not intend to authorise the police to make disproportionate interferences with private life that violated Article 8. Furthermore, there was no reason why Parliament should not delegate to the police the power to regulate the retention of DNA profiles, so a declaration of incompatibility was not constitutionally necessary: section 3 was not being taken beyond its interpretative purposes and being used to legislate. The minority, on the other hand, read section 64 PACE as requiring the retention of data in breach of Article 8, and so a declaration of incompatibility was the proper step for the court to take.

 DISCUSSION TOPIC

The balance between courts and Parliament in the Human Rights Act

The HRA creates a particular constitutional balance between Parliament (dominated by the government) and the courts. Has the right balance in terms of both effectiveness and legitimacy been achieved? Does the Act create foundations for proper mutual respect between Parliament and the courts? To consider this issue, it is necessary both to consider matters in this chapter but also the broader theoretical issues about 'bills of rights' raised in Chapter 1.

Issue 1: There is no full 'legislative review'. Incompatible legislation remains valid. If Parliament wishes to violate human rights it may do so, so long as it expresses that intention clearly.

Arguments such as the following can be considered:

- The absence of full legislative review is acceptable. It does not mean that Parliament can or will act oppressively (political culture, the House of Lords as 'watchdog of the constitution', the need for regular elections, will normally see to that). It recognises that human rights (or at least some of the rights) are not absolute but are subject to reasonable restrictions which reflect complex judgments about the public interest (see *R v A*, the rape shield case, discussed at section 4.4.7, as an example). Such judgments are best made by Parliament or by ministers accountable to Parliament.

- The absence of full legislative review is unacceptable. The essence of human rights, the point of their being valued, is that they represent a form of higher law which is binding on legislatures such as Parliament, as much as on governments. Reliance on political culture, the House of Lords, and elections is insufficient. This will not give proper protection to unpopular minorities. Human rights protection requires institutions which are independent of government and the popular will: we call these courts.

Issue 2: The Act gives the courts too much influence on what are essentially political questions. These include identifying what may or may not be 'necessary in a democratic society' (a phrase found in the Convention when identifying the grounds on which rights such as the right to freedom of expression can be restricted by law). Section 3 HRA leaves the courts reluctant to issue declarations of incompatibility and thus return an issue to

Parliament. On the contrary, they feel licensed to depart from the clear and unambiguous words of statutes in order to re-draft them to make them compatible with Convention rights. Arguments such as the following can be considered:

- The role of the courts in the Act is unacceptable. Difficult moral or political issues should be decided by the elected Parliament and the accountable government, not by the unelected and unaccountable courts. Furthermore, interpreting section 3 as they have, the courts have increased legal uncertainty—we are now bound not by what an Act of Parliament says but by what the courts think the 'underlying thrust' of the policy of the Act is.

- The role of the courts is acceptable. Human rights express limits on the exercise of state power. To apply these limits, impartial bodies, independent of government, are necessary—we call these courts and tribunals. Otherwise, government becomes judge in its own cause. In any case, the courts are strongly aware of the need to respect the will of Parliament where appropriate and have developed the notion of 'deference' by which they give way to political judgment on issues like national security.

Issue 3: Some commentators believe the courts should be more willing to use declarations of incompatibility. They argue that declarations both allow the democratic will of Parliament to prevail but also allow the courts to register human rights concerns and return the matter to Parliament for reconsideration. There is thus a type of dialogue or debate between the courts and Parliament and the executive through which fruitful answers to the usually complex and controversial matters to which human rights law relates, may emerge.

- See, for example: Nicol, D. 'Law and Politics after the Human Rights Act' [2006] *Public Law* 722–751; cf Hickman, T. 'The Courts and Politics after the Human Rights Act' [2008] *Public Law* 84–100.

4.5 The duty on public authorities: sections 6, 7, and 8

4.5.1 Introduction

Sections 6, 7, and 8 concern the second of the two principal ways in which the HRA gives further effect to the Convention rights in UK law. These sections impose a duty on public authorities:

- section 6 makes it unlawful for a 'public authority' (as that term is understood in the Act) to act incompatibly with the Convention rights in Schedule 1 HRA, unless it is required to do so by a valid Act of Parliament;

- section 7 creates rights to bring proceedings against public authorities if they act unlawfully under section 6; and

- section 8 identifies the remedies that courts can order.

4.5.2 The identification of a public authority: UK responsibility at Strasbourg

With two important exceptions (Parliament and the courts) the Act does not define a public authority. Whether Convention rights apply to particular bodies and institutions is left to the courts. Other Acts, such as the Freedom of Information Act 2000 or the Parliamentary Commissioner Act 1967 (which creates the Ombudsman), take a different approach and list by name or type all the public authorities that are covered (with a provision for the list to be amended).

The general idea of the HRA is that if a person could take a case to the ECtHR in Strasbourg they should, under the Act, be able to take the same case to UK courts. 'Public authorities', therefore, are those bodies for which the United Kingdom, as a state, would be responsible under the Convention.

> The purpose is that those bodies for whose acts the state is answerable before the European Court of Human Rights shall in future be subject to a domestic law obligation not to act incompatibly with convention rights.
>
> (*Aston Cantlow* v *Wallbank* [2003] UKHL 37, para 6)

▶ CROSS REFERENCE

State responsibility under the Convention is discussed in Chapter 2, section 2.4.2.

Although the basic approach is to leave the identification of public authorities to the courts, the Act does specify the status of two institutions.

4.5.3 Parliament

Parliament, including both the House of Lords and House of Commons, is not a public authority, nor is any one exercising functions in connection with 'proceedings in Parliament' (other activities connected with Parliament over which Parliament has sole control) (section 6(3)(b) HRA). Excluding Parliament from the reach of section 6 is a necessary consequence of parliamentary supremacy and of section 3 HRA, which clearly recognises that Parliament can make valid and effective law even though it is incompatible with Convention rights.

4.5.4 The courts

Courts and tribunals are specifically identified, in section 6(3)(a) HRA, as public authorities bound by the HRA. Included in this is the Supreme Court of the United Kingdom (and previously the House of Lords in its judicial capacity). The consequences of this are discussed in sections 4.6 and 4.7.

4.5.5 Defining and identifying 'public authorities'

Section 6(1) HRA says:

> It is unlawful for a public authority to act in a way which is incompatible with a Convention right.

The section does not define a public authority. This is left to the courts as they interpret those words. Though reference may be made to the type of body which is amenable to ordinary judicial review and to bodies which are 'emanations of the state' for the purposes of European Union law, the test for 'public authority' under the HRA is independent of both of these.

The leading case for identifying public authorities is *Aston Cantlow Parochial Church Council* v *Wallbank*.

🔍 CASE-CLOSE UP

Aston Cantlow Parochial Church Council v Wallbank [2003] UKHL 37

Mr and Mrs Wallbank purchased a property that was subject to a traditional duty which required them to pay for the upkeep and repair of the chancel of the local parish church (the area of a church used by the clergy). This duty to repair was enforced by the local Parochial Church Council (PCC) exercising statutory powers. Mr and Mrs Wallbank argued that the enforcement of this duty was arbitrary and involved a violation of their right to the peaceful enjoyment of possessions under Article 1 of the First Protocol (a scheduled Convention right). The PCC would only be bound by the provisions of Article 1 if it was a public authority under section 6.

The House of Lords held that the PCC was not a public authority. They also held that even if Article 1 had been engaged, the enforcement of the duty to repair would not have been a violation.

The Law Lords said the central characteristic pointing towards a body being a public authority is that its nature is 'governmental in a broad sense of that expression' (*Aston Cantlow*, para 7).

The reason for this definition is that the HRA aims to provide a remedy in a UK court if, and only if, such a remedy would also be available from the ECtHR in Strasbourg. Article 34 ECHR says that 'non-governmental' bodies can bring cases before the ECtHR and so, by inference, governmental bodies cannot bring cases, they do not have 'human rights'. Governmental bodies, therefore, are those bodies for which the state (the UK) has responsibility and which have the duty, in their spheres, of putting the UK's obligations to secure human rights for all into effect.

> **CROSS REFERENCE**
> This is an example of the mirror principle; see section 4.3.2.

'Intuitive' public authorities

But what are governmental bodies? Some bodies are obviously part of 'government' and are public authorities without argument. In *Aston Cantlow*, the House of Lords identified government departments, local authorities, the police, and the armed forces as being 'intuitively' governmental. HM Revenue and Customs can easily be added to this list. It needs to be recalled that the civil service is no longer organised in single bureaucratic departments of state but is structured as a number of relatively free-standing agencies, such as the Prison Service or the Immigration Service. Since these are the organisational structures adopted by government departments, they clearly come within the definition of governmental. Scottish ministers, exercising devolved powers based on the Scotland Act 1998 are 'public authorities' (*Somerville v Scottish Ministers* [2007] UKHL 44).

General characteristics

Many other bodies will be governmental and, therefore, public authorities. There is no definitive list but the House of Lords (adopting proposals by Professor Dawn Oliver) suggested features such as the following:

- the possession of special powers (i.e. powers given by an Act of Parliament which enable the body concerned to regulate, take decisions, and in other ways exercise authority over others);
- democratic accountability (e.g. to Parliament or other representative assembly or its committees or to a minister responsible to Parliament);
- public funding in whole or in part;

- a statutory constitution (i.e. the body is established under statute for purposes given in the statute and for no other);
- an obligation to act only in the public interest (i.e. there are no additional or complementary private interests).

Two other factors were listed in a Scottish case, *Grampian University Hospitals NHS Trust* v *Procurator Fiscal* [2004] HRLR 18, at paras 9 and 19, which may have general relevance:

- a body established by the executive with functions specified by the executive, a legal duty to comply with directions given by the executive, and which is funded by the executive and dissolvable by the executive (it is not clear whether the reference to 'the executive' is confined to the Scottish Executive);
- bodies which are 'wholly under the supervision of the state' and 'very far from being an entity distinct from or independent of the State'.

Quangos or NDGOs

These general principles mean that public authorities will probably include 'quangos' or 'non-departmental governing organisations' (NDGOs). These are bodies, normally established by Act of Parliament, which perform a wide range of functions and duties. These can include, for example, regulating or inspecting a particular area of governmental, social, or economic activity. They all have different characteristics from each other. They are, to varying degrees, independent of central government but are also, to varying degrees, subject to direction or supervision by central government. They are, however, wholly 'public' in the sense of not having a significant charitable or commercial side to their activities. Examples include the Commission for Equality and Human Rights, the Office of Communications (Ofcom), the Financial Conduct Authority, the various Directors General responsible for regulating the utility companies (Ofgas, Ofwat, etc.), and the Chief Inspector of Prisons. Such bodies (and there are many of them) are likely to fit at least some of the criteria for being a public authority. If they do, it needs to be remembered that, whilst they are themselves bound to act compatibly with Convention rights, they do not themselves have Convention rights which they might otherwise use to challenge a minister's direction.

Service providers

What of service providers, for example the maintained education sector (from play school to university) and the National Health Service? These are governmental in the sense that the state, through the government, accepts responsibility for, and funds, the bulk of educational and health provision in the United Kingdom (universities less so). They also have special powers: school education in the UK is compulsory, universities have special authority to issue degrees, and the distribution of health care involves the exercise of power.

- In *Ali* v *Head Teacher and Governors of Lord Grey School* [2006] UKHL 14, a state-maintained school (acting through the governors and the head teacher) was 'undoubtedly' a public authority under section 6(1) (see para 79).
- In *R (Munjaz)* v *Mersey Care NHS Trust* [2005] UKHL 58, there was 'no doubt' that the NHS Trust in question was a public authority under section 6(1) (see para 7).

In neither case was the issue subject to much discussion. A focus on the provision of services could lead to the conclusion that schools and hospitals are not governmental and so only bound by human rights when exercising their special powers, rather than in all they do. This would make them 'functional' authorities, see section 4.5.6. This does not seem to be the case. In *Copland* v *UK* (2007) 45 EHRR 37, the UK accepted that it had state responsibility for the actions of a further education college in respect of one of its administrative employees.

Where a body is defined as a public authority by section 6(1) alone it can be referred to as a 'core' or 'standard' authority.

4.5.6 **Any person exercising public functions**

Public functions

Some of the difficulties about whether a body is a public authority are resolved by section 6(3)(b) and (5) HRA. Section 6(3)(b) says that 'public authority' includes:

> any person certain of whose functions are functions of a public nature.

Thus anyone, an individual, a business, a charity or a public organisation such as a university or the BBC, can be bound by Convention rights in so far as they are exercising public functions. These non-governmental bodies performing public functions can be referred to as 'functional' authorities. They are subject to the HRA in respect of their public functions but not in respect of any other commercial or charitable activities they may perform (section 6(5)). At least in respect of these non-public functions they have rights under the HRA.

There is no definitive test for a public function in this context. In *Aston Cantlow*, the House of Lords said that the matter was to be decided on the facts of each case (a Parochial Church Council was not a 'functional authority'—though Lord Nicholls dissented on the point). Guidance on the matter in *Aston Cantlow* has been built on by the House of Lords in *YL* v *Birmingham City Council* [2007] UKHL 27—in which a majority of their Lordships decided that a private care home, providing care to elderly people under contract with a local authority, was not performing functions of a public nature. In *YL* Lord Neuberger suggested the following (paras 156–169):

- Applying section 6(3)(b) should not result in persons and organisations having human rights responsibilities under the HRA even though the United Kingdom does not have responsibility for such persons or organisations at Strasbourg.

- A pointer to functions being 'public' is that they are 'governmental' in character.

- The simple fact that the state has accepted responsibility for a service (such as health, education, or pensions) does not mean that particular providers are necessarily performing public functions.

- Public funding of a service as a whole points to the provision of that service being a public function; this should be distinguished from particular payments to particular individuals.

- Of 'particular importance' is that a function is likely to be public when it involves the exercise of coercive or other particular and intrusive powers, based usually but not necessarily on statute.

- A function is unlikely to be 'public' if it is exercised on the basis of a private, contractual relationship rather than one arising from statute.

Section 6(3)(b) recognises one of the important features of the way public functions are dealt with in the modern state of the twenty-first century. Examples are:

- Commercial companies running public services, such as prisons or transportation of prisoners. These involve the exercise of special powers at the behest of a core authority. In *Yarl's Wood Immigration Ltd* v *Bedfordshire Police* [2009] EWCA Civ 1110, it was held that

Group 4, running an immigration detention centre on behalf of the Home Office, was a functional authority 'in many circumstances'.

- Commercial companies exercising regulatory and supervisory powers. For example, commercial operators of airports and docks have some responsibilities for safety; airlines have duties as regards immigration.

- Charities when they have a specific statutory role (as the NSPCC does under the Children Act 1989). In *RSPCA v Attorney General* [2001] 3 All ER 530, on the other hand, it was held that the famous animal charity did not perform public functions (para 37).

- The professional regulatory bodies, such as the Solicitors Regulation Authority. Professional disciplinary decisions may be taken, ultimately, by a tribunal, which is expressly a public authority (see *Virdi* v *Law Society* [2010] EWCA Civ 100). In *Tehrani* v *United Kingdom Central Council for Nursing, Midwifery and Health Visiting* [2001] IRLR 208 (a Scottish case), the Professional Conduct Committee of the nurses' professional body was, when exercising its disciplinary function, performing functions of a public nature.

- Independent schools can be subject to the HRA since the UK has state responsibility over, for example, their use of punishment (this issue is discussed in section 4.7).

Sporting regulators such as the Football Association are normally not considered to be exercising public functions (*Stretford* v *FA* [2006] EWHC 479). Likewise informal systems of cooperation, such as a pub watch scheme, in which pub landlords cooperated over the banning of undesirable customers, are unlikely to involve the exercise of a public function (*R (Boyle)* v *Haverhill Pub Watch* [2009] EWHC 2441).

Private acts

6(5) In relation to a particular act, a person is not a public authority by virtue only of subsection (3)(b) if the nature of the act is private.

Persons and organisations discussed in the previous sections, i.e. those which are not governmental but that perform public functions, are not bound by Convention rights in respect of their 'private' acts. Private acts are likely to include matters connected with contracts of employment, property matters, and matters relating to internal management (see the *RSPCA* case, this section). In particular, such non-governmental public authorities are likely to have extensive private functions (e.g. their commercial or charitable activities) and actions connected with these are likely to be private acts and, therefore, not subject to the HRA.

The issue of the private acts of a body performing public functions can be complex. In *R (Weaver)* v *London and Quadrant Housing Trust* [2009] EWCA Civ 587, it was conceded that a charitable housing trust, in receipt of large project grants and central to the chosen means by which government policy on affordable housing was pursued, was exercising public functions and was a public authority by virtue of section 6(3)(b). The issue was then whether the individual action of evicting W, a tenant, was a 'private act'. Taking into account the circumstances, the Court of Appeal decided that the eviction was part of the exercise of the public function and not a private act.

The position of a functional authority is different in principle from a core, governmental, public authority. The latter are taken to be subject to human rights in all they do. Their employment and property relations are at least arguably subject to the HRA. In a series of cases the UKHL/UKSC has, following Strasbourg principles, held that public landlords (e.g. local authorities) do not have the freedom of private landlords when exercising statutory powers of eviction.

4.5.7 **Contracting out and the 'welfare gap'**

These days it is normal for standard public authorities, such as local councils, to contract out the provision of services. A local council, exercising statutory powers and duties, will decide whether, for example, an elderly person is entitled to care, but the care itself will be provided by a commercial or charitable organisation on the basis of a contract. The nature and quality of care can raise issues under, for example, Article 8 of the Convention (the right to respect for a person's home) and the question arises whether the private or charitable organisation providing the service is a functional authority and so subject to the HRA.

YL (at section 4.5.6) indicates that a body that simply delivers a service on a contract with a core public authority, such as a local council, does not have obligations under the Convention. In the court's view the simple provision of a service to individuals (as distinct from the decision that they are entitled to it) is not within the concept of public function in section 6(3)(b) (see section 4.5.6). The provider's rights and duties are private: they are founded on a contract with the core authority rather than a statutory scheme. Convention rights may apply, however, if the provider is closely tied, institutionally and organisationally, with the core authority (see *Poplar Housing and Regeneration Community Association Ltd* v *Donoghue* [2001] EWCA Civ 595).

This position is controversial. It seemed to leave vulnerable people (such as the old and the homeless) unable to bring human rights claims even though they may have suffered degrading treatment (raising issues under Article 3) or interferences with their sense of selfhood and autonomy (raising issues under Article 8); in particular they lose the chance to claim that their right to a home (in Article 8) has been violated if the accommodation they have grown used to is suddenly closed. Critics argue that it is arbitrary to make the rights of vulnerable people in such situations depend on issues of political fashion—whether services are provided directly (as they often were into the 1980s) or by being contracted out (as they normally are today). So far as care homes are concerned (the issue in *YL* at section 4.5.6), the matter has now been resolved by Parliament. Under section 73 Care Act 2014, the provision of accommodation coupled with nursing or personal care in a care home involves exercising a public function. But the problem of a 'gap' in human rights protection for the vulnerable remains in others areas, such as provision for the homeless.

The courts have, however, made it clear that the public authority that contracts with the mere service provider retains its statutory obligations under the HRA and this may involve responsibilities for the human rights of the vulnerable to be secured through direct regulation or by the terms of the contract with the provider.

 DISCUSSION TOPIC

The definition of a 'public function'

At the heart of the matter is a deep-seated disagreement over what is a public function, and this, in turn, raises questions about the role of the state.

- On one view, public functions are to do with the exercise of coercive authority based on special powers: a public function is to do with the exercise of power, restricting people's liberty in the public interest, regulating, etc. The provision of services does not involve these things. Responsibility, including funding, should lie with public authorities properly so-called and they should ensure that service providers meet high standards. A particular advantage of this view, under the Act, is that it permits organisations, such as universities and care homes, to enjoy Convention rights. If they were public authorities they might not have standing to bring cases.

- Alternatively it is argued that the failure of families and of civil society to deal with a range of social problems, such as poverty, adequate education, care of the mentally ill, etc. has meant that (since the mid-nineteenth century if not before) these have increasingly become state responsibilities. Where programmes originate in legislation and government action they should be recognised as public functions. It is arbitrary to withhold Convention rights from people merely because of the current administrative fashions.

Leading texts on this debate include: House of Lords, House of Commons Joint Committee on Human Rights Seventh Report of the Session 2003–2004, *The Meaning of a Public Authority under the Human Rights Act* and Oliver, D. 'Functions of a Public Nature under the Human Rights Act' [2004] *Public Law* (Summer), 329; cf Craig, P. 'Contracting out, the Human Rights Act and the Scope of Judicial Review' (2002) 118 *LQR* 551–568. The debate is reflected in their Lordships' disagreements in *YL* v *Birmingham City Council* [2007] UKHL 27.

4.5.8 Public authorities defence, section 6(2)

Public authorities do not act unlawfully if statute requires them to act in a way which is incompatible with Convention rights (i.e. the statute cannot be read and given effect in a compatible way, see the discussion of section 3 HRA, at section 4.4.2). Section 6(2) says:

Subsection (1) does not apply if—

(a) as the result of one or more provisions of primary legislation the authority could not have acted differently; or

(b) in the case of one or more provisions of, or made under, primary legislation which cannot be read or given effect in a way which is compatible with the Convention rights, the authority was acting so as to give effect to or enforce those provisions.

Section 6(2) has been discussed by the House of Lords.

 CASE CLOSE-UP

R (Hooper) v *Secretary of State for Work and Pensions* [2005] UKHL 29

Various welfare payments and pensions were, according to the Social Security Contributions and Benefits Act 1992 (now repealed), only available to widows and not widowers. This was sex discrimination in respect to property rights and incompatible with the Convention (see Chapter 7, section 7.1). The legislation could not, under section 3, be read for compatibility. The claimants had asked the Secretary of State (a public authority) to make equivalent non-statutory payments to widowers but the Secretary refused to do so. The House of Lords held that the Secretary was protected by section 6(2) and had not acted unlawfully.

Though in *Hooper* the Law Lords disagreed between themselves about the precise application of section 6(2), broadly it can be said that:

- if the legislation prevents a Convention-compatible action (here the making of non-statutory payments), then section 6(2)(a) protects the public authority that does not act;
- if the legislation does not expressly prevent Convention-compatible actions but, to make them, involves a public authority going against the clear purpose of the legislation, then section 6(2)(b) protects the public authority.

Thus section 6(2) protects a public authority not only when it is acting in accordance with the express requirements of the statute (performing a duty), but also when it is acting compatibly with the statute even though it could, legally, act differently. In other words, the public authority has chosen to exercise a discretion which can only be exercised in a non-compatible way. In *Doherty* v *Birmingham City Council* [2008] UKHL 57, the House of Lords upheld the right of a local authority to evict tenants in breach of Convention rights. The local authority had the statutory power (discretion) to evict in breach of Article 8 and was protected by section 6(2)(b) when it chose to do so.

4.5.9 **Actions against public authorities**

Sections 7, 8, and 9 of the HRA deal with enforcement: with the way Convention rights can be asserted against public authorities in UK courts and the remedies that can be obtained from the courts. This important matter is dealt with in Chapter 5.

4.6 The courts and the Human Rights Act: proportionality and deference

The job of the UK courts is to apply Convention rights in cases involving statutes or the actions of public authorities. In doing so they will often have to assess the 'proportionality' of a public authority's actions. This is because proportionality pervades the way Convention rights are applied (see Chapter 6, section 6.5). Proportionality can involve the courts in assessing the relative importance of an individual's Convention rights measured against the rights of others or the general public interest.

4.6.1 **The test for proportionality**

 CASE CLOSE-UP

***Bank Mellat (2)* v *The Treasury* [2013] UKSC 39**

Using powers under the Counter-Terrorism Act 2008, HM Treasury made orders prohibiting a large Iranian bank from undertaking business in the UK. Part of the Bank's legal challenge to these orders was that they were a disproportionate interference with its right

❯ CROSS REFERENCE

Article 1 of the First Protocol is discussed in Chapter 23.

to the peaceful enjoyment of possessions under HRA Schedule 1, Article 1 of the First Protocol. Lords Reed and Sumption included discussions of the idea of proportionality in their judgments which have been widely followed (paras 20 and 68 passim). The European idea of proportionality focuses on reviewing whether the authorities have achieved a 'fair balance' between the rights of the individual and the rights of others or the common good. In this they have a (variable) margin of appreciation. Margin of appreciation does not apply in domestic law and so a structured approach is required.

This more structured approach is based upon an 'exacting analysis' by the domestic court of the factual case advanced by the authorities in defence of the measure (usually a piece of legislation itself or the actions of the executive taken on the alleged authority of some legislation). The aim of this analysis is to determine:

(i) whether the objective of the measure is sufficiently important to justify the limitation of a fundamental right;

(ii) whether the content of the measure is rationally connected to the objective—is in a sensible way capable of achieving the objective;

(iii) whether a less intrusive measure could have been used. This provision is controversial because if a judge, for other reasons, wanted to find the measure disproportionate, it is usually possible for him or her to come up with an alternative less intrusive approach. So this is not an absolute requirement. Rather, the judge must be satisfied that the limitation on the right was one which it was reasonable for the legislature to impose (see Lord Reed para 75); and

(iv) whether, having regard to these matters and to the severity of the consequences, a fair balance has been struck between the rights of the individual and the interests of the community. Thus even if an outcome is sufficiently serious to justify limiting rights and the measure used to do this is not obviously more drastic than available alternatives, it may still be the case that its specific impact on the applicant's rights is so severe that it is disproportionate to the alleged benefits.

These four requirements are logically separate, but in practice they inevitably overlap because the same facts are likely to be relevant to more than one of them.

 THINKING POINT

Consider why, though Lords Sumption and Reed agreed on the nature of the proportionality test, they disagreed on its application in the case.

This is different from the approach in ordinary administrative law. Traditionally this was concerned with whether a decision maker had taken all relevant matters into account and not taken irrelevant matters into account. If this was so, assessment of the weight and significance of these matters tended to be for the decision maker and not the courts. In human rights adjudication, on the other hand, 'the court is concerned with whether the human rights of the claimant have in fact been infringed, not with whether the administrative decision-maker took them into account' (*Miss Behavin' Ltd* v *Belfast City Council* [2007] UKHL 19, para 31, per Baroness Hale).

4.6.2 **Deference**

A judgment of proportionality puts the burden on the court, on the judges, to assess the balance of interests the decision taker has struck and, perhaps, to assess for itself the weight and significance that needs to be given to the different interests involved. In doing this the courts may be accused of so-called 'merits review'—that they are substituting their own view of a policy matter for that of the executive or Parliament.

Separation of powers. This raises, first, a constitutional issue about the separation of powers. Does the constitutional position of the courts require them to respect and follow the decisions of the executive or respect the will of Parliament? Here the HRA has made a difference to the traditional position. The Act discloses the intention of Parliament that the judges have, as their overriding duty, the protection of individual's human rights: 'the court's role under the 1998 Act [the HRA] is as the guardian of human rights. It cannot abdicate this responsibility' (Simon Brown LJ, as he then was, *International Transport Roth GmbH* v *Secretary of State for the Home Department* [2003] QB 728, para 27. It follows that, in human rights cases, the traditional reticence of the courts to evaluate the executive's position, should be dispensed with in so far as this reticence is thought to embody the constitutional role of the courts and the separation of powers. Even on issues traditionally associated with the executive, such as national security and foreign policy, the court is entitled to subject any matter to its scrutiny and evaluation which is relevant and necessary to determining whether a person's human rights are violated (Lord Sumption in *R (Carlile)* v *Secretary of State for the Home Department* [2014] UKSC 60, paras 27–31). There are no 'no-go areas' which, on separation of powers grounds, are simply outside the jurisdiction of the courts when it comes to human rights.

Institutional competence. However, there remain important questions about the 'institutional competence' of the courts. The fact that, in a human rights context, there is no constitutional barrier to a court forming a judgment for itself on the weight to be given to relevant factors, does not mean that, in the circumstances of a case, a court can do this in a credible way in practice. The argument about 'institutional competence' concerns whether, pragmatically, a court has the resources to evaluate the executive's judgment which has led to the action or decision being challenged on human rights grounds. For example:

- The courts may not have access to the information and expertise that the authorities have. For this reason it may be necessary to give considerable respect to the judgments of those who do. The government may have almost a monopoly on information about threats to national security or best conduct of foreign policy to which the courts may have reason to defer. This information is part of the justification for interfering with someone's rights. Likewise, where an executive or regulatory body has been created with expertise over a particular matter, again the courts may need to give its views considerable respect.

- The courts adjudicate—they settle disputes on the basis of evidence provided by the parties. This means that they may not be in a position to challenge an assessment made by the authorities on the basis of a wide range of views and ideas.

- Similarly the courts may be in no better position than anyone else to make judgments about future outcomes; yet doing this is the very stuff of much political judgment (see *Carlile*).

The judicial role. But in the human rights context, constitutional duty and institutional competence can be hard to separate. This is because the degree of deference also depends on the nature of the human right in issue in a case. The ban on torture (Article 3) is absolute even if torture might lead to desirable outcomes. This means that there can be no justifications based on information, expertise, or future outcomes that needs to be assessed. On the other hand, other rights (such as freedom of expression) do allow justification on such grounds. There are also some matters on which the courts themselves have a constitutionally acknowledged role which entitles them to exercise intensive scrutiny of justifications for interference with rights—individual liberty (Article 5) and fair trials and hearings (Article 6) are two examples.

Parliament and democratic legitimacy: many human rights cases, of course, are concerned with a judgment made by Parliament. The courts can issue a declaration of incompatibility in respect of an Act of Parliament which authorises or allows a breach of human rights. The issues of institutional competence discussed earlier in this section are relevant. At stake are the balancing of interests accepted by Parliament in legislating as it has. But there is an additional factor: how much deference is owed on the grounds of democratic legitimacy—to the fact that an Act of Parliament is an expression of the will of the people's representatives and may have been in the governing party's manifesto; or what weight should be given to the fact that an administrative action has been expressly endorsed by Parliament.

One view is that human rights apply to and limit the freedom of Parliament as much as the executive and so no additional deference should be shown. There is sufficient deference inherent in the HRA itself, given that it does not allow courts to invalidate an incompatible Act.

The other view is that, in a democracy, some deference is owed particularly on those questions where an Act embodies a particular way of weighing conflicting interests and the issue is justification.

In *R (Nicklinson)* v *Ministry of Justice* [2014] UKSC 38 (discussed in Chapter 15), the issue for the court was whether section 2 Suicide Act, which bans assisting someone's suicide, infringes the Article 8 rights of the person unable, thereby, to die at a time of their choice. The majority held that the UKSC had the right to determine this question; it was not solely and constitutionally just a matter for Parliament. However, the court declined to exercise its power because of 'institutional competence' matters—it did not have access to the full range of ideas and information necessary for an effective decision. Deference was shown to Parliament at least to the extent that Parliament should have the opportunity for a full debate on the issue.

Nicklinson was subject to strong dissents, with four justices (out of a court of nine) arguing that the issue was fundamentally one for Parliament and the courts should not interfere.

4.7 The courts and the Human Rights Act: the Convention and private law

Courts and tribunals are public authorities.

> 6(3)(b) In this section 'public authority' includes—
>
> (a) a court or tribunal.

This means that courts and tribunals must ensure that in all they do in hearing cases and granting remedies, etc. they act compatibly with the Convention rights.

4.7.1 **The impact on private parties**

The main point of the ECHR is to provide rights against the state acting through its agents such as the police and civil service (thus section 6 HRA is confined to 'public authorities'). Treating courts and tribunals as public authorities and requiring them to act compatibly with Convention rights, raises the question of the impact of Convention rights on private law (the legal relations between private parties—individuals, commercial companies, charities, etc.). The courts deal with private law (contract, tort, etc.) and the duty under section 6(3)(b) must apply to this as much as to public law.

 BIGGER PICTURE

For authoritative discussion see Sir William Wade, 'Horizons of Horizontality' (2000) 116 *LQR* (April) 217–224 and criticised by The Rt Hon. Sir Richard Buxton, 'The Human Rights Act and Private Law' (2000) 116 *LQR* (January) 48–65.

Horizontal effect

'Horizontal effect' means the effect on the relations between private parties as distinct from 'vertical effect', which refers to the relationship between the individual and the state.

No direct horizontal effect

The Act does not provide for 'direct' horizontal effect. Sections 6 and 7 only permit cases to be brought against public authorities and not against private companies and other bodies. For example, newspapers, which in the United Kingdom are owned by commercial companies, are not public authorities under section 6 and so cannot be directly sued under section 7. Nevertheless there are a number of ways in which Convention rights will apply to private parties. This is sometimes known as 'indirect horizontal effect'.

Section 3 applies in both a public and a private context

The duty under section 3 of the HRA to interpret statutes so far as possible for compatibility applies to all statutes, including those which govern private relations. Nothing in the Act suggests that it is only statutes governing public authorities that need to be so interpreted.

 CASE CLOSE-UP

X v *Y* [2004] EWCA Civ 662

X went to the lavatory in a transport café where he had a sexual encounter with another man. Police were undertaking surveillance and X was arrested and then cautioned for an offence under section 13 of the Sexual Offences Act 1956 (gross indecency between men, now repealed). As a consequence of the caution, X's name was placed on the sex offenders' register and this became known to his employer. He was dismissed because he had failed to disclose the offence to his employer. He brought an action for unfair dismissal under the Employment Rights Act 1996. Under section 98 the employer must (broadly speaking) prove that the dismissal was fair. X argued that fairness in relation to section 98 should be interpreted so as to secure his right to privacy.

> The Court of Appeal held that section 98 of the Employment Rights Act should be interpreted for compatibility with Convention rights. It held that the encounter did not take place in a private place, and so, on the facts, Article 8 was not engaged (Brooke LJ dissented on this point).

Positive obligations/duties

These points, of course, raise the question of how Convention rights can affect the actions and decisions of private parties. Courts' duties under sections 3 and 6(3)(b) HRA are to seek compatibility with Convention rights. They do not imply that the courts should impose new kinds of duties and obligations which are not found in Convention rights.

- The Convention does not directly place duties on individuals, private companies, etc. Rather, duties are imposed on the state to secure the rights for all (Article 1) and provide effective remedies (Article 13).

- Nevertheless the ECtHR has said many times that securing Convention rights and freedoms for all may involve the state in taking positive steps. These can include changing the law or regulatory regime that applies to private parties. For example, the law governing the relations between newspapers and the public must be capable of guaranteeing that a proper balance between freedom of expression and private life is struck. Similarly, employment law should enable a tribunal to balance employees' rights to freedom of expression against employers' interests when private sector employees are dismissed for things they have said or written (see *Sanchez* v *Spain* App 28955/06, Grand Chamber judgment of 12 September 2011, paras 57 and 60). As state institutions, the courts can be expected to give effect to these positive obligations in the way they develop the law.

- These positive obligations, however, remain obligations on the state, so they do not impose obligations on private bodies directly.

> **CROSS REFERENCE**
>
> Positive duties are discussed in Chapter 6, section 6.6.

- The extent to which the language of positive obligations really does authorise the imposition of Convention rights on private parties should not be overstated. Under the Convention, states have a wide margin of appreciation on the way positive obligations are achieved.

Developing the common law

Convention rights have clearly influenced the way in which some aspects of the common law governing private relations has developed. Nothing in the HRA authorises courts directly to impose Convention duties on private parties or to create new remedies and causes of action. Nevertheless, as was expected during the Act's passage through Parliament, the Convention has influenced the way in which private law has developed. The values inherent in the Convention have, in some areas, been absorbed as values of the common law.

This was a process that occurred before the HRA came into effect: see Chapter 3, sections 3.3.3 and 3.5.2. A good example of this process of absorption is found in cases where the courts have developed the common law concept of breach of confidence in order to protect celebrities' reasonable expectations of privacy against the press. Convention rights are not directly in issue, since newspapers are not public authorities and no Act of Parliament is being relied upon. Nevertheless, in *Campbell* v *MGN* [2004]

UKHL 22, the House of Lords held that Convention rights provided 'values' and gave 'important guidance' for the common law and dealt with the issue in terms of a balancing of Articles 8 and 10.

But the issue is within the discretion of the courts. In *Smith v Chief Constable of Sussex Police* [2008] UKHL 50, for instance, a majority of the House of Lords expressly refused to strengthen the common law liability of the police for damages in a way that would have endorsed Article 2 (see paras 136–139).

CROSS REFERENCE
The 'celebrity' cases are discussed in Chapter 22.

4.8 Free speech and freedom of religion

During the passage through Parliament of the HRA, concern was expressed that there could be detrimental effects on freedom of expression and religious freedom. It was feared, for example, that freedom of the press would be unduly restricted by the need to respect private life (under Article 8) or that religious schools would be unable to defend themselves by dismissing teachers whose behaviour was incompatible with the school's ethos. Though these concerns were probably exaggerated, sections 12 and 13 of the Act require courts to have 'particular regard' to freedom of expression and freedom of religion.

CROSS REFERENCE
For section 12 see Chapter 17, section 17.3; for section 13 see Chapter 16, section 16.1.3.

4.9 Ministers and Parliament

4.9.1 Ministers and human rights culture

The HRA embodies a particular constitutional balance between the courts, Parliament, and ministers over the proper way to protect human rights in the United Kingdom. Obviously the primary duties lie with the courts, specifically regarding the interpretation of statutes and the legally enforceable duty on public authorities. However, a significant role for Parliament and ministers is allowed for under the Act.

- Ministers of the Crown (and equivalents from the devolved assemblies) are entitled to be joined as a party to the proceedings if a court is considering whether or not to make a declaration of incompatibility (section 5 HRA).

- If the courts do award a declaration of incompatibility, it is then up to ministers (and Parliament) to decide what is the best course of action (see section 4.4.4).

The 'Ministerial Code', in which Prime Ministers express the general standards which ministers should meet when performing their duties and obligations, refers to the 'overarching duty on Ministers to comply with the law' (2015 version, para 1.2). This duty involves respecting human rights, including the ECHR (the 2015 version removed an additional reference to international law).

The Act is also an important part of an effort to develop a 'human rights culture' in government by which all actions and decisions are considered for compatibility with human rights.

> **BIGGER PICTURE**
>
> The 'Human Rights Inquiry' produced by the Equality and Human Rights Commission in 2012 contains a detailed exploration of the extent to which a human rights culture has been successfully embedded in public authorities.

4.9.2 **Section 19 HRA**

The Act requires ministers to consider compatibility with human rights when promoting legislation before Parliament.

Statement of compatibility

19(1) A Minister of the Crown in charge of a Bill in either House of Parliament must, before Second Reading of the Bill—

(a) make a statement to the effect that in his view the provisions of the Bill are compatible with the Convention rights ('a statement of compatibility'); or

(b) make a statement to the effect that although he is unable to make a statement of compatibility the government nevertheless wishes the House to proceed with the Bill.

(2) The statement must be in writing and be published in such manner as the Minister making it considers appropriate.

These statements have no legal effect and are not binding on the courts. Section 19 does not require ministers to give reasons for their view. A typical statement is one or two lines long, simply stating that, in the minister's view, the bill is compatible. Where a minister thinks the bill is not compatible, he or she is legally required merely to say whether or not the bill should be proceeded with. The way section 19 is put into effect is left to the discretion of ministers.

It is, however, common, these days, for major bills to be accompanied by 'explanatory notes' produced by the department, which may contain explanations in some detail.

Section 19 only applies to the time prior to the second reading of a bill. Amendments made after that, such as in committee, do not, by law, have to have a statement of compatibility. It is perfectly possible for bills to be significantly amended after the second reading with provisions that raise human rights issues.

Most bills are stated to be compatible. An exception was the Communications Bill 2003. This was a vast bill which reorganised the regulations of broadcasting and telecommunications. The Secretary of State (the minister) made the following statement under section 19:

> I am unable (but only because of clause 309) to make a statement that, in my view, the provisions of the Communications Bill are compatible with the Convention rights. However, the government nevertheless wishes the House to proceed with the bill.

Clause 309 was a total ban on political advertising and may have been incompatible with Article 10 (but see *R (Animal Defenders International)* v *Secretary of State for Culture Media and Sport* [2008] UKHL 15, discussed in Chapter 17, section 17.8.3). No reason is given in the section 19 statement, but the 'explanatory notes' accompanying the bill gave an explanation (see explanatory notes on the Communications Bill, paras 631–634, on clause 309).

4.9.3 *Pepper v Hart*

Ministerial statements made during the parliamentary process can be used to assist statutory interpretation under the rule in *Pepper v Hart*. On limited occasions, such statements can be used to determine the Convention compatibility of legislation under section 3 HRA. Such statements can only be used to provide background information (such as on the mischief the legislation aims to remedy) to assist the courts. However, it remains the job of the courts to make their own judgment on whether or not the legislation is compatible with Convention rights, see *Wilson v First County Trust (No 2)* [2003] UKHL 40, para 67.

4.9.4 **Parliament and the Joint Select Committee on Human Rights**

A human rights culture and proper adherence to human rights values should involve legislators. The HRA does not expressly require anything of legislators (indeed, as we have seen, it permits Parliament to legislate incompatibly with Convention rights). Nevertheless, Parliament responded to the Act by establishing a Joint Committee on Human Rights. This is a select committee of MPs and peers established under the rules and standing orders of both Houses. It has cross-party membership of six backbench MPs and six peers. The Committee has a staff and a legal advisor. The committee has a broad remit to 'consider matters relating to human rights in the United Kingdom'. It does not deal with individual cases. The Committee has the following duties:

- The Committee reports to Parliament on the compatibility of bills with Convention rights. The Committee examines all bills before Parliament and brings the attention of Parliament to any problems of compatibility there may be. The Committee's reports contain detailed examination of issues and are an impressive and authoritative source of information and ideas.

- The Committee examines any remedial orders made under section 10 of the Act.

- The Committee produces ad hoc reports on themes and issues relevant to human rights generally and the HRA in particular. It has, for example, conducted its own report into deaths in custody in the United Kingdom as well as producing an influential report on the definition of a public authority under the Act and whether this should include private and charitable bodies providing welfare services at the behest of local councils. As currently operating, the Committee provides a strong parliamentary voice contributing to the development and protection of human rights in the UK, often in opposition to the government.

BIGGER PICTURE

The reports of the Joint Committee are available on the internet via the Parliament website http://www.publications.parliament.uk/pa/jt/jtrights.htm (UK Parliament/ Publications and Records/Committee Reports/Select Committee Publications/Joint Committee/Human Rights).

4.10 Equality and Human Rights Commission

The HRA did not set up a public authority with a brief to promote human rights and, perhaps, to aid individuals in bringing human rights cases. Northern Ireland does have a Human Rights Commission. In the rest of the United Kingdom such bodies had been set up only in the context of sex, race, and disability discrimination. One of the reasons for not establishing a specific human rights commission at the time of the Act was opposition from these established bodies, coupled with the fear that there would be difficult 'turf wars' between them and the human rights body, and that difficult questions of priority between, say, racial discrimination and other human rights might occur.

Under the Equality Act 2006, the Equal Opportunities Commission, the Commission for Racial Equality, and the Disability Rights Commission were abolished and replaced by a single agency, the Equality and Human Rights Commission. (Scotland and Wales have their own Commissions.) On the basis of its powers, the Commission works to eliminate discrimination in disability, age, gender, religion or belief, sexual orientation, and race. The Commission has important powers to promote human rights (including rights not in the Convention) generally and, with public authorities, to monitor the effectiveness of the law and advise on change. It can, exceptionally and subject to the Lord Chancellor's order, assist some individual human rights claimants (section 28(7)(c)).

 BIGGER PICTURE

For further detail on the Commission see http://www.equalityhumanrights.com.

4.11 Where does the Human Rights Act apply?

The HRA is an Act of the United Kingdom, which applies, therefore, to the law in England, Wales, Scotland, and Northern Ireland. The laws in these four countries can be very different. Scotland and Northern Ireland have their own legal systems.

4.11.1 Devolution

Devolution is the process through which political and legal powers have been transferred to Scotland, Northern Ireland, and Wales.

The Scotland Act 1998 created a Scottish Parliament and Scottish Executive, which have primary law-making and governing authority over all matters relating to Scotland which have not been expressly held back for the UK Parliament and government. The Scottish Parliament and Executive are established by, and derive their power from, the Scotland Act 1998 and nowhere else. The Scotland Act 1998 makes it clear that it is unlawful for Parliament or the executive to legislate or act incompatibly with Convention rights. If they do so, they can be challenged before the Scottish courts. Appeal is to the UKSC. Thus Acts of the Scottish Parliament can be held to be void if they are incompatible with Convention rights (unlike the Acts of the UK Parliament, which remain valid); and a minister of the Scottish Executive who violates Convention rights has acted *ultra vires*, outside his powers. Ministers of the Scottish Executive, as public authorities, are also subject to actions under sections 6 and 7 HRA. This was confirmed in *Somerville* v *Scottish Ministers* [2007] UKHL 44. Human rights actions can be brought under either the Scotland Act 1998 or section 7 HRA—different remedies are available and this will determine an applicant's choice.

In *Axa* v *Lord Advocate* [2011] UKSC 46, for example, the UKSC held that an Act of the Scottish Parliament was not incompatible with insurers' rights to possessions under Article 1 of the First Protocol. The Act reversed an earlier judicial decision and stated that pleural plaques (possible indicators of future asbestosis) could be the basis for actionable claims for negligence against employers. Employers' insurance companies challenged the validity of the Act.

 BIGGER PICTURE

For discussion of human rights law in the context of devolution, see Lord Hope, 'Devolution and Human Rights' [1998] 4 *EHRLR* 367–379.

In the past there was the possibility of inconsistency between the way human rights apply in Scotland and England because, in respect of Scotland, devolution matters (which include human rights) were decided by the Judicial Committee of the Privy Council, rather than the House of Lords. Inconsistency is now less likely since the Supreme Court has taken over jurisdiction on devolution matters. This has not lessened controversy, however, as it can lead to Scottish concern that matters of Scottish law are being decided south of the border. These arose, for example, in *Fraser* v *HM Advocate (Scotland)* [2011] UKSC, when the UKSC reversed the Scottish courts on a point of human rights relating to Scottish criminal law and procedure.

Devolution to Northern Ireland and Wales is different in detail and context from Scotland. Nevertheless, the basic principle, that the devolved assemblies and executives cannot lawfully act incompatibly with Convention rights, remains.

4.11.2 Territories for which the United Kingdom is responsible

The HRA applies to the United Kingdom. Here we have to distinguish between the UK's obligations under the ECHR (a matter of international law) and the obligations of the British government and public authorities under the HRA (a matter of national law). The United Kingdom has extended, under Article 56 ECHR, the protection of the Convention to many of its overseas territories (areas still under the ultimate control of the United Kingdom) and other places, like the Channel Islands, for which the United Kingdom had accepted foreign policy responsibilities. Such places are not part of the United Kingdom. The HRA has not been expressly extended to them. This is confirmed in *R (Barclay)* v *Secretary of State for Justice* [2014] UKSC 54. Convention rights apply in Guernsey by virtue of an Order in Council giving further effect to Convention rights in the Bailiwick, not by virtue of the HRA. Human rights challenges should be pursued in the Guernsey courts. Though the UKSC did have jurisdiction to review the making of the Order in Council, this was not a proper way to pursue a human rights claim.

Their populations can, however, take cases against the United Kingdom to the ECtHR in Strasbourg—so long as the Convention right or freedom they allege has been violated has been extended to them (as in *Matthews v United Kingdom* (1999) 28 EHRR 361—applying the right to vote (Article 3 of the First Protocol) to a Gibraltarian, see Chapter 25).

4.11.3 **UK actions overseas**

The question can arise whether the HRA applies in respect of the action of UK officials abroad. For example, are soldiers in Iraq or Afghanistan bound to act compatibly with Convention rights and do those foreigners affected by what the soldiers do have a right of action in UK courts under the Act?

The normal principle is that UK statutes, such as the HRA, do not, in the absence of express words, apply to actions done outside the jurisdiction of the United Kingdom. However, in order to ensure remedies that would be available in Strasbourg are also available under the HRA, the jurisdiction of the UK had to be interpreted in the same way as by the ECtHR.

 CROSS REFERENCE

Al-Skeini v United Kingdom is discussed in Chapter 2, 2.4.5.

The leading Strasbourg case is *Al-Skeini v United Kingdom* (2011) 53 EHRR 18. Here the ECtHR, building on earlier cases, held that normally a state's responsibility under the ECHR applied only to its actions within its territory but that there were exceptions.

These related to where the state was exercising some form of control over the situation in which the alleged breach occurred. The test is predominantly factual.

Foreigners as the 'victims'

In *R (Al-Skeini) v Secretary of State for Defence* [2007] UKHL 26, a number of Iraqis alleged a failure by the United Kingdom properly to investigate whether the deaths of their relatives killed by British forces occupying Basra in southern Iraq was a breach of Article 2. The House of Lords held that the HRA applied only in respect of one of the six victims, Baha Mousa, who had died whilst in a British military prison in Basra.

It is clear, however, that, following *Al-Skeini v UK*, this approach is too narrow. 'Control', as understood in *Al-Skeini*, includes where the state's officials and military exercise effective administrative control, directly or through local agencies, of a territory. In such circumstances the UK's duty was to ensure the full range of Convention rights, including the investigative duty under Article 2.

But the HRA may give a victim rights even if the UK is not in administrative control. If UK troops mistreat a prisoner, there may be a breach of Article 3. This would be based on the physical power and control being exercised over the prisoner. Since *Al-Skeini*, human rights can be divided and tailored. The soldiers would not need to secure all Convention rights for the prisoner.

BIGGER PICTURE

Cases by Iraqis against United Kingdom forces have tended to be subsumed by official inquiries and reports, in particular:

- *Report of the Baha Mousa Public Inquiry* (www.bahamousainquiry.org) (which found serious abuse, see Chapter 9); and

- *Al-Sweady Inquiry* https://www.gov.uk/government/publications/al-sweady-inquiry-report (which found the most serious allegations to be unfounded).

Control is a matter of fact rather than legal authority. In *R (Al-Saadoon)* v *Secretary of State for Defence* [2009] EWCA Civ 7, the HRA was said not to apply to the Secretary of State's decision to transfer the applicant, who had been detained in Iraq by UK troops, to the Iraqi authorities. The HRA did not apply because civil legal authority was with the Iraqis not the UK. However, the ECtHR, in *Al-Saadoon* v *UK* (2009) 49 EHRR SE11, focused on the fact of control (rather than its legal basis) and held that Convention rights did apply.

Soldiers fighting abroad as victims

 CASE CLOSE-UP

Smith v *Ministry of Defence* [2013] UKSC 41

Relatives of soldiers killed in Iraq sought damages from the Ministry of Defence based on breaches of Convention rights (as well as under common law).

The Supreme Court held, unanimously, that rights guaranteed by the HRA could apply to soldiers operating abroad. *Al-Skeini* (discussed earlier) was followed. The troops were clearly under the control of the UK at all times and so came under the exceptions, listed and confirmed in *Al-Skeini*, to the general principle that Convention rights mainly apply in the national territory. This applied even when the troops were outside their base (in this finding the UKSC set aside its earlier, pre-*Al-Skeini* decision in *R (Smith)* v *Oxfordshire Coroner* [2010] UKSC 29).

The substantive issue, the application of the right to life in this context, is discussed in Chapter 8, section 8.3.5.

UK troops themselves will still enjoy Convention rights relating to decisions affecting them made in the United Kingdom. In *R (Gentle)* v *Prime Minister* [2008] UKHL 20, it was held that there was no duty owed by the UK government under the HRA and Article 2 not to send UK troops to war without reliable legal advice on the legality of the war. No such duty could be read into Article 2.

Another *Al-Skeini* exception relates to actions by diplomatic and consular officials. In *R (Sandiford)* v *Secretary of State for the Foreign and Commonwealth Office* [2014] UKSC 44, the UKSC has accepted this under the HRA. S argued she had a Convention right (under Article 6, fair trial) to legal assistance in Indonesia where she was sentenced to death. However, there was no relevant act by such officials on which the denial of legal aid was based.

 ## Summary

- The HRA creates the legal framework in terms of which the content of the rights and freedoms in the ECHR are given further effect in UK law.
- There are two principal ways in which the Act does this: by imposing a duty on the courts to interpret legislation 'so far as it is possible to do so' for compatibility with Convention rights, and by putting a legally enforceable duty on 'public authorities' to act compatibly with the Convention rights.

- Anyone can be a public authority to the extent that they are performing public functions. Otherwise the Act does not impose duties on private individuals or companies directly.

- The courts are public authorities. They may be influenced by the Convention when developing the common law, including in areas that relate to the rights and obligations of private parties.

- The Act creates a particular constitutional balance between the courts, Parliament, and the government. If its intention is quite clear, Parliament may enact legislation that violates human rights. In such circumstances the courts can make a 'declaration of incompatibility'. If so, ministers must decide whether to seek a change in the law from Parliament. Where there are 'compelling reasons', ministers may change the law themselves; although they need the consent of Parliament, there is no need for a full Act of Parliament. When introducing a bill to Parliament, ministers are required to certify that they have considered the impact of the bill on human rights.

? Self-test questions

1. What would you say was the principal reason for enacting the HRA?

2. What is the 'mirror' principle governing the relationship with Strasbourg under the HRA and what are the major exceptions to it?

3. When should section 3 HRA be used rather than 'ordinary' canons of statutory interpretation when a court is applying a statute?

4. What is a 'declaration of incompatibility' and what consequences does it have?

5. When would a UK court be likely to use a declaration of incompatibility rather than use section 3 HRA to find a Convention-compliant meaning to a statute?

6. What are the main indicators that a body is a 'public authority' or is exercising a 'public function'?

7. Under what circumstances can a person bring an action under section 7 of the HRA?

8. What remedies are available under the HRA for breach of a Convention right by a public authority?

9. What is the responsibility of a minister introducing a Bill to Parliament under the HRA?

10. When, if at all, does the HRA impose obligations on UK officials for actions taken overseas?

 For suggested approaches, please visit the Online Resource Centre.

? Exam questions

1. The Human Rights Act should be replaced. It does not go far enough and give full and complete protection to people in the UK from statutes or executive practices which are capable of and do violate the rights in the ECHR which the UK, as a state, has agreed to guarantee.

   By reference to the terms of the HRA, explain this statement and give reasons for agreeing or disagreeing with it.

2. The Ministry of Justice decides to introduce a new, severe regime into some of the nation's prisons. There are good grounds for thinking that aspects of this new regime are so tough that they may violate Article 8 (private life), perhaps even Article 3 (inhuman and degrading treatment).

   Advise the following on whether the UK courts would be able to hear the following cases:

   (a) Prisoners in prisons directly operated by the Prison Service (an executive agency of the Ministry of Justice; in effect a part of the civil service) bring a case against the Prison Service and the Minister of Justice alleging a violation of Articles 3 and 8.

   (b) Prisoners in prisons operated by Bars R Us, a (fictitious) security company which runs a number of prisons under contract from the Prison Service, bring a similar case.

   (c) An employee of Bars R Us speaks to the press about the issues and is sacked for being in breach of a 'gagging' clause in his contract of employment. He claims that, because of Article 10 (the right to freedom of expression), his dismissal is unfair.

 For suggested approaches, please visit the Online Resource Centre.

Further reading

Amos, M. (see Preface) Parts 1–5

Bamforth, N. 'The Application of the Human Rights Act 1998 to Public Authorities and Private Bodies' (1999) 58(1) *CLJ* (March) 159–170

Edwards, R. 'Judicial Deference under the Human Rights Act' (2002) 65 *MLR* 859–882

Gearty, C. *Principles of Human Rights Adjudication* (2004) Oxford: OUP

Hickman, T. *Public Law after the Human Rights Act* (2010) Oxford: Hart Publishing

Kavanagh, A. *Constitutional Review under the UK Human Rights Act* (2009) Cambridge: CUP

Lester, A., Pannick, D., and Herberg, J. (see Preface) Chapters 2 and 3

Oliver, D. 'The Frontiers of the State: Public Authorities and Public Functions under the Human Rights Act' [2000] *Public Law* 476–493

Annex: Repeal of the HRA

 For updates on the repeal of the Human Rights Act, please visit the Online Resource Centre www.oxfordtextbooks.co.uk/orc/davis_directions4e/

The government intends to repeal the Human Rights Act and replace it with a 'British Bill of Rights' (BBoR). According to the Conservative manifesto of 2015 (on which the election was won), this will break the formal link with the ECtHR and allow the UKSC to have the final word on UK human rights law. This reflects considerable concern at the consequences of the Act which have been taken up by the Conservative Party.

Reasons

Prisoners, criminals, and other unpopular people have human rights. From early on there was concern and some degree of popular resentment reflected in some of the media that the Act was undermining public safety. A report into the workings of the Act in 2006 found that many concerns were exaggerated, though there was some evidence that officials had sometimes allowed individuals' rights to outweigh public safety.

Nevertheless, concern and controversy continued. The Conservative Manifesto of 2010 contained a promise to replace the HRA with a British Bill of Rights, but coalition with the Liberal Democrats meant that there was no legislative progress. A Commission on a Bill of Rights reported in 2012. The majority accepted the idea of a BBoR but, crucially, on the assumption this would build on the HRA and, therefore, offer a package of rights that was as extensive, perhaps more extensive, than those found in the ECHR.

But Conservative criticism became more strident in the final years of the Coalition. In particular Teresa May, Home Secretary, expressed her frustration at being unable to deport 'Abu Qatada'.

The Conservative government was elected in 2015 with a similar manifesto commitment as in 2010. However, no Bill is to be brought forward for enactment in the parliamentary session 2015–2016, but there is an intention to consult on changes in 2016.

By January 2016 there was no government consultation document, let alone any legislative proposals. There has, however, been huge amounts of political, journalistic, NGO, and academic discussion, including by some senior judges. The matter is controversial and major support for the HRA from human rights organisations such as Liberty continues.

The basic issues reflecting the concerns that have motivated the Conservative's desire for change are reasonably clear. These have been reflected in 'Protecting Human Rights in the UK', published by the Conservative Party in October 2014 (2014 Proposals). Though it is clearly a party political document published with the May 2015 election in mind, it provides a framework for considering issues. It may well be taken into account by the post-2015 government but, emphatically, it does not necessarily indicate what will eventually be brought forward as legislation.

Discussion

The government's proposals, when brought forward, are likely to involve a weakening of the authority of ECtHR. At the heart of reform, is, first, a desire to protect the sovereignty of the UK Parliament over the laws of the UK which is seen, rightly or wrongly, as having been weakened by the HRA; second is the sense that the ECtHR's concept of the Convention as a 'living instrument' which evolves (see Chapter 6, section 6.1.6) has caused it to expand human rights beyond what the Convention text can bear and this, in the case of prisoners for example, is a major cause of dissatisfaction.

1. **Repeal of the HRA**. This is easily done. In theory it just requires a majority of one in the House of Commons and avoiding the House of Lords (assuming the Parliament Act 1911/ 1949 is used).

2. **The British Bill of Rights (BBoR): still based on ECHR**. The 2014 Proposals suggest that, at its heart, the BBoR will contain the rights in the ECHR. This is important. There is no intention for radical departure from the rights in the Convention. To that extent UK law will continue to recognise and enforce the basic international human rights norms built on the UNDHR. This is consistent with the Commission's view that any reform of human rights law should continue to have the norms in the Convention as their basis.

3. **BBoR: less generous provisions?** However, if the 2014 proposals are a guide, the BBoR is likely to contain specific limitations on rights and in particular contexts, which are not found at Strasbourg. These may reflect the causes of the discontent (popular, media-based, ministerial, and parliamentary) that have stimulated the Conservative government to repeal the HRA. For example, in the context of facilitating deportation, the BBoR might include provisions about the application of terms such as 'private life' (Article 8) or 'degrading treatment' (Article 3) which the courts will be required to follow (rather than the Strasbourg interpretations). Something like this has already been done in relation to the application of Article 8 by immigration tribunals by Pt 5A Immigration and Asylum Act 2002. Of course the courts may seek to resist such measures if any mandatory guidance seems to interfere with their role of statutory interpretation. Another example is an express ban on prisoners voting—it is after all one of the main issues that have motivated these changes.

   If there are less extensive provisions, victims will still want to pursue their rights before the ECtHR.

4. **BBoR: additional provisions?** The BBoR is also an opportunity to extend basic rights, particularly if these are in some sense important in the UK's constitutional culture. The example that has been given (e.g. by the minister, Michael Gove, appearing before the House of Lords Constitutional Committee in December 2015) is a strengthened right to trial by jury. There may be other rights put in. Given the financial burdens and Parliament's ultimate authority over social policy, these are unlikely to be the kinds of economic, social, and environmental rights which are only weakly and indirectly found in the ECHR (see Chapter 1, section 1.3.2).

5. **Lesser influence of ECtHR on domestic human rights law.** A core principle of the BBoR is to lessen the influence of the ECtHR in UK law. The idea is that the rights in the BBoR will be interpreted and applied by the UK courts, ultimately the UKSC, on the basis of its independent interpretation and analysis of human rights. Therefore, there is unlikely to be any provision, echoing section 2 HRA, requiring UK domestic courts to take into account the rulings of the ECtHR.

   However, such a change might not be as radical as is perhaps hoped.

   - UK courts may still allow themselves to be influenced by Strasbourg rulings.
   - In any case, as discussed in sections 4.3.6 and 4.3.7, the effect of section 2 HRA is already on the wane—judges are increasingly willing to depart from the 'mirror' Strasbourg principle and prefer to ground a decision on common law.

- In any event, the large body of law derived from the HRA will not disappear and will be the basis of new decisions under the BBoR.

6. **Parliamentary sovereignty and the Supreme Court.** An important aim of HRA repeal is to protect the ultimate sovereignty of Parliament. The HRA does this anyway, since courts do not have the power to invalidate an Act of Parliament (see sections 4.4.2 and 4.4.3). It will be of great interest to see what the relationship between the courts and Parliament will be in the BBoR. Options include the following:

   - An equivalent to section 3 HRA, which allows the courts to 'strain' the meaning of statutory words in order to obtain a meaning which is compatible with the rights in the BBoR (see section 4.4). But this can set up conflict with Parliament, and the freedom that section 3 HRA allows the courts has been a point of criticism.

   - No section 3 equivalent. Acts of Parliament would be interpreted on ordinary canons of statutory interpretation with any resulting incompatibility being lawful. But this creates very weak human rights protection.

However, it is likely that the courts will simply transfer the approaches to statutory interpretation adopted under section 3 HRA to the interpretation of the BBoR. Indeed, if the BBoR ends up over-endorsing parliamentary sovereignty and giving only weak protection of human rights, more judges might move in the direction of direct enforcement of (specifically) human rights treaties to which the UK is a party, including the ECHR (see Lord Kerr in *R (SG)* v *Secretary of State for Work and Pensions* [2015] UKSC 16). Statutory interpretation is a matter of common law.

The other point which is quite unclear is the nature of dialogue, if any, between the courts and Parliament and the executive. It remains to be seen whether there will be an equivalent to the 'declaration of incompatibility' measure under the BBoR. Again, on this turns the strength of human rights protection in the UK and, as suggested above, the attitude of the courts.

The claim of the Conservative reformers is to maintain strong and effective human rights protection in the UK. So it is likely that provisions similar to sections 3 and 4 HRA will be in the BBoR; likewise, provisions equivalent to sections 6 and 7 HRA (the duties on public authorities, see section 4.5). If this is true in both cases, the tensions that exist today, on deportation, etc., will continue under the BBoR.

The BBoR might even enhance the power of the UKSC by a stronger declaration of incompatibility which requires Parliament and the executive to change incompatible legal provisions. The UKSC would become something close to a full constitutional court, interpreting the BBoR as if it were a written, preeminent, part of the constitution.

Disconnecting the ECtHR. None of this, however, affects the international obligations on the UK (on Parliament, the executive, and the judiciary) to give effect to the rulings of the ECtHR.

- A declaration (as in Germany and, since 2015, Russia) that ultimate sovereignty lies with Parliament is fine, but makes no difference. The international obligations remain in place. It would simply affirm the current situation—the ECHR is not a directly effective part of UK domestic law (see Chapter 3).

- Removing the right of individual application to Strasbourg (Chapter 2, section 2.5.2) or renouncing the duty under Article 46 to give effect to ECtHR judgments (Chapter 2, section 2.4.2) would violate the Convention and place the UK in breach of its international law obligations.

- The 2014 Proposals suggest making ECtHR rulings merely 'advisory' to be followed only if the UK Parliament approves. Unless the acceptability of this can be negotiated with Strasbourg (most unlikely), the UK will still be in breach of Article 46 if Parliament refuses to make the necessary changes. This, of course, is the case under the HRA—demonstrated by the continuing problem of votes for prisoners (see Chapter 25, section 25.3.2).

The 2014 Proposals talk of an ultimate willingness of the UK to renounce the ECHR and withdraw from the Council of Europe altogether. It is highly unlikely that there is a political consensus within the Parliamentary Conservative Party for this.

If this is so, the continuation of the right of individual application and of the UK's obligations under Article 46 mean that the effect of the BBoR will be limited and the ultimate reach of the Strasbourg Court will remain.

EU. Continued membership of the EU is hard to reconcile with reform, especially if it involves withdrawing from the Council of Europe. The EU Charter of Fundamental Rights (Chapter 3, section 3.4) is already part of UK law dealing with EU matters. The Court of Justice of the European Union (whose interpretations must be followed by UK courts) must, when interpreting the Charter, either follow the ECtHR or give more extensive rights protection. Furthermore, the EU is supposed to become bound by the ECHR (though see Chapter 3, section 3.4), so even if it were possible to remain in the EU and not be in the Council of Europe, the ECtHR's rulings on Convention rights would still have to be followed in the UK if relating to EU law.

The significance of this will depend on the outcome of the referendum on continued UK membership of the EU, in June 2016.

Devolution. Even though the protection of human rights is ultimately a matter for the UK, the current system (HRA and ECHR) may be thought to be a fundamental part of the devolution settlement—the political inspiration which underlies the devolution laws. By constitutional convention, the UK must obtain the consent of the devolved institutions (e.g. the Scottish Parliament). Not only the enactment of a BBoR, but also any moves to separate or weaken the current role of the ECtHR will, politically at least, need the consent of the devolved institutions.

All the above suggests that effective, noticeable change will be hard to achieve. The sense of a 'home grown' protection for rights which, for that reason, will enjoy the support of the British people may be achieved. What will be harder to achieve will be any enhancement of parliamentary sovereignty beyond that already there in the HRA and any significant weakening of the ultimate influence of the ECtHR on UK law and its international obligations.

5 The Human Rights Act 1998 (2): proceedings and remedies

☐ **LEARNING OBJECTIVES**

● Article 13, the right to a remedy, and the Human Rights Act 1998 (HRA).

● Procedures and remedies under section 3 HRA (interpretation of statutes).

● Procedures and remedies against public authorities (sections 7, 8, and 9 HRA).

● Rules of 'standing' (who is entitled to bring a Human Rights Act case): section 7 HRA and Article 34 of the Convention.

● Damages ('just satisfaction') and the HRA.

Introduction

Rights without effective remedies are meaningless. European history is full of examples of constitutions guaranteeing basic rights and liberties ignored by governments because there was no proper system of remedies. Many of the liberal constitutions of nineteenth-century Europe were, from time to time, ignored or set aside by emergency clauses; Stalin's famous constitution of 1936 purported to guarantee social and economic rights but exercised little restraint on the dictator; Hitler came to power on the basis of exceptional provisions of what was otherwise an impeccably liberal constitution.

From earliest cases the European Court of Human Rights (ECtHR) has asserted the need to ensure the Convention provides effective protection for individuals and their rights. This means in particular that it will focus on the position of specific individuals and their rights (rather than deal with abstract, political, concerns that a country's laws or policy may be inconsistent with rights). An essential part of this is that such individuals get some sort of remedy from the Court. This same principle, that rights should be real and effective, translates itself into the law of the United Kingdom under the Human Rights Act 1998.

5.1 Article 13 and the need for a remedy

Article 13 Right to an effective remedy

Everyone whose rights and freedoms as set forth in this Convention are violated shall have an effective remedy before a national authority notwithstanding that the violation has been committed by persons acting in an official capacity.

In Chapter 2, on the ECHR itself, we see that the major strength of the Strasbourg system lies in the opportunity it gives to individuals to take their case to the ECtHR and, if successful, to obtain a remedy which the states of the Council of Europe generally accept. People can do this if they feel that the political and legal system in their own country has failed to secure their ECHR rights and freedoms.

The Court's purpose is to provide a remedy when national systems have failed. By accepting Article 13, a state agrees to ensure that effective remedies for breaches of the Convention are available through its own legal system and from its own national courts. People should only have to go to Strasbourg if, after a full and proper examination of all the human rights issues by their national courts, they feel they still have good grounds for claiming that their Convention rights and freedoms have not been secured. There needs to be a full willingness of national governments to accept the judgments of their own courts on these issues.

> **CROSS REFERENCE**
> The right of individual application is discussed in Chapter 2, section 2.5.2.

5.1.1 Article 13 and the HRA

The need for a remedy from the national courts is recognised by Article 13 of the Convention. Article 13 is not one of the Convention rights in Schedule 1 HRA. The government's principal explanation for not allowing UK courts to ensure that there are adequate remedies, as Article 13 requires, was that it was unnecessary. The HRA itself provided effective remedies. This means that even if it appears to a court that the remedies available are inadequate, courts are not able directly to create a new, more effective remedy. If the ineffective remedy is embodied in statute, the courts must accept it. If Article 13 had been included, a court in the UK would have been able to create a new remedy or, at least, issue a declaration of incompatibility, in certain areas where existing remedies might not be satisfactory. Remedies for people who think they have been the victim of unlawful surveillance by the Intelligence Services (who must use the Investigatory Powers Tribunal) or who are to be deported from the country in the public interest (who must use the Special Immigration Appeal Tribunal) are possible examples.

The courts are 'public authorities' under section 6 HRA and are bound to act compatibly with Convention rights unless compelled otherwise by primary legislation. In this regard, though they cannot create new remedies, they are able to adjust and develop existing remedies in order to secure Convention rights. See Chapter 4, section 4.7.

> **CROSS REFERENCE**
> Declaration of incompatibility is defined in Chapter 4, section 4.4.3.

It is helpful, therefore, to consider the requirements of Article 13 in order to assess whether the HRA really does meet its requirements.

5.1.2 **Article 13 in summary**

Article 13 obliges states to provide:

- Adequate procedures. The national law must allow for access to a court or other appropriate forum which is properly independent and able to deal, under its rules of procedure and evidence, with all the points raised by a human rights claim.

- Adequate remedies. The court or other forum must have sufficient authority to provide an adequate remedy. For example, if an award of damages is necessary to compensate for the breach of human rights, then the court must be able to make such an award; if someone is deprived of their liberty in breach of Article 5 of the Convention, the court or tribunal must have the power to order his or her release.

The right to a remedy may be integrated into some of the substantive rights, with Article 13 adding little to what is already required. Article 5(4) ECHR already gives a person deprived of his or her liberty a right to challenge before a judicial body the basis of their detention and, as a requirement of Article 2 (right to life), the ECtHR has made it clear that deaths in custody should be properly investigated (see Chapter 8, section 8.5).

5.1.3 **Arguable claim or complaint**

❱ CROSS REFERENCE

Admissibility is discussed in Chapter 2, section 2.7.2.

Article 13 requires states to provide a procedure and a remedy by which 'arguable claims' or 'complaints' (both terms are used) that the Convention has been violated can be tested in a national forum (a court, etc.) and, if the complaint is proved, a suitable remedy granted—*Klass v Germany* (1979–80) 2 EHRR 214, para 64.

The test for 'arguable' claim or complaint is not clear. It is likely to be linked to the question of whether a matter is admissible before the ECtHR. The lack of such a procedure in the national courts to deal with cases that would be admissible before the Strasbourg court can mean that Article 13 has been violated. It is not necessary to show that the case would have succeeded and that some other Convention right has also been violated (e.g. *Hatton v UK* (2003) 37 EHRR 28, para 137).

5.1.4 **An effective remedy**

The available procedure and remedy must be 'effective' both in law and, importantly, in practice (*De Souza Ribeiro* v France [2014] 59 EHRR 10, para 78). It need not be from a fully judicial body such as a 'court'. In the UK, for example, it can be from tribunals (such as First Tier Tribunal (Mental Health) hearing claims by the mentally ill that they should not be detained in hospital) and, in principle, any other body capable of meeting the requirements of Article 13. In particular, though:

- the body providing the remedy needs to be properly independent of the government or other agency, such as the police, whose actions are being questioned—the independence of non-judicial bodies may need proper scrutiny (*De Souza Ribeiro*, para 79);

❱ CROSS REFERENCE

Fairness is defined by reference to the requirements of Article 6 (right to a fair trial) and Article 5(4): see Chapters 12 and 11, section 11.8, respectively.

- the procedure must be fair, giving proper opportunities to the alleged victim to put his or her case;

- the body must be able to give an effective remedy (e.g. to order the release of a person detained in violation of Article 5);

- the body must be able to hear evidence on, and deal with, all the issues of fact and law which relate to the alleged Convention violation.

An example of the United Kingdom being in breach of Article 13 is *Peck* v *United Kingdom*.

CASE CLOSE-UP

Peck v United Kingdom (2003) 36 EHRR 41

P attempted suicide in part of a town centre. The attempt was caught on CCTV. The images were distributed by the local authority (which controlled the CCTV) to the local media, and stories, illustrated by the images, were run on TV and in the local press. The attempts to blank out P's identity were unsuccessful. P made various attempts to obtain redress but these were only partially successful. The ECtHR held that there had been a breach of Articles 8 and 13.

The ECtHR noted that Article 13 did not require a particular form of remedy, and there is a margin of appreciation afforded the states on this matter. Legal systems, including in the United Kingdom, tend to have a complex range of institutions dealing with the redress of grievances against public bodies. In *Peck* the principal remedies for the applicant were complaint to a media regulator, a private law action, or judicial review of the actions of the local authority. In Peck's circumstances all were inadequate.

5.2 Redress of grievances in the United Kingdom

As was made clear in *Peck*, securing human rights through legally enforceable remedies need not be confined to the courts. In the United Kingdom, like all other modern countries, a wide and variable range of institutions may be able to provide different forms of redress of grievances. These institutions all have an important part to play in ensuring that individuals' human rights are properly protected. Examples from the United Kingdom include the following.

5.2.1 The courts of law

These include both the civil courts dealing with private law matters and public law disputes (in the Administrative Court) and the criminal courts, such as the Crown Court and Magistrates' Courts.

Judicial review by the High Court (Administrative Court)

Judicial review, involving public law actions brought against public authorities, is outlined in Chapter 3, section 3.3.2. In some contexts it has been doubted whether judicial review can provide adequate remedies for violations of the Convention. This is because, put simply, judicial review is focused on the manner in which a public decision is taken rather than with the outcome of the decision. Again, put simply, the High Court, traditionally, would not interfere with a properly taken decision even if the result might have been a violation of the Convention. The court, in judicial review, is mainly concerned with issues of law rather than fact and so again, it can be difficult for all the issues bearing on whether Convention rights and freedoms have been secured, to be fully aired. These were the main reasons why judicial review was held to be an inadequate remedy by the ECtHR in *Peck*.

CROSS REFERENCE

For other examples see Chapter 3, section 3.3.2.

In fact, following adverse decisions from Strasbourg, but mainly in order for the High Court to perform its duties as a 'public authority' under the HRA (and thus put Article 13 into effect), judicial review tends now to be flexible. Depending on the facts and on the matters raised by the Convention right in issue in a case, judicial review is normally capable of allowing a full examination of all the issues, of fact and law, to enable a judicial judgment to be made on whether or not there has been a breach of a Convention right. This was the view taken by the House of Lords in *R (Alconbury Developments Ltd)* v *Secretary of State for the Environment, Transport and the Regions* [2001] UKHL 23, in respect of challenges to the planning system based on the requirements of a fair hearing in Article 6. The moving together of the grounds of judicial review and Convention rights was noticed and discussed by the House of Lords in *Doherty* v *Birmingham City Council* [2008] UKHL 57, e.g. para 135.

Private law

CROSS REFERENCE

See Chapter 4, section 4.7.1 for the impact of the HRA on private law.

Private law actions (breach of contract or tort) can be brought against both private and public parties. These will not necessarily provide adequate remedies. In *Peck*, an action for breach of confidentiality was thought, by the ECtHR, to be inadequate since it was not (reliably) available for a simple invasion of privacy. There have been significant legal developments in this area (see Chapters 15 and 22).

5.2.2 **Tribunals**

Tribunals are court-like bodies that have statutory powers to provide remedies in specific areas. Matters dealt with by tribunals can involve both basically private law (such as Employment Tribunals, which deal with disputes over employment rights) or public law (such as First Tier Tribunals (Mental Health), which have powers to release patients who are detained in mental hospitals).

5.2.3 **Inspectorates, regulators, and commissions of various kinds**

CROSS REFERENCE

See Chapter 22, 22.2.1 for press regulation.

These bodies can perform a range of functions such as investigating problems, regulating activities, and adjudicating disputes. They may provide a suitable remedy themselves. The media regulator, Ofcom, has a range of remedies which might, in some circumstances, be adequate for a violation of the right to respect for private life under Article 8 (though in *Peck* the ECtHR held that the inability of the predecessors of Ofcom to award financial compensation meant that they did not satisfy Article 13).

The Independent Police Complaints Commission (IPCC) investigates, for example, police killings, which are possible violations of Article 2. The investigation is a requirement of Article 2. The Commission can also instigate other remedies by, for example, sending reports to the prosecuting authorities and so be a part of what is necessary for Article 13. One of the reasons for creating the Commission was to satisfy Article 13 by creating a body that was (unlike its predecessor) properly independent of the police and the executive.

5.2.4 **Ombudsman systems**

There are a number of Ombudsmen dealing with, for example, central government, local government, and prisons. They can investigate and suggest ways of remedying so-called 'maladministration'. The Ombudsman's inability to make a binding order (the Ombudsman makes findings and recommendations) can mean that it may not be an adequate remedy, see, e.g., *E* v *United Kingdom* (2003) 36 EHRR 31, a case involving compensation for victims of violent crime.

5.2.5 **Access to the courts**

Inspectorates, regulators, commissions, and Ombudsmen are just some of a complex range of different bodies operating in different areas of social, economic, and political life in the United Kingdom. They can offer a wide range of remedies, specific to the area they deal with. Not all the remedies will, in all situations, be sufficient to satisfy Article 13 or other Convention requirements. Where this is so, access to the courts, often to the High Court for judicial review, becomes important. It may be only because the decisions of such bodies can be challenged in the courts that there is no violation of the Convention.

5.3 Remedies: section 3 and legislation

5.3.1 **The duty under section 3**

The duty under section 3 HRA to interpret legislation, so far as it is possible to do so, to make its meaning compatible with Convention rights applies not only to courts and tribunals but also to any other institutions or organisations whose powers and functions depend upon Acts of Parliament. These may be government, police, public bodies, commercial organisations, charities, private individuals, etc. The duty applies in both public law and private law.

> **CROSS REFERENCE**
> For discussion of section 3 see Chapter 4, section 4.4.

There is no direct remedy provided by section 3 HRA. The point is that everyone who is affected by an Act of Parliament has a right that the Act be interpreted, if it is possible to do so, for compatibility with Convention rights. If the matter goes to a court or tribunal, whether it is private law (e.g. an action for breach of contract) or public law (e.g. a judicial review or a complaint to the IPCC), there is a duty on the court, tribunal, etc. hearing the case to interpret the legislation in a manner that it thinks is required by the Convention. Failure to do this is a basis on which an appeal could be made.

5.3.2 **Declaration of incompatibility**

As discussed in Chapter 4, section 4 HRA authorises senior courts to make a 'declaration of incompatibility' if it is not 'possible' to read and give effect to legislation in a way that is compatible with Convention rights. It is not necessary to show that the statute can only operate incompatibly but that it can so operate and has done so (*T* v *Secretary of State for the Home Department* [2014] UKSC 35, para 52).

> **CROSS REFERENCE**
> For declaration of incompatibility see Chapter 4, section 4.4.3.

The fact that a UK court cannot invalidate (make of no legal effect) an Act of Parliament that it is not possible to interpret for compatibility, is not, as such, a violation of Article 13. The ECtHR has held that Article 13 does not require US-style procedures through which national courts can set aside primary legislation on the grounds that it violates the Convention (*James* v *United*

Kingdom (1986) 8 EHRR 123, para 85). The ECtHR has cast doubt on the effectiveness of the declaration as a remedy but acknowledged that it could be accepted as effective so long as the government's response was always to remedy the defect (*Burden* v *United Kingdom* (2008) 47 EHRR 38, paras 40–44).

▶ **CROSS REFERENCE**
The identification of a 'victim' for the purposes of the HRA and the Convention is discussed at section 5.4.4.

Normally only a person who alleges they are a victim of a human rights violation (directly and detrimentally affected by the legislation in question) can seek a declaration of incompatibility. In *Re S* [2002] UKHL 10, a case involving child care, the House of Lords said: 'Ordinarily the court will grant such relief [a declaration of incompatibility] only to a person who is a victim of an actual or proposed breach of a Convention right' (para 88). In *Chester* v *Secretary of State for Justice* [2013] UKSC 63, the UKSC accepted that the blanket ban on prisoner voting violated Convention rights (see Chapter 25) but refused a declaration of incompatibility partly for the reason that the applicant prisoners had been convicted of serious offences and so would still be excluded from a Convention compliant scheme (which would probably exclude serious offenders).

But context is all. The courts are reluctant to allow themselves to be used as part of an abstract political battle but, on the other hand, do not want to prevent important cases, involving the rule of law, from getting to court. In *R (Rusbridger)* v *Attorney General* [2003] UKHL 38, a majority agreed with Lord Steyn that there was no need for the applicant to prove that he had been a 'victim' of the legislation (the Treason Felony Act 1848) in order to seek a declaration (see para 21).

A declaration of incompatibility is not available in respect of subordinate legislation if the parent Act does not prevent the removal of the incompatibility, HRA section 4(4)(b), see *T* (discussed earlier), para 54.

Furthermore, the remedy (like most remedies under the HRA) is discretionary. There may be all sorts of reasons why a declaration might not be appropriate, such as the practical and perhaps retrospective impact it would have, or because the government is already proposing to change the law.

5.4 Actions against public authorities

▶ **CROSS REFERENCE**
Section 6 HRA is discussed in Chapter 4, section 4.5.

Section 6 of the HRA requires public authorities to act compatibly with Convention rights unless required otherwise by primary legislation.

Sections 7 and 8 provide statutory procedures and remedies in order to enable a person to uphold his or her Convention rights against the actions of a public authority.

Under section 7(1):

a person who claims that a public authority has acted (or proposes to act) in a way which is made unlawful by section 6(1) may—

(a) bring proceedings against the authority under this Act in the appropriate court or tribunal, or

(b) rely on the Convention right or rights concerned in any legal proceedings

Thus remedies for breach of the Convention by a public authority can be sought in one of two ways:

- in an action originated by the person alleging the breach (section 7(1)(a)); or
- in any legal proceedings of any kind in which the victim is involved—whether as claimant or defendant (section 7(1)(b)). This could be, for example, alleging Convention violations by the police as part of a defence in criminal proceedings; using Convention rights as a defence to eviction proceedings brought, in the County Court, by a local authority; or using Convention rights as part of tribunal proceedings against a public authority.

5.4.1 Appropriate court or tribunal

In respect of section 7(1)(a), where the alleged victim brings the case him or herself, the Act stipulates that the case must be brought before the 'appropriate tribunal'. The appropriate tribunal is identified by 'rules' made by a Secretary of State or the Lord Chancellor (section 7(9)). For England and Wales judicial review (see section 5.2.1) is the normal procedure. The Civil Procedure Rules (CPR) (the rules governing all aspects of civil procedure) have been amended to facilitate actions brought under section 7 (see CPR Part 7). Scotland has its own particular code of rules dealing with HRA cases.

In some situations there are special rules which identify a particular court or tribunal which, alone, can hear human rights claims. For example: allegations that Convention rights have been breached in respect of surveillance by the security services are determined only by the Investigatory Powers Tribunal established by Part IV of the Regulation of Investigatory Powers Act 2000 (RIPA). This is required by section 65(2) RIPA.

The absence of rules designating a court of tribunal as capable of hearing HRA cases can mean that an argument that a Convention right has been violated cannot be brought. Thus in *MBA v Merton LBC* [2013] EWCA Civ 1562, it was suggested (obiter) that an Employment Tribunal had not been so designated and so that part of the employee's case based on a violation of Article 9 (freedom of belief) could not be heard by the Tribunal.

5.4.2 Judicial actions and decisions

Often what is complained about as a violation of the Convention will be a judicial act (e.g. a magistrate committing a person to prison allegedly in breach of Article 5 (right to liberty and security)). Here the appropriate way of pursuing a human rights case is by exercising any existing right of appeal (section 9(1) HRA). For example, an appeal against a criminal conviction from Crown Court to the Court of Appeal (Criminal Division), an appeal from most statutory tribunals to the Upper Tribunal, by judicial review (this can be the way to challenge some decisions of magistrates and also other tribunals, particularly those such as the Parole Board for which there is no other form of appeal), or by any other form of appeal allowed by law. There are specific provisions which apply to whether damages can be awarded in respect of judicial decisions, which are discussed in section 5.5.3.

5.4.3 Time limits

Section 7 requires a person to bring an action within one year unless rules require a shorter period or fairness requires a longer period (section 7(5)). Under the Civil Procedure Rules relating to judicial review, cases must be brought 'promptly' and, at most, not more than three months from the time of the decision or action complained about. If a person is seeking a remedy that is only available through judicial review (e.g. a 'prerogative order' quashing (i.e. cancelling) a public authority's decision), then the case must be brought according to the judicial review rules. Where, on the other hand, the human rights case is made directly under section 7, the one year with possible extension for fairness rule applies.

CASE CLOSE-UP

Rabone v Pennine Care NHS Foundation Trust [2012] UKSC 2

R brought proceedings based on section 7(1)(a) HRA alleging a breach of Article 2 (the right to life) by the defendant hospital in respect of the death of his daughter. The proceedings were issued nearly sixteen months after the daughter's death. The Supreme Court, exercising discretion under section 7(5), allowed the case to be brought. Issues to be weighed by a court included the degree of prejudice likely to be suffered by the public authority; and the length and reasons for the delay. However, the 'most important' reason was the merit of the case—that there had been a violation.

The Supreme Court confirmed the view in *Dunn* v *Parole Board* [2008] EWCA Civ 374 that factors relating to extensions of time in ordinary civil proceedings (in section 33(3) Limitation Act 1980) can be taken into account but are not decisive as regards section 7(5) HRA.

The one-year rule under the HRA can be compared with the position at Strasbourg. Article 35 of the Convention requires an application to be made within six months of domestic remedies being exhausted.

5.4.4 Standing: the victim test

These are the rules developed by the law which define who is entitled to bring cases in various types of procedure. To bring an action for breach of contract, for instance, you normally have to be a party to the contract; to bring a judicial review against a public body, the law requires you to have 'sufficient interest' in the case.

THINKING POINT

Compare the approach to 'standing' under the HRA with that for ordinary domestic judicial review. Which is the better and why?

Under section 7 HRA only a person who would be able to bring a case before the ECtHR can bring a case in the UK courts alleging a breach by a public authority of its duty under section 6 HRA to act compatibly with Convention rights.

To bring a case before the ECtHR, a person must be a 'victim' as defined in respect of Article 34 ECHR (section 7(7) HRA). Application to the UK courts therefore mirrors the rules before Strasbourg and demonstrate, again, the primary purpose of the HRA, which is to make rights available in the UK courts if they would also be available before the ECtHR.

The test for being a 'victim' at Strasbourg and, therefore, for being able to bring a case under section 7 HRA, is discussed in Chapter 2, section 2.7.1.

5.5 Remedies: sections 8 and 9

5.5.1 **General**

Sections 8 and 9 HRA deal with the remedies that can be given when a court in the United Kingdom finds that a public authority has violated a Convention right. The sections indicate what orders can be made and when financial compensation can be awarded.

Section 8(1) allows a court or tribunal to grant whatever remedy it considers 'just and appropriate', provided that the remedy proposed is one it is authorised to impose.

Section 8 does not, therefore, allow courts and tribunals to create new remedies that they do not have the power to grant (a Crown Court, for example, still cannot award damages). UK courts can, however, fashion the remedies they are allowed to grant in ways that are appropriate to the Convention violation. Financial compensation (discussed at section 5.5.2) can be awarded, but only by a civil court which already has the power to award damages (section 8(2)).

Since sections 6, 7, and 8 HRA involve actions against public authorities, the remedy will often be sought by way of judicial review (see section 5.2.1). The High Court can issue certain remedies (known as 'prerogative orders') which are only available by way of judicial review:

- a quashing order cancels a decision made by a public body and may require that decision to be taken again on a proper legal basis;
- a mandatory order requires a public body to perform a legal duty;
- a prohibitory order requires that a public body desist from a proposed action;
- the High Court, in judicial review proceedings, can also award private law remedies such as injunctions and, but only if there is a legal basis, damages. In particular the High Court can make a 'declaration' which does not order anyone to do anything but declares what the law is; public bodies characteristically obey the law.

Public authorities can also be the subject of private law actions (e.g. against the police for false imprisonment) and the section 6 duty can be relevant to these. Examples of remedies based on section 7 include:

- In *R (Amin)* v *Secretary of State for the Home Department* [2003] UKHL 51, the House of Lords held that there had been a breach of Article 2 (right to life) in respect of the investigation carried out by the Home Office into the death of a prisoner. The remedy was an order requiring a proper investigation that met the standards of Article 2.
- In *A* v *Secretary of State for the Home Department* [2004] UKHL 56, the House of Lords first quashed a government order purporting to derogate from Article 5 in order to allow the detention without trial of foreign terrorist suspects; then, second, made a declaration of incompatibility regarding the legislation under which the detentions had been authorised.
- In *R (K)* v *Secretary of State for the Home Department* [2009] EWCA Civ 219, the Court of Appeal issued a declaration that the Home Secretary should have investigated alleged violations of Article 3 regarding a privately run immigration detention centre.

Courts and tribunals, being public authorities, are themselves subject to the section 6 HRA duty. When dealing with, for example, private, common law matters (like contract and tort) they are required, by section 6, to act compatibly with Convention rights and this can have an

> **CROSS REFERENCE**
> The private law ('horizontal') impact of the HRA is discussed in Chapter 4, section 4.7.

impact not only on the way the law develops but also on the way the remedies and the situations in which they are available are developed.

5.5.2 Damages

General

Damages can be awarded against a public authority for breach of its duty under section 6 HRA by a UK court. Damages can only be awarded if:

- the court is one with powers to award damages or compensation in civil proceedings. This can include, for example, the High Court but excludes the Crown Court (which tries serious criminal cases);
- in all the circumstances the award of damages is necessary to afford 'just satisfaction' to the applicant.

In deciding whether or not to award damages and, if so, how much, section 8(4) HRA requires the UK to take into account the Strasbourg case law on just satisfaction under Article 41 of the Convention.

 BIGGER PICTURE

A full and detailed summary of the Convention position has been produced by the Law Commission: *Damages under the Human Rights Act 1998* Report 266.

Article 41 allows the ECtHR to compensate for the failure of national courts to provide an adequate remedy by affording, if necessary, 'just satisfaction to the injured party'. The following principles, derived from the Strasbourg case law, were accepted by the House of Lords as guiding the way in which section 8 HRA should be applied by UK courts (see *R (Greenfield)* v *Secretary of State for the Home Department* [2005] UKHL 14).

Finding of a violation often sufficient

The principal aim is to remedy violations rather than focus on the financial compensation of the victim. The ECtHR frequently holds that a finding in favour of the applicant is sufficient satisfaction and no further remedy is required.

Restorative principle

If a financial payment is necessary, the underlying principle of Article 41 is *restitutio in integrum* (restored in full)—the principle of returning the person, as far as possible, to the situation he or she would have been in had his or her Convention rights not been violated. Primary responsibility for this lies with the state. The ECtHR may make an award if the state has not remedied the situation or its purported remedy is inadequate.

Causative link

Compensation is confined to those losses attributable to the public authority's breach of the Convention. Unlike under the common law, the ECtHR does not award 'exemplary' or 'punitive' damages. These recognise particularly reprehensible behaviour by the respondent authority by imposing a higher award than restitution strictly requires. Nevertheless, it is clear that the ECtHR does take context into account and this can include the conduct of the parties. The

Court awards non-pecuniary damages on an 'equitable basis' without going into detail on how the equity is assessed. There are often considerable gaps between amounts claimed by applicants and the amount the Court is prepared to award.

Pecuniary losses

Convention breaches directly causing monetary loss, such as loss of income, welfare benefits, or valuable property, can be compensated under Article 41. In *Smith and Grady* v *United Kingdom* [2001] 31 EHRR 24, £59,000 and £40,000 respectively were awarded for loss of salary due to being dismissed from the armed forces in breach of Article 8.

Violations of Article 1 of the First Protocol (the right to peaceful enjoyment of possessions) can commonly lead to significant, even massive, awards. In *Yukos* v *Russia* App 14902/04, judgment of 31 July 2014, pecuniary losses were assessed at nearly two billion euros (€1,866,104,634)—see Chapter 23, section 23.8.1.

Non-pecuniary losses

These cover intangible matters such as distress, anxiety, and psychological trauma. Thus the applicants in *Smith and Grady* also received £19,000 each to compensate for the distress and destabilisation caused by the investigation into their sexual lives, which then triggered their dismissal (see Chapter 3, section 3.3.2). Awards for breaches of Article 2 have been between €5,000 and €60,000 (see *Rabone*, at section 5.4.3, para 85). The award of non-pecuniary damages does seem to be based partly on an unstated ethical assessment of the case. Thus those convicted of criminal offences or who are terrorist suspects may find that a finding in their favour is sufficient just satisfaction and an award for non-pecuniary damages is denied. The graver the violation, the more likely it is that significant non-pecuniary losses will be recognised and compensated. Underlying the Convention jurisprudence is, as always, the need to establish a 'fair balance' between individual interests and public good.

Costs and expenses

These are legal costs and expenses incurred in bringing the case to Strasbourg. They do not normally cover costs incurred whilst exhausting domestic remedies in the national courts, though they might include extra costs incurred in trying to persuade a national court not to act incompatibly with the Convention. It is common to find that an applicant is not awarded any financial just satisfaction but is awarded a considerable sum to cover actual costs and expenses. Perhaps the most controversial instance is *McCann* v *United Kingdom* [1996] 21 EHRR 97. The ECtHR found a violation of Article 2 in the case of the shooting by British forces of members of an IRA active service unit in Gibraltar. No damages were awarded in 'just satisfaction' but the relatives who brought the case received £38,700 (from which legal aid of about £4,000 already received was deducted) in costs and expenses.

Damages and the HRA

Damages under section 8 HRA are discretionary, not a matter of right. The principles governing the exercise of this discretion for the law of England and Wales have been discussed by the House of Lords in *R (Greenfield)* v *Secretary of State for the Home Office* [2005] UKHL 14 (see section 5.5.4). This case relates to just satisfaction for a breach of Article 6, but it also deals with just satisfaction more generally. The overall requirement is that UK principles mirror those of the ECtHR and, perhaps, to lessen expectations and opportunities for major financial awards following a breach of Convention rights.

The House of Lords made clear that UK courts needed to follow the general principles of the Strasbourg court (outlined earlier in this section) when considering just satisfaction. Their lordships disapproved of deciding amounts of just satisfaction by reference to domestic law, such as tort or by Ombudsmen or the Criminal Injuries Compensation Board (see *Greenfield*, para 19). UK courts should look to Strasbourg for guidance (*Rabone*, section 5.4.3, para 82).

In particular:

- The priority under the HRA is the protection of human rights rather than compensation for harm caused. Even where a finding of a violation is not sufficient, it is still a matter of weight whose value needs to be subtracted, as it were, from the amount of damages that would be awarded under tort principles.

- In *Anufrijeva* v *Southwark* LBC [2003] EWCA Civ 1406, it was also pointed out that in human rights cases the need is often to balance personal and public interests, a task that is much less relevant in a tort context.

- The point of the HRA, enshrined in section 8(4), is to enable victims to obtain from UK courts what they could get from Strasbourg—no less but also no more.

 CASE CLOSE-UP

D v *Commissioner of Police for the Metropolis* [2014] EWHC 2493

The High Court considered the quantum of damages to be paid to two women who would not have been raped were it not for serious investigative failures by the police in breach of the procedural limb of Article 3. The court accepted that HRA damages could be in addition to other civil awards, given that the human rights breach by the police had its distinct consequences for the victims (the victims had received awards in a civil claim from the rapist and from the Criminal Injuries Compensation Board). The court applied the principles mentioned above and considered similar awards by the ECtHR. Factors such as the nature of the harm, treatment costs, duration of the breach by the police, the nature of their failings, and whether these were systematic or indicated bad faith were taken into consideration. The court awarded damages of £19,000 and £22,250 respectively.

5.5.3 Just satisfaction and Article 5

Article 5(5) creates a right to compensation for anyone arrested or detained in contravention of Article 5 (the right to liberty). It may be that the applicant will also have been a victim of 'false imprisonment' (a tort) and so the award will be based on common law principles (e.g. *R (Kambadzi)* v *Secretary of State for the Home Department* [2011] UKSC 23).

Generally, under English law, there is absolute immunity for members of the senior judiciary; legal protection against claims for damages in respect of good faith decisions of magistrates is found in sections 31 and 32 of the Courts Act 2003. These principles are found in section 9(3) HRA, which does not allow an action for damages in respect of a 'judicial act done in good faith' by a judge, magistrate, or tribunal member. An express exception is made for the purposes of Article 5(5). Awards for damages against judges etc. for breach of Article 5(5) are paid from public funds.

Damages may also be paid in respect of deprivations of liberty consequent on breaches of Article 5(4) (judicial supervision).

 CASE CLOSE-UP

R v (Faulkner) v Parole Board [2013] UKSC 47

Article 5(4) was breached due to error and delay in reviewing the cases of two prisoners (Faulkner and Sturnham).

The UKSC considered the basis on which damages should be awarded under section 8 HRA.

- Damages should normally be awarded where deprivation of liberty was a consequence of a breach of Article 5(4) (as in F's case).
- Any pecuniary losses should be compensated in full.
- Quantum of non-pecuniary losses would depend on the context and UK courts should consider comparable awards made by the ECtHR.
- There was a strong presumption that prisoners would suffer significant stress and frustration (as in S's case) which should be (modestly) compensated.
- Faulkner received £6,500 for delayed release and Sturnham £300 for stress and anxiety.

5.5.4 **Just satisfaction and Article 6**

The issue of just satisfaction if there has been a violation of Article 6, the right to a fair trial, raises a particular problem. If, as a result of the breach, the claimant was denied a full and proper opportunity to make his or her case, should the court, in considering whether to award just satisfaction, speculate on what the outcome of the original trial would have been had it been conducted in line with Article 6? The issue has been discussed in *Greenfield*.

 CASE CLOSE-UP

R (Greenfield) v Secretary of State for the Home Office [2005] UKHL 14

G, a serving prisoner, was sentenced to 21 additional days in prison as a result of a disciplinary process in which, in breach of Article 6, he was denied representation. The House of Lords held that the finding of a violation was sufficient and that no financial award should be made.

The House of Lords reviewed the general principles governing awards for just satisfaction (see section 5.5.2). The judgment is, however, focused on a breach of Article 6. Regarding such breaches the House of Lords noted that:

- The ECtHR does not normally speculate on what the outcome of a trial would have been (see, for example, *Ezeh and Connors* v *United Kingdom* (2004) 39 EHRR 1, para 141 of the Grand Chamber's judgment adopting paras 112–114 of the Chamber's judgment). The exception is where a national court has itself indicated that a different outcome would have been likely had the trial been fair. In that situation, damages might be awarded. An example is *Perks* v *United Kingdom* (2000) 30 EHRR 33, where the ECtHR accepted that the applicant would probably not have been imprisoned if, as fair trial procedures dictated, they were told about his personal circumstances (he was awarded £5,500).

- Non-pecuniary damages for physical and mental suffering caused by failures in the fairness of a trial are sometimes awarded under Article 42, and this is done without reference to the likely outcome of the trial. Such damages are invariably of small amounts (see, e.g. *Stephen Jordan* v *United Kingdom (No 2)* (2002) App 49771/99, judgment of 10 December 2002).

Delay in a criminal or civil trial can be a violation of Article 6. Here an additional question arises: should the delayed trial proceed? There is now clear authority from the House of Lords that the delayed trial should proceed unless, for additional reasons, it would be unjust to continue. The violation of Article 6 can be recognised by appropriate measures such as release on bail (if delay is recognised before the trial) or a lesser sentence or payment of compensation (if recognised during or after the trial) (*Attorney General's Reference (No 2 of 2001)* [2003] UKHL 68 (before a panel of nine Law Lords)).

 ## Summary

- Effective human rights require effective remedies.
- Under the HRA, people can seek the protection of their human rights either by persuading a court or tribunal to interpret a relevant Act of Parliament in the way that protects their human rights or by bringing or defending cases on the grounds that a public authority has acted in a way that violates Convention rights.
- Various procedural issues have to be borne in mind—particularly that, in cases involving public authorities, a person must show that he or she was a 'victim' and could, therefore, have brought a case to the ECtHR.
- Remedies available under the HRA are English law remedies fashioned to reflect the remedies available in Strasbourg. In particular, these are a finding that the Convention has been violated and 'just satisfaction' in terms of financial compensation (damages) for pecuniary and non-pecuniary losses. The principles for awarding damages are complex but need to be distinguished from ordinary tort actions.

? Self-test questions

1. What makes a remedy 'effective' under Article 13?
2. Why might the Ombudsman, by herself, not be able to provide an effective remedy for human rights breaches?
3. Explain the two ways in which, under section 7, a person may allege their human rights have been breached by a public authority.

4. What are the rules under which a person can obtain 'standing' to bring a human rights case under section 7 HRA?

5. What are the general principles governing a court's choice of remedies under the HRA?

6. When might a court choose to award damages (just satisfaction) for a breach of section 6 HRA?

 For suggested approaches, please visit the Online Resource Centre.

? Exam questions

1. The BBC is intending to produce a programme about the activities of the Security Services. The Home Secretary, acting under powers in the Communications Act 2003, has announced she will ban the programme. The BBC think it would be a clear breach of their rights under Article 10 (free expression)

   Assuming that the BBC's case under Article 10 is strong, advise the BBC on whether it could bring a case against the Home Secretary under the HRA (you are not required to consider the substance of the Article 10 issue).

2. The ECtHR makes financial awards in 'just satisfaction' on the basis of the overall equity of the case. What factors are taken into account by the Court? How are these adapted by UK courts for the purposes of the HRA?

 For suggested approaches, please visit the Online Resource Centre.

≡ Further reading

Amos, M. (see Preface) Part 1, Chapter 6

Lester, A., Pannick, D., and Herberg, J. (see Preface) Chapter 2, Chapter 4, Article 13

Standing and the 'victim' test

Miles, J. 'Standing under the Human Rights Act 1998: Theories of Public Rights Enforcement and the Nature of Public Law Adjudication' (2000) 59(1) *CLJ* 133–167

Just satisfaction

Mowbray, A. 'The European Court of Human Right's Approach to Just Satisfaction' [1997] *Public Law* (Winter) 647–659

6

Convention law: pervasive themes

☐ **LEARNING OBJECTIVES**

● Concepts and background values which apply generally and pervade the Convention and the way it is interpreted.

● These include legality and the rule of law, 'margin of appreciation', democracy, proportionality.

● The obligation of states to take positive steps to secure Convention rights for all.

Introduction

The European Convention on Human Rights (ECHR) is a constitutional document. The words and phrases in it are written in highly abstract and general terms which need interpretation if they are to be applied to the particular facts and situations of individual cases. There are a number of general principles, concepts, and values which pervade the Convention (that is, they are relevant to all or most of the Convention's Articles). Some of these principles, concepts and values are derived from the text of the Convention (e.g. the importance of 'democracy'), others derive from international law generally. Whatever the source, the pervasive principles originate in the European Court of Human Rights' (ECtHR) own conception of its duty—it is an international court, so it must respect the sovereignty of states; yet it is applying an international instrument whose purpose is to give effective, individual protection to human rights, usually when these are threatened by the actions or inactivity of states.

CROSS REFERENCE
On section 2 HRA, see Chapter 4, section 4.3.

Under section 2 HRA these pervasive principles have to be taken into account by UK courts interpreting Convention rights in domestic law setting.

The application of these pervasive principles can be controversial. For example, the ECtHR's insistence that the Convention is a 'living instrument' which must evolve with the times can, for opponents, seem like judicial law making (the controversy over voting rights for prisoners (see Chapter 25, section 25.3.2) is a prime example.

6.1 International law

The Convention is an international treaty and the ECtHR is an international court.

6.1.1 The Vienna Convention

The United Nations Vienna Convention on the Law of Treaties 1969 is a treaty about treaties. It contains a range of general principles, agreed by states, on how the treaties they enter into should be interpreted. From the earliest cases the ECtHR accepted that it should be guided by the Vienna Convention (*Golder* v *United Kingdom* (1979–80) 1 EHRR 524, para 29). Article 31 of the Vienna Treaty, for instance, requires that treaties should be interpreted by reference to their 'context' and 'object and purposes'. Time and again the ECtHR emphasises that it interprets and applies the ECHR in a way that recognises its purpose as being to give effective human rights protection to individuals.

6.1.2 Other UN treaties etc.

Other treaties bearing on human rights issues can influence the way in which the ECtHR interprets the Convention (both the Vienna Convention and the Preamble to the ECHR itself authorise this). General human rights treaties, such as the International Covenant on Civil and Political Rights (ICCPR) (Chapter 1, section 1.4.4) assist the ECtHR, as do more focused treaties such as the UN Convention against Torture (see *Selmouni* v *France* (2000) 29 EHRR 403, Chapter 9, section 9.2.2).

In *R (SG)* v *Secretary of State for Work and Pensions* [2015] UKSC 16, the Supreme Court of the United Kingdon (UKSC) considered the United Nations Convention on the Rights of the Child 1990 in the context of assessing the compatibility of the statutory cap on welfare benefits with Convention rights.

6.1.3 Subsequent documents from Council of Europe

The Council of Europe (of which the ECtHR is part) produces a vast range of documents relating to human rights issues. These include other Conventions (which have the force of law) and a range of 'Recommendations' and 'Resolutions' which have persuasive authority.

6.1.4 Convention materials

Travaux préparatoires

The *travaux préparatoires* are the records of the process of writing and agreeing the Convention in 1950. The Court may refer to the *travaux préparatoires*. However, the ECtHR reads the Convention as a 'living instrument', evolving with the times, which means that the influence of these early documents can be limited.

6.1.5 Preamble and Article 1

These are both part of the Convention. Neither can be the basis of a decision but both can influence the way the Convention is interpreted.

The Preamble

The Vienna Convention allows courts to refer to the Preamble of a treaty for interpretative purposes. The Preamble of the ECHR is a significant source of guidance for the Court. It permits it, for example, to:

- refer to international law;
- insist on the importance of democracy and the rule of law; and
- invoke the 'common heritage' of European political traditions.

Under Protocol 15, references to the primary responsibility of states to secure human rights and to the margin of appreciation enjoyed and to the principle of subsidiarity will be added to the Preamble.

Article 1

Article 1 (along with Article 46) expresses the basic duties undertaken by states when they sign the Convention. They are discussed in Chapter 2, section 2.4.2.

6.1.6 The evolutive approach and precedent

The evolutive principle

The ECtHR treats the ECHR as a 'living instrument' and not as something whose meaning was set for all time by the drafters in 1950. The aim is to ensure that the application of the Convention can evolve as European society, culture, and values change.

The evolutive approach means that the Court has a relatively weak idea of precedent. It tends to follow the principles and decisions found in its earlier decisions, but is perfectly willing to depart from these in order to provide an effective protection of human rights in the modern age. Examples, found in this book, include *Goodwin* v *United Kingdom* (2002) 35 EHRR 18 (transgender: see Chapter 19, section 19.5) and *Stec* v *United Kingdom* (2005) 41 EHRR SE 18 ECHR (welfare rights: see Chapter 23, sections 23.2.3).

 THE BIGGER PICTURE

A good discussion of the evolutive approach is in *Stafford* v *United Kingdom* (see especially paras 68–80).

6.2 Legality and the rule of law

6.2.1 The idea of the rule of law

The duties and responsibilities the ECHR imposes on its signatory states must be exercised only on the basis of law. The 'rule of law' is a golden thread that runs through the Convention.

The rule of law is a foundation principle of modern national constitutional law, though its origins lie back in classical times. As an abstract principle it is fully recognised in the constitutional law of the United Kingdom (see *R* v *Goldstein* [2005] UKHL 63, para 32, for quotations). It is a principle found in international law and in 'liberal' political theory.

The general idea of the rule of law is that state power should only be exercised on the basis of laws—general rules for the regulation of conduct, both of individuals and the state's own agents. The rule of law is usually contrasted with 'arbitrary' or 'tyrannical' government found in dictatorships of various kinds. Under such systems individuals have no security: the activities of government are not controlled by rules and it is not possible to predict what actions are going to be penalised.

The problem is that there is nothing in the nature of rules which prevents their being used for oppressive purposes. Historically, therefore, the rule of law has come to be associated with certain values believed to underlie good government. In particular, it has come to embody certain 'procedural' values—such as the need for rules to be publicised; not to be applied retrospectively; to be sufficiently clear and certain so that they can be put into effect; and, above all, the right of access to the courts. Other accounts equate the rule of law with part or all of the full range of human rights.

Binding officials to obey rules may mean, in some situations, they are unable to do the right and best thing in any particular situation. The tension between rule following and exercising 'discretion' (choice of action) is one of the ongoing issues about the rule of law and is demonstrated in the understanding of that concept developed by the ECtHR.

6.2.2 The place of law in the Convention

References to 'law' are found throughout the Convention.

- The Preamble describes the rule of law as part of the common heritage of Europe.
- Restrictions on personal liberty and other freedoms can only be compatible with the Convention if authorised by law (see, for example, Articles 5 and 9–11).
- Rights and freedoms, such as the right to life, must be secured by law (see, for example, Articles 2 and 6).
- The requirement that criminal punishment must be based on the rule of law is expressly found in Article 7.

6.2.3 The autonomous Convention concept of law

Law and legality has an 'autonomous' meaning in the Convention. Autonomous concepts are concepts, found in the Convention, which have a particular meaning given to them by the ECtHR for Convention purposes. This meaning is autonomous in the sense that it does not depend on the way concepts are defined in national laws.

The seminal ECHR case is *Sunday Times* v *United Kingdom* (1979–80) 2 EHRR 245, para 49. The principles have been referred to by the ECtHR in countless cases (e.g. *Perincek* v *Switzerland* App 27510/08, Grand Chamber judgment of 15 October 2015, paras 131–136) and they have been summarised for the purposes of English law under the HRA in *R* v *Shayler* [2002] UKHL 11 (Lord Hope, para 56).

- There must be a legal basis for the state's action in the domestic law.
- Accessibility—the law or rule in question must be sufficiently accessible to the individuals who are affected by the restriction.

- Foreseeability—the law or rule in question must be sufficiently precise to enable the individuals affected to understand its scope and foresee the consequences of their actions so that they can regulate their conduct without breaking the law.
- The law must not have been applied in an arbitrary way.

Legal basis

Lawless action by a state in an area covered by human rights is likely to be a violation.

Accessibility—identifying the law

> First, the law must be adequately accessible: the citizen must be able to have an indication that is adequate in the circumstances of the legal rules applicable to a given case.
>
> (*Sunday Times*, para 49)

An individual, or at least her or his legal advisor, must be able to identify the legal rules on the basis of which the state has allegedly interfered with their Convention rights.

In *R (Gillan)* v *Commissioner of Police for the Metropolis* [2006] UKHL 12, the Terrorism Act 2000 allowed police to stop and search people even though there was no reasonable suspicion against those people. This could only be done if an 'authorisation' had been made in respect of the locality where the stops and searches are made. Such an authorisation was made in respect of the London area, but its existence was not made known to the public. The House of Lords held that the use of stop and search powers, given the context of the terrorist threat, satisfied the legality provision in Article 5.

Accessibility—what counts as 'law'

What counts as a 'law' depends on the particular legal system. In the *Sunday Times* case, the Court had to deal with the judge-made common law (the rules on contempt of court). The ECtHR had no difficulty in holding that 'unwritten', non-statutory law, such as English case law, was properly thought of as law. Enactment in a statute or code of law is not a requirement. Sources of law, therefore, include any rules which have the rule-like quality of generality and are accepted as such by the national courts. In the United Kingdom, for example, as well as case law, Acts of Parliament, and delegated legislation, there are also 'codes of practice', 'rules', 'regulations', 'guidelines' of various kinds, and many other forms in which general rules applying in different places and contexts are expressed. The legal force of such documents are a matter of domestic law and the ECtHR, it seems, will accept these as sources of law in so far as they are so accepted by the national courts. 'In sum, the "law" is the provision in force as the competent courts have interpreted it', *Sahin* v *Turkey* (2007) 44 EHRR 5, para 88, Grand Chamber.

A so-called law which does not have general application but which only applies to a particular individual or purpose does not meet the Convention test of law. 'Such an act is valid for one specific purpose only and is not intended to prescribe a general rule of conduct for recurrent applications', *Amat-G* v *Georgia* (2007) 45 EHRR 35, para 61.

Foreseeability, the absence of regulation

> Secondly, a norm cannot be regarded as a 'law' unless it is formulated with sufficient precision to enable the citizen to regulate his conduct: he must be able—if need be with appropriate advice—to foresee, to a degree that is reasonable in the circumstances, the consequences which a given action may entail.
>
> (*Sunday Times*, para 49)

In order for individuals to foresee (or predict) the circumstances in which the might of the state may be used against them, it is sometimes necessary for there to be a proper, sufficiently detailed body of law and regulations dealing with a particular matter. The absence of this in a matter touching on human rights can be a violation.

In *Malone* v *United Kingdom* (1985) 7 EHRR 14, the ECtHR held there was a breach of Article 8 (the right to private life) in a phone tapping case. In the United Kingdom, at the time, there was no statute-based regulatory regime dealing with phone tapping by the police. Surveillance seemed to be predominantly a matter of official discretion, a position which had been accepted by the UK courts (see, in particular, para 67).

Foreseeability and discretion

In many areas, officials need 'discretion', the freedom to decide policies and take decisions. The more precise and demanding the rules, the less discretion officials enjoy. The advantage of discretion is that it enables officials to take actions appropriate to the particular situation; the disadvantage, of course, is that it lessens certainty about what is acceptable or unacceptable under the law. There is no simple answer to this issue, which goes to the heart of questions about the nature of legitimate government.

The ECtHR takes a view which is circumstance and context dependent.

> The Court reiterates that the scope of the notion of foreseeability depends to a considerable degree on the content of the instrument in question, the field it is designed to cover and the number and status of those to whom it is addressed.
>
> (*Sahin* v *Turkey* (2007) 44 EHRR 5, para 91)

Laws drafted with too much precision may be too rigid and be unable to keep pace with changing circumstances. For this reason laws are 'inevitably couched in terms which, to a greater or lesser extent, are vague' (*Kokkinakis* v *Greece* (1994) 17 EHRR 397, para 40).

In *R (Purdy)* v *DPP* [2009] UKHL 45, the House of Lords held that guidelines, produced by the Director of Public Prosecutions did not, in the context of assisted suicide, differentiate clearly enough between different situations and motives. They failed, therefore, the 'foreseeability' test.

Non-arbitrariness and safeguards.

Law governing the exercise of state power will only satisfy the Convention if its provisions are sufficient to prevent arbitrary action by officials. The discretion, the powers, enjoyed by officials under the law must not be so wide as to allow them to act as they wish. The application of this point depends on context. In some situations, such as surveillance, non-arbitrariness requires there to be proper and sufficient safeguards in the law governing the exercise of these powers.

▶ CROSS REFERENCE
See Chapter 15, section 15.10.2, for a discussion of surveillance.

6.2.4 States themselves must obey legal orders

The rule of law requires governments to follow the law and obey court orders. In a number of cases the national courts have, for example, ordered the state to pay compensation. The response of simply refusing to pay (as in *Amat-G Ltd* v *Georgia*, earlier in this section) or of refusing to release a person from custody despite a court order (as in *Goral* v *Poland* App 38654/97, judgment of 30 October 2003) are all likely to be violations.

6.3 Margin of appreciation

The ECtHR has recognised, from its earliest cases, the need to take into account the different conditions and standards that apply in different countries. States have the primary duty to secure human rights and they are allowed a degree of freedom of choice over the measures they take regarding the issues that are the subject matter of the different articles in the Convention. The term given to this degree of freedom for states in the way Convention rights and freedoms are secured is 'margin of appreciation'.

A margin of appreciation is often recognised in respect of the power of states to restrict the exercise of freedoms found in the second paragraphs of Articles 8–11 (private life; thought, conscience, and religion; expression; assembly and association). It is not, however, confined to these Articles.

The margin of appreciation doctrine has been recognised from the earliest cases (see, in particular, *Handyside* v *United Kingdom* (1979–80) 1 EHRR 737, para 48). For a Grand Chamber restatement of the basic principles see *Marper/S* v *United Kingdom* (2009) 48 EHRR 50, para 102.

The basic points are:

- primary duty to protect human rights lies with the nation states;
- the role of the ECtHR is subsidiary and supervisory;
- the national authorities are in principle better placed than an international court to evaluate local needs and conditions. They have 'direct democratic legitimation' (*Hatton* v *United Kingdom* (2003) 37 EHRR 28, para 97) and so it is for the national authorities to make the initial assessment of the 'necessity' for an interference with a Convention right or freedom;
- this applies both to the laws and to the particular measure of implementation complained about;
- however, although a margin of appreciation is thereby left to the national authorities, their decision remains subject to review by the Court for conformity with the requirements of the Convention. Even a wide margin of appreciation is subject to limits based on the Court's assessment of the minimum required to uphold a right (its 'essence' or core).

The existence and extent of a margin of appreciation is variable. It is a matter for the ECtHR based on a range of relevant matters such as:

- the importance and nature of the right guaranteed—there is less room for a margin of appreciation in respect of absolute or unqualified rights like Article 3, than in respect of those rights, like Articles 8–11, which expressly require a balance to be struck between competing interests;
- the importance of the matter for the individual—where what is at stake is the effective enjoyment of 'intimate or key' rights, such as sexuality (*Dudgeon* v *UK* (1982) 4 EHRR 149, para 52), the margin will be less; likewise where a particularly important 'facet of an individual's existence or identity' is at stake (*Hämäläinen* v *Finland* App 37359/09, judgment of 16 July 2014, para 67);
- the nature of the activities which have been restricted—factors such as 'the circumstances, the subject matter and its background' (*Fretté* v *France* (2004) 38 EHRR 21, para 40);

- the nature of the interference and the purpose being pursued by the state;
- the lack of any consensus between the states on the importance of the issue or the best means of protecting it, indicates a wide margin of appreciation.

The margin of appreciation is a concept relevant only to an international court. Domestic courts may have reason to 'defer' to the judgments of the legislature or executive on the 'fair balance' of interests in a case (see Chapter 4, section 4.6).

6.3.1 Matters over which states have little or no margin of appreciation

Convention relevant matters which indicate no margin of appreciation or only a very narrow one, include the following:

- Where the Convention standard is 'objective', and its application more straightforward than one which is open to debate and disagreement. Torture and inhuman treatment, prohibited by Article 3 is an example.
- Where the Court feels able to identify a clear European consensus. In *Goodwin* v *United Kingdom* (2002) 35 EHRR 18, the Court decided that a general European cultural and medical consensus on the rights of transsexuals had developed and so, where before there had been a margin of appreciation, this was now greatly reduced.

  > **CROSS REFERENCE**
  > Goodwin is discussed in Chapter 19, section 19.5.

- Where an important Convention principle needs to be upheld. For example, the importance of political democracy means that there is very little margin of appreciation for states to restrict political speech (protected by Article 10).

6.3.2 Matters over which states have a wide margin of appreciation

Issues over which the states are likely to have a wide margin of appreciation include:

- Matters of controversy and diverging views, particularly in respect of 'moral' issues. In cases involving, for example, sadomasochism (*Laskey, Jaggard and Brown* v *United Kingdom* (1997) 24 EHRR 39) or obscenity (*Müller* v *Switzerland* (1991) 13 EHRR 212), a wide margin of appreciation is allowed. But even the most profound moral views may sometimes be outweighed by the need to protect individual rights. See, for example, *Open Door Counselling and Dublin Well Woman* v *Ireland* (1993) 15 EHRR 244, Chapter 17, section 17.6.3.
- Matters of social policy, such as housing, health care, or the environment. These are issues that are very dependant on the social, economic, and political factors prevailing in a country and are the sorts of matter over which there is reasonable disagreement between people, often expressed in the differences between political parties and going to the very heart of democratic debate. See, for example, *James* v *United Kingdom* 1986 8 EHRR 123 (housing policy, Chapter 23, section 23.6.1) or *Hatton* v *United Kingdom* (2003) 37 EHRR 28 (night flying at Heathrow, Chapter 15, section 15.10.1).
- Matters over which states are assumed to have special, exclusive knowledge. This can involve the existence and seriousness of threats to national security and the methods needed to deal with them. Even here, though, the ECtHR expects states to protect the core of the individual rights in issue (e.g. an early surveillance case: *Klass* v *Germany* (1979–80) 2 EHRR 214, paras 49–50).

6.3.3 **Criticisms of the doctrine**

The margin of appreciation can be a controversial doctrine because it appears to undermine the universal nature of human rights and, in the name of diversity, may allow oppressive government actions to go unchallenged. In particular it introduces an unwarranted level of flexibility into a Convention which already, in its express terms, is highly flexible.

> **THINKING POINT**
>
> Consider abortion and euthanasia cases (Chapter 15, sections 15.10.4 and 15.10.5). Do you approve of the wide margin allowed?

Defenders of the margin of appreciation see it as recognising the reality of the existence of different cultural and political standards in different countries. Such recognition is necessary to ensure the continuing support of the Convention amongst governments and people. It also supports the Convention value of democracy by ensuring that, where appropriate, decisions are taken by elected or accountable political bodies rather than handed over to judges.

In any event the ECtHR retains its reviewing role and, even where the margin is at its widest, has a duty to ensure that the 'essence' of a right is not undermined.

6.4 Democracy

6.4.1 **The importance of democracy**

Under the Convention, protecting human rights means upholding political democracy. As the ECtHR has said on more than one occasion:

> democracy is the only political model contemplated by the Convention and, accordingly, the only one compatible with it.
>
> (*United Communist Party of Turkey* v *Turkey* (1998) 26 EHRR 121, para 45)

This central importance of political democracy is affirmed by the Court in, for example, cases involving the banning of political parties (as in *United Communist Party of Turkey*, see para 45) or the imposition of restrictions on political participation (as in *Zdanoka* v *Latvia* (2007) 45 EHRR 17, Grand Chamber, see para 98).

The importance of democracy for the Convention flows, first, from the Preamble, which asserts that human rights are best protected in a democratic society.

The Preamble also refers to the European 'common heritage of political traditions': these the ECtHR takes as embodying democracy. There is, of course, a problem with the 'common heritage' argument. Until the last decade of the twentieth century, Europe was divided. States in Eastern Europe were not members of the Council of Europe and their governments were not 'democratic' or respectful of human rights in the Convention sense. In reality it is the concept of democracy, as developed by liberalism as a political theory and justified by abstract principles, that is maintained by the Convention. These principles may have been widely adopted in Western Europe after the Second World War, but they have hardly been 'common' to Europe as a whole.

'Democracy' is specifically referred to in Articles 8 to 11. These deal with respecting private life and protecting the freedoms of thought, conscience, and religion; expression; and assembly and association.

These freedoms can be restricted by the state but only on certain conditions, and one of these conditions is that the restriction be 'necessary in a democratic society'. In other words, restrictions on a person's private life, religion, expression, etc. are only justified if they spring from the needs of a democratic society (see, for example, *Gorzelik* v *Poland* (2005) 40 EHRR 4, Grand Chamber, para 89).

6.4.2 **The Convention concept of democracy**

Democracy has many meanings. Virtually all states claim in one sense or other to be democratic. The ECtHR, interpreting the Convention, has developed a general sense of democracy.

No particular political system

The Convention does not specify any particular form of government. The only specific reference to the political system is in Article 3 of the First Protocol. This places a duty on states to hold elections and, as interpreted by the ECtHR, gives individuals rights to vote, to stand in elections, and to take their seats in the legislature if elected. From this can be inferred that the Convention requires some system of representative democracy based upon an elected legislature; but little else.

There is little, if any, requirement in the Convention that would support a conception of democracy based on participation in the public life of the nation. The Convention appears to be narrower on this than international law generally. Article 25 ICCPR, in particular, refers to direct or indirect participation in 'the conduct of public affairs'. Systems of direct democracy, by which citizens have rights to be directly involved in the political decisions that affect them, gain no support from the ECHR. A passive democracy, based on no more than the peoples' choices, from time to time, of representative legislators, is all that the Convention requires by way of the political system.

> **CROSS REFERENCE**
> Political participation is, of course, secured by the rights to freedom of belief (Article 9), freedom of expression (Article 10), and freedom of association and assembly (Article 11). See Chapters 16–18.

The limits to majority rule—pluralism, tolerance, and broadmindedness

A concept of democracy based solely on majority rule or on the decisions of representative and accountable institutions is incompatible with the Convention. Human rights are to be enjoyed by all, including unpopular minorities and individuals. It is not permissible, for example, to deprive someone of his or her liberty or to stop someone exercising freedom of speech just because it is the wish of the majority that this be so. This can, for majoritarians (those who believe the essence of democracy is majority rule) make human rights themselves seem undemocratic.

The idea of democracy developed by the ECtHR involves a number of non-majoritarian elements. In particular democracy requires society to be pluralist, tolerant, and broadminded. This issue is discussed further in Chapter 1, section 1.1.

Pluralism means that the legal and constitutional system must accept and allow for the existence of different groups based, for example, on ethnic, religious, social, political, or other differences. This applies even if such groups are unpopular with the majority in society and their representatives. In particular:

- The state and legal system cannot impose a particular religious, ideological or other belief system on society as a whole.

CROSS REFERENCE

Pluralism is discussed further in Chapter 18, on Article 11, in particular section 18.7.1.

CROSS REFERENCE

Issues of tolerance and broadmindedness are discussed further in Chapter 15 (Article 8 private life) and Chapter 17 (Article 10 freedom of expression).

- The state and legal system must allow people to express and further their different ways of life through associations and groups. In particular people must be free to form and join political parties which can compete effectively for state power.

On tolerance and broadmindedness, the Convention requires society to tolerate minorities of whom the majority may disapprove, in particular, where the minority's behaviour is (to use an often repeated phrase) 'offensive, shocking or disturbing'. This is true especially in the context of freedom of expression (Article 10) but is also relevant to other Articles such as the right to private life in Article 8. Speech or behaviour which is opposed solely because it shocks, offends, or disturbs ought to be protected under the Convention. If, however, the expression or behaviour not only shocks, offends, and disturbs but also interferes with the lives of others or with the legitimate interests of state and society, then legal restriction may be necessary and acceptable under the Convention.

6.4.3 **Protecting democracy**

Political democracy sometimes needs defending against political groups seeking to undermine its institutions and values. The ECtHR, from its earliest cases, has accepted that it can be compatible with the Convention for governments to ban or restrict the activities of groups which pose credible threats to the democratic quality of their society. The basis for this was discussed by a Grand Chamber in *Zdanoka*, which affirms a degree of militancy inherent in Convention democracy.

🔍 CASE CLOSE-UP

Zdanoka v Latvia(2007) 45 EHRR 17, Grand Chamber

Latvia obtained independence from the Soviet Union in 1991. Just before, there was (it was alleged) an unsuccessful, pro-Soviet, attempted *coup d'etat*. Latvian election law banned ex-communists and pro-Soviet sympathisers who may have been implicated in the coup from standing for the independent Latvian Parliament. Z was banned under this provision. The party she would have sat for won 19 per cent of the vote and had 25 per cent of the seats. The ECtHR (a Grand Chamber reversing the previous Chamber decision) held that there had not been a violation of Article 3 of the First Protocol (which includes a right to stand in elections for the legislature).

- Democracy is the only political system acceptable to the Convention.

- The danger that individuals, groups, or parties may seek to use their Convention rights in order to undermine the rights of others cannot be ruled out and Article 17 (discussed in Chapter 7) is designed to deal with this: the Convention concept of democracy is one that is 'capable of defending itself'.

- The state is entitled to take special measures in order to safeguard its democratic values. In the context of genuine threats to a democratic society, individuals may have to accept restraints on their political or other freedoms in order to uphold common interest in effective democracy.

- A proper balance will need to be achieved between such restraints and the social good. Restrictions on political freedom in the name of the greater good need the most careful evaluation (which is ultimately under the supervision of the ECtHR).

- Pre-emption: a state is entitled to take pre-emptive measures to prevent an established threat to democratic institutions from occurring. Subject to rigorous European supervision, a state may 'reasonably forestall the execution of such a policy which is incompatible with the Convention's provisions, before an attempt is made to implement it through concrete steps that might prejudice civil peace and the country's democratic regime'. A dramatic example is *Refah Partisi* v *Turkey* (2003) 37 EHRR 1, discussed in Chapter 18, 18.7.2.

This idea of 'militant democracy' (Harvey, see Discussion Topic in this section) is problematic. There is no clear and uncontested conception of democracy available. There is a danger, therefore, that this approach allows the suppression of political views on the grounds of being undemocratic when, in fact, they are simply inconsistent with one conception of democracy but consistent with another.

Likewise there is the danger that states can silence their more radical critics simply by labelling them anti-democratic. This is, for example, an allegation made in respect of the *Refah Partisi* case, where some critics claimed there was no real evidence of anti-democratic intentions by the Islamist party.

> **CROSS REFERENCE**
> Article 17 is the topic of Chapter 7, section 7.3.

 DISCUSSION TOPIC

Conception of democracy

In an age in which the power of states is increasingly subordinated to the demands of global capitalism and corporate power, is there a need for a more effective and active conception of democracy to be protected by human rights?

Three articles may be helpful as further reading:

- Harvey, P. 'Militant Democracy and the European Convention on Human Rights' (2004) 29(3) *European Law Review* 407–420.
- Mowbray, A. 'The Role of the European Court of Human Rights in the Promotion of Democracy' [1999] *Public Law* (Winter) 703–725.
- O'Connell, R. 'Towards a Stronger Conception of Democracy in the Strasbourg Convention' [2006] 3 *EHRLR* 281–293.

6.5 Proportionality

6.5.1 **The idea of proportionality**

In applying the text of the Convention to individual cases, the ECtHR seeks 'proportionality'. The basic question is whether or not the interference with an individual's rights in the case can be justified by the social good or gain to others that the interference aims at. This depends on a balancing assessment between, on the one hand, the importance of the human right in question and, on the other hand, the benefit that the interference is likely to achieve. The point has been made emphatically and continuously by the Court, from some of its earliest cases:

> the Court must determine whether a fair balance was struck between the demands of the general interest of the community and the requirements of the protection of the individual's fundamental rights . . . The search for this balance is inherent in the whole of the Convention.

(Sporrong and Lönnroth v Sweden (1983) 5 EHRR 35, para 61)

The term 'proportionality' does not appear in the text of the Convention. It is a principle developed by the ECtHR for the purpose of interpreting and applying the Convention. It is a concept with a long history both in public international law and in some European national jurisdictions (German administrative law, for example), but not English common law.

Proportionality applies to all the Convention articles. For example, a balancing judgment of proportionality is needed in situations such as the following:

- whether restrictions on various freedoms guaranteed by Articles 8 to 11 ECHR are 'necessary in a democratic society' to achieve certain purposes;

- whether a use of lethal force by police or military was 'no more than absolutely necessary'. If so there will have been no violation of Article 2 ECHR (right to life);

- whether a deprivation of liberty is arbitrary or not (this judgment goes to the heart of Article 5 ECHR);

- whether 'treatment' of a person by the state meets a threshold of seriousness so that it is 'inhuman or degrading' and thus a violation of Article 3 ECHR.

6.5.2 **Fair balance**

What is or is not proportionate and a fair balance will depend on the facts of the case. A range of considerations, such as those listed in this section, have been taken into account by the ECtHR when determining proportionality.

State actions may be held disproportionate in situations including the following:

- Less restrictive alternatives. If there were alternative, less restrictive ways of achieving a legitimate purpose (see, for example, *Hentrich v France* (1994) 18 EHRR 440).

- Absolute rules. If rights were restricted by putting into effect an absolute rule, one which does not allow for the exercise of individual discretion (see, for example, *Hirst v United Kingdom* (2006) 42 EHRR 41).

- Inappropriate reasons. If the reasons given for an action by the state do not properly justify what is done (see, for example, *Stafford v United Kingdom* (2002) 35 EHRR 32).

- Flawed or inadequate procedural protections and safeguards. These include rights of access to independent and impartial courts and fair trials. The nature of such protections can depend on the context and the justifications for the restriction (see, for example, *Klass v Germany* (1979–80) 2 EHRR 214).

CROSS REFERENCE

The impact of proportionality on the UK courts under the HRA is discussed in Chapter 4, section 4.6.

- Maintaining the 'essence' of a right. In some circumstances the ECtHR will allow restrictions and qualifications of rights so long as the essence of the right is maintained: it must still be possible to exercise the right even though the restrictions and qualifications may make it harder or less effective in individual cases.

6.6 Positive duties

'Securing' Convention rights and freedoms places on the state parties both negative and positive duties.

6.6.1 **Negative duty**

A negative duty obliges a state not to do certain things. Examples of negative duties on states include not to torture people or subject them to inhuman treatment (Article 3); not to use deadly force intentionally, save in certain situations (Article 2); not to detain people other than in the circumstances laid down in Article 5; and not to restrict freedom of expression other than in the circumstances laid down in Article 10. The negative approach tends to dominate human rights thinking: the point of classical human rights is to protect individuals from oppressive and arbitrary actions by those in political power.

6.6.2 **Positive duties**

A positive duty obliges a state to take the necessary steps to secure the Convention rights and freedoms. The point is that Convention rights and freedoms cannot be effectively secured unless such steps are taken. These 'positive duties' can involve significant expenditure of money, official time, and resources.

> **CROSS REFERENCE**
> See Chapter 8, section 8.3, for example.

Some Articles, by their very nature, require positive steps and expenditure. Under Article 6, for example, states have to establish a system of courts, judges, a regulated legal profession, etc. in order to satisfy even the most minimum requirements of a 'fair trial'; similarly, securing the right to life under Article 2 requires states to have an effective criminal justice system with an organised police force, a prosecution service, a system of criminal courts and a prison service, and so on. Furthermore, none of that would be effective unless there was also a positive duty to investigate deaths.

Positive duties can also be owed to individuals. Thus if a state agency (e.g. the police) know of a specific threat to an individual's Convention rights, such as the right to life, there may be a positive obligation to take appropriate steps to protect that person.

Positive duties can also require states to alter private law, the law dealing with the relations between private persons (such as contract and tort in England and Wales). This duty is particularly relevant in respect of the right to respect for private and family life under Article 8.

> **CROSS REFERENCE**
> See Chapter 15, section 15.2.2 and Chapter 4, section 4.7.

Positive duties, particularly where implied, tend not to impose absolute obligations on states. Depending on the circumstances, and because states have limited resources and must decide their priorities, the burden on the state is only to do what is reasonable in the circumstances. Sometimes positive duties give rise to strict obligations, such as the duty to provide an effective investigation of deaths of prisoners and others who died under the control of the state

Increasingly the ECtHR recognises that distinguishing positive from negative actions can be quite unreal. Rather the approach is to ask whether the position the applicant is in engages state responsibility under the Convention. If it does, the principles which govern the question whether the interference is compatible with the Convention are the same whether state responsibility is couched in negative or positive terms, or both:

> In both contexts regard must be had to the fair balance to be struck between the competing interests of the individual and of the community as a whole.

(*Broniowski* v *Poland* (2005) 40 EHRR 21, para 144, a case involving the right to possessions)

 Summary

- A number of concepts pervade the Convention and are used by the ECtHR in interpreting the Convention (and so will be adopted by UK courts under the HRA).
- They are relevant to the way all the Articles are understood, either as interpretive devices (e.g. 'margin of appreciation') or as background values (e.g. 'democracy').

? **Self-test questions**

1. What is the importance of the Vienna Convention 1969 on the way in which the ECHR is interpreted?

2. What is the implication of calling the ECHR a 'living instrument'?

3. Explain the term 'margin of appreciation'.

4. Distinguish 'negative' and 'positive' duties—can they really be distinguished?

5. What concepts go to make up the Convention idea of 'democracy'?

 For suggested approaches, please visit the Online Resource Centre.

? **Exam questions**

1. How does 'proportionality' affect the way Convention rights and freedoms are applied?

2. Able, taking part in a demonstration, has been arrested and detained by the police under a general power to 'take necessary steps to prevent breaches of the peace'. She was released without charge but her personal details and the fact of her arrest are held on a police data base. The authority for the police to store and use this data (e.g. in the investigation of later crimes) is contained in an unpublished memorandum from the Home Secretary to the various forces which says that they can store the data and that they should take whatever measures they think appropriate to keep it safe.

   Able has approached your law firm arguing that his rights under the Convention have been breached. You are required to produce a briefing paper on the single issue of whether, in Convention terms, the Police have acted lawfully.

 For suggested approaches, please visit the Online Resource Centre.

Further reading

Bingham, T. *The Rule of Law* (2010) London: Allen Lane

Fredman, S. 'Human Rights Transformed: Positive Duties and Positive Rights' [2006] *Public Law* 498–520

Lester, A., Pannick, D. and Herberg, J. (see Preface) Chapter 3

Rivers, J. 'Proportionality and Variable Intensity of Review' (2006) 65(1) *CLJ* 174–207

See also reading on 'Conception of democracy', Discussion Topic, section 6.4.3

PART 2

SUBSTANTIVE RIGHTS AND THEIR APPLICATION IN THE UNITED KINGDOM

7 Ancillary rights

◻ **LEARNING OBJECTIVES**

● Important 'ancillary' rights in Part 1 of the Convention which affect the way the main rights are put into effect. These are:

  ● Article 14 (discrimination);

  ● Article 15 (derogation);

  ● Article 17 (abuse of rights);

  ● Article 16 (restraints on aliens); and

  ● Article 18 (limiting restriction on rights).

Introduction

Part One of the European Convention on Human Rights (ECHR) includes the substantive Articles which secure the human rights to life: the prohibition on torture, the right to a fair trial, etc. Part One also contains a number of Articles which are ancillary in the sense that they do not in themselves establish any human rights but are relevant to the way the substantive Articles are put into effect. In particular, the rights in the Convention must be applied without discrimination (Article 14) and not in a way which allows a person to undermine the rights of others (Article 17). Article 15 allows states, when under threat, to suspend some of the substantive rights (Article 15).

7.1 Article 14

Article 14 Prohibition of discrimination

The enjoyment of the rights and freedoms set forth in this Convention shall be secured without discrimination on any ground such as sex, race, colour, language, religion, political or other opinion, national or social origin, association with a national minority, property, birth or other status.

7.1.1 **Introduction**

Article 14 is the anti-discrimination provision in the ECHR. As will be shown, its scope is limited: it only deals with discrimination in the way a state gives effect to its obligations under the Convention.

It needs, therefore, to be placed in the context of anti-discrimination law more generally. In its modern form this can be traced back, in the UK, to the Sex Discrimination Act 1975 and the Race Relations Acts from 1975. These sought to prohibit both direct discrimination (not justifiable) and indirect discrimination (which could be justified) on the grounds of sex and race in the contexts of employment and the provision of services. Since then there has been a great expansion. The coverage of the law has widened (e.g. to people with disabilities, or on the grounds of religion or sexual orientation), as has the context of legal enforcement (e.g. beyond employment and services to include education and other public services). Likewise concern with anti-discrimination (dealing with comparatively less favourable treatment) has been complemented with a more general concern with equality (e.g. ensuring the opportunity to participate on equal terms in employment). The European Community, now European Union, is, and has been, a major driving force behind this. UK law gives effect to Treaty provisions and, in particular, EU directives in this field.

The Equality Act 2010 is the major UK legislation dealing with anti-discrimination and the promotion of equality. It repeals most of the existing legislation (Acts of Parliament like the Sex Discrimination Act 1975 and Regulations like the Equality Act 2006 (Sexual Orientation) Regulations 2007) and restates them in a single Act. It also enacts new provisions which extend equality law in various ways.

- It stipulates age, disability, gender reassignment, marriage and civil partnership, pregnancy and maternity, race, religion or belief, sex and sexual orientation as 'protected characteristics' to which equality law applies.

- It defines different ways in which it is unlawful to treat someone unequally—by discriminating against them (treating them less favourably, this can be done directly or indirectly), harassing or victimising them, or failing to make, in respect of a person with a disability, a reasonable adjustment.

- It defines the areas in which such prohibitions, differently, apply (e.g. in employment, the provision of goods and services, in schools, and in private associations).

- It extends the law in various ways such as by stipulating situations in which equality must be promoted. Of particular importance is the duty, in Part 11, on public authorities and those exercising public functions, to have 'due regard' to the need to eliminate discrimination and advance equality of opportunity and in other ways to seek to overcome disadvantage suffered by persons who share a protected characteristic.

- It defines the circumstances in which positive action may, lawfully, be taken to eliminate disadvantages or recognise different needs of those who share a protected characteristic (i.e. where that might otherwise be discrimination against those who do not share the protected characteristic).

- It deals with enforcement of these provisions, mainly, though not exclusively, in an Employment Tribunal or County Court.

There are other provisions which deal with equality and discrimination in various ways. It is a massive and highly complex piece of legislation and it is outside the scope of this book to deal with it in any detail. It is subject to any directly effective EU rights enjoyed by individuals and, like any UK legislation, must, under the Human Rights Act 1998 (HRA), be interpreted compatibly with Convention rights.

The Equality Act 2006 created and empowered the Equality and Human Rights Commission. This took over the roles of the Equal Opportunities Commission and the Commission for Racial Equality. Its job is to promote anti-discrimination, equality, and human rights in various ways.

BIGGER PICTURE

On the Equality Act 2010 see Wadham, J. (ed) et al *Blackstone's Guide to the Equality Act 2010* 2nd edn (2012) Oxford: OUP.

On the Equality and Human Rights Commission see http://www.equalityhumanrights.com

7.1.2 Article 14: general principles

The general principles of Article 14 were laid down by the ECtHR in the so-called *'Belgian Linguistics'* case.

CASE CLOSE-UP

Case Relating to Certain Aspects of the Laws on the Use of Languages in Education in Belgium (Belgian Linguistics Case (No 2)) (1979–80) 1 EHRR 252

Under Belgian education laws, the language of publicly funded education provision depended on the dominant language of the area. French-speaking parents, some living in Dutch-speaking areas and some in an area where no language predominated, challenged these laws because they meant that their children would not be taught in French. The case was argued on the basis of language discrimination in the way the right to education (in Article 2 of the First Protocol) was put into effect. The European Court of Human Rights (ECtHR) (in this important early case) upheld the laws regarding their impact on the predominantly Dutch-speaking areas but, in the case of an area where no language predominated, held that there was a breach.

The principles discussed in the next section derive from the ECtHR's reasoning in this case.

7.1.3 Article 14 relates solely to the 'rights and freedoms set forth in this Convention'

Article 14 applies only to discrimination in the way Convention rights and freedoms are secured. For this reason there cannot be a violation of Article 14 in isolation. Any alleged violation must be of Article 14, linked to one of the other Articles. In the case law of the Court, Article 14 tends to play a subordinate role and normally will only be considered separately if 'a clear inequality of treatment in the enjoyment of the right in question is a fundamental aspect of the case' (*Chassagnou v France* (2000) 29 EHRR 615, para 89).

Article 14 can be compared with Protocol 12 ECHR, which prohibits discrimination in respect of 'any right set forth in law'. The Protocol came into force on 1 April 2005 but the United

Kingdom is not a signatory. Likewise the EU Charter of Fundamental Rights also has an unqualified anti-discrimination provision (Article 21)—see Chapter 3, section 3.4.

7.1.4 No need for a breach of the linked Article

It is not, however, necessary for there to have been a breach of the substantive Article to which Article 14 is linked. What is necessary is that the discriminatory actions must have fallen 'within the ambit' of one of the Convention rights. It must relate to a matter that is covered by a substantive Article (be 'linked to the exercise of a right guaranteed' by the Convention). So, even if there is no breach of the substantive Article, there can still be a breach of Article 14.

The Convention

In *Abdulaziz, Cabales and Balkandali* v *United Kingdom* (1985) 7 EHRR 471, the ECtHR held that part of British immigration law was in breach of Article 14. Women were treated less favourably than men on the issue of the rights of spouses to enter the country. This touched on Article 8 ECHR (right to family life). There was no breach of Article 8 since the United Kingdom was entitled to regulate immigration. Only Article 14 was violated; but Article 14 was only in issue because the matter related to Article 8.

A matter can be within the ambit of a Convention right even if it is the provision of a service by the state that it has no Convention duty to provide. Examples given in *Belgian Linguistics* were the provision of a particular kind of educational provision (e.g. grammar schools) and a system of appeal courts (not required by Article 6). If states do choose to provide such services, Article 14 can still be violated if they are provided in a discriminatory way.

In *Stec* v *United Kingdom* (2006) 43 EHRR 47, a Grand Chamber held that although the Convention does not require states to provide welfare payments and pensions, if they are provided, they are 'possessions' within the ambit of Article 1 of the First Protocol and Article 14 means they must be provided without discrimination.

The HRA

In giving effect to anti-discrimination principles for UK law under the HRA, the House of Lords has expressed concern at the uncertainty of the scope of Article 14.

 CASE CLOSE-UP

***M v Secretary of State for Work and Pensions* [2006] UKHL 11**

M lived in a homosexual relationship with another woman. She was separated from her husband. Her children were looked after by her husband. Her contributions to the maintenance of her children under the Child Support Act 1991 were greater than they would have been had she been living in a heterosexual relationship. The House of Lords rejected the argument that there was a violation of Article 14 linked to Article 8.

The House of Lords held that 'ambit' was a very loose expression. For Article 14 to be engaged, there has to be something more than a tenuous (weak) link. The difference in treatment must be such as to undermine the core, underlying values inherent in the article in issue (here Article 8). Here the difference in treatment meant that M was financially worse off but it did not affect her ability to have and enjoy a family life.

7.1.5 What is 'discrimination': objective and reasonable justification

The Convention

As *Belgian Linguistics* made clear, Article 14 is not violated if a state can show that treating someone differently for a reason based on their sex, race, nationality, etc. is a legitimate way of solving a particular problem or of correcting 'factual inequalities' between groups. In *DH v Czech Republic* (2008) 47 EHRR 3, a Grand Chamber summarised the core meaning of discrimination in Article 14: 'discrimination means treating differently, without an objective and reasonable justification, persons in relevantly similar situations' (para 175).

All forms of different treatment are in principle capable of justification. In some situations, indeed, a state may be under a positive duty to treat people differently on 'status' grounds where this is necessary to correct an unjust inequality.

In *Thlimmenos* v *Greece* (2001) 31 EHRR 15, the ECtHR held that the failure of Greek law to distinguish between convicted conscientious objectors and ordinary criminals when it came to the rules governing entrance to the professions, violated Article 14 linked to Article 9 (freedom of thought, conscience and religion).

The existence of an 'objective and reasonable justification' depends upon two factors:

- Does the difference in treatment have a legitimate aim?
- Is there a relationship of proportionality between the aim and the discriminatory means used?

Intensity of justification

The depth and degree of justification depends upon the nature of the issue. In its case law the ECtHR has indicated that whilst some differences in treatment may only require a rational explanation, other differences in treatment require enhanced, 'very weighty' justification. In *AL (Serbia)* v *Secretary of State for the Home Department* [2008] UKHL 42, Baroness Hale identified differences based on the following characteristics as requiring, according to Strasbourg, such increased justification:

- race, colour, or ethnic origin (*DH* v *Czech* (2008) 47 EHRR 3, Grand Chamber, para 196);
- sex (*Abdulaziz*, para 78);
- sexual orientation (*EB* v *France* App 43546/02, para 91);
- birth or adopted status (*Inze* v *Austria* (1987) 10 EHRR 394);
- nationality (*Gaygusuz* v *Austria* (1996) 23 EHRR 364).

Partly these reflect grounds of long-standing historical subordination and contempt which human rights law must seek to overcome. But the Strasbourg jurisprudence seems to go further. Weighty justification is required for differences in treatment based upon 'personal characteristics of an individual which he cannot or should not be asked to change' (*AL (Serbia)*, para 31).

On the other hand, differences in treatment which relate to measures of 'economic or social strategy' (involving social and economic policies whose impact may depend on a person's status) require a less demanding scrutiny by the Court. A rational justification (that the means used are likely to achieve a legitimate purpose) is likely to be accepted: Strasbourg allows a wide margin of appreciation.

> ### 🔍 CASE CLOSE-UP
>
> ***Stec* v *United Kingdom*** (2006) 43 EHRR 47, Grand Chamber
>
> A number of applicants, some men, some women, received welfare benefits that were lower than would have been received by the opposite sex. The underlying reason for all the claims was the difference in the retirement age between men and women at the relevant time. A Grand Chamber dealt with the case by applying Article 14 linked to Article 1 of the First Protocol. It held that there was no violation of Article 14 because there was an objective and reasonable justification for the different pension age enjoyed by men and women.

It was held (para 66) that:

- at the time it was introduced a difference in pension age had an objective and reasonable justification which recognised the 'traditional' economically inactive role of women which the pension system sought to compensate for;
- the economic role of women has, of course, changed greatly over the years. At some point the justification for differential pension ages no longer applied (indeed they have been held to be incompatible with EU law) and change was necessary. States, however, have a wide margin of appreciation over the pace and nature of that change, which the United Kingdom had not exceeded.

The HRA

In adopting the need for objective and reasonable justification for differences in treatment into UK law, the House of Lords/Supreme Court has recognised the distinction, made by the ECtHR and referred to earlier in this section, between differences flowing from social policies and differences requiring more intense scrutiny. Article 14 embodies something more than just an objection to differences in treatment. The point of Article 14 is to uphold (in Lord Hoffmann's words) the 'Enlightenment value that every human being is entitled to equal respect and to be treated as an end and not a means' (*R (Carson) v Secretary of State for Work and Pensions* [2005] UKHL 37, para 15). Article 14 requires that differences in treatment that offend our sense of equal respect must be justified by the state and the justification subjected to intense scrutiny by the courts. However, *AL (Serbia)*, mentioned earlier, is less focused on Enlightenment values. It clarifies the issue by placing the court's attention on differences of treatment based on personal characteristics (see Baroness Hale's list, under Intensity of justification, earlier in this section) and avoids the language of 'suspect classifications' based upon historical subordination.

> ### 🔍 CASE CLOSE-UP
>
> ***R (SG) v Secretary of State for Work and Pensions*** [2015] UKSC 16
>
> This was a challenge to regulations imposing a 'benefits cap' by which the total of benefits that could be paid to persons working less than 16 hours per week was capped at £500 per week irrespective of needs. It was conceded by the government that there could be indirect discrimination against women with dependent children and living in high rent areas; also, possibly, women seeking refuge from domestic violence.

Following *Stec* (discussed earlier), benefits can be 'possessions' and so it was argued that the benefits cap breached Article 14 read with Article 1 of the First Protocol. Given the concession the issue was justification.

The test was whether the justification was 'manifestly without reasonable foundations' (i.e. a low intensity of review by the court). The justification was made out: there had been full parliamentary debate, and it was not manifestly unreasonable to say that the cap advanced fairness between workers and non-workers, generated financial savings, and incentivised work.

There were strong dissents focused on the impact on children and whether this was compatible with the UN Convention of the Rights of Children given its relevance to the justification issue. There was no breach of Article 14 with Article 1 of the First Protocol.

The easily satisfied test, in a social welfare context, of manifestly without reasonable foundations can contrasted with *A* v *Secretary of State for the Home Department* [2004] UKHL 56. Here the House of Lords had no difficulty in finding incompatibility with Article 14 linked to Article 5. Foreign-born terrorist suspects were deprived of their liberty whilst suspects who were UK nationals were not. The matter was subjected to intense review.

7.1.6 **The victims of discrimination: 'status'**

Unlike many anti-discrimination provisions found in national and international law, Article 14 is not restricted to a specific range of types of victim. The given list includes many of the main victim groups whose suffering of discrimination has disfigured European history in the twentieth century and beyond. But the term 'or other status' means that the list is not closed. Other forms of discrimination that have only affected the public conscience after the Convention came into effect or which reflect new ways of living, can be included. Sexual orientation is an obvious example (see *Salgueiro da Silva Mouta* v *Portugal* (2001) 31 EHRR 47, para 28).

In *Kjeldsen* v *Denmark* (1979–80) 1 EHRR 711, the ECtHR sought to limit 'other status' to a personal characteristic. In *Clift* v *UK* App 7205/07, judgment of 13 July 2010, the Court made it clear that this term is to be given a broad and inclusive meaning that was not necessarily *ejusdem generis* the list in Article 14 and not confined to characteristics which are innate or inherent (paras 54–59). In the case, it held that differences in the treatment of long-term prisoners was a difference based on status.

Examples of matters accepted as going to status for the purposes of Article 14 by UK courts include:

- being a resident in a foreign country: *Carson* (section 7.1.5);
- being an unmarried couple treated differently from a married couple in the context of adoption law: *Re G (Adoption: Unmarried Couple)* [2008] UKHL 38;
- being homeless and therefore denied benefits available to others (*R (RJM)* v *Secretary of State for Work and Pensions* [2008] UKHL 63 (their Lordships rejected the view that if a state of affairs had been voluntarily chosen it was less likely to be a personal characteristic, para 47)).

An example of a characteristic which was not accepted:

- being innocent but involved in a criminal investigation and, in respect of the retention of DNA samples taken, treated differently from those not so involved: *R (Marper)* v *Chief Constable of South Yorkshire* [2004] UKHL 39.

> ### THINKING POINT
>
> Caste is not one of the 'protected characteristics' on which the Equality Act 2010 is based. Is it appropriate to consider it as a matter of 'other status' in Article 14?

7.1.7 The Human Rights Act and Article 14

In *SG* (discussed in section 7.1.5), Lord Reed summarised the judgments to be made by the domestic court (adopting the position in *Carson* v *United Kingdom*, para 61).

In relation to actions within the ambit of a Convention right and in respect of someone's 'status', as defined earlier:

- Has there been a difference in treatment between persons in relatively similar positions (or a failure to treat different people differently which can also be a violation). In *AL (Serbia)* (section 7.1.5), Baroness Hale compared Article 14 with domestic law? Article 14 focuses on justification for differences in treatment and, unlike domestic anti-discrimination law, is less concerned with the precise identification of some other group or individual for comparison, though the argument for discrimination is often supported by the identification of a general comparator.
- Does the difference in treatment pursue a legitimate aim?
- Is there a relationship of proportionality between the means employed and the aim?

The state must prove that the restriction is a proportionate way of meeting a legitimate purpose. The degree of scrutiny by the court, as indicated earlier, depends on the context. Judicial scrutiny will be more intense the more the differences in treatment embody a lack of respect on traditional grounds or, perhaps, important rights such as those of children—recognised as warranting close scrutiny by Baroness Hale in *AL (Serbia)* and also in *SG*.

7.2 Article 15

Article 15 Derogation in time of emergency

(1) In time of war or other public emergency threatening the life of the nation any High Contracting Party may take measures derogating from its obligations under this Convention to the extent strictly required by the exigencies of the situation, provided that such measures are not inconsistent with its other obligations under international law.

(2) No derogation from Article 2, except in respect of deaths resulting from lawful acts of war, or from Articles 3, 4 (paragraph 1) and 7 shall be made under this paragraph.

(3) Any High Contracting Party availing itself of this right of derogation shall keep the Secretary General of the Council of Europe fully informed of the measures which it

has taken and the reasons therefore. It shall also inform the Secretary General of the Council of Europe when such measures have ceased to operate and the provisions of the Convention are again being fully executed.

7.2.1 Derogation

Derogation means to repeal or to lessen the force of something, such as a law. The effect of the law is cancelled for the time being.

States can be faced with political movements who believe the end justifies the means and who are prepared to use violence, including the kind of violence aimed at civilians that, today, we call 'terrorism'. Because such movements are likely to hold the existing laws in contempt and because they are intentionally and deliberately seeking to undermine the established order, states can feel vulnerable and in need of special powers. These are powers that make it easier for the police and security services to operate—to do things like enter property and search it, arrest and detain suspects, ban organisations, make it easier to secure convictions, and so on.

Such powers are likely to be incompatible with some of the rights and freedoms in the Convention. Article 15, therefore, allows states to 'derogate' from (or suspend) most, though not all, of the articles. For example, suspending the operation of all or parts of Article 5 (the right to liberty), a state may detain people on suspicion, without their being suspected, or convicted, of a criminal offence and without full judicial supervision of the grounds on which they are detained (as happened in the United Kingdom between 2002 and 2005).

Derogation is, of course, highly controversial. It means that at precisely the time when suspects need greatest protection of their basic rights, that protection is removed. The alternative to derogation is the position that tends to be adopted by international bodies such as the Council of Europe (e.g. in various documents it has produced in the context of anti-terrorism laws). This position recognises that states may need to deal with genuine threats by the use of special measures but that such special measures should be compatible with Convention rights. Convention rights are not inflexible. Their application usually involves seeking a 'fair balance' between the rights of individuals and the legitimate requirements of society. They can then be given effect in ways that recognise the problems faced by states dealing with terrorism, insurrection, etc. The need is to ensure that the minimum, or the 'essence' of the right is preserved.

7.2.2 Derogations and the HRA

Under the HRA, Convention rights are to take effect subject to any derogations made by the United Kingdom (section 1(2): see Chapter 4, section 4.2.4).

7.2.3 Main points of Article 15

Article 15 allows derogation:

- only if there is a 'war or other emergency facing the life of the nation';
- only if the measures which require derogation are strictly necessary to deal with the emergency and are not more extensive than is necessary for that purpose;
- where the measures taken are not incompatible with other international obligations;
- where the Council of Europe, through its Secretary General, is informed of the measures taken and why they are necessary, and is told when the measures are no longer in effect and the derogation is ended.

7.2.4 **Limits to derogation**

States cannot derogate from the following Articles:

- Article 2, the right to life. The claim that there is an emergency cannot be used to allow a loosening of the rules regarding the use of deadly force. Even at such a time, the use of deadly force by the police etc. needs to be justified under the terms of Article 2(2) (e.g. that the force is 'strictly necessary' to quell a riot or insurrection). There is an exception: Article 2 can be disregarded in the context of 'lawful war'. The war needs to be 'lawful' (today this probably means that it is sanctioned in some way by the United Nations). Furthermore, the measures taken need to be compatible with other international obligations, and so any actions must be compatible with the Geneva Convention and other international 'laws of war'.

- Article 3, the prohibition of torture. The existence of a war or emergency does not provide justification for the use of torture or inhuman or degrading treatment or punishment. The ban on torture etc. is 'absolute' in the sense that it must not be done no matter how strong the justification in any particular instance. The likelihood of saving the lives of others is not a factor that can be weighed against the prohibition on torture.

- Article 4(1), prohibition of slavery and forced labour. The necessities of war or public emergency cannot justify the enslavement of captives or a population. The ban on forced or compulsory labour in Article 4(2) can, however, be suspended under Article 15. It should be noted that military service is not considered as forced or compulsory labour.

- Article 7, no punishment without law. The criminal law cannot be changed and used retrospectively against those alleged to be involved in war, insurrection, terrorism, etc. It should be noted that nothing in Article 7 prevents the prosecution and conviction of people for war crimes and crimes against humanity.

7.2.5 **'War or other public emergency facing the life of the nation'**

There can be no derogation unless there is a 'war or other public emergency facing the life of the nation'. This means that there is:

> an exceptional situation of crisis or emergency which affects the whole population and constitutes a threat to the organised life of the community of which the State is composed.
>
> (*Lawless* v *Ireland No 3* (1979–80) 1 EHRR 15, para 28)

In the *Greek Case* (1969) 12 YB 1, the Court identified the following characteristics of a public emergency:

> (1) It must be actual or imminent. (2) Its effects must involve the whole nation. (3) The continuance of the organised life of the community must be threatened. (4) The crisis or danger must be exceptional, in that the normal measures or restrictions, permitted by the Convention for the maintenance of public safety, health and order, are plainly inadequate.

The ECtHR allows states a wide margin of appreciation on the question of the existence of the threat. The IRA campaign against the British in Northern Ireland was recognised as such an emergency (see *Lawless* v *Ireland* and, for the period 1968–98, *Brannigan and McBride* v *United Kingdom* (1994) 17 EHRR 539); similarly the Kurdish insurrection against Turkey in the late twentieth century (*Aksoy* v *Turkey* (1997) 23 EHRR 553).

The HRA

Article 15 was given full consideration by the House of Lords in a landmark case involving the detention, without conviction, of a number of foreign terrorist suspects.

CASE CLOSE-UP

A v Secretary of State for the Home Department [2004] UKHL 56

Part IV of the Anti-terrorism, Crime and Security Act 2001, enacted in the aftermath of the '9/11' attacks in New York and Washington, allowed the Home Secretary to certify a foreigner (someone without permanent rights of residence in the United Kingdom) as a terrorist suspect. Normally such a person would be deported. Article 3 of the Convention prohibits deportation if there are grounds for thinking that the person would be tortured or treated inhumanely in the country to which he or she is deported. Article 3 cannot be derogated from. Rather than release terrorist suspects, the government decided that they should be detained in prison, and some were sent to Belmarsh Prison (thus the case is referred to as 'the Belmarsh case'), a maximum security prison in London. Detention for this reason involves a breach of Article 5. Article 5, however, can be derogated from. This the British government did, using Article 15. The grounds of the derogation were challenged by the detainees. The House of Lords held that the derogation was not 'strictly necessary' and so it was not lawful. In particular, it involved discrimination against foreigners in breach of Article 14. Therefore the detentions were incompatible with Article 5. The derogation was quashed (cancelled) and a 'declaration of incompatibility' under the HRA was made in respect of Articles 5 and 14. The detainees were released about three months later and made subject to 'control orders'. Part IV was repealed.

> **CROSS REFERENCE**
>
> Control order and subsequent measures are discussed in Chapter 26, sections 26.3.3 and 26.7.2).

> **CROSS REFERENCE**
>
> Declarations of incompatibility and their effects are explained in Chapter 4, section 4.4.3.

On the issue of the existence of a threat (international jihadist terrorism), Lord Bingham applied the *Greek Case* criteria but, with the majority of Law Lords, he accepted that the courts could not easily interfere with the government's assessment of the risk. Deference to the government by UK courts (see Chapter 4, section 4.6.2) mirrors the margin of appreciation states have under the Convention.

Lord Hoffmann's dissent

In the *Belmarsh* case, Lord Hoffmann dissented on the issue of the existence of a public emergency. In an eloquent passage (paras 91–96) he argued that a 'public emergency facing the life of the nation' must involve a threat to the democratic institutions and way of life of the country. Jihadist terrorism of the twenty-first century might lead to a significant number of deaths but does not threaten the life of the nation or its institutions (though an over-reaction by government might begin to do just that).

> I do not underestimate the ability of fanatical groups of terrorists to kill and destroy, but they do not threaten the life of the nation. Whether we would survive Hitler hung in the balance, but there is no doubt that we shall survive Al-Qa'ida.
>
> (para 96)

 THINKING POINT

A v SSHD left open the question of what should be done with foreign terrorist suspects. Would this have been a relevant issue for a court?

7.2.6 'to the extent strictly required by the exigencies of the situation'

Though a wide margin of appreciation is left to the states on the issue of the existence of an emergency, the question whether the measures taken, measures which require derogation, are 'strictly required' is treated differently. Article 15 requires that these measures are no more than what is strictly required to deal with the emergency. Any derogation is incompatible with Article 15 in so far as it purports to authorise measures which are not needed or which are not reasonable means of dealing with the emergency. On this issue the states still have a margin of appreciation but that must be subject, first, to effective supervision by national bodies (e.g. individuals must be able to test the legality of the way they are applied in the national courts), and second, to supervision by the ECtHR (see *Aksoy* v *Turkey* (1997) 23 EHRR 553 para 68).

In *Aksoy* v *Turkey* (1997) 23 EHRR 553, the ECtHR stressed the need for proper procedures. The detention of an individual, in that case for 14 days, without access to lawyers or courts, was disproportionate, even in the circumstances of deadly terrorism, and so was not covered by any purported derogation. In *A* (see section 7.2.5), the House of Lords found that the measures were more than 'strictly required' because they treated dangerous foreign terrorist suspects (subject to detention without trial) differently from equally dangerous British nationals (who were not subjected to control). The government's justifications for this difference in treatment (based on immigration law) were not accepted by the court. Since it was not necessary to detain British nationals, there was no reason for detaining equally dangerous foreigners and so the derogation did more than was necessary.

7.2.7 International law

The derogation must be compatible with international law. It must not authorise behaviour which is inconsistent with other international obligations of a state. United Nations conventions against discrimination on sexual or racial grounds, for example, must be adhered to; likewise the International Covenant on Civil and Political Rights whose provisions are similar to the European Convention. Like the Convention, Article 4 of the Covenant allows derogation on similar terms to Article 15 supplemented by the Siracusa Principles of 1984.

7.2.8 Information

The Council of Europe must be kept informed by the state seeking to derogate from the measures being taken which are incompatible with the Convention and the reasons which explain and justify them. Although not expressly in Article 15, it seems that some form of announcement or proclamation of the existence of an emergency may be necessary.

7.3 Article 17

Article 17 Prohibition of abuse of rights

Nothing in this Convention may be interpreted as implying for any State, group or person any right to engage in any activity or perform any act aimed at the destruction of any of the rights and freedoms set forth herein or at their limitation to a greater extent than is provided for in the Convention.

Article 17 expresses the great dilemma of a liberal society. A liberal society is one in which pluralism, tolerance, and political freedom are fundamental values. How can such a society defend itself against intolerance and various types of political extremism without, at the same time, fatally undermining these values?

The need for a provision such as Article 17 seemed very clear to the drafters of the Convention. It underscored the point that one of the Convention's main purposes was (and is) to prevent totalitarianism ever again scarring Europe's governments and politics.

From its inception the ECtHR has had to deal with cases in which states have taken steps to ban or restrict political parties or individuals. For example:

- bans after the Second World War of Nazi and fascist parties and their successors, e.g. *X v Italy* (1976) DR 5, 83;

- bans, during the 'Cold War', on Communist parties, on the grounds that they sought to impose dictatorship (see *German Communist Party (KPD) v Germany* (1957) App 250/57, 1 YB 222). There were also bans on individual communists working in the public sector, which the Court upheld in *Glasenapp v Germany* (1987) 9 EHRR 25, but then took a more tolerant position in later cases such as *Vogt v Germany* (1996) 21 EHRR 205 (both cases were decided on the basis of Article 10(2) rather than Article 17).

The HRA

Under the HRA, UK courts must read the Convention rights in the light of Article 17 (see Chapter 4, section 4.2.1). In cases where it has arisen, the attitude of UK courts is that Article 17 adds little to what is already allowed by Article 10 etc. (see, for example, the Scottish case of *Whaley v Lord Advocate* 2004 SC 78, paras 46–47.

General principles

A Grand Chamber of the ECtHR affirmed the following principles as regards Article 17 in relation to admissibility in *Paksas v Lithuania* (paras 85–89).

 CASE CLOSE-UP

Paksas v Lithuania (2014) 59 EHRR 30 Grand Chamber

P, who had been president of Lithuania, had been impeached on grounds of corruption and breach of his oath of office. He alleged that being subsequently prevented from standing in elections for the presidency and the legislature violated his rights under Article 3 of the First Protocol (see Chapter 25).

The Grand Chamber rejected the government's argument that the case was inadmissible on Article 17 grounds.

- The general point of Article 17 was to prevent groups with 'totalitarian aims' from exploiting the Convention.

- Therefore, as the case law indicates, it is to be used only exceptionally (usually the Court will rely on justification for alleged breaches of a qualified right such as Article 10) and in extreme cases (usually in respect of extremist organisations seeking to undermine the values of the Convention).

- It can apply, in the context of Article 10 (freedom of expression) to remarks which 'are directed against the Convention's underlying values' of justice and peace. An example is Holocaust denial, see 'Current issues'.

- It applies, therefore, to statements by people trying to 'deflect Article 10 from its real purpose' so that they can engage in activities contrary to the text and spirit of the Convention.

Current issues

Early twenty-first-century issues which involve the defence of democracy include:

- Racist political parties. In *Glimmerveen and Hagenbeek v The Netherlands* (1982) 4 EHRR 260, the Commission applied Article 17 in accepting that a ban on racist politicians from standing in an election did not violate the Convention. The applicants would have used their candidatures to propagate racist views.

- Holocaust denial. In *Garaudy v France* App 65831/01, admissibility decision of 24 June 2003, the ECtHR said that the denial of clearly established political facts, specifically denial that the Holocaust occurred, would be speech which, because of Article 17, would not be protected by the right to freedom of speech in Article 10 (see also *Lehideux v France* (2000) 30 EHRR 665).

- Violent Islamic militancy. In *Hizb ut-Tahrir v Germany* (2012) 55 EHRR SE12, an organisation advocating the violent overthrow of governments in the Muslim world and their replacement by an Islamic State (Caliphate) which was banned by the German government had their application to the ECtHR declared inadmissible on Article 17 grounds.

Applying the general idea behind Article 17, militant democracy, the idea of democracy defending itself by measures which are, on their face, undemocratic, is fraught with danger. For this reason, as made clear in *Paksas* and illustrated in *Perincek v Switzerland* App 27510/08, Grand Chamber judgment of 15 October 2015, para 115, the ECtHR prefers analysing a restraint on political freedom by exploring its justification in terms of the more specific and particular language of the second paragraphs of Articles 10 and 11. In this way the Court can consider the applicant's rights rather than avoid them. Usually cases can be dealt with under Article 11 (freedom of association), Article 10 (freedom of expression), or Article 3 of Protocol 1 (free elections). These three Articles allow proportionate restrictions on political freedom and these, as in *Refah Partisi*, for example, are normally sufficient for the effective protection of political democracy.

▶ **CROSS REFERENCE**

Refah Partisi is fully discussed in Chapter 18, section 18.7.2. and *Perincek* in Chapter 17.

7.4 Article 18

Article 18 Limitation on use of restrictions on rights

The restrictions permitted under this Convention to the said rights and freedoms shall not be applied for any purpose other than those for which they have been prescribed.

Many of the Convention Articles permit limits, qualifications, and restrictions on an individual's freedom. The point of Article 18 is to ensure that rights and freedoms are only restricted for the purposes allowed for in the Articles and not for other purposes that the state may consider important. Article 18 reinforces the other, substantive Articles. Like Article 14, it requires a link to the other Article to be established, but, also like Article 14, there does not need to be a breach of that other Article for there to be a breach of Article 18. Article 18 is not widely used (although see *Gusinskiy* v *Russia* App 70276/01, judgment of 19 May 2004, para 73).

7.5 Article 16

Article 16 Restrictions on political activity of aliens

Nothing in Articles 10, 11 and 14 shall be regarded as preventing the High Contracting Parties from imposing restrictions on the political activity of aliens.

Article 16 is an anomaly whose continued presence in the Convention is widely criticised. It allows restrictions on the political freedom of aliens (foreigners) and, as such, is at odds with Article 1, which insists that the rights and freedoms in it are to be secured for 'everyone' (not just citizens); and it seems to contradict Article 14, which requires that the Convention Articles should be applied to everyone without discrimination on various grounds including 'national...origin'. Both the ECtHR and UK courts have avoided basing their judgments on Article 16 (see *Piermont* v *France* (1995) 20 EHRR 301 and *R (Farrakhan)* v *Secretary of State for the Home Department* [2002] EWCA Civ 606). In *Perincek* v *Switzerland*, Article 16 was narrowly interpreted and said to apply only to activities by foreigners which 'directly affect the political process'.

 Summary

- Article 14 prohibits discrimination in the way Convention rights and freedoms are secured. Differences in treatment can be justified if there is an objective and reasonable justification but intense scrutiny is required of certain suspect classifications such as race and sex.

- Article 15 allows states to derogate from their responsibilities under the Convention in times of 'war or other public emergency facing the life of the nation'. Any derogation must only be to the extent strictly required by the emergency (a matter over which courts have an important scrutinising role). Some Convention rights cannot be derogated from.

- Article 16 allows states to restrict the political activities of aliens. It is incompatible with the spirit of the Convention and is little used.

- Article 17 authorises the ECtHR and national courts to refuse to uphold the rights of those, like racists, who would use their rights to undermine the rights of others. It does not mean that such people have no Convention rights at all.

- Article 18 insists that rights and freedoms in the Convention can be restricted and qualified but only for the purposes allowed by the Convention.

? Self-test questions

1. Article 14 is not a free-standing anti-discrimination right (unlike Protocol 12). In what situations does it apply?

2. What is meant by 'other status' in respect of discrimination covered by Article 14?

3. How did the House of Lords interpret and apply Article 15 in *A* v *SSHD* [2004] UKHL 56?

4. Does Article 15 apply equally to all Convention rights?

5. When dealing with restrictions on inflammatory speech by a radical group, why would a court use Article 17 rather than the qualifying provisions of substantive rights (such as Articles 8–11)?

6. What does Article 16 provide and should it be removed from the Convention?

 For suggested approaches, please visit the Online Resource Centre.

? Exam questions

1. Is it possible, compatibly with the Convention, to have laws which restrict the political activities of groups and individuals whose aim is to impose an authoritarian government on a country?

2. Proposals are made under which only women candidates can be chosen for at least half of the seats contested by a political party. Men candidates will be barred. Men who lose out complain that they have been discriminated against in respect of their rights to stand for election found in Article 3 of the First Protocol.

   Advise some disappointed potential male candidates on whether Article 14 might be of assistance to them.

 For suggested approaches, please visit the Online Resource Centre.

≡ Further reading

Amos, M. (see Preface) Chapter 15

Lester, A, Pannick, D., and Herberg, J. (see Preface) Chapter 4, Articles 14–18

On Article 14

Baker, A. 'The Enjoyment of Rights and Freedoms: A New Conception of the "Ambit" under Article 14 ECHR' (2006) 69(5) *Modern Law Review* 714–737

8 Article 2: right to life

Article 2 Right to Life

(1) Everyone's right to life shall be protected by law. No one shall be deprived of his life intentionally save in the execution of a sentence of a court following his conviction of a crime for which the penalty is provided by law.

(2) Deprivation of life shall not be regarded as inflicted in contravention of this Article when it results from the use of force which is no more than absolutely necessary

    (a) in defence of any person from unlawful violence;

    (b) in order to effect a lawful arrest or to prevent the escape of a person lawfully detained;

    (c) in action lawfully taken for the purpose of quelling a riot or insurrection.

Introduction

The right to life is morally fundamental. Respect for life is the condition, the basic presumption, of moral thinking and belief—without respect for life the idea of individual human autonomy and dignity is meaningless. Article 2 does not establish the right to life but imposes on states the duty to protect life. It gives specific, enforceable, legal form to the first duty on states which is to protect the physical security of all those within their jurisdiction. A government that fails to protect the lives of its citizens has no justification and so no authority over the citizens.

There are all sorts of ways in which the duty to preserve and protect life can be in question. For example, in the context of the threat of terrorism, Article 2 requires states to take proportionate measures to protect its population from threats of death. But it is also part of the legal framework relating to how governments respond. The lawfulness of assassination of terrorist suspects operating abroad (e.g. in Syria in 2015), for example, will depend on questions such as whether these killings are a necessary way of protecting the rights of others. These questions derive from Article 2 (as well as from other aspects of international law).

States also have to protect the lives of those who, for good reason or bad, are the subject of popular hatred. Advocates of terrorism, child murderers, paedophiles, but also police and members of the armed forces who participated in shootings (such as 'Bloody Sunday' in Northern Ireland in 1972) can all be the victims of threatening hate campaigns. Article 2 may require steps for their protection to be taken.

But Article 2 is also relevant to some of the most profound questions about life and its value that arise in the context of modern medical science. Issues such as abortion, assisted suicide and euthanasia, and the withdrawal of treatment from both competent and incompetent patients all raise questions about the responsibility of states to protect life or to allow clinical death to occur perhaps earlier than it otherwise would (these questions also arise in respect to Article 8 and the right of personal autonomy).

8.1 General principles

In interpreting and applying Article 2, the European Court of Human Rights (ECtHR) has identified and developed a number of general principles to which the domestic laws of signatory states must adhere. These have been adopted into the law of the United Kingdom in, for example, *Rabone* v *Pennine Care NHS* [2012] UKSC 2, para 12.

- **A fundamental duty.** Securing the right to life is a fundamental, primary duty on states. It enshrines one of the basic values of a democratic society. It cannot be derogated from under Article 15 (except in times of lawful war) and it applies 'absolutely' in the sense that the terms of Article 2 do not permit a balancing with the public interest.

  It must also be borne in mind that, as a provision which not only safeguards the right to life but sets out the circumstances when the deprivation of life may be justified, Article 2 ranks as one of the most fundamental provisions in the Convention—indeed one which, in peacetime, admits of no derogation under Article 15. Together with Article 3 of the Convention, it also enshrines one of the basic values of the democratic societies making up the Council of Europe.

  (*McCann* v *United Kingdom* (1996) 21 EHRR 97, para 147)

- **Effectiveness.** Article 2 must be interpreted and applied by the courts to ensure that its safeguards are made practical and effective.

- **The 'negative' duty.** States must refrain from the intentional taking of life except under the conditions in Article 2(2).

- **The 'positive' duties.** In order to ensure that 'everyone's life is protected by law', states must take positive measures of various kinds. Thus the impact of Article 2 goes beyond the deliberate use of force by the state and it can include duties, of various degrees of specificity, in areas such as environmental protection and medical practice. The ECtHR has been careful, however, to describe a positive duty in terms of what is reasonable in the circumstances and to allow a wide margin of appreciation to states. The positive duties can be summarised as:

(a) **Provision of an adequate legal and administrative framework.** There must be an adequate system of criminal law with appropriate offences such as murder and manslaughter, and with an adequate police force and court structure through which the criminal laws are made effective and capable of deterring threats to life. The specific nature of the national offences, and the structures and powers of the police, prosecution, and court system are not matters for the ECtHR so long as they meet the requirements of Article 2. In some circumstances the availability of a civil remedy may be sufficient. The absence of an effective civil remedy for damages against the police etc. can be the basis of a breach of Article 13 (see *Bubbins* v *United Kingdom* (2005) 41 EHRR 24; see Chapter 5, section 5.1 on Article 13).

(b) **Operational duty.** The need to take appropriate, protective, action in respect of risks to particular individuals or groups who are in danger (see section 8.3).

(c) **Investigation.** States must undertake full and adequate investigations into deaths that are within the scope of the Article. This applies not only to deaths caused by state agents but also to the deaths of persons, such as prisoners, for whom the state has assumed responsibility; likewise the duty to investigate relates not only to intentional killing but also to unintended deaths.

In its case law the ECtHR refers to the 'substantive' and 'procedural' limbs of Article 2. The **substantive limb** relates to the duty to secure life and prevent the disproportionate use of force; the **procedural limb** refers to the provision of adequate remedies and, in particular, a state'sduty to investigate well founded allegations that Article 2 has been breached.

 BIGGER PICTURE

These general principles have been asserted by the ECtHR in important cases such as *McCann* v *United Kingdom* (1996) 21 EHRR 97, paras 146–150 and *Giuliani* v *Italy* (2012) 54 EHRR 10, paras 174–182, 208–210, 244–251, and 298–306 (a Grand Chamber judgment).

8.1.1 The scope of Article 2 and other Convention rights

Article 2 can be invoked in situations such as the use of lethal force by police and other state agencies, the treatment of prisoners and others in the custody of the state, and respecting medical issues such as consent to treatment. Other Articles, such as Article 3 (prohibition of torture etc.) or Article 8 (respect for private life) are also applicable to such situations. As will become plain, a frequent problem is to identify the relative significance or weight of the right to life when measured against these other rights or against state imperatives concerning the maintenance of order and the suppression of crime.

8.1.2 Standing (who can bring a case)

Usually (though not always) the person whose right to life has been allegedly violated will be dead. Under general rules relating to standing before the ECtHR (which also apply to UK cases brought under section 7 HRA), close relatives can bring and sustain cases on behalf of

⟩ CROSS REFERENCE

See Chapter 2, section 2.7.1 in respect of Article 34 and indirect victims; see also section 7 HRA, Chapter 5, section 5.4.4.

deceased victims, especially where there is a strong case that the deceased person's right to life has been violated.

8.2 The intentional use of force by police, military, and other state agents

8.2.1 General principles

Article 2 deals with the intentional use of lethal force (though it is not confined to this). From Article 2(1) it can be inferred that states must have adequate laws, police forces, and systems for investigation, prosecution, trial, and punishment of anyone, civilians or officials, who might have used force in a manner likely to result in death. Article 2(2), however, defines the exclusive circumstances in which these laws and practices may permit the intentional use of lethal force. Issues involving the legal justification for the use of force characteristically focus on actions taken by state agents: the police, the military, and other security forces.

The leading case in which the ECtHR first laid down the general principles that apply to the use of lethal force by the military, police, and security forces is *McCann* v *United Kingdom* (1996) 21 EHRR 97. The ECtHR found, by a majority of 10–9, that there had been a violation of Article 2 when members of the SAS shot three members of an IRA active service unit as they were leaving Gibraltar. The case was one of the most controversial ever decided by the Court and it led to a degree of tension between the British government of the time and the Court.

🔍 CASE CLOSE-UP

McCann v *United Kingdom* (1996) 21 EHRR 97

British security officials had intelligence indicating a possible IRA attack on the British army in Gibraltar. Three members of an active service unit of the IRA, two with convictions for explosives offences and one believed to be an explosives expert, were identified at Malaga and followed through Spain and not stopped from entering Gibraltar. Military intelligence officers were convinced that a remote control device was a likely form of attack and one of the suspects was seen parking a car in the area in Gibraltar where the attack was likely; this was reported back to the military commanders as a 'suspect car bomb'. The three IRA members were shot dead by soldiers from the SAS as they were walking towards the Spanish border well away from the area of attack. The evidence of the soldiers was that they believed their actions were necessary to avoid the suspects detonating what they believed to be a car bomb. Other witnesses, however, suggested that the suspects were shot whilst attempting to surrender and that the geographical circumstances of the shooting made it impossible for a remote control bomb to be detonated. After the shooting it was found that, in fact, the suspects were unarmed and there was no bomb in the parked car.

The ECtHR held there was a violation of Article 2, not in respect of the decision to shoot taken by the soldiers but in respect of the decision to allow the suspects to continue their journey into Gibraltar, the certainty with which intelligence assessments were communicated to the soldiers, and the fact that the soldiers automatically shot to kill rather than disable. These factors, for the majority, meant that the killings were more than was 'absolutely necessary' in the circumstances. The large minority of judges entered a strong dissenting judgment in which they dissected and criticised the reasoning of the majority. In particular the minority insisted on the need for a court to avoid the benefits of hindsight and to discount the tactical advantage of the suspects: that the security forces were required to operate within the rule of law whilst the suspects operated outside such constraints with no need to take steps to preserve innocent lives.

 CASE CLOSE-UP

Giuliani and Gaggio v Italy (2012) 54 EHRR 10

Police shot dead a demonstrator who appeared to be attacking them with lethal intent in the context of a violent political protest (the G8 summit, in 2001 in Genoa). A majority of a Grand Chamber held that there was no violation of Article 2 in its various aspects.

The following principles from *McCann* have been developed and applied in later cases, such as *Giuliani*, which involve the use of lethal force by agents of the state.

Not confined to intentional killing

Article 2 includes intentional killing but also can apply whenever force is used which 'may result, as an unintended outcome', in a person's death. This includes the use of force which is not intended to be lethal but does result in a killing; it also can include the use of force that puts a person's life at risk even if no death actually results.

In *Makaratzis* v *Greece* (2005) 41 EHRR 49, the applicant had broken through a police road block and was pursued by police who fired at him many times. Though wounded, he survived. The ECtHR held that Article 2 was applicable (para 55).

Allegations of brutality and abuse against the police and security services which, even though serious and life threatening, did not result in death will normally be approached in terms of Article 3 ('No one shall be subjected to torture or to inhuman or degrading treatment or punishment').

In *Ilhan* v *Turkey* (2002) 34 EHRR 36, the applicant's brother had been detained by Turkish police. He suffered serious brain damage as a consequence, at least, of being struck on the head by a rifle butt. The ECtHR held that there had been no violation of Article 2; there had been a violation of Article 3.

> **CROSS REFERENCE**
> Article 3 and ill-treatment is discussed in Chapter 9, section 9.5.

The reason why Article 2 was relevant in *Makaratzis* but not in *Ilhan* is, presumably, to do with the nature and intentions behind the violence; guns were fired in *Makaratzis* and so there is, perhaps, more reason to suppose an intention to kill and a likelihood of death.

Strict test for absolute necessity

▶ **CROSS REFERENCE**
Justification in respect of Articles 8–11 is discussed in Chapter 14, section 14.4.

The force used must be no more than is absolutely necessary. This is a demanding requirement. It is harder for the state to justify the use of lethal force by showing its absolute necessity than it is for the state to justify an interference with one of the freedoms in Articles 8–11 by showing the interference was 'necessary in a democratic society'. It is easier to justify the latter in terms of balancing an individual's freedom with the public good.

Strict scrutiny of justifications

The absolute necessity test means that the justifications for the use of force in Article 2(2) must be subjected to the strictest scrutiny. Article 2(2) will only justify a use of lethal force, or non-lethal force which nevertheless threatens a person's right to life, if it was 'strictly proportionate' in all the circumstances. A non-proportionate use of force, even if done for one of the purposes in Article 2(2), will not be justifiable under Article 2(2).

Planning and control

The strict scrutiny required must include not only a consideration of the particular actions and decisions taken by those directly responsible for the use of force but also the 'surrounding circumstances including such matters as the planning and control of the actions under examination'. It was failures in the planning and control of the operation, not the actions of the SAS soldiers, that was the basis of the finding of a violation in *McCann*. Issues that arise can include, for example:

- Allowing a situation to develop in which lethal force might be necessary. In *McCann* one of the reasons for finding a violation of Article 2 was the decision taken by the British authorities to allow the suspects to enter Gibraltar and plant what was believed to be a bomb. A reason for not arresting the suspects at the border was that there was, at the time, insufficient evidence on which 'reasonable suspicion' of an offence (the basis of a lawful arrest) could be based and so the suspects would have had to be released. In the Court's view this problem was not sufficient to outweigh the threat to the lives of people in Gibraltar, which was, after all, the threat which justified the decision of the soldiers to shoot and kill.

- Inadequacies in the intelligence and information given to the police or soldiers on the ground. In *McCann*, for example, all sorts of assumptions about the intentions of the suspects were communicated to the soldiers as factual certainties.

- Training and techniques used by security forces. The soldiers in *McCann* had been trained to shoot to kill rather than disable and this inflexibility in response pointed to a violation. In *Giuliani*, on the other hand, the training, in the circumstances of a mass protest, was adequate (para 255).

- The planning and control of the incident. The decisions taken by the authorities on using force, the nature of the operation, the type of force that is used, the timing, the existence of effective alternatives and so on are all matters that can be in issue. The legal basis for the exercise of force is also relevant. In *Giuliani*, the Court examined the relevant legislation and found that, since it only authorised lethal force as a last resort, it was compatible with Article 2. In *Makaratzis v Greece* (2005) 41 EHRR 49, by contrast, there was an unplanned and uncoordinated chase, involving the firing by the chasing police of many shots at a driver who had driven through a number of road blocks. Greek law and police practice had not, at the time, developed an adequate set of rules and systems for control and management of situations in which lethal force might be used and this was an important reason for the finding of a violation of Article 2.

Honest but mistaken belief

Where the particular decision to use force is based on a mistaken but honest belief that, in the circumstances, lethal force is necessary, there will not be a violation of Article 2. Lethal force used on the basis of a mistaken belief that it is necessary in self-defence or to save the lives of others, for example, is not necessarily a breach of Article 2. The belief must not only be honestly held (a subjective matter relating to the state of mind of the officer involved) but there must also have been 'good reasons' for the officer, at the time, to have believed the circumstances to be what he or she thought they were (a more objective matter). The ECtHR in *McCann* said

> the use of force by agents of the State in pursuit of one of the aims delineated in paragraph 2 of Article 2 (art. 2–2) of the Convention may be justified under this provision (art. 2–2) where it is based on an honest belief which is perceived, for good reasons, to be valid at the time but which subsequently turns out to be mistaken. To hold otherwise would be to impose an unrealistic burden on the State and its law-enforcement personnel in the execution of their duty, perhaps to the detriment of their lives and those of others.

(para 200)

This is confirmed in *Giuliani*, para 178.

In *Bubbins v United Kingdom* (2005) 41 EHRR 24, police shot dead the applicant's brother in the belief that he was armed and holding a woman hostage. In fact it turned out that the gun was only a replica. The ECtHR held that, given the honest but mistaken belief about the gun, and given the circumstances of being confronted by an apparently armed man, the use of force was not disproportionate (paras 138–140).

Proving responsibility

A court may be faced with a situation in which troops, police, or unidentifiable armed men have arrived at a village, people have been stopped and questioned, and perhaps arrested and taken away. Sometimes people have disappeared and never been seen again; other times they have turned up later dead or badly injured. In such circumstances the facts are often disputed, with the state denying responsibility.

However the Court is aware that human rights protection must be effective. The importance of the right to life means that allegations of breaches of Article 2 must be examined by the Court with the 'most careful scrutiny' (see, for example, *Khashiyev v Russia* (2006) 42 EHRR 20, paras 131–135). In situations where the direct victim was in the custody of the state prior to his or her disappearance, it may be impossible for the applicant to discharge the burden of proving the case beyond reasonable doubt. In such situations, however, the ECtHR is prepared to examine a wide range of available contextual evidence (which might be provided by NGO investigations, media reports, or open source government documents, for example) and draw its own conclusions. In doing this it will also take into account the behaviour of the parties, particularly the respondent state, at the time of seeking the evidence. It is prepared to make certain presumptions as to state responsibility for the violation of the direct victim's rights based, for example, on the failure of the state to conduct a full and proper investigation into the disappearances or on the state's failure, possibly in breach of Article 38, to cooperate with the ECtHR's investigation. Reasonable doubt is an 'autonomous' Convention concept (not to be related to the idea in domestic law) and the ECtHR is prepared to find a case proved to that standard on the basis of 'sufficiently strong, clear and concordant inferences or of similar unrebutted presumptions of fact'.

▶ CROSS REFERENCE

For examples, in relation to breaches of Article 3, see case close-up 'extraordinary rendition', Chapter 9, section 9.4.3.

> **BIGGER PICTURE**

For a full discussion of this approach, albeit in the context of Article 3, see *Husayn (Abu Zubaydah)* v *Poland* App 7511/13, judgment of 24 July 2014, paras 393–400.

A presumption of state responsibility is particularly likely where it is established beyond a reasonable doubt (based on inferences from the evidence of witnesses, for example) that the deceased or disappeared person was in the custody of the authorities. In *Ikincisoy* v *Turkey* App 26144/95, judgment of 15 December 2004, the applicant's son was arrested by police after a violent episode in which a police officer had been killed. The applicant's son was never seen again. The Turkish authorities claimed he had been in an armed clash. The ECtHR held that, since there was clear evidence that the son had been taken into custody, there was a strong, resulting presumption that he had been killed whilst in custody. The presumption could only be rebutted by proof to the contrary, which the state, Turkey, had failed to provide (see para 69).

▶ CROSS REFERENCE

The duty to investigate deaths (which is not confined to the use of lethal force by state agents) is discussed at section 8.5.

Where there is this presumption, the ECtHR, characteristically, will also find a violation of the procedural limb of Article 2—the state's failure adequately to investigate the killings; and perhaps also of Article 13, the right to a remedy. The fact that the state alleges that it was not responsible for the killings does not assist since the duty to investigate applies to all suspicious deaths.

The willingness of the ECtHR carefully to draw conclusions from contextual evidence and to make presumptions from state inactivity is extremely important. In situations where the state and its agents are complicit in the most serious human rights violations but also have a monopoly of direct knowledge of the events, the ECtHR is able to make full and authoritative determinations of the facts. In doing so it can help to meet the need of victims to know the truth about happened to their loved ones.

8.2.2 Justifications for the intentional use of force, Article 2(2)

Use of force by police or security forces which causes death or is likely to do so, will not be a violation of Article 2 if it is justified under the terms of Article 2(2). However, the fact that the use of lethal force is for one of the purposes listed in Article 2(2) is not sufficient. Measured by the relevant circumstances, the use of force for the purpose must be no more than is absolutely necessary.

Article 2(2)(a): 'in defence of any person from unlawful violence'

This includes both actions taken in self-defence, and actions taken to prevent a person causing death or injury to others. As *McCann* and *Giuliani* make clear, in both situations the principle that police or military can act on the basis of an honest but reasonable mistake as to the need to exercise force is accepted. The absolute necessity for the amount of force used is to be judged in respect of the situation as understood, albeit mistakenly, at the time. Nevertheless the force used must be proportionate (absolutely necessary) to the situation as understood at the time.

In *Giuliani*, video evidence showed an 'unlawful and very violent attack' on the police vehicle which was trying to leave the scene and which posed no threat to the demonstrators. In these circumstances, the officers inside could reasonably fear they might be lynched (para 187). Their use of force was justified.

Article 2(2)(b): 'in order to effect a lawful arrest or to prevent the escape of a person lawfully detained'

The requirement of absolute necessity is very important here. Article 2(2)(b) cannot justify the use of lethal force to enforce a lawful arrest where, if the arrest was not made or the person was allowed to escape, no serious danger to others will result. This view has been confirmed by a Grand Chamber of the ECtHR in *Nachova v Bulgaria*.

CASE CLOSE-UP

Nachova v Bulgaria (2006) 42 EHRR 43, Grand Chamber

Bulgarian military police shot and killed two conscripts who had gone absent without leave and, on being discovered by the police hiding out in a barn, had tried to escape. The men presented no threat and were not violent. The ECtHR held there had been a violation of Article 2. The conscripts were of Roma origin and the Court also found a violation of Article 14 (discrimination) linked to Article 2, regarding failures of investigation.

In *Nachova* the Grand Chamber said (at para 95):

> Accordingly, and with reference to Art. 2(2)(b) of the Convention, the legitimate aim of effecting a lawful arrest can only justify putting human life at risk in circumstances of absolute necessity. The Court considers that in principle there can be no such necessity where it is known that the person to be arrested poses no threat to life or limb and is not suspected of having committed a violent offence, even if a failure to use lethal force may result in the opportunity to arrest the fugitive being lost.

In *Streletz, Kessler and Krenz v Germany* (2001) 33 EHRR 31, and *K-HW v Germany* (2003) 36 EHRR 59, the ECtHR made it clear that the shooting by border guards of people trying to escape from (what was then) East Germany (German Democratic Republic) to West Germany (German Federal Republic) could not be justified by reference to Article 2(2) (see paras 96 and 98 respectively).

Article 2(2)(c): 'in action lawfully taken for the purpose of quelling a riot or insurrection'

The use of potentially lethal force by police and security forces in the context of quelling a riot or insurrection must meet the test of being absolutely necessary. The ECtHR will take into account the general difficulties of the authorities in such situations, such as their need to act on the basis of the situation as they reasonably understand it to be at the time, even if that belief is mistaken, and their need to use the weapons and equipment available to them, even if it increases the likelihood of death. The latter point, though perhaps justifying the use of lethal force by those directly responsible, is relevant to an assessment of whether the actions involved were properly planned and organised.

In *Stewart v United Kingdom* App 10044/82 (1984) 39 DR 162, the Commission of Human Rights reported that, on the particular facts, there was no violation of Article 2 when troops used 'plastic bullets' in the course of quelling a riot which resulted in the death of the applicant's 13-year-old son. The case turned on the Commission's assessment of circumstances in which the bullets were fired and the view that the statistical evidence indicated that the weapon was less dangerous than alleged.

In *Gülec* v *Turkey* (1999) 28 EHRR 121, Turkish security forces used a machine gun to disperse a crowd of demonstrators. The bullets were not deliberately aimed at the demonstrators but the applicant's son was killed by a ricochet. The ECtHR held that Article 2 had been violated.

8.2.3 **Lawfulness**

For the use of force to be justified under Article 2(2) it must be 'lawful'. This term is specifically mentioned in Article 2(2) but is also pervasive through the Convention.

Under the Convention, state actions are only lawful if they are not only compatible with national law but also meet the Convention tests of being 'accessible' and 'foreseeable'.

▶ CROSS REFERENCE

The Convention concept of law and legality is introduced in Chapter 6, section 6.2.

If the security services can use potentially lethal force on the basis of national law which appears to provide a near unlimited and unchallengeable discretion to the authorities, the necessary legal basis may not be compatible with the Convention.

In *Makaratzis* v *Greece* (2005) 41 EHRR 49, mentioned earlier, the Greek law on the use of firearms by the police had been enacted by the Nazis in 1943. It enabled state officials to use firearms, for example, in order 'to enforce the laws, decrees and decisions of the relevant authorities or to disperse public gatherings or suppress mutinies'. The ECtHR held that this (even after later changes to the law requiring any use of force to meet the test of necessity) did not create an adequate legal framework.

8.2.4 **The duty to hold a full and adequate investigation**

Under Article 2 the intentional use of force by state agents that results in death requires a full investigation. This important requirement, because it applies to other situations in which deaths may occur, is discussed later in the chapter, section 8.5.

8.2.5 **The law of England and Wales**

Compatibly with Article 2, nothing in the law of England and Wales prevents the full weight of the criminal law from being used against officials such as the police. Police and civilians alike are protected in so far as the law permits the use of 'reasonable force' in order to prevent crime or to effect or assist in the lawful arrest of offenders, suspected offenders, or persons unlawfully at large (section 3 Criminal Law Act 1967). Reasonable force includes the right of self-defence against unlawful attack (the prevention of crime) and this right is recognised in the permitted defences to murder and manslaughter in English law. Police officers ('constables') may also use 'reasonable force, if necessary' when exercising their powers under the Police and Criminal Evidence Act 1984, such as stop and search, arrest, and entry into premises (section 117).

▶ CROSS REFERENCE

Section 3 HRA is discussed in Chapter 4, section 4.4.

Section 3 HRA requires that these statutory references to 'reasonable' force should be 'read and given effect' to be compatible with the Convention standard of force that is 'no more than is absolutely necessary'. Following *McCann* v *United Kingdom*, the courts of England and Wales accept that there is no difference between the two standards (see *R (Bennet)* v *HM Coroner* [2007] EWCA Civ 617, para 3, quoting Collins J in [2006] EWHC 196, para 25).

For the purposes of criminal law (including murder), reasonableness is measured in terms of how the defendant (e.g. a police officer) honestly understood the situation he or she was in at the time. Honest mistakes of fact, even if unreasonable, do not alter this (see *R v Williams (Gladstone)* [1987] 3 All ER 411. This has been given statutory force by section 76 Criminal

Justice and Immigration Act 2008). The full compatibility of this with Article 2 needs to be tested since, as mentioned previously, *McCann* requires mistakes of fact to be based on 'good reasons' if there is not to be a violation of Article 2.

Civil actions (e.g. for damages) which arise out of the use of lethal force are treated differently from criminal prosecutions. Any mistake of fact must also have been a reasonable one to have made if it is to succeed as a defence (*Ashley* v *Chief Constable of Sussex Police* [2008] UKHL 25). This may be enough to satisfy Article 2.

THINKING POINT

What is it about civil actions as distinct from criminal prosecutions which explains and (you might think) justifies this distinction in *Ashley?*

The duty to ensure proper management and control of actions by armed forces and police and the duty to establish an effective investigation is not always explicitly or even implicitly found in UK law. Under the HRA it is now a requirement of the law.

DISCUSSION TOPIC

The use of lethal force by police and army

Is the view that police and security forces are merely civilians in uniform who are able to use lethal force, on the basis of the same general principles of law that apply to civilians, a sound position? At the moment differences between civilians and police and military are recognised only in the judgments of fact that, for example, juries make when assessing the 'reasonableness' of or 'necessity' for an act of force. Is this enough or should the law be developed to accommodate not only the special difficulties and dangers that the police and security forces face, but also the special responsibilities they have, given their licence to use force?

Issues such as the following are relevant:

- Should police and security forces be able to rely on an honest mistake as to the facts even if the mistake was not based on reasonable grounds (section 76(4)(b)(ii) Criminal Justice and Immigration Act 2008)?

- Is it reasonable that the proportionality of the use of force can depend upon the nature of the weapons that the security forces have available to them? Is it acceptable that standard issue, high-velocity rifles should be used by the military when dealing with civil disorder (see the *Gülec* case)?

- The planning of operations must be taken into account in any assessment of whether a use of force was absolutely necessary (e.g. *McCann*; see also *Andronicou* v *Cyprus* (1997) 25 EHRR 491); ought this to mean that an officer responsible for inadequacies in the planning etc. of an operation that results in death could be held personally criminally liable? Should it mean at least civil liability either for individuals or for their forces? This issue was central in the case of Jean Charles de Menezes. He was an innocent man, mistaken for a suicide bomber, who (in the immediate aftermath of the London tube bombings of July 2005) was deliberately shot by police in an underground train on his way to work. The investigation disclosed a degree of confusion among those controlling the police operation, and the Metropolitan Police Service was convicted under the Health and Safety at Work etc. Act; a jury which heard the evidence expressly recommended that the officer in charge should not be censored. The results of this case are discussed at section 8.5.1, The use of force by police, army, or other state agents.

- Should the common law's famous refusal to acknowledge a defence of obedience to 'superior orders' (see *R* v *Clegg* [1995] 1 AC 482) still apply? The Rome Statute, which creates the International Criminal Court with jurisdiction over 'crimes against humanity', 'war crimes', and 'genocide' limits the defence, under Article 33, to occasions where a soldier had a legal obligation to obey orders, did not know that the order was unlawful, and the order was not obviously unlawful.

8.3 The positive duty on states to take adequate steps to protect life

8.3.1 Introduction

CROSS REFERENCE

For positive duties in general, see Chapter 6, section 6.6.

Article 2 is not confined to situations in which force has been deliberately used by state agents such as police and military. On the basis of the first sentence of Article 2, that 'everyone's life shall be protected by law', the ECtHR has applied the Article in such a way as to impose on states 'positive duties' to take 'appropriate steps' to safeguard peoples lives in various circumstances. There can, therefore, be an issue, which will be considered in terms of Article 2, if states fail to develop laws and practices by which people are protected from various risks of death. These positive duties apply particularly, but not only, when people are under the direct responsibility of the state.

The scope of these positive duties and the burden they place upon the authorities is not precisely determined, and a 'margin of appreciation' (see Chapter 6, section 6.3) is accorded the states. The duties include, depending on the situation, the need for:

- a system of criminal law and procedures (police, prosecutors, courts, prisons, etc.): 'putting in place effective criminal law provisions to deter the commission of offences against the person backed up by law enforcement machinery ' (*Osman*, para 115, see section 8.3.2);
- civil procedures to provide remedies resulting from carelessness and errors of judgment;
- criminal penalties in more serious situations such as where officials know of dangers and their powers to act, but do nothing;
- ensuring the provision of adequate information to the public;
- ensuring there is adequate investigation of deaths so that proper responsibility can be identified and attributed, and the criminal, civil, and administrative remedies made effective.

The duty is not absolute. It is to take appropriate and reasonable measures in the circumstances and the ECtHR may give a wide margin of appreciation to states on the issue of what is reasonable.

Thus in *LCB v United Kingdom* (1999) 27 EHRR 212, the ECtHR held, on the basis of Article 2(1), that a state could be under a positive duty to take appropriate steps to 'safeguard the lives of those within its jurisdiction'. In this case, the ECtHR had to consider whether this required the state to provide information on radiation risks and to continue to monitor the health of armed forces personnel who had been involved with the UK's nuclear testing programme in 1957–58 and their families. The ECtHR, taking into account the state of knowledge and understanding at the time generally, held that the state had discharged its duty under Article 2(1) in this context.

8.3.2 **Specific threat to individuals: the *Osman* duty**

Positive duties were initially developed in respect of threats to specific individuals.

 CASE CLOSE-UP

Osman v United Kingdom (2000) 29 EHRR 245

Ahmet Osman, a school pupil, became an object of obsession of one of his teachers, Paget-Lewis. The problem was recognised by the school authorities and reported to the police who interviewed some of the parties but did not take action directly against Paget-Lewis. The obsession manifested itself in increasingly violent incidents. Eventually Paget-Lewis, armed with a shotgun, went to Ahmet Osman's home and seriously wounded him and killed his father, going on to injure the deputy headmaster of the school and kill his son. The Court of Appeal, following earlier authority of the House of Lords, held that the police did not, as a matter of law, owe a duty of care to the Osman family. Thus the family had no legal remedy available to them against the police. The family took the case to the ECtHR alleging a violation of Articles 2, 8, and 6.

The ECtHR held that there had not been a violation of Article 2. Although the state had positive obligations to protect the right to life, these had been discharged since the police had done all that could be reasonably expected of them and there was no evidence that the police knew or ought to have known that the lives of the Osman family were at real and immediate risk from Paget-Lewis. On similar grounds it was held that there was no violation of Article 8.

In *Osman,* the Court (at paras 115 and 116) established the existence of positive duties in general terms. It went on to develop a specific duty on the authorities, in 'certain well-defined circumstances':

> to take preventative operational measures to protect an individual whose life is at risk from the criminal acts of another individual.

> (para 115)

This duty arises when:

> the authorities knew or ought to have known at the time of the existence of a real and immediate risk to the life of an identified individual or individuals from the criminal acts of a third party.

The duty is to:

> take measures within the scope of their powers which, judged reasonably, might have been
> expected to avoid that risk.

(para 116)

This duty involves a higher standard than the avoidance of gross negligence but is a long way
from being absolute:

> such an obligation must be interpreted in a way that does not impose an impossible or dis-
> proportionate burden on the authorities.

On the facts in *Osman*, there was no breach of the duty.

8.3.3 The *Osman* duty and the HRA

The positive duty on the authorities to take reasonable steps to protect the lives of specific
individuals has, through the HRA, been utilised and amended for the purposes of English law.

 CASE CLOSE-UP

Re Officer L [2007] UKHL 36

The Robert Hamill Inquiry was investigating allegations of police involvement in the alleged sectarian killing of Robert Hamill in Northern Ireland in 1997. The Court of Appeal
had allowed a claim by the police officers involved that they were entitled to anonymity
and to be screened from view when giving evidence. The Inquiry appealed this decision
to the House of Lords. The House of Lords allowed the appeal and established the basic
principles on which the Article 2 duty applied.

- When is the duty triggered? When there is a risk to life which is 'real and immediate'.
  'Real' in the sense of being verifiable and not just based on the subjective fears of
  the person involved. 'Immediate' in the sense of being present and continuing. The
  risk must be one created or increased by the matter in hand (e.g. giving evidence). In
  Re L the risk was already there and was not increased by involvement in the Inquiry.

- The evidence of a real and immediate risk must be strong: proving a real and immediate risk is not easily done. There was no assumption of a lower degree of proof
  in respect of activities the authorities are themselves contemplating (removing a
  prisoner from solitary confinement, for example).

- The duty of the authorities is to do what is reasonable and proportionate and they
  are not expected to undertake obligations that are unduly burdensome in proportion to the risk. Circumstances, resources, and the ease of taking protective measures are all relevant to compatibility with Article 2. In *Van Colle* v *Chief Constable of
  Hertforshire Police* [2008] UKHL 50, the House of Lords held that assessment of the
  Osman duty must be based on the knowledge and understanding of the risk to the
  applicant that the police had or ought to have had at the time; there is no breach of
  the duty if the facts as the police reasonably understood them at the time did not
  disclose a real and immediate risk.

In *Venables* v *News Group Newspapers* [2001] All ER 908 (Family Division), an injunction was
issued to protect the anonymity of two men who, as 10-year-old children, had murdered a

two-year-old child. In the views of some the punishment had not been sufficient and there had been credible threats that the lives of the two men might be threatened after their release. Awarding an injunction, such as in *Venables*, involves the court in seeking a balance between Article 2 and the right, under Article 10, to freedom of expression enjoyed by both the media and the population at large. Where the threat is real and serious, an injunction may be a pro-portionate restriction on freedom of expression, which is done to protect the rights, under Article 2, of the potential victims. Section 12 HRA requires the UK courts to have 'particular regard to the Convention right of freedom of expression' when considering the issuing of injunctions.

⟩ CROSS REFERENCE

Section 12 HRA is discussed further in Chapter 17, section 17.3.

8.3.4 **Prisoners and others under direct state control**

The ECtHR has recognised that the state has special responsibilities to protect the lives of those who are under its direct control. *LCB* (discussed earlier) refers to members of the armed forces and in other cases the special position of prisoners has been recognised.

The position of prisoners is is discussed in Chapter 21, sections 21.4, 21.5, and 21.6.

8.3.5 **Dangerous activities and environments**

The positive duty to 'safeguard the lives of those within its jurisdiction' has been extended on a case by case basis.

BIGGER PICTURE

According to Lord Rodger it is a 'tralatician jurisprudence'—one which is handed down. He provides a useful survey of positive obligations in *Savage* v *South Essex NHS Foundation Trust* [2008] UKHL 74, paras 18–50.

The duty includes securing the safety and right to life of individuals who may be affected by hazardous activities that it undertakes where there is clear evidence that the state knew or should have known of a serious risk to the health and life of the applicant.

Under the HRA, in the United Kingdom, this duty has been applied, in a limited fashion, to decisions made in the context of military combat overseas.

CASE CLOSE-UP

Smith v Ministry of Defence [2013] UKSC 41

The claimants were next of kin of of soldiers killed by roadside bombs in Iraq between 2003 and 2009 (after formal hostilities had ceased) or by 'friendly fire' during hostilities. The claims alleged that deaths had resulted from the MoD's failure to provide effective equipment which could protect against roadside bombs or from the failure to provide technology capable of preventing 'friendly fire' incidents.

In part these were claims alleging a breach of the positive duty in Article 2. However, the UKSC was not concerned with the merits of the cases (i.e. whether there had been breaches of Article 2) but whether the claims were obviously without merit and so should be 'struck out' (i.e. whether or not a court could find that there had been breaches of Article 2).

By a majority the UKSC held that, depending on the facts of the case, a breach of Article 2 was possible. The majority accepted that there was a middle ground between two kinds of decision which were non-justiciable and incapable of legal challenge. Firstly, big policy decisions about procurement of military equipment (these were matters of military and budgetary judgments that are for politicians to make, not the courts); and, secondly, direct combat decisions (which involved difficult and dangerous situations quite unsuitable for judicial re-assessment). The facts of an individual case involving equipment, training, etc. might not necessarily involve either of these 'no-go' areas and so they could be subject to judicial assessment in terms of the positive obligation in Article 2. These were for courts hearing the cases to decide. To strike out any such claim in principle would go too far and undermine the essence of the duty in Article 2 for states to take reasonable mesures to protect the lives of those under their control..

⟩ CROSS REFERENCE

Smith also involves an important discussion of the whether the HRA applies to actions outside the United Kingdom—see Chapter 4, section 4.11.3.

But Article 2 can also be the basis of positive duties towards the population at large regarding environmental dangers caused by private and commercial activities. Environmental issues are usually dealt with under Article 8 ECHR (private life), which involves the Court in seeking a fair balance between the impact on individuals and the public good.

Article 2 can be relevant where there has been a death consequent to the behaviour of the authorities; usually their lack of action.

🔍 CASE CLOSE-UP

Oneryildiz v *Turkey* (2005) 41 EHRR 20

Local authorities were responsible for and used a rubbish tip. After the authorities started using the tip, slum dwellings, involving illegal occupancy, had developed in the vicinity of the tip. An expert's report indicated that the tip was not in conformity with safety regulations and there was a potential danger to the slum dwellers. No action was taken. There was a methane gas explosion on the site which killed members of the applicant's family who were in occupation of one of the slum dwellings. Though there was an investigation, resulting in criminal prosecutions of two mayors, a report attributed official responsibility more widely. Furthermore, judgment in the applicant's favour for compensation was never paid.

Held, by a Grand Chamber, that there had been a violation of Article 2.

⟩ CROSS REFERENCE

The application of Article 8 to environmental issues is discussed in Chapter 15, sections 15.8 and 15.10.1.

In *Oneryildiz*, in the context of the regulation of dangerous activities, the Grand Chamber emphasised (see paras 89–96):

- The need for a proper regulatory system which is geared to the particular dangers, including procedures for making information available to the public.
- Where the threat to life involves officials knowing of the dangers but disregarding the powers they have to take remedial action, then the situation is akin to the unjustified use

of lethal force. National courts must be willing and able to impose, if justified, a criminal penalty on those responsible. This is necessary in order to maintain public confidence, ensure the maintenance of the rule of law, and prevent any official collusion in unlawful actions.

- A lesser degree of official culpability (blameworthiness) may only require a civil remedy against the authority.

- A proper investigation, capable of identifying, attributing, and measuring fault and re-sponsibility is vital.

If the system fails to meet these essential requirements, there will be a violation of Article 2.

8.4 Medical treatment

Article 2 applies in the context of health care; this includes both the substantive and proce-dural aspects and the positive and negative duties. States, for example, have positive duties to ensure that both public (e.g. NHS) and private hospitals 'adopt appropriate measures for the protection of patient's lives' (see *Vo* v *France* (2005) 40 EHRR 12, para 89). This objective is to be pursued through appropriate regulations and the availability of civil remedies and, in proper cases, criminal remedies (see, for example, *Calvelli* v *Italy* App 32967/96, judgment of 17 January 2002, concerning allegations of negligence against Italian doctors). Article 2, therefore, is relevant to the law that applies to morally complex issues such as withdrawal of treatment from the terminally ill or voluntary euthanasia.

8.4.1 **Medical treatment and the HRA**

Medical treatment in England and Wales must be compatible with Convention rights.

- NHS Trusts are 'public authorities' for the purposes of section 6 HRA (*R (Munjaz)* v *Mersey Care NHS Trust* [2005] UKHL 58, para 7). States have positive duties in the medical context which may apply to private treatment, too.

- Relevant statutes must be interpreted with regard to section 3 HRA.

- Courts are public authorities under the Act and they are involved in some of the most pressing issues, such as the extent of the duty of care owed by a doctor to his or her patients or whether the withdrawal of treatment is lawful.

Medical professionals in making decisions must, therefore, act compatibly with their patients' rights to life under Article 2 (which, amongst other things, imposes a positive duty to protect life) and Article 3 (which prohibits treatment causing a person to suffer inhuman or degrading treatment). However, in the medical context, even these rights may have to give ground to the principle, found in Article 8, of patient autonomy (the right of a mentally competent patient to consent or refuse consent to treatment). This is also a fundamental principle of common law. Autonomy is so important it can outweigh concerns, under Article 2, that a patient's decisions will lead to his or her death or to their being left in a condition that violates Article 3 (see, for example, *NHS Trust A* [2001] 1 All ER 801, paras 25–26). It must be remembered, however, that interferences with Article 8(1) rights, including the right to autonomy, can be justified under the terms of Article 8(2). No such justification is possible if the complaint is of a violation of Article 3.

▶ CROSS REFERENCE
For Article 3 see Chapter 9, section 9.7.2 and Article 8 see Chapter 15, section 15.4.1.

8.4.2 **Normal treatment**

Normal, therapeutically sensible treatment administered to a consenting patient in good faith is unlikely to raise Convention issues. Even where treatment is administered negligently, it is likely that the state will have discharged its duties under the Convention if there is an adequate system of civil remedies—an action for negligence, for example.

8.4.3 **Resources**

The possibilities but also the costs of medical treatments are ever expanding and very hard questions about the affordability of treatments, especially in the context of a publicly funded health service, can arise. Article 2 imposes positive duties on states to secure the right to life and this must involve a burden on resources. However, in *Keenan* v *United Kingdom* (2001) 33 EHRR 38, the ECtHR said, in relation to Article 2:

> the scope of the positive obligation must be interpreted in a way which does not impose an impossible or disproportionate burden on the authorities.

Where treatments have significant resource implications it is unlikely that Article 2 will compel health authorities to fund treatments whatever the impact this may have on their budgets generally (see, for example, a pre-HRA case: *R* v *Cambridge Health Authority ex parte B* [1995] 2 All ER 129).

In *R (Rogers)* v *Swindon Primary Health Care Trust* [2006] EWCA Civ 392, a health authority refused to fund Herceptin, an expensive breast cancer drug, which had been prescribed for R by her doctor. The Administrative Court had held that the claimant's Article 2 rights had not been violated. On appeal, the Court of Appeal did not consider the impact of Article 2 but subjected the health authority's decision to intense scrutiny on ordinary public law grounds. It held that the authority's policy was unlawful and needed to be reconsidered, but it did not order the drug to be funded.

8.4.4 **Operational duty to particular patients**

The *Osman* duty (mentioned in section 8.3.3) has been applied, under the HRA, in respect of the duty of hospitals to their patients.

 CASE CLOSE-UP

***Rabone* v *Pennine Care NHS Foundation Trust* [2012] UKSC 2**

Melanie Rabone, 24, agreed to voluntary admission to a mental hospital. The hospital agreed to her request to go on home leave, despite the concerns of her parents. Whilst on home leave she committed suicide. The hospital admitted negligence.

The Supreme Court took the view that M's situation was one of those 'circumstances' which gave rise to the *Osman* ('operational') duty, mentioned in section 8.3.3. Her situation was different from 'ordinary' medical situations in which mere negligence leading to death will not violate Article 2 (assuming that civil remedies are available). In *Savage* v *South Essex Partnership NHS Trust* [2008] UKHL 74, the House of Lords had imposed the duty in the circumstances of a non-voluntary patient detained under the Mental Health Act 1983 who had been able to leave and who had committed suicide. The Supreme

Court extended the circumstances in which the duty arises to voluntary patients, being persuaded that the differences with non-voluntary patients were not decisive. Both types are vulnerable and require the special protection of the authorities. There was a real and immediate risk to M's life which the hospital should have appreciated and sought to prevent by taking appropriate measures.

8.4.5 Refusal of medical treatment by a competent patient

The general situation of competent patients regarding their Convention rights has been summarised by the Court of Appeal in *R (Burke)* v *General Medical Council* [2005] EWCA Civ 1003, paras 32–34.

- Patients are owed a duty of care by medical staff to take 'such steps as are reasonable' to keep them alive.

- However, a competent patient can refuse such treatment on the grounds of his or her autonomy.

- Withdrawal of treatment from a consenting competent patient does not violate Article 2 and may even be required, for a competent patient, in order to prevent inhuman or degrading treatment, prohibited by Article 3 (paras 38–39)—an example is *Re JT (Adult: Refusal of Medical Treatment)* [1998] 1 FLR 48 (refusal of renal treatment).

- Article 2 ECHR would be violated, however, if doctors withdrew life-prolonging treatment from a competent patient who did not consent, even if it meant the patient would suffer degrading treatment etc. (*Burke* para 39).

8.4.6 Withdrawal of medical treatment from an incompetent patient

Article 2 may be in issue when what is proposed is the withdrawal of treatment from an incompetent patient. The basic approach of English law is that withdrawal of treatment in these circumstances is lawful if it is in the 'best interests' of the patient (*Airedale NHS Trust* v *Bland* [1993] AC 789). In *NHS Trust A* v *M* [2001] 1 All ER 801, this test was held to be compatible with Article 2 under HRA 1998. The High Court issued a declaration that treatment could lawfully be withdrawn from two patients in a 'permanent vegetative state' (a clinical condition defined by a complete lack of awareness of self and of the environment). Withdrawal of treatment would result in death. The positive obligations of the state under Article 2 were discharged when a responsible medical decision was taken that continuance of treatment was not in the patients' best interests.

There are Guidelines produced by the General Medical Council which contain principles and also procedures for dealing with cases of withdrawal of treatment. They can be subject to legal assessment in the light of Article 2.

 BIGGER PICTURE

See www.gmc-uk.org/guidance for GMC guidance. 'Treatment and care towards the end of life: good practice in decision making' was produced in 2010. Earlier guidance was reviewed by the courts in *R (Burke)* v *General Medical Council* [2005] EWCA Civ 1003.

The existence of proper procedure and guidance is important to ensure compliance with Article 2.

CROSS REFERENCE

Lambert contains significant discussion on standing to bring a Convention case and is also discussed in Chapter 2, section 2.7.1.

In *Lambert* v *France* App 46043/14, Grand Chamber judgment of 25 June 2015, a Grand Chamber considered compliance with Article 2 in the case of a 41-year-old man in a permanent vegetative state who would die if the proposal to withdraw nutrition and hydration was allowed. In accepting that the proposed course of action was compatible with Article 2, the majority emphasised that there was no European consensus (moral, legal, political, etc.) on the beginning and ending of life. Therefore states enjoyed a significant, though not unlimited, margin of appreciation. French law and procedures on the matter were effective in the sense of allowing a properly balanced view, taking into account all interests, to prevail. There was no breach of Article 2 (the decision was subject to a strongly worded dissenting opinion).

Article 2 may, however, be of little assistance when appalling choices have to be made between lives. Nothing in Article 2 suggests that one life can be of lesser value than another. In *Re A (Children) (Conjoined Twins: Surgical Separation)* [2000] 4 All ER 961, the Court of Appeal upheld the right of doctors, against the wishes of the parents, to separate conjoined twins even though the inevitable result was the death of the weaker twin. Without separation both twins would die. A choice had to be made between two equal claims to life. The doctrine of necessity (a common law doctrine), rather than Article 2, was the basis of the decision. Article 2 was, however, understood to be compatible with such a decision.

8.4.7 Deaths in hospital

Deaths in hospital may, depending on the circumstances, require an investigation under the procedural aspect of Article 2: see section 8.5.

8.4.8 Assisted suicide

Euthanasia, in the sense of allowing one person to assist another in the latter's voluntary decision to die, is controversial and, in many countries (including the United Kingdom) would involve a crime, perhaps murder, by the person assisting. **The issue raises significant issues under Article 8 and is discussed in Chapter 15, 15.10.5.**

As regards Article 2, the general principle is that Article 2 is the right to life and the obverse, a right to die, is not to be implied from it. States are not, therefore, obliged to have laws permitting euthanasia (though nor is it a breach of Article 2 to have laws permitting euthanasia). Article 2 does not require any minimum standard of the quality of life. These principles can be derived, for example, from *Pretty* v *United Kingdom* (2002) 35 EHRR 1 (discussed further in Chapter 15).

8.4.9 Abortion

Abortion is a profoundly controversial issue on which, in its moral aspect, irreconcilable positions are adopted. In its barest essentials there is, on the one hand, the claim that a foetus, from conception, is a life, equivalent to post-natal life, and should be protected by Article 2 to the same extent as a post-natal life. On the other hand, there is the claim that a foetus is clearly distinguishable from a post-natal life and has no claims that can legitimately interfere with a woman's right to autonomy over her body and reproductive activity, protected by Article 8. There is, of course, a full range of more modulated intermediate positions.

Since the principle focus is on Article 8, abortion is discussed in Chapter 15, section 15.10.4.

8.5 Article 2 and the need for a full investigation— the procedural obligation

Since *McCann v United Kingdom* (see section 8.2.1), the ECtHR has insisted that states have a duty to provide an effective official investigation into deaths covered by Article 2, particularly, but not exclusively, when these result from the use of force by state agents. This is the 'procedural' limb of Article 2 and is implied from the text of Article 2. A full Grand Chamber summary of the obligation, confirming the points made in this section, is in *Giuliani* (section 8.2.1) paras 298–306. The duty has been adopted into UK law: *R (Amin) v Secretary of State for the Home Department* [2003] UKHL 51, see, in particular, paras 20–21.

- An investigation is necessary to ensure that the national laws and procedures dealing with the right to life can be effectively implemented. In *Amin* (discussed earlier) Lord Bingham described the purposes of an investigation as:

  To ensure as far as possible that the full facts are brought to light; that culpable and discreditable conduct is exposed and brought to public notice; that suspicion of deliberate wrongdoing (if unjustified) is allayed; that dangerous practices and procedures are rectified; and that those who have lost their relative may at least have the satisfaction of knowing that lessons learned from his death may save the lives of others.

  (para 31)

- An investigation is necessary to ensure that there is proper accountability by officials for their actions including, if necessary, criminal prosecution (UK courts have added that an investigation is necessary to learn lessons for the future—*R (JL) v Secretary of State for Justice* [2008] UKHL 68).

- An investigation must be adequate to this purpose and so the precise nature and scope of the duty to investigate will depend upon the circumstances of different cases. Regarding 'ordinary' murder (intentional killing), a police investigation followed by prosecution and a proper criminal trial is likely to be sufficient to discharge the duty. Where death results from alleged negligence (failing to guard against risks) the existence of a system of civil courts and remedies may be sufficient (see *R (Goodson) v Bedfordshire and Luton Coroner* [2004] EWHC 2931). Where the authorities have, themselves, some degree of responsibility for the death, a more intensive and independent requirement may be required.

8.5.1 The existence of the duty

The duty of investigation is not confined to intentional killing by security forces: it includes all deaths covered by the positive duty to secure life although, as indicated previously, the independence and intensity of the investigation will depend on circumstances. Furthermore it exists even in times of war and emergency. States cannot avoid their duties on the grounds of the difficult times they are experiencing (see, for example, *Mocanu v Romania* (2015) 60 EHRR 19, 319).

Independent of the substantive limb

The procedural obligation, the obligation to undertake an effective investigation, can arise even if there is no breach by the state of its substantive duties to protect life under Article 2. Thus the failure of the state to investigate can arise in respect of deaths for which the present state was not responsible or for deaths which occured before the state signed the Convention and accepted the obligations therein. The issue has arisen in the context of 'transitional justice' in Eastern Europe and the investigation of atrocities committed by the communist dictatorships. The state may have obligations, under Article 2, to investigate killings and other atrocities that occurred before the Convention came into force. This is a limited obligation the extent of which has been summarised and clarified by a Grand Chamber in *Janowiec v Russia* (2014) 58 EHRR 30 (in which it found no breach by Russia in respect of the Katyn massacres of 1940).

- There is no obligation, based on Article 2, on states to open up new investigations of past events or create an historical account and record of past atrocities.

- Any obligation based on Article 2 must relate to specific criminal, civil, or other proceedings aimed at vindicating the Convention rights of specific victims and also at identifying and perhaps punishing those responsible.

- The obligation to investigate past events requires a 'genuine connection' between the deaths in issue and the coming into force of the Convention. This refers to proceedings that were or should have been started or mainly conducted after the Convention came into force in the country. The emergence of new, credible evidence about past events might trigger such an obligation to investigate. The ECtHR has also laid down an absolute time limit of 10 years between the entry into force of the Convention and the deaths to which they relate.

- In exceptional circumstances the ECtHR could insist on an effective investigation in respect of deaths occurring before the Convention came into force and where there was no 'genuine connection'. These would be in respect of the most serious allegations, such as war crimes, genocide, or crimes against humanity where the fundamental values of the Convention were in issue.

The position in the UK, under the HRA, is unsettled. In *Re McKerr* [2004] UKHL 12, the House of Lords held that an obligation to initiate an investigation under Article 2 only applied to deaths occurring after the HRA came into force in 2000. This was perhaps doubted in *McCaughey's Application* [2011] UKSC 20, a decision which took into account much of the Strasbourg case law mentioned earlier. But *McCaughey* concerned the nature of an inquest that was already taking place. In *R (Keyu)* v *Secretary of State for Foreign and Commonwealth Affairs* [2015] UKSC 69 (concerning an effective investigation into an alleged massacre by British troop in Malaya in 1948), the Supreme Court applied the principles in *Janoviec* and held that, on the facts and the timings of the case, there was no duty to hold an investigation under Article 2. Since this was the case, they declined to rule on whether, for the purposes of applying the investigative duty in the UK under the HRA, the principle in *Re McKerr* (that for domestic law purposes under the HRA, the procedural limb of Article 2 applies to deaths after the HRA only) should be re-assessed.

The use of force by police, army, or other state agents

- **The use of lethal force.** The duty to investigate applies when deaths occur following the deliberate use of force by state agencies. In *McCann v United Kingdom* (1996) 21 EHRR 97, for instance, the ECtHR held that the duty had been discharged by the coroner's hearing in Gibraltar in which all relevant matters had been fully dealt with (see paras 157–163).

An example is the shooting by police of Jean Charles de Menezes in July 2005 (mistaken for a suicide bomber) which clearly engaged state responsibility. It led to an investigation and report from the Independent Police Complaints Commission (IPCC) ('Stockwell 1'), which identified issues for the Crown Prosecution Service to examine when considering the need for criminal prosecutions against the police. The Crown Prosecution Service decided that there was insufficient evidence for criminal prosecutions against police officers involved (a decision upheld by the High Court in *R (Silva)* v *DPP* [2006] EWHC 3204 (Admin)). The Metropolitan Police, as an organisation, was prosecuted and convicted under the Health and Safety at Work etc. Act 1974 for endangering the public and fined £175,000. The IPCC did not require any officers to face internal disciplinary proceedings. The inquest, the first public examination of the case, opened in September 2008. For inquests to be compatible with Article 2, they must be able to explore the circumstances surrounding the death (see section 8.5.3). The jury returned an 'open verdict' (they were not allowed to consider 'unlawful killing'). The IPCC also investigated early inaccuracies in the information released by the police and criticised a named police officer ('Stockwell 2').

- **Unexplained deaths.** The duty to investigate can be very important where the precise facts about a person's death are unclear and disputed but there are well-founded allegations that the person was in the custody of the police or security forces at the time. In such circumstances an effective investigation to establish the facts and responsibilities is essential. As *Ikincisoy* v *Turkey* (discussed in section 8.2.1) indicates, the ECtHR has been prepared to presume state responsibility for the death from the fact of the deceased being in custody, which only a sufficient investigation leading to a convincing alternative explanation, can rebut.

- **Allegations of security forces' involvement in deaths.** The duty to investigate applies to unexplained killings where there are allegations of direct or indirect involvement of the security forces. The mere denial of responsibility by the state is not enough. There will be a breach of Article 2 if the allegations are not fully and effectively investigated as part of the investigation of the death. This principle has been important in the context of allegations made of unofficial collusion between security forces and armed groups.

Deaths of persons for whom the state is directly responsible

The duty to investigate under Article 2 ECHR extends to deaths of those, such as prisoners, who are under the care of the state. There must be an adequate investigation where, for example, prisoners die whilst in custody, either intentionally killed by other prisoners (see *Edwards* v *United Kingdom* (2002) 35 EHRR 19) or by committing suicide (such as *Keenan* v *United Kingdom* (2001) 33 EHRR 38).

The matter has been of great importance under the HRA.

 CASE CLOSE-UP

***R (Amin)* v *Secretary of State for the Home Department* [2003] UKHL 51**

A British Asian man, serving a sentence in a young offender's institution, was placed by the Prison Service in the same cell as a prisoner with known racist tendencies, who subsequently murdered him. The House of Lords held that there was a duty under Article 2 of a proper investigation, which the state had not discharged (the inadequacies are identified at section 8.5.2).

The duty to undertake an enhanced investigation as required by Article 2 can apply to deaths in custody without, first, proving state liability for the death, though the extent and nature of the investigation will depend on the circumstances, including the degree of state responsibility (*R (JL)* v *Secretary of State for Justice* [2008] UKHL 68).

Deaths in hospital

Deaths in hospital must be properly investigated (see *Calvelli* v *Italy*, section 8.4, paras 49–51). As we have seen, the substantive limb of Article 2 will not be violated by mere hospital negligence—unless special circumstances give rise to the *Osman*/'operational' duty (see *Rabone*, discussed at section 8.4.4). Under the HRA, the issue has been considered by the Court of Appeal in *R (Takoushis)* v *Inner London North Coroner* [2005] EWCA Civ 1440, paras 70–109. The case involved a mental patient who was not stopped by a hospital from leaving its accident and emergency department and who then killed himself. The Court of Appeal found:

- Article 2 required an effective investigation into hospital deaths.
- This does not necessarily require a particular, state initiated investigation. In normal situations the availability of an inquest (whose conduct, as here, can be challenged in the courts) and the availability of a civil action for negligence, is likely to satisfy this duty (see, for example, *R (Goodson)* v *Bedfordshire and Luton Coroner* [2004] EWHC 2931.
- In other circumstances a more demanding investigation may be required (such as where the operational duty has arisen).

Death in a safe-environment context

As mentioned previously (see section 8.3.5) the 'substantive' aspect of Article 2 includes a duty on states to take reasonable steps to protect against dangerous environmental conditions. The duty to investigate also applies in such circumstances. In *Oneryildiz* v *Turkey* (see section 8.3.5), where death was caused by an explosion at a rubbish tip, the ECtHR said (at para 94):

> Where lives are lost as a result of a dangerous activity . . . the competent authorities must act with exemplary diligence and promptness and must of their own motion initiate investigations capable of, firstly, ascertaining the circumstances in which the incident took place and any shortcomings in the operation of the regulatory system and, secondly, identifying the state officials or authorities involved in whatever capacity in the chain of events in issue.

8.5.2 The nature of the duty: an effective investigation

The investigation must be effective. What this requires will depend on the circumstances. Where the state is not directly responsible for a death, the requirements of Article 2 may be significantly less onerous (see, in relation to rail safety, *R (Main)* v *Minister for Legal Aid* [2007] EWCA Civ 1147). Where there is direct state responsibility for the death, or the death is of a prisoner or person under state control, the investigation must be able to determine, in detail, how the deceased died and to allocate responsibility, including amongst officials. Any special, official investigations are in addition to the availability of more general legal proceedings such as criminal trials, if necessary, or civil actions in the courts. The official investigation should provide facts on which such other proceedings can be based.

The requirements of an effective investigation

With reference to earlier cases, a Grand Chamber has summarised the requirements of an effective investigation in *Mocanu* v *Romania* (2015) 60 EHRR 19. In this case the ECtHR found, *inter alia*, a violation of Article 2 in respect of the failure of the current government of Romania to carry out an effective investigation into police action against demonstrators at the time of transition from dictatorship to democracy. The ECtHR insists that the procedural obligation applies even when the state is facing difficult security conditions (para 319).

 THINKING POINT

Consider why the ECtHR thought it had jurisdiction (see *Janowiec* v *Russia*, discussed earlier). The killing was in 1990; the Convention came into force in Romania in 1994.

- **Initiation.** The authorities must initiate the investigation and not leave it to others, such as next of kin (in England and Wales this includes through the system of coroners and inquests).

- **Independence.** The investigators must be fully independent of those officials who are implicated in the investigation.

- **Authority.** To be effective, the investigation must have sufficient authority to be able to do its job of determining the facts. In particular it must be capable of considering justification and allocating responsibility of state officials. In *Jordan* v *UK* (2003) 37 EHRR 2, the Court held that this included being able secure the evidence (forensic and medical evidence, for example) and the appearance of witnesses (para 107).

- **Promptness.** The investigation must be conducted with reasonable promptness; this is essential for retaining confidence in the rule of law.

- **Family involvement.** States have a duty to involve the close family (next of kin) in the investigation, by making information available and by giving full reasons for decisions taken. Involvement of the family must be 'to the extent necessary to safeguard his or her legitimate interests' (para 109). In some circumstances this may require publicly funded representation (see, for example, *R (Khan)* v *Secretary of State for Health* [2003] EWCA 1129).

- **Thoroughness.** The investigation must be thorough and based on an open mind, rather than completed swiftly on the basis of hasty or ill-founded conclusions.

- **Public scrutiny.** Confidence in the rule of law may also require an 'element of public scrutiny' (*Jordan* v *UK* para 109; though this is not in the *Mocanu* summary.) Public confidence requires that there should be an element of openness in the investigation process. The degree of openness will depend on the circumstances and the ECtHR recognises that there can be exceptional reasons for limiting scrutiny. In *Taylor* v *UK* (1994) 79-A DR 127, for example, there was no breach of Article 2 when the government refused to set up a public inquiry into killings of patients by a hospital nurse.

In *Amin* (see section 8.5.1) the House of Lords found that the investigation into the prisoner's murder was inadequate: there was no inquest, the police investigation (properly) did not involve the family, the advice not to prosecute prison officers was not made available, the Prison Service's own inquiry was not independent, it was conducted in private and was not published, and an inquiry by the Commission for Racial Equality only focused on race issues (paras 33–37). As a result, following *Amin* a public inquiry was held which identified major failings by named individuals in the Prison Service, see *Report of the Zahid Mubarak Inquiry* (2006) HC 1082-I.

Whether there has been an adequate investigation depends on the circumstances.

- In *R (D)* v *Secretary of State for the Home Department* [2006] EWCA Civ143, D, a prisoner, had attempted suicide. The Court of Appeal held that an adequate investigation under Article 2 required evidence to be taken in public: an inquiry by the Prison Ombudsman was not sufficient. The involvement of D was required but this did not give him a right to cross-examine witnesses. (See further *R (JL)* v *Secretary of State for Justice* [2008] UKHL 68.)

- In *Ramsahai* v *Netherlands* (2008) 46 EHRR 43, a Grand Chamber found that the investigation of a controversial police shooting had not been effective. For example, police officers involved had not been separated from each other, not properly tested, there were no photographs of the body, and the setting up of the independent investigation was delayed.

The purpose of the investigation remains that of exploring the reasons for the death. Courts are likely to resist using Article 2 to require a wider exploration of, for example, the background political policies that formed the context in which the death took place. In *R (Gentle)* v *Prime Minister* [2008] UKHL 20, mothers of two soldiers killed in Iraq argued that Article 2 required the government to take reasonable steps to be satisfied that the war was lawful. The House of Lords rejected the argument on various grounds. In particular, that an effective investigation was an implied, not an express, duty and so it should not be given a scope beyond what the draftsmen and governments of the time (at the end of the Second World War) would have had in mind. States would not have obligated themselves to the possibility of such a wide-ranging investigation that would both second-guess the United Nations and also hand over matters of high politics to an investigation that was neither representative nor accountable to Parliament. (Baroness Hale adopted this position but with reluctance: see paras 55–57.)

8.5.3 **Coroners in England and Wales**

The duty to investigate is one of the areas in which the Convention has had a significant impact on UK law. In particular, cases brought before the English courts have cast doubt on whether the **coroner** system for investigating deaths satisfies Article 2.

A coroner's court, because of the limitations on juries in the Coroner's Rules, may not have sufficient authority to allocate responsibility for deaths. The House of Lords found that such inadequacies existed in *R (Middleton)* v *West Somerset Coroner* [2004] UKHL 10 and *R (Sacker)* v *West Yorkshire Coroner* [2004] UKHL 11. Both cases involved prisoners who had committed suicide. In both cases the coroner's jury formed the view that neglect by the Prison Service was a contributory factor. Under the Coroners Act 1988, such findings could not be accepted or, if accepted, could not be included in the coroner's findings. The House of Lords held that this was incompatible with the investigative duty in Article 2 in respect of a death that occurred after October 2000 and engaged state responsibility. For these deaths the Coroners Act could be read and given effect to make it compatible with Article 2. In doing this the House of Lords exercised its interpretative obligation under section 3 HRA. Section 11(5)(b)(ii) of the Coroners Act 1988 (now repealed) required coroners to determine 'how, when and where the deceased came by his death'. In *Middleton* and *Sacker,* the House of Lords read 'how' to mean not only 'by what means' the deceased died (a narrow meaning given in earlier cases) but also 'in what circumstances' (giving the term a wider meaning in order to accommodate the Article 2 duty of investigation and allow, for example, consideration of allegations of negligence by public authorities).

8.6 Death penalty

Article 2(1) expressly reserves the possibility that states may have the death penalty. However, Protocol 13 of the European Convention, which is a scheduled right under the HRA, requires abolition in all circumstances including time of war. In the United Kingdom the death penalty has been progressively abolished, for murder in 1965, piracy and treason in 1998, and for military offences in the face of the enemy by section 21 HRA.

8.7 War

Article 2 does not give an exemption to states for acts of war, which involve intentional killing. It will apply, therefore, to acts of war which are within a state's 'jurisdiction' (as required by Article 1 ECHR).

Derogation from Article 2 in respect of 'deaths resulting from lawful acts of war' is allowed under Article 15 ECHR. This places great emphasis on the legality of the war, a matter determined by the principles of international law and is outside the scope of this book.

If the Convention does not apply, the armed forces involved will still be subject to the laws of war and also, if their nations, like the United Kingdom, are signatories to the Rome Statute, they will be subject to the jurisdiction of the International Criminal Court. Both these issues are outside the scope of this book.

The application of the Convention outside the territory of a signatory state is discussed in Chapter 2, section 2.4.5 and the application outside the United Kingdom of the HRA is discussed in Chapter 4, section 4.11.3.

For Article 15 in general, see Chapter 7, section 7.2.

 Summary

- Article 2 expresses one of the most fundamental of the Convention rights, one that is not subject to derogation, in peacetime, under Article 15.

- Article 2 requires states to ensure that the use of intentional force that causes death is unlawful except under the specific circumstances allowed for under Article 2(2).

- Article 2(1) requires that everyone's right to life shall be protected and this has led the ECtHR to impose 'positive duties' on states to provide a proper framework of law, regulation, and administrative practice. These duties include the provision of a proper system of criminal law, enforced by a system of police, prosecutors, and courts; access to civil remedies may be enough in some circumstances.

- Positive duties apply to dangerous activities generally, including, for example, medical treatments in hospitals and environmental dangers.

- Perhaps the most important duty on states is the procedural obligation to ensure that deaths are properly investigated.

? Self-test questions

1. In what circumstances may states have laws which authorise the use of lethal force?

2. In what circumstances, if any, can Article 2 be subject to derogation under Article 15?

3. What positive duties do states have, generally, under Article 2?

4. In what circumstances might a state have positive duties to protect the life of an identi-fied individual?

5. How do the courts balance the duty to preserve life in Article 2 with other rights a patient may have?

6. How, if at all, might Article 2 affect the decisions taken by politicians, civil servants, and the military in respect of the safety of soldiers in a combat zone?

7. When does the duty to investigate deaths arise as a result of Article 2?

8. What are the requirements of an effective investigation under Article 2?

 For suggested approaches, please visit the Online Resource Centre.

? Exam questions

1. An armed man is holding a woman hostage. The police end the siege violently, caus-ing the death of both the armed man and his victim. The victim's family are seeking a remedy from the courts alleging a breach of Article 2.

   Advise the family on the principles, based on Article 2, which should have governed the way the issue was handled by the authorities.

2. Evaluate the extent to which Article 2 places a duty on states to bring about a safe environment; or is it merely confined to providing remedies after deaths have occured?

 For suggested approaches, please visit the Online Resource Centre.

☰ Further reading

Chevalier-Watts, J. 'Effective Investigation under Article 2 ECHR: Securing the Right to Life or an Onerous Burden on a State?' (2010) 21(3) *EJIL* 701–721

Lester, A., Pannick, D., and Herberg, J. (see Preface) Chapter 4, Article 2

Leverick, F. 'Is English Self-defence Law Incompatible with Article 2 ECHR?' [2002] *Crim LR* 347–362

Sweeney, J.A. *The European Court of Human Rights in the Post-Cold War Era* (2015) London: Rourtledge

9 Article 3: prohibition of torture

LEARNING OBJECTIVES

- The absolute nature of Article 3.
- The definitions of torture and inhuman and degrading treatment and punishment.
- State responsibility to secure Article 3 rights.
- The unlawfulness of torture.
- Article 3 and punishment.
- Article 3 and unintended suffering.

Article 3 Prohibition of torture

No one shall be subjected to torture or to inhuman or degrading treatment or punishment.

Introduction

The ban on torture and on inhuman treatment and punishment is as near to a legal absolute as can be found. The use of torture etc. is not lawful no matter how compelling the proposed excuse or justification. Nevertheless it appears to be widespread throughout the world. States and their officials may use it when they think it is likely to yield valuable information but it can also, apparently, fulfil some human need to hurt, humiliate, and degrade enemies and demonstrate superiority through harming and de-humanising those who are under complete control.

Article 3 did not prevent some Council of Europe states cooperating in torture in the context of the US led 'war on terror' after '9/11' 2001. Nor did it prevent some dreadful brutality during the invasion of Iraq. But, after the event, it has provided an important basis on which victims have been able to obtain remedies, particularly to have the story told and the activities condemned by authoritative judicial rulings. It has also prevented deportations to countries where torture is widespread.

But Article 3 also has an important impact outside the torture chamber. States have duties to ensure that people are not subject to treatment by others that violates Article 3 and that people are not left in conditions that are so intolerable they are inhuman or degrading. Thus Article 3 establishes a minimum standard that can be relevant in contexts such as the treatment of prisoners in prisons and police stations but also in hospitals and in the context of welfare. But it is only a minimum standard and the minimum is set by the context and can sometimes seem to tolerate some very severe treatment (as in the acceptance that the conditions in US maximum security prisons are not below the standard). Where the issue is not the deliberate infliction of pain, Article 3 can often be of less direct significance than Article 8, the right to private life; but Article 8, unlike Article 3, does allow a balancing of the impact on the individual with the rights of others or the common good.

9.1 The fundamental nature of Article 3

Article 3 of the European Convention on Human Rights (ECHR) is expressed in absolute terms. There are no qualifying terms (as there are in the second paragraph of Article 8, for example) which would allow torture or inhuman or degrading treatment if it was a proportionate way of achieving a pressing social need, such as public safety (see *Ahmed* v *Austria* (1997) 24 EHRR 278, para 40) or saving the lives of others (see *Gäfgen*, at section 9.1.1). Likewise the text of Article 3 does not identify any general purposes for which torture, etc. can be justified (unlike, for example, Article 2, the right to life, which permits intentional killing in the circumstances defined in its second paragraph, see Chapter 8, section 8.2.2). If the treatment comes within the definitions in Article 3, it is illegal under the Convention.

CROSS REFERENCE

Derogation (suspending rights) is discussed in Chapter 7, section 7.2.

The fundamental nature of Article 3 is confirmed by its being an Article from which states may not, under Article 15, derogate from even in times of war and public emergency. Again, it can be contrasted with Article 2 which does allow derogation in respect of deaths occurring as a result of 'lawful acts of war' (see Chapter 8, section 8.7).

The ECtHR has emphasised that treatment which violates Article 3 cannot be justified in terms of public benefit. In *Balogh* v *Hungary* App 47940/99, judgment of 20 July 2004, at para 44, for example, the Court said:

> Even in the most difficult of circumstances, such as the fight against terrorism or crime, the Convention prohibits in absolute terms torture or inhuman or degrading treatment or punishment. Unlike most of the substantive clauses of the Convention and of Protocols Nos 1 and 4, Article 3 makes no provision for exceptions and no derogation from it is permissible under Article 15 even in the event of a public emergency threatening the life of the nation.

Ill-treating a suspect on the basis of a well-founded likelihood of obtaining information which will save, in a proximate way, the lives of identifiable people, is banned under Article 3. Likewise winning the 'wars' on crime or terrorism do not justify raising the threshold of severity for what counts as a breach of Article 3 so that states can use tough methods of interrogation without violating Article 3 (see *Tomasi* v *France* (1993) 15 EHRR 1, para 115). Nor can a 'noble purpose' be a matter of weight in deciding whether treatment prohibited by Article 3 is 'torture' or something less.

THINKING POINT

Do you accept the reasons for the ban on torture and inhuman and degrading treatment and punishment to be absolute?

9.1.1 Article 3 and the rights of others

The absolute nature of Article 3 means it cannot be violated even in order to secure the Convention rights of others. The argument that torture should be used against the terrorist suspect, for example, to secure the right to life of others (even if convincing) is not acceptable.

- In *Gäfgen* v *Germany* (2011) 52 EHRR 1, police threatened a suspect with physical harm in order to get him to disclose the whereabouts of a kidnapped and murdered child, which he did. A breach of Article 3 was not disputed, however the Grand Chamber held that the small suspended fine imposed by the German courts was an insufficient response to the breach, whatever its motive.

In hospital cases, it may be wrong to continue with treatments which might prolong life but which would be inhuman or degrading for the patient (subject to patient autonomy). Humiliating cross-examination in order for the defendant to have a fair trial under Article 6 (sometimes alleged in rape trials) could be challenged on Article 3 grounds, for example.

9.1.2 Minimum level of severity

Treatment can only violate Article 3 if it reaches a minimum level of severity. In *Tarakhel* v *Switzerland* [2015] 60 EHRR 28 (concerning the conditions in reception centres in Italy to which the applicants, asylum seekers in Switzerland, might be returned), a Grand Chamber, recapitulating well-established general principles, said:

> to fall within the scope of Article 3 the ill-treatment must attain a minimum level of severity. The assessment of this minimum is relative; it depends on all the circumstances of the case, such as the duration of the treatment and its physical or mental effects and, in some instances, the sex, age and state of health of the victim.

It can depend on the individual characteristics of the individual involved—treatment of a vulnerable person may cross the threshold when it might not for a person of ordinary robustness. The purpose of the treatment may be important at least to the extent that the suffering and humiliation inherent in normal, legitimate, imprisonment will not breach the threshold.

UK courts have been more explicit than the ECtHR in suggesting that the 'circumstances of the case' means that the threshold is not determined solely by the degree of severity in the abstract. UK courts, evaluating the Strasbourg case law, consider that whether treatment is inhuman or degrading may depend, also, on the legitimacy of the purpose behind, and the proportionality of, the actions taken against the individual. Imprisoning a person in order to humiliate them may breach Article 3, whilst arguably greater suffering in the context of legitimately imposing restrictions, proportionate in the circumstances, on a terrorist suspect might not (see *DD* v *Secretary of State for the Home Department* [2014] EWHC 3820, para 116 (the decision was changed on the facts in [2015] EWHC 1681, but the general purposive approach was confirmed, para 74). Considering the 'circumstances' of treatment may, therefore, inescapably involve a court in considering the proportionality of state actions. Thus, even in respect of Article 3, some need to weigh competing interests may be required of a court.

In *Re A (A Child) (Family Proceedings: Disclosure of Information)* [2012] UKSC 60, for example, the UKSC held that the effect on the alleged victim of disclosing, against her wishes, confidential allegations she had made of sexual abuse, would not cross the threshold of severity. The UKSC balanced the public interest in open justice (the disclosures were part of legal proceedings) with the fact that the alleged victim enjoyed significant professional support.

9.1.3 **Article 3 and Article 8**

▶ **CROSS REFERENCE**

See Chapter 15 for a full discussion of Article 8.

There is overlap between Article 3 and Article 8, the right to respect for private and family life. Treatment of a person that is within Article 3 is also likely to involve a failure to respect a person's physical or psychological integrity and thus give rise to an alternative action under Article 8; likewise treatment that does not meet the minimum level of severity needed for Article 3 may come within the scope of Article 8. There is, however, an important difference between the two Articles. Unlike under Article 3, treatment that comes within the scope of Article 8 can be justified by the state and, if so, does not involve a breach of the Convention. The state has to prove that the interference was in accordance with the law, for one of the purposes listed in Article 8(2) and necessary in a democratic society in the sense of being a proportionate way of achieving a pressing social need.

Consequently, if only an Article 8 case is available, the applicant is vulnerable to the state successfully justifying the interference—which is not possible under Article 3. Thus in *Pretty v United Kingdom* (2002) 35 EHRR 1 (the facts are given in section 9.2.3), the failure of English law to allow assisted suicide was not 'treatment' that violated Article 3. On the other hand, the ECtHR accepted that it might be an interference with the applicant's private life; however, if so, it was a justified interference in terms of the second paragraph of Article 8, as it was a proportionate way of protecting the vulnerable from possible abuse (see paras 61–78).

9.2 Definitions: 'torture'; 'inhuman and degrading treatment and punishment'

9.2.1 **Torture and inhuman treatment**

In *Ireland v United Kingdom* (1979–80) 2 EHRR 25, the ECtHR defined torture as 'deliberate inhuman treatment causing very serious and cruel suffering' (para 167). Inhuman treatment, the case suggests, is treatment or punishment that is:

- likely to cause actual bodily injury or intense physical and mental suffering including acute psychiatric disturbance (the causing of bodily injury is not necessary) (see also *Pretty v United Kingdom* (2002) 35 EHRR 1, para 52);
- premeditated and intentional;
- applied for long periods at a time.

Given that Article 3 can apply to inhuman treatment which is unintended (see section 9.7), the last two bullet points are not necessary to every application of Article 3.

BIGGER PICTURE

In *Ireland* v *United Kingdom*, the ECtHR had held that the interrogation techniques of hooding, subjection to continuous loud, hissing noises, sleep deprivation, reduced diet, and being made to stand against a wall in a painful posture for a long period of time, applied with premeditation and for hours at a stretch, amounted to inhuman treatment which violated Article 3 and were unlawful. Consider, however, the report into the death of Baha Mousa (an Iraqi detainee who, in 2003, was beaten to death by British troops— see *Al Skeini* v *Secretary of State for Defence* [2007] UKHL 26). This showed that similar 'conditioning techniques' had been used against detainees in Iraq after 2003. However, the Ministry of Defence had failed to take proper, effective, and publicised steps to ban them in the armed forces (see *The Report of the Baha Mousa Public Inquiry* https://www. gov.uk/government/publications/the-baha-mousa-public-inquiry-report, Volume III, Summary, para 270).

9.2.2 **The special case of torture**

In *Ireland*, the Court's view was that Article 3 expressly distinguishes 'torture' from other forms of inhuman and degrading treatment. Torture is a particularly serious form of inhuman treatment, distinguished by the degree of suffering caused and the deliberateness with which it is applied. Consequently it is behaviour to which a special stigma is attached. An example is given in the case close-up.

CASE CLOSE-UP

***Aksoy* v *Turkey* (1997) 23 EHRR 553**

The applicant was subjected to 'Palestinian hanging' by Turkish security forces. He was stripped naked, with his arms tied together behind his back, and suspended by his arms. The ECtHR found this to be torture because:

- it was deliberately inflicted and must have involved preparation and exertion on the part of the torturers;
- it was administered in order to obtain information or admissions from the victim;
- it caused severe pain with some long-lasting consequences.

The Court considers that this treatment was of such a serious and cruel nature that it can only be described as torture.

The UN Convention

There is a special UN Convention dealing with torture, the UN Convention Against Torture and Other Cruel, Inhuman or Degrading Treatment or Punishment (UNCAT). UNCAT has been used by the ECtHR to determine the border between 'torture' and 'inhuman treatment' (as in *Selmouni* v *France* (2000) 29 EHRR 403).

Article 1 UNCAT defines 'torture' in relation to:

- the degree and nature of suffering—that severe pain or suffering is inflicted that can be physical or mental;
- intentional acts of public officials—the pain and suffering is intentionally inflicted by a public official or with, at least, the acquiescence of a public official;
- purpose—the pain or suffering is inflicted for a purpose such as: obtaining information or a confession, punishment, intimidation or coercion, or for a reason based on some form of discrimination.

Whether some form of brutal treatment by officials has attached to it the particular stigma of being 'torture' is a matter of judgment for a court. In *Selmouni* (mentioned earlier), the ECtHR held that, in distinguishing torture from inhuman or degrading treatment, it would recognise changing values and the higher standards required to protect human rights than might have applied in the past (para 101).

9.2.3 'Degrading treatment'

Article 3 prohibits 'degrading' treatment or punishment. The meaning of 'degrading' has been discussed in general terms in *Pretty v UK*.

 CASE CLOSE-UP

Pretty v United Kingdom (2002) 35 EHRR 1

Diane Pretty suffered from motor neurone disease. Under English law it was unlawful for her husband to assist her in dying at a time and in a manner of her choice. She sought a finding from the ECtHR that this was incompatible with the Convention. Her argument, in relation to Article 3, was that being able to die at a time and in a manner of her choosing would enable her to die with some dignity and less suffering. By refusing her this right she was condemned to suffer in a way that was inhuman and degrading.

The ECtHR found no violation of Article 3 and held that the refusal of the state to sanction assisted suicide did not amount to 'treatment' nor could there be a positive duty on the state to assist a person's suicide by a change in the law.

In *Pretty*, degrading treatment was defined:

. . . Where treatment humiliates or debases an individual showing a lack of respect for, or diminishing, his or her human dignity or arouses feelings of fear, anguish or inferiority capable of breaking an individual's moral and physical resistance, it may be characterised as degrading and also fall within the prohibition of Article 3.

(para 52)

Thus treatment or punishment is degrading if it is likely to:

- arouse in victims feelings of fear, anguish, and inferiority which is humiliating and debasing and is capable of breaking physical and moral resistance;
- in considering whether treatment is degrading, the Court will consider the motive behind the treatment, but a motive to degrade or humiliate is not a necessary requirement;

- discrimination on certain grounds is capable of being degrading. This has been recognised as a possibility by the ECtHR in respect of racial discrimination and discrimination based on sexual orientation.

▶ CROSS REFERENCE

Pretty is also discussed in Chapter 15, the right to private life.

9.3 State responsibility and positive duties

Where officials, such as police, military, security officials, or prison officers, torture people or intentionally subject them to other degrees of ill-treatment, the state is responsible under Article 3. States must ensure that there are proper laws and effective administrative and judicial processes and sufficient punishments (see *Gäfgen*, at section 9.1.1) by which the perpetrators, even though officials, can be brought to justice by the criminal law. Both Article 1 and, in particular, Article 13, which requires effective remedies 'notwithstanding that the violation has been committed by persons acting in an official capacity', will otherwise be violated. If effective legal remedies against officials are not available, the requirement that a victim must, if taking their case to Strasbourg, exhaust his or her domestic remedies (see Chapter 2, section 2.7.2) can be waived.

9.3.1 The scope of Article 3

The definitions of 'torture' and 'inhuman or degrading treatment or punishment' include but are not confined to treatment meted out or supervised by state officials such as police or members of the security services. Unlike under UNCAT (which requires at least the acquiescence of officials, see section 9.2.2), the definition of torture in Article 3 ECHR does not expressly require official involvement. Likewise, the definition of inhuman and degrading treatment or punishment extends to actions by private individuals such as a parent beating his child (as in *A v United Kingdom* (1999) 27 EHRR 611) or a teacher slippering one of his pupils (see *Costello-Roberts v United Kingdom* (1995) 19 EHRR 112). *Pretty*, in particular, makes it clear that Article 3 can apply to treatment which was not intended to cause suffering and was not aimed at obtaining information, punishment, or intimidation, etc. but is, nevertheless, treatment for which the state can be made responsible. Hospital treatment, treatment of prisoners, and state responsibility for welfare are examples. Article 3 bases liability on a general approach to state responsibility. There may be a violation if the state has failed in its duty to produce an adequate framework of laws and procedures to protect individuals from behaviour by anyone that causes them to suffer in ways that are incompatible with Article 3. In the context of welfare provision, the *Pretty* definition has been adopted into the law of England and Wales, under the HRA 1998, in *R (Limbuela) v Secretary of State for the Home Department* [2005] UKHL 66, see paras 7 and 54 (see section 9.7.1). The existence of reasonably well-resourced systems of police and criminal justice, of civil law by which compensation may be obtained, systems of health care, child protection and so on, will go a long way towards discharging the duty.

9.3.2 Positive duties

As well as the general duty to provide such adequate systems of civil and criminal law, the state may be under a wider 'positive' duty to respond effectively to particular threats against identifiable individuals and groups which, if they materialise, might violate Article 3. This aspect of state responsibility under Article 3 can be similar to the *Osman* duty, discussed in Chapter 8, section 8.3.3. The duty is owed where the state is aware or ought to have been aware that someone in the jurisdiction is in danger of suffering above the Article 3 threshold. The duty is to take preventive actions but the extent of these actions is not required to be such as would 'impose an impossible or disproportionate burden on the authorities'. Nevertheless, the duty is context dependent. Failure to give adequate protection to children, for example, may give rise to a violation, as in *Z* v *United Kingdom* (2002) 34 EHRR 3 (failure by local authority social workers to protect the applicant children from abuse and neglect). In *E* v *Chief Constable of the RUC* [2008] UKHL 66, children going to a Catholic primary school in Belfast were subjected to hostile and violent abuse by Loyalists. The House of Lords held that the police's positive duty to protect children from treatment by others that violated Article 3 was not absolute. The positive duty was to do all that could be reasonably expected of them, in the circumstances; this the police had done.

9.3.3 Investigation

As with Article 2, the state has a duty to ensure that there is an 'effective official investigation' of credible assertions of a breach of Article 3. In *Mocanu* v *Romania* (2015) 60 EHRR 19, a Grand Chamber confirmed the duty in general terms and linked Article 2 and Article 3. An investigation is necessary in order that the right to life and the prohibition on torture should be 'effective and practical' safeguards. The aim is to ensure that the domestic laws by which freedom from torture etc. is guaranteed are given effect and that, in addition to any compensation, those responsible can be identified and, if necessary, punished. As with Article 2, the investigation needs to be independent, state originated, capable of identifying those responsible, broad enough to take surrounding circumstances into effect, promptly put into effect, expeditiously carried out, to involve the victim, thorough and not pre-judged, and not hindered by amnesties or pardons for officials (see paras 314–326).

Examples of the duty being applied are *Assenov* v *Bulgaria* (1999) 28 EHRR 652 (alleged police mistreatment) and *Labita* v *Italy* (2008) 46 EHRR 50 (alleged mistreatment of prisoners), though the duty is not, in principle, confined to allegations of abuse by police and other officials (see *Secic* v *Croatia* App 40116/02, judgment of 31 May 2007, paras 53–54).

 BIGGER PICTURE

In *Mocanu* the ECtHR applied the investigative duty in the context of 'transitional justice' (the question of how, in the present, Eastern European members of the Council of Europe should deal with their past as oppressive dictatorships). Other examples are:

- *Mocanu* v *Romania* (2015) 60 EHRR 19: Romania's transition from dictatorship to democracy;
- *Zdanoka* v *Latvia* (2007) 45 EHRR 17: Latvia's transition from being a part of the Soviet Union to an independent state;
- *Janowiec* v *Russia* (2014) 58 EHRR 30: the Katyn massacre 1940 (here the ECtHR held it did not have jurisdiction to hear a complaint of an inadequate investigation by the current Russian authorities).

See: Sweeney, J.A. *The European Court of Human Rights in the Post-Cold War Era* (2013) London: Routledge.

The duty to investigate allegations of a breach of Article 3 may be satisfied by established procedures (e.g. in the UK, an investigation by or supervised by the Independent Police Complaints Commission); if these are inadequate when judged against these requirements, a special, independent inquiry may be required.

Under the HRA, the duty to investigate required by Article 3 has been accepted by UK courts in *R (Green) v Police Complaints Authority* [2004] UKHL 6 (para 59). In *R (AM) SSHD* [2009] EWCA Civ 219, a breach of Article 3 was declared because the Home Secretary, alerted to possible breaches of Article 3 in a commercially run immigration detention centre, failed to hold an effective investigation.

9.3.4 Proof of state responsibility

Torture and ill-treatment cases often involve disputes over the facts; in particular the state may deny that its agents were responsible for a victim's suffering. The ECtHR starts with the normal position that the burden of proof is on the applicant to prove the case (e.g. against state officials) beyond a reasonable doubt. However 'reasonable doubt' is an autonomous Convention concept. The ECtHR is prepared to make presumptions of state responsibility which it is then up to the state to rebut. These presumptions are based on, for example, the state's refusal to cooperate with the ECtHR (itself a breach of Article 38 which requires state cooperation with the court's own investigations) or on the absence of an effective inquiry by the state or on the fact that the applicant was arrested in a good physical state but emerged from state custody injured (see, for example, *Toteva v Bulgaria* App 42027/98, judgment of 19 May 2004). For examples, consider the case close-ups concerning extraordinary rendition, in section 9.4.3.

> ▶ **CROSS REFERENCE**
> Similar, and relevant, approaches are adopted in the context of the right to life—see Chapter 8, section 8.2.1 'Proving Responsibility'.

9.4 Torture

Torture has come in for the special condemnation of mankind. As the ECtHR recognises there is a particular shame for a state shown to conduct torture. Most, if not all, states condemn it and make it unlawful. However, most states have officials who have practised, and continue to practise, torture.

Article 3 is by no means the only basis on which torture is unlawful internationally and in the UK.

9.4.1 International law

Jus cogens erga omnes

Prohibition of torture is a 'peremptory norm' of international law and is part of the common law of England, enforceable in the courts. It is *jus cogens* (compelling law) and imposes a general obligation on states to act against torture wherever it is found (*erga omnes*). It represents perhaps the highest and most universally recognised obligation on states. As well as torture, the prohibition on slavery and genocide are other accepted examples of *jus cogens*. Compulsory law not only requires states to desist from torture themselves but also empowers them (if they wish), to act lawfully against it wherever committed (*erga omnes*—in relation to everyone).

UN Conventions

■ CROSS REFERENCE

See Chapter 1 for a general discussion of the ICCPR and enforcement mechanisms, section 1.4.4.

The outlawing of torture and inhuman and degrading treatment and punishment is found widely in international law, not just in Article 3. Article 5 of the UNDHR said that 'No one shall be subjected to torture or to cruel, inhuman or degrading treatment or punishment'. These words are reproduced in Article 7 of the IPPCR which adds, 'In particular, no one shall be subjected without his free consent to medical or scientific experimentation.'

UN Convention against torture

The special UN Convention dealing with torture, the UN Convention Against Torture and other Cruel, Inhuman or Degrading Treatment or Punishment (UNCAT), has been mentioned previously. The obligations on signatory states include:

* establishing effective laws and procedures so that torture is outlawed as a crime in their jurisdiction in all circumstances;

* not expelling persons to countries where they might be tortured;

* investigating and, if necessary, prosecuting persons in their territory against whom well-founded allegations of involvement in torture have been made.

Torture has a severity and also a link to official sanction that distinguishes it from 'ordinary' brutality and ill-treatment (see *A v UK*, mentioned in section 9.3.1, para 53). The problem is that making this distinction may enable states to treat suspects in inhuman or degrading ways without attracting full legal condemnation. The routine hooding of detainees in Iraq in 2003 may be an instance of this.

European Convention for the Prevention of Torture and Inhuman or Degrading Treatment or Punishment

The Council of Europe has strengthened it measures against torture in the European Convention for the Prevention of Torture and Inhuman or Degrading Treatment or Punishment. This creates the European Committee for the Prevention of Torture and Inhuman or Degrading Treatment or Punishment. The Committee makes regular visits to the signatory states and reports on a range of matters, such as prison conditions.

9.4.2 Law of the United Kingdom

Torture has been illegal in England since 1640 (when the King's claim to use torture under the prerogative was ended) and, in Scotland, by section 5 of the Treason Act 1708.

The UK's obligations under UNCAT are given effect by section 134 of the Criminal Justice Act 1988, which makes 'torture', as defined by UNCAT, a crime under UK law wherever in the world it is committed and by whoever it is committed, including officials and including an ex-head of state (see *R v Bow Street Metropolitan Stipendiary Magistrate ex parte Pinochet Ugarte (No 3)* [2000] 1 AC 147). Torture will also involve a range of ordinary offences for which anyone, including officials, can be prosecuted.

9.4.3 Using the product of torture in courts

Prohibition of torture is one thing, the use of evidence obtained by torture performed by others raises different issues. Article 15 of UNCAT expressly bans the use of evidence obtained by torture in any proceedings.

In *A v Secretary of State for the Home Department* [2005] UKHL 71), the House of Lords considered whether evidence that might have been obtained by torture, conducted in foreign countries, could be admissible before courts in the United Kingdom dealing with anti-terrorism cases.

The House of Lords made it clear that the use of torture evidence in UK courts is illegal. The reasons for this are, in part, the unreliability of torture. More importantly, it is that the use of torture evidence would shock the conscience of the court. Torture, even where effective and productive of reliable information, is unlawful; it is incompatible with the dignity of the law. The only exception (in recognition of parliamentary supremacy) would be if an Act of Parliament expressly provided for the use of torture—any such statute would violate international law.

In *A*, the Law Lords disagreed on the burden of proof. All judges agreed that a prisoner alleging torture did not have to prove his or her case. This would be impossible to do. If the applicant could raise a reasonable suspicion that there was torture evidence being relied upon, then the court (in *A* the court was the SIAC) had a duty to investigate.

- The minority view. The evidence allegedly obtained by torture should be rejected unless the court was satisfied, on a balance of probabilities, that the evidence was not the product of torture.
- The majority view. The evidence allegedly obtained by torture should be accepted (so long as it was thought reliable and otherwise admissible) unless, on a balance of probabilities, the court was satisfied that torture had been used.

In other words, the majority took the view that where doubt persisted on whether there had been torture, the evidence should be admitted, if reliable.

> **CROSS REFERENCE**
> For discussion in the context of deportation see Chapter 12, 12.16.

A refers to evidence admissible in courts. The House of Lords accepted that the Secretary of State can use torture evidence in his or her executive role, in deciding whether a person should be arrested, whether to take action to protect individuals or the public, etc.

 BIGGER PICTURE

For further discussion of *jus cogens* see *Prosecutor v Furundzija* [1998] ICTY 3, paras 147–157 (a case of the International Criminal Tribunal for the Former Yugoslavia), quoted in *A*, discussed earlier, para 33.

In *A v Secretary of State for the Home Department* (see above in this section), the House of Lords not only outlawed the use of evidence obtained by torture but also condemned torture in no uncertain terms and reviewed the various ways in which torture was unlawful (see paras 11–13, 30–33, and 103–111 in particular).

See also an article by one of the judges, Lord Hope: Hope, D. 'Torture' (2004) *ICLQ* 807.

 DISCUSSION TOPIC

Can torture ever be justified?

- The arguments against torture are clear. Persons under the absolute control of others must be treated properly and without abuse and oppression. To torture someone is to deny their very humanity; they are not treated as a 'person' but merely as an object. Even the most dangerous or most unpleasant persons must be accorded this basic respect. The ban on torture is, perhaps, the strongest principle of both international and common law.

- Opposition to torture is partly a 'deontological' argument (an argument about what is 'right' rather than what is useful). It is based on the conception of the person and 'trumps' all other arguments—i.e. you can achieve outcomes that are in the public interest (e.g. public safety) but only if, in doing so, you also safeguard the basic rights of individuals not to be tortured, etc. A 'consequentialist' argument, on the other hand, is one that weighs the full range of arguments for and against and looks at the overall outcome.

- There are arguments that might concede the legitimacy of torture in some circumstances (though some argue that even to raise the issue is to concede too much).

  - Giving an absolute priority of one right over another may lead to serious consequences for others. In particular, can states fulfil their obligations under Article 2 to protect life if they cannot torture, for example, the alleged bomber (consider *Gäfgen*, discussed earlier)?

  - States always claim not to engage in torture. Nevertheless intelligence services throughout the world seem to find inflicting pain and fear on their prisoners an effective way of obtaining information. It is better to accept this and put it on a legal basis. Torture would still be barred but lesser, still serious, forms of physical treatment of detainees could then be undertaken on the basis of a regulated legal structure with defined limits. It is better to regulate dangerous activities that are going to happen anyway; they are more dangerous if unregulated.

For a summary of the arguments see: Rumney, P. and O'Boyle, M. 'The Torture Debate' (2007) 157 *NLJ* 1566.

Q CASE CLOSE-UP

Extraordinary rendition

The ECtHR has given a robust reaction to the complicity of some European states to the US programme, after '9/11', of secretly (and without clear legal authority) violently kidnapping terrorist suspects, transferring them to secret prisons within or outside Europe, and then subjecting them to harsh interrogation measures which were so severe as to amount to torture (the 'standard' and 'enhanced' forms of which are described at paras 53–70 in *Al Nashiri* and *Husayn*, discussed immediately below). Two applicants subjected to this treatment brought cases before the ECtHR. In *Al Nashiri* v *Poland* (2015) 60 EHRR 16, the applicant was suspected by the US authorities of involvement in terrorist bombings; and in *Husayn* v *Poland* (2015) 60 EHRR 16, the applicant was suspected of being a leading figure in Al-Qaida. The ECtHR found violations by Poland of Article 3 and other cases. In particular, the Court:

- made it clear that these actions were outside the rule of law;

- provided an authoritative, detailed account, based on a range of official and unofficial sources, of the events. Though building on Council of Europe investigations, CIA disclosures, NGO campaigns, and journalistic enquiries, it is the authoritative and judicial basis of the Court's findings that make them important. The Court also made specific findings of fact concerning the applicants' treatment (e.g. *Husayn*, paras 408, 415, and 417);

- made rulings that parts of the treatment suffered by the applicants amounted to 'torture', not just inhuman treatment (e.g. *Al Nashiri*, para 516);

- held that Poland did know or at least ought to have known what was going on in the secret prisons on its territory and its failure to take action, its facilitation of unlawful rendition, its 'acquiescence and connivance' with the CIA, was a breach of its duty to prohibit torture under Article 3;

- held that there was also a breach of the procedural aspect of Article 3, Poland had failed to conduct an adequate investigation into the allegations. Also Poland had failed in its duty under Article 38 ECHR to assist the ECtHR in its investigations. The fact that important national security issues were involved did not relieve the state of its duties under these Articles;

- held there were also violations of Article 5 (the right to liberty), Article 8 (private life), Article 6(1) (the right to a fair trial), and Article 13 (the right to a remedy).

In an earlier case, *El-Masri* v *Former Yugoslav Republic of Macedonia* (2013) 57 EHRR 25, the applicant was unlawfully detained, incommunicado, in Macedonia for 23 days and then handed over to the USA at the airport where he was physically beaten and 'stripped and sodomised with an object. He was placed in a nappy and dressed in a dark blue short-sleeved tracksuit. Shackled and hooded, and subjected to total sensory deprivation, the applicant was forcibly marched to a CIA aircraft where he was forcibly tranquilised and chained to the floor' (para 205). This treatment amounted, in the circumstances, to torture (para 211).

These cases represent some of the most authoritative and forthright declarations that the policy of 'extraordinary rendition' was incompatible with the rule of law and that enhanced interrogation techniques amounted to torture. Of course the USA and CIA were not before the court and the ECtHR has none of the procedural and substantive constraints that might apply to a domestic court dealing with the domestic legal balance between judiciary and executive. Nevertheless, it is quite clear that, even in the context of counter-terrorism and the need to support a powerful ally, European states cannot surrender the basic obligations found in the Convention.

9.5 Deliberate ill-treatment by officials

Allegations of abuse of prisoners detained by police, military, or other security forces are normally to be considered in the light of Article 3. This is so even if the use of force alleged also threatened the right to life (as in *Ilhan* v *Turkey* (2002) 34 EHRR 36, mentioned in Chapter 8, section 8.2.1).

The ECtHR has made the position very clear. Persons detained by the police etc. must be treated properly and not be subjected to treatment which violates Article 3 (see *Ribitsch* v *Austria* (1996) 21 EHRR 573). Suspects are entirely within the control of the state, they have little autonomy (few choices), and they are vulnerable to the will and the prejudices of their captors. The use of force against detainees is limited to that required by the suspect's own behaviour and that which is 'strictly necessary' to keep him or her under proper control in custody. The threshold of severity is low in respect of detainees since even a minor beating is incompatible with a prisoner's basic dignity. The duty to hold an effective investigation is particularly pressing in respect of people who are apparently injured whilst in the custody of the police or other officials.

Not all physical treatment of suspects will meet the threshold of severity. The normal use of handcuffs and other forms of restraint, for example, can be compatible with Article 3. Such restraints are both below the threshold of severity and for a legitimate purpose consequent on arrest and detention (see *Raninen* v *Sweden* (1998) 26 EHRR 563). Similarly, such restraints are also unlikely to violate Article 8. It needs to be stressed, however, that Article 3 may be breached if, for example, the aim of a particular use of restraining devices is to humiliate or degrade or if the person is young or otherwise vulnerable and such restraint is, given the circumstances, above the minimal level of severity necessary to engage Article 3.

In *FGP* v *Serco* [2012] EWHC 1804, the claimant was detained at an immigration removal centre. When taken to hospital for examination and treatment he was handcuffed and restrained by long chains at all times. The High Court held that the continual use of restraint, in particular whilst he was being treated, was unnecessary, disproportionate, and violated Article 3 (*Mouisel* v *France* (2004) 38 EHRR 34 was followed).

9.6 Punishment

Lawful punishment must be compatible with Article 3.

9.6.1 **Corporal punishment**

The Convention sets its face against corporal punishments (beating etc.) and has had a significant influence on the law in England and Wales. Physical punishments for criminal offences were abolished in the UK in 1948 and it is clear that any restoration would be likely to be incompatible with the Convention. In *Tyrer* v *United Kingdom* (1979–80) 2 EHRR 1 (in relation to the retention of birching in the Isle of Man), the ECtHR found that the punishment was degrading, in breach of Article 3, principally because of its character as 'institutionalised violence': carried out impersonally by police officers in a police station with complete physical control over the victim.

Corporal punishment in schools, on the other hand, may not necessarily reach the threshold of severity to violate Article 3 ECHR (e.g. *Campbell and Cosans* v *United Kingdom* (1982)

4 EHRR 293), though there have been indications of a lack of approval (e.g. *Y v United Kingdom* (1994) 17 EHRR 238). Corporal punishment is now unlawful in all schools, state or independent, in the United Kingdom (section 548 Education Act 1996). School punishment also raises issues under Article 2 of the First Protocol, which gives parents a right that their children be educated in line with their broad philosophical and religious beliefs: see Chapter 24, section 24.4.1.

Parents and carers

The state is responsible for ensuring that punishment imposed on children and others, even by their parents and carers, does not go beyond the level of severity permitted under Articles 3 and 8. The Convention imposes a positive duty on the state to ensure that the criminal law is available to deter and punish those, including private individuals, who inflict such punishment.

 CASE CLOSE-UP

A v United Kingdom (1999) 27 EHRR 611

Between the ages of six and nine years A was frequently punished by his stepfather who beat him with a garden cane, causing bodily marks indicative of serious injury. The stepfather was prosecuted for assault occasioning actual bodily harm but was acquitted. The jury accepted his defence, available to him under English law, that he had done no more than administer 'reasonable chastisement' of a child.

The ECtHR held that, in the circumstances, the punishment reached the level of severity required for a breach of Article 3 and that the state had failed to provide an adequate legal framework for protecting A's Article 3 rights.

Though the judgment in *A* is not clear on the point, the failure of the United Kingdom seems to have been that the law left it to the prejudices of a jury to decide whether or not a punishment was reasonable. The Court also mentioned the fact that the burden of proof was on the prosecution to prove that the beating went beyond what was reasonable. Partly as a consequence of this case, section 58 of the Children Act 2004 removes the defence of reasonable punishment from those accused of offences involving the causing of various degrees of bodily harm or of cruelty to children. The defence remains available for lesser forms of physical punishment of children (such as a common assault or battery not causing bodily harm). This means there is (in England) no outright ban on 'smacking' children; nor, as *Costello-Roberts* indicates, is such an outright ban required under the Convention.

9.6.2 Prisoners' rights under Article 3

Article 3 has a significant impact on the rights of prisoners, particularly in regard to the general conditions they experience, their medical treatment, and the types of punishment and security measures they can be subjected to. These are considered in Chapter 21.

9.7 Unintended suffering and hardship

⟩ **CROSS REFERENCE**

For authority see section 9.3 (the discussion on 'positive duties', especially section 9.3.2).

The ban in Article 3 extends to 'inhuman and degrading treatment'. This means that the effect of Article 3 extends beyond the torture chamber and the prison. It applies to action taken where suffering is not intended but is a consequence of entirely lawful decisions and actions which have nothing to do with punishment or with extracting information. Civil servants, for example, may take welfare decisions affecting individuals. If, as a consequence of such otherwise legitimate activity, a person ends up in a situation in which they suffer bodily injury, intense physical or mental suffering, or a situation in which they are humiliated or debased or in which feelings of fear, anguish, or inferiority are aroused so that their moral or physical resistance is broken, they may have a right under Article 3. Likewise, the state has positive duties under Article 3 to ensure that the activities of others for which it has responsibilities (e.g. health care and education) are conducted in ways which avoid causing suffering which, in context, goes above the Article 3 threshold of severity. As is made clear in section 9.7.1, the 'threshold of severity' in cases that do not involve the deliberate infliction of suffering, can be high.

9.7.1 Asylum seekers and welfare under the HRA

The duty on states not to treat people in a way that, unintentionally, may cause suffering which, in context, is above the Article 3 threshold, has become an important issue in English law, particularly in respect of what duties the state has towards people seeking political asylum (foreigners seeking refuge in the United Kingdom on the grounds of a well-grounded fear, which they have yet to prove, of persecution in their own country).

Citizens, and those entitled to reside in the United Kingdom, have access to the welfare state. Other people, such as asylum seekers, who are in the country may have no such right and so the question arises whether there is any duty under the HRA on the state to provide at least a minimum level of subsistence to prevent destitution. Article 3 is not the only Convention right potentially involved: Article 2 can be invoked if the state's refusal to provide accommodation and subsistence is likely to lead to death. Article 8 can be invoked if the state's refusal will lead to circumstances in which a person could be said no longer to be an autonomous person (though the Court of Appeal has suggested that there is no positive duty on the states to provide welfare in respect only of a possible a breach of Article 8 by itself (*Anufrijeva* v *Southwark LBC* [2003] EWCA Civ 1406, para 43)).

Although Article 3 does not require states to provide welfare to a certain level, being left in extremely poor conditions could violate Article 3, especially where domestic legal entitlements are not made available (*MSS* v *Greece and Belgium* (2011) 53 EHRR 2). The issue of the extent of the duty under Article 3 of the state towards asylum seekers has come before the UK courts.

🔍 CASE CLOSE-UP

R (Limbuela) v *Secretary of State for the Home Department* [2005] UKHL 66

Asylum seekers are not entitled to the ordinary range of welfare benefits. Nor are they permitted to work. It is also accepted that charitable provision, though available, can be hard to come by.

Section 95 of the Immigration and Asylum Act 1999 permits the Secretary of State to provide welfare support to 'destitute' asylum seekers. However, section 55(1) of the Nationality, Immigration and Asylum Act 2002 prevents the provision of welfare to late applicants, defined as those who had not claimed asylum 'as soon as reasonably practicable after arriving in the United Kingdom'. Nevertheless, the Act gives the Secretary of State the power to grant welfare payments to late applicants if this is necessary to avoid a breach of an applicant's Convention rights, including those under Article 3. Cases were brought by three late-applying asylum seekers who had been denied benefits. The question was whether the Home Office's understanding of the threshold of severity, when Article 3 would require some form of welfare support, was, in the three cases, correct. The House of Lords approached the matter on these principles:

- In the context of treatment that does not involve the deliberate infliction of pain, the threshold of severity of the suffering involved is high (though their Lordships rejected the Court of Appeal's analysis in so far as it had suggested that a higher degree of suffering needed to be shown than for deliberately inflicted suffering).

- 'Treatment' means that Article 3 is only involved when the state has taken specific action. Article 3 does not provide a general duty to house the homeless or provide for the destitute. However, there can be 'treatment' where the state takes a decision about an individual, the consequences of which involves suffering above the Article 3 threshold. In *R v Altham* [2006] EWCA Crim 7, in contrast, the defendant had used cannabis to alleviate severe pain consequent to a road accident. The Court of Appeal held that the authorities had done nothing to cause the defendant's pain and so had no positive duty under Article 3 to take steps (such as making the defence of necessity available to him) to alleviate it.

- Treatment is inhuman or degrading if 'to a seriously detrimental extent, it denies the most basic needs of any human being'. The threshold of severity may be crossed if a person with no alternative means available to him is 'by the deliberate action of the state, denied shelter, food or the most basic necessities of life'.

On these principles the House of Lords held that there had been a violation of Article 3 in all three cases.

Adam: He claimed to have sought asylum the day after he arrived in the United Kingdom. He was denied benefits. He had to sleep rough in a car park though he had access to Refugee Council premises during the day and could wash himself and his clothes. He was eventually recognised as a genuine refugee.

Limbuela: He claimed to have sought asylum on the day he arrived in the United Kingdom but not at the place of entry. He was denied benefits and had to sleep rough and beg for food (unsuccessfully). He had no access to washing facilities and became ill. His asylum claim failed.

Tesema: He claimed asylum the day after his arrival in the United Kingdom. He was denied benefits. He lived in a hostel but if evicted would have had to sleep rough. He was eventually recognised as a genuine refugee.

(See paras 18–33 for each individual's situation.)

The House of Lords was careful not to lay down a general rule; nevertheless, these cases suggest that an official would violate the duty under section 6 HRA if he or she made a decision which left a person with no food, shelter, or means of subsistence.

9.7.2 **Medical treatment**

State duties

CROSS REFERENCE

On the application of the HRA in a medical context see Chapter 8, section 8.4.

States have responsibilities under the Convention to ensure that medical treatment is given in ways which are compatible with Article 3. Likewise the HRA applies to lawfulness of medical treatment in the UK.

States have positive duties under Article 3 to ensure that the suffering that flows from illness etc. is not made worse by measures taken which engage state responsibility (*Pretty* v UK (2002) 35 EHRR 1, para 52). State responsibility can be engaged in acute situations, situations involving vulnerable people, or where the state's monopoly over legitimate force is in issue (such as imprisonment, deportation, or forcible treatment).

Normal, therapeutic treatment, aimed at curing the disease or curing the symptoms, administered by competent professionals who are supported by a well-resourced health system is unlikely to violate Article 3. The ECtHR said in *Herczegfalvy* v *Austria* (1993) 15 EHRR 437, 'as a general rule, a measure which is a therapeutic necessity cannot be regarded as inhuman or degrading' (para 82).

Medical treatment is also likely to engage Article 8 (respect for private life etc.). It must be remembered that whilst an interference with, say, a patient's private life can be justified under the terms of Article 8(2), treating someone in an inhuman or degrading way which crosses the threshold of severity will violate Article 3 irrespective of any alleged justification. Article 3, therefore, is likely to apply in the most serious cases (though, as said previously, the threshold of severity depends on a range of contextual factors).

A competent patient, of course, can refuse treatment even against his or her acknowledged best interests. Patient autonomy is overriding even if, it may appear, the patient is left in a degrading position. Conversely, a withdrawal, consented to by the patient, of highly invasive treatment may be justified by Article 3 (death being preferred to the severe, degrading consequences of the treatment)—see *R (Burke)* v *GMC* [2005] EWCA Civ 1003, paras 38–39.

CROSS REFERENCE

Withdrawal of treatment leading to death is discussed in Chapter 8, section 8.4.

Decisions relating to incompetent patients are based on an assessment of the patient's best interests. Such patients are to be treated with dignity. A properly taken medical decision, taking into account all the factors from which a patient's best interests are indicated, including a decision to withdraw life-saving treatment, will not give rise to a breach of Article 3 (*Re M (Adult Treatment)* [2011] EWHC 2443, para 92).

Forcible treatment

Forcible treatment is treatment imposed, against his or her will, on a patient who is competent enough to give consent for medical treatment. Clearly, this engages the state's monopoly of legitimate force. In England and Wales, for instance, such treatment is permitted under the Mental Health Act 1983 where the treatment is for the patient's mental condition (see section 63, read with sections 57, 58, and 58A). In *Herczegfalvy* v *Austria* (1992) 15 EHRR 437 (the forced feeding of a mental patient on hunger strike), the Court required that the need for the forced treatment must be demonstrated and must relate to convincing therapeutic grounds not, for example, just the desire to maintain physical dominance and control over a patient. The position of inferiority and powerlessness of patients in psychiatric hospital calls for particular vigilance and the patients retain the protection of Article 3. Since the Court did not insist that forced treatment must be for the mental condition, the Convention, perhaps, has a lower standard than under English law.

Whether treatment is 'forced' may depend upon the degree that consent was freely given on the basis of full information; the lack of such full and free consent to a sterilisation procedure was the basis of a violation of Article 3 in *VC* v *Slovakia* App 18968/07, judgment of 8 November 2011.

Under the HRA courts will examine, with 'increased vigilance' which must be judicially tested through a properly adversarial procedure, proposals for non-voluntary treatment under the Mental Health Act 1983 (as in *(Wilkinson)* v *Responsible Medical Officer, Broadmoor Hospital* [2001] EWCA Civ 1545).

Article 8 can also be engaged by forcible treatment. In *YF* v *Turkey* (2004) 39 EHRR 34, a forced gynaecological examination done, apparently, to forestall allegations of rape, was a violation of Article 8.

9.8 Deportations—'foreign cases'

9.8.1 **The legal basis of deportation etc.**

People who are not British citizens may, on various grounds, be required to leave the UK.

Deportation. Persons lawfully in the UK but who are not British citizens may be 'deported'. This can be done under the Immigration Act 1971 and other legislation. There are two principal grounds of deportation: as a consequence of conviction and punishment for a serious offence (section 3(6) Immigration Act 1971); or where in the view of the government the presence of the person (and family members) in the UK is not 'conducive to the public good' because they represent a threat to national security, for example (section 3(5) Immigration Act 1971).

Removal. Persons who are not in the UK lawfully may be 'removed'. Over-stayers, illegal entrants, former refugees, etc. are subject to summary removal by immigration officials exercising powers under section 10 Immigration and Asylum Act 1999.

Extradition. Anyone living in the UK, including British citizens, can sent to another country that is seeking to try them for a serious criminal offence. Extradition is based on treaty arrangements between the UK and other states and is brought into effect through the Extradition Act 2003; within the EU the European Arrest Warrant applies.

9.8.2 **Real risk of a violation of Article 2 or 3 in the receiving state**

The fundamental nature of Articles 2 and 3 means that it is a violation of the Convention to deport, extradite, or otherwise remove a person to a country in which there is a 'real risk' that they might be killed, tortured, or suffer other ill-treatment prohibited by Articles 2 and 3. This applies even though the receiving country is not a member of the Council of Europe. The principle was first developed in *Soering* v *United Kingdom* (1989) 11 EHRR 439. It was held that the proposed extradition of a West German national to the United States to face a murder charge would be a violation of Article 3. If he was sentenced to death, the intensity and duration of suffering associated with being on 'death row' was such that it crossed the Article 3 threshold of severity. The violation stems not from actions of the United States (which is not a signatory to the Convention) but from actions by the United Kingdom in complying with the extradition request.

CASE CLOSE-UP

Chahal v United Kingdom (1997) 23 EHRR 413

Chahal was an Indian citizen resident in the United Kingdom. He was politically involved in the movement for a separate Sikh state in Indian Punjab and was suspected by UK authorities of involvement in terrorism in India and violence in the United Kingdom. The Home Secretary sought to deport him back to India on public interest grounds. The ECtHR found, on the facts (particularly Amnesty International reports), that there was a real risk that Chahal would suffer torture at the hands of Punjab security forces and others and that deportation would, therefore, violate Article 3.

In coming to this decision the Court established a number of important general principles:

- States have the right to control the entry, residence, and expulsion of aliens (para 73).

- However, the right must be exercised in full recognition of the absolute and fundamental requirements of Article 3.

- Under Article 3 there was an unqualified duty on states not to remove a person who would face 'a real risk of being subjected to treatment contrary to Article 3 in the receiving country' (para 74).

- The obligation is absolute in the sense that it applies where the risk of torture etc. is 'real'. There is no balance to be struck between the public interest served by the removal and the degree of likelihood that the real risk will materialise (para 76): 'the national interests of the State could not be invoked to override the interests of the individual where substantial grounds had been shown for believing that he would be subjected to ill-treatment if expelled' (para 78).

Under Protocol 13, there is an absolute ban on capital punishment (at the time of *Soering* the death penalty was an exception to the ban on intentional killing in Article 2). This means that it is a breach of the Convention to extradite (or deport or remove) someone to a country in which there are 'substantial grounds' for believing there is a 'real risk' of the death penalty. It is a direct breach of Article 2 and also a breach of Article 3 based on the 'intense psychological suffering' inevitably experienced (confirmed by a Grand Chamber in *Al-Nashiri* v *Poland* [2015] 60 EHRR 16, paras 576, 577, and 579; the court interpreted Articles 2 and 3 in the light of the ban of the death penalty in Protocol 6 now replaced by the absolute ban in Protocol 13).

CROSS REFERENCE

Life sentences are further discussed in Chapter 21, section 21.3.

Fear of or experience of lesser punishments is less likely to cause a breach of Article 3. The suffering must go beyond that inevitably associated with imprisonment. Whether there would be a breach will depend upon individual circumstances. In *Ahmad* v UK (2013) 56 EHRR 1, the 'highly restrictive' conditions in a particular Federal US prison did not cross the threshold of severity so as to prevent extradition. A real risk of a life sentence with no hope of parole might violate Article 3 unless some other procedure, such as executive clemency, was, even though unlikely, available (*R (Wellington)* v *Secretary of State for the Home Department* [2008] UKHL 72).

Article 3 has also been considered in relation to unintended suffering that the individual is likely to experience in the receiving country. The ECtHR has found a violation because of the poverty, destitution, official indifference, and danger likely to be experienced in the receiving country (e.g. *Sufi* v *United Kingdom* (2011 54 EHRR 209), in particular where this contradicts the duty owed to refugees (see *MSS* v *Belgium* (2011) 53 EHRR 28). But Article 3 is unlikely to be violated where someone who is ill is deported to a country with inferior health services and consequently may suffer and have a shortened life. In *N* v *Secretary of State for the Home Department* [2005] UKHL 31, the UKHL did not prevent the deportation of a woman suffering from Aids who would experience a quicker and more painful death in the receiving country than she would if allowed to remain in the UK. Only in 'death bed' cases might inadequate medical treatment in the receiving country justify stopping a deportation (see *D* v *United Kingdom* (1997) 24 EHRR 423). The principle here (which distinguishes the medical cases from *MSS*) is that Article 3 does not require states to provide medical care to persons not entitled to be in the country.

Deportation and other Articles

Deportation and other forms of removal raise issues under other Articles of the Convention. These are considered in the appropriate chapters. Thus the effect of family ties in the UK is considered in Chapter 15, section 15.10.7 (Article 8) and the issue of the fairness of a trial in the receiving country is considered in Chapter 12, section 12.16 (Article 6). Important issues respecting the deportation of terrorist suspects, including reliance on diplomatic assurances, are addressed in Chapter 26, section 26.7.3.

 ## Summary

- Article 3 is fundamental. It applies absolutely in the sense that torture and inhuman and degrading treatment or punishment is prohibited no matter how strong the public interests which purport to justify it.

- Treatment prohibited by Article 3 must, however, meet a threshold of severity. This threshold is context dependent, so what counts as a violation of Article 3 depends upon a range of factors.

- Torture is defined in terms of the deliberate infliction of severe suffering in order to obtain information or a confession, or to punish, or simply to abuse. Characteristically, it is imposed by state agents but the Convention does not require this.

- Inhuman and degrading treatment and punishment involves suffering that is less severe than torture and not necessarily for the purposes of torture.

- The jurisprudence of the ECtHR has extended the notion of 'treatment' for which the state is responsible into fields such as education, health care, prisons, and deportation. Suffering which meets the Article 3 threshold but which is not imposed deliberately and for which the state agents may not be the direct cause may still engage state responsibility and lead to violations of Article 3.

Self-test questions

1. What makes Article 3 an 'absolute' right?

2. Define 'torture' and 'inhuman treatment'; compare with the definition in UNCAT.

3. Define 'degrading treatment'.

4. In what circumstances, if at all, does an investigative duty, similar to that in Article 2, arise in respect of Article 3?

5. What made the ECtHR hold that the applicants were 'tortured' in *El Masri* and other 'extraordinary rendition' cases?

6. In what circumstances might Article 3 require states to support asylum seekers and other destitute people?

7. How can a state's duties towards medical patients under Article 3 be balanced with their duties under Article 2?

8. On what grounds can Article 3 be used to prevent the deportation of a person from the UK to another country which is not a signatory of the ECHR?

 For suggested approaches, please visit the Online Resource Centre.

? | Exam questions

1. Discuss and evaluate the requirements of Article 3 regarding a duty on states to provide for public safety in respect of the use by the police and the military of firearms in public places.

2. A suspected child kidnapper is detained by police. On good grounds they believe he has an accomplice who is holding the child and that the suspect knows where the child is. They believe the child to be in serious danger. The police subject the suspect to loud noise, he is denied food and sleep, and made to stand for hours on end in an uncomfortable posture.

    As a lawyer for the police, advise them on the principles that a court would take into account in considering whether there has been a violation of Article 3.

 For suggested approaches, please visit the Online Resource Centre.

☰ | Further reading

Articles dealing with issues under Article 3

Grief, N. and Addo, M. 'Does Article 3 ECHR Enshrine Absolute Rights?' (1998) 9(3) *European Journal of International Law* 510–524

Palmer, S. 'A Wrong Turning: Article 3 ECHR and Proportionality' (2006) 65(2) *Cambridge Law Journal* 438–451

On torture

Articles in [2006] 2 *EHRLR* (special issue on torture)

Evans, M.D. and Morgan, R. *Preventing Torture* (1998) Oxford: OUP, especially Chapters 1 and 2

Sands, P. *Lawless World* (2005) London: Penguin, Chapter V

Wadham, J. 'Rendition, Detention and Torture in Europe: territorial responsibility and the right to truth' (2014) 5 *EHRLR* 519–526

10

Article 4: prohibition of slavery and forced labour

LEARNING OBJECTIVES

● The absolute ban on 'slavery' and 'servitude' (Article 4(1)).

● The prohibition of 'forced or compulsory labour' (Article 4(2)).

● Exceptions to the prohibition on forced or compulsory labour in respect of various forms of work that people may be required to do (Article 4(3)).

Article 4 Prohibition of slavery and forced labour

(1) No one shall be held in slavery or servitude.

(2) No one shall be required to perform forced or compulsory labour.

(3) For the purpose of this article the term 'forced or compulsory labour' shall not include:

   (a) any work required to be done in the ordinary course of detention imposed according to the provisions of Article 5 of this Convention or during conditional release from such detention;

   (b) any service of a military character or, in case of conscientious objectors in countries where they are recognised, service exacted instead of compulsory military service;

   (c) any service exacted in case of an emergency or calamity threatening the life or well-being of the community;

   (d) any work or service which forms part of normal civic obligations.

Introduction

In a way, 'slavery' can no longer exist—it means the legal ownership of a person by another with all the freedoms the owner enjoys over his or her property—of buying and selling, using, and destroying. In this strictly legal sense there are few, if any, slaves left in the world because slavery is illegal under most, if not all, legal systems. But that is not the point. Millions of men, women, and children throughout the world are treated like slaves or reduced in all but name to the condition of slavery. Anti-Slavery International defines slavery in terms of working under threat and coercion, being 'controlled' by abuse or threatened abuse, being treated as a commodity, and being physically restrained in various ways. In this sense slavery is as great a problem throughout the world as it ever was. In the UK and Europe the focus is on 'modern slavery' and, in particular, the business of trafficking men, women, and children into Europe to, amongst other things, provide cheap manual labour, service the sex trade, and perform the duties of domestic servants; and to do so under oppressive conditions of subordination and discrimination. This has become a major concern of governments internationally which, in the UK, has culminated in the Modern Slavery Act 2015. Human trafficking is likely to be a form of servitude or forced or compulsory labour, and therefore within the reach of Article 4. But the Article is not specific about the laws and remedies necessary to deal with the problem. These have been addressed by a range of other international instruments dealing with the matter. But Article 4 is one of the foundations on which this law of modern slavery has been built.

 BIGGER PICTURE

See the website of Anti-Slavery International http://www.antislavery.org/

10.1 The ban on slavery and servitude

10.1.1 The illegality of slavery

Slavery in Britain, in the sense of a claim by one person to have absolute control over the life of another, seems to have been illegal at common law since at least the sixteenth century. However, where the law of other countries, including British colonies, permitted slavery, English law would uphold contractual and property rights (for example, between buyer and seller of slaves). The rights of the master over the slave, once in England, were a different matter. The famous words, 'the air of England is too pure for a slave to breath' may have originated in a decision of the Court of Star Chamber in the time of Elizabeth I in which the claim of a slave owner to beat his Russian slave with impunity was denied (see *Oxford Dictionary of Quotations*, 4th edn (1992) Oxford: OUP, p 17; Sedley J. 'Human Rights: A Twenty-First Century Agenda' [1995] *Public Law* (Autumn) 386–400, 392–393).

Somerset's 1772 case was understood to confirm that slavery in England was illegal (exactly what Lord Mansfield said or meant remains unclear).

 CASE CLOSE-UP

***Somerset* v *Stewart* (1772) Lofft 1; 98 ER 499**

The court was concerned with the liberty of a runaway slave (James Somerset), who had been recaptured and was being held on board ship in London awaiting transport to Jamaica. Lord Mansfield ordered his release. No clear rule of law permitted the detention of Somerset and, because slavery was 'so odious that nothing can be suffered to support it but positive law', the detention was illegal and his release was ordered.

But, as the quotation makes clear, slavery can still be legal if expressly allowed by 'positive law' (definite rules of law such as are laid down in statute). Slavery in the West Indian colonies was recognised by English courts who denied, for example, that the presence of a slave in England meant that he or she remained free on returning to their home country (see *The Slave Grace* (1827) 2 St Tr (NS) 273). It was up to nation states and, later, the international community, to make slavery illegal by 'positive law'. Important dates include:

- 1807—Parliament made British involvement in the slave trade illegal.
- 1833—slavery in the British colonies ended.
- 1863—ending of slavery of African-Americans in the United States by constitutional amendment after the Civil War.
- Second half of the nineteenth century—increasingly, European courts would free slaves brought within their jurisdiction and bilateral treaties between states were made aimed at suppression of the slave trade.
- 1885—the Treaty of Berlin made the slave trade illegal at international law.
- 1926—the Slavery Convention committed the international community to 'prevent and suppress the slave trade' and 'to bring about, progressively and as soon as possible, the complete abolition of slavery in all its forms'.
- 1936–45—the use of slave labour under the Nazi and Japanese dictatorships (Russian also) before and during the Second World War was a spur to further international action. In 1953 the Slavery Convention was extended to seek the abolition of 'practices similar to slavery' such as serfdom and debt bondage.

10.1.2 The Prohibition of Slavery and Servitude, Article 4(1)

Slavery and servitude are not defined in the Convention.

Slavery

In *Siliadin v France* (2006) 43 EHRR 16, the European Court of Human Rights (ECtHR) accepted the 'classic' definition of slavery found in the 1926 Convention:

> Slavery is the status or condition of a person over whom any or all of the powers attaching to the right of ownership are exercised.

> (Article 1(1))

In the strict sense, based on legally recognised ownership, slavery is not found in Europe and is unlikely to reappear. This is not to deny that trafficking of men, women, and children into Europe and the UK takes place and that such persons may be horribly exploited in slave-like ways. This issue, in relation to Article 4, is discussed later.

Servitude

Unlike 'slavery', 'servitude' does not imply ownership. In *Van Droogenbroeck v Belgium* (1982) 4 EHRR 443, the Commission of Human Rights identified the central point of servitude as including 'the obligation on the part of the "serf" to live on another's property and the impossibility of changing his condition'.

The utility of such a concept, in dealing with modern conditions of trafficking and exploitation, depends upon a realistic rather than legal understanding of the nature of the 'obligation' a person is under. Work is 'servitude' if it is imposed on another in a way that involves a 'particularly serious . . . violation of freedom' (*Van Droogenbroeck*, para 58). Under Article 4(3), as discussed in section 10.3, it is acceptable under the ECHR to require work from prisoners, soldiers, and others. But such work must be 'normal' in the context. If the work is normal it is unlikely to be servitude: see *W, X, Y and Z* v *United Kingdom* App 3435/67, Commission decision of 19 July 1968 (military service) and *Van Droogenbroeck* v *Belgium* (1982) 4 EHRR 443 (prison work).

10.2 Forced or compulsory labour, Article 4(2)

The concept of forced or compulsory labour was discussed by the ECtHR in *Van der Mussele* v *Belgium*.

CASE CLOSE-UP

Van der Mussele v *Belgium* (1984) 6 EHRR 163

The Belgium legal profession, putting into effect requirements of Belgian law for a form of legal aid, required some trainees (pupil 'avocats') to act for poor clients without payment. The ECtHR held that there was not a violation of Article 4. The obligation on trainees had to be considered in context: the trainee gained the valuable right of membership of the profession with exclusive rights of audience in the courts; the required work enabled the trainee to add to his or her experience and professional reputation. Given also that the trainees had opportunities for paid work, the obligation was a proportionate requirement imposed on those who were voluntarily seeking professional membership.

The ECtHR took as its starting point the definition of forced labour in the International Labour Organization Convention of 1930:

> all work or service which is exacted from any person under the menace of any penalty and for which he has not offered himself voluntarily.

The ECtHR went on to refine the meaning of these terms for the purposes of Article 4 ECHR.

- 'Labour' means all kinds of work or service and is not confined to physical work (para 33).
- 'Forced' implies a 'physical or mental constraint' (para 34).
- 'Compulsory' means 'work exacted . . . under the menace of a penalty' and 'performed against the will of the person concerned'. Labour is not 'compulsory' just because it is based on a contract freely entered into and breach of the contract would have legal consequences.

- Voluntary. The ECtHR does not accept that the fact that a person has consented to the obligation necessarily makes it voluntary. *Van der Mussele* illustrates the situation where an organisation has monopolistic control over the provision of a benefit (e.g. a professional body controlling entry to a profession) and the body imposes costs and burdens on a person seeking the benefit. The fact that the person, after weighing the advantages against the burdens, chooses to obtain the benefit and accept the burden, does not mean that the burden is accepted voluntarily: in the Court's view there is no real choice (para 36).

- Need not be 'unjust' etc. In *Van der Mussele* the ECtHR did not directly endorse the Commission's view that forced or compulsory labour needed to be 'unjust', 'oppressive', 'an avoidable hardship', 'needlessly distressing', or 'somewhat harassing' (para 37) (see *Iversen* v *Norway* (as *X* v *Austria*) App 1452/62, Commission decision of 18 December 1963).

In *Van der Mussele* the ECtHR accepted that there is no simple test for forced or compulsory labour. Its existence depends on a range of circumstances, in particular:

- the nature of the work involved;
- the existence of a penalty or of a burden comparable to a penalty;
- the fact of consent (lack of consent does not, alone, mean the labour was forced or compelled);
- the benefits that may accrue to the individual;
- the degree of oppression and hardship involved; and
- the general circumstances.

The legal test is proportionality: whether, in the circumstances, the burden is excessive and disproportionate in relation to any benefit or advantage enjoyed (see *Van der Mussele*, para 38). Article 4(3) (discussed at section 10.3) stipulates that certain obligations to work are not 'forced or compulsory labour'. The principles underlying these exemptions help the Court in defining identifying forced labour and servitude and distinguishing this from other kinds of work which, for various reasons people are, reasonably, required to do. In *Reilly* v *Secretary of State for Work and Pensions* [2013] UKSC 68, the UKSC identified some element of exploitation as going to the heart of forced labour (see section 10.4).

10.3 Article 4(3) exclusions

Article 4(3) expressly excludes from 'forced or compulsory labour' certain work done under conditions of compulsion. In particular:

- **Prisoners.** Work that is imposed upon prisoners as part of their punishment or as part of a scheme of rehabilitation. It must be 'ordinary', part of normal, lawful, imprisonment. What is normal prison work will depend upon different national customs and develop over time. Thus working unpaid for private companies was considered normal and so not a violation of Article 4 in the late 1960s (*21 Detained Persons* v *Germany* App 3134/67, Commission decision of 6 April 1968). In *Stummer* v *Austria* (2012) 54 EHRR 11, it was held that, in the early twenty-first century, states were not required to allow prison work to count towards entitlement to the old age pension.

  In *R* v *Clarke* [2008] EWCA Crim 893, such punishment was said to be justified under Article 4(3)(a).

▶ **CROSS REFERENCE**
Conscientious objection
may involve Article 9 and
is discussed in Chapter 16,
section 16.4.6.

- **Military service.** Compulsory military service ('conscription') is still found in some European states. But conscripts undertaking the normal demands of military life are not, thereby, subject to forced labour or servitude (*W, X, Y, Z* v *United Kingdom* App 3435/67, admissibility decision of 19 July 1968). If, however, conscripts were subject to burdens of work unlike those normally expected of military service, there could be a violation of Article 4(2), or of Article 4(1) if abnormal work so restricted freedom that it amounted to servitude.

  Article 4 does not require states to grant rights of conscientious objection to citizens. If, however, conscientious objection to military conscription is recognised by law, any alternative service that may be required cannot be regarded as forced or compulsory labour unless wholly disproportionate and unusual in its demands, or sufficiently oppressive to count as servitude.

- **Emergency service.** The principle of social solidarity means that proportionate, though compulsory, demands on individuals can be made as a means of dealing with 'an emergency or calamity threatening the life or well-being of the community', Article 4(3)(c). *Iversen* v *Norway* (as *X* v *Austria*) App 1452/62, Commission decision of 18 December 1963, involved dentists who were required to work in the public dental service in order to deal with a crisis shortage of dentists in parts of Norway. The Commission declared the case to be inadmissible—there was no arguable breach of Article 4.

- **Normal civic obligations.** On the principle of 'solidarity', Article 4(3)(d) exempts compulsory work which is part of 'normal civic obligations' from being forced or compulsory labour. What counts as a 'normal' civic obligation will depend on the circumstances and the context. Such obligations may be required in order for society, through the state, to discharge its duties to the least well-off and those in need: *Van Mussele* and *Iversen* (discussed earlier) concerned, respectively, legal aid and free dentistry. Compulsory jury service is a normal civic obligation (*Adami* v *Malta* (2007) 44 EHRR 3). In the United Kingdom, under the HRA, it has been held that procedures and penalties connected with the payment of taxes do not disclose a violation of Article 4 (*Murat* v *Inland Revenue Commissioners* [2004] EWHC 3123).

10.4 Identifying forced labour

The interpretation of Article 4 indicates, therefore, that mere compulsion is not enough. There must be the added element of burdens that are disproportionate. The principles underlying the Article 4(3) exclusions help to identify what is or is not a disproportionate obligation to work. These principles are said to be the 'general interest, social solidarity and what is in the normal or ordinary course of affairs' (see *Van der Mussele*, para 38). They embody the sense that, in some circumstances, an obligation to work can be a reasonable expression of social membership.

This approach was adopted, under the HRA, by the UKSC in *Reilly* v *Secretary of State for Work and Pensions* [2013] UKSC 68. Here the UKSC held that requiring a person receiving Job Seeker's Allowance to do unpaid work experience as a condition for receiving the benefit, did not breach Article 4. Interpreting *Van der Mussele* (and appearing to follow the Commission's view), the UKSC held that the essence of forced labour was 'exploitation'.

Likewise Article 4(2) is unlikely to be relevant in respect of claims about poor conditions for those working under normal contracts of employment in the United Kingdom. Such matters are more likely to raise issues under health and safety and employment protection legislation (including from the European Union); or be dealt with by trade unions and collective bargaining. Nor does non-payment of lawfully due wages engage Article 4 (*Vorana* v *Ukraine* App 44372/02, judgment of 9 November 2006).

10.5 Modern slavery

As a consequence of the global economy trafficking in men, women, and children is widespread. Victims may be unlawfully (or even lawfully) brought into the country and then subjected to slave-like use as manual labourers, sex workers, domestic servants, etc. It is clear that these people may be victims of servitude or forced labour in breach of Article 4.

States have positive duties under Article 4 to ensure that there are adequate criminal penalties and civil remedies to punish those guilty or practices in breach of Article 4 (*Siliadin*, mentioned earlier, para 89). In *Allen* v *Hounga* [2014] UKSC 47, for instance, the UKSC refused to allow an employer to rely on the fact that the employee was unlawfully in the country in order to defeat the employee's sex discrimination case. The employee had probably been trafficked and Article 4 required her to have a remedy.

The issue of trafficking is a global and complex issue which has been the subject of a number of specific, focused, international conventions which impose particular positive obligations on states. The United Nations, the Council of Europe, and the European Union have produced such agreements (see the Further reading section at the end of this chapter).

On the basis of these and other instruments, and compatibly with Article 4, the Modern Slavery Act 2015 has been enacted in the United Kingdom. It is a major piece of legislation which is now the framework for seeking to combat trafficking in the UK. Amongst its provisions are:

- the creation of a range of criminal offences including slavery, servitude, and forced or compulsory labour;
- giving courts a range of powers to make various prevention orders;
- creating the office of Independent Anti-Slavery Commissioner;
- providing for the protection of victims in various ways.

The success of this important piece of legislation remains to be seen.

 Summary

- Article 4 requires a total ban on slavery and servitude.
- There is also a total ban on forced or compulsory labour, but the meaning of these two terms excludes any work a person is legally obliged to do as a lawful prisoner, as a member of the armed forces, to assist in an emergency, or as part of established civic obligations, so long as such work is normal in the context.

? Self-test questions

1. What if anything was decided by 'Somersett's case'?

2. Give examples of two types of compulsory labour that is not 'forced' labour.

3. Compare the ECtHR's definition of slavery with that of Anti-Slavery International.

 For suggested approaches, please visit the Online Resource Centre.

? Exam questions

1. How have the Commission and ECtHR defined 'slavery', 'servitude', and 'forced or compulsory labour'? Are these concepts sufficient to be the legal basis for dealing with the exploitation of men, women, and children associated with 'people trafficking' in the twenty-first century?

2. Prepare a briefing note for civil servants, police, and social workers on the way in which the Modern Slavery Act 2015 helps to fulfil the UK's obligations under Article 4 (you are not required to explore all the provisions of the Act).

 For suggested approaches, please visit the Online Resource Centre.

☰ Further reading

The UN and Council of Europe conventions on people trafficking are:

The Protocol to Suppress and Punish Trafficking in Persons Especially Women and Children (the UN Convention against Transnational Organized Crime)

The Council of Europe Convention on Action against Trafficking in Human Beings (in force in the UK from 1 April 2009)

European Union Directive on preventing and combating trafficking in human beings (Directive 2011/36/EU.

General texts

Lester, A., Pannick, D., and Herberg, J. (see Preface) Chapter 4, Article 4

11 Article 5: right to liberty and security

Article 5 Right to liberty and security

(1) Everyone has the right to liberty and security of person. No one shall be deprived of his liberty save in the following cases and in accordance with a procedure prescribed by law:

   (a) the lawful detention of a person after conviction by a competent court;

   (b) the lawful arrest or detention of a person for non-compliance with the lawful order of a court or in order to secure the fulfilment of any obligation prescribed by law;

   (c) the lawful arrest or detention of a person effected for the purpose of bringing him before the competent legal authority on reasonable suspicion of having committed an offence or when it is reasonably considered necessary to prevent his committing an offence or fleeing after having done so;

   (d) the detention of a minor by lawful order for the purpose of educational supervision or his lawful detention for the purpose of bringing him before the competent legal authority;

   (e) the lawful detention of persons for the prevention of the spreading of infectious diseases, of persons of unsound mind, alcoholics or drug addicts or vagrants;

   (f) the lawful arrest or detention of a person to prevent his effecting unauthorised entry into the country or of a person against whom action is being taken with a view to deportation or extradition.

(2) Everyone who is arrested shall be informed promptly, in a language which he understands, of the reasons for his arrest and of any charge against him.

(3) Everyone arrested or detained in accordance with the provisions of paragraph 1(c) of this article shall be brought promptly before a judge or other officer authorised by law

to exercise judicial power and shall be entitled to trial within a reasonable time or to release pending trial. Release may be conditioned by guarantees to appear for trial.

(4) Everyone who is deprived of his liberty by arrest or detention shall be entitled to take proceedings by which the lawfulness of his detention shall be decided speedily by a court and his release ordered if the detention is not lawful.

(5) Everyone who has been the victim of arrest or detention in contravention of the provisions of this article shall have an enforceable right to compensation.

Introduction

Article 5 deals with freedom of the person, with 'liberty' in the sense of not to be under the direct physical control of another. As the European Court of Human Rights (ECtHR) said in *Engel* v *The Netherlands* (1979–80) 1 EHRR 647, para 58, Article 5 deals with 'individual liberty in its classic sense, that is to say the physical liberty of the person'. It is not to do with broader ideas of liberty, such as the sense of personal autonomy and the lack of psychological or social subordination.

The core examples of restriction of liberty in this sense are arrest and detention by the police, imprisonment after conviction, detention of the mentally ill in hospitals, and detention of foreigners in the context of immigration and asylum. Article 5 expressly allows the state to take away liberty in these contexts. However, because its focus is on the fact of the deprivation of liberty only, the impact of Article 5 can seem quite limited. Thus, in the context of the continuing struggle against terrorism, Article 5 has stopped the government in the UK from imprisoning terrorist suspects on suspicion in order to prevent them from committing outrages. It does not, however, apply to Terrorist Prevention and Investigation Measures (TPIMs) since these, as a matter of law, must not involve depriving a person of his or her liberty. Nevertheless TPIMs can have a significant and negative impact on an individual's freedom in the sense of the ability to live life as he or she wants (the matter is also discussed in Chapter 23).

Likewise, in the context of policing, the power of stop and search has been widely resented and, perhaps, improperly used, especially against young black males. Again, although the person stopped and searched may well feel that their liberty has been restricted, Article 5 tends not to apply because of the relatively short time for which a person is stopped.

There is currently great concern at the detention of persons who are going to be deported. These may include some very vulnerable and frightened people such as victims of traffickers. Indeed there is an on-going campaign aimed at the closure of one such centre—Yarl's Wood. But, again, detention in this context is unlikely to raise questions under Article 5 since deportation is one of the reasons which Article 5 allows for depriving people of their liberty.

Despite these issues, Article 5 has great significance. It prevents the state from taking away liberty in situations not allowed for by its text. Above all, it requires the state to act in non-arbitrary ways, according to law, and under independent and effective supervision by courts or other bodies with a judicial character. Thus decisions to release murderers on licence from prison must be taken by the Parole Board which is independent of the Home Secretary. Likewise, people detained in mental hospitals must have access to an independent tribunal which can release them if the grounds for detaining them no longer exist. This fundamental principle, that liberty, its loss, and its being regained, is a judicial matter, a matter of law and not of policy, is at the heart of Article 5.

11.1 The right to liberty

11.1.1 The right to liberty and the law of England and Wales

The importance of physical liberty has been long recognised in English law. Lord Bingham has referred to:

> the long libertarian tradition of English law, dating back to chapter 39 of Magna Carta 1215, given effect in the ancient remedy of habeas corpus, declared in the Petition of Right 1628, upheld in a series of landmark decisions down the centuries and embodied in the substance and procedure of the law to our own day.

(A v Secretary of State for the Home Department [2004] UKHL 56, para 36)

Article 5 can be enforced directly against a public authority in the UK (e.g. the Home Secretary or a prison governor) by using section 7 Human Rights Act 1998 (HRA). But this is in addition to a number of long-standing remedies, protecting liberty, already recognised in the law of England and Wales (and also, differently, in Scotland and Northern Ireland). Many Acts of Parliament permit restrictions on liberty (e.g. the Police and Criminal Evidence Act 1984); under section 3 HRA, such Acts must be interpreted, as far as possible, for compatibility with Article 5. In English law the right to liberty can be given effect in various ways such as:

- *Habeas corpus.* By means of the writ a person alleging they have been unlawfully detained can seek from the High Court an order for their immediate release by whoever is detaining them. The Court has no discretion and must issue the writ if it finds that the detention is unlawful. The writ can be issued against state agents such as the police or immigration officers as well as private parties. Though developed by the judges, the availability of the writ has been strengthened by Habeas Corpus Acts dating back to 1679.

- Courts, tribunals, and judicial review. *Habeas corpus* tends to be a back-stop remedy. It is rarely going to be appropriate where a person is detained on the basis of detailed rules in an Act of Parliament (such as being detained by the police under the Police and Criminal Evidence Act 1984 (PACE 1984), or in a mental hospital under the Mental Health Act 1983). In such contexts legal challenge is most likely to be based, first, on the procedures for challenge provided for in the Act and, second, by a judicial review challenge to the legality of the decisions made by the officials or tribunal involved. There is a legal presumption in favour of liberty so any intention by Parliament that a statute will allow a deprivation of liberty must be clear and unambiguous (*R (Kelly)* v *Secretary of State for Justice* [2008] EWCA Civ 177, para 26).

- A civil action for damages in the tort of false imprisonment. The claimant needs to prove that he or she was directly and intentionally imprisoned by the defendant; the tort is proved unless the defendant can show lawful justification. There is no need to prove other loss (*Lumba* v *Secretary of State for the Home Department* [2012] UKSC 12, paras 64–65). A justified false imprisonment cannot also be a violation of Article 5, and vice versa (*Austin* v *Metropolitan Police Commissioner* [2009] UKHL 5).

CROSS REFERENCE

Section 7 HRA is discussed in Chapter 5, section 5.4.

CROSS REFERENCE

Judicial review is outlined in Chapter 5, section 5.2.1.

> CROSS REFERENCE

On the validity of
incompatible statutes see
Chapter 4, section 4.4.2.

A key point is that courts in England and Wales cannot order release or award damages if the deprivation of liberty is clearly permitted by the law. Under the HRA, if the clear policy of legislation is to permit detention on grounds which are incompatible with Article 5, then nothing in the Act or *habeas corpus* or any of the other remedies outlined earlier will require a person's release. An example is the detention without trial of foreign terrorist suspects between 2001 and 2005. The House of Lords declared that this was incompatible with Article 5 but had no power to order release because the detention was clearly allowed for by legislation (see Chapter 26, section 26.3.2 and Chapter 7, section 7.2.5).

11.2 Deprivation of liberty

11.2.1 Deprivation of liberty or restriction on movement

The general aim of Article 5 is to provide a general guarantee against the arbitrary (unprincipled or oppressive) interference with liberty (see *Creanga* v *Romania* (2013) 56 EHRR 11, para 84 for a general summary, and section 11.3).

This general guarantee underlies the specific requirements of Article 5 and these (the requirements of Article 5(1)(a)–(f) and Article 5(2)–(5)) apply only when there has been a 'deprivation of liberty'. This is a legal term. Not all restrictions imposed by the state on individuals' movements are within the ambit of Article 5. 'Deprivation of liberty', in Article 5, needs to be distinguished from general restrictions on movement and interferences with normal life—such as when a person is banned from entering a geographically defined area but whose freedom of movement is otherwise not restricted. 'Restrictions on movement' which are not 'deprivations of liberty' are within the ambit of Article 2(1) of Protocol 4 ECHR (freedom of movement). Since the United Kingdom has signed but not ratified this Protocol, it is not in Schedule 1 HRA. In any case, Article 2(3) of the Protocol allows proportionate restrictions on movement where the state can show these are necessary.

Though imprisonment is the obvious example of a deprivation of liberty, the ECtHR has made it clear that the term has a wider meaning. The existence of a deprivation of liberty is a matter of judgment based on all the circumstances. The leading case on the distinction between deprivation of liberty and restrictions on movement is *Guzzardi* v *Italy* (1980) 3 EHRR 333.

 CASE CLOSE-UP

***Guzzardi* v *Italy* (1981) 3 EHRR 333**

A mafiosi suspect was required to live and be supervised in a small village on a small island off Sardinia. The village had an area of about 2.5 square kilometres. The ECtHR held that Article 5 was engaged. A range of factors, such as being under a curfew, being unable to mingle with the bulk of the island's population and being subject to punishment for breach of these and other conditions were, when taken together, sufficient to amount to a deprivation of liberty.

The ECtHR held (in paras 93 and 95) that:

- 'The difference between deprivation of and restriction upon liberty is nonetheless merely one of degree of intensity, and not one of nature or substance'.

- Deprivation of liberty is not confined to 'classic detention in prison' but may take 'numerous other forms' which cannot be identified in abstract.

- The Court is required to take 'account . . . of the whole range of criteria such as the type, duration, effects and manner of implementation of the measure in question' in determining whether or not a 'deprivation of liberty' has occurred. (In the case of the 'mentally disordered', placed in institutions, deprivation of liberty may also depend on whether there has been 'valid consent'—*Stanev* v *Bulgaria* (2012) 55 EHRR 22, 115–117.

 BIGGER PICTURE

See also *Engel* v *Netherlands* (1979–80) 1 EHRR 647 where the ECtHR distinguished between military punishments which involved a deprivation of liberty and those which did not.

The *Guzzardi* approach has been broadly adopted by the UK courts. But the decisive principle is not entirely clear. This is not surprising, as the ECtHR said in *Stanev*, para 115, distinguishing deprivations of liberty from mere restrictions on movement is 'no easy task' and in difficult cases may amount to 'pure opinion'. Nevertheless the judgment has to be made since Article 5 depends upon it.

In *JJ* v *Secretary of State for the Home Department* [2007] UKHL 45, the UKHL had to decide whether a control order which imposed 18 hours house arrest on a terrorist suspect and a whole range of other restrictions on the way he could live, deprived him of his liberty. A majority (3–2) held that there had been a deprivation of liberty.

- All agreed that there had to be a core element of physical confinement. But disagreed on its relative importance. Lord Brown, for the majority, thought that this needed to be a minimum of 16 hours—without at least that, there would be no deprivation (though this rule-based approach has not been followed).

- Lord Bingham, for the majority, suggested that there could be a deprivation of liberty where the person was left in a situation similar to a prisoner in an open prison.

- Lady Hale held that where there are severe restrictions on ordinary life, in addition to the core element of confinement, there can be a deprivation of liberty.

- The two dissenters (Lords Carswell and Hoffmann) argued that confinement, being in a prison-like situation, was the defining principle. Here JJ had six hours of freedom so he was not in a prison-like situation and no amount of restrictions on normal life applying to those six hours could alter the fact that he was not deprived of his liberty.

> **CROSS REFERENCE**
> See Chapter 26 for Terrorism Prevention and Investigation orders.

It is clear, therefore, that a person can be deprived or his or her liberty who is not in prison. For such a person there has to be a significant element of physical confinement coupled with significant restrictions on the life that can be lived when not confined.

In *Austin* v *Commissioner of Police of the Metropolis* (2009) UKHL 5 (where police had confined, 'kettled', some political demonstrators in order to control them and prevent outbreaks of violence), the House of Lords suggested that whether there has been a deprivation of liberty may depend, not on the circumstances in which people find themselves, but on the purpose for which the confinement takes place. This 'purposive' approach was rejected by the ECtHR in *Austin v United Kingdom* (2012) 55 EHRR 14. The person's circumstances remain the fundamental issue. Nevertheless, the courts can take into account the 'type' of measure imposed and its 'manner of implementation'. 'Kettling', such as occurred in Austin, could be a type of measure which, if implemented proportionately, would not amount to a deprivation of liberty.

Deprivation of liberty, therefore, involves focusing on the circumstances that people are placed in rather than the purpose or intention behind their treatment. *Cheshire West v P* [2014] UKSC 14, involved the difficult problem of highly vulnerable people with little mental capacity to choose for themselves, who are looked after in various care situations which, though very supportive and caring, nevertheless involve a considerable, if not constant, degree of control and supervision. The majority agreed that the key test was whether the person is 'under continuous supervision and control and was not free to leave' (para 49 following *HL v United Kingdom* (2005) 40 EHRR 761, para 91). If so they were 'deprived of their liberty' (and certain regulations therefore came into effect, see section 11.4.5) even if they happily complied with the control exercised over them and despite the fact that the purpose of the control was to care for them and allow them the best kind of life available. The dissenters took the view that to talk about deprivation of liberty in the context of caring for the vulnerable in care homes or foster homes was an unjustified extension of the term.

 DISCUSSION TOPIC

Should the United Kingdom ratify Protocol 4. If it did so, would it make any difference? Note that, in England, persons can be subject to restrictions on their ability to live a normal life (such as ASBOs or football banning orders).

11.2.2 **Voluntary detention**

Persons who choose to give themselves into the hands of the authorities or who choose to stay under confinement when they are technically free to leave, may still enjoy the protection of Article 5, especially if there are significant non-voluntary aspects to their circumstances.

> **CROSS REFERENCE**
>
> As with the foreign terrorist suspects in *A* v *Secretary of State for the Home Department* [2004] UKHL 56—see Chapter 26, section 26.3.2 and Chapter 7, section 7.2.5.

The ECtHR has recognised that 'temporary distress or misery' may cause a person to give themselves up to the authorities but that the importance of the right to liberty is such that a detained person should not lose the protection of Article 5 simply because he or she voluntarily surrendered to the authorities (see the 'vagrants' case, *De Wilde, Ooms and Versyp v Belgium* (1979–80) 1 EHRR 373).

The point is particularly important in respect of asylum seekers. They should not (and do not) lose the protection of Article 5 just because they are free to accept the risk of leaving the host country. In *Amuur* v *France* (1996) 22 EHRR 533, the applicants were kept in the transit lounge of an airport for 20 days whilst their application for asylum was being considered. They were free to leave France but not to enter the country during that period. The ECtHR held that they had suffered a deprivation of liberty under Article 5.

11.3 'Procedure prescribed by law': non-arbitrariness

Time and again the ECtHR has emphasised that the point of Article 5 is to ensure that any 'deprivation of liberty' must not be arbitrary and a court dealing with detention must satisfy itself that this is so. The general principles are summarised in *Saadi* v *United Kingdom* (2008) 47 EHRR 17, where a Grand Chamber, in paras 67–70, made it clear that, whilst there is no definitive list of what makes a decision 'arbitrary', the case law indicates a number of factors.

11.3.1 **Lawfulness**

A main protection from 'arbitrariness' is the requirement that any deprivation of liberty must be 'in accordance with a procedure prescribed by law'.

The authorities (police, etc.) need to act lawfully in terms of their own national law. The ECtHR normally accepts the national courts' interpretations of the national law. If there is compelling evidence that a deprivation of liberty was not consistent with national law or lacked the continuing authority of the national law, the Court will find a violation. For example, the detention of a person for a psychiatric examination despite the absence of legal power to detain for that purpose in the national law violated Article 5 (*Kepenerov* v *Bulgaria* (2004) 38 EHRR 33).

But conformity with national law is not 'decisive'. The law authorising detention must also meet the Convention's concept of law: it must meet the standards of 'accessibility', 'certainty', and 'foreseeability' that are at the heart of the Convention concept of the rule of law and the avoidance of arbitrary power.

> **CROSS REFERENCE**
>
> The Convention concept of law is introduced and discussed in Chapter 6, section 6.1.

> It is therefore essential that the conditions for deprivation of liberty under domestic law be clearly defined and that the law itself be foreseeable in its application, so that it meets the standard of 'lawfulness' set by the Convention, a standard which requires that all law be sufficiently precise to allow the person—if need be, with appropriate advice—to foresee, to a degree that is reasonable in the circumstances, the consequences which a given action may entail.
>
> (*Jecius* v *Lithuania* (2002) 35 EHRR 16)

In *R (Lumba)* v *Secretary of State for the Home Department* [2011] UKSC 12, the claimants, on completion of a prison sentence, were due to be deported. They were detained on the basis of an unpublished policy which required the blanket detention of all such persons. This was inconsistent with the published policy, which required detention only in certain circumstances. The UKSC held that the detention was unlawful both at common law and for violating the 'prescribed by law' requirement of Article 5.

11.3.2 **Illegal acts by the authorities**

Arbitrariness is also found where the authorities detain people on a basis of dubious legality or a breach of good faith and so deny the persons involved the substantive and procedural rights that the law provides. For example, in *Conka* v *Belgium* (2002) 34 EHRR 54, the police persuaded a group of Slovakians of Romany origin to attend a police station in order to complete the formalities of their asylum application. In fact the Belgium authorities had turned down their application. They were then arrested and deported. The ECtHR held that there had been a violation of Article 5; they had been subject to an 'administrative ruse' and thereby treated in an arbitrary fashion.

11.3.3 **Purpose and conditions**

The deprivation of liberty must genuinely relate to one of the purposes listed in Article 5(1)(a)–(f), which are the only purposes for which the state may deprive a person of his or her liberty. Also, the conditions under which a person is detained must be governed by the purpose to be served (it would be wrong to detain a harmless mentally ill person in a maximum security prison, for example).

11.3.4 **Necessity**

Deprivation of liberty is so serious that, for most purposes, it can only be justified as a last resort where other, less severe, measures have been considered and rejected. (This does not apply when someone is detained with a view to their deportation, see Article 5(1)(f), below.)

11.3.5 **Records**

> **CROSS REFERENCE**
>
> Disappearances may engage Articles 2 and 3. For discussion see Chapter 8, section 8.2.1, proving responsibility.

The requirement that a deprivation of liberty must not be arbitrary and must be in accordance with a 'procedure prescribed by law' places a positive duty on states to ensure that all deprivations of liberty are properly acknowledged and that adequate records are kept. Adequate records assist states in their duty to conduct proper investigations into alleged disappearances. In *Cyprus v Turkey* (2002) 35 EHRR 30, the ECtHR held that the continuing refusal of Turkey to investigate alleged disappearances of men last seen in the custody of its troops following their invasion of Cyprus in 1974 (which, in 1992, had been held to be a violation of Article 5) was a further violation of Article 5.

11.3.6 **Legal supervision and an effective investigation**

Deprivations of liberty must be properly supervised by the national courts. This principle is enshrined in Article 5(3) and (4), and is discussed at sections 11.7 and 11.8. Linked to this is a procedural aspect which requires effective investigations of credible claims that Article 5 rights have been violated.

Q CASE CLOSE-UP

El Masri v Macedonia (2013) 57 EHRR 25

The 'unlawful rendition' cases (also discussed in Chapter 9) involved not only torture and inhuman treatment but also arbitrary detentions. El Masri was secretly detained without any legal authority and kept incommunicado by the Macedonian authorities acting in cooperation with the CIA. There was no judicial supervision of his detention or removal from the country. On his return to Macedonia the authorities there made no serious and independent attempt to investigate his credible allegations that his Article 5 rights had been breached. The ECtHR stressed the need for judicial supervision precisely to prevent the kind of abuses visited on El Masri. Furthermore, there is a procedural aspect to Article 5. Credible violations must be promptly and effectively investigated. This did not happen. There was a breach of both the substantive and procedural aspect of Article 5.

11.4 The purposes of lawful deprivation of liberty

Even if 'prescribed by law' a deprivation of liberty can only be compatible with the Convention if it is for one of the six purposes listed in Article 5(1)(a)–(e). These are exclusive; depriving a person of their liberty for some other purpose violates Article 5.

11.4.1 Article 5(1)(a)

> the lawful detention of a person after conviction by a competent court

Normal imprisonment following conviction for a criminal offence is a deprivation of liberty that does not violate Article 5. A court is 'competent' if it is able to provide the procedural protections of a fair trial. The lawfulness of the conviction is normally a matter for the national courts, though if the ECtHR finds that there has been a blatant disregard of the national law by the convicting court, it may find a violation of the Convention on that ground (see *Tsirlis* v *Greece* (1998) 25 EHRR 198, for example).

Release on appeal

A person who is convicted, imprisoned, and then released after a successful appeal has not thereby been a victim of a violation of Article 5 since all those stages are lawful. If, however, the ground of appeal is that the court had no legal jurisdiction to imprison, for example the person was imprisoned for an offence that did not carry a prison sentence as a possible punishment, then a violation of Article 5 can be argued.

The proportionality of the punishment

The 'detention' must be 'lawful'. Lawfulness includes the requirement that a period of imprisonment must be proportionate to the offence. Specifically, there needs to be a 'causal relationship' between the nature of the offence, the sentence passed, and the purpose for which a convicted person is actually kept in prison. In *Stafford* v *United Kingdom* (2002) 35 EHRR 32, for example, a convicted murderer was not released on licence for fear that he might commit non-violent offences such as theft and fraud. This violated Article 5 since there was no causal connection between Stafford's continued detention for fear of non-violent offences and the purpose of the original life sentence, which was a punishment for a murder, a violent offence.

11.4.2 Article 5(1)(b)

> non-compliance with the lawful order of a court or in order to secure the fulfilment of any obligation prescribed by law.

Non-compliance with the lawful order of a court

Article 5 also allows lawful deprivation of liberty for breach of a court order requiring certain behaviour or some event to occur. For example a court might order that a person pay a tax demand or require a person to undergo a blood test to establish paternity. If, under the national law, such orders can be enforced by the threat of prison (or some other form of deprivation of liberty) then, so long as any sentence is proportionate, enforcing the order will not be a violation of Article 5 (e.g. *Harkman* v *Estonia* App 2192/03 judgment of 11 July 2006). Where breaching a court order is itself a distinct offence (as, under English law, with the breaching of an Anti-Social Behaviour Order) then Article 5(1)(a) is engaged and recourse to Article 5(1)(b) is unnecessary. The person must have the opportunity to perform the order (e.g. *O.G.* v *Latvia* App 66095/09 judgment of 23 September 2014).

Secure the fulfilment of any obligation prescribed by law

The ECtHR has made it clear (e.g. in *Engel* v *The Netherlands* (1979–80) 1 EHRR 647, para 69) that this part of Article 5(1)(b) needs to be interpreted narrowly. Any national law which permits someone to be detained in order to obtain from them the performance of a legal duty must:

- relate to a 'specific and concrete' legal obligation and not be just a way of compelling general obedience to the law;
- have as its purpose the obtaining of the performance of the obligation and not the punishment of a person for failing to perform the obligation.

In *Ostendorf* v *Germany* App 15598/08, judgment of 7 March 2013, the ECtHR gave examples such as the duty to comply with a banning order or a statutory duty to give evidence. The case involved the detention of an alleged football hooligan. The Court accepted that detention was aimed at the fulfilment of a negative duty—not to organise a riot in respect of a particular match.

In most cases a deprivation of liberty should follow a deliberate or neglectful failure to perform the obligation. The person under the obligation should know of the duty and have had an opportunity to perform it in his or her own time. However, this is not an absolute requirement. In special circumstances the ECtHR has accepted the compatibility with Article 5(1)(b) of national laws which permit the detention of a person so that the obligation can be performed in the first place. Rules aimed at the prevention of terrorism provide such circumstances (as in *McVeigh et al* v *United Kingdom* (1983) 5 EHRR 71, see in particular, paras 188–196).

11.4.3 Article 5(1)(c)

> the lawful arrest or detention of a person effected for the purpose of bringing him before the competent legal authority on reasonable suspicion of having committed an offence or when it is reasonably considered necessary to prevent his committing an offence or fleeing after having done so.

Any legal system must permit its police force to arrest and detain those who are suspected of a crime. Equally important is that such powers are only exercised under careful legal control and that those who are so detained enjoy certain basic rights and protections reflecting the presumption of their innocence. Article 5(3), discussed at section 11.7, provides additional, express rights for persons arrested for the purposes of Article 5(1)(c).

'the lawful arrest . . .'

CROSS REFERENCE

Arrest under the law of England and Wales is generally thought compatible with Article 5(1)(c) and is discussed in Chapter 20, section 20.3.

Any arrest must be on the basis of the national law. The question of lawfulness is for the national courts in the first place but, as stated earlier, the ECtHR can review the national law and find a breach of the Convention if that law fails to meet the Convention standard of legality or fails to prevent arbitrary arrest.

Article 5(1)(c) contains three separate grounds for deprivation of liberty.

1. '. . . reasonable suspicion of having committed an offence . . .'

The person who is deprived of his or her liberty must be reasonably suspected of having committed an 'offence' under the state's domestic law. Classification of the matter as a crime under domestic law is an important indicator; however, even if a matter is not so classified it may, nevertheless, be accepted as an 'offence' for the purpose of Article 5(1)(c).

In *Brogan* v *United Kingdom* (1989) 11 EHRR 117, the applicants had been arrested on suspicion of 'terrorism' related to Northern Ireland. There is no offence of 'terrorism' as such; however, the term implies suspicion of criminal activities of various kinds and, in fact, the applicants, after being detained, had been questioned about particular offences. The ECtHR held that, in the circumstances, they had been arrested for an offence. This point is clearly relevant to the long periods of pre-charge detention allowed under the UK's anti-terrorism laws, which are discussed in Chapter 26.

In *Steel* v *United Kingdom* (1999) 28 EHRR 603, Steel was arrested (and detained for 44 hours) for a breach of the peace when she walked in front of a 'gun' during a grouse shoot and so prevented him from enjoying his lawful sport. Breach of the peace is not an offence. The facts to which it relates may be offences for which the person may be subsequently charged (Steel was charged under the section 5 of the Public Order Act 1986) or, as also happened to Steel, a person can be 'bound over' to keep the peace for a period of time on the security of a sum of money. For the ECtHR, arrest for breach of the peace had all the characteristics of arrest for an offence.

The suspicion relating to the offence must be 'reasonable'. The ECtHR has identified (e.g. in *O'Hara* v *United Kingdom* (2002) 34 EHRR 32, paras 34–36) the main requirements of a 'reasonable suspicion' and emphasised the importance of this requirement as part of the general protection against arbitrary arrest afforded by Article 5.

- The suspicion must be honestly held, an arrest in bad faith would be incompatible with the Convention.

- But an honest belief is not enough. For a suspicion to be 'reasonable' there must be in existence 'facts or information which would satisfy an objective observer that the person concerned may have committed the offence in question' (see *Fox, Campbell and Hartley* v *United Kingdom* (1991) 13 EHRR 157, para 32). What is sufficient to satisfy this test will depend on the circumstances, and reasonableness depends on the facts or information as understood by the arresting officer at the time of the arrest. The reasonableness of an arrest cannot be retrospectively validated by new facts or information unknown at the time (see *Stogmuller* v *Austria* (1979–80) 1 EHRR 155).

- Furthermore, the state must be prepared to disclose sufficient facts and information on which the arrest was based so that a court (or at least the ECtHR) can be satisfied that the reasonable suspicion test has been met (see *O'Hara* v *United Kingdom* (2002) 34 EHRR 32, para 35).

- Nevertheless, so long as the evidence suggests the suspect 'may have' committed the offence, he or she can be arrested. Reasonable suspicion does not require that there is, at the time of arrest, enough evidence on which to bring charges (see *O'Hara* v *United Kingdom* (2002) 34 EHRR 32, para 36).

2. '. . . when it is reasonably considered necessary to prevent him committing an offence . . .'

A person can be deprived of their liberty to prevent them committing an offence. This is an offence as defined in Convention terms, so can include detention for breach of the peace (as in

Steel, discussed earlier). However, from earliest cases (*Lawless v Ireland* (1979–80) 1 EHRR 15, paras 13–14), the ECtHR has held that this provision permits neither internment (executive detention of persons considered to threaten national security) nor preventive detention directed against those with a propensity to crime (*Guzzardi v Italy* (1981) 3 EHRR 333, para 102; see also *Al-Jedda v UK* (2011) 53 EHRR 23, para 100). A preventive element in a criminal punishment following conviction, such as indeterminate sentences in the United Kingdom where prisoners serve a period for punishment but are only subsequently released if the Parole Board consider them no longer a threat, are compatible with Article 5(1)(a).

3. '. . . or fleeing after having done so'

The third aspect to Article 5(1)(c) refers to a person who has committed a criminal offence but who is evading arrest.

'. . . bringing him before the competent legal authority'

Since *Lawless* (para 14) the case law is clear: an arrest or detention under any of the three aspects of Article 5(1)(c) must be effected for the purpose of bringing the person before a competent legal authority such as a magistrate. This is one of the central safeguards to prevent internment or merely preventive detention.

▶ **CROSS REFERENCE**

Section 2 HRA is discussed in Chapter 4, section 4.3

There is some uncertainty as to what the police's intention should be at the time of arrest. In *Ostendorf v Germany* (discussed earlier), the ECtHR has appeared to rule that, under Article 5(1)(c), the intention must be to bring the person before the court so that the alleged offence can be tried. This appears to depart from the earlier view, first argued in *Lawless* (para 14), that the intention at the time of arrest should be to take the arrested person to court irrespective of which of the three grounds justified the arrest. The implication of this is that the role of the court is to supervise the legality of the detention, not necessarily to try an offence. In *R v Hicks* [2014] EWCA Civ 3, the Court of Appeal, under the HRA, held that the detention of demonstrators against the Royal Wedding was to prevent an apprehended breach of the peace. The intention at the time had been to bring the demonstrators before a magistrate who would determine whether their detention was lawful or would order their release. The fact that, later, they were released without going to court did not affect the intention at the time of arrest. The Court of Appeal, following section 2 HRA, declined to follow the *Ostendorf* understanding.

Proportionality

The decision to arrest or detain, under any of the three grounds, must be a proportionate response (see, for example, *Shishkov v Bulgaria* App 38822/97, judgment of 9 January 2003). There must be a proper balance between the interest served by the arrest and the impact on the individual. A disproportionate detention will be a violation of Article 5(1), see for example *Vasileva v Denmark* (2005) 40 EHRR 27.

Furthermore, an original reasonable suspicion will cease, after a certain time, to be a sufficient justification for detention. There will need to be other grounds to justify the deprivation of liberty (e.g. *Ilkin v Russia* App 12436/11, judgment of 22 September 2015, para 59).

11.4.4 Article 5(1)(d)

the detention of a minor by lawful order for the purpose of educational supervision or his lawful detention for the purpose of bringing him before the competent legal authority.

Parental rights of custody over children are recognised so that, for example, parents may decide, compatibly with national law, that the best interests of their children require treatment in a hospital or other establishment and, given a fair balance in the law between parental rights and the autonomy of children, it is unlikely that the ECtHR will find that there has been a deprivation of the child's liberty (see, for example, *Nielsen v Denmark* (1989) 11 EHRR 175, regarding the placing of a child in a child psychiatric ward by his mother).

Nothing in Article 5(1)(a)–(c) prevents the detention of children after conviction of a crime or after arrest on reasonable suspicion. Article 5(1)(d) identifies extra grounds on which children can be lawfully deprived of their liberty: educational supervision or being brought before the competent legal authority.

'educational supervision'

 CASE CLOSE-UP

DG v Ireland (2002) 35 EHRR 33

DG was a child with a serious personality disorder who was made subject to a court order requiring 'high support therapeutic care'. He had not been convicted of an offence. The Irish authorities were unable to find a place where appropriate intensive and expensive care could be given. As the 'least offensive' alternative, the High Court ordered DG to be detained in a prison environment whilst a proper placement was found. The prison did not provide the 'high support' required or, indeed, much by way of even basic education. DG absconded and was returned to the prison environment. He was held in the prison for just over a month.

The ECtHR in *DG* held that there had been a violation of Article 5(1).

- The ECtHR insists that 'educational supervision' must mean more than providing just 'class room teaching'. It must 'embrace many aspects of the exercise, by the authority, of parental rights for the benefit and protection of the person concerned' (*DG*, para 80, *Ichin v Ukraine* App 28189/04, judgment of 21 December 2011, para 38).

- Appropriate care may not be immediately available and the Court accepted that temporary accommodation in an unsuitable environment does not in itself violate Article 5. If this happens, the state must act with diligence to provide an appropriate placement.

- The Court is not sympathetic to a lack of resources argument. The states are required to fund and resource the system of child protection they have chosen to adopt:

[the Irish state] was obliged to put in place appropriate institutional facilities which met the security and educational demands of [the system chosen to deal with juvenile delinquency], para 79.

'. . . the purpose of bringing him before the competent legal authority'

Article 5(1)(d) also permits the remanding of a minor in custody in the context of legal proceedings. These might be on remand awaiting criminal trial or after sentence awaiting social reports, for example. The usual Convention principles, such as the need for lawfulness and for proportionality, apply. The educational requirement, however, does not apply.

11.4.5 Article 5(1)(e)

the lawful detention of persons for the prevention of the spreading of infectious diseases, of persons of unsound mind, alcoholics or drug addicts or vagrants

General principles

Depriving a person with a mental disability of his or her liberty must be compatible with Article 5(1)(e). In *Hutchison Reid* v *United Kingdom* (2003) 37 EHRR 9, paras 46–48, the ECtHR summarised the general principles; these are now discussed.

Lawfulness

Any detention must be 'lawful' as that term is understood in Convention terms (see section 11.3). The national law must not permit arbitrary detentions of the mentally ill (see, for example, *Kepenerov* v *Bulgaria* (2004) 38 EHRR 33).

In England and Wales, the Mental Health Act 1983, as amended by the Mental Health Act 2007, permits persons to be detained for assessment or in order to receive 'appropriate medical treatment' (it no longer needs to be treatment that can cure or ameliorate their condition). Persons unfit to stand trial for serious criminal offences because of mental incapacity can also be detained under other measures. These provisions are likely to meet the 'lawfulness' requirement of Article 5.

Persons who lack mental capacity (who are unable to make decisions for themselves because of mental impairment) can also (independently of the Mental Health Act) be cared for in conditions that may deprive them of their liberty. This is allowed under common law if necessary for the patient's 'best interests'. In *HL* v *United Kingdom* (2005) 40 EHRR 32, the ECtHR held that the lack of a formalised admission system, the total reliance on professional judgment as to the patient's best interests, and the lack of adequate safeguards and remedies violated Article 5. The Mental Capacity Act 2005 (as amended by the Mental Health Act 2007) now forbids deprivation of liberty except as allowed for in the Act (section 4A) (the 'deprivation of liberty safeguards'). Specifically: Schedule A1 authorises the managing authority of a hospital or care home to deprive a person of his or her liberty under specific conditions and if this is in the patient's 'best interests' (the Act lays down procedures and criteria for determining these). It provides a detailed procedure for hospitals and care homes to follow. A system of review is created, with the Court of Protection having ultimate supervisory authority.

 THINKING POINT

Consider the impact of the finding in *Cheshire* (see section 11.2.1) that there had been a deprivation of liberty. Was this necessary for the proper protection of the vulnerable?

The Court of Protection itself has the power to order a deprivation of liberty if necessary for a person's welfare (section 16).

The *Winterwerp* conditions

Any detention must satisfy the three conditions laid down in *Winterwerp* v *The Netherlands* (1979–80) 2 EHRR 387, at para 39.

- The person must be shown to be of 'unsound mind'. There is no Convention definition of this term. It implies some form of mental disorder. States are allowed a margin of appreciation over the forms this might take. However, depriving a person of his or her liberty on the basis of behaviour which is merely 'deviant' cannot be permitted under Article 5(1)(d).

- The mental disorder must be sufficiently serious in its effects to 'warrant' compulsory confinement in hospital. Later case law suggests that this understates the position: any detention must be necessary, in the sense that less severe alternatives have been considered and found to be inadequate.

- The validity of continuing detention requires the persistence of the mental disorder.

Need for a therapeutic environment

A person detained in relation to Article 5(1)(e) must be provided with a suitable therapeutic environment (i.e. one which is aimed at providing treatment rather than punishment). However, so long as the treatment is therapeutic, Article 5 does not require anything more regarding the suitability of the treatment for the patient.

 CASE CLOSE-UP

Ashingdane v _United Kingdom_ (1985) 7 EHRR 528

A (who had been convicted of various offences) was placed in a high security special hospital. His condition improved but, for administrative reasons, the Home Secretary would not authorise his transfer to a local mental hospital. The ECtHR held that Article 5 had not been violated.

The ECtHR said (para 44):

> The Court would further accept that there must be some relationship between the ground of permitted deprivation of liberty relied on and the place and conditions of detention. In principle, the 'detention' of a person as a mental health patient will only be 'lawful' for the purposes of sub-paragraph (e) of paragraph 1 if effected in a hospital, clinic or other appropriate institution authorised for that purpose. However, subject to the foregoing, Article 5(1)(e) is not in principle concerned with suitable treatment or conditions.

In _LB_ v _Belgium_ App 22831/08, judgment of 2 October 2012, for example, the applicant was detained for seven years in the psychiatric wing of a prison rather than in a more appropriate mental health institution. There was a breach of Article 5(1)(e).

This position has been confirmed for English law under the HRA 1998.

 CASE CLOSE-UP

_R (B)_ v _Ashworth Hospital Authority_ [2005] UKHL 20 (see para 34)

B was a compulsorily detained mental patient. He sought to prevent the hospital transferring him from a ward in which he was being successfully treated for schizophrenia to one specialising in psychotic personality disorders. The House of Lords allowed the transfer. It made it clear that there was no breach of Article 5(1)(e). (The case was mainly about whether the Mental Health Act 1983 allowed a person detained for one type of illness to be treated, whilst detained, for another.)

Need for treatment

The Convention does not require a lawful deprivation of liberty to have the treatment of a treatable mental illness as its purpose. National laws may authorise detention of persons of unsound mind for other purposes which can be compatible with the Convention. In *Hutchison Reid* v *United Kingdom* (2003) 37 EHRR 9, the ECtHR held that there could be a deprivation of liberty under Article 5(1)(e) even if a person cannot be treated for a cure but 'needs control and supervision to prevent him, for example, causing harm to himself or other persons' (para 51).

Immediate release

A person no longer needing to be detained (e.g. because no longer suffering from a mental disorder) should be released. However, sensible transitional and rehabilitative arrangements, which delay release, are not necessarily incompatible with Article 5 (see, for example, *Johnson* v *United Kingdom* (1999) 27 EHRR 296, paras 61–63).

If a tribunal thinks that a patient should be released but only subject to conditions (e.g. effective care in the community) and these conditions cannot be met, he or she can continue to be detained. If the conditions are not met, the grounds justifying detention remain. This approach was adopted in English law in *R (IH)* v *Secretary of State for Health* [2003] UKHL 59. The House of Lords did, however, find a breach of Article 5(4) (see section 11.8) because IH had no right to effective legal review of the possibility of meeting the conditions.

The basic approach in *IH*, to both Article 5(1)(e) and 5(4), was agreed with by the ECtHR in a similar case: *Kolanis* v *United Kingdom* (2006) 42 EHRR 12.

11.4.6 '. . . spreading of infectious diseases . . . alcoholics or drug addicts or vagrants'

There is little case law on these issues. The most important point is their range—to what kinds and conditions of persons do they apply. The Court has held that the term 'alcoholics' in Article 5 is not confined to persons in a 'clinical state of "alcoholism" '. It extends to laws which permit the taking into custody of persons who, under the influence of drink, pose, through their behaviour, a threat to public order, or to themselves. What is not permitted is the taking into custody of a person merely because of being drunk rather than because of their behaviour (see *Litwa* v *Poland* (2001) 33 EHRR 53, paras 60–61).

As regards the term 'vagrants', the ECtHR accepted the definition in Belgium national law: 'persons who have no fixed abode, no means of subsistence and no regular trade or profession' (*De Wilde, Ooms and Versyp* v *Belgium* (1979–80) 1 EHRR 373, para 33, see section 11.2.2).

11.4.7 Article 5(1)(f)

the lawful arrest or detention of a person to prevent his effecting unauthorised entry into the country or of a person against whom action is being taken with a view to deportation or extradition.

CROSS REFERENCE

'Removal', 'deportation', 'extradition' are legally significant terms which apply in very different situations; see Chapter 9, section 9.8.1.

States, dealing with mass migration into Europe, may wish to detain some migrants with a view, for example, to deciding if they are entitled to enter the country. Likewise states may wish to detain non-citizens with a view to removing them from the country.

In *Saadi* v *UK* (2008) 47 EHRR 17, the Grand Chamber found the UK's policy of detaining some asylum seekers, those whose applications for asylum could be speedily dealt with, was compatible with Article 5(1)(f) (asylum seekers are people who a state is obliged to accept if they can be shown to be fleeing persecution; a failed asylum seeker, with no other basis to be lawfully in the country, can be 'removed').

The Grand Chamber laid down some important general principles which have been expanded on in later cases. They are:

- The first limb of Article 5(1)(f) clearly allows the detention of persons who are lawfully seeking entry to a country; the second limb allows the detention of deportees or those seeking to evade entry requirements.

- So long as done in good faith with a view to lawful deportation/removal, there is no need to show detention is otherwise necessary (e.g. as the only means available to prevent the detainees absconding). Thus the normal Article 5 requirement that any deprivation of liberty should be necessary is less stringently applied in the immigration context than under, in particular, Article 5(1)(b), (d), and (e).

- Detention should only be allowed if deportation is being actively undertaken. As the ECtHR said in *Chahal* v *United Kingdom* (1997) 23 EHRR 413, at para 113:

  If such proceedings are not pursued with due diligence, the detention will cease to be permissible under art 5(1)(f).

When deportation is legally impossible (e.g. because it would breach the Convention) detention cannot be justified under Article 5(1)(f).

In *Nabil* v *Hungary* App 62116/12, judgment of 22 September 2015, the ECtHR has considered these principles (see paras 26–35). The Court stressed that, in addition, any detention must not be 'arbitrary'. This means:

- Domestic law must allow for detention of deportees etc. Since a failure to follow domestic law is, itself, a breach of the convention, the ECtHR will review the domestic law to ensure that it does not authorise arbitrary or unreasonable executive actions. Therefore the domestic law is measured against the Convention standard of non-arbitrariness (thus detention could be lawful under domestic law but still breach Article 5).

- Non-arbitrariness has not been exclusively defined but includes the idea that the state must act in good faith and, importantly, that the place and conditions of detention should be appropriate (e.g. to detainees who may be innocent of any crime and may have been the victims of horrific experiences).

A clear implication of the stress on lawfulness is that there must be an adequate, domestic, judicial procedure available for testing the legality of the grounds for detention. In *Nabil*, the applicant was originally detained on grounds that satisfied the above principles; but his continued detention was not properly scrutinised by the courts and so there was a violation of Article 5.

 DISCUSSION TOPIC

Was *Saadi* v *United Kingdom* correctly decided? Is it an executive-friendly decision which fails to recognise the position and difficulties of asylum seekers who are some of the most vulnerable people in the world (see a strong dissent supported by a minority of judges in the Grand Chamber)?

11.5 The right to be informed, Article 5(2)

Article 5(1)(a)–(f) specifies the purposes of legitimate deprivation of liberty. The remaining provisions of Article 5 identify basic rights of those deprived of their liberty.

11.5.1 **Article 5(2)**

> Everyone who is arrested shall be informed promptly, in a language which he understands, of the reasons for his arrest and of any charge against him

The right to be informed applies only where there has been an 'arrest' (usually a deprivation of liberty justified under Article 5(1)(c)). It will not necessarily apply to other deprivations of liberty allowed by Article 5 which are not based on an 'arrest', such as some detentions for treatment of persons with mental incapacity.

Knowledge of why they have been arrested enables the detained person to realise the degree of seriousness of his or her situation and to take practical steps, such as obtaining appropriate legal advice, if the situation warrants it. Precise details of the offence need not be given nor need the full information be given at the time of arrest. The test for the nature of the requirement was laid out in *Fox, Campbell and Hartley* v *United Kingdom* (1991) 13 EHRR 157, para 40:

> . . . any person arrested must be told, in simple, non-technical language that he can understand, the essential legal and factual grounds for his arrest, so as to be able, if he sees fit, to apply to a court to challenge its lawfulness in accordance with paragraph 4 . . . Whilst this information must be conveyed 'promptly' . . . it need not be related in its entirety by the arresting officer at the very moment of arrest. Whether the content and promptness of the information conveyed were sufficient is to be assessed in each case according to its special features . . . .

> ❱ **CROSS REFERENCE**
>
> The law of England and Wales on the right to be informed is discussed in Chapter 20, section 20.3.5.

In *Saadi* v *United Kingdom* (see section 11.4.7) a Grand Chamber held that Article 5(2) had been violated because it took 76 hours to inform the applicant why he, as an individual, was being detained. The fact that general statements about the detention of some asylum seekers had been made in Parliament was insufficient.

Article 5(2) also requires that the information is given in a language the arrested person understands and this may require the speedy presence of interpreters at police stations (see, as an example, *Ladent* v *Poland* App 11036/03, judgment of 18 March 2008).

11.6 Judicial supervision of deprivation of liberty: introduction

Deprivation of liberty must be compatible with the rule of law. Article 5 requires adequate and proper judicial supervision of decisions taken by the authorities to detain a person.

Article 5(3) applies only to persons arrested and detained on reasonable suspicion of having committed an offence as allowed by Article 5(1)(c). It applies mainly to people held by the police prior to being charged, e.g. someone who has been lawfully arrested and detained by the police for questioning.

Article 5(4) applies to all deprivations of liberty allowed by Article 5(1)(a)–(f). For example: those held on remand awaiting trial or people detained for long periods (e.g. in mental hospitals) when the circumstances justifying their original detention may change.

The specific way these provisions are put into effect varies according to the nature and provisions of the different legal systems in Council of Europe countries.

11.7 Judicial supervision prior to trial, Article 5(3)

Everyone arrested or detained in accordance with the provisions of paragraph 1(c) of this article shall be brought promptly before a judge or other officer authorised by law to exercise judicial power and shall be entitled to trial within a reasonable time or to release pending trial. Release may be conditioned by guarantees to appear for trial.

11.7.1 **'Shall be brought promptly'**

The idea that a person should languish for days in police cells being subject to questioning, perhaps torture, with no access to the courts, is anathema. In the ECtHR's language, it is 'arbitrary' detention. Where someone has been detained by the police following arrest on reasonable suspicion, Article 5(3) requires prompt judicial supervision as a safeguard against abuse of power This must be automatic and not require an application by the detained person (*McKay v United Kingdom* [2007] 44 EHRR 41, para 32).

The ECtHR has always been very reluctant to determine in advance any specific time limits. It prefers to judge matters according to the particular circumstances of the case. Nevertheless the word 'promptly' which, in the French text ('aussitot') is more like 'immediately', does not permit flexibility.

 CASE CLOSE-UP

Brogan v United Kingdom (1989) 11 EHRR 117

Brogan and three others were arrested under the Prevention of Terrorism (Temporary Provisions) Act 1984 (now repealed) on suspicion of terrorist activities and detained for between four days and six hours, and six days and 16 hours. Under the Act police could detain individuals, for up to a week, with the authority of the Home Secretary (a member of the executive, not a magistrate or judge) being required for any period beyond two days. The applicants were questioned about terrorist offences and were then all released without charge.

The ECtHR held that there had been a violation of Article 5(3) in all the cases.

CROSS REFERENCE
The law of England and Wales on police detention is discussed in Chapter 20, section 20.5.

The significance of *Brogan* is that it concerns a terrorist investigation and, as discussed in Chapter 26, the ECtHR permits states a certain leeway in that context. In a non-terrorist context, four days' detention without being brought before a court is likely to be beyond what is permitted unless there are extraordinary circumstances that explain a longer period. A period of 10 days before being brought before a judge, even in a terrorist context, is clearly a breach (see *Yildirim* v *Turkey* App 40518/98, judgment of 29 July 2004).

11.7.2 Bail or remand in custody?

The second part of the first sentence of Article 5(3) concerns the situation following a suspect being charged with a criminal offence. This raises different issues from pre-charge detention. The authorities must decide whether a person who has been arrested on reasonable suspicion and then charged with a criminal offence should be released pending the trial (released on bail) or kept in custody (held on remand). The basic principles regarding custody or bail have been summarised by the ECtHR in, for example, *Smirnova* v *Russia* (2004) 39 EHRR 22, at paras 56–64.

- Under Article 5(3), a person who is remanded in custody is entitled to trial within a 'reasonable time'.

- Under Article 6(1) (the right to a fair trial), those who are released on bail are also entitled to trial within a 'reasonable time' (see Chapter 12, section 12.10).

- Article 5(3) creates a presumption in favour of release after a person has been charged.

    A person charged with an offence must always be released unless the State can show that there are 'relevant and sufficient' reasons to justify the continued detention.

    (see *Wemhoff* v *Germany* (1979–80) 1 EHRR 55, para 12)

Relevant reasons

The ECtHR has identified the 'relevant' reasons for refusing bail. There must be evidence the following:

- The accused might abscond and not appear for trial. Personal factors of the accused, such as the 'character of the person involved, his morals, his assets, his links with the State in which he is being prosecuted and his international contacts' are relevant (*Smirnova* v *Russia* (2004) 39 EHRR 22, para 60).

- If released, the accused will take action which prejudices the administration of justice, for example, intimidate witnesses or destroy evidence.

- If released, the accused is likely to commit further offences.

- The release of the accused could create a danger to public order. This reason applies only in exceptional circumstances where release of an unpopular accused person might trigger an adverse public reaction.

These reasons must be properly established, on evidence, produced by the state (it should not be up to the accused to prove the absence of these factors). The seriousness of the offence or of the likely sentence is not, of itself, a basis for justifying pre-trial detention.

Sufficient reasons

The 'relevant' reasons must also be 'sufficient' to justify remand in custody in the individual case. To justify remand, the national courts must be satisfied that there is a genuine reason, found in the particular circumstances of the case, which outweighs the force of the presumption of innocence and the respect for the individual liberty of the suspect. It follows from this that the courts must make their decisions on the basis of the individual circumstances of the case. Laws which require the automatic refusal of bail because of the severity of the offence or the previous record of the accused person, are likely to breach the Convention.

Review

The situation of a person who is detained rather than released on bail must be kept under review by the authorities. It is not up to the detained person to seek such reviews, although he or she should be entitled to do this under the provisions of Article 5(4), discussed later. If the reasons which had previously justified detention no longer exist or if the grounds for reasonable suspicion on which the original arrest was made have also diminished, it may be necessary to bail the accused. Failure to do this will be a breach of Article 5(3).

In *Labita v Italy* (2008) 46 EHRR 50, Grand Chamber, a mafia suspect was held in custody on remand for two years and seven months. There was a breach of Article 5(3) because the initial grounds on which reasonable suspicion was based had faded away and were never very strong in the first place. Labita's arrest had been based on the hearsay of 'pentiti' (mafia members now cooperating with the authorities), at least one of whom was dead.

Diligence

The ECtHR refuses to lay down, '*in abstracto*' (in general terms) the periods of detention, prior to trial, that the national authorities must abide by. It does insist that the prosecution authorities display 'special diligence' in preparing the case and bringing it to trial.

 CASE CLOSE-UP

Erdem v _Germany_ (2002) 35 EHRR 15

The German authorities detained Erdem, a leading member of the PKK (the leading Kurdish separatist organisation). Erdem was detained awaiting trial for five years and eleven months. The ECtHR held that there had been a breach of Article 5(3). It stressed:

- the need for individual assessment of the need for remand in custody;
- the need for significant reasons why the public interest requires detention;
- these reasons must relate to the specific situation of the individual (i.e. not just because he or she is a particular type of defendant);
- these reasons must persist throughout the time of the detention and the state must realise the likelihood that they will lessen over time.

The Court found that although many of the reasons which explained the delay in the trial—involving the complexity of the case and the actions of the defendant—were reasonable, there was a violation of Article 5(3) because the authorities failed to show 'special diligence' in the way they pursued the case.

Judicial supervision

Article 5(3) requires that the decisions taken authorising detention by the police during investigation or in prison or house arrest whilst awaiting trial, must be taken by a 'judge or other officer authorised by law to exercise judicial power'—a court or similar body having a judicial character. The court must have sufficient authority in law, be properly independent and impartial, and conduct itself with proper procedural safeguards for the defendant. In England and Wales such decisions are taken, in respect of regular offences, by magistrates. In the context of anti-terrorism, specially designated District Judges are involved (see Chapter 26, section 26.7.2). As *Brogan* (discussed earlier) demonstrates, detention authorised for more than a few days solely by the executive (e.g. police or Home Secretary) will violate Article 5(3).

Authority—the power to order release

The court supervising the custody decisions must have the power to order the release of the suspect. Merely being able to recommend release or make declarations as to the lawfulness of detention is not enough (see *Sabeur Ben Ali* v *Malta* (2002) 34 EHRR 26, for instance).

Impartiality and independence

The court supervising the custody decisions must be independent and impartial. Effective independence from the executive and from the parties to the criminal process is essential.

In *Boyle* v *United Kingdom* (2008) 47 EHRR 19, there was a breach of Article 5(3) when a commanding officer ordered the detention of a suspect soldier prior to trial by court martial. The commanding officer was not sufficiently impartial and independent because of his general responsibilities for discipline at the base.

Fair procedure

The court supervising custody decisions must have a fair procedure. In particular the procedure must allow 'equality of arms' and proper participation by the accused. Decisions about bail, which are taken in the absence of defendants or their representatives, or decisions based on evidence that the accused has been unable to challenge, are likely to be breaches of Article 5(3).

Further detail on fair procedures, relevant to Article 5(3), is given at section 11.8, in respect of Article 5(4).

 BIGGER PICTURE

These requirements for judicial supervision under Article 5(3), in respect of both pre- and post-charge detention, have been summarised by a Grand Chamber of the ECtHR in *McKay* v *United Kingdom* (2007) 44 EHRR 41, paras 30–47.

11.8 Judicial supervision of persons deprived of their liberty, Article 5(4)

Everyone who is deprived of his liberty by arrest or detention shall be entitled to take proceedings by which the lawfulness of his detention shall be decided speedily by a court and his release ordered if the detention is not lawful.

11.8.1 Introduction

The principles of non-arbitrariness and the rule of law require that anyone deprived of their liberty is entitled to go to a court or tribunal to challenge the lawfulness of his or her detention and be released if continued detention is unlawful or incompatible with Article 5. This right applies to those detained for any of the purposes in Article 5(1)(a)–(f) (including mental patients and deportees, for instance). This is a judicial function—it must be performed by a court or, if not, by a body which has proper independence from government and a fair procedure.

'Lawfulness' means not only that the domestic law has been properly applied but also that the domestic law meets Convention standards of non-arbitrariness (the same as under Article 5(1), see section 11.3 and *Musa* v *Malta* (2015) 60 EHRR 23, para 50).

11.8.2 The remedy must be real and effective

Article 5(4) requires access to court to be effective and not just a right that is never enforced.

In *Ocalan* v *Turkey* (2005) 41 EHRR 45, O was taken to Turkey and held incommunicado for 10 days in police custody. Under Turkish law there was a legal right of access to the court by persons detained by the police but no evidence that the remedy was effective in practice. One of the findings of a Grand Chamber in this complicated and important case was that there was a violation of Article 5(4) (paras 68–72).

11.8.3 Criminal sentences

For normal criminal sentences the requirements of Article 5(4) are satisfied by the decision of the convicting and sentencing court; continual review of determinate prison sentences (where the prisoner is released after a certain term) is not required. Where a court passes an indeterminate sentence (where a prisoner may only be released if it is safe to do so), the processes for determining the time of release must be compatible with Article 5(4).

> **CROSS REFERENCE**
> The situation of prisoners with an indeterminate sentence in England and Wales is discussed further in Chapter 21, section 21.3.2.

11.8.4 A 'court' and its authority: England and Wales.

The body to which the detained person can apply must have the authority, under the national law, to deal with all the issues that bear on the question of the deprivation of liberty, including the merits of the decision to detain and its compatibility with Article 5. Above all, the body must be able to order the detained person's release.

The law of England Wales has been significantly amended to ensure compatibility with Article 5(4). *Habeas corpus* and judicial review (discussed earlier, at section 11.1) provide generally available procedures for determining the legality of a deprivation of liberty and ordering release. (The availability of a civil action for damages based on, for instance, false imprisonment or negligence, may provide compensation but does not meet the Article 5(4) requirement for ordering release.) However, *habeas corpus* and judicial review may not always be enough to satisfy Article 5(4).

In *HL* v *United Kingdom* (2005) 40 EHRR 761, the applicant had been detained in a mental hospital, but not on the basis of the Mental Health Act 1983. Consequently he had no access to a tribunal which could have ordered his release. The ECtHR held that there were inadequate remedies available to HL and so there had been a breach of Article 5(4). Following this decision, under the Mental Capacity Act 2005, such patients now have access to a review procedure and can challenge the deprivation decision in the Court of Protection.

HL suggests that general remedies in English law, such as *habeas corpus* or judicial review may sometimes be inadequate. Neither remedy may give the High Court sufficient scope to consider all the factual issues bearing on the merits of the decision to detain. Furthermore, the test for proving the lawfulness of a detention may be too easy to satisfy and not allow the court to make its own, rigorous, evaluation of the need to detain. *Habeas corpus* was also found, by the ECtHR, to be inadequate for dealing with deprivations of liberty based on national security concerns (see *Chahal*, section 11.4.7).

Under the HRA, these remedies are either adjusted to meet the requirements of the Convention (see Chapter 3, sections 3.3.2 and 3.3.3) or detained persons can pursue the remedies available to them directly under section 7 HRA (see Chapter 5, section 5.4).

There are other judicial (court-like) bodies which deal with deprivations of liberty and whose procedures must be compatible with Article 5(4). For example:

- The Parole Board determines the release date for prisoners serving a life sentence and other indeterminate sentences.

- The First Tier Tribunal (Mental Health) hears cases brought by persons detained for treatment under the Mental Health Act 1983 in England and Wales. Following an adverse decision from the ECtHR, such tribunals (whose powers used to be only advisory) have the power to order a person's release from detention.

- Some immigration detainees have a right to seek bail from the Asylum and Immigration Tribunal.

11.8.5 Procedure

A court which meets the requirements of Article 5(4) must have a proper judicial procedure. It is not necessary to provide the full range of procedural guarantees found in Article 6 for criminal trials (see Chapter 12), since the purpose of a trial is different from the issues raised by Article 5(4) (see the discussion in *DPP* v *Havering Magistrates Court* (2001) 3 All ER 997, para 35). Nevertheless the basic requirements of access to the courts, independence, impartiality, and fairness, must be secured. The precise nature of the procedural requirements required under Article 5(4) depends upon the facts and circumstances of the case. As some of the cases below illustrate, English courts, under the HRA, are prepared to accept that procedural rights are context dependent and flexible (see, for example, *Roberts* v *Parole Board* [2005] UKHL 45.

Access to court

The law must enable detained people to take their case to court. States have positive duties to make this possible.

- Under the Mental Health Act 1983, mental patients who are challenging certain aspects of their situation cannot, whilst the issue is being resolved, apply to the First Tier Tribunal. In *R (H)* v *Secretary of State for Health* [2005] UKHL 60, the House of Lords declined to issue a declaration of incompatibility. Aspects of the law, particularly the power enjoyed by the Secretary of State to refer a matter to a tribunal on his or her own motion, satisfied Article 5(4).

- In *Allen* v *UK* (2010) 51 EHRR 22, the ECtHR held that the normal practice of denying a remand prisoner the right to be present whilst a prosecution appeal against bail is heard, violates Article 5(4).

Delay

The importance of liberty means that the hearings should not be delayed. In *R (Johnson* v *Secretary of State for the Home Department* [2007] EWCA Civ 427, delays in Parole Board hearings involved violations of Article 5(4). In *R (KB)* v *Mental Health Review Tribunal* [2002] EWHC 639, delays and postponements in hearing mental health cases involved violations of Article 5(4).

'Equality of arms'

Both parties must be in the same position as regards access to the court and access to the materials on which the court will decide. *R (Roberts)* v *Parole Board* (discussed earlier) raised the question whether the Parole Board could, in principle, make a decision on the basis of a prejudicial letter about a prisoner seeking parole which was neither known about nor disclosed to the prisoner or to his lawyers. A majority of the House of Lords, illustrating the flexibility of procedural rights, agreed that this course of action could be compatible with Article 5(4) in certain circumstances, such as the existence of a credible threat against the writer of the letter. The use of a 'special advocate' (who would represent the prisoner without consulting him) was also, in principle, compatible.

Oral hearing

The importance of liberty means that an oral hearing will often be necessary (as for many Parole Board decisions; see *R (Osborn)* v *Parole Board* [2013] UKSC 61).

Burden of proof

The state or public agency (such as a mental hospital) must prove the need to detain. Original provisions in the Mental Health Act 1983 put the burden of proof on the applicant appearing before a Mental Health Review Tribunal (as then called). This was the subject of a 'declaration of incompatibility' under section 4 HRA by the House of Lords and the rules were changed by 'remedial action' under section 10 HRA.

> **CROSS REFERENCE**
> For remedial action, see Chapter 4, section 4.4.4.

11.8.6 Remedy by appeal: 'decided speedily'?

Failures by a court or tribunal hearing to meet Article 5 standards can, in principle, be remedied by an appeal court. However, this may not be sufficient to satisfy Article 5(4) if the process of appeal takes too long and so the issue is not decided 'speedily'.

 BIGGER PICTURE

The general principles dealing with procedure have been summarised in *Megyeri* v *Germany* (1993) 15 EHRR 584, paras 22 and 23.

11.9 Article 5(5) compensation

Article 5(5) requires national laws to make provision for the compensation of someone who has been deprived of their liberty in contravention of Article 5. Compensation is not required just because there has been a miscarriage of justice; it is, specifically, required for breach of any of the provisions of Article 5 (*Wassink* v *The Netherlands* App 12535/86, judgment of 27 September 1990, para 38).

What is required is compensation ordered by the national courts and this is provided, in the UK, on the basis of section 8 HRA, which permits damages in 'just satisfaction' for breach of any Convention right.

There is fuller discussion of Article 5(5) in Chapter 5, section 5.5.3.

BIGGER PICTURE

Compare Article 5(5) with, for example, awarding damages for false imprisonment, against the police or under section 133 Criminal Justice Act 1988, for miscarriages of justice (miscarriage of justice is defined in *R (Adams)* v *SSJ* [2011] UKSC 18).

Summary

- Article 5 gives effect to the right to physical liberty, specifically the right not to be detained ('deprived of liberty') in an arbitrary manner.

- Article 5(1)(a)–(e) identifies the exclusive purposes for which a person can be deprived of his or her liberty.

- Article 5(2) requires a proper explanation to be given to arrested persons.

- Of great importance is that the grounds on which a person is detained, and on which he or she continues to be detained, must be judicially supervised by a court with full powers (see Article 5(3) and (4)).

Self-test questions

1. What are the exclusive purposes for which a person can be deprived of her or his liberty compatibly with Article 5?

2. How does the ECtHR define 'deprivation of liberty' in contrast with restrictions on movement?

3. Does the power of 'stop and search' raise issues under Article 5?

4. What, in the context of Article 5(1)(c) is meant by 'reasonable suspicion'?

5. How does the ECtHR define non-arbitrariness in the context of Article 5?

6. How specific is the information that needs to be given to meet the requirements of Article 5(2)?

7. What are the main requirements for judicial supervision of a deprivation of liberty?

8. In *Brogan* v *UK*, the courts discussed the time scale of being brought before a competent judicial authority—what is the judicial approach to 'promptness'?

9. Explain the grounds on which bail can be refused compatibly with Article 5.

10. On what grounds is compensation to be paid under Article 5(5)—is it for any miscarriage of justice?

 For suggested approaches, please visit the Online Resource Centre.

? | Exam questions

1. Advise the relevant officials about the implications of Article 5 in respect of:

    (a) Able, who is detained under Mental Health legislation. He was showing signs of great anxiety. He is detained in a maximum security mental hospital.

    (b) Baker, who is taking part in a political demonstration. The police decide to cordon off demonstrators into a small area. This is because they, the police, are concerned that, in an hour, a counter-demonstration may take place and violence result.

    (c) Charlie is an unlawful entrant into the United Kingdom. The government intend to remove him but are unable to do this because he might be tortured in his home country. The government, believing him to be dangerous, decide to detain him.

2. Critically evaluate the provisions of Article 5 in respect of the detention of people on the grounds of mental illness. Consider in particular whether they meet the demands of modern approaches to mental illness.

For suggested approaches, please visit the Online Resource Centre.

☰ | Further reading

General texts

- Lester, A. and Pannick, D. (see Preface) Chapter 4, Article 5

- Amos, M. (see Preface) Chapter 9

- Stone, R. 'Deprivation of Liberty: the Scope of Article 5 of the European Convention on Human Rights' [2012] EHRLR 46–58

12 Article 6: right to a fair trial

LEARNING OBJECTIVES

- The importance of fair trials and the rule of law.
- The scope of Article 6: trials 'determining' 'civil rights and obligations' or a 'criminal charge'.
- The general right to a fair trial: express and implied rights found in Article 6(1) which apply to both civil and criminal trials (e.g. equality of arms and access to the courts).
- Fair trial rights that are specific to criminal trials (Article 6(2) and (3)).
- The general character of Article 6 rights: flexibility and the importance of context.

Article 6 Right to a Fair Trial

(1) In the determination of his civil rights and obligations or of any criminal charge against him, everyone is entitled to a fair and public hearing within a reasonable time by an independent and impartial tribunal established by law. Judgment shall be pronounced publicly but the press and public may be excluded from all or part of the trial in the interests of morals, public order or national security in a democratic society, where the interests of juveniles or the protection of the private life of the parties so requires, or to the extent strictly necessary in the opinion of the court in special circumstances where publicity would prejudice the interests of justice.

(2) Everyone charged with a criminal offence shall be presumed innocent until proved guilty according to law.

(3) Everyone charged with a criminal offence has the following minimum rights:

    (a) to be informed promptly, in a language which he understands and in detail, of the nature and cause of the accusation against him;

    (b) to have adequate time and facilities for the preparation of his defence;

    (c) to defend himself in person or through legal assistance of his own choosing or, if he has not sufficient means to pay for legal assistance, to be given it free when the interests of justice so require;

(d) to examine or have examined witnesses against him and to obtain the attendance and examination of witnesses on his behalf under the same conditions as witnesses against him;

(e) to have the free assistance of an interpreter if he cannot understand or speak the language used in court.

Introduction

Article 6 might be thought dry and procedural. This is misleading. In some areas, such as terrorism (dealt with in Chapter 26), serious crime, drug dealing, even drink driving and speed cameras, the prosecution of alleged offenders or civil actions can be difficult because of the nature of the evidence, intimidation, the wish to protect police and security service procedures, issues of national security, and so on. These difficulties can lead to a tension with the need for trials to be fair and public. The question arises: should a trial be stopped if the ordinary legal requirements of fairness cannot be met? If so, it may be that dangerous people are released or laws promoting important social interests become unenforceable. The alternative is to adjust the concept of 'fairness' to the circumstances with the equal and opposite danger that the innocent are at greater danger of conviction. These problems are at the heart of the Article 6 case law.

12.1 Article 6 and legal systems

12.1.1 The role of the European Court of Human Rights (ECtHR)

The Convention does not require fair trials to take a particular form. In Europe there are major differences between different legal systems and court procedures. How the fairness of trials is obtained is, principally, up to the national governments and judiciary. The ECtHR, therefore, accepts a wide margin of appreciation on the issue of what makes a fair trial. Its role is to judge the overall fairness of individual trials by measuring the application of national laws and procedures, whatever they happen to be, in the particular case against the terms of Article 6.

> **CROSS REFERENCE**
> For margin of appreciation see Chapter 6, section 6.3.

Fair trials and procedures are at the heart of the traditional role of the courts under the separation of powers. Article 6 cases, therefore, are likely to be decided by the domestic courts acting, on judicial principles, without much, if any, 'deference' to the views of the executive.

> **CROSS REFERENCE**
> For deference see Chapter 4, section 4.6.2.

To say this, however, is not to suggest that the courts do not accept that the needs of social policy or national security may require, in context, qualifications and limitations in the application of Article 6. This is true, for example, in relation to the disclosure in court of sensitive information (see section 12.11.3).

12.1.2 English law and fair trials

In England, irrational forms of trial, such as trial by ordeal, were abolished in the thirteenth century (though aspects, including 'dunking for witches', seem to have survived into the seventeenth century)—see *Blackstone's Commentaries*, http://avalon.law.yale.edu/subject_menus/blackstone.asp Book IV, Chapter 27, paras 1–3, for examples of irrational modes of trial.

Fundamental requirements of a fair trial, such as the presumption of innocence in criminal trials, have been practised under English law for centuries. However, some fundamentally important rules were not introduced until comparatively recently. The rule which prevented a defendant from giving evidence on oath was not altered until the late nineteenth century, for example.

Today the fairness of trials (both criminal and civil) is protected by rules such as the following:

- Laws of evidence. These include important statutory rules such as, for criminal trials, sections 76 and 78 of the Police and Criminal Evidence Act 1984 (PACE), which impose on judges the duty to exclude confessions obtained by oppression and give judges the discretion to exclude any evidence which is likely to have 'an adverse effect on the fairness of the proceedings'.

- The law on contempt of court. This prevents the publication of stories and other actions which might undermine fair trials.

- Rules of 'natural justice'. These are rules of fairness which apply to criminal trials (such as those in magistrates' courts) and to non-criminal procedures in courts, tribunals, and administrative and professional bodies.

- Civil Procedure Rules. These are the detailed rules of procedure governing the conduct of civil trials and procedures. The Rules have an 'overriding objective', which is to ensure that cases are dealt with 'justly'.

Under the Human Rights Act 1998 (HRA), such laws and procedures need to be applied in a way that is compatible with Article 6 of the European Convention on Human Rights (ECHR). Generally there is a high level of compatibility, although, as we shall see, there are a number of important and controversial areas where compatibility is, to say the least, strained.

12.1.3 International Covenant on Civil and Political Rights (ICCPR)

The right to a fair trial in Article 14 of the ICCPR (see Chapter 1, section 1.4.4) contains a number of provisions that are not found, at least as express rights, in Article 6. These include the right not to be compelled to confess guilt, the right of appeal in criminal cases, and the right to compensation for a miscarriage of justice.

The substance of these rights is already recognised in the domestic law of the United Kingdom. They are also found in Protocol 7 ECHR, but the United Kingdom has neither signed nor ratified this and so it is not in the HRA. It can be taken into account by UK courts, as in *R (Mullen) v Secretary of State for the Home Department* [2004] UKHL 18.

For England and Wales, the Criminal Justice Act 2003 (CJA 2003) allows for the retrial of someone previously acquitted of murder if there is 'new' and 'compelling' evidence. This is in tension with the traditional principle against 'double jeopardy' (being tried twice for the same offence), a principle which is not in Article 6 ECHR but is in Article 14 ICCPR; it is in Protocol 7 ECHR but with exceptions that would allow CJA 2003 (see *R* v *Dunlop* [2006] EWCA Crim 1354).

12.2 The application of Article 6: introduction

12.2.1 Article 6 does not apply to all types of trial

For Article 6 to apply the 'trial' must be one which 'determines' either:

- 'civil rights and obligations', or
- a 'criminal charge'.

Therefore, not all trial-like procedures are covered by Article 6 (see section 12.3.4).

If Article 6 does apply, it is a matter of significance whether it is a 'criminal charge' or 'civil rights and obligations' that are being determined. Both criminal and civil trials have the rights based on Article 6(1), but only criminal trials must accord with the rights listed in Article 6(2) and (3). Deciding whether a matter is 'criminal' or 'civil' can be difficult (see, for example, *International Transport Roth GmbH* v *Secretary of State for the Home Department* [2002] EWCA Civ 158, where the Court of Appeal divided on the matter).

12.2.2 Other fair trial Articles

Even if Article 6 does not apply, a person may have other fair trial rights under the Convention. In particular there are rights under Article 5(3) and (4) (testing the legality of a deprivation of liberty) and Article 13 (the right to a remedy). In both contexts fair procedures appropriate to the different contexts are required. In *R (Smith)* v *Parole Board* [2005] UKHL 1, for example, the House of Lords held that Article 6 did not apply to decisions of the Parole Board but that Article 5(4) did (see paras 40–41; 37).

There is a lot of common ground between what is required by Article 6 and by Article 5(4). Nevertheless, the two rights are not necessarily the same. The purposes of a trial subject to Article 6 (e.g. to determine guilt or innocence) and a hearing subject to Article 5(4) (e.g. to determine whether it is safe to release a person into the community) are very different and the content of the rights that each Article secures relates to that purpose (for discussion see *R (DPP)* v *Havering Magistrates Court* [2001] 3 All ER 997).

> ⟫ **CROSS REFERENCE**
> For Article 5(4), see Chapter 11, section 11.8; for Article 13, see Chapter 5, section 5.1.

12.3 The scope of Article 6: 'civil rights and obligations'

The term 'civil rights and obligations' is not defined in Article 6. It has an 'autonomous' meaning (see Chapter 6, section 6.2.3) and is not dependant on whether a right or obligation is categorised as civil in the domestic law. The person claiming fair trial rights under Article 6 must have a substantive legal right, recognised by national law, which the trial is determining (see *R (Kehoe)* v *Secretary of State for Work and Pensions* [2005] UKHL 48).

12.3.1 'Private law' rights

The core meaning of civil rights and obligations relates to trials dealing with ordinary 'private law' rights. Thus, in terms of the law of England and Wales, trials determining contracts, torts, real and personal property, etc. come within the core meaning of civil rights and obligations.

Employment law and professional discipline

The rights under a contract of employment, and the right to practise a profession or remain employable are also 'civil rights' (*Le Compte* v *Belgium* (1982) 4 EHRR 1; *R (Wright)* v *Secretary of State for Health* [2009] UKHL 3). Generally, however, an employer's internal disciplinary processes, which result in dismissal, will not engage Article 6 and so those processes need not be fully independent or grant rights, such as representation, to the employee. Such proceedings are seen (by UK courts following *Le Compte* and other cases) to be just the exercise by the employer of an alleged contractual right to dismiss. The civil right involved is not being 'determined' by these proceedings (though see the next paragraph). This 'determination' takes place in an Employment Tribunal or County Court if the employee chooses to challenge the lawfulness of the employer's actions. Article 6 rights must be available in the tribunal or court (*Mattu* v *University Hospitals* [2012] EWCA Civ 641, paras 76 and 102).

Decisions taken by disciplinary bodies (e.g. of the professions) that prevent a person working in their chosen profession, 'determine' the right to remain employable and will engage Article 6(1) (*Le Compte; Wright*). Where the internal, employer's, procedures, referred to earlier, also have a 'substantial influence or effect' on the disciplinary body's decision, then, contrary to what has been said earlier, Article 6 rights may also be required of the employer's procedures. Usually, though, a disciplinary body will make its own, fully independent, assessment. If so, the employer is not bound by Article 6 (*R (G)* v *Governors of X School* [2011] UKSC 30); and if the employer's decision merely makes it harder for an employee to be employed by someone else, then Article 6 is probably not engaged for the reasons given in the previous paragraph (*Mattu*).

12.3.2 The determination of 'Convention rights'

Some, but not all, Convention rights are likely to be civil rights and so courts and tribunals deciding them have to meet Article 6 standards. The House of Lords has suggested that disputes about Article 8 (private and family life) and Articles 10 and 11 (freedom of expression and freedom of assembly and association) involve civil rights, see *R (McCann)* v *Crown Court at Manchester* [2002] UKHL 39, paras 78–79. Trials relating to serious restrictions on liberty, whether or not they engage Article 5, are likely to involve civil rights and so come within the scope of Article 6 (*Aerts* v *Belgium* (2000) 29 EHRR 50 and, under HRA, *R (MB)* v *Secretary of State for the Home Department* [2007] UKHL 46, para 24). Some Convention rights certainly are not civil rights, e.g. the right to free and fair elections under Article 3 of Protocol 1.

12.3.3 The individual and the state

The notion of 'civil rights and obligations' is based on a distinction found in continental legal systems (such as in France) between 'private' and 'public' law. Public law, dealing with the relationship of individual and state, raises complex policy questions which cannot be dealt with on the same basis as private law. Disputes may be dealt with by administrative courts or tribunals on the basis of principles of public law. The intention of the Convention's drafters in 1950 was to introduce a separate body of fair procedure rights to deal with the individual–state relationship, but this has not happened (see *Begum* v *Tower Hamlets LBC* [2003] UKHL 5, para 28).

12.3.4 **Public law rights**

Article 6(1) does not apply to public law rights in the absence of any direct implication for private rights.

Political rights

Determination of rights which are 'political', in the narrow sense that they are concerned with rights of political participation, such as rights under election laws and other laws dealing with direct participation in the political processes, are outside the scope of Article 6 (even though these rights may engage Article 3 of Protocol 1) (see *Pierre-Bloch* v *France* (1998) 26 EHRR 202).

Civic status and duties

Disputes over status and basic civic obligations may not engage Article 6(1). Two examples are immigration and taxation.

- In *Maaouia* v *France* (2001) 33 EHRR 42, the ECtHR confirmed that decisions about 'entry, stay or deportation', are not determinations of a person's civil rights and obligations. This has been followed under the HRA in *R (Ullah)* v *Immigration Appeal Tribunal* [2003] EWCA Civ 1366, para 20.
- In *Ferrazzini* v *Italy* (2002) 34 EHRR 45, the ECtHR confirmed that disputes about tax demands were outside the scope of Article 6: 'tax matters still form part of the hard core of public-authority prerogatives, with the public nature of the relationship between the taxpayer and the community remaining predominant'.

12.3.5 **Public law decisions decisive of private rights**

State officials and agencies exercise a vast range of regulatory powers involving economic and social life. They take decisions which directly affect the significance and value of individual's private rights such as rights under contract or property. These may, for example, be decisions about planning applications for permission to build or the granting of economically valuable licences to sell products. Such decisions should be taken on the basis of fair trial rights in Article 6(1) or, at least, be subject to effective review by courts or tribunals that provide Article 6(1) rights (e.g. *Tre Traktörer Aktiebolag* v *Sweden* (1991) 13 EHRR 309, licence to sell alcohol).

12.3.6 **Welfare state benefits**

Article 6(1) is now applied to disputes with government agencies about social welfare provision. In the past the ECtHR would only grant Article 6 rights where the welfare scheme was contributory and so had features similar to private insurance (e.g. *Feldbrugge* v *The Netherlands* (1986) 8 EHRR 425). However, this position is now changed. In *Schuler-Zgraggen* v *Switzerland* (1993) 16 EHRR 405, the Court held that 'the general rule is that Article 6(1) does apply in the field of social insurance, including even welfare assistance' (para 46) and in *Salesi* v *Italy* (1998) 26 EHRR 187 (involving a state disability pension), the ECtHR held that similarity with private insurance may not be necessary. Article 6(1) can apply to any dispute over 'a specific economic

> **CROSS REFERENCE**
Welfare benefits may also be 'possessions' secured by Article 1 of the First Protocol—see Chapter 23, 23.2.3.

right flowing from a statute'. Disputes over entirely non-contributory benefits, especially if they are discretionary, may still be outside the scope of Article 6(1).

12.3.7 Administrative decisions

Decisions, like those mentioned in sections 12.3.4, 12.3.5, and 12.3.6, are amongst the thousands taken all the time by civil servants, local council officers, and other officials. These decisions may give public money and extend public services to individuals. They involve the application of complex legislation, both primary and secondary, to individuals. They give effect to government policy often in the general context of the welfare state. They are made on the basis of complex factual assessments, in the light of policy objectives, and take into account resources and the public interest. They are the ultimate responsibility of elected bodies. Obviously, such decisions are of great importance to the individuals involved. However, they are rarely taken on the basis of a full hearing, with full procedural rights presided over by fully independent officers. They are 'administrative' not 'judicial' decisions. The question is whether such decisions need to be taken in line with Article 6.

Two issues need to be determined.

The first is whether the decision is one which determines civil rights and obligations. This is a context-sensitive matter. In *Bryan* v *UK* (1996) 21 EHRR 342, the ECtHR held that planning decisions may well determine civil rights since they affect property interests. In *Tsfayo* v *United Kingdom* (2009) 48 EHRR 18, a welfare dispute about the amount of housing benefit owed to the applicant also came within the scope of Article 6.

British courts, working with decisions such as these, have explored the underlying principles.

 CASE CLOSE-UP

Ali v *Birmingham City Council* [2010] UKSC 8

The case involved the decisions made by local authority housing departments. The legal issue was whether the decision of a local authority that it has discharged its duty to secure accommodation for homeless persons is a decision which determines the homeless person's civil rights and so needs be taken independently and otherwise in accordance with Article 6.

The Supreme Court noted that, whilst Convention case law has accepted that welfare state decisions can involve civil rights (see sections 12.3.5 and 12.3.6), it has never been proposed that all administrative decisions affecting individuals should be covered by Article 6. This is partly a matter of principle: the public/private distinction inherent in Article 6 (referred to at section 12.3.3); it is also a recognition of the practical problems and costs which would result if welfare administration was 'judicialised' and had to be reorganised to allow hearings, rehearings, and appeals to conform to Article 6.

The Justices made a distinction between:

- benefits to which the claimant has a specific entitlement based upon the clear words of a statute; here Article 6 is likely to apply; and
- benefits which are more discretionary—they are 'dependent upon a series of evaluative judgements by the provider as to whether statutory criteria are satisfied' and how best to meet the claimant's needs; here Article 6 is unlikely to apply.

> **THINKING POINT**
>
> How easy is this distinction to make in practice? Consider, for example, *M* v *Secretary of State for Health* [2012] UKUT 474.

Determinations of planning applications can be examples in the first category (see *Bryan*, at section 12.3.7, followed by *R (Alconbury)* v *Secretary of State for the Environment* [2001] UKHL 23). Decisions about the housing by local authorities of children in need are examples of the second, see *R (A)* v *Croydon LBC* [2009] UKSC 8. The decision in *Ali* is likely to reduce significantly the extent to which Article 6 rights can intrude into administrative decision taking.

If, however, a decision does relate to a specified right (it is in the first category and Article 6 is engaged), then the second issue arises: whether Article 6 has been violated. Internal reviews and appeals of the decision, in particular, are unlikely to be properly 'independent' and 'impartial' as required by Article 6. If internal processes do not satisfy Article 6, the approach of the ECtHR is that Article 6 is not violated so long as the claimant has a right of appeal or review to a court or tribunal that does satisfy Article 6 and has 'full jurisdiction' to hear all the matters of fact and law that are in dispute (*Albert* v *Belgium* (1983) 5 EHRR 533, para 29). Whether such a court or tribunal has full jurisdiction will depend on context. The High Court, through 'judicial review', for example, may not be able to deal with predominantly factual disputes (as in *Tsfayo*, at section 12.3.7).

> **CROSS REFERENCE**
>
> Judicial review is summarised in Chapter 5, section 5.2.1.

In *Alconbury*, mentioned earlier in this section, on the other hand, the dispute was more a matter of fact and law and the High Court, through judicial review, did have full jurisdiction. In a housing case, *Begum* v *Tower Hamlets LBC* [2003] UKHL 5, the right of the applicant to appeal the housing department's decision to the County Court was held, by the House of Lords, to satisfy Article 6 (the application of Article 6 was presumed).

12.4 The application of Article 6: 'criminal charge'

12.4.1 **Criminal charge**

A trial which determines a 'criminal charge' must accord not only with the fair trial rights in Article 6(1) but also those additional and more specific rights in Article 6(2) and (3). As with civil rights and obligations, the concept of a 'criminal charge' is autonomous to the Convention (see Chapter 6, section 6.2.3).

> **CASE CLOSE-UP**
>
> ***Engel* v *The Netherlands* (1979–80) 1 EHRR 647**
>
> E and others were Dutch conscripts subjected to a range of military disciplinary measures of varying degrees of severity. One issue was whether these measures were criminal charges that had been imposed in breach of Article 6.

In *Engel*, the ECtHR identified three principal criteria for deciding whether or not a legal procedure involved the determination of a criminal charge (see paras 82–83).

- National classification. If the matter is classified as 'criminal' under national law, this is conclusive that the full range of Article 6 rights apply.

What matters are the realities of the situation. Where a matter is not classified as criminal (but is, for example, called a disciplinary or administrative offence) there may still be a criminal charge for Convention purposes. This depends on two things:

- The nature of the offence. Does it have criminal characteristics such as a whether there is a requirement for **mens rea** (the guilty mind or intention) or whether the process results in a finding of guilt. How other countries deal with the problem can also be relevant.

- The point of proceedings is punishment. This is the most important matter. If the point of the proceedings is to punish (retribution or deterrence) in non-trivial ways, then there is a strong inference that a criminal charge is being determined.

These principles have been discussed and adopted under the HRA by the House of Lords in *R (McCann)* v *Manchester Crown Court* [2002] UKHL 39: see section 12.4.3.

12.4.2 Examples of 'criminal charges'

Applying these principles, the ECtHR has held that a criminal charge is being determined in relation to, for example:

- 'administrative offences': regulations enforced by penalties applied in contexts such as road traffic, food quality, the environment (e.g. *Mauer* v *Austria* (1998) 25 EHRR 91, involving minor traffic offences);

- military discipline: trials by courts martial of members of the armed forces for serious military offences are likely to involve a criminal charge (e.g. *Findlay* v *United Kingdom* (1997) 24 EHRR 221, discussed at section 12.7.2, Independence and the United Kingdom); and

- prison discipline: prisoners who break Prison Rules can be disciplined by the Prison Service. Where such hearings can lead to significant punishment, including extra days in prison, the matter is likely to involve the determination of a criminal charge (e.g. *Ezeh* v *United Kingdom* (2004) 39 EHRR 1).

12.4.3 Non-punitive procedures—not 'criminal charges'

In the United Kingdom, as in other societies, there are legal procedures that can result in significant detriment for the individuals affected but which do not have punishment as their aim. They have some other purpose such as the protection of the public. Such procedures are likely not to involve the determination of a criminal charge. Examples include:

- Professional bodies, working through independent tribunals, such as the Solicitors Disciplinary Tribunal or the Medical Practitioners Tribunal Service, holding disciplinary hearings. These hearings aim to protect the public from incompetent or wicked practitioners, and not at punishment. (Their decisions, which may lead to 'striking off', are likely to be determining civil rights and obligations (see *Le Compte*, at section 12.3.1.)

- Disqualification from public office, such as in *Pierre-Bloch* v *France* (section 12.3.4).

- In relation to UK law, the UKSC held that a person questioned under Schedule 7 Terrorism Act 2000 (which permits questioning of people possibly implicated in terrorism at ports and airports) had not been 'charged' with a criminal offence, and hence the privilege against self-incrimination, implied in Article 6(2) (see section 12.14.1) did not apply; *Beghal* v *DPP* [2015] UKSC 49.

Measures of public protection

States may have laws and procedures which aim at protecting the public from dangerous or anti-social persons. For example, in the United Kingdom, the Parole Board decides whether certain prisoners (e.g. murderers serving a life sentence) who have served the punishment part of their sentence, are safe to release. The Board is concerned not with punishment but public safety, *R (Smith)* v *Parole Board* [2005] UKHL 1. Prisoners enjoy the procedural protection of Article 5(4) (see Chapter 11, section 11.8) and they may have civil rights, see *Smith*, para 44.

Entry on the 'sex offenders' register' (in effect a duty to report to the police) may, in some circumstances, be an alternative to punishment or it may be a consequence of a criminal conviction, but its purpose is to enhance the safety of the public, not to punish (see *Jones* v *Greater Manchester Police Authority* [2001] EWHC 189 (Admin) and *R (R)* v *Durham Constabulary* [2005] UKHL 21).

 DISCUSSION TOPIC

Should those threatened with anti-social behaviour measures have full rights to a fair trial guaranteed in Article 6?

There are a variety of powers available to courts to deal with anti-social behaviour. For example, under Part 1 Anti-social Behaviour, Crime and Policing Act 2014, Youth Courts (amongst others) may issue injunctions imposing prohibitions or requirements. This is where, on a balance of probabilities, the court is satisfied that a young person is involved in anti-social behaviour. These prohibitions or requirements may have a significant impact on an individual, such as restricting where they may go and whom they may associate with. Breaches of the order can lead to significant penalties being imposed, such as a detention order.

The question is whether it is fair to impose such orders on the basis of a civil procedure which, for example, may permit hearsay evidence which might not be admissible in criminal proceedings (see Article 6(2)–(3)) and which is difficult to challenge in court.

Arguments in favour of avoiding full criminal trial procedures include the following:

- Victims of anti-social behaviour need to feel safe from possible retribution before they will come forward.
- Injunctions do not involve punishment; all they do is to require a person to stop behaving in an anti-social way.
- Injunctions do not involve a criminal record.

Arguments in favour of full criminal safeguards include:

- An injunction is likely to seem like punishment to the person involved.
- Breach of an injunction is in effect criminal and can lead to imprisonment.
- Criminal procedure might minimise the danger of the disproportionate application of injunctions.

In *R (McCann)* v *Manchester Crown Court* [2002] UKHL 39, the House of Lords considered Anti-social Behaviour Orders (ASBOs, replaced by the injunctions discussed earlier). It held that since ASBOs did not have punishment as their purpose they did not involve the determination of a criminal charge. Courts might, however, be determining civil rights. In *McCann*, the UKHL went on to insist that, though a civil measure, the court issuing the ASBO must be satisfied to the criminal standard of proof (beyond reasonable doubt) that the person was responsible for anti-social behaviour (para 37). In relation to injunctions, however, a balance of probabilities test is required by statute.

12.5 Express rights, implied rights, and qualifications

Sections 12.2–12.4 deal with the circumstances in which a person is able to claim rights based on Article 6. The next issue is to identify what rights Article 6 secures. It is important to stress that the substance of criminal law and of trial procedures are primarily matters for the states. The ECtHR's role is to ensure that, whatever system is adopted in a country, the essence of a fair trial is assured.

- Pervasive fairness. The concept of a 'fair trial' in Article 6(1) is the governing idea in Article 6. This idea must influence the way the express and implied rights in Article 6 are given effect.

- Express rights. Particular rights are expressed in Article 6(1) (e.g. the right to an independent tribunal) and, for those facing criminal charges, express rights are also found in Article 6(2) and (3).

- Inherent rights. Various rights have been identified by the ECtHR as inherent in, or implied by, the concept of a fair trial, e.g. the right of access to a court. These are not expressed as such in Article 6 but will apply, in context, to both civil and criminal trials.

- Qualifications and context dependency. What counts as 'fair' will depend upon circumstances and context and upon the particular system adopted in the state. Article 6 rights, especially inherent rights, have a certain flexibility. What is fair can depend upon a range of factors including, given the situation, the need to balance fairness to individuals with the rights and interests of others and even with the general public interest. As Lord Bingham said in *Brown* v *Stott (Procurator Fiscal)* [2003] 1 AC 681, 704:

   The jurisprudence of the European Court very clearly establishes that while the overall fairness of a criminal trial cannot be compromised, the constituent rights comprised, whether expressly or implicitly, within art 6 are not themselves absolute. Limited qualification of these rights is acceptable if reasonably directed by national authorities towards a clear and proper public objective and if representing no greater qualification than the situation calls for . . . The case law shows that the court has paid very close attention to the facts of particular cases coming before it, giving effect to factual differences and recognising differences of degree . . . The court has also recognised the need for a fair balance between the general interest of the community and the personal rights of the individual, the search for which balance has been described as inherent in the whole of the convention.

- Overall fairness. Any limitations or qualifications must, nevertheless, be compatible with the overall fairness of a trial, otherwise there will be a breach of Article 6. There is little, if any, 'deference' by the courts to the views of Parliament or the government on fairness.

12.6 Article 6(1): access to court

Perhaps the most important right in Article 6 is the right of a person to be able to take his or her case to court for a fair hearing. This right is inherent in the concept of a fair trial in Article 6(1). It is recognised as 'fundamental' by English common law, to be departed from only by clear statutory words—*Pyx Granite Co* v *Ministry of Housing and Local Government* [1960] AC 260.

12.6.1 Criminal law and the right of appeal

Since the state initiates proceedings, the right of access to court is of lesser significance in respect of criminal charges. The Convention itself does not give a person convicted after a fair trial a right to appeal. Such a right is found in Article 2 of the Seventh Protocol; but this has not been signed or ratified by the United Kingdom.

12.6.2 Civil rights and obligations

The general principle

> **CASE CLOSE-UP**
>
> ***Golder* v *United Kingdom*** (1979–80) 1 EHRR 524
>
> G was accused by a prison officer of participation in a prison disturbance. The allegation was later withdrawn but not removed from his record. G's letters to his MP concerning his circumstances and his attempt to consult a solicitor with a view to an action for defamation against the officer were stopped by the governor exercising powers under the prison rules.
>
> The ECtHR held that there had been a breach of Article 6(1).

For the Court, the right of a person to go to court in order both to assert or defend his or her civil rights and obligations was fundamental. It was rooted in the commitment of the signatory states to the rule of law and it also follows from the general requirement that Convention rights need to be effective:

> And in civil matters one can scarcely conceive of the rule of law without there being the possibility of having access to the courts.

(para 35)

A qualified right

As with all implied rights, the right of access to the courts is not absolute and may be subject to qualifications over which states have a considerable margin of appreciation. Any restrictions must pursue a legitimate aim, have a proportionate effect in particular cases, and not undermine the very essence of the right (see, for example, *Fayed* v *United Kingdom* (1994) 18 EHRR 393, para 65). Examples of accepted restrictions include those on children, persons of unsound mind, 'vexatious litigants', bankrupts, and those defamed by Members of Parliament speaking with the protection of parliamentary privilege.

In *Ashingdane* v *United Kingdom* (1985) 7 EHRR 528, the ECtHR upheld a statutory restriction which prevented mental patients suing their carers. The Court accepted that preventing unfair harassment of staff by patients was a legitimate aim (paras 56–59).

In *Seal* v *Chief Constable of South Wales Police* [2007] UKHL 31, the House of Lords upheld a clear statutory requirement that mental patients must obtain the leave of the High Court before they could bring a legal challenge to contest certain decisions made about them. Article 6 was not mentioned. The ECtHR then held, on margin of appreciation grounds, that there was no violation of Article 6 (*Seal* v *UK* (2012) 54 EHRR 6).

Procedural bars

A right of access to court can be in issue if procedural rules or rules of evidence are such as to make any court action pointless. If, for example, national security considerations prevent crucial evidence from being admitted or challenged, then a person may have no effective access to court (e.g. *Tinnelly* v *United Kingdom* (1998) 27 EHRR 249).

Traditionally, under international law, states and their senior officials enjoy a wide immunity from being sued in the domestic courts of other countries. This immunity has been generally accepted by the ECtHR as serving a legitimate purpose.

In *Al-Adsani* v *UK* (2002) 34 EHRR 11, the ECtHR upheld the principle of state immunity even in the context of allegations of torture—there was no developed legal consensus that state immunity did not apply to civil actions alleging torture. This view was followed by the House of Lords in *Jones* v *Ministry of the Interior* [2006] UKHL 26, a tort action brought, in English courts, against Saudi Arabian officials and alleging torture.

It is clear, however, that state immunity, as a barrier to access to court, is not absolute.

Q CASE CLOSE-UP

Sabeh el Leil v *France* [2012] 54 EHRR 14

The applicant was an accountant for the Kuwait Embassy in Paris. He brought a case for unfair dismissal under French law. The French courts dismissed the case on grounds that, as an embassy worker, the state had immunity.

The ECtHR, Grand Chamber, held:

- the right of access to the court was not absolute and could be limited by rules which pursued a legitimate aim and which were proportionately applied;
- applying recognised rules of international law (such as state immunity) would not normally breach Article 6;
- however state immunity was not an absolute principle;
- on the facts the applicant was not employed to perform diplomatic or governmental tasks, and so
- by refusing to hear his case the French courts had violated his right of access to the courts.

Procedural bars or substantive rights?

The right of access to court requires that the individual must, arguably, have a substantive right to be heard and determined in the court. In respect of negligence (under English law), for example, an injured person only has a right of action if the person who injured them owed them a 'duty of care'. This is a matter of law to be decided by the courts. The English courts have sometimes denied that various public officials owe duties of care to the people they deal with (e.g. the police to some victims of crime in *Hill* v *Chief Constable of West Yorkshire* (1989) AC 53). Those people, though allegedly harmed by the actions of the officials, do not have a right of action and so have no right to go to court and sue. The lack of a right to go to court is because they have no right, not because there is a procedural barrier preventing them suing to uphold a right. In *Z* v *United Kingdom* (2002) 34 EHRR 3, the ECtHR made it clear that Article 6(1) is not concerned with substance (what rights people have) but with the procedure for dealing with disputes about these rights (*R* v *G* [2008] UKHL 37, para 4).

Legal aid in civil cases

In criminal cases, the provision of free legal aid is virtually a requirement of the Convention, based on Article 6(3)(c) (see section 12.15.3). In civil cases, the situation is much less clear. How the right to a fair trial is achieved is a matter, in the first instance, for the national authorities: it is not for the ECtHR to insist on the provision of legal aid in all circumstances. In some cases, for example, the right of a litigant to appear in person may satisfy the requirements of a fair trial; in others it will not (see *Airey* v *Ireland* (1979–80) 2 EHRR 305).

In the UK there is now little civil legal aid. Instead there have been statutory changes to the way fees and costs are allocated, for example, 'no win no fee'—conditional fee arrangements—in the Access to Justice Act 1999. Whilst the aim of these changes has been to improve access to justice for persons with meritorious claims, they do act to the detriment of some litigants, such as defendants with strong cases who settle early. In *Coventry* v *Lawrence* [2015] UKSC 50, the UKSC found that, although there were other ways in which the aim could have been put into effect so as to protect the position of 'non-rich' litigants, the scheme was, on balance, a proportionate way of achieving the aim and, hence, compatible with Article 6.

12.7 Article 6(1): an 'independent and impartial tribunal'

12.7.1 Introduction

The judicial function

A court, tribunal, etc. determining civil rights and obligations or a criminal charge must be and must appear to be 'independent and impartial'. These values are, of course, at the heart of any known conception of judicial procedure and decision taking. They imply that the proper application of the law in individual cases excludes reasons such as the personal advancement of the judge, the promotion of political policies, or discrimination against particular groups represented by a litigant. Independence and impartiality embody the constitutional principle of the separation of powers: that the application of the laws in individual cases (the judicial function) needs to be separated from the making of the laws (the legislative function) and policy making and enforcement (the executive function).

A matter of appearance

There is no need to prove that a court or tribunal has been biased or prejudiced in the way it actually decided the case. Appearance of lack of independence or impartiality is enough.

Natural justice

CROSS REFERENCE

See Chapter 5, section 5.2.1 for a description of judicial review.

Under English law, the principle that courts, tribunals, and other bodies should appear to be unbiased is part of general administrative law. There are rules of natural justice which can be given effect through judicial review and other proceedings. Natural justice has a strong and effective rule against the appearance of bias.

For the ECtHR, independence and impartiality are closely linked ideas. Nevertheless it is possible to identify distinct general features of each concept.

12.7.2 Independence

General features of independence

The general idea of independence is that bodies determining civil and criminal cases should do so on the basis of their own judgment and not act under the influence of the executive or other outside pressures. Independence is a matter of fact. The ECtHR has suggested that independence can be measured by factors such as the following (see *Findlay* v *United Kingdom* (1997) 24 EHRR 221, para 73):

- the manner of appointment of the members of a court or tribunal;
- their term of office;
- the existence of guarantees against outside pressures; and
- whether it presents an appearance of independence.

Independence and the United Kingdom

As discussed at section 12.3.7, those administrative procedures which also determine civil rights and obligations, such as executive involvement in the planning process, are unlikely to be independent (e.g. *Alconbury*). But, so long as the applicant has access to an Article 6 compliant court or tribunal which has 'full jurisdiction' to deal with disputed issues of law and fact that arise, there will be no violation of Article 6.

Difficulties about independence, therefore, tend to arise in respect of courts and tribunals that perform judicial, not administrative, functions.

 CASE CLOSE-UP

Findlay v United Kingdom (1997) 24 EHRR 221

F, a soldier, was charged with a number of offences arising out of a shooting incident in his barracks. His defence was that, as a result of his participation in the Falklands War, he was suffering post-traumatic stress disorder. He was tried and convicted by a

Court Martial, which was held properly according to the rules and procedures then in place. The applicant alleged he had been denied a fair hearing before an independent tribunal.

The ECtHR held that there had been a violation of Article 6. Under the rules, the decision on the charges to be brought, the type of court martial, the membership of the court, and the choice of the prosecuting and defending officers were the responsibility of the 'convening officer'. This officer also had other links with the prosecution (his consent was necessary if the prosecution were to accept a lesser charge, for example) and it was the convening officer who confirmed the sentence. The convening officer, therefore, played a major organising role but it was one linked to the prosecution. The members of the court were subordinate in rank to the convening officer and were within his chain of command. For this reason the ECtHR held that F had grounds to fear a lack of independence in the court.

Following *Findlay*, the court martial system was reformed to meet the requirements of Article 6. UK courts and the ECtHR have accepted the compatibility of the new system (*R v Spear* [2002] UKHL 31 and *Cooper v United Kingdom* (2004) 39 EHRR 8).

The concept of independence has had a practical impact in a number of UK cases such as:

- *Starrs v Ruxton* 2000 SLT 42, where the Scottish High Court of Justiciary held that the system of using temporary sheriffs in the Scottish summary justice system was incompatible with Article 6. The Lord Advocate played an important role in the appointment of these sheriffs and their make-up to a full-time position was subject to his judgment. The Lord Advocate, however, was also ultimately responsible for criminal prosecutions.
- *Scanfuture UK v Secretary of State for Trade and Industry* [2001] IRLR 416, where the independence of employment tribunals was successfully challenged before the English courts regarding cases where the Secretary of State was a party. The Secretary of State was responsible for appointing the tribunal members (the system has now been changed).

12.7.3 Impartiality

The general approach under the Convention

Impartiality is linked to independence but shows its own distinctive focus of concerns. The ECtHR considers impartiality in terms of an objective and subjective test. This approach is summarised in *Morice v France* App 29369/10, Grand Chamber judgment of 23 April 2015.

The subjective test considers reasons relating to characteristics of a judge and whether these are sufficient both to set aside the presumption of judicial impartiality and, also, to render the trial unfair. Matters such as political prejudices and personal links with the prosecution are relevant here.

The objective test focuses on external factors which may undermine public confidence in the impartiality of the trial. Objective factors can lead to a violation of Article 6 even in the absence of evidence of subjective bias. On the objective test, the question of 'appearances' is important. Objective bias must itself be decided objectively, from the standpoint of an impartial and informed observer: the standpoint of the defendant is not enough.

The HRA

The rules of natural justice, in the law of England and Wales, recognise two tests for bias by a judicial body.

- **Direct personal interests**. Where a judge or tribunal member has a personal interest in the outcome of the trial, he or she should be automatically removed from the case. This was originally focused on the judge having a 'pecuniary' (financial) interest in the case.

 CASE CLOSE-UP

***R v Bow Street Magistrates ex parte Pinochet (No 2)* [2000] 1 AC 119**

Lord Hoffmann's decision decided the outcome of a case concerning whether General Pinochet, the former dictator of Chile, should be extradited to Spain to face charges of torture. Lord Hoffmann was a director of a charitable wing of Amnesty International who were interveners in the case. This was not known at the time of the case. A different House of Lords held that the decision should be set aside and reheard by a different committee of Law Lords.

The House of Lords, determining English law in a manner consistent with Article 6, extended the need for automatic removal to cases in which a judge's other political, moral, intellectual, etc. interests might be in issue. Later cases, however, have made it clear that the barrier to prove the appearance of bias on these grounds is very high (see *Locabail* v *Bayfield* [2000] 1 All ER 65).

Bias cannot, for example, be based on the fact that judge and defendant are of different faiths (*Seer Technologies* v *Abbas* The Times, 16 March 2000; *Helow* v *Advocate General for Scotland* [2008] UKHL 62 provides a clear affirmation of judicial detachment).

In *Hoekstra* v *HM Advocate* 2000 JC 391, a case involving HRA issues was set aside because of the appearance of bias. One of the judges (Lord McCluskey, a very senior judge and author on legal affairs) had published an article in a Sunday newspaper that was highly critical of the Convention and its incorporation into Scots law.

- **Objective factors**

CASE CLOSE-UP

***Porter* v *Magill* [2001] UKHL 67**

The Leader and Deputy Leader of Westminster Council had been removed from office by the District Auditor and surcharged for wilful misconduct in office. They challenged the auditor's impartiality. The House of Lords held that the auditor had not breached Article 6(1).

In *Porter*, the House of Lords confirmed the test, based on objective factors, for the appearance of bias:

> The question is whether the fair-minded and informed observer, having considered the facts [the facts relating, for and against, to the issue of bias] would conclude there was a real possibility that the tribunal was biased.

(para 100)

Factors such as links to those previously involved in the case (*R (Chief Constable of Lancashire Constabulary) v Crown Court at Preston* [2001] EWHC 928 (Admin)), or friendship with witnesses (*AWG Group v Morrison* [2006] EWCA Civ 6) can be grounds for finding bias.

Particular difficulties in England and Wales arise in respect of tribunals. These are often chaired by a lawyer who is assisted by two experts in the area the tribunal deals with. Expert members of the tribunal may also, in different cases, appear before the tribunal as an expert witness. Depending on the facts, there may be bias (as in *SSWP v Cunningham* 2004 SLT 1007). The matter has been discussed by the House of Lords in *Gillies v SSW&P* [2006] UKHL 2.

Juries

Juries do not give reasons for their decisions. Under the Contempt of Court Act 1981, their deliberations must be kept secret. Allegations are sometimes made that the jury has been racist or has used irrational ways of deciding cases, like the use of an ouija board (*R v Young* (1995) QB 324). The ECtHR requires allegations of racism to be taken seriously by the judge and action taken which is sufficient to deal with the allegations (compare *Gregory v United Kingdom* (1998) 25 EHRR 577 with *Sander v United Kingdom* (2001) 31 EHRR 44). In *R v Mirza* [2004] UKHL 2, the House of Lords upheld the approach of the ECtHR but insisted that action taken in the face of well-founded allegations must not compromise the underlying secrecy of jury deliberations.

12.8 Public hearing

12.8.1 **Introduction**

Trials that are covered by Article 6 must generally be held in public. But a public hearing is by no means an absolute right and the second sentence of Article 6(1) permits the exclusion of press and public in a wide range of circumstances, discussed in section 12.8.2.

A public hearing protects litigants and defendants against secret trials: one of the evils of a totalitarian system. It helps to maintain public confidence in the courts. Publicity also deters inappropriate behaviour by the court, maintains public confidence that the courts are impartial, and can result in evidence being available which would otherwise not be known. See *Diennet v France* (1996) 21 EHRR 554, para 33 and *R v Legal Aid Board ex parte Kaim Todner* [1998] 3 All ER 541, 549–50.

12.8.2 **Exceptions**

Article 6(1) permits exceptions to the principle of public trials:

- where the exclusion of the press or public serves the interests of morals, public order, or national security as these terms are understood in a democratic society;
- where the exclusion is necessary to protect the interests of juveniles or the private life of the parties;
- where publicity would, in the opinion of the court, prejudice the interests of justice.

These exclusions have had an important impact on the development of English law under the HRA.

Juveniles and private life

Restrictions on public access to court and on media publicity are found in the law of England and Wales (both statute and common law) in respect of juvenile justice, both civil and criminal. They are also found in respect of many issues of family and matrimonial law. Such restrictions are likely to be consistent with Article 6(1).

Difficulties can arise when the principle of public trials and the protection of private life under Article 8 ECHR come into tension.

 CASE CLOSE-UP

Re S [2004] UKHL 47

S was charged with the murder of one of her children. An order was made prohibiting the publication of information and photographs that might lead to the identification of her other child. At the behest of newspapers the order was varied to allow the publication of the names and photographs of the parents and the deceased child. The other child challenged the variation. The House of Lords held that, weighing Article 8 and Article 10 in the facts of the case, the variation of the order should stay.

Although Article 6 was not directly involved (the other child was not on trial), the principle of open justice in Article 6(1) was the starting point. The House of Lords held that neither media freedom nor respect for private life had priority over the other. The court undertook a 'balancing' exercise (see para 17) of those rights in the context of open justice. Where there are good grounds for thinking that publicity might lead to a witness or defendant being killed or otherwise threatened, their rights under Article 2 may override the presumption in favour of publicity.

▶ **CROSS REFERENCE**

For Article 2 see Chapter 8, section 8.3.3.

Prisoners and detainees

Prison disciplinary hearings have been accepted as exceptions to the rule in favour of open justice. Privacy can be justified as a proportionate means of securing 'public order' and security (see *Campbell and Fell* v *United Kingdom* (1985) 7 EHRR 165, paras 86–88).

In *AH* v *West London MHT* [2010] UKUT 264, the Upper Tribunal accepted that the claimant (who had been detained in a special hospital for 23 years) had a right to a public hearing before a mental health tribunal. The 'interests of justice', interpreted in the light of Article 6, meant that the norm of private hearings should be departed from.

National security

Article 6 permits restrictions on the public nature of trials in the context of national security. In the UK, courts have discretion to hear matters in private ('*in camera*') with a right of appeal to the Court of Appeal.

In *R* v *A* [2006] EWCA Crim 4, the applicant was charged with conspiracy to cause explosions in the UK. He alleged he had been tortured before being brought to the UK. The trial judge held that evidence about torture which the prosecution might have to disclose would be heard *in camera*. The Court of Appeal accepted that *in camera* orders in this criminal law context did not violate Article 6(1). Questions of disclosure in a civil context are discussed at section 12.11.3.

Contempt of court

The law on contempt of court permits restrictions on media publicity in order to protect the fairness of a trial. In England and Wales the law is found in the Contempt of Court Act 1981 and also in common law. Such rules are not only compatible with Article 6(1) but are likely to be compatible with Article 10, the right to freedom of expression, as being a proportionate way of protecting the rights of defendants and of maintaining the 'authority and impartiality of the judiciary'. Legal rules aimed at restricting the publication of articles that might prejudice the outcome of a trial were upheld as being compatible with both Article 6 and Article 10 in *Worm* v *Austria* (1998) 25 EHRR 454.

12.9 Pronounced publicly

Even where the trial itself has been conducted in private or secretly, there is a strong presumption that judgment should be given in open court or at least be available to public knowledge. Otherwise the fact that there has been a trial at all could be withheld. The Court, therefore, takes a strict view of the grounds on which the judgment itself can be withheld from the public (see *Campbell and Fell* v *United Kingdom* (1985) 7 EHRR 165). The parties themselves have a right to the full judgment (not just a summary) in order to consider whether there are grounds for appeal (e.g. *Ryakib Biryukov* v *Russia* App 14810/02, judgment of 17 January 2008).

The need for publicity can lead to tensions between Article 6 and other Convention Articles, particularly Articles 8 (private life) and Article 10 (freedom of expression, including media freedom).

In *Blunkett* v *Quinn* [2004] EWHC 2816, the judge, in family proceedings involving David Blunkett, the former Home Secretary, decided that the proportionate balance between Articles 6, 8, and 10 was to pronounce judgment in open court if only to correct inaccuracies in the massive press coverage that the case had generated.

12.10 Trial within a reasonable time

It is a denial of justice to allow unreasonable delays in the judicial processes by which civil rights and obligations and criminal charges are determined. Article 6 requires a trial within a 'reasonable time'. A complementary provision is found in Article 5(3), which provides, in effect, that everyone charged with a criminal offence must be released on bail or, if they need to be remanded in custody, must be tried within a reasonable time. What is a reasonable time to await trial is likely (depending on all the circumstances) to be shortest in respect of a person on remand and is primarily dealt with under Article 5(3); trials of such prisoners should be a priority for the state, which must display 'special diligence'.

CROSS REFERENCE
For Article 5(3) see Chapter 11, section 11.7.

Longer periods are acceptable under Article 6 for defendants on bail and for civil litigation.

The unfairness of delay does not mean that the trial must be stayed. Delay can be remedied by other means such as public recognition of the delay, a lowering of sentence, or compensation

(*Attorney General's Reference (No 2 of 2001)* [2003] UKHL 68 and (for Scotland) *Spiers v Ruddy* [2007] UKPC D2).

12.10.1 **Starting and finishing times**

The reasonableness of the time in criminal cases is measured from the time of the 'charge'. This has an autonomous Convention meaning and was defined in *Corigliano v Italy* (1983) 5 EHRR 334 as 'the official notification given to an individual by the competent authority of an allegation that he has committed a criminal offence'. In England and Wales 'official notification' runs from the time of being charged or summonsed (*Attorney General's Reference (No 2 of 2001)* [2003] UKHL 68, para 29).

For civil actions, official notification is likely to be from the time that proceedings are instituted, for example the issuing of a writ.

These are the times from which the specific right to a trial 'within a reasonable time' is measured. The state's obligations to secure the other rights which inhere in the right to a fair trial generally can kick in earlier. For example, the right to legal advice (an aspect of Article 6(1) as well as Article 6(3)(c), see section 12.15.3) may arise when the police are questioning a suspect, not just after the suspect is charged (see *O'Neill v HM Advocate* [2013] UKSC 36), and the fairness of a trial can depend on the way evidence has been obtained (see *Ludi v Switzerland* (1993) 15 EHRR 173, at section 12.11.5).

For both criminal and civil cases, the period of time in issue ends with the final determination of the case, which will usually be after all appeal procedures have been exhausted. Delay concerns 'the entirety of the proceedings in issue, including any appeals' (*Poiss v Austria* (1988) 10 EHRR 231, para 50).

12.10.2 **Reasonableness**

The reasonableness of the time the authorities take to complete a trial process depends upon the particular facts and circumstances of the case. In assessing this, matters such as the following are taken into account (see *Philis v Greece (No 2)* (1998) 25 EHRR 417):

- the complexity of the case;
- the conduct of the applicant;
- the conduct of the authorities; and
- the importance of the case for the applicant.

Examples of unreasonable delay in Convention cases include:

- over four years to determine a straightforward dispute on costs: *Robins v United Kingdom* (1998) 26 EHRR 527;
- eight years, 11 months in a complex fraud case. The applicant bore considerable responsibility for the delay but the authorities had not pursued the matter diligently: *Eastaway v United Kingdom* (2005) 40 EHRR 17;
- periods of up to seven years in determining claims for compensation brought by haemophiliacs infected with HIV from blood transfusions with contaminated blood; the authorities had not been sufficiently diligent and the issue was of life and death importance to the applicants: *A v Denmark* (1996) 22 EHRR 458.

In the United Kingdom, the Privy Council, applying the HRA in Scottish devolution cases, held that two years, four months' delay in the trial of a 13-year-old boy for serious sexual offences was too long, the need for particular diligence where children are concerned had not been met. On the other hand, a period of one year and 10 months to deal with a trial of police officers for perjury was not unreasonable (*Dyer* v *Watson* [2002] UKPC D1).

12.11 Article 6(1): the nature of a fair hearing

12.11.1 Introduction

Under Article 6, criminal and civil trials must be fair overall. This, as we have seen, includes their being conducted without unreasonable delay, usually conducted in public, and decided by judges who are independent and impartial.

Article 6 says nothing particular about what makes the hearing itself, criminal or civil, a fair one. A number of general rights and characteristics of a fair hearing have been identified by the ECtHR as being inherent in the idea of a fair trial. These 'inherent' or 'implied' rights of a fair hearing may be subject to context-related qualifications, though any such qualifications are limited by the overriding principle that the trial be fair overall (see section 12.5). These general characteristics of a fair hearing are discussed in this section.

The general right to a fair hearing in Article 6(1) applies to both civil and criminal trials. Article 6(2) and (3) gives additional more specific rights to criminal defendants.

12.11.2 Participation

There is a general right to effective participation in a trial. This applies to both civil and criminal trials, though in relation to the latter the right is enhanced by various, more specific entitlements in Article 6(3). In criminal trials especially there is a strong presumption that the defendant should attend the trial (though a trial *in absentia* is not necessarily a violation).

Effective participation can, depending on context, mean a right to an oral hearing.

 CASE CLOSE-UP

R (Wright) v Secretary of State for Health [2009] UKHL 3

Under the Care Standards Act 2000, care workers, against whom allegations of abuse had been made, could be put, immediately, on an interim list which prevented them from working with vulnerable adults. After being on the list for nine months, the care worker could apply to an independent tribunal. Listing was by the Secretary of State who allowed care workers to be put on the list without the opportunity to be heard. The House of Lords held that civil rights were engaged and the lack of an opportunity to make representations prior to listing violated Article 6. A declaration of incompatibility was made.

CROSS REFERENCE
'Civil rights' are defined at section 12.3; 'declarations of incompatibility' are discussed in Chapter 4, section 4.4.3.

See also *R (Hammond) v Secretary of State for the Home Department* [2005] UKHL 69, in Chapter 4, section 4.4.7.

Participation means not only being present but also being able to follow the proceedings, at least in general terms. What is required for effective participation must be appropriate to the person concerned.

CASE CLOSE-UP

T v United Kingdom (2000) 30 EHRR 121

An 11-year-old boy was, along with another boy, V, accused of murder. The victim was two years old, the murder was brutal and shocking and, as a result, there was intense national and international media attention. T and V were tried in an adult court, which retained adult procedures and formalities. Various measures were taken to assist T and V to understand the trial process.

The ECtHR held that there had been a violation of Article 6(1).

In this famous case the ECtHR made it clear that the right to participate in the trial means, in the case of a child:

that it is essential that a child charged with an offence is dealt with in a manner which takes full account of his age, level of maturity and intellectual and emotional capacities, and that steps are taken to promote his ability to understand and participate in the proceedings.

Although a number of things had been done to assist T in understanding the proceedings, the ECtHR held that these were was not enough (indeed some, such as the placing of the defendant on a raised platform so he could better see the proceedings, may have contributed to his feeling of discomfort and being under pressure) and that in all the circumstances, including the intense and sometimes hostile media scrutiny, there had been a breach of Article 6(1) (see paras 84–85).

12.11.3 Equality of arms

The concept of equality of arms

Hearings involving civil rights and obligations and criminal charges must be adversarial. The principle of equality of arms is an aspect of an adversarial hearing which applies to both civil and criminal trials. The idea is that, both in reality and appearance, the parties should be treated equally and have equal rights in the trial process. In particular this can require:

- equal access to the evidence;
- equal participation in the procedures through which the matter is determined by the court;
- the equal treatment of witnesses (see *Dombo Beheer v The Netherlands* (1994) 18 EHRR 213);
- the right of a person to see and comment upon all the evidence on which the court or tribunal's decision will be made. Thus in *McMichael v United Kingdom* (1995) 20 EHRR 205, there was a breach of Article 6(1) in respect of a mother denied access to various social reports about her on which her ability to have the care of her child was determined;
- if an official advises the court, like a magistrate's clerk or as advocate general, their advice, if it may influence the way the court decides, must be open to challenge by the defence

(see *Borgers v Belgium* (1993) 15 EHRR 92 and *Clark (Procurator Fiscal, Kirkcaldy) v Kelly* [2003] UKPC D1).

Disclosure and public interest immunity

The general principle in a criminal trial is that the prosecution must disclose evidence to the defence which is likely to undermine the prosecution or assist the defence. In civil cases the court can order the disclosure of evidence if one of the parties is reluctant to agree full disclosure. There may, however, be reasons why, in the 'public interest', evidence which should otherwise be disclosed, should be kept secret; for example, to protect a police informant, or maintain the operational effectiveness of surveillance devices. Of particular importance is the government's duty to maintain national security.

This raises an important dilemma for the courts: is it best to stand on an important principle (justice can only be done on the basis of full disclosure, publicly, in court) even though the consequence may be that the trial is stopped and, therefore, justice in the particular case is not done? On the other hand, is it best to compromise on the principle of full open disclosure in order that the trial can take place and justice done in the particular case?

The approach of the ECtHR is that Article 6(1) (the general principle of a fair trial in civil and criminal cases) does require full disclosure by both sides and an opportunity for both sides (e.g. prosecution and defence in a criminal trial) to know and challenge this disclosed material. Nevertheless this duty of full disclosure is not absolute and may be qualified if, first, this is necessary to protect important competing interests such as the fundamental rights of third parties (e.g. the right to life of a witness) or to preserve important public interests such as national security; and, secondly, if the hearing cannot go ahead without the material being shown to a judge. However, these qualifications must be 'strictly necessary' (i.e. for legitimate purposes, proportionate and consistent with the overall fairness of the trial). Vitally, the judicial authorities must develop adequate safeguards aimed at reducing the impact on the defendant and which have the effect of 'counterbalancing' the difficulties caused by the restriction on rights. Safeguards can include:

- the giving of a 'gist' or summary of the closed material; or
- the use of 'special counsel'.

Without these safeguards applying to the main features of the case, it will not normally be possible for the hearing to proceed (but compare *Al-Khawaja* at section 12.15.4, the sole or decisive rule).

These principles have been articulated in a number of Strasbourg cases including *Rowe and Davis v United Kingdom* (2000) 30 EHRR 1 (a murder trial), *Chahal v United Kingdom* (deportation proceedings), and *A v United* (detention without trial of terrorist suspects). They are adopted into UK law and have been summarised in *Bank Mellat v The Treasury (No 1)* (section 12.11.3), paras 5–8.

In the United Kingdom the courts accept that 'Public Interest Immunity' (PII) may justify non-disclosure and a procedure to deal with such cases (both criminal and civil) has been developed. The evidence is disclosed to the judge in chambers who decides whether its disclosure is necessary to proceed with the case. The proceeding may be *ex parte* (without the defence being present or even knowing of the hearing). If the defence are not present when the evidence is disclosed to the judge, counter-weighting measures, in particular 'special counsel', may be used. Special counsel are security cleared advocates. They represent the defendant, but once they have seen the 'closed material' concerning the defendant they may no longer discuss the case or take instructions from the defendant or his or her lawyers.

CASE CLOSE-UP

R v H [2004] UKHL 3

In a drugs case the prosecution sought to withhold evidence, requested by the defence, on PII grounds. Prior to his scrutiny of the evidence, the judge ruled that special counsel could be appointed.

HELD: appointing special counsel at this stage was premature.

The main point of the case was to establish, in UK law, the main principles for ensuring that the PII procedure, at least in the criminal law context, was compatible with Article 6. It was held that:

- the golden rule, the starting point, is full disclosure under the Act;
- however, departure from the golden rule is permissible if important public interests are at stake; but
- any departure must be the minimum necessary to secure the public interest; and
- the judge was required to consider a range of factors such as the possibility of protecting both the defendant's rights and the public interest without full disclosure (such as through limited, partial, disclosure or by giving the 'gist' of the evidence to the defendant;
- factors that might be considered could include special counsel, but only as a last resort;
- overall, though, the general fairness of the trial must not be imperilled. If the trial cannot be fair it may have to be stayed.

Disclosure and national security cases

Similar issues arise in civil cases involving national security. Again, the issue is whether, and if so how, a trial can proceed, justice under the law be done, when the case requires the state to disclose sensitive national security information (e.g. information given on the understanding that it will not be disclosed).

In the national security context, however, the government's objective goes beyond PII. The PII procedure leaves the last word on disclosure to the judge and if the judge orders disclosure (as in *Al Rawi*, below), the government may judge that they are unable to proceed with the case and defend the lawfulness of their actions. In this context the government sought full 'closed material procedures' (CMP) which include holding part or all of the trial in secret without the claimants being present or seeing all the evidence.

CASE CLOSE-UP

Al Rawi v Security Services [2011] UKSC 24

The Court of Appeal, refusing a PII claim (discussed earlier), had ordered the government to disclose evidence that could prove that a one-time Guantanamo Bay detainee (BM) had been tortured. The evidence had originally been obtained in confidence from the US government. BM then sought to use this and other evidence in a civil action for damages against the Security Services. The government, wishing to defend itself, sought to have important sections of the trial heard in secret.

The Supreme Court, by a majority, denied this. It affirmed the principles of open justice and full access to the evidence as fundamental to the common law. These fundamental principles could be subject to PII and qualified by 'gisting', special counsel etc (see *R* v *H*, discussed earlier) but not any further. Full CMP (trial in secret without the presence of the parties) would require statutory authorisation.

As a consequence the government reached an out-of-court settlement with BM.

 CASE CLOSE-UP

Bank Mellat v The Treasury (No 1) [2013] UKSC 38

Bank Mellat (an Iranian bank operating in London) challenged a Treasury direction preventing them from conducting financial business in London. The government believed that the Bank was assisting the alleged Iranian nuclear weapons programme. The direction was made under the Counter Terrorism Act 2008 and this Act, under sections 66 and 67, authorised, if necessary in the public interest, the use of CMPs, including holding trials in private without the presence of the claimant.

The majority, in a strongly contested judgment, held that the Supreme Court did have the authority to hold a secret hearing. Unlike in *Al Rawi* (discussed earlier) there was statutory authority for so doing. The implication of both the 2008 Act and also the Constitutional Reform Act 2005, which established the Supreme Court, was that such hearings could and should be held if necessary. The minority held, on the contrary, that only express statutory terms (not just implications) could authorise such a drastic departure from the fundamental principle of open justice.

These issues are now, to some extent, resolved by the Justice and Security Act 2013 Part 2, which introduces closed material procedures into ordinary civil actions (not criminal cases) where preventing the disclosure of sensitive material might prevent the trial from proceeding. Senior courts (i.e. the High Court, Court of Appeal, and Supreme Court, and, in Scotland, the Court of Session) can grant an application (by any person, but normally the government) to use CMP. These include the use of special counsel, gisting, and (section 11(2)(e)) closed hearings. The court must be satisfied that the case requires the disclosure of sensitive material and that closed procedures would be in the interest of the fair and effective administration of justice.

This allows the case to proceed. Critics point to the way this institutionalises the unfairness of secret procedures.

12.11.4 **Representation**

The value of legal representation is that the relevant points of a case are properly understood by the court, the evidence is properly tested, and, as a result, a just outcome emerges. Many people, through lacking legal knowledge, being inarticulate, or lacking other skills, will be unable to present their case with its due strength without professional assistance. Defendants and civil litigants may also believe, with good reason, that their chances of winning are greater if they are represented.

Criminal trials

Defendants in criminal trials have a strong right to representation under Article 6(3)(c), which is discussed in section 12.15.3.

Civil trials

There is no equivalent right for civil litigants. Representation may be an inherent right, required in order to achieve a fair trial in the circumstances.

 CASE CLOSE-UP

P, C and S v United Kingdom (2002) 35 EHRR 31

P and C were involved in complex and emotionally charged family proceedings involving the fate of their youngest child, S. During the care proceedings, P and C's legal representatives withdrew because they felt they were being asked to conduct the case unreasonably, and P and C represented themselves. P and C lost the care proceedings and, consequently, an action to free S for adoption was begun by the local authority. P and C were denied legal representation in these adoption proceedings. Subsequently S was adopted and all contact with P and C was ended.

The ECtHR held that the lack of legal representation was a breach of Article 6(1).

The ECtHR said that under Article 6(1) (see paras 88–91):

- There is no automatic right, under the Convention, to representation in civil proceedings.
- However, representation might be necessary to ensure access to court and the fact and appearance of a fair trial.
- A range of relevant factors include: whether representation is compulsory (under some legal systems representation is necessary before the higher courts); the complexity of the case; and the degree of emotional involvement, which might undermine the degree of objectivity necessary for effective representation and the seriousness of the matter for the applicant (see also *Airey* v *Ireland* (1979–80) 2 EHRR 305, paras 26–28 for examples).
- Like all rights implied from the overarching right in Article 6(1), representation and access to the court is subject to proportionate restrictions and these can be justified by a range of factors relating to the administration of justice, including costs and the need to expedite some kinds of hearing.

Under the law in England and Wales, a right to representation will be found in the rules of courts and tribunals. Inferior courts, tribunals, or other bodies which, consistent with their rules, deny a right of representation, can be challenged by judicial review. The High Court denies a general legal rule requiring representation but it is unlawful (a breach of natural justice) for a tribunal to refuse representation if it is needed because of circumstances, such as the seriousness and complexity of the case, the capabilities of the parties, or the consequences for the litigants.

In *Perotti* v *Collyer-Bristow* [2003] EWCA Civ 1521, the Court of Appeal recognised that Article 6 imposed a lesser requirement in civil cases than criminal cases. The test for whether representation was necessary was whether, without representation, a court would be unable to do justice in the case. The mere fact that a case might be poorly presented was not sufficient.

12.11.5 Illegally or improperly obtained evidence

General principles

As has been said before, the law on criminal procedure, including the admissibility of evidence, is a matter for the national authorities. The law of England and Wales, like most legal systems, does not have a rule of law banning the admissibility of illegally or improperly obtained evidence. Section 78 PACE gives judges discretion to exclude evidence it would be unfair to admit and this includes on grounds relating to 'the circumstances in which the evidence was obtained'.

Nothing in Article 6(1) requires an absolute exclusion rule. The ECtHR accepts the existence of discretion under national laws to admit illegally obtained evidence so long as the overall trial remains fair. Of particular importance is the need to maintain the rights of the defence. In *Khan* v *United Kingdom* (2000) 31 EHRR 45, even evidence obtained in breach of a Convention right (Article 8) was accepted in the circumstances. What is important is that there should be adequate remedies to deal with illegal or oppressive actions by the police. These principles have been followed by English courts, in relation to the HRA, in *R* v *P* [2001] 2 All ER 58, 67–70.

 DISCUSSION TOPIC

Should unlawfully obtained evidence always be inadmissible?

In favour of general inadmissibility is the deterrent effect this would have on police and other officials who might, often from public interest motives, break the law in order to convict alleged criminals.

In favour of allowing admissibility is that the unlawfully obtained evidence may be true or have a high value in helping to convict dangerous criminals. Law breaking by the police, from this point of view, should be dealt with in other ways such as by police complaints, disciplinary actions, or civil actions.

Oppressive confessions

Confessions obtained by oppression should be inadmissible as a matter of law (indeed section 76 PACE gives judges no discretion: once a judge has decided there has been oppression he or she must exclude the evidence). Article 6(1) rights would be violated if it was left to a jury to consider whether or not there had been oppression (see *R* v *Mushtaq* [2005] UKHL 25).

Evidence obtained in breach of Article 3, i.e. by torture or inhuman treatment, must be excluded both under international law (Article 15 of the UN Convention against Torture) and English law (section 76 PACE 1984 and, in particular, *A* v *Secretary of State for the Home Department* [2005] UKHL 71, discussed in Chapter 9, section 9.4.3).

Entrapment

Despite the absence of a general rule banning illegally or improperly obtained evidence, the ECtHR has held in a number of cases that the way in which evidence is obtained can affect the overall fairness of a trial (see, for example, *Ludi* v *Switzerland* (1993) 15 EHRR 173).

The use of surveillance and undercover officers does not in itself violate Article 6. However, if the undercover officers do more than merely conduct surveillance and make reports, a violation of Article 6 can occur. In particular, there may be a violation of Article 6 where there has been 'entrapment'. This is where police or other authorities act in a way which incites the commission of a crime. The principles of the leading Convention case, *Teixeira de Castro* v *Portugal* (1999) 28 EHRR 101, have been adopted by the House of Lords.

🔍 CASE CLOSE-UP

R v *Looseley; Attorney General's Reference (No 3 of 2000)* [2001] UKHL 53

One defendant (L) was convicted of supplying drugs. He alleged entrapment. The other defendant's trial was stayed (stopped) by the judge on the grounds of entrapment. In L's case the House of Lords held there was no entrapment because undercover officers had merely presented themselves to him as ideal customers. In the other case the judge was right to stay proceedings because the police had encouraged the defendant to commit a crime he would not otherwise have committed.

The House of Lords made a strongly worded attack on entrapment.

* The law must set its face against 'state created crime'. This is an abuse of process and an affront to the public conscience.

* Police are not required only to be passive observers of crime. They can play a 'proactive' role but must not overstep the boundary and behave in a way which brings the administration of justice into disrepute.

* Issues for a court to consider are the nature of the offence, the reasons for the police operation, and the nature and extent of police participation.

* It will not be unlawful for the police to behave as an ordinary customer of an illegal trade, nor to give the defendant an unexceptional opportunity to commit a crime. In *R* v *Jones* [2007] EWCA Crim 1118, for example, a police officer pretended, on the internet, to be a child to whom J willingly made unlawful sexual overtures. There was no entrapment.

* There must be evidence to support police suspicion of the defendant, more than a criminal record and a disposition to commit crimes.

These basic principles reflect the Convention law and represent a toughening of English law. Judicial disapproval means that, where there has been entrapment, a trial should normally be stayed, rather than the evidence considered for exclusion under section 78 PACE.

12.12 Additional rights relating only to criminal trials

Criminal defendants enjoy the full range of rights under Article 6(1). Articles 6(2) and (3) provide them with an additional range of rights. Frequently the same issue in a case can be dealt with under the general idea of fair trial involving Article 6(1) or under one of the more specific rights found in Article 6(2) or (3). The ECtHR characteristically resolves the case under Article 6(1) unless there are additional issues that can only be dealt with in terms of Article 6(2) or (3). The rights expressed in Article 6(2) and (3) are subject to reasonable restrictions and limitations, which serve legitimate purposes and which are proportionate in respect of the individual and the particular context.

12.13 Article 6(2): the presumption of innocence

The presumption of innocence is perhaps the most fundamental principle governing a criminal trial and it has a long history, certainly in European legal systems, as the principal idea in terms of which the fairness of a trial is recognised. The state, in whose name the prosecution is brought, has the burden of proving the guilt of the accused. The accused should not be required to prove his or her innocence and should, therefore, not be compelled to give evidence and cannot be compelled to incriminate him or herself. The principle is so important that it warrants an express section in Article 6 (though the presumption of innocence is also inherent in Article 6(1)).

12.13.1 **Strict liability and reverse burdens of proof**

Most European legal systems, including that of the United Kingdom, have offences in which guilt is fully or partially based on a finding of fact rather having to go further and prove the defendant's 'guilty mind' or a particular intention or state of knowledge. It is sometimes alleged that such offences violate Article 6(2). The ECtHR has not taken a strict, absolutist approach to such cases. The Court outlined its position in *Salabiaku* v *France* (1991) 13 EHRR 379 (see paras 27–28):

- Subject to not violating other Convention rights, the content of the criminal law is up to the states.
- Presumptions of fact or law, in the way crimes are defined, are not, in themselves, prohibited under the Convention (they are commonly found in European legal systems).
- But these presumptions must be kept within reasonable limits 'which take into account the importance of what is at stake and maintain the rights of the defence'.

12.13.2 **Reverse burden defences: evidential and legal burdens**

The most serious cases have involved so-called 'reverse burden' or 'reverse onus' defences. This is where guilt can be based on a presumption which the defendant is then left to disprove. For example, a person occupying premises in which terrorist articles are found may be presumed to be in 'possession' of the article and, therefore, can be convicted of an offence unless they can prove that they did not know the articles were on the premises (as in *R* v *DPP ex parte Kebilene* [1994] 4 All ER 801; see now section 57 Terrorism Act 2000). On the basis of the *Salabiaku* principles, such reverse burden defences are not in principle incompatible with Article 6(2) so long as they are justifiable.

Following *Kebilene*, UK law distinguishes between reverse burden offences which impose an 'evidential burden' and those which impose a 'legal burden' of proof on the defendant. Whether it is an evidential or legal burden is either expressly stipulated in the Act (as is the case with some of the anti-terrorism offences) or is a matter of statutory interpretation for the courts. Since the HRA, of course, such interpretation must seek compatibility with Article 6(2).

- 'Evidential burdens' do not alter the burden of proof and so do not violate Article 6(2). An evidential burden merely requires the defendant to raise a matter which, because of the statutory defence, it is relevant for the court to consider. For example, it can be an offence under anti-terrorism legislation not to disclose certain information to the police and some such offences have a 'reasonable excuse' defence. A journalist, for example, might raise the fact that he or she is investigating terrorist groups as a reasonable excuse. If, on a literal reading of the statute, the burden is 'evidential', simply raising the issue establishes the defence. There should be an acquittal unless the prosecution, to whom the burden of proof now returns, can prove, beyond reasonable doubt, that in the circumstances the matter raised does not assist the defendant (e.g. that being a journalist is no defence). Article 6(2) is not in issue.

- A 'legal burden' requires the defendant to prove, at least on a balance of probabilities, one of the matters specified in the defence. This does reverse the burden of proof and so raises an Article 6(2) issue.

- If on 'ordinary' principles of statutory interpretation, it is a legal burden, section 3 HRA requires the courts, if possible, to 'read down' the defence to turn it into an evidential burden. If this is not 'possible' the court must consider whether Article 6(2) is violated. *Salabiaku* is taken to mean that departures from a strict application of the presumption of innocence are compatible with Article 6(2) if they can be justified (*R* v *Lambert* [2002] 2 AC 545, para 88). Proportionality is at the heart of the matter. It requires a fair balance between the fundamental rights of the individual and the social interest in the suppression of crime. Issues such as the seriousness of the punishment, the extent and nature of the issues that the defendant must prove (e.g. whether they are matters over which he has personal knowledge) are relevant to proportionality (see, in particular, *Sheldrake* v *DPP* [2004] UKHL 43, para 21).

🔍 CASE CLOSE-UP

Sheldrake v DPP; Attorney General's Reference (No 4 of 2002) [2004] UKHL 43

Sheldrake: S was convicted, under the Road Traffic Act 1988, of being drunk and in charge of a motor vehicle, which, at the time, was parked. There was a defence for him to prove that there was no likelihood of his actually driving the car whilst over the statutory limit. The House of Lords held that the defence imposed a legal burden on the defendant. The burden was reasonable and not a violation of Article 6(2) since the offence served a reasonable purpose (road safety) and it was not unfair to expect the defendant to discharge the burden, since he or she would be well placed to provide the necessary evidence.

AG's Reference: the defendant had been prosecuted for membership of a part of Hamas, a proscribed (banned) terrorist organisation. The legislation allowed a defence if the defendant could prove that the organisation was not banned when he joined and that he had not taken part in any of its activities since it was banned. The House of Lords held that, on ordinary statutory construction, the defence imposed a legal burden on the accused. This could be unfair, however, since the defence would be difficult to prove and a wholly innocent person might be put in an impossible position. Therefore, 'reading down' the statute on the basis of section 3 of the HRA, the defence would be interpreted as requiring only an evidential burden and thus potential conflicts with Article 6(2) would be avoided.

BIGGER PICTURE

UK law on reverse defences is summarised by Lord Philips in *R v Keogh* [2007] EWCA Crim 528, paras 4–12 (concerning the Official Secrets Act 1989); see also *R v Johnstone* [2003] UKHL 28 (concerning selling bootleg CDs).

12.14 Article 6(2): the right to silence

The right to silence is considered here in relation to Article 6(2). It involves the general right to a fair trial and so cases may relate to Article 6(1) alone or Article 6(1) read in the light of Article 6(2).

The presumption of innocence means that the prosecution should have the burden of proving the guilt of the accused who need say or do nothing and, specifically, who cannot be required to incriminate him or herself. There are two aspects to the right.

- Compelled evidence. The accused should not be required, on pain of punishment, to answer questions whose answers are used to convict.
- Drawing inferences. The courts should not be able to infer guilt from the accused person's silence either when being questioned by the police or at his or her trial.

The general position under the Convention (reflecting the ECtHR's unwillingness to adopt absolutist positions) is: the right to silence is at the heart of the protection offered by Article 6, however, the rule is not absolute and qualifications are acceptable so long as they do not undermine the essence of a fair trial.

12.14.1 Compelled evidence

A fair trial issue under Article 6(1) (read with Article 6(2)) is raised if a person is prosecuted for a criminal offence on the basis of evidence which, through other legally based procedures, he or she was required by law to provide.

CASE CLOSE-UP

Saunders v United Kingdom (1997) 23 EHRR 313

Statute required S to answer questions from government inspectors inquiring into a city takeover battle. Failure to answer could lead to contempt of court proceedings and

> punishment. S was later prosecuted and convicted for theft, false accounting, and conspiracy, and transcripts of evidence given by S to the inspectors was used by the prosecution in the criminal case. The ECtHR, following its decision in *Funke v France* I1993) 16 EHRR 297, held that there had been a breach of Article 6(1).

The Court asserted:

- The importance of the right to silence and the right not to incriminate oneself as inherent in the idea of a fair trial and as closely linked to Article 6(2) and the presumption of innocence.
- Its justification is to prevent the use by the authorities of improper compulsion. The argument is that this is likely to increase the likelihood of a fair trial.
- The right does not extend to material whose existence is independent of the accused person's will—nothing in Article 6 restricts the powers of the state to compel the production of documents, blood samples, etc. and for these to be used in court.
- The violation of Article 6 results from the use in a criminal trial of the compelled evidence: the legal duty to answer investigator's questions does not of itself violate Article 6 (see *IJL v United Kingdom* (2001) 33 EHRR 11, para 100).

However, *Saunders* should not be read as imposing an absolute right not to incriminate oneself. The right is implied and subject to proportionate and reasonable restrictions serving a legitimate purpose which is compatible with the overall fairness of the trial; e.g. speed camera cases such as *O'Halloran and Francis v United Kingdom* (2008) 46 EHRR 21.

12.14.2 **Drawing inferences**

The right to silence is also protected by forbidding the court from drawing inferences of guilt from the fact that an accused person chooses to remain silent. In Northern Ireland since 1988 and England and Wales since 1994, magistrates and juries (and judges in special courts in Northern Ireland) have been able to draw such inferences in certain circumstances. This has been tested against Article 6.

 CASE CLOSE-UP

***Murray* v *United Kingdom* (1996) 22 EHRR 29**

M had been arrested in the house where the IRA had held an informer captive. M remained silent under police questioning. He was convicted of aiding and abetting the false imprisonment of the informer and sentenced to eight years' imprisonment. The judge (who determined guilt) made adverse inferences from M's silence. The ECtHR held that there was no violation of Article 6.

In *Murray*, the ECtHR stated that the right to silence was not absolute. All the circumstances of the case needed to be taken into account. In particular in a situation which 'clearly calls for an explanation', the drawing of an adverse inference was reasonable. However, it was essential that the basis of a fair trial is not displaced. A system, for example, in which guilt could be based on silence alone, i.e. with no other evidence, would violate Article 6. Preventing improper inferences was strongest in respect of jury trial.

In *Condron* v *United Kingdom* (2001) 31 EHRR 1, two heroin addicts remained silent in interviews on the advice of their solicitor. The ECtHR held that there had been a violation of Article 6(1).

Condron suggests that the proportionality of any restriction on the right to silence includes consideration of the plausibility of the reasons for silence. This has been followed in English law in *R* v *Betts* [2001] EWCA Crim 224. The Court of Appeal held that it was incompatible with Article 6 to allow a jury to draw an adverse inference even though they found the explanation for silence to be plausible.

 DISCUSSION TOPIC

The right to silence is not necessary to a fair trial?

The right to silence is controversial and, as indicated previously, has been restricted.

The right to silence is defended on grounds that include:

- The best way to maintain the fundamental dimensions of a fair trial is by a simple rule placing, unambiguously, the burden of proof onto the prosecution.
- It discourages improper compulsion of defendants and so helps to avoid miscarriages of justice.
- There may be many legitimate reasons why a person would be best advised to keep silent.

The arguments of critics of the right include:

- There is no need for such a rule since 'innocence proclaims itself'.
- The rule is abused by skilled criminals and their advisors.
- So long as a conviction cannot be based solely on silence, the real burden of proof remains with the prosecution.
- In respect of compelled evidence, some defendants are in a special situation. People such as company directors are in legally defined positions of power and responsibility on which others rely. They should be expected to answer truthfully questions relating to their responsibility; there is no reason why answers given should not also be used in related criminal proceedings. See further: Sedley, S. *Ashes and Sparks* (2011) Cambridge: CUP, Chapter 9.

12.15 Article 6(3): the rights of the defence

Article 6(3) contains a number of specific rights that the defence in a criminal trial should enjoy in order to secure a fair trial. These are free-standing rights but they may also be aspects of the overarching right to a fair trial in Article 6(1). (Some of the issues raised have already been discussed earlier in the chapter.) Though express rights, they are not absolute and may be subject to reasonable and proportionate restriction so long as the overall fairness of the trial is not compromised.

12.15.1 **The right to be informed, Article 6(3)(a)**

Persons charged with criminal offences have the right to be informed of the nature and cause of the accusations against them. It is impossible to answer an unknown charge or one which is imprecisely formulated. The information must be precise enough for the accused to be able to formulate a relevant defence.

> **CROSS REFERENCE**

Article 5(2)—an arrested person must be informed of the charge against them, discussed in Chapter 11, section 11.5 and Chapter 20, section 20.3.5.

UK laws on arrest and court procedures normally meet these information requirements. Note that they only apply to a person 'charged with a criminal offence'. In relation to other coercive actions the state may take, Article 6 does not, expressly at least, require states to provide information, though, if detained, such information might be required under Article 5(2).

12.15.2 **Time and facilities for the defence, Article 6(3)(b)**

Article 6(3)(b) requires that the national law and procedures give the defendant an adequate opportunity to prepare his or her defence. Too swift a trial, for example, would violate this provision. In some circumstances the state may be under a positive duty to delay a trial or allow an adjournment if, for example, there is new evidence to be assessed or late changes in legal representation (as in *Goddi* v *Italy* (1984) 6 EHRR 457).

As ever, the ECtHR refuses to lay down as rules any specific time periods. Whether time and facilities are adequate will depend upon the circumstances of the case, such as its legal complexity, the length of documents to be considered, and changes in personnel.

12.15.3 **The right to defend oneself, Article 6(3)(c)**

Article 6(3)(c) requires states to ensure that any defendant in a criminal trial is able to defend him or herself either in person or on the basis of legal representation. Such a general right is, of course, part of the overall right to a fair trial but, again, a criminal defendant has a specific and express right to rely on whilst a civil litigant must argue in terms of rights inherent in a 'fair hearing'. The terms of the express rights in Article 6(3)(c) are open to interpretation and exactly what they do or do not require will, typically of Article 6, be subject to proportionate, context-based, restriction.

A number of specific issues have arisen in the context of Article 6(3)(c) either standing alone or read in tandem with Article 6(1).

The right to attend

In the ECtHR's view it is difficult to make sense of the various rights of the defence in Article 6(1) and (3) without the defendant's presence (*Sejdovic* v *Italy* App 56581/00, Grand Chamber judgment of 1 March 2006). States have positive duties to ensure that a defendant is able to attend and failure to allow prisoners to come to court, or have adequate facilities to participate, can lead to a violation of Article 6 (see *Brozicek* v *Italy* (1990) 12 EHRR 371).

A trial in the absence of the defendant (*in absentia*) can be compatible with Article 6, especially when this is due to the intentional actions of the defendant. The court must ensure that the defendant is treated as fairly as possible (a second trial with the defendant may be necessary, see *Sejdovic*, mentioned earlier in this section).

In *R* v *Jones (Anthony)* [2002] UKHL 5, the House of Lords held that the holding of J's trial, despite his having absconded and, also, despite his not being represented at the trial, was compatible with Article 6 so long as the court acted with great caution and ensured that the trial was as fair as the circumstances allowed.

Access to a lawyer and legal advice

Criminal punishment must be based on the breach of a legal rule which is accessible and fore-seeable in its application (see Article 7, Chapter 13). Legal advice must be available so that this principle, inherent in the rule of law, can be effective. The presence of lawyers helps accused persons understand their situation, what rights they have, and what issues are relevant to any defence they may have. It also helps to ensure that, both at the trial and before, the proper procedures necessary to fairness are followed. Where the right to silence has been limited, as in the United Kingdom, access to a lawyer is particularly important (see *Murray* v *United Kingdom* (1996) 22 EHRR 29). The right to legal advice (as distinct from legal representation) is an implied right that is, like all implied rights, subject to restrictions for a legitimate purpose ('a good cause') so long as the overall objective of a fair trial is maintained (e.g. *Brennan* v *United Kingdom* (2002) 34 EHRR 18, para 45). The right to legal advice can apply to pre-trial events, such as the questioning of the accused by the police (as in *Murray*, earlier in this section).

Under English law, section 58 PACE (exercised in line with Code C) provides a right of persons detained for questioning to have access to a solicitor, but the exercise of this right can be postponed for up to 36 hours in respect of serious crimes and on the authority of a senior police officer.

Legal representation

Article 6(3)(c) gives a criminal defendant:

- the right to defend him or herself in person if they wish, or
- the right to legal assistance of his or her own choosing, and
- the right to legal aid 'when the interests of justice so require'.

(See *Pakelli* v *Germany* (1984) 6 EHRR 1, para 31.)

There is, therefore, an unqualified right to representation in criminal cases. This is much stronger than the right to representation regarding civil cases. If, in the law of England and Wales, civil proceedings might result in a person being committed to prison for breach of a court order, representation is likely to be necessary, as in *Hammerton* v *Hammerton* [2007] EWCA Civ 248.

The right of prisoners to representation at disciplinary hearings which could result in a longer stay in prison, has been strongly upheld by the ECtHR in *Ezeh* v *United Kingdom* (2004) 39 EHRR 1, and is discussed in Chapter 21, section 21.8.4.

> **CROSS REFERENCE**
> The right to representation in civil cases is discussed in section 12.11.4.

Legal aid in criminal cases.

In order to meet the representation requirements of Article 6, the state may be under a positive duty to provide free legal assistance including representation. This will be so if the defend-ant lacks means (there is no requirement for legal aid of a defendant who can afford his own lawyers) and 'if the interests of justice so require'. It represents a much stronger right to legal aid than is required in respect of civil cases.

> **CROSS REFERENCE**
> For legal aid in civil cases, see section 12.6.2.

Benham v *United Kingdom* (1996) 22 EHRR 293 suggests that legal aid, along with representa-tion, is necessary in cases involving a person's liberty (the case was followed in *Hammerton*, mentioned earlier in this section.

12.15.4 Examination of witnesses, Article 6(3)(d)

Article 6(3)(d) provides a right of the defence to be able to test, usually by cross-examination, the prosecution's evidence. Conviction on the basis of evidence that the court can rely on, but that the defendant cannot test, is likely to be a breach of Article 6(3)(d) and also of Article 6(1) (the principle of 'equality of arms').

There may be circumstances in which restrictions on the right to examine witnesses may be legitimate. It may be necessary to use evidence statements by deceased witnesses, witnesses may be intimidated and need protection (indeed their Convention rights may need protection), the prosecution may wish to protect the identity of an informer, and the identity of a security service witness may need to be withheld for reasons of national security. Thus rules of evidence may allow criminal trials to be conducted using anonymous witnesses or on the basis of hearsay (where someone, such as a police officer, gives a third party's evidence against the defendant).

The basic approach of the ECtHR, found in numerous cases (a good example is *Doorson v Netherlands* (1996) 22 EHRR 330, paras 68–76) is:

- Rules of evidence are primarily for the domestic law to determine; the role of the ECtHR is supervisory, not to insist on particular procedures.
- Article 6 requires, normally, that evidence must be produced in open court, in the presence of the accused and be fully testable.
- However, there can be exceptions based on the need to protect victims, witnesses, and also public interests.
- Restrictions on the capacity of the defence fully to test the evidence must be proportionate. There need to be effective counter-balancing procedures aimed at protecting the rights of the defence so far as possible. The job of the ECtHR is to evaluate the overall fairness of the trial.

The 'sole or decisive' rule

> **CROSS REFERENCE**

The 'sole or decisive' rule in the context of counter-terrorism measures is discussed in Chapter 26, section 26.9.

In this criminal context the ECtHR has also said, in a number of cases, that a decision based 'solely or decisively' on evidence the defendant cannot test will, for that reason, violate Article 6. This led to a 'dialogue' between the UK Supreme Court and the ECtHR.

Q   CASE CLOSE-UP

R v Horncastle [2009] UKSC 14; *Al-Khawaja and T v UK* (2012) 54 EHRR 23

In *Horncastle*, criminal convictions were secured on the basis of hearsay: statements by witnesses who could not be cross examined because they had died prior to the trial or were too frightened to attend the trial. The evidence was admitted on the basis of section 116 Criminal Justice Act 2003, which gives the judge discretion to admit such evidence.

In *Al-Khawaja v UK* (2009) 49 EHRR 1, an ECtHR Chamber held that the convictions of A-K and T, also based on hearsay evidence admitted under section 116, violated Article 6. They were 'solely or to a decisive degree' based on the untested evidence, and Article 6 imposed an absolute ban on convictions in those circumstances.

In *Horncastle*, the Supreme Court disputed the jurisprudential basis of the absolute nature of the 'sole or decisive' rule. It ruled that English law provided sufficient safeguards, in section 116 and in judicial discretion, to protect the defendant and ensure the overall fairness of the trial.

In *Al-Khawaja & T v UK* (2012) 54 EHRR 23, a Grand Chamber reconsidered the Chamber judgment. It upheld the sole or decisive rule but not as an absolute provision (para 147).

If there is careful scrutiny and strong procedural safeguards there will not, necessarily, be a breach of Article 6. In *Al-Khawaja* there was some corroborating evidence so no breach of Article 6; in *T*, however, there was little corroborating evidence and insufficient safeguards—the breach of Article 6 remained.

In *R v Davis* [2008] UKHL 36, the House of Lords held that in England and Wales, the admission of hearsay evidence and anonymous witnesses must be done by statute: the tradition of open justice is too rooted in the common law to allow such radical departures. Importantly, though, any legislation that allows convictions solely or decisively based on such evidence can be compatible with Article 6 if there are sufficient safeguards (per Lord Mance, para 88).

The evidence of vulnerable people

These principles are relevant when court procedures, which inhibit the rights of the defence, are aimed at protecting children and vulnerable persons. The ECtHR accepts such restrictions subject to the need for adequate balancing of the rights of the defence. In *R (D) v Camberwell Green Youth Court* [2005] UKHL 4, the House of Lords upheld, as compatible with Article 6, the use of video-link when evidence is given by child witnesses in cases of a sexual nature or those involving violence.

12.15.5 Interpreter

Article 6(3)(e) imposes a positive duty on a criminal court to provide an interpreter for any defendant who cannot understand the language of the court. The extent of the duty, what it requires of the authorities, will depend upon the circumstances of particular cases.

12.16 Deportation and Article 6

We have seen that there is an absolute ban on deporting someone where there is a real risk that they will be killed or suffer torture or inhuman treatment, in violation of Articles 2 and 3 respectively.

Regarding other rights, the House of Lords in *R (Ullah) v Special Adjudicator* [2004] UKHL 26 held (following Strasbourg case law) that deportation should not take place if the risked violation would be 'flagrant'. So a person should not be deported to face a trial in a foreign country if there is a real risk not just that the trial, if held in a European country, would violate Article 6, but that the trial would be flagrantly unfair.

> **CROSS REFERENCE**
> The grounds of deportation are discussed in Chapter 9, section 9.8.1.

Q **CASE CLOSE-UP**

Othman v United Kingdom (2012) 55 EHRR 1

The British government sought to deport O to Jordan on the grounds that his presence in the UK was inconsistent with the public interest. O alleged he would be tried on the basis of torture evidence. The House of Lords (*OO (Jordan) v Secretary of State for the Home*

Department [2009] UKHL 10) had held that there would only be a 'flagrant' denial of justice if the evidence was that the outcome of the trial would involve a flagrant miscarriage of justice. The real risk of torture evidence was not simply and of itself enough to say there would be a flagrant breach of Article 6 rights.

The ECtHR disagreed. It held:

- A 'flagrant' denial of justice went beyond mere irregularities: it meant the nullification or destruction of the essence of the rights protected by Article 6 (para 260).
- The admission of torture evidence would be a flagrant denial of justice (para 267).
- Evidence of a 'real risk' was sufficient to refuse deportation given the difficulties of proof to a higher standard such as balance of probabilities.

Therefore the deportation of O by the United Kingdom would violate Article 6 (on the basis of subsequent agreement between the UK and Jordan, O agreed to return voluntarily).

▶ CROSS REFERENCE

Othman raises other important points about deportation in a counter-terrorist context which are discussed in Chapter 26, section 26.7.3.

⟲ Summary

- The right to a fair trial is an essential element in ensuring people's effective protection of their legal rights, including their human rights.
- Article 6 establishes rights to a fair trial which apply only where a civil right or obligation, or a criminal charge is being determined. These are autonomous terms not dependant on national laws. Limiting fair trial rights to these kinds of trials means that some legal processes are not subject to its terms.
- Article 6(1) applies to both civil and criminal trials. It lays down a generic right to a fair trial, from which more specific rights can be implied and it makes specific requirements concerning speed, publicity, independence, and impartiality.
- Article 6(2) and (3) applies only to criminal trials and preserves the presumption of innocence and a range of other rights of the defence.
- The application of Article 6 rights may depend on context, but any limitations should not undermine the essence of a fair trial.

? Self-test questions

1. Define the term 'civil rights and obligations'.
2. Define the term 'criminal charge'.
3. How does *Findlay* v *United Kingdom* demonstrate the requirements of an independent hearing?
4. What does the term 'equality of arms' mean?

5. Must trials and hearings always be in public to satisfy Article 6; if not, give two circumstances when they may be in private?

6. Explain the right of 'access to a court' and give two examples of situations in which it has been necessary to assert this right.

7. When, if at all, can Article 6 rights come into play before any trial or hearing commences?

8. How does Article 6 control undercover policing that is aimed at getting evidence of criminal activity?

9. Can compelled evidence ever the admissible in a criminal trial?

10. What is meant by the 'sole or decisive' rule—and is it absolute?

 For suggested approaches, please visit the Online Resource Centre.

? Exam questions

1. Describe and discuss the scope of the right to a fair hearing in Article 6. Consider whether it is satisfactory or whether it should be widened to include a wider range of hearings.

2. The Prison Service is creating an entirely new set of procedures dealing with prison discipline and you, as a Ministry of Justice lawyer, have been charged with ensuring compliance with Article 6 for the system to be used in the prisons housing the most dangerous prisoners. You are asked to advise on (a) whether Article 6 is involved and, if so, in which situations; (b) what specific rights Article 6 provides; and (c) whether those rights can be restricted to prevent, for example, the intimidation of one prisoner by another.

 For suggested approaches, please visit the Online Resource Centre.

≡ Further reading

Leading texts on Article 6

Amos, M. (see Preface) Chapter 10

Jacobs, F. 'The Right to a Fair Trial in European Law' [1999] 2 *EHRLR* 141–156

Lester, A., Pannick, D., and Herberg, J. (see Preface) Chapter 4, Article 6

Critical analysis

Craig, P. 'The Human Rights Act, Article 6 and Procedural Rights' [2003] *Public Law* (Winter) 753–773

Masterman, R. 'Determinative in the Abstract? Article 6(1) and the Separation of Powers' [2005] 6 *EHRLR* 628–648

13 Article 7: no punishment without law

□ **LEARNING OBJECTIVES**

● The rule of law and the principle that criminal laws should not be applied retrospectively and should embody legal certainty.

● The principle that a person should not be convicted for offences that did not exist at the time of the person's actions.

● The principle that a convicted person should not be subjected to more severe punishments than could, lawfully, have been imposed at the time the offence was committed.

● The exception for internationally recognised offences, such as crimes against humanity.

Article 7 No punishment without law

(1) No one shall be held guilty of any criminal offence on account of any act or omission which did not constitute a criminal offence under national or international law at the time when it was committed. Nor shall a heavier penalty be imposed than the one that was applicable at the time the criminal offence was committed.

(2) This article shall not prejudice the trial and punishment of any person for any act or omission which, at the time when it was committed, was criminal according to the general principles of law recognised by civilised nations.

Introduction

Article 7 requires that states do not apply their criminal law and their approach to sentencing in retrospective ways. This principle is fundamental to the rule of law—people should not be punished for breaking laws that were not in force at the time nor be punished more severely than the law allowed at the time.

Nevertheless there can be significant issues that arise. For example: whether changing attitudes towards crimes can be reflected in sentencing decisions (e.g. those convicted of historic sexual offences). Article 7 can be also be relevant in respect of difficult issues of transitional justice (moving from dictatorship to democracy). Is it fair to prosecute and punish officials of dictatorial regimes who committed cruel actions which were not properly recognised as crimes by the regime?

13.1 *Nullum crimen, nulla poena sine lege*

Article 7 embodies a general principle of law, found in most legal systems and in international law: this is the principle of *'nullum crimen, nulla poena sine lege'* (no crime, no punishment without law). It means that there should be no crimes and no punishments other than on the basis of law. States act in an arbitrary manner, and will be caught by Article 7, if they impose a penalty on a person which has no effective legal basis. The Convention standard of legality must be met: any legal rule on which a criminal penalty is based should be sufficiently clear and precise in its potential application so that individuals can know in advance whether any proposed action is likely to be criminal or not.

CROSS REFERENCE
See Chapter 6, section 6.2, for the Convention concept of 'law'.

The justification for the *nullum crimen, nulla poena sine lege* principle is that the rule of law requires that people be able to know and follow (or choose to break) the law that applies to them at the time they act. Otherwise states act arbitrarily and people suffer unjustly. Historically it is clear that majorities, or those in power, can create laws and apply them retrospectively as a way of discriminating against, and subordinating, minorities and powerless groups, who are often the defeated in a civil war or conflict.

13.1.1 **Common law**

Nullum crimen, nulla poena sine lege is a long-established principle of English common law.

English courts will interpret criminal legislation on the presumption that it is not intended to apply retrospectively. In *Waddington v Miah* (1974) 59 Cr App Rep 149, 151 and 152, Lord Reid said:

> There has for a very long time been a strong feeling against making legislation, and particularly criminal legislation, retrospective . . . I use retrospective in the sense of authorising people being punished for what they did before the Act came into force.

Of course Parliament can, in constitutional theory, enact criminal legislation with retrospective effect. To do so, it must express itself with sufficient clarity and precision on the point not only to displace the presumption but also to escape the interpretative obligation placed on the courts by section 3 Human Rights Act 1998 (HRA) (see Chapter 4, section 4.4).

The courts no longer allow themselves to create new criminal offences. Under the system of judicial precedent, such offences apply retrospectively, at least the first time they are pronounced (see *R v Withers* [1975] AC 842).

There is a strong steer from the courts against the expansion of existing common law offences into new areas and applications.

In *R* v *Goldstein; R* v *Rimmington* [2005] UKHL 63 (a rich source of quotations on the common law), the House of Lords refused to allow the common law offence of public nuisance to be redefined so that it was no longer necessary for the prosecution to prove that the defendant had acted in a way which interfered with the public at large and so the offence could be used against a person who harassed particular, identifiable individuals rather than the general public. The House of Lords' refusal was based on the *nullum crimen* principle and Article 7.

There are, therefore, unlikely to be many difficulties of achieving compatibility of English and Convention law on this issue. As is indicated later in the chapter, the main issues have arisen over retrospective changes to burdens placed on persons convicted of offences (e.g. whether they can be made to pay compensation) and whether such burdens amount to a punishment or not.

13.2 General principles governing Article 7(1)

The general principles guiding the application of Article 7 are discussed in sections 13.2.1–13.2.6. They have been recently confirmed by a Grand Chamber in *Kononov* v *Latvia* (2011) 52 EHRR 21 (paras 185–186).

13.2.1 Article 7 is an important feature of the rule of law

The guarantees in Article 7 are an essential element of the rule of law and, as such they occupy a prominent place in the Convention system of protection.

13.2.2 'Law' means the same in Article 7 as in other Articles

The concept of legality and law pervades the Convention. This is the same notion of 'law' as is applied through Article 7. As discussed in Chapter 6, section 6.2, to be a law, for Convention purposes, a rule must:

- be accepted as law by the national courts (in England, for instance, it must be a rule found in an Act of Parliament, in the common law or equity and occasionally in custom);
- be 'accessible' (the laws which apply can be identified) and 'foreseeable' (the applicable laws are sufficiently clear and precise to be able to guide a person's conduct).

Conviction and punishment on the basis of criminal laws that do not meet this test will be a violation of Article 7.

13.2.3 A safeguard against arbitrary action

Article 7 should be construed and applied so as to provide an effective safeguard against arbitrary prosecution, conviction, and punishment. This is, in any case, part of how the European Court of Human Rights (ECtHR) understands the rule of law. That this is the underlying point of Article 7 is shown by the fact that the ECtHR will not allow its guarantees to be used in a way which contradicts the rule of law and which gives protection to lawless, oppressive state actions.

> **Q** | **CASE CLOSE-UP**

Streletz, Kessler and Krenz v Germany (2001) 33 EHRR 31

The unification of Germany after 1989 led to some prosecutions in Germany of officials of the former German Democratic Republic (GDR). S and others (political leaders of the GDR) were prosecuted in 1993 for authorising shoot to kill policies and practices against East German civilians who were trying to cross the border into West Germany (the Federal Republic of Germany)—the policies called for the 'annihilation' of escapers if they could not be arrested. S was prosecuted for breaking laws of the GDR which were in force at the time (1971–89) but which, partly at S's behest, were disregarded by, and not enforced against, the border police. S argued that a prosecution in the 1970s and 1980s was not foreseeable; therefore his later prosecution, in 1993, violated Article 7. The ECtHR rejected this argument. S was claiming that the policies and practices were the relevant law of the time; yet they were the opposite of law, they emptied the enacted law of all meaning. Article 7(1) seeks to uphold the rule of law; the applicants, on the other hand, were seeking to uphold lawless and brutal practices.

In *Kononov* v *Latvia* (2011) 52 EHRR 21, a Grand Chamber, disagreeing with the Chamber, held that the prosecution by Latvia (now independent; formerly part of the USSR) of the commander of a Red Army Partisan (fighting the Nazis) group did not violate Article 7. The defendant was found guilty of allowing the ill-treatment and killing of villagers in Latvia who, allegedly, had been cooperating with the Nazis. The Court reviewed the state of international law as it was in 1944 and found that attacks on civilians who were not engaged in combat were clearly defined, in a range of treaties, as war crimes. These international war crimes applied to the individual responsibility of a commander, and, although they had not been promulgated in the Soviet Union, a 'cursory reflection' by the commander would have alerted him at least to the possibility that not forbidding the attacks might be a war crime.

13.2.4 **Article 7 is non-derogable**

The central place of the rule of law in the Convention system means that Article 7 is one of the rights which cannot be derogated from by states in time of 'war or other public emergency facing the life of the nation'.

> **⟩ CROSS REFERENCE**
> Derogation under Article 15 is discussed in Chapter 7, section 7.2.

13.2.5 **Article 7 prohibits retrospective criminal law and punishment**

The express words of Article 7 bar the retrospective application of the criminal law to the disadvantage of an accused person. In *Coëme* v *Belgium* App 32492/96, judgment of 22 June 2000, the ECtHR said:

> The Court must therefore verify that at the time when the accused person performed the act which led to his being prosecuted and convicted there was in force a legal provision which made that act punishable and that the punishment imposed did not exceed the limits fixed by that provision.

(para 145)

It is important to note that Article 7 only prohibits retrospective criminal law. Retrospective provisions in civil law, such as private or administrative law, are not barred by Article 7. They might be barred by the application of other provisions such as the right to peaceful enjoyment of property in Article 1 of the First Protocol. This could happen, for example, if the legislature enacts legislation which retrospectively changes the effects of a court decision (as in *Pressos Compania Naviera SA* v *Belgium* (1996) 21 EHRR 301, discussed in Chapter 23, section 23.7.4).

13.2.6 **Article 7 guarantees go beyond just retrospective criminal law**

Article 7's place as one of the guarantors of the rule of law means that it has a wider application than just a bar to retrospective criminal prosecutions. As noted previously, it is taken as embodying the *nullum crimen* principle, which clearly includes something more than just a ban on retrospective law. Article 7 also includes the following principles:

- There can be no crimes and no punishments unless these are found in the law.
- Offences must be clearly defined in the law.
- The criminal law must not be construed to the accused's detriment.

In *Scoppola* v *Italy* (2010) 51 EHRR 12, a Grand Chamber, went further. By majority it departed from its earlier case law and introduced the principle of *lex mitior*—that changes to the law allowing for a more lenient penalty should applied even if the changes took place after the offence was committed. The Court considered that this principle, which is found in international law (e.g. Article 15 ICCPR and Article 49 of the EU Charter of Fundamental Rights) and some national laws, should now be seen as a 'fundamental principle of criminal law'.

THINKING POINT

Consider *R* v *Docherty* [2014] EWCA Crim 1197—why was *lex mitior* not applied in the case? See in particular paras 38–60.

13.3 Article 7(1) and offences (the first sentence)

The first sentence of Article 7(1) requires that, if a person is convicted of a criminal offence, there must be:

- a clearly defined criminal offence, that was
- in force at the time the alleged crime was committed, and which
- covered, within its terms, the actions for which the defendant was convicted.

The essence of this is that changes to the criminal law and procedure cannot be used to prosecute people in respect of their actions performed before the changes came into effect (as in, for example, *Veeber* v *Estonia* (2004) 39 EHRR 6).

13.3.1 **What counts as a criminal offence?**

Article 7(1) only applies to the application of the rules of criminal law. Whether legal rules are 'criminal' or not for Article 7 purposes is a matter of autonomous Convention law (i.e. it is not solely dependent on the way the matter is classified under national law). The obvious link would be to the concept of a 'criminal charge' found in Article 6, but the ECtHR has not had occasion to make this clear. In most cases the fact that there has been a criminal conviction under the national law is sufficient, and without it, Article 7 may not apply.

⟩ CROSS REFERENCE

See Chapter 12, section 12.4.

The need for a criminal conviction means that the retrospective application of laws in the area of, for example, immigration or deportation may not raise Article 7 issues. Despite the seriousness of the matter for the individuals involved, they do not involve a criminal conviction.

 CASE CLOSE-UP

Lawless v United Kingdom (No 3) (1979–80) 1 EHRR 15

L was interned under an Irish law brought into force in 1957. His internment was based on his activities before that date. The ECtHR held that Article 7 did not apply (para 19).

Limiting Article 7 to criminal offences makes sense given the Article's wording. But it might be thought to weaken the protection for the rule of law that is the essence of Article 7. It allows the retrospective application of laws and procedures in a wide range of issues, like internment, which have a severe impact on the lives of the individuals and which might embody state oppression of political opponents or unpopular minorities.

13.3.2 **Clarity with flexibility**

Clarity

Article 7 requires that the criminal offence for which a person is prosecuted and convicted must be clearly defined in the national law. This means that:

> the individual can know from the wording of the relevant provision and, if need be, with the assistance of the court's interpretation of it, what acts and omissions will make him criminally liable.
>
> (*Cantoni* v *France* App 17862/91, Grand Chamber judgment of 22 October 1996, para 29)

The ECtHR accepts that the offence may be found in unwritten law, though the requirement for certainty may be all the more demanding.

Flexibility

The notion of a law implies a rule of general application—laws regulate the conduct of the public or a class of the public and do so over a period of time. Laws, in this sense, are different from judicial decisions, which apply the law to individuals. Under the separation of powers, legislatures are not normally permitted to enact legislation which relates only to an individual or to a specific event.

Characteristically laws are couched in general terms. This implies some degree of vagueness and imprecision which requires interpretation before being applied to particular circumstances. The ECtHR accepts this, not only in the context of Article 7 but also in respect of its pervasive concept of law. This 'open-textured' nature of law (as the British legal philosopher H.L.A. Hart called it) is necessary to ensure that laws are not over-rigid and unable to develop with time and changing contexts. The danger, of course, is that individuals will end up being convicted on the basis of new developments or applications of the law which could not be foreseen.

Where general words in a statute have been interpreted by courts and a settled body of case law created, the ECtHR is likely to find that the certainty requirement has been satisfied. This acceptance of the necessary flexibility in legal rules is illustrated in the matrimonial rape case: *SW v United Kingdom* (see also *CR v United Kingdom*).

 CASE CLOSE-UP

SW v United Kingdom (1996) 21 EHRR 363

In 1990 SW was convicted of the rape (having sexual intercourse without consent) of his wife. At that time there was an accepted common law rule that a husband could not be convicted of the rape of his wife since, by agreeing to marriage, the wife was held to have agreed, once and for all, to sexual intercourse with her husband. In *R v R* [1991] 2 All ER 257, decided in 1991, the House of Lords held that the common law rule was no longer the law of England. SW argued, unsuccessfully, that he should be tried under the law of rape as it stood at the time of the alleged offence (prior to *R v R*) and that to apply *R v R* would be to impose a change in the law retrospectively. After conviction, SW applied to the ECtHR, which held there had not been a violation of Article 7.

The Court said:

> There will always be need for elucidation [clarification] of doubtful points and for adaptation to changing circumstances . . . Article 7 of the Convention cannot be read as outlawing the gradual clarification of the rules of criminal liability through judicial interpretation from case to case, provided that the resultant development is consistent with the essence of the offence and could reasonably be foreseen. (para 36/34)

- In *R v R* the House of Lords had not created a new offence but extended an existing offence to new circumstances (husbands having sex with their wives) without changing the essence of the offence (lack of consent to sex).
- This legal development was foreseeable because it continued an identifiable line of case law (e.g. that the immunity of husbands did not apply when the parties were separated).
- Given the debasing nature of rape, to have allowed the husband to succeed would be using Article 7 against its own purpose and that of the Convention.

13.3.3 **UK cases**

UK courts have applied Article 7, or at least referred to it as a complement to domestic law, in a number of cases dealing with the question whether crimes are defined with adequate clarity. For example:

- In *Webster (Procurator Fiscal) v Dominick* 2003 SCCR 525, Scottish courts held that the Scottish common law offence of 'shameless indecency' had not been defined with sufficient clarity to meet the test in Article 7.
- In *R v Remington; R v Goldstein* [2005] UKHL 63, the House of Lords held that the offence of public nuisance was, in its traditional definition, defined with adequate clarity (but rejected its extension in the way outlined earlier in this chapter).

13.3.4 **International law**

The first sentence of Article 7(1) makes it clear that a conviction can be compatible with Article 7 if the crime in issue is defined under international law. International offences are crimes that have been defined by the international community and which states may (or, in some cases, must) prosecute if an alleged offender is in their custody, even if the crimes were committed elsewhere. Such offences include torture, drug trafficking, and aircraft sabotage. The Rome Statute of the International Criminal Court 1998 gives detailed definitions of the offences of 'genocide', 'crimes against humanity', and 'war crimes' and, since 2010, 'aggression'.

Some international crimes, such as torture, are part of the compulsory law of nations ('*jus cogens*') and apply irrespective of specific agreements.

▶ CROSS REFERENCE
Jus cogens is defined in Chapter 9, section 9.4.1.

Other offences (such as those under the Rome Statute) only apply where a country has expressly signed a treaty recognising the offence. A prosecution might be brought by a new regime against officials of the predecessor regime (as in *Streletz, Kessler and Krenz* v *Germany* (2001) 33 EHRR 31, mentioned at section 13.2.3). In such a situation Article 7 allows prosecutions based on *jus cogens*, because this contains general duties applicable to all states independent of their wills. It is not clear whether a prosecution could be based on the retrospective application of a treaty-defined offence which the predecessor state had not signed up to.

13.4 Article 7(1) and punishment (the second sentence)

The courts must not impose a heavier sentence on a convicted criminal than was available to the courts at the time the offences were committed. A clear case of this is *Ecer* v *Turkey* (2002) 35 EHRR 26, in which the applicant was convicted of national security offences committed between 1988 and 1989 but given a punishment that was not introduced until 1991.

13.4.1 **Retrospective changes to sentencing practice.**

Commonly, statute law will establish the maximum sentence that a prisoner can serve in respect of a particular offence but leave it to the judge in the case to decide the length of sentence in relation to the maximum. The question is then raised whether Article 7 can be invoked if, by retrospective changes in practice, a person is given a more severe punishment than he or she might have expected at the time they committed the crimes, even though this more severe punishment is still within the maximum laid down in the statute which applied at that time. In *Coëme* v *Belgium* (section 13.2.5), the ECtHR defined the task of a court dealing with an Article 7 challenge as to:

> verify that at the time when an accused person performed the act which led to his being prosecuted and convicted there was in force a legal provision which made that act punishable, and that the punishment imposed did not exceed the limits fixed by that provision.

(para 145)

In the United Kingdom, the House of Lords has interpreted these words to mean that (in the words of the Article) the 'penalty . . . that was applicable at the time the criminal offence was committed' is the maximum which under the law could have been imposed as distinct from that which was, at the time, normally imposed.

> ### 🔍 CASE CLOSE-UP
>
> **R (Uttley) v Secretary of State for the Home Department** [2004] UKHL 38
>
> U committed three rapes in a period ending in 1983. He was not convicted until 1995. In 1983 the maximum sentence for rape was life imprisonment. U was sentenced to 12 years' imprisonment. If given 12 years in 1983 he would, subject to good behaviour, have been unconditionally released after eight years. Under changes introduced in 1991, he was still entitled (with good behaviour) to be released after eight years but his release was subject to various conditions which put him at risk of being recalled to prison if he breached them. The House of Lords held that there had not been a breach of Article 7(1) since it was clearly the case that the sentence imposed, though more severe than the sentence that would have been expected in 1983, was still less severe than the maximum (life imprisonment with a longer jail term than 12 years) that could have been imposed in 1983. Uttley's application to the ECtHR was inadmissible.

Thus *Uttley* permits retrospective, detrimental, changes in sentence, so long as they are within the statutory range applicable at the time of the offence. In *R v Clifford* [2014] EWCA Crim 2245, Clifford was sentenced in 2014 for sexual offences against teenage girls committed between 1977 and 1984. He was sentenced to the maximum available in the 1980s (a more severe sentence than might have been imposed then) in order to reflect the more serious attitude to such offences taken today. It was held that a sentencing court was entitled to take into account modern attitudes to historic offences and there was no breach of Article 7.

13.4.2 Retrospective changes to sentence management.

After sentence, the length of time a prisoner spends in prison can depend on various policy factors such as the conditions for early release. These factors may change after the original sentence was passed. The ECtHR distinguishes between retrospective changes that affect the 'scope' of the penalty, and which may breach Article 7, and those (more commonly) which relate only to the 'manner of its execution', and so do not breach Article 7.

A detrimental post-sentence change which amounts to a redefinition of the sentence in a way that was not foreseeable at the time of sentencing will affect the 'scope' of the sentence.

> ### 🔍 CASE CLOSE-UP
>
> **Del Rio Prada v Spain** (2014) 58 EHRR 37
>
> In the late 1980s DRP was sentenced to long periods of imprisonment for a range of terrorist offences. Based on established approaches, confirmed to her in 2000, she could expect to serve a 30-year sentence reduced to take into account prison work undertaken.

In 2008, however, the Spanish Supreme Court changed the approach to early release to the detriment of DRP.

The ECtHR, Grand Chamber, held that these changes were not foreseeable, affected the scope of the sentence, and so their retrospective application violated Article 7.

13.4.3 **What is a 'penalty'?**

Convention principles

The second sentence of Article 7(1) only applies to the retrospective application of a 'penalty'. Measures which are not penalties may be applied retrospectively to the detriment of a convicted person, without coming within Article 7. Such other measures can include, for example, orders for compensation or orders aimed at prevention of crime and the protection of the public.

The concept of 'penalty' is autonomous, it has a particular meaning for the purpose of the Convention and does not depend on how the matter is defined in national law.

 CASE CLOSE-UP

Welch v United Kingdom (1995) 20 EHRR 247

W was convicted in 1988 for drug offences committed prior to 1987. He was sentenced to 22 years' imprisonment and made subject to a confiscation of property order. This required him to surrender to the state a high proportion of his property on the grounds that it was the proceeds of selling drugs. Failure to hand over the property could be punished by extra years in prison. Confiscation orders were introduced in 1987 (after W had committed the offences) but their application was expressly made retrospective (see the Drug Trafficking Offences Act 1986). W alleged a breach of Article 7. It was agreed that the confiscation orders had been retrospectively introduced; the issue for the ECtHR was whether these orders were a penalty. The Court held that they were a penalty and that there had been a violation of Article 7.

In *Welch* the ECtHR suggested five criteria for identifying whether a measure is a penalty. The essential point is whether or not it is, in reality, a punishment.

(1) A penalty is imposed following a conviction for a crime.

    However, just because a measure is imposed following criminal conviction, it does not follow that this is a penalty. Conversely, if a measure is imposed without there being a criminal conviction, it is unlikely that Article 7 will be of assistance.

    In considering whether a measure is a 'penalty' a court must consider these other factors:

(2) A penalty aims at punishment rather than solely prevention or compensation.

(3) The way a measure is defined in national law is of weight, but is not decisive.

(4) The fact that a measure can only be imposed on the basis of trial procedures that recognise the rights of the defence is evidence pointing to the fact that it is a penalty.

(5) Penalties are relatively severe. The more severe the measure, the more likely it is that it will be a penalty.

THINKING POINT

Note similarities with the definition of a 'criminal charge' for Article 6 purposes (see Chapter 12, section 12.4) and consider whether protective measure such as Football Banning Orders (see *Gough and Smith* v *Chief Constable of Derbyshire* [2002] EWCA Civ 351) and Anti-Social Behaviour injunctions are unlikely to be 'penalties' and so will not enjoy the protection of Article 7 any more than they come within the criminal charge limb of Article 6.

13.5 Article 7(2) war crimes exception

The Nuremburg trials of the Nazi leaders at the end of the Second World War involved, in a sense, retrospective justice. Herman Goring and others were tried for actions that, probably, were 'lawful' under German law at the time they were committed. However, the justification for these Nuremburg trials was that the Nazis were tried for crimes already established in international law either in custom or treaty. The great advance made at Nuremberg was the codification of these war crimes, their application to the political leaders as well as to lesser figures, and the principle of individual responsibility.

With the ending of the 'Cold War' the Nuremberg principles could be revived. Under UN auspices, specific tribunals have been established for the trials of persons involved in atrocities committed in, for example, the former Yugoslavia and in Rwanda. The International Criminal Court has also been established with a more general jurisdiction, but it can only deal with crimes committed after 2002. Of equal, if not greater, importance is the gradual acceptance by many states, including European states, that they have a duty to try and punish alleged war criminals and perpetrators of crimes against humanity who may be within their control—the national law is applying internationally defined crimes. In the UK, for instance, section 51 of the International Criminal Court Act 2001 makes it an offence, under the domestic law of England and Wales to commit 'genocide, a crime against humanity or a war crime'.

Article 7(2), therefore, exempts such international and national proceedings from the ban on retrospective law. This is not the endorsement of 'victor's justice'. The claim is that such trials do not really involve retrospective law because all that is done is to try people according to norms and standards which had already been recognised internationally before the deeds in question were committed.

There has been little serious discussion by the ECtHR on the impact of Article 7(2). *Streletz, Kessler and Krenz* v *Germany* (see section 13.2.3) and *Kononov* (see section 13.2.3) were both decided on the basis of Article 7(1) alone. The question for the court was whether, in the circumstances of the cases, there was applicable law, domestic or national, which was accessible and foreseeable and which meant the perpetrator could be held criminally responsible for his actions. Given the positive answers to these questions, the prosecutions did not involve arbitrary, retrospective applications of the criminal law. Hence the provisions of Article 7(2) did not need to be considered.

Summary

- Article 7(1) prohibits the retrospective application of criminal laws: a person should not be convicted for an offence that did not exist at the time he or she committed the acts in question, nor should any punishment they receive be one that was not available to the courts at that time. Article 7 recognises an exception in relation to internationally recognised offences.

- Article 7 also embodies the principle of legal certainty at least in the context of criminal law. People must be able to know the laws that apply to them and be able to foresee the circumstances in which laws will be applied. They can then adjust their conduct accordingly.

- As the case law indicates, Article 7 permits considerable flexibility in the way these principles are applied.

? **Self-test questions**

1. In relation to Article 7 explain why the common law no longer creates new criminal offences.

2. Why was the so-called 'matrimonial rape' prosecution (*SW v UK*) not a violation of Article 7?

3. Define the idea of 'law' inherent in Article 7.

4. What is meant by the term 'penalty' in Article 7?

 For suggested approaches, please visit the Online Resource Centre.

? **Exam questions**

1. Able is accused of historical child abuse offences. The legal definition of the crimes he may have committed has changed since the time of the alleged offences so, under the current law, he could be charged with more serious offences than were open to prosecutors at the time of the offences. Furthermore, the punishments available today are more severe; in addition, a judge, today, is likely to treat the same facts more seriously than at the time of the offences and, therefore, punish at the higher end of the range of punishments available.

   Advise the Crown Prosecution Service on the effect of Article 7 on the decisions they must make regarding the offences to prosecute and, if there is a conviction, the punishment that might be argued for.

2. Critically evaluate Article 7(2)—which, in essence, states that Article 7 does not prevent prosecutions for international crimes.

 For suggested approaches, please visit the Online Resource Centre.

Further reading

Atrill, S. *'Nulla Poena Sine Lege* in Comparative Perspective: Retrospectivity under the ECHR and the US Constitution' [2005] *Public Law* 107–131

Lester, A., Pannick, D., and Herberg, J. (see Preface) Chapter 4, Article 7

14 Introduction to Articles 8–11

☐ **LEARNING OBJECTIVES**

● The common features of Articles 8, 9, 10, and 11.

● Identifying the basic right (first paragraphs).

● Identifying the exclusive circumstances under which states can restrict those rights (second paragraphs).

Introduction

This is a brief summary chapter in which the main terms of Articles 8–11 are introduced.

Articles 8, 9, 10, and 11 deal with individual freedoms: private and family life (Article 8); belief (Article 9); freedom of expression, including the freedom of the media (Article 10); freedom to 'assemble' (to hold meetings, to march, to protest, etc.) and to 'associate' (to form, join, and participate in trade unions and pressure groups, etc. (Article 11)).

The exercise of these freedoms can have a significant impact on the lives and freedoms of others and on the exercise of important public interests. This can be controversial. We can agree, for example, that freedom of speech is not absolute and there are circumstances in which any reasonable society is entitled to restrict expression: the protection of military and defence secrets, for example. However, there is likely to be deep disagreement on its practical application in particular situations. Likewise, in relation to the right to private and family life, serious disputes can arise over the extent to which someone's rights can interfere with the exercise of government policy (e.g. over deportation), restrict the rights of the media to publish stories the people want to hear, and even compel changes in the law (as, perhaps, over euthanasia).

14.1 The structure of Articles 8–11

Articles 8–11 provide a structure for resolving these kinds of dilemmas.

- First paragraph: the Articles establish the freedoms (private life, religious belief, expression, etc.) as rights that the states which have signed the Convention must secure for everyone.

- Second paragraph: the Articles state the conditions which must be satisfied if these freedoms are to be restricted. The freedoms can only be restricted, or interfered with, if these conditions are satisfied.

14.2 The scope of the first paragraph

A court must, first, decide whether the facts of the case disclose that the applicant has been exercising a freedom which is protected by the first paragraph of Article 8, 9, 10, or 11. This is often obvious, but not always. For example, is 'private life' (protected by Article 8) in issue when a person is photographed in the street, are political demonstrations covered by Article 10, does the right of association in Article 11 include a right not to be legally or economically compelled to join a trade association or union?

14.3 Whether there has been an interference for which the state is responsible

Next, a court must decide whether the exercise of a freedom protected by Articles 8–11 has been interfered with. Again, this is generally obvious. The principal issue for a court, including the European Court of Human Rights (ECtHR), is whether the interference is one for which the state has responsibility.

Frequently a person will be complaining about some interference with his or her freedom (of private life, belief, speech, etc.) which has been imposed by a state official putting into effect a legal rule. Thus demonstrators may have been arrested by the police, a political party refused registration by an election official, or a group of religious believers prevented from building a church by a planning decision taken by a local council. In such circumstances, the responsibility of the state is direct and the question of whether it can justify its action under the terms of the second paragraph must then be considered.

At other times a person will be complaining about an interference with his or her freedom which has been directly brought about not by a state official but by some private person or organisation (an individual, a commercial body, or a charity, for example). Here the question is whether the state has responsibility for what has happened. Only if it does is it necessary then to consider its possible liability for a breach of one of the Articles. The ECtHR refers to the state having 'positive duties' to regulate, to take official action, or to change the law, in order to prevent the type of interference with a person's freedom that is in issue.

> CROSS REFERENCE

Positive duties are discussed in Chapter 6, section 6.6.

14.4 Justification (the second paragraph)

Once state responsibility for an interference with one of the freedoms protected by Articles 8–11 is established, the next issue is whether the state is able to justify the interference. It can only do this by reference to the terms in the second paragraphs of these Articles. Interferences must be

- on the basis of 'law',
- for a legitimate purpose, and they must
- be 'necessary in a democratic society'.

14.4.1 **'Law'**

Any interference must be 'in accordance with the law' (Article 8) or 'prescribed by law' (Articles 9, 10, and 11). The Convention concept of 'law' means not only that the interference must be lawful in terms of the national law, but the national law also has to be 'accessible' (capable of being identified) and 'foreseeable' (people subject to the law can know or be advised on the likely application of the law); it must also be non-arbitrary and consistent with rule of law values.

> CROSS REFERENCE

For the Convention concept of 'law' see Chapter 6, section 6.2.

14.4.2 **Legitimate purpose**

Restrictions on the freedoms protected by Articles 8–11 can only be compatible with the Convention if they pursue one of the purposes listed in the relevant second paragraph. Article 18 ECHR makes it clear that any restrictions on rights and freedoms that are allowed under the Convention can only be for the purposes allowed by the Convention.

> CROSS REFERENCE

For Article 18 see Chapter 7, section 7.4.

Each of the Articles has its own particular list of purposes. Some purposes are common to all four Articles: all of the freedoms can be restricted to protect the 'rights of others'. This broad concept includes background rights that have not been precisely established in law (examples are given in Chapter 17, section 17.6.3, 'protection of the ... rights of others').

Other purposes are only found in respect of one or some but not all of the four Articles. Thus it is possible to interfere with private and family life (Article 8) if this is in the interests of the 'economic well being of the country', but such a trade-off between economic wealth and individual rights and freedoms is not permitted under Article 9, 10, or 11. Similarly, 'national security' can justify restrictions on private and family life, expression, assembly, and association, but not interferences with the way a person manifests his or her religion.

States normally find it relatively easy to show that a restriction on a freedom serves one of the listed purposes. The purposes are expressed in very open-textured language and it is easy to establish some kind of instrumental link between the interference and the purpose.

14.4.3 Necessary in a democratic society

Many cases involving Articles 8–11 are resolved in relation to the third requirement of the second paragraph: that any interference must be 'necessary in a democratic society'.

A judicial assessment of whether an interference is necessary in a democratic society involves factors such as the following:

- Whether, as well as serving one of the purposes listed in the second paragraph of the Article concerned, there is also a 'pressing social need' for the particular action taken.

> **CROSS REFERENCE**
>
> Ideas of 'democracy' and 'proportionality' pervade the Convention. See Chapter 6, sections 6.4 and 6.5 respectively.

- Whether there is clear evidence that the state has made a careful assessment of the situation and arrived at reasonable conclusions which take into account the impact of its decisions on the parties concerned. At the heart of the issue is 'proportionality'. There must be a 'fair balance' between the various private and public interests affected by the issue.

It is important to distinguish the role of the ECtHR from a national court, such as a court in England and Wales dealing with a case under the Human Rights Act 1998 (HRA).

> **CROSS REFERENCE**
>
> 'Margin of appreciation' is discussed in Chapter 6, section 6.3. Deference by UK courts is discussed in Chapter 4, section 4.6.2.

The role of the ECtHR is a reviewing one. What is 'necessary' in a democratic society is likely to involve questions about what is for the good of the public and society. In this context, the ECtHR may accept, depending on context, that states enjoy a 'margin of appreciation', which, as an international court, it must respect. National courts, such as courts in the United Kingdom, acting under the HRA, will have to consider whether and to what extent the 'necessary in a democratic society' issue requires them to 'defer' to Parliament or to executive bodies on what is proportional, or whether the issues of fair balance and proportionality are ones they must answer for themselves. It is clear that necessary in a democratic society is dependent on context.

⟲ Summary

Articles 8–11 have a similar, two-paragraph structure which requires the courts to decide, first, whether some action for which the state is responsible interferes with a protected freedom and, if it does, whether the state has shown that the interference is justified in terms of the second paragraph of the Article involved.

In the chapters that follow each Article will be looked at in detail.

? Self-test questions

1. Compare and contrast the lists of legitimate purposes in Articles 8, 9, 10, and 11.

2. By reference to Chapter 6, section 6.2, define the concept of 'law' used in the Convention.

3. By reference to Chapter 6, section 6.5, define the concept of 'proportionality' used in the Convention.

 For suggested approaches, please visit the Online Resource Centre.

? Exam questions

1. A court order restrains the media from publishing a story. What general questions will an appeal court judge have to ask him or herself when deciding whether the order is compatible with the Convention?

2. Discuss the reasons for some rights being 'qualified rights' and compare this with the reasons for other rights being non-qualified.

 For suggested approaches, please visit the Online Resource Centre.

≡ Further reading

See Further Reading in Chapters 15–18

15 Article 8: right to respect for private and family life

LEARNING OBJECTIVES

- The basic structure of Article 8.
- The state's obligations under Article 8.
- The concepts of 'private life', 'family life', 'home', and 'correspondence' and some of the situations to which they can be relevant (Article 8(1)).
- The grounds on which states may lawfully interfere with 'private life' etc. (Article 8(2)).
- Some specific issues such as environmental law, surveillance and the protection of personal information.

Article 8 Right to respect for private and family life

(1) Everyone has the right to respect for his private and family life, his home and his correspondence.

(2) There shall be no interference by a public authority with the exercise of this right except such as is in accordance with the law and is necessary in a democratic society in the interests of national security, public safety or the economic well-being of the country, for the prevention of disorder or crime, for the protection of health or morals, or for the protection of the rights and freedoms of others.

Introduction

Any non-totalitarian society must recognise there are some matters which are personal, over which individuals are sovereign, and with which the state should not interfere. 'Autonomy' (self-directedness) is at the heart of human rights. Article 8 seeks to protect this area of freedom from improper state interference. But in doing so it is involved in some deeply intractable and controversial problems. For example, should the law allow assisted suicide, should justified deportations be prevented just because the deportee has established a family life in the UK, or are there sufficient protections for personal information in the context, for instance, of police action in combating crime. The difficulties inherent in these questions are recognised in the structure of Article 8.

15.1 Article 8: general issues

15.1.1 Article 8 and the two-paragraph structure

The dilemmas and tensions exemplified above explain why Article 8 is a qualified right. It establishes the right to respect for private life, etc. but then goes on to allow interferences with those rights so long as certain conditions are followed.

The first paragraph identifies 'private life', 'family life', 'home', and 'correspondence' as the general concepts in terms of which this sphere of the personal is to be protected under the European Convention on Human Rights (ECHR). The second paragraph permits interferences but only if they can be justified. To be justified, they must be done only with the authority of law, only for one or more of the purposes listed in the second paragraph, and only if it is necessary in a democratic society to make the interference and, in the instant case, the interference represents a fair balance between the interests of the individual and the interests of others or of society that the interference aims to protect.

> **CROSS REFERENCE**
> The general principles governing qualified rights have been discussed in Chapter 14.

15.1.2 A right to privacy in English law

No general right to privacy has been developed by English common law. Different aspects of privacy are protected in a number of different ways. Thus 'home' and property can be protected by laws of property and the tort of trespass to land; bodily integrity is protected by the criminal law and the tort of trespass to the person; confidences by an action for breach of confidence; reputation by an action for defamation, and so on. In *Wainwright v Home Office* [2003] UKHL 53, the House of Lords refused to develop a general tort (a civil wrong not directly based on a breach of contract) of privacy. It saw this as a pointless abstraction. The existing remedies gave specific and effective remedies. Any 'gaps' could be met by the Human Rights Act 1998 (HRA) (see Lord Hoffmann's analysis, paras 15–51). And, indeed, Article 8 has been the inspiration for developing the common law tort of breach of confidence so that it includes an action which is based on a reasonable expectation of privacy.

> **CROSS REFERENCE**
> The right to privacy is explored in Chapter 22, section 22.5.

15.1.3 Article 8 and other rights

Issues involving Article 8 often also raise issues under other Articles of the Convention such as Article 12, the right to marry (see Chapter 19), and Article 1 of the First Protocol, protection of property (see Chapter 23).

Furthermore, issues about discrimination (e.g. on grounds of sexuality) frequently involve Article 14 (prohibition of discrimination) linked to Article 8 (see, on Article 14, Chapter 7, section 7.1).

It can also be necessary to weigh the importance to an individual of his or her rights under Article 8 with the importance to others of their rights under a different Convention Article. This is common in respect of invasions of privacy by the media (the media have rights to freedom of expression under Article 10).

CROSS REFERENCE
On Article 3, see Chapter 9, particularly, section 9.1.3.

Particularly difficult questions involve the relations between Article 8 and Article 3, the prohibition of torture and inhuman and degrading treatment, and punishment. Treatment which reaches the threshold of severity to violate Article 3 cannot be justified no matter how compelling are the gains to the common good or to the rights of others. Treatment which is not so severe can still be an interference with Article 8(1) but, in that case, it is open to the state to justify the treatment in the terms allowed by Article 8(2).

15.2 The states' obligations and positive duties

15.2.1 Respect

Article 8 requires states to 'respect' private and family life etc. There is no obligation on states to provide these things in the first place. For example, states are not required to ensure that everyone has a home, rather to respect what rights to a home people have (this is discussed later in the chapter). Respect may also imply a threshold of seriousness. Non-serious interferences or interferences which do not imply a lack of respect may be outside the ambit of Article 8(1) altogether (see Lord Walker's discussion of the case law in *M* v *Secretary of State for Work and Pensions* [2006] UKHL 11, paras 62–83).

15.2.2 Positive duties

Under the Convention

In *Belgian Linguistics Case (No 2)* (1979–80) 1 EHRR 252, the European Court of Human Rights (ECtHR) stated that the 'essential' purpose of Article 8 is negative, it requires the state to desist from arbitrary interferences with private life etc. However, since that case, the Court has frequently said that Article 8 may require states to take positive steps to ensure that private life etc. is respected. States must not only desist from interfering unreasonably in private life, but also they may have a legal duty to do things, like change the laws or take particular administrative steps.

The classic statement by the ECtHR is from *X and Y* v *The Netherlands* (1986) 8 EHRR 235, para 23:

CROSS REFERENCE
Positive duties are found throughout the Convention, see Chapter 6, section 6.6.

> The Court recalls that although the object of Article 8 is essentially that of protecting the individual against arbitrary interference by the public authorities, it does not merely compel the State to abstain from such interference: in addition to this primarily negative undertaking, there may be positive obligations inherent in an effective respect for private or family life. These obligations may involve the adoption of measures designed to secure respect for private life even in the sphere of the relations of individuals between themselves.

In the context of Article 8 positive duties have been found in contexts such as the following:

- To ensure that there are adequate legal remedies available to those whose Article 8 rights have been interfered with.
- To provide information and ensure proper access to personal information.
- To undertake a proper investigation of allegations of a breach of Article 8.

Interferences by private companies and individuals

As the quote from *X and Y* v *The Netherlands* indicates, Article 8 requires states to ensure that private and family life etc. is respected even where the intrusions come from non-state sources. The ECtHR, therefore, reads Article 8, as meaning:

- there is to be proper respect for private life, and that

- the only acceptable interferences with private life are those by public authorities which can be justified under Article 8(2). Other interferences are not acceptable.

To secure this, the state may have to prevent or regulate interferences with private life etc. that come from non-state sources (part of the 'horizontal effect' of the Convention).

The obvious example is the media. TV and broadcasting is (with the exception of the BBC) commercially owned and so not directly covered by the HRA. Nevertheless, media intrusions into the personal lives of individuals, including celebrities, may need to be regulated in order to ensure that press and TV give proper respect to their private and family lives. The law must enable a balance to be drawn between the media's rights to freedom of expression and a person's right to respect for private life; and it must guarantee adequate remedies if Article 8 rights are not respected. In the United Kingdom this is achieved through a combination of protection through the courts (e.g. damages or an injunction for breach of confidentiality), with media regulation through bodies such as Ofcom (for commercial television), the BBC Trust, and the Independent Press Standards Organisation. The courts are designated as 'public authorities' by section 6 HRA and so must act compatibly with Convention rights such as Article 8; likewise the regulators must so act since they perform public functions.

Media regulation is discussed further in Chapter 22, section 22.2.

CROSS REFERENCE
For 'horizontal effect' see Chapter 4, section 4.7.1.

CROSS REFERENCE
The definition of 'public authority' is discussed in Chapter 4, section 4.5.

15.3 The approach of courts to Article 8

15.3.1 **Scope and interference**

The first issue for a court dealing with an Article 8 claim is to decide whether there has been an interference with a person's 'private' life, 'family life', 'home', or 'correspondence'. These are open-textured and controversial terms which need interpretation by the courts. Are you 'private' when in a public place, does 'family' include unmarried or same-sex couples? It is only if the courts, interpreting the Convention, answer 'yes' that Article 8 is relevant (these matters are discussed in the next section). In the UK, under the HRA, the trigger for the engagement of Article 8 in respect of private life is whether, in the context, there is a 'reasonable expectation of privacy' (confirmed in *JR38's application for judicial review* [2015] UKSC 42).

The second issue is whether there has been an 'interference' amounting to a failure to 'respect' private life, etc. Again, judgment by the courts is called for. Does taking photographs or keeping records amount to an interference? The interference must be by the state (directly) or indirectly through a failure to perform a positive duty.

15.3.2 **Justification**

If there is an issue within the scope of Article 8(1) and an interference, it still does not follow that the complainant's rights under Article 8 have been violated. Courts dealing with Article 8 must go on to consider whether the interference can be justified under the terms of Article 8(2). There is only a breach of the Convention if the answer to the latter question is 'no'.

Where the state has interfered with a person's private or family life etc., the approach of the courts to justification is to check through Article 8(2) in order to form a judgment on whether the interference is justified. Where the issue is the failure to perform a positive duty, the approach has to be different (there has been no interference to be justified). The ECtHR, in such circumstances, approaches the matter in terms of proportionality: has there been a 'fair balance' between the interests of individuals and those of society. The Court dislikes overly formal distinctions and the difference between positive and negative duties may not always be clear. The overriding concern, in either context, is to ensure the fair balance.

▶ **CROSS REFERENCE**

Proportionality is discussed in Chapter 6, section 6.5.

15.3.3 **Margin of appreciation and deference**

▶ **CROSS REFERENCE**

Deference by UK courts is discussed in Chapter 4, section 4.6.2. 'Margin of appreciation' is discussed in Chapter 6, section 6.3.

Striking a fair balance between individual entitlements and legitimate social values and benefits can involve complex questions of policy and controversial questions of what common goods are valuable and worthwhile. The ECtHR acknowledges that, depending on the issue, nation states enjoy a wide margin of appreciation on many issues. The margin is focused on the issue of justification under Article 8(2), especially on the need for an interference in a democratic society. Under the HRA, for the same types of reason, courts in the United Kingdom are willing to 'defer', and, on the issue of justification, give weight to the decisions of Parliament (expressed in the policies inherent in Acts of Parliament) and of the executive and the administration.

15.4 'Private . . . life'

▶ **CROSS REFERENCE**

Pretty is further discussed at section 15.10.5.

The ECtHR has developed a wide, inclusive understanding of 'private life'. *Pretty* v *United Kingdom* (2002) 35 EHRR 1, involved the question whether the right to a private life could include the right to choose the time of one's own death.

The ECtHR stressed that 'the concept of "private life" is a broad term not susceptible to exhaustive definition' (see paras 61–62):

> It covers the physical and psychological integrity of a person. It can sometimes embrace aspects of an individual's physical and social identity. Elements such as, for example, gender identification, name and sexual orientation and sexual life fall within the personal sphere protected by Article 8. Article 8 also protects a right to personal development, and the right to establish and develop relationships with other human beings and the outside world . . . the Court considers that the notion of personal autonomy is an important principle underlying the interpretation of its guarantees.

Private life includes the idea of being left alone. However, as *Pretty* shows, it also extends to concepts of self-development and autonomy. UK courts have adopted this definition under the HRA. Nevertheless, doubt has been expressed about the concepts of 'identity' and 'personal development', referred to in *Pretty*. In *R (Razgar)* v *Secretary of State for the Home Department* [2004] UKHL 27, Lord Walker, at para 34, suggested that the meaning of these words was unclear and that the rights developed out of Article 8 could be 'abstract and volatile' in character.

15.4.1 **Physical integrity**

ECHR

States must have laws and procedures which give adequate protection to those who have suffered physical abuse or been subject to physical, bodily, interference: see, for example, *X and Y v The Netherlands*, at section 15.2.2. The suffering must reach an appropriate level of severity to engage Article 8(1), but this level is lower than that required for a breach of Article 3 (*Bensaid v United Kingdom* (2001) 33 EHRR 10, para 46). Treatment covered by Article 8(1), unlike under Article 3, may be acceptable if it is justified under Article 8(2) as being proportionate to the achievement of a social good. For example, forcible medical interventions (see Chapter 9, section 9.7.2) and requiring a person to undergo a strip search (*Wainwright* v *United Kingdom* (2007) 44 EHRR 40) engage Article 8(1) and therefore require justification under Article 8(2).

HRA

 CASE CLOSE-UP

Evans v Amicus Healthcare Ltd [2004] EWCA Civ 727

Under the Human Fertilisation and Embryology Act 1990, in vitro fertilisation treatment could only be given on the basis of the consent of both parties to the fertilisation. The claimant's former partner withdrew his consent. The claimant sought an injunction to compel her former partner to restore his consent and a declaration that the Act was incompatible with her rights under Article 8.

It was held by the Court of Appeal that the claimant's Article 8 rights were engaged but the requirement for continued consent, insisted on by Parliament, was proportionate and so was justified under Article 8(2).

The Court of Appeal found both that refusal of treatment by the clinic and the question of when a person can become pregnant engaged Article 8(1). In *Burke* v *General Medical Council* [2005] EWCA Civ 1003, it was accepted that Article 8 was likely to be engaged on issues concerning consent to medical treatment.

15.4.2 **Psychological or moral integrity**

States also need to have laws and procedures to protect citizens from abuse causing psychological harm and threats to what is called 'moral integrity'. Moral integrity is something less than psychological illness. It can include, for instance, the humiliation and degradation of the person that can accompany physical abuse and ill-treatment. On these grounds Article 8 can be relevant in the context of abusive prison conditions and other forms of detention (see, for example, *Raninen* v *Finland* (1998) 26 EHRR 563, para 63).

Article 8 might involve duties on states to ensure adequate treatment for those suffering mental illness, though the extent of such a positive duty is unclear.

In *Bensaid* v *United Kingdom* (2001) 33 EHRR 10, the applicant sought to resist deportation on the grounds that, as a sufferer from schizophrenia, his treatment in Algeria, the country he was to be deported to, would be so inadequate as to violate his right to private life under Article 8. The ECtHR held that 'mental health must . . . be regarded as a crucial part of private life associated with the aspect of moral integrity' (para 47); though, on the facts, the alleged deprivations were probably not so serious as to come within the protection of Article 8 and, even if they did, the deportation could be justified under Article 8(2).

15.4.3 **Personal and social identity**

Names

Legal restrictions on the names that people are entitled to adopt can engage Article 8(1) (as in *Johansson v Finland* (2008) 47 EHRR 14).

Gender

▶ **CROSS REFERENCE**
The human rights of transgendered persons are considered in Chapter 19, section 19.5.

A person's sense of identity is closely related to their gender. Article 8(1) (as well as Article 12) has frequently been engaged in respect of national laws which discriminate against transgendered persons who have gone through a psychological and, often, a physical process of gender reassignment. In *Goodwin v United Kingdom* (2002) 35 EHRR 18, the ECtHR held that legal barriers imposed on a transgendered person violated their rights to private life.

Reputation

A person's reputation is an aspect of private life protected by Article 8. Thus rights and remedies to protect reputation (such as common law 'defamation') must be available (e.g. *Clift v Slough BC* [2010] EWCA Civ 1484) and, likewise, courts, when considering whether to allow parties or witnesses to be anonymous, must act compatibly with Article 8. The issue is discussed in *Re Guardian News and Media* [2010] UKSC 1, paras 37–42, which cites *Pfeifer v Austria* (2007) 48 EHRR 175, para 35.

15.4.4 **Sexual orientation and sexual freedom**

Private life 'includes . . . sexual life' (*Dudgeon v United Kingdom*(1982) 4 EHRR 149, para 41). Laws regulating or restricting sexual orientation and sexual freedom deal with a person's most intimate feelings and relationships and engage Article 8. Cases such as *Dudgeon* (criminalised male homosexual activity), *BB v United Kingdom* (2004) 39 EHRR 30 (age of consent), *ADT v United Kingdom* (2001) 31 EHRR 33 (group sex and privacy) make it clear that laws which treat homosexuals less favourably than heterosexuals cannot be justified under Article 8(2).

A remaining issue under the Convention is whether states are required to give full and equal recognition to same-sex partnerships (this is discussed at section 15.5.3).

15.4.5 **Personal information**

Access to personal information

A full sense of identity involves knowing the central facts about who one is and where one came from. For some people, crucial pieces of information may be held by public authorities and be unavailable under the law. Although Article 10 (the right to freedom of expression) includes a right to 'receive . . . information', the ECtHR has held that this does not create an obligation on the unwilling party (e.g. the authorities) to divulge secret information (*Leander v Sweden* (1987) 9 EHRR 433, para 74). However, the Court has accepted that there may be a right to receive information in the context of Article 8. This right has been asserted in respect of:

- access to social work files where this is necessary for the applicant to have knowledge about his early childhood (*Gaskin* v *United Kingdom* (1980) 12 EHRR 36);

- information pertaining to the health risks of those involved in dangerous activities (*McGinley* v *United Kingdom* (1999) 27 EHRR 1);

- information for adopted children about their natural parents (*Odievre* v *France* (2004) 38 EHRR 43).

Protection of personal information

Making personal information available to the public without the person's consent raises an issue under Article 8(1). There have been a number of cases under the HRA.

In *R (Robertson)* v *Wakefield Metropolitan District Council* [2001] EWHC 915 (Admin), the sale to a commercial buyer of personal information contained in the electoral register without the right of an individual to refuse, was held to engage Article 8(1) and not be justified under Article 8(2). It also violated EU law on data protection.

>> CROSS REFERENCE

Cases involving celebrities are discussed in Chapter 22, section 22.5.

Police records and samples

Under various powers in the Police and Criminal Evidence Act 1984 (PACE) and other statutes, the police have powers to take and retain fingerprints and body samples from suspects. **This raises important issues, which are discussed in Chapter 20, sections 20.6.1 and 20.6.2.**

15.4.6 **Public places**

As *von Hannover* v *Germany* (2005) 40 EHRR 1 (see section 15.4.8, Freedom) makes clear, the simple fact that a person is in a public place, such as a street, does not mean that they have thereby lost all rights to private life. After all, private life, in its positive aspect, includes the idea of being able to interact with others and it would be arbitrary if that freedom could only be exercised in private places. It is the nature of the activity and the circumstances that are important. Being photographed by police whilst engaged in a political demonstration (whose point is public awareness) is unlikely to engage Article 8(1) (see *Friedl* v *Austria* (1996) 21 EHRR 83). On the other hand, there was a breach of Article 8 when CCTV footage of a man attempting suicide in a town centre was used by the media without his full consent (see *Peck* v *United Kingdom* (2003) 36 EHRR 41). The Court distinguished between the simple monitoring of people in public places, which will not normally engage Article 8, and the keeping of personal records or other uses of the information which may well do so.

>> CROSS REFERENCE

There is further discussion of *Peck* in Chapter 5, section 5.1.4.

In *R (Countryside Alliance)* v *Attorney General* [2007] UKHL 52, all the Law Lords agreed that the public and spectacular nature of hunting made it impossible for Article 8(1) to be engaged.

15.4.7 **Surveillance**

Surveillance activities, by police, security services, and others, engage Article 8(1). Justification for surveillance is discussed later in this chapter, section 15.10.2.

15.4.8 Personal development, autonomy, and freedom

Personal development

The extent of the protection given by Article 8(1) is unclear. The summary in *Pretty* (paras 61–62 quoted at section 15.4) refers to 'personal development'. This gives protection beyond merely the right to be left alone:

> It also secures to the individual a sphere within which he or she can freely pursue the development and fulfilment of his or her personality.

> (*Brüggerman and Scheuten v Germany* (1977) DR 10, para 55)

CROSS REFERENCE

Prisoners' rights are discussed in Chapter 21. For ASBOs see Chapter 12, section 12.4.3, Discussion topic. For TPIMs see Chapter 26, section 26.7.2.

Thus Article 8(1) is engaged when laws or official practices limit a person's ability to establish and develop relationships with other people and the outside world generally. In the United Kingdom, prisoners held in solitary confinement, persons under Anti-social Behaviour Orders, or terrorist suspects subject to Terrorism Prevention and Investigation Measures (TPIMs), if they suffer significant restrictions on their right to meet and associate with whom they please, could, if the restrictions are sufficiently severe, find that their Article 8 rights are in issue.

Autonomy

In *Pretty* (see section 15.4), the Court also referred to personal autonomy, the idea that a person should, given their circumstances, be able to control his or her life and make important decisions for themselves, is an important guiding principle in Article 8.

In *Pretty* the ECtHR would 'not . . . exclude' the possibility that autonomy included, at least in the circumstances of the case, a right to choose to die (para 67). For UK law the application of Article 8(1) in 'right to die' cases was affirmed by the House of Lords in *R (Purdy)* v *DPP* [2009] UKHL 45. In *Haas* v *Switzerland* (2011) 53 EHRR 33, the right of a competent person to commit suicide (without assistance) was clearly brought within the scope of Article 8(1).

Freedom

The scope of these concepts of self-development and autonomy is not clear. First, Article 8(1) seems to extend to a person's right to go about his or her daily business and ordinary life without unjustifiable interference. Thus in *von Hannover* v *Germany* (2005) 40 EHRR 1, Princess Caroline of Monaco was able to assert a right to private life, which the German courts should have protected, against being hassled by paparazzi when doing ordinary things like shopping and playing tennis. Some senior UK judges would like this to go further and for private life to include activities that are of core importance to an individual's sense of him or herself, or they would like Article 8 to embody a general right to freedom. On this basis, legal restrictions on a person's freedom of action that are not based on harm to others but on, for example, facilitating a policy that benefits others or stopping actions considered to be immoral or disgusting, will engage Article 8(1), and therefore need justification before the judges.

 DISCUSSION TOPIC

Should there be a right to freedom?

Should Article 8(1) express a right to freedom? The argument mentioned previously was developed, *obiter dicta,* by Lords Rodger and Brown in *R (Countryside Alliance)* v *Attorney*

General [2007] UKHL 52, an unsuccessful challenge to the ban on hunting in England and Wales. All their Lordships accepted that the ban on fox hunting could not be sufficiently justified on the grounds of suppression of cruelty to animals (since alternatives to fox hunting are also cruel) and so part of the justification was a moral revulsion, on behalf of a majority of MPs, to fox hunting.

The views of Lords Rodger and Brown ('Why should it [Article 8(1)] not encompass a broad philosophy of live and let live ') are at paras 95–101 and 137–141; and can be compared with the view of Baroness Hale ('In my view there is no human right to be left alone to do as one likes') at paras 110–116. Lords Rodger and Brown both accepted that the Article 8 case law had not gone as far as they would like.

15.4.9 **Private life and economic activity**

The idea of personal development can make Article 8 significant in respect of legal barriers that prevent people from leading normal lives, such as refusing passports or creating legal barriers to people working in their chosen careers (e.g. *Sidabras and Dziautas* v *Lithuania* (2006) 42 EHRR 6, where barriers to former members of the KGB working violated Article 14 linked to Article 8).

The concept of 'private life' is indeterminate in scope and could be applied in a commercial and professional context, as in *Niemietz* (see section 15.6.1). Individuals construct their lives in ways in which there is intermingling of the private and the public.

15.5 'Family life'

15.5.1 **Introduction**

States have duties not to interfere in arbitrary ways with those close, personal, and psychologically important relationships which are contained in the concept of 'family'. Interferences with the relationships between close blood relations, husband and wife, parents and children, and parents and their adopted children will all come within the scope of Article 8(1). In *Huang* v *Secretary of State for the Home Department* [2007] UKHL 11, Baroness Hale, summarising Strasbourg case law, defined family in terms of deep social, emotional, and financial dependency (para 18).

15.5.2 **Family and informal relationships**

From early days the ECtHR has sought to define the idea of a family relationship in a way that recognises social change and development and which does not allow legal forms (e.g. marriage) to prevail over 'biological and social reality' (*Kroon* v *The Netherlands* (1995) 19 EHRR 263, para 40). So-called 'ad hoc' relationships are recognised. These relationships are not defined in advance. Their acceptance by the Court as being family relationships depends on 'real' (as distinct from legal) factors, such as whether there is sufficient closeness and longevity for it to be familial in quality. If so it must be respected by the national laws. Laws and official practices which discriminate between legitimate and illegitimate children (*Marckx* v *Belgium* (1979–80) 2 EHRR 330) or which base family life solely on marriage, or which focus on legal formalities rather than personal realities (*Abdulaziz, Cabbales and Balkandali v United Kingdom* (1985) 7 EHRR 471) are likely to raise Article 8(1) issues and require justification under Article 8(2).

🔍 CASE CLOSE-UP

Kroon v The Netherlands (1995) 19 EHRR 263

Before being divorced from her husband, K formed a relationship with A. It was a stable relationship although K and A did not live together. They had a child but, under The Netherlands' law, the child could not be registered as A's child because only the husband could authorise legal steps which denied the legitimacy of his wife's children. The ECtHR held that there was a violation of Article 8.

Various points follow from this case:

- Familial relationships, which the laws must respect, do not depend on marriage.
- Given factors of strength and stability, a relationship can be familial even if the couple are living apart.
- Relationships between parents and children must be protected by national laws, and legal presumptions (here about legitimacy) must not be allowed to interfere with the biological and social realities.

15.5.3 **Same-sex relationships**

Same-sex relationships are included in family relationships and are protected by Article 8(1), *Schalk and Kopf v Austria* (2011) 53 EHRR 20, paras 90–94). This involves a deliberate change by the ECtHR from its earlier rulings. There is not yet a positive duty on states to provide for homosexual marriage or 'civil partnership', though the latter, at least, is a discernable trend in European societies.

15.5.4 **Social policy**

There are a number of areas of social policy in which states, acting in pursuit of legitimate policy objectives, take actions which interfere with family life, given its broad definition. These include the following:

- Steps taken to protect children, by taking them from their parents and placing them in the care of the local authority, who then make important decisions about whom the children are to live with and whether the biological parents have rights of access etc. These actions must respect the rights to family life of those involved including the children themselves and the biological parents (*C v United Kingdom* App 14858/03, admissibility decision of 14 December 2004).
- Immigration. Under the Convention it is recognised that states are entitled to take steps to control immigration. Immigration policies on who may enter the country or who is to be deported may involve decisions about whether family members can be together. Such actions must respect the rights to family life of those involved (*Abdulaziz, Cabalas and Balkandali v United Kingdom* (1985) 7 EHRR 471, para 57).

15.6 'Home'

15.6.1 **The concept of 'home'**

Under Article 8, states have obligations not to interfere in arbitrary ways with a person's 'home'. 'Home' is not defined but the implication is that it is the place where a person lives or intends to live on a settled basis.

 CASE CLOSE-UP

Buckley v United Kingdom (1997) 23 EHRR 101

B was a gypsy who, for two years, had lived in caravans placed on land that she owned. She sought retrospective planning permission for herself and her family. The application was refused by the local authority. B was offered a place on an official site, which she turned down. The local authority issued enforcement notices requiring the caravans to be removed. She alleged a breach of Article 8. The ECtHR held that the refusal to grant planning permission was an interference with B's home but it was one which was within the margin of appreciation of the United Kingdom's planning authorities and hence was justified under the terms of Article 8(2).

In finding that Article 8 was engaged, the ECtHR adopted a Convention specific, 'autonomous' meaning of home. In particular:

- A person's home exists independently of whether or not it is 'lawful' under the national laws.
- No abstract definition of home is provided.
- The main issue involves the intentions and attitude of the applicant towards the land in issue—an intention now or in the future to treat the place as home.
- It is not necessary for a person to have lived all the time on the land in question—a home is not lost just because a person is living abroad for a while. But it is necessary to show sufficient, continuous links with the place in issue and, perhaps, that no other permanent home has been established.

In *Giacomelli* v *Italy* (2007) 45 EHRR 38, the ECtHR described a home as 'the place, the physically defined area, where private and family life develops', para 76. This is clearly not a complete definition since home can include company offices (*Société Colas Est v France* (2004) 39 EHRR 17) and the place where an individual works.

 CASE CLOSE-UP

Niemietz v Germany (1993) 16 EHRR 97

A lawyer's offices were searched by the police acting on the basis of a warrant. The ECtHR held that a person's place of work could be considered as part of their home. Because of the intermingling of the private and the professional in the way individuals construct and value their lives, such a broad definition of home was necessary given that the underlying purpose of Article 8 is to prevent arbitrary interference by states in individual lives. The search was not justified under Article 8(2), and so there was a breach of Article 8.

15.6.2 Respect for a home

 CROSS REFERENCE

Peaceful enjoyment of possessions is also a right under Article 1 of the First Protocol, see Chapter 23.

Article 8 places a duty on states to 'respect' a person's home. This can mean, for example, that states must ensure access and a right to live in their home (such as did not happen in *Gillow* v *United Kingdom* (1989) 11 EHRR 335); that states must protect a person's peaceful enjoyment of their property (taking reasonable steps to prevent harassment, for example, as in *Whiteside* v *United Kingdom* (1994) 18 EHRR CD126).

Right to a home?

Article 8 does not mean that states have general social duties to house the homeless and provide secure accommodation to people who do not have, or have lost through lawful eviction, a place they can call home.

Article 8 applies to evictions by public landlords.

🔍 CASE CLOSE-UP

McCann v United Kingdom (2008) 47 EHRR 40

M's wife left him because of alleged domestic violence. M lost his legal right to remain in the family home and the local authority landlord successfully evicted him. The legal procedure it used gave M no opportunity to argue that, on the basis of his personal circumstances, eviction was unlawful. The ECtHR found that there was a breach of Article 8.

In *McCann* the ECtHR said that eviction was 'a most extreme form of interference with the right to respect for the home' (para 50). Even though the tenant had no legal right to remain it should still, 'in principle', be possible for the proportionality of the eviction to be measured by a court that had a jurisdiction to deal with all the relevant factual as well as legal issues.

The principle in *McCann* has now been adopted into the law of England and Wales under the HRA.

🔍 CASE CLOSE-UP

Manchester CC v Pinnock [2010] UKSC 45

P lived in a property let by MCC as a 'demoted tenant'. This meant, in essence, that MCC could seek a possession order from the County Court, which would be granted on the sufficient grounds that he had breached the terms of the demoted tenancy and that the authority had followed a statutory procedure (i.e. the County Court was not required to consider whether it was reasonable to evict in the circumstances). Continued anti-social behaviour by P's children led to his eviction. The Supreme Court applied Article 8 to the eviction:

- Article 8(1) is engaged when public landlords exercise lawful powers to evict people from their homes.

- Section 3 HRA could be used to read into the statutory duties of the County Court the power to consider justification for the eviction under Article 8(2).
- The tenant must raise the issue of proportionality; otherwise public landlords can proceed on the assumption that Article 8 is complied with.
- There was a high threshold for the tenant to cross. Fair balance, required by 'proportionality' (Article 8(2)), would give great weight to public landlords' legal rights and also to their judgment on housing policy and balancing the various interests engaged by social housing (though the court refused to say that disproportionate eviction would be 'exceptional').
- The case has no implications for private landlords.

There may even be extreme examples where the Convention does impose a duty to provide a home. In *R v North East Devon Health Authority ex parte Coughlan* [2001] QB 213, a Health Authority promised a severely disabled young woman a 'home for life' in a specially built facility. Under English administrative law the promise established a 'legitimate expectation', but the question for the courts was whether this was merely a legitimate expectation to be consulted about any proposed changes to her situation or whether it gave her a right to go on living in the facility. The Court of Appeal took the latter view and, in part, saw this as giving effect to Coughlan's Article 8 rights.

15.7 'Correspondence'

The term 'correspondence', like private life, is given a wide definition under the Convention. Both terms can embrace interferences with personal communications in all their forms: letters and telephone calls and, presumably, other methods such as fax and e-mail (see *Klass v Germany* (1979–80) 2 EHRR 214, para 41).

As with private life and home, the ECtHR recognises that it not possible to make a clear distinction between the private sphere and other aspects of a person's life such as their working life.

In *Halford v United Kingdom* (1997) 24 EHRR 523, a senior police officer, who was bringing a sex discrimination case against her force, had both her home telephone and her office telephone bugged by the police authority. The ECtHR held that Article 8 applied both to the interceptions on her home phone and the office phone (see also *Copland v United Kingdom* (2007) 45 EHRR 37).

'Respect' for correspondence means that states must justify, under Article 8(2), actions such as opening and reading letters or e-mails, metering and tapping phones, censoring correspondence, and so on. States may have positive duties to ensure adequate access to communication by vulnerable groups, including prisoners.

15.8 Environmental law

No provision in the Convention expressly requires environmental rights; there are, for instance, no express rights to clean air or a quiet environment.

CROSS REFERENCE

The applicability of the Convention to the modern political agenda is discussed in Chapter 2, section 2.3.5.

Despite this, the ECtHR has implied environmental rights into Article 8(1). Where environmental damage has a serious direct effect upon a person's private and family life or their home, there can be an issue raised under Article 8.

In *López Ostra* v *Spain* (1995) 20 EHRR 277, the ECtHR held that there had been a breach of Article 8 in respect of the authority's failure adequately to deal with a waste treatment plant built only 12 metres from the applicant's home and which was responsible for fumes, bad smells, and contamination causing health problems.

CROSS REFERENCE

Environmental failures causing death can engage Article 2, see Chapter 8, section 8.3.5.

In *Guerra* v *Italy* (1998) 26 EHRR 357, the applicant lived one kilometre from a chemical factory which had released highly toxic substances into the atmosphere, which were responsible for serious poisoning of the population. The ECtHR held that there had been a violation of Article 8 in respect of both the failure properly to regulate the factory and also the failure to make proper information available to the population.

In *Moreno Gomez* v *Spain* (2005) 41 EHRR 40, noise pollution from night clubs raised an Article 8 issue.

The general principles are summarised in *Fadeyeva* v *Russia*.

🔍 CASE CLOSE-UP

Fadeyeva v *Russia* (2007) 45 EHRR 10

F was one of thousands of people who lived within a 1000-metre buffer zone that was supposed to isolate the biggest steel smelter in Russia from any residential area. The smelter, which was old and inefficient, was the cause of major air pollution which caused serious respiratory and blood illnesses amongst many of the population. Schemes to re-house the residents were not put into full effect. The resident was one who was not rehoused. No remedy was available to her from the Russian courts. The ECtHR held that there had been a violation of Article 8.

- Though there is no explicit right to a clean environment in the Convention, Article 8 is engaged if pollution has a direct effect on a person's private and family life, or on his or her home.

- Pollution will only engage Article 8(1) if it surpasses a minimum level of severity. This level depends on the particular circumstances, such as the intensity and duration of the pollution.

- The facts must be proved. The standard of proof is beyond a reasonable doubt; the burden of proof is on the applicant but, given the fact that obtaining information may be difficult and that much of the information will be controlled by the authorities, the Court adopts a flexible approach. It will make inferences and work on the basis of presumptions about the responsibilities of the authorities if direct causal evidence of the effects on the applicant is not available.

The need for significant severity in pollution before Article 8 is engaged has been emphasised for the purposes of domestic UK law in *Barr* v *Biffa Waste Services* [2011] EWHC 1003 (see paras 305–310 for a summary of cases).

It is rarely the state itself which does the polluting. In *Fadeyeva*, as in all the cases mentioned, the pollution was done by a commercial company. In the environmental context, therefore, states have 'positive duties' to regulate commercial industrial processes to the extent necessary to protect private and family lives and people's homes. Positive duties are not absolute. The ECtHR must be satisfied that the state has achieved a fair balance between the interests of the applicant, other parties involved (e.g. the commercial owners of the plant), and the wider public interest. Factors explicit in Article 8(2) can be relevant to such a judgment.

It is emphatically not the Court's job to determine a state's environmental laws and policies. The Court's role is to ensure that the states have given due weight to the applicant's Article 8 rights and not just ignored them. States have a wide margin of appreciation. Only in exceptional circumstances will the Court be prepared to find that the states, acting lawfully, in good faith, and giving full weight to individual's rights, have made a wrong judgment on where the fair balance lies.

> **CROSS REFERENCE**
> For margin of appreciation see Chapter 6, section 6.3.

15.9 Article 8(2)

How individuals wish to lead their private and family lives and what they may wish to do regarding their homes and correspondence can have a significant impact on others and on the interests of the public. Under the Convention a state, acting through public authorities, can restrict the private and family lives, the right of access to, and enjoyment of, home, and the correspondence, of individuals. But such restriction or interference is only possible if it is:

- done for one of the purposes listed in Article 8(2) and not for any other purpose;
- done 'in accordance with the law', i.e. is based on law and is compatible with the rule of law;
- 'necessary in a democratic society'—it is a proportionate way of meeting a pressing social need.

15.9.1 **Public authorities and positive duties**

Article 8(2) refers only to 'interference by a public authority'. This term refers to the full range of executive and administrative bodies through which the authority of the state is exercised (ministers and civil service, police, local councils, 'quangos', etc.) and also to other bodies for which the state is responsible, such as the FE college in *Copland* v *United Kingdom* (2007) 45 EHRR 37.

> **CROSS REFERENCE**
> For a fuller discussion of the 'state' see Chapter 2, section 2.4.3.

States may also have positive duties to regulate interferences with the Article 8 freedoms which come from private sources such as the media or private landlords. States may have to alter national laws, including those, such as laws of contract and property, which govern private relations; or establish regulatory agencies which control the activities of private or commercial bodies. Likewise the UK courts, public authorities under the HRA, need to fashion the private law in ways that recognise Article 8 rights.

Where an interference is based on a freely entered into contract, Article 8(1) may not be engaged at all (there will have been no interference as recognised under the Convention) or it will be easily justified under Article 8(2) as being to protect the rights of others, namely the rights under the contract of the other party. Thus, while states may have positive duties to regulate the private media in order to protect privacy, it is less likely that the same will apply to private landlords whose power over tenants is entirely contractual (see *Pinnock* at section 15.6.2). Nevertheless, context means a lot under the Convention and there may be

> **CROSS REFERENCE**
> For positive duties see section 15.2.2, and Chapter 6, section 6.6.

circumstances where this is not true (as in *Ghaidan* v *Godin-Mendoza* [2004] UKHL 30, discussed in Chapter 4, section 4.4.7).

15.9.2 'In accordance with the law'

CROSS REFERENCE

The pervasive concept of law and legality is discussed in Chapter 6, section 6.2.

Under Article 8(2) any interference with the freedom in Article 8(1) must be 'in accordance with the law'.

The concept of law and legality which pervades the Convention applies in respect of Article 8(2).

That is, the interference must be:

- in accordance with the national law as determined by the national courts;
- the national law must also meet the Convention requirements of 'accessibility' and 'foreseeability' (see Chapter 6, section 6.2);
- legality also requires that the applicant's rights are protected by a fair, adversarial, legal procedure. The applicant must have an opportunity to assert his or her fundamental rights and this applies, albeit subject to context, even in situations such as where the state acts to protect national security (see, for example, *Al Nashif* v *Bulgaria* (2003) 36 EHRR 37, paras 123–124).

Officials may exercise **discretion**.

> **discretion** Often the law identifies a general purpose officials (like police officers or civil servants) are to pursue but says little about the ways and means for doing this. The matter is left to the officials who thereby exercise 'discretion'.

Where this is so, the law must indicate the scope and limits of discretion. Otherwise the application of the laws by officials may not be sufficiently 'foreseeble'. Whether the legality test is met will depend upon contextual factors such as the purpose being pursued and the availability of adequate safeguards. The protection of children, for example, may justify wider discretion than that enjoyed by officials in the context of surveillance and national security.

15.9.3 Legitimate purposes

An interference with private life etc. must not only be in accordance with the law but can be only for one or more of the purposes listed in Article 8(2). It is often (though not always) easy for the state to prove that it is acting for a legitimate purpose.

'In the interests of national security'

'National security' has been accepted by the Court as justifying interferences with private and family life, home, and correspondence in a number of circumstances such as surveillance by security services and information gathering (e.g. *Klass* v *Germany* (1979–80) 2 EHRR 214, para 46).

Historically it has been all too easy for states to invoke national security to justify their actions and national courts have been reluctant to allow this claim to be challenged before them. Under the Convention, however, national law and procedures must give an opportunity for the government's claims to be tested to ensure that they have some reasonable basis. The person whose private life has been interfered with must be able, under national law, to:

challenge the executive's assertion that national security is at stake. While the executive's assessment of what poses a threat to national security will naturally be of significant weight, the independent authority [i.e. a court] must be able to react in cases where invoking that concept has no reasonable basis in the facts or reveals an interpretation of 'national security' that is unlawful or contrary to common sense and arbitrary.

(*Al-Nashif* v *Bulgaria* (2003) 36 EHRR 37, para 124)

BIGGER PICTURE

UK courts do require the government to give a proper explanation of why national security is at stake, though they also recognise that the government is the primary decision taker and, on this matter above all, is in possession of the main evidence, all or much of which may legitimately be secret or only available to special tribunals. On such a matter, context, including the nature of the burden on the individual, is all-important. See, for example, *A* v *Secretary of State for the Home Department* [2004] UKHL 56, para 177, per Lord Rodger.

'In the interests of . . . public safety'

This purpose seldom stands in its own right but is more likely to be linked with other purposes such as the prevention of crime. The purpose may justify, for example, public disclosure by the police or other authorities of personal information.

'In the interests of . . . the economic well-being of the country'

This phrase is unique to Article 8 and, unlike most of the others, does not appear in Article 9(2), 10(2), or 11(2). It appears to have been inserted at the behest of the (old) Labour government in the United Kingdom, which was concerned that Article 8 rights might be used to inhibit the programme of nationalisation (government ownership of basic industries) they were pursuing.

It is, in principle, hard to explain a situation in which an individual's rights can be restricted in order to promote the general wealth of the community since one of the central aims of human rights is to ensure that individuals and minorities are protected as society pursues its collective interests. Nevertheless this category has been used in the context of cases that involve the deportations of foreigners who have established family links and also environmental protection cases.

'for the prevention of disorder or crime'

This category can justify surveillance by the police and security services; it has also been accepted by the ECtHR as a legitimate purpose underlying the deportation of foreigners with criminal offences.

'for the protection of health'

Article 8(1) can be in issue in respect of a range of difficult issues relating to health and medical treatment. Respect for private life may be interfered with by, for example, the withdrawal of treatment or by forced treatment. The state may seek to justify such measures as being 'for the protection of health' but cannot do so if the measures were merely to exercise physical control. Issues about the care and custody of children may also fall to be considered as being for the protection of health.

'for the protection of . . . morals'

Governments and Parliaments may wish to restrict personal behaviour on the grounds that it is immoral in itself or harmful to the person involved or harmful to others. Such restrictions on personal behaviour may be found in respect, for example, of sexual behaviour or sexual orientation.

'for the protection of the rights and freedoms of others'

This is a broad and inclusive category, which is often linked with other purposes when states are seeking to justify interferences with Article 8(1) rights. The 'rights and freedoms' are not just those secured in the Convention but the term is used more generally to include legal rights and other freedoms that the ECtHR recognises. Similarly, the right to private life under Article 8(1) is itself a 'right' which can be asserted against, for example, the claims of the media to publish or broadcast personally intrusive stories.

15.9.4 'Necessary in a democratic society'

▶ CROSS REFERENCE
See Chapter 14, section 14.4.3 for general discussion.

By signing the Convention, the states agree that they will not interfere with the private lives of their population unless each and every individual interference meets the test of being 'necessary in a democratic society'. This involves courts in a judgment of proportionality and whether a fair balance has, in the detail of the case, been achieved between the various private and public interests involved. This is often the central issue in cases including those discussed in this chapter.

15.10 Particular interferences

Article 8 has an important impact on many important aspects of social, economic, and political life. Where there has been a direct interference by a public authority it must be justified in terms of Article 8(2). Where it is state inaction that is in issue, justification is in terms of the fair balance between maintaining the essence of Article 8 rights and the competing individual and collective interests that are at stake.

In the last part of this chapter a number of topics will be discussed in relation to justification directly under the Convention or, for UK law, the HRA.

15.10.1 Environmental law

ECHR

Environmental hazards or state policies to protect the environment can raise issues under Article 8 (see section 15.8).

Where, for example, pollution affects private and family life then a state's failure to enforce its own anti-pollution laws may mean a violation of Article 8 (as in *López Ostra* v *Spain* (1995) 20 EHRR 277, section 15.8). However, where an interference comes as a consequence of a carefully conceived, lawful regulatory regime, the ECtHR may be persuaded that a fair balance has been achieved.

In *Hatton* v *United Kingdom* (2003) 37 EHRR 28, a Grand Chamber reversed the Chamber's decision and held that the night flying regulations at Heathrow were proportionate interferences with the private and family life of the applicants and in the interests of the economic well-being of the country.

In *Hatton*, the Court gave considerable weight to the fact that noise pollution from night flying at Heathrow Airport served the economic interests of the nation, a legitimate purpose allowed under Article 8(2). Such a purpose is, of course, capable of supporting the claims of most industrial and commercial polluters. The concern is that decisions such as *Hatton* seriously weaken the environmental protection allowed under the Convention. *Fadeyeva v Russia* (section 15.8), however, may indicate that the Court is still prepared to find important environmental protection in the Convention for the worst cases.

HRA

Environmental issues under Article 8 have arisen in a number of contexts. For example:

- Noise pollution was considered in *Dennis v Ministry of Defence* [2003] EWHC 793: very loud aircraft noise from a nearby RAF base interfered with D's enjoyment of his home. The High Court held that any fair balance of D's rights under Article 8(1) with the public interest in an effective air force could only be achieved on the basis of (considerable) financial compensation.

- In *Marcic v Thames Water* [2003] UKHL 66, M's home and garden were repeatedly flooded and affected by sewage discharge. The cause was pipes which needed to be replaced. The water company, acting under a statutory scheme, had a system of priorities for replacing pipes and M was a low priority. The House of Lords held that the statutory scheme was a fair balance between the different interests. (*Hatton*, discussed earlier in this section, was followed.)

15.10.2 **Surveillance**

Surveillance and other forms of secret investigation engage Article 8(1) (see section 15.4.8).

ECHR

From its earliest cases the ECtHR has accepted that states may conduct secret surveillance (*Klass v Federal Republic of Germany* (1979–80) 2 EHRR 214). The surveillance must be strictly necessary to protect democratic institutions from threats to national security (as in *Klass*) but can also be used for the prevention of crime (e.g. *Valenzuela Contreras v Spain* (1999) 28 ECHR 483). For example, in *Erdem v Germany* (2002) 35 EHRR 15, the ECtHR accepted that the monitoring of the correspondence of a terrorist suspect was for the legitimate purpose of protecting national security (para 60).

The Court continues to stress the need for proper legal regulation of surveillance and of effective review.

 CASE CLOSE-UP

Zakharov v Russia **App 47143/06, Grand Chamber judgment of 4 December 2015.**

Z was a publisher and chair of a free press pressure group who claimed that his mobile phone had been intercepted on the basis of a secret order which allowed interception without prior judicial authorisation. Russian courts refused a remedy. In essence Z challenged the legal basis of surveillance in Russia at that time (2003).

In its assessment, the Grand Chamber confirmed the general principles relating to conformity of secret surveillance with Article 8.

- Surveillance involves an interference with private life, therefore the issue in the case is whether there is justification.

- **'In accordance with the law'.** As the Grand Chamber recognised, this raises particular problems. Generally the domestic 'law' which authorises surveillance must be 'accessible' to the applicant and 'foreseeable' in its effects (see Chapter 6, section 6.2). But in the context of surveillance, 'foreseeability' cannot (without destroying secrecy) mean that a person should be able foresee when he or she will be subject to surveillance. Laws on surveillance did not aim to restrict the behaviour of individuals but, rather, to regulate the behaviour of officials. Legal 'forseeability' did not mean that a person is entitled to know when his or her phone was likely to be tapped. In this context 'in accordance with the law' means that the law must be sufficiently clear in its terms to give citizens an adequate indication as to the circumstances in which and the conditions on which public authorities are empowered to resort to secret surveillance. Given the technical complexity of modern surveillance, this 'indication' is only adequate if the legal regime contains 'clear detailed rules' (para 229).

- **Law requires safeguards.** There is an obvious danger of arbitrary action by officials. Therefore, for an interference by surveillance to be in accordance with the law, there must be proper safeguards against abuse. In particular, there needs to be effective review of surveillance decisions by a judicial-type body which is independent, impartial, and based on proper procedures. In *Zakharov*, building on earlier cases, the Grand Chamber identified the 'minimum safeguards' which legal regulation of surveillance must contain. The law must identify:

  - the categories of people who might be subject to surveillance (e.g. those suspected of spying or terrorism);

  - the criminal offences for the prosecution of which surveillance might be used;

  - time limits on any particular authorisation;

  - the procedures for examining, using, and restoring the product of surveillance;

  - the precautions followed when giving others access to the data; and

  - provision for the destruction of such information.

- **Legitimate purpose.** As said previously, national security and the prevention of crime are legitimate purposes that may justify surveillance.

- **'Necessary in a legitimate society'.** The adequacy of safeguards can arise when the proportionality, the balance of security and freedom, of any act of surveillance is being assessed. States have a margin of appreciation over this (unlike the minimum safeguards inherent in the law) but even so, the Court must be satisfied that, on issues like the process for authorising warrants, there is protection from abuse. The Court says that it is 'in principle desirable' for there to be supervision by a judge or at least by a process independent of the executive.

The United Kingdom

In the United Kingdom the legal regime for surveillance is currently found in statutes such as the Regulation of Investigatory Powers Act 2000 (interception of communications) and both the Police Act 1997 and the Intelligence Services Act 1994, which deal with other forms of surveillance which would, without a warrant, be unlawful. These provisions are supplemented by Codes of Practice. A major safeguard is the Investigatory Powers Tribunal (IPT), which provides a degree of judicial supervision over the surveillance activities of the security services. In *Kennedy* v *United Kingdom* (2011) 52 EHRR 4, the ECtHR considered significant aspects of the legal, administrative, and judicial system governing surveillance in the UK and found, overall, that it was compatible with Article 8.

However, the system in the UK remains controversial generally and in respect of Article 8. For example: in *Liberty* v *GCHQ* [2014] UKIPT 13_77-H (5 December 2014) and later hearings, the Tribunal considered the system by which GCHQ (which conducts national security surveillance in the UK) acquires data from the USA which has been obtained through the vast, general, surveillance undertaken in that country (part of what was revealed by Edward Snowden). A challenge was brought under Article 8. The IPT held that 'in accordance with the law' required proper public disclosure of the safeguards that apply when such data was obtained. It was only after this disclosure was made that it could be said that GCHQ was complying with Article 8.

One of the issues which has caused disagreement is whether surveillance warrants need prior judicial authorisation or whether after the event judicial supervision is satisfactory. Article 8 ECHR does not specifically require prior judicial authorisation of warrants (authorisation by the Home Secretary was accepted in *Kennedy* v *United Kingdom*, discussed earlier). However, EU law is relevant here. The EU Charter of Fundamental Rights provides for data protection (in its Article 8) and the Court of Justice of the European Union, in *'Digital Rights Ireland'* [2015] QB 127, seemed to suggest that national laws on surveillance need to have prior judicial authorisation of warrants. This would mean that EU law protection would be different, perhaps stronger, than that required under Article 8 ECHR. It remains to be confirmed whether this really is mandatory.

In the United Kingdom a draft Investigatory Powers Bill was published in November 2015. It will be scrutinised, perhaps amended, and then new legislation will be put to Parliament. It still permits some warrants to be issued by a minister but goes on to require judicial approval before the warrant can be exercised.

THINKING POINT

Is prior judicial authorisation of surveillance warrants necessary to provide proper safeguards? Consider, for example, the discussion in David Anderson QC's review of surveillance (*A Question of Trust*), in particular paras 14.47 *passim*. Is the new Investigatory Powers Bill (which received its Second Reading in March 2016) adequate in this regard?

Journalists and others may undertake secret surveillance. Whilst intercepting communications is likely to be unlawful in English law, other forms of surveillance, like secret filming, will not necessarily be so unless it involves trespass or some other form of illegality. Where invasions of privacy are committed by the media, complaints to the appropriate regulator (Ofcom, for instance) may be appropriate.

In *Jones* v *Warwick University* [2003] EWCA Civ 151, the Court of Appeal accepted that secret filming by an employer's insurer aimed at testing an employee's claim to be unable to work, engaged Article 8(1). The invasion of privacy was by the employer's insurers, a private body. For the Court the issue was whether to admit the evidence. Was it justified in doing so, under Article 8(2)? On the one hand, the secret filming was 'improper and not justified'; on the other hand, the employee's behaviour was outrageous. Overall it was in the interests of justice to admit the evidence.

15.10.3 **Abortion**

The ECtHR has consistently refused to rule that a foetus is directly protected by Article 2. Article 2 does not define when 'life' begins. There is no legal, moral, or scientific consensus in Europe on these matters. A wide margin of appreciation is to be allowed to the states (see, in particular, *Vo* v *France* (2005) 40 EHRR 12, paras 75–82 and, in particular paras 80 and 82). Under the HRA the position in English law is similar—a foetus is not recognised as having a 'life' (*Evans* v *Amicus Healthcare* [2004] EWCA Civ 727, paras 174–179).

But there are limits. An absolute ban on abortion when the mother's life was in danger, particularly in the early stages of pregnancy, could be incompatible with the right to life of the mother (*Vo* para 75, endorsing an earlier Commission case); but allowing mothers to go abroad for terminations may satisfy this (see *A, B, C* v *Ireland* below).

Abortion engages the mother's right to private life (*Tysiac* v *Poland* (2007) 45 EHRR 42, para 107). However, this does not mean that a woman has an unlimited 'right to choose' (*Brüggemann and Scheuten* v *Germany* (1977) 3 EHRR 244). Her private life is closely connected with the foetus and must be weighed against other competing rights and freedoms, including those of the foetus (see *A, B, C*, para 213). A wide margin of appreciation is allowed to states and even severe legal restrictions on abortion are likely to be justified under Article 8(2).

CASE CLOSE-UP

A, B, C v *Ireland* (2011) 53 EHRR 13

Ireland's constitution banned abortion unless it was necessary to protect the mother's life. Two women (whose lives were not in danger but who both had serious health and social problems) travelled to the UK for abortions and alleged the Irish ban on abortion had detrimental consequences for their subsequent care. They challenged the Irish law. The Grand Chamber, held that:

- The Irish ban on abortions for reasons of health and well-being was an interference with the women's private lives and needed justification. The Convention neither imposes a positive duty on states to allow women the right to choose, nor, on the other hand, does it give states an entirely free hand to restrict abortion.

- The ban was in accordance with the law.

- It served a moral purpose.

- On the issue of proportionality, of balancing the competing rights and freedoms, the Court has the final word. However, a wide margin of appreciation is allowed to the states. Even though most European states have more liberal laws than Ireland, this does not narrow the margin of appreciation. This is because proportionality involves weighing the interests of mother and foetus and there is no consensus on whether the latter counts as a life. The Irish people still retained a profound moral opposition to abortion and this was an important factor in the fair balance. There was no breach of Article 8.

But it remains for the courts to decide whether limits to abortion are justified and proportionate. In the *Northern Ireland Human Rights Commission's Application* [2015] NIQB 96, the Belfast High Court decided that the law on abortion in Northern Ireland was not compatible with Article 8 in so far as it did not permit abortion for healthy mothers carrying babies with fatal abnormalities or which were conceived by rape.

Of great importance is that decisions about abortion should be taken in accordance with the law—on the basis of proper procedures rather than the whim of doctors (*Tysiac*, section 15.10.3, where a refusal to allow an abortion caused the mother to go blind). States have a positive duty to enshrine, in accessible and foreseeable legal rules, the abortion rights that women do have. The third applicant in *A, B, C* succeeded in showing a violation of Article 8. The Irish constitution allowed abortion to protect a mother's life, but this provision had not been given specific enactment. Doctors and women were unable to be certain about what was legally permissible.

15.10.4 Euthanasia (assisted suicide)

Whilst committing suicide is not unlawful, most European countries, including the UK, make it a crime to assist another's suicide (in the UK: section 2 Suicide Act 1961). As discussed in Chapter 8, such crimes do not violate Article 2, since the right to life does not imply a right to die. A more significant issue is whether a ban on assisting another's suicide may violate Article 8.

 CASE CLOSE-UP

Pretty* v *United Kingdom (2002) 35 EHRR 1

The applicant, Diane Pretty, suffered from Motor Neurone Disease, which involved progressive muscular deterioration and would lead inevitably to a death that would be distressing and undignified. Pretty's mental faculties were unimpaired. She was frightened by the prospect of her death and wanted, instead, to die at a time and in a manner of her own choosing. For this she needed the assistance of another and her husband was willing to assist her. Such action would, however, be likely to involve the husband in committing the crime of assisting another's suicide (section 2(1) Suicide Act 1961). The Director of Public Prosecutions refused to give any undertaking that her husband would not be prosecuted. The House of Lords refused to hold that the DPP had acted unlawfully.

The ECtHR held that issues concerning quality of life could engage Article 8. In this context the principle of autonomy, an aspect of a private life, meant that the DPP's refusal interfered with Mrs Pretty's rights in Article 8(1). However, the inclusion of assisted suicide within the definition of 'murder' was justified under Article 8(2). It was necessary to protect the rights of others, in particular ill people who might be pressurised by relatives to choose to die.

Countries have a considerable margin of appreciation over the question of justification and nothing in *Pretty* or subsequent judgments suggests that states have a duty to allow assisted suicide.

In *Haas* v *Switzerland* (2011) 53 EHRR 33, the ECtHR removed any doubt and made it clear that interferences with a person's ability to choose their time of death do interfere with Article 8(1) and so needed justification under Article 8(2). The wide margin of appreciation regarding justification remains. A complete failure even to consider an Article 8 claim in these circumstances may be a violation (see *Koch* v *Germany* (2012) 56 EHRR 195) but that is not because the ECtHR has decided that such cases must be decided in a particular way.

Following this case in *Purdy*, the UKHL accepted that the right to autonomy, inherent in Article 8(1), was interfered with by the ban on assisted suicide. However, Article 8(2) required that such interference be 'in accordance with the law' and not arbitrary. On this basis a patient was entitled to foresee the circumstances in which her assister might be prosecuted. The guidelines issued by the DPP failed to do this with sufficient clarity and so Article 8(2) was not satisfied.

 CASE CLOSE-UP

***Nicklinson* v *Ministry of Justice* [2014] UKSC 38**

- Two men whose paralysis was so complete that they could hardly communicate at all and who had a 'voluntary, clear, settled and informed' wish to die, challenged the prohibition on assisted suicide. The UKSC held:

  (a) The criminalisation of assisted suicide in section 2 Suicide Act was not necessarily outside the margin of appreciation allowed under Article 8(2).

  (b) But, given the width of the margin, other results were possible. The question was what state institution should have final responsibility.

  (c) The majority thought that, given the authority found in the HRA, it would not be constitutionally improper for the courts to determine the issue. However, it should decline to do so because there was insufficient evidence and, also, a very high level of deference was owed to Parliament.

  (d) One minority agreed but thought there was sufficient evidence to make a declaration of incompatibility.

  (e) A second minority thought this was essentially a matter for Parliament and not the courts.

 CROSS REFERENCE

The constitutional issues in Nicklinson are further discussed in Chapter 4, section 4.6.2.

Parliament debated the issue in September 2015 and resolved to keep the situation unchanged.

 THINKING POINT

Consider how you would have decided *Nicklinson*.

15.10.5 Child care

Under the Convention

States accept legal responsibilities to protect and care for children in need. In England and Wales local authorities have various powers under the Children Act 1989 to identify children in need and, by court order, assume parental responsibilities for them. Local authorities exercise a range of powers including removing a child from his or her parents under a 'care order'. The exercise of such powers engages the Article 8 rights of the children, the parents, and others.

CASE CLOSE-UP

Haase v *Germany* [2005] 40 EHRR 19

The applicants' children, one of which was newborn, were removed into care without a hearing and on the basis of what turned out to be flawed expert evidence. The ECtHR held that the removal failed the 'necessary in a democratic society' test and so violated Article 8.

Some general principles emerge from paras 82–94:

- Protection of children involves interferences with their private and family life which must be justified in terms of Article 8(2).

- Laws aiming at the protection of children are likely to give officials quite a wide discretion over how they act. Given the fact that the situations in which children may be harmed are impossible to predict in advance, such discretion is likely to be in accordance with the law (see *Eriksson* v *Sweden* (1990) 12 EHRR 183, paras 59–60).

- Care orders etc. can be necessary to protect the health and morals, and the rights and freedoms of children.

- A decision may be proportionate if based on the 'best interests' of the child.

- An international court must respect the decisions of the national authorities but it must be satisfied that the national authorities have acted for sufficient reasons and on the basis of proper procedures. The removal of a newborn child from his or her parents requires 'extraordinarily compelling' reasons.

 BIGGER PICTURE

See also *P, C and S* v *United Kingdom* [2002] 35 EHRR 31, paras 113–138.

Under the HRA

The Children Act 1989 does not contain provisions that are necessarily incompatible with Article 8: see *Re V (A Child) (Care Proceedings: Human Rights Claims)* [2004] EWCA Civ 54. In particular, the court said, section 1(3) of the Act has a list of factors to be taken into account when identifying the best interests of the child. Following this list enables an authority to give proper weight to the competing Article 8 rights of the child and other parties (see para 8). Where a local authority makes a judgment in good faith about a child's best interests, it is unlikely that an Article 8 challenge will succeed on the issue of the need for the order proposed (see, for example, *Re G* [2006] UKHL 43, in which the House of Lords assessed a child's best interests in a residency dispute without mentioning Article 8).

 BIGGER PICTURE

In *Re S* [2002] UKHL 10, the House of Lords held that the relatively limited rights of parents under the Act did not necessarily conflict with their Article 8 rights. In *S* v *L* [2012] UKSC 30, the Supreme Court held that statutory rules allowing a court to dispense with parental consent to adoption were not incompatible with the parent's Convention rights.

Social workers and others have powers under the Act that not only can but must be exercised compatibly with Convention rights.

In *Langley* v *Liverpool CC* [2005] EWCA Civ 1173, an emergency protection order was obtained to protect children from their father who, though registered blind, persisted in driving. The police, exercising powers to assist social workers, forcibly removed one of the children after he had gone to bed. The Court of Appeal held the police action was unlawful and a breach of Article 8.

15.10.6 Protection of personal information

Disclosure of personal or confidential information about a person engages Article 8(1) and so must be justified under Article 8(2). Any system which involves the storing and release of information and which fails to allow adequate means for the information to be challenged for accuracy, will raise issues under Article 8(1).

In *Leander* v *Sweden* (1987) 9 EHRR 433, a system of security vetting for people working in a naval dockyard was accepted as a justified restriction on Article 8(1) rights.

Under the HRA, the protection of personal information under Article 8 has been significant in a number of areas.

Police records

Taking fingerprints and other samples is an interference with respect for private life. If it is done according to the procedures in the PACE and Codes of Practice, it is likely easily to be justified under Article 8(2). Retention raises other issues. **These are discussed in Chapter 20, sections 20.6.1 and 20.6.2.**

Health records

Disclosure of health records must be justified under Article 8(2). The ECtHR weighs a person's right to confidentiality in this area very highly—it is of fundamental importance not only to protect a person's private life but also general confidence in a willingness to use a country's health service (see *Z* v *Finland* (1998) 25 EHRR 371, para 95). Any interference can only be justified by weighty reasons.

 CASE CLOSE-UP

Ashworth Hospital Authority* v *MGN Ltd [2002] UKHL 29

The *Daily Mirror* published articles clearly based on the medical records of Ian Brady, a notorious murderer serving a life sentence in a secure mental hospital. The House of Lords considered that the right to medical confidentiality was one of the reasons (para 63) which outweighed freedom of the press and the principle that journalists should not be compelled to disclose their sources. The order that the newspaper disclose its source was confirmed.

The newspaper disclosed that its source was a freelance journalist. In subsequent proceedings, however, the Court of Appeal refused to order the freelance to disclose his original source. Given the passage of time and other factors and given the importance of press freedom under Article 10, the need for disclosure was no longer pressing; nevertheless the general principle of protecting medical records was strongly endorsed (*Mersey Care NHS Trust* v *Ackroyd (No 2)* [2007] EWCA Civ 101).

Disclosure of confidential information

Disclosure by the authorities of information about individuals can engage Article 8 rights and so the courts must decide whether any interference is justified.

This important matter is considered in respect of police disclosures in Chapter 20, section 20.6.3.

15.10.7 Deportation and Article 8

We have seen that Convention rights, being applied in the UK, can prevent removals, deportations, and extraditions if there is a real risk of death, torture, or inhuman treatment in the receiving country (discussed in Chapter 9, section 9.8).

Likewise a real risk of a 'flagrant' denial of other rights in the receiving country should prevent a deportation or extradition, and this includes a risk that the person will be tried on the basis of evidence obtained by torture (discussed in Chapter 12, section 12.16).

Deportations can engage Article 8 rights. A distinction is drawn between 'foreign' and 'domestic' cases.

Foreign cases concern the conditions in the receiving country.

> **CROSS REFERENCE**
>
> See Chapter 9, section 9.8.1 for definition and legal grounds of extradition, deportation, and removal.

CASE CLOSE-UP

R (Razgar) v *Secretary of State for the Home Department* [2004] UKHL 27

R's application for asylum failed. He feared that, if removed to Germany and perhaps back to Iraq, his mental health would seriously deteriorate. The House of Lords, following Strasbourg principles (see *Bensaid* v *United Kingdom* (2001) 33 EHRR 10), held that R might have a claim to resist deportation under Article 8 even if the consequences were not so severe as to engage Article 3. The evidence should show that the denial of Article 8(1) rights will be flagrant (para 72). The Secretary of State had acted unlawfully in deciding that his Article 8 claim was hopeless. An immigration adjudicator might have found it justified.

'Domestic cases' concern the family ties that have been established in the deporting country.

CASE CLOSE-UP

Üner v *The Netherlands* (2007) 45 EHRR 14

A Turkish national was deported from the Netherlands as a consequence of his conviction for serious crimes. On account of his relationship with his partner and sons he alleged there would be a violation of his Article 8 rights if he was deported.

A Grand Chamber confirmed:

- that states may control immigration, including by expelling aliens;

- however, actions must be compatible with Convention rights and there are circumstances in which an expulsion (removal, extradition, deportation) can engage Article 8(1) and require justification under Article 8;

- relevant criteria, which courts must consider in seeking a fair balance between the public interests served by immigration control and the interests of the person being removed, are listed (following *Boultif* v *Switzerland* (2001) 33 EHRR 50) at para 57 and 58. They include the length of time the applicant has been in the country; the seriousness of offences committed by the applicant; the applicant's family situation, such as the length of marriage, age of children, the seriousness of difficulties that the family may experience in the receiving country; the interests of children and the relative solidity of ties with the host and receiving country (para 60).

These principles have been followed and adapted by UK courts under the HRA.

 CASE CLOSE-UP

R (H) v *Deputy Prosecutor of the Italian Republic* [2012] UKSC 25

Three individuals appealed against the decision to extradite them from the UK on the basis of a European arrest warrant. They claimed that extradition would have a serious effect on their family life.

The Supreme Court weighed the various interests (based on the *Üner* criteria, considered earlier) and allowed one of the three appeals on the grounds of the very severe consequences for family life. The court emphasised:

- The weight to be given to the public interest might be different as between extradition (involving criminal punishment for serious crime) and deportation (the removal of undesirable aliens), but in all cases that weighing of interests was central to Article 8.

- Of particular importance were the rights of children. The Supreme Court, building on *Üner* and other Strasbourg case law, and other sources such as the UN Convention on the Rights of the Child, held that the best interests of the children were 'a primary consideration'—very important but not 'the' primary or 'the paramount' consideration. They were, therefore, capable of being outweighed by the public interests involved in a deportation or extradition.

As with Article 3 (see Chapter 9, section 9.8.2), Article 8 is unlikely to be the basis for preventing deportation on the grounds of the relatively inadequate medical treatment the deportee is likely to obtain in the receiving country (see the discussion in *GS (India)* v *Secretary of State for the Home Department* [2015] EWCA Civ 40, where the Court of Appeal found nothing in Article 8 to prevent the deportation of six men suffering from serious and terminal illnesses).

It is clear that these issues of removal, deportation, or extradition involve a complex weighing of interests. In England and Wales this is to be done by the tribunal or court hearing an appeal. The tribunal should decide for itself, giving little deference to the authorities (*Huang* v *Secretary of State for the Home Department* [2007] UKHL 11). Deportation decisions have been highly controversial, especially those involving 'domestic cases'. The government has argued that it is too easy for undesirable persons to resist deportation on the basis of family connections established in the UK sometimes after the events for which they are to be deported. Part 5A Immigration and Asylum Act 2002 (amended in 2014) tries to instruct a court or tribunal on how to apply Article 8. The constitutional propriety of this is questionable.

15.10.8 **Privacy and the media**

A person's desire for privacy may conflict with the desire of the media to publish stories about them. Such conflicts involve the balancing of the person's rights under Article 8 and the media's rights to freedom of expression under Article 10. **This issue is explored in Chapter 22.**

 Summary

- Article 8 requires states to respect people's private life, family life, home, and correspondence.
- These terms (private life etc.) are given a wide and inclusive definition.
- States may have positive duties to ensure that Article 8 rights are effective.
- There are many circumstances in which it is reasonable and in the public interest for private life etc. to be interfered with.
- Article 8 allows such interferences but only if they are by a public authority and only if they are lawful (as that term is understood by the Convention), necessary in a democratic society (a proportionate means of achieving a pressing social need), and only for one or more of the purposes listed in Article 8(2).

? **Self-test questions**

1. What does it mean to refer to Article 8 as a qualified right?

2. What are the main steps, the process of legal reasoning, a court must undertake when dealing with a claim that Article 8 rights have been interfered with?

3. In the context of Article 8, define 'positive duties' and give two examples of their effect.

4. Give three examples of factors inherent in the idea of 'private life'.

5. What is a 'family' for the purposes of Article 8?

6. In what sense, if at all, does Article 8 guarantee a right to a home?

7. In what circumstances might Article 8(1) rights be qualified by action taken in the interests of the economic well-being of the country?

8. How does Article 8 potentially inhibit the executive's right to deport a person from the United Kingdom?

 For suggested approaches, please visit the Online Resource Centre.

? Exam questions

1. What is meant by 'private life' in the context of Article 8? Do you agree that, as developed by the ECtHR, the term is imprecise and there is a lack of certainty over what is encompassed by it?

2. As a consequence of adverse decisions by both the European Court of Human Rights and, in respect of EU law, the Court of Justice of the European Union, the UK government needs to reconsider the law on surveillance and data retention. Your advice is sought on the principles of law that apply if the law is to be compatible with Article 8.

 For suggested approaches, please visit the Online Resource Centre.

≡ Further reading

Leading texts on Article 8

Amos, M. (see Preface) Chapters 11–13

Harris, D. et al (eds), *Harris, O'Boyle and Warbrick: Law of the ECHR* 2nd edn (2009) Oxford: OUP, Chapters 8 and 9 (by Warbrick and Kilkelly)

Lester, A., Pannick, D. and Herberg, J. (see Preface) Chapter 4, Article 8

Moreham, N. 'The Right to Respect for Private Life in the European Convention on Human Rights: A Re-examination' [2008] 1 *EHRLR* 44–79

16

Article 9: freedom of thought, conscience, and religion

Article 9 Freedom of thought, conscience and religion

(1) Everyone has the right to freedom of thought, conscience and religion; this right includes freedom to change his religion or belief and freedom, either alone or in community with others and in public or private, to manifest his religion or belief, in worship, teaching, practice and observance.

(2) Freedom to manifest one's religion or beliefs shall be subject only to such limitations as are prescribed by law and are necessary in a democratic society in the interests of public safety, for the protection of public order, health or morals, or for the protection of the rights and freedoms of others.

Introduction

A hallmark of a totalitarian state is its attempt to control the thoughts, beliefs, and ideas of its citizens and to insist that only officially sanctioned ideas and attitudes are allowed. Mind control may be attempted by, for example, endless propaganda or by imposing a particular curriculum on schools. More usually, the totalitarian state simply closes down the places of worship, the societies, the university departments, the trade unions, etc. where unwelcome ideas and beliefs are expressed. Article 9 is one of the Articles which embodies the 'pluralism' inherent in the Convention: states are not allowed to enforce particular ideologies or religions on their population; these are matters for individuals and the state must accept, tolerate, and protect a plurality of beliefs.

The assertion of beliefs in public ('manifestations of belief') can interfere with the rights and freedoms of others or with important public interests. In the early years of the twenty-first century there is, perhaps, a sense that, for many, religion is ceasing to be a matter of a private relationship with God, albeit mediated by a church, and is, in some circumstances, being 'politicised'. Matters of the school science curriculum, sex education, abortion, the performance of plays, and, above all, the dress of women, have involved not just claims of individual wish and conscience but also the exercise of political and social power by religious groups. Religion, for many, must be asserted publicly and powerfully, involving adjustments to their lives by others. In this context we can expect Article 9 to have an increasing emphasis in the modern world.

16.1 General

16.1.1 **The structure of Article 9**

Article 9(1) establishes:

- A general right to freedom of 'thought, conscience and religion' which cannot be restricted by the state.
- A right to 'manifest' (demonstrate) religion or belief in 'worship, teaching, practice and observance'. The Convention recognises that there can be circumstances in which it is reasonable to restrict the manifestation of a belief and these circumstances are identified, in abstract terms, in the second paragraph, Article 9(2).

The job of a court dealing with an Article 9 issue is:

- To decide whether there has been an interference, for which the state is responsible, which either restricts a person in holding religious beliefs or which restricts the manifestation of belief.
- If it is a restriction on the holding of belief, then the restriction is a violation of Article 9(1). There is no question of justification.
- If it is a restriction on a manifestation of belief, the court must decide whether the state has demonstrated that the restriction is justified under the terms of Article 9(2): it has been imposed on the basis of 'law', it is for one of the purposes listed in Article 9(2), and that the particular restriction was 'necessary in a democratic society'.

These principles are summarised and applied, for example, in *Church of Bessarabia* v *Moldova* (2002) 35 EHRR 13, paras 101–119.

CROSS REFERENCE

The common features of Articles 8, 9, 10, and 11 have been introduced in Chapter 14.

Thus the approach to Article 9 is similar to that to Articles 8, 10, and 11.

> **BIGGER PICTURE**
>
> Under Article 34 of the European Convention on Human Rights (ECHR), and therefore section 7 Human Rights Act 1998 (HRA), a church or other religious organisation can bring actions in order to protect the Article 9 rights of its believers (*Church of Bessarabia* v *Moldova* (2002) 35 EHRR 13, para 101).

16.1.2 Links with other rights

Article 9 can often be invoked in tandem with other Convention rights which also help to secure freedom of religion and belief. Thus, Article 10 can be engaged where there are restrictions on religious expression, Article 11 may be relevant to restrictions on religious organisations and associations and Article 8 can be involved if restrictions on religion interfere with a person's private life. Where the issue centres on manifestations of religion, Article 9 is likely to be the Court's focus, with the other Articles being relevant only if they raise serious and distinct issues.

The most important other right relevant to freedom of belief is Article 2 of the First Protocol. This gives a right to parents (not to anyone else) that the education of their children shall be 'in conformity with their own religious and philosophical convictions'. A restriction on a manifestation of religion that is justified under Article 9(1) is likely to be also compatible with Article 2 of the First Protocol. This is because Article 2 is not an absolute right: it, too, is subject to reasonable restrictions.

> **CROSS REFERENCE**
> Article 2 of the First Protocol is the topic of Chapter 24.

16.1.3 Section 13 HRA

During its passage through Parliament, the Human Rights Bill came under criticism from religious groups who feared that the Act would impose unreasonable restraints on their freedom to conduct their affairs in the ways that enabled them to preserve their religious and moral ethos. For example, there was a concern the Act would make it hard to employ only people with a sufficient degree of religious belief or acceptable moral rectitude. Though these fears were probably groundless, the government conceded a special provision in the Act for the protection of religion.

Section 13 Freedom of Thought, Conscience and Religion

(1) If a court's determination of any question arising under this Act might affect the exercise by a religious organisation (itself or its members collectively) of the Convention right to freedom of thought, conscience and religion, it must have particular regard to the importance of that right.

(2) In this section 'court' includes a tribunal.

Whether this provision has any significance at all, or was just a sop to religious groups when the bill was going through Parliament, is debatable. It requires no more of a court than it is already required to do—to consider the proper significance of Article 9 in the situation before it. It does not give Article 9 any priority or greater weight or importance in respect of other rights and freedoms.

16.2 Article 9(1): the unrestrictable right to thought, conscience, and religion

The right to freedom of thought, conscience, and religion, including the right to change religion, cannot be restricted under the terms of the Convention (though a derogation is possible under Article 15 (see Chapter 7, section 7.2). Manifestations of religion or belief, on the other hand, can be restricted if the state can show it was necessary so to do under the terms of Article 9(2). It can be important, therefore, to distinguish between actions which are a necessary consequence of having a belief and actions which involve the manifestation of that belief. Restrictions on the former cannot be allowed. Thus, for example, restrictions on movement which prevent a person getting to his place of worship may be a simple breach of Article 9 without there being any need to consider whether the restriction was justified.

16.2.1 The importance of religion and belief

The great importance of freedom of thought, conscience and religion is recognised by the European Court of Human Rights (ECtHR).

> [Freedom of thought, conscience, and religion] is, in its religious dimension, one of the most vital elements that go to make up the identity of believers and their conception of life, but it is also a precious asset for atheists, agnostics, sceptics and the unconcerned. The pluralism indissociable from a democratic society, which has been dearly won over the centuries, depends on it.

(Kokkinakis v Greece (1994) 17 EHRR 397)

In *R (Williamson)* v *Secretary of State for Education and Employment* [2005] UKHL 15, the House of Lords called beliefs, religious or not, 'part of the humanity of every individual. They are an integral part of his personality and individuality' (para 15, per Lord Nicholls—the case is discussed later in the chapter). Time and again the ECtHR emphasises that the Convention acknowledges only one general form of government: a plural and liberal democracy. All states must support, through their laws, the diversity of people's religious, moral, and political views, and recognise that, in any society, people will hold many different views of how best to live and what to believe. Article 9 is clearly central to this.

16.2.2 'Thought, conscience and religion'

Religion

Religion includes the major, organised, world religions such as Buddhism, Christianity, Hinduism, Islam, Judaism, and Sikhism, and the various traditions, denominations, and sects that make up their parts. Other beliefs which claim, in one way or another, to be 'religious' have also been recognised. Druid ceremony, for example, was recognised by the Commission as being religious in nature in *Arthur Pendragon* v *United Kingdom* App 31416/96, admissibility decision of 19 October 1998. Under the HRA, English courts have accepted that Rastafarianism is a religion (*R* v *Taylor* [2001] EWCA Civ 2263). There is no need for an abstract discussion of the nature of religion by the Court since if a matter is not religious it is likely, nevertheless, to be a 'belief' and so enjoy the same protection.

Thought and conscience, non-religious beliefs

Article 9 is not confined to religion. Freedom of belief is a 'precious asset' for atheists (who deny the existence of God), agnostics (who accept the possibility of the non-existence of God), and sceptics (who doubt the claims of religion). Belief is also defined widely to include specific social and moral ideas that have direct consequences for people's actions. Pacifism (*Arrowsmith* v *United Kingdom* (1981) 3 EHRR 218) and 'vegetarianism and temperance' (*Williamson* (section 16.4.5)) have been accepted as beliefs for the purposes of Article 9. This approach was followed in *Grainger* v *Nicolson* [2010] ICR 360 (paras 20–31), where Article 9 jurisprudence was followed in holding that a belief in climate change could be a 'philosophical belief' (for the purposes of domestic law on discrimination) if genuinely held as a serious belief, not a mere opinion, and worthy of respect in a democratic society (see Evaluation of beliefs, section 16.3).

It also protects the 'unconcerned'—those who are indifferent and lack political or other beliefs or those whose quietness is taken, by the regime, to signify hostility (see *KM v SSHD* [2012] UKSC 38).

16.2.3 **The role of the state**

Neutrality

Article 9 presupposes a pluralist, liberal democracy. In that context the role of the state is to be neutral, not to promote one religion over another, and not to act on the basis that a particular belief is false or lacks credibility or is in some way bad.

In *Hasan v Bulgaria* (2002) 34 EHRR 55, the ECtHR held that there was a violation of Article 9 when the Bulgarian government intervened in a dispute between Bulgarian Muslims over who should be their national leader in post-Communist Bulgaria. The state had ceased to be neutral over a religious matter (see, in particular, para 78). However, when it comes to the manifestation of belief, the state may be entitled to form of judgment about the content of the belief (see section 16.3, Evaluation of beliefs).

Established religion

Article 9 does not forbid state or **established** religions.

> **establishment** An established religion is one that has been recognised by law as, in some sense, the religion of the state. The Church of England is the established religion in the UK. Some states, such as the USA, are constitutionally banned from establishing a religion. The old Reformation principle *cuius regio, eius religio* (whose rule, his religion) by which the religion of the ruler was imposed on the people, can no longer apply. Any attempt to impose religion on the population would violate the Convention.

But establishment does not justify propaganda through the education system (see Chapter 24 on the right to education). Nor can adherence to a particular religion or doctrine be a requirement of public office.

In *Buscarini v San Marino* (2000) 30 EHRR 208, the ECtHR found that Article 9 was violated when Parliamentarians were required to take a religious oath before taking their seats.

 DISCUSSION TOPIC

In the United Kingdom, the monarch, by law, must not be a Roman Catholic. Does this violate Article 9?

Legal recognition

If a state refuses or unreasonably delays the legal recognition of a religious group (so that it cannot enjoy legal protection of its assets and advantages such as tax breaks), the approach of the ECtHR is to consider the matter under Article 9 with due regard to Article 11 (freedom of association). An unjustified refusal or delay may violate either Article read in the light of the other;

e.g. *Moscow Branch of the Salvation Army* v *Russia* (2007) 44 EHRR 46 (violation of Article 11); *Religionsgemeinschaft der Zeugen Jehovas* v *Austria* (2009) 48 EHRR 17 (violation of Article 9).

Positive duties

States may have positive duties under Article 9 to protect believers, particularly religious believers, from the intolerance, contempt, and hatred of others (see *97 Members of the Gldani Congregation of Jehovah's Witnesses* v *Georgia* (2008) 46 EHRR 30. Here the indifference of the authorities in the face of attacks on Jehovah Witnesses was a breach of Article 9).

16.2.4 Freedom to change religion

Article 9 provides an 'absolute' right (a right that cannot be restricted in terms of Article 9(2)), to change religion and beliefs. States cannot have laws which compel people to have particular beliefs or which punish a person who renounces beliefs. Nor can atheism or agnosticism be crimes. Islamic states (of which there are none in Europe) can have difficulties with this provision as found in international law since 'apostasy' (the renunciation of a particular religion) may be contrary to some of the traditions on which Islamic law is based and may, indeed, invite the death penalty. However, there is no unanimity by Islamic jurists on the point.

BIGGER PICTURE

For discussion, see Baderin, M. *International Human Rights and Islamic Law* (2003) Oxford: OUP, Chapter 4, pp 123–125.

16.3 Article 9(1): the manifestation of religion

Under Article 9 a person has the right to manifest his or her religion or belief. This can be done 'alone or in community with others and in public or private'. Manifestation can be 'in worship, teaching, practice or observance'. A clear instance of this is where the state prevents people worshipping by, for example, refusing to give the necessary legal recognition to a religious organisation, as in *Church of Bessarabia* v *Moldova* (2002) 35 EHRR 13.

Definition and examples of manifestations of belief

Manifestation goes further than just acts of worship. It includes actions which are 'intimately linked' to the belief. The action must be a direct expression of the belief, though it need not be a definite, universally acknowledged, requirement. Examples of manifestations of belief are:

- forms of dress (such as the Islamic headscarf in *Leyla Sahin* v *Turkey* (2007) 44 EHRR 5);
- dietary requirements (such as ritual slaughter of animals as required by Judaism in *Cha'are Shalom Ve Tsedek* v *France* App 27417/95, judgment of 27 June 2000);
- views on school punishment, including corporal punishment (such as in ECHR case *Campbell and Cosans* v *UK* (1982) 4 EHRR 293 and the HRA case *R (Williamson)* v *Secretary of State for Education and Employment* [2005] UKHL 15, see section 16.4.5).

English courts have considered the matter under the HRA. For example:

- Burial in a cemetery recognised by the religion was treated as a manifestation of belief (the disinterment of a Jew, buried in a Christian cemetery at the behest of his Christian wife (now deceased), to be reinterred in a Jewish cemetery in accordance with the wishes of his Jewish relatives), *Re Durrington Cemetery* [2001] Fam 33.

On the other hand:

- A conscientious objector who refused to return to duty was not manifesting his belief (see *Khan* v *RAF Summary Appeal Court* [2004] EWHC 2230 (Admin); see further, section 16.4.6).

Manifestation, not just motivation

An action that is merely motivated by religious belief or individual conscience is not a manifestation of that belief (see *Arrowsmith* v *United Kingdom* (1981) 3 EHRR 218, para 71).

The following are examples of conduct motivated by a religious or other belief that the Strasbourg authorities (Court or Commission of Human Rights) have held not to be manifestations of religious belief, protected by Article 9, but actions merely motivated by religious belief for which the Article gives no protection.

- The distribution of pacifist leaflets to soldiers (*Arrowsmith*, section 16.2.2).
- Refusing to sell contraceptives that had been prescribed to women (*Pichon and Sajous* v *France* App 49853/99, admissibility decision of 2 October 2001).
- Assisting in another's suicide (as in *Pretty* v *United Kingdom* (2002) 35 EHRR 1, para 82).
- Commercial advertising to promote a belief (as in *X and Church of Scientology* v *Sweden* [1979] ECC 511, para 14).

Article 9 does not therefore protect the right of a person to behave in public situations in a manner dictated by religious belief.

> Article 9 does not always guarantee a right to behave in a manner governed by religious belief . . . and does not confer on people who do so the right to disregard rules that have proved to be justified.
>
> (*Leyla Sahin* v *Turkey* (2007) 44 EHRR 5, para 121)

The right to 'manifest belief' does not, for example, mean that a person can use his or her religious beliefs as a defence for what would otherwise be a criminal offence (such as drugs offences). Nor does a religious motivation entitle a person to avoid duties and obligations that they have voluntarily accepted or that have been embodied in rules and practices (e.g. school rules) that are justified and proportionate.

Under the HRA these principles have been confirmed by the House of Lords in *R (Williamson)* v *Secretary of State for Education and Employment* [2005] UKHL 15 (see section 16.4.5) and followed in *R (Boughton)* v *Her Majesty's Treasury* [2006] EWCA Civ 504. Here the Court of Appeal (following clear Strasbourg authority) rejected a claim by a group of tax payers that the Treasury had a duty, based on Article 9, to set up a fund into which those with conscientious objections to defence spending could pay their taxes.

Of course actions motivated by political, religious, or other belief, though outside Article 9, may be protected by Article 10 (freedom of expression) or Article 11 (freedom of assembly and association).

Evaluation of beliefs

What about the manifestation of extreme or utterly eccentric beliefs, religious or otherwise? In some of its statements the ECtHR has suggested that, regarding manifestations of belief, states may depart from the position of neutrality. In *Campbell and Cosans v United Kingdom* (1982) 4 EHRR 293, the ECtHR suggested that Convention protection might be confined to 'views which attained a certain level of cogency, seriousness, cohesion and importance' and to 'convictions as are worthy of respect in a "democratic society" . . . and are not incompatible with human dignity'. *Campbell and Cosans* involved Article 2 of the First Protocol, which requires states to respect the 'religious and philosophical convictions' of parents in educational provision (see Chapter 24). Nevertheless, the Court's view refers to the basic values of the Convention and might be thought to extend to Article 9.

This view appears to give state officials and courts the power to make controversial judgments about which beliefs are worthy or not of respect in a democracy. In the HRA case *Williamson* (see section 16.4.5), Lord Walker found the prospect 'alarming', arguing that courts are not equipped to evaluate religious and other beliefs in this way and that the ECtHR begged too many questions. In fact, there are few, if any, cases in which the Court has evaluated the worth of a belief; and there are many cases in which it has asserted the need for state neutrality on matters of belief.

16.4 Article 9(2): restrictions on the manifestation of religion or belief

Genuine manifestations of religion or belief, such as those given above, can be restricted by the state under the terms of Article 9(2). The right to have such beliefs and the right to change religion cannot be restricted. Restrictions on manifestations of religion may be necessary to protect a plural, democratic society in which peoples of different religions, beliefs, and interests live together.

> in democratic societies, in which several freedoms coexist within one and the same population, it may be necessary to place restrictions on this freedom in order to reconcile the interests of the various groups and ensure that everyone's beliefs are respected.
>
> (*Kokkinakis v Greece* (1994) 17 EHRR 397, para 33)

The second paragraph to Article 9 has the same structure as that of Articles 8, 10, and 11.

16.4.1 The existence of an interference

If a state takes actions which interfere with the manifestation of a belief, then possible justification under Article 9(2) is relevant. This must be distinguished from the situations in which Article 9(2) is not relevant such as:

- where states interfere with or fail to secure the general right to freedom of thought, conscience, and religion (there will be an unjustifiable violation of Article 9(1));
- where the state interferes with an action which is motivated by religion but which is not a manifestation of it (Article 9 is not engaged at all).

16.4.2 'Prescribed by law'

The interference imposed on the manifestation of a belief must meet the Convention test of lawfulness: the interference must not only be based on a provision of national law but that provision must be 'accessible' and 'foreseeable' and compatible with the rule of law.

In *Kokkinakis* v *Greece* (1994) 17 EHRR 397, the ECtHR accepted that the Greek laws on pros-elytism (seeking converts), despite the general way they were expressed, were sufficiently precise and developed by a body of known and accessible case law to satisfy the Convention requirements.

▶ CROSS REFERENCE
The Convention concept of 'law' is discussed in Chapter 6, section 6.2.

16.4.3 The restriction is for a legitimate purpose

Restrictions by the state of a manifestation of religion or belief can only be for one of the pur-poses listed in the second paragraph of Article 9, and not, as Article 18 makes clear, for any other purpose. The purposes in Article 9(2) (public safety, public order, health, morals, or the rights and freedoms of others) are the same as in Article 18 of the International Covenant on Civil and Political Rights (ICCPR). It is not possible to argue that manifestations of religion can be restricted in order to advance the economic interests of society (as is possible for restricting the right to private life) or to protect national security (as is possible for justifying restrictions under Articles 8, 10, and 11) nor to protect the reputations of others (as can justify a restriction on freedom of expression under Article 10). In practice it is normally not difficult for the state to relate its reasons for restriction to one of the listed purposes. In *Kokkinakis* v *Greece* (1994) 17 EHRR 397, for example, the ECtHR accepted that one of the 'rights of others' was the right to be free of attempts by others at conversion, at least in so far as this involved 'immoral or deceitful means' (see para 46).

16.4.4 'Necessary in a democratic society'

A restriction on the manifestation of religion must also be 'necessary in a democratic society', and this is the issue on which much of the case law depends. The general approach is identified by the ECtHR in *Kokkinakis* v *Greece*.

> The Court has consistently held that a certain margin of appreciation is to be left to the Contracting States in assessing the existence and extent of the necessity of an interference, but this margin is subject to European supervision, embracing both the legislation and the decisions applying it, even those given by an independent court. The Court's task is to determine whether the measures taken at national level were justified in principle and proportionate.
>
> (para 47)

Essentially a court (including a national court such as in the United Kingdom under the HRA) must examine:

- whether the state's actions were justified in general terms (e.g. that the state had suf-ficiently and properly worked out reasons for laws restricting manifestations of religious or other belief and that these laws were options that the state could reasonably adopt in its circumstances); and
- whether the application of the laws in the particular case represented a 'fair balance' (was 'proportionate') between the freedom of the individual and the benefit to others or to society generally that the restricting law aimed to achieve.

🔍 CASE CLOSE-UP

Surayanda* v *The Welsh Ministers [2007] EWCA Civ 893

S represented a Hindu community for whom the killing of cows was akin to killing a human being. It was held that Welsh Ministers were entitled to order the slaughter of Shambo, the community's bullock, as part of a campaign to prevent the spread of bovine tuberculosis. The minister's decision not to make an exception under Article 9(1) was justified under Article 9(2).

16.4.5 **Corporal punishment in schools**

CROSS REFERENCE

See also Chapter 24, section 24.4, on Article 2 of the First Protocol.

Parental views about school discipline, including the use or non-use of corporal punishment ('beating' or 'smacking', depending on your views), engage Convention rights in at least two ways: as a manifestation of a belief that, parents argue, should be protected by Article 9, and as a 'religious or philosophical conviction' that, under Article 2 of the First Protocol, should be respected by the state in the education of children.

The issue has come before the House of Lords under the HRA.

🔍 CASE CLOSE-UP

R (Williamson)* v *Secretary of State for Education and Employment [2005] UKHL 15

Parents and teachers in Christian schools challenged the ban on corporal punishment in all schools, state or independent, by section 548 of the Education Act 1996. They alleged that their rights under Article 9 (as well as Article 2 of the First Protocol) had been violated. The House of Lords held that there had been an interference with the manifestation by the parents of their beliefs. It was, therefore, necessary to consider whether the interference was justified under Article 9(2). They held that the interference was prescribed by law (it was found in a clear statutory rule). It was for a legitimate purpose: the rights of others, in particular the rights of children to protection. Finally, it was necessary in a democratic society: states had a wide margin of appreciation and a ban on corporal punishment was an appropriate way of achieving this and one which a legislature was entitled to choose.

▢ BIGGER PICTURE

Corporal punishment has also been in issue in respect of Article 3, see Chapter 9, section 9.6.1; school cases include *Costello-Roberts* v *United Kingdom* (1995) 19 EHRR 112; *Warwick* v *United Kingdom* App 9471/81, Commission Report of 18 July 1986 and *Y* v *United Kingdom* (1994) 17 EHRR 238.

16.4.6 **Conscientious objection**

Many countries in the world, including in Europe, have military conscription (this ended in the United Kingdom in the 1960s). Many, but not all, recognise a right of conscientious objection. This usually requires an objector to perform substitute social service and authorises punishment if the objector refuses. It is much rarer for a society to recognise a right to conscientious objection in the full sense of allowing a person, on grounds of conscience, to avoid military or substitute social service altogether without punishment. Similarly, it is quite common for conscientious objection to be recognised in respect of military service generally but not in respect of particular wars and causes.

For a long while the ECtHR was unwilling to read Article 9 as guaranteeing a right to conscientious objection, at least to military service. This was because Article 9 had to be read in the light of Article 4(3)(b) which expressly exempts normal military conscription or substitute forms of social service, from the ban on forced or compulsory labour (see Chapter 10). In the UK, as late as 2003, following this approach (and other international treaties) the UKHL held that there was not yet established an internationally recognised human right to conscientious objection (*Sepet* v *Secretary of State for the Home Department* [2003] UKHL 15).

However, there has been a clear tendency in Europe to phase out conscription and permit conscientious objection. Likewise, there has been a strong movement towards recognising a right to conscientious objection at the international and European level. In particular, the EU's Charter of Fundamental Rights explicitly recognises conscientious objection (Article 10). Recognising these developments, the ECtHR shifted its position.

 CASE CLOSE-UP

Bayatyan **v** *Armenia* **(2012) 54 EHRR 15**

The applicant was a Jehovah's Witness who declined, for conscientious reasons, to do compulsory military service. He was sentenced to two-and-a-half years in prison. A Grand Chamber held that there had been a violation of Article 9.

- Because of international developments favouring conscientious objection and phasing out of conscription, Article 9 should no longer be limited in its application by reading it in conjunction with Article 4(3)(b).

- Although Article 9 does not expressly mention conscientious objection, opposition to military service motivated by a 'serious and insurmountable conflict between the obligation to serve in the army and a person's conscience or his deeply and genuinely held religious beliefs' could come within the protection of Article 9.

- Whether there has been a violation will depend on justification under Article 9(2), in particular proportionality.

- Because of European developments, the margin of appreciation for states is limited.

- In the circumstances of the case the ban was disproportionate.

> **CROSS REFERENCE**
Bayatyan is a good example of the Convention as a 'living instrument' (see Chapter 6, section 6.1.6.

It is important to stress that *Bayatyan* simply makes it possible for Article 9 to apply to conscientious objectors; the question of justification remains.

> **Q** **CASE CLOSE-UP**

R v Lyons [2011] EWCA Crim 2808, Courts-Martial Appeal Court

L voluntarily joined the Royal Navy. He formed the view that UK involvement in Afghanistan was morally wrong. He refused to obey orders to be trained in order to be sent there. He was court-martialled and convicted. Following *Bayatyan* the Courts-Martial Appeal Court held:

- Article 9 could apply to volunteers as well as conscripts.
- Nevertheless, being a volunteer would affect the balancing exercise under Article 9(2).
- Nothing in Article 9 requires a conscientious objector to be immediately removed from duty.
- The Navy's procedures meant that all the issues under Article 9(2) were properly considered. There was no violation.

16.4.7 Conscience, dress, and employment rights

▶ CROSS REFERENCE

For more on the Equality Act 2010 see Chapter 7, section 7.1.1.

Though there are no express rights to employment in the ECHR, states have positive duties to ensure that Article 9 rights are secured in the context of commercial employment. The Equality Act 2010 (based on EU law) makes discrimination, including on grounds of 'religion or belief', unlawful in respect of employment (and also the provision of public services).

Employment and equality legislation must be interpreted in accordance with section 3 HRA (see Chapter 4) and nothing in the Act makes it impossible to apply in ways which are compatible with Article 9.

▶ CROSS REFERENCE

For public authorities see Chapter 4, section 4.5.

Employers who are core 'public authorities' have a similar duty towards their employees based on their duty in section 6 HRA.

The application of discrimination law can lead to claims that rights protected by Article 9 have been violated. Employees or office holders may be dismissed for refusing to work on their Sabbath or to do duties that they think are otherwise inconsistent with their religious beliefs. However, the ECtHR applies a wide margin of appreciation in this context. Therefore, so long as the employers' actions serve a legitimate purpose, such as protecting the rights of others, the Convention, and therefore the HRA, gives such employees little support. One important point is that the restrictions which are related to the requirements of their employment or office do not (and should not) interfere with their freedom to manifest their beliefs outside these roles (see *R (Begum)* v *Governors of Denbigh High School* [2006] UKHL 15, para 23, discussed at section 16.4.8).

> **Q** **CASE CLOSE-UP**

Eweida and others v United Kingdom (2013) 57 EHRR 8

E worked for British Airways. Her desire to wear a cross as an expression of belief and in a way visible to others was incompatible with the uniform policy. She was suspended until the policy was changed. BA refused to compensate her for her time under suspension and she brought a case in the UK courts alleging discrimination and a breach of her right to manifest her religious beliefs. Eventually the Court of Appeal found against her. The issue before the ECtHR was whether UK employment law gave sufficient protection for a person in E's position.

The ECtHR held that Article 9 had been violated. In all the circumstances there was no evidence that the ban was necessary or served to protect the interests of others and hence it was disproportionate.

However, in the other cases the ECtHR found that there was sufficient evidence to justify the actions taken, given the wide margin of appreciation enjoyed by states in this context.

Chaplin was a nurse and the ban on her wearing a cross was to protect health and safety on the ward.

Lavelle was a Registrar, a public official, whose eventual dismissal for refusing to register civil partnerships was justified given the consequences for the rights of others of her refusal.

MacFarlane was a Relate counsellor who was dismissed for refusing to give sex counselling to same-sex couples. Again the ECtHR felt that this was justified, within the margin of appreciation, given the need to provide counselling without discrimination.

In all the cases apart from *Eweida*, the ECtHR endorsed the decisions of the domestic courts indicating that the general approach of the UK courts correctly gives effect to Article 9. In *Eweida* the ECtHR accepted that UK courts had properly understood the requirement of Article 9—they just took a different view of the proportionality of the interference with E's right to manifest her religious beliefs.

16.4.8 General restrictions on religious dress

 DISCUSSION TOPIC

Freedom to manifest religion and religious dress

Should Article 9 secure the right of Muslim women, who so wish, to wear headscarves and whatever other forms of dress, including veils, they believe to be appropriate for, or required by, their religious beliefs?

This is a topic of great controversy in a number of European countries.

Arguments in favour of the view that women have a right to wear headscarves etc., which the Convention should protect, include:

- A number of Muslim women feel that such dress is a requirement of their religion or at least it feels appropriate to wear it as an aspect of their religious identity; this feeling needs to be respected.
- The Convention embodies the values of tolerance and broadmindedness.
- Adult women should be allowed to choose for themselves what they wear.
- Other religious symbols, such as crucifixes worn as neck pendants, are allowed.

- The alleged problems caused are exaggerated. There is no necessary connection between religious dress and problems such as extremism. Dress harms no one. If a person wishes to wear something that others think is a badge of subordination, so be it: that someone is 'harming' themselves is their business and not grounds for the state to interfere.

Where state laws, or institutional practices within states, have restricted headscarves and other forms of Islamic dress for women, the arguments for restriction include:

- In a context of religious diversity, states and institutions are entitled to take steps to preserve secularism (the idea that public institutions should not embody the beliefs of any religion).

- The wearing of a headscarf may, in some contexts, be associated with 'proselytism' (putting pressure on others to conform to a particular set of religious beliefs), particularly if it is alleged to be a requirement of the religion. Some restriction may be reasonable to protect the freedom of others not to wear the dress.

- The argument that it is only women but not men who are subjected to a dress code may be hard to square with gender equality, highly valued under the Convention.

The issue has come before the ECtHR in a number of different contexts. Bans on (usually) Muslim dress are treated as interferences with Article 9 and therefore the issue for the Court is justification under Article 9(2).

In *Leyla Sahin* v *Turkey* (2007) 44 EHRR 5, a Grand Chamber of the ECtHR found that a ban, imposed by a Turkish university, on its female students wearing headscarves, did not violate Article 9. There was an interference with the applicant's rights under Article 9(1) but it was justified in the terms of Article 9(2). Turkey has a large Muslim population. Specifically:

- Turkey is a secular state committed to secularism and gender equality.
- The university's ban was 'prescribed by law' since it was in its regulations.
- The ban served legitimate purposes, including protecting the rights of others and public order.
- The ban was proportionate. It resulted from a careful weighing of the issues and interests of all those involved. The university, and the Turkish courts that found in its favour, had acted within the state's margin of appreciation, being best placed to decide the matter in context. (See also *Dahlab* v *Switzerland* App 42393/98, judgment 15 February 2001.)

France has banned women wearing niqab or burqa in public places; it is a criminal offence.

 CASE CLOSE-UP

SAS v France (2015) 60 EHRR 11

S objected to the ban on the grounds that it interfered with her freedom to choose whether or not to wear niqab or burqa as an expression of her religious views. She brought the case on the day the law entered into force. However the Grand Chamber accepted that, since she was at risk of prosecution, she was a 'victim' under Article 35 ECHR (see Chapter 2, section 2.7.1) and that the clarity of the law meant she did not have to exhaust domestic remedies. Furthermore it would be wrong to test the sincerity of her views in terms of Islamic law and practice.

The Grand Chamber accepted that the ban interfered with her right to manifest religion under Article 9. On justification under Article 9(2) the court found:

- The ban was prescribed by law.
- Purpose. Unusually this was significant for the decision. As aspects of the 'rights and freedoms of others', the Court was unconvinced that the ban could be justified by gender equality since this was a woman trying to exercise her rights; nor could this expression of cultural values be banned to promote 'human dignity'. But the Court did accept that the ban had a legitimate purpose in terms of the right of human community, of 'living together'.
- Proportionality. The Grand Chamber found that the ban was seen by France as necessary to the values of its Republic and so it was within the margin of appreciation that applied.

 THINKING POINT

There were two strong dissents to this case which challenged the majority on both purpose and legitimacy. Who persuades you more—majority or minority?

The United Kingdom has not banned niqab or burqa. Rather the issue has focused on whether the law should or should not support various bodies who, in the context of their activities, have reasons for prohibiting these garments (e.g. in the context of defendants or witness in criminal or civil trials). The approach focuses on proportionality and whether, in the factual and legal context of the case, there is a fair balance between the wishes of the individual and the rights of others or the social good that is served by the reasons for the ban.

 CASE CLOSE-UP

R (Begum) v _Governors of Denbigh High School_ [2006] UKHL 15

The UKHL held that the exclusion of SB, a Muslim girl, from her school (a public authority under the HRA) was compatible with Article 9. She was excluded because she insisted, for religious reasons, on wearing a more concealing form of dress (jilbab) than was permitted under the school's rules (shalwa kameeze). The purpose of the uniform rules was to protect the majority of Muslim female pupils (who were happy with the uniform policy) from pressure being exerted on them to adopt a more fundamentalist conception of their religion. The House of Lords followed Strasbourg case law. The restriction was prescribed by law (a carefully thought out uniform policy), its purpose was to protect the rights and freedoms of others (other pupils), and its application to SB was proportionate (in particular SB did have the opportunity to go to other schools in which the jilbab was permitted). The school had striven to achieve a fair balance of different interests to which a court had to defer.

Other cases include:

- _R (Playfoot)_ v _Millais School_ [2007] EWHC 1698—banning a pupil from wearing a purity ring did not violate Article 9.

- *R (Watkins-Singh)* v *Aberdare High School* [2008] EWHC 1865—where there was unlawful discrimination of a pupil excluded for insisting on wearing a Kara (Sikh bracelet)—*Begum* was distinguished on the facts.

16.5 Blasphemy

The ECtHR has been not unsympathetic to national laws which criminalise blasphemous expression (i.e. words which seriously insult or offend religious believers). The issue is dealt with, normally, on the basis of a claim under Article 10 (freedom of expression) brought by the broadcaster, film maker, etc. who is subjected to a blasphemy law. Under Article 10(2) restrictions on expression may be justified if done to protect the rights of others. These can include the rights to freedom of religion in Article 9, which can legitimately be protected by blasphemy laws applied in a lawful and proportionate manner. This position has been adopted by the ECtHR in cases such as *Wingrove* v *United Kingdom* (1997) 24 EHRR 1 and *Otto-Preminger Institute* v *Austria* (1995) 19 EHRR 34. The Court makes it clear, however, that the laws must not be applied in ways that prevent religious beliefs from being denied or criticised. Indeed, there is a reciprocal duty of the religious to tolerate criticism. By reference to the 'duties and responsibilities' provision in Article 10(2), however, states can place legal limits requiring appropriate respect in the manner of such criticism (the prosecution in *Wingrove* could be justified because of the highly offensive nature of the video). It should be noted that, at least according to the Commission (*Choudhury* v *United Kingdom* App 17439/90, Commission admissibility decision of 5 March 1991), nothing in Article 9 places a positive duty on states to adopt general laws against blasphemy.

In the United Kingdom the common law offences of blasphemy and blasphemous libel were abolished for England and Wales by section 79 of the Criminal Justice and Immigration Act 2008. They were replaced by laws which criminalise expressions of religious hatred which are distinguished from expressions of 'antipathy, dislike, ridicule, insult or abuse', section 29J, Part IIIA of the Public Order Act 1986.

 Summary

- The protection of belief itself is absolute in the sense that, unless there are grounds for derogation under Article 15, the state cannot interfere with religious and other beliefs and may have a duty to secure religious freedom.

- Manifestations of belief can be restricted by the state subject to the provisions of Article 9(2). The important point here is to distinguish between actions which manifest belief and those which simply are motivated by belief. The latter do not raise issues under Article 9.

- Nothing in Article 9 allows a person to manifest their beliefs whenever they wish and so Article 9 gives little support to conscientious objection in the employment context.

? Self-test questions

1. How does the ECtHR distinguish a manifestation of a belief from an action motivated by a belief?

2. For what kinds of purpose is it legitimate to restrict a person's manifestation of belief?

3. In what circumstances, if any, will a court evaluate the nature, quality, and credibility of beliefs for the purpose of Article 9?

4. Contrast Article 9 with the right of parents under Article 2 of the First Protocol to have their religious and philosophical convictions respected by the state in supplying education.

5. How does the ECtHR approach cases dealing with laws against blasphemy and their compatibility with Article 9?

6. Identify three cases in which the ECtHR has considered issues of the compatibility of bans on religious dress or symbols with Article 9 (see also Exam question 1, below).

 For suggested approaches, please visit the Online Resource Centre.

? Exam questions

1. In *SAS* v *France* (above) the ECtHR accepted the compatibility of France's ban on the burqa with Article 9.

   Critically evaluate the reasons for the decision and discuss whether they provide a reasonable basis for protecting the right to manifest belief of some Muslim women.

2. Able and Baker are both civil servants working for the transport division of the Ministry of Defence. They are to be sent to Syria to support British forces which, under a UN Mandate, are there to attack and defeat rebels holding the north of the country. Both object to being sent.

   Able's objection is religious—he is a devout Christian and pacifist.

   Baker's objection is political—he believes that the army he will be supporting is likely to be doing enormous environmental damage in Syria.

   Although their terms of employment suggest that the Civil Service can send them anywhere in the world, they both assert they have a rights based on Article 9 not to be sent and that alternative employment should be found.

   Advise the Secretary of State for Defence who must decide whether to compel them to go. Your advice should be strictly limited to the issues raised by Article 9.

 For suggested approaches, please visit the Online Resource Centre.

Further reading

Addison, N. *Religious Discrimination and Hatred Law* (2007) London: Routledge-Cavendish

Ahdar, R. and Leigh, F. *Religious Freedom in the Liberal State* (2005) Oxford: OUP

Brownlee, K. *Conscience and Conviction: the case for civil disobedience* (2012) Oxford: OUP

Lester, A., Pannick, D., and Herberg, J. (see Preface) Chapter 4, Article 9

Taylor, P. *Freedom of Religion* (2005) Cambridge: CUP

17 Article 10: freedom of expression

LEARNING OBJECTIVES

- The importance of freedom of expression.
- 'Expression' and the scope of Article 10(1).
- Media freedom.
- Restrictions on freedom of expression as permitted under Article 10(2).
- Political speech (which has the highest levels of protection).
- Permissible restrictions of political speech.
- Artistic speech.
- Commercial speech.

Article 10 Freedom of Expression

(1) Everyone has the right to freedom of expression. This right shall include freedom to hold opinions and to receive and impart information and ideas without interference by public authority and regardless of frontiers. This article shall not prevent states from requiring the licensing of broadcasting, television or cinema enterprises.

(2) The exercise of these freedoms, since it carries with it duties and responsibilities, may be subject to such formalities, conditions, restrictions or penalties as are prescribed by law and are necessary in a democratic society, in the interests of national security, territorial integrity or public safety, for the prevention of disorder or crime, for the protection of health or morals, for the protection of the reputation or rights of others, for preventing the disclosure of information received in confidence, or for maintaining the authority and impartiality of the judiciary.

Introduction

Freedom of expression is widely acknowledged as a fundamental right in a liberal, democratic society. There are, however, important and legitimate reasons why freedom of expression may need to be restricted in order to protect other important rights, freedoms, and interests. The protection of national security and right of an individual to have a fair trial are both areas in which freedom of expression might, legitimately, be restricted. Protecting the rights of others can also involve restricting, for example, advertisements with controversial content or the entry into the country of individuals with controversial views. Such questions involve weighing such rights and interests with the restricted person's right to express him or herself or the right of the rest of us to receive information and ideas. The two-paragraph structure of Article 10 provides the procedure by which this balancing can be judicially undertaken.

17.1 Freedom of expression as a value in common law

Freedom of expression is a well-recognised principle of the common law (the basic judge-made law of England and Wales) which had been established before, and independently of, the Human Rights Act 1998 (HRA). British judges have, on a number of occasions, insisted that there is no incompatibility between the degree of protection afforded expression under the common law with the protection under Article 10: there is simply a difference of approach. The following quote, from Lord Goff in one of the *Spycatcher* cases of the 1980s, expresses the point.

> I can see no inconsistency between English law on this subject and art 10 [ECHR]. This is scarcely surprising, since we may pride ourselves on the fact that freedom of speech has existed in this country perhaps as long as, if not longer than, it has existed in any other country in the world. The only difference is that, whereas art 10 of the convention, in accordance with its avowed purpose, proceeds to state a fundamental right and then to qualify it, we in this country (where everybody is free to do anything, subject only to the provisions of the law) proceed rather on an assumption of freedom of speech, and turn to our law to discover the established exceptions to it.
>
> (*Attorney General* v *Guardian Newspapers (No 2)* [1988] 3 All ER 545, 659)

The importance of freedom of expression in common law continues to be asserted by the judges. It has been recognised by Law Lords as attaining 'the status of a constitutional right with attendant high normative force' (*McCartan Turkington Breen* v *Times Newspapers* [2000] 4 All ER 913, 926). There is a good summary of the law and importance of freedom of expression in English law, taking Article 10 into account and including references to significant cases, see *R (BBC)* v *Secretary of State for Justice* [2012] EWHC 13, paras 35–54.

Under the law of England and Wales issues of freedom of speech can arise, for example:

- in 'defamation' proceedings where a person seeks damages for false statements made which damage their reputation;
- to protect confidential information through an action for 'breach of confidence';
- to protect intellectual property rights such as copyright and trade marks;
- in the criminal law, such as public order offences which may have been committed by political demonstrators.

Some of these issues will involve the HRA directly, for example where the interpretation of an Act of Parliament is involved or where it is alleged that the police or some other public authority have failed to respect freedom of expression. Where, like defamation or breach of confidence, it is essentially a matter of private law, freedom of expression is still relevant, either because the courts are public authorities required to act compatibly with Convention rights or, irrespective of the HRA, because freedom of expression is a long-standing value in the common law. As Lord Steyn said, in *Reynolds* v *Times Newspapers Ltd* [1999] 4 All ER 609, 628, 'freedom of expression is the rule and regulation of speech is the exception requiring justification'.

17.2 Article 10: general issues

17.2.1 Importance

From one of its earliest cases, *Handyside* v *United Kingdom* (1979–80) 1 EHRR 737, onwards the European Court of Human Rights (ECtHR) has continuously recognised the importance of the right to freedom of expression within the Convention scheme (see para 49). In *Pentikäinen* v *Finland* App 11882/10, judgment of 20 October 2015, a Grand Chamber, reiterating earlier cases, confirmed that freedom of expression is both:

- an essential foundation of a democratic society. A democratic society, characterised by pluralism, tolerance, and broadmindedness, is a necessary condition in which human rights can be protected and justice and peace can flourish; and

- necessary for individual self-fulfilment.

17.2.2 General structure

Despite this importance, the text of Article 10 makes it clear that there is no absolute right to freedom of expression. Freedom of expression, like the freedoms in Articles 8, 9, and 11, can be restricted if certain conditions are present. The nature and scope of freedom of expression is established in the first paragraph (Article 10(1)), and the exclusive conditions under which that freedom can be restricted are identified in the second (Article 10(2)). Thus the approach of the ECtHR (or any national court) to freedom of expression cases is to ask itself:

- is an act of speech, writing, or some other type of expression in issue in the case? If it is, then:

- is it a type of expression that is protected under the terms of the first paragraph of Article 10? If it is, then:

- has the speech etc. been restricted (usually this will have been by a court or by a state agency such as the police)? If so, then:

- has the state shown that the restriction is justified in terms of Article 10(2), i.e. that it was imposed 'by law', that it aimed to achieve one of the purposes listed in paragraph 2 and that it was 'necessary in a democratic society' in the sense of being a proportionate means of meeting a pressing social need?

Following this approach, a court's job involves balancing freedom of expression with the arguments for restricting expression. The latter may be in terms of the collective good or the rights of other individuals that restricting speech promotes or protects. In this balancing exercise the ECtHR gives greatest weight to political speech, broadly defined as speech involving the discussion of public and social affairs; only the most compelling reasons will justify restrictions.

Other forms of speech, such as commercial or artistic speech, are still within the scope of the protection of the first paragraph, but restrictions are more easily brought within the terms of the second paragraph.

17.2.3 The judicial role in protecting free expression

European Court of Human Rights

The ECtHR has the final say on whether any restriction on freedom of expression is compatible with Article 10. National laws permitting restriction must be narrowly construed and government actions be subject to close scrutiny. On the issue of the need for an interference with free expression, the Court has summarised its role in this way (similar wording is used in many cases):

> The Court's task, in exercising its supervisory jurisdiction, is not to take the place of the competent national courts but rather to review under Article 10 the decisions they delivered in the exercise of the power of appreciation. This does not mean that the supervision is limited to ascertaining whether the respondent State exercised its discretion reasonably, carefully and in good faith; what the Court has to do is to look at the interference complained of in the light of the case as a whole and determine whether it was 'proportionate to the legitimate aim pursued' and whether the reasons adduced by the national authorities to justify it are 'relevant and sufficient'.
>
> (*Association Ekin* v *France* (2002) 35 EHRR 35, para 56)

Depending on the issue, the ECtHR allows a margin of appreciation to states (wide on moral questions, very narrow for political speech).

UK courts

CROSS REFERENCE

For 'deference' see Chapter 4, section 4.6.2.

Under the HRA the question of the degree to which UK courts should defer to the way Parliament, the executive or various administrative bodies have balanced free speech with other interests, arises. Since freedom of expression is an important legal value, the courts will often show little deference to the authorities, even to Parliament.

 CASE CLOSE-UP

Ashdown v Telegraph Group Ltd [2001] EWCA Civ 1142

A, who had been leader of the Liberal Democrats, alleged breach of copyright by the *Daily Telegraph*. The newspaper had published, without his permission, excerpts from his diary detailing meetings with the Prime Minister. Under the Copyright, Designs and Patents Act 1988 there is a defence of 'fair dealing', but this was not available to the *Telegraph*. The question was whether the *Telegraph* could rely on wider rights to free expression under Article 10. The Court of Appeal expressly rejected the view that the 'fair dealing' defence was Parliament's way of dealing with the freedom of expression issue and that the courts should defer to this. Rather it was the court's duty to make its own assessment of whether there were overriding public interests which justified publication. On the facts there were not.

There are exceptions if, for example, there is a body with particular expertise—see the majority position in *Pro-Life Alliance* v *BBC* [2003] UKHL 23, discussed at section 17.8.3.

17.2.4 Positive duties or obligations

National authorities have limited obligations to take positive steps to protect freedom of expression. In *Palomo Sánchez* v *Spain* (2012) 54 EHRR 24, a Grand Chamber found no violation of Article 10 when domestic Spanish employment law allowed the sacking of trade unionists, by their private employer, for publishing defamatory cartoons of managers. Confirming earlier cases, the Court held that 'in certain cases the State has a positive obligation to protect the right to freedom of expression, even against interference by private persons' (para 59). The case, which, because of the trade union connection, also involved Article 11, was an example. Whether it means that Article 10 applies generally to dismissals on the basis of expressions by the employee, is unclear.

Positive duties are not absolute, a positive obligation should not be 'interpreted in such a way as to impose an impossible or disproportionate burden on the authorities', *Özgür Gündem* v *Turkey* (2001) 31 EHRR 49, para 43. In *Özgür Gündem* there was a breach of Article 10 because of the state's inadequate investigation of violence and harassment against the owners and editors of a newspaper.

CROSS REFERENCE

For 'positive duties' see Chapter 6, section 6.6.

17.2.5 Prior restraint

One of the debates about the law of freedom of expression generally is whether the law should be used to prevent publication in the first place (e.g. through an injunction) or whether freedom of expression is best protected by allowing publication even of material which, after publication, can be the subject of legal action against the speaker.

The main argument in favour of banning prior restraint orders is that it maintains the 'hearers' interests' in the content of the expression. In particular, it makes it difficult for government and powerful individuals or groups to prevent information and ideas getting into the public domain.

The main argument for allowing prior restraints is that some legitimate restrictions on speech would lose their force altogether if publication were allowed. If, for example, the point of a legitimate restriction on free speech is to protect information obtained in confidence, there is little point if the law cannot protect the confidence by restraining publication.

Two examples from English law are given here.

- Defamation. Following *Bonnard* v *Perryman* [1891] 2 Ch 269, English courts will not, other than exceptionally, issue an injunction to prevent a publication which impugns a person's reputation, particularly where, in legal proceedings for defamation, the defence would claim justification. The legal approach is 'publish and be damned'. (The rule has been held to be compatible with Convention rights in *Greene* v *Associated Newspapers* [2004] EWCA Civ 1462.)

- Breach of confidence. An injunction is more easily available where a newspaper, for example, intends to publish information obtained in confidence (whether true or false, whether defamatory or not). If the law accepts that some information is legitimately confidential (such as medical records or trade secrets) then it will protect it by issuing an injunction. The underlying issue is whether, on balance, the public interest justifies publication or secrecy; see, for example, the refusal of the Court of Appeal to issue a temporary injunction to preserve the confidentiality (in reality the privacy) of the Michael Douglas–Catherine Zeta-Jones wedding photographs: *Douglas* v *Hello!* [2001] 2 All ER 289.

Prior restraint is not incompatible with the ECHR (see *Markt Intern Verlag GmbH* v *Germany* (1990) 12 EHRR 161, for example). Nevertheless, the inherent dangers call 'for the most careful scrutiny on the part of the Court', particularly in restraining the media in news reporting: 'for news is a perishable commodity and to delay its publication, even for a short period, may well deprive it of all its value and interest' (*Association Ekin* v *France* (2002) 35 EHRR 35, para 56).

17.3 Freedom of expression and section 12 HRA

During the passage of the HRA, Parliament expressed concern that some Convention rights, in particular the right to privacy in Article 8, might be used to limit freedom of expression, especially media freedom, more than was acceptable. Section 12 was introduced and applies whenever a UK court is considering whether to grant a civil remedy (including an injunction prior to publication or damages after publication) which affects the exercise of freedom of expression.

Section 12(2) requires that, unless there are compelling reasons to the contrary, a remedy affecting freedom of speech should only be granted if the person against whom the injunction is made is present or represented.

Section 12(3) deals with interim injunctions. These are holding injunctions whose effect is to prevent publication of a matter in the period before the full trial to decide whether or not the law permits publication is held. An interim injunction can be issued on the basis of a 'balance of convenience', which does not deal with the legal rights and wrongs but relates to the issue of whether it is the applicant or respondent who has most to lose if publication is allowed in this interim period. Given the 'perishable nature' of much news and information, issuing an interim injunction can have the effect of stopping the story once and for all. For this reason, under section 12(3) an interim injunction affecting freedom of expression can only be issued if the court goes beyond the balance of convenience and considers, by reference to the merits of the case, that the claimant would 'probably' (more likely than not) succeed at the final trial. The degree of probability required depends on the circumstances (*Cream Holdings Ltd* v *Banerjee* [2004] UKHL 44, para 22).

Section 12(4) requires a court to have 'particular regard' to the importance of Article 10. In respect of matters affecting journalistic, literary, or artistic material, the court must consider the extent to which the material is or is about to be available to the public, whether publication is or would be in the public interest, and 'any relevant privacy code' (e.g. in the context of the media, the Codes of Practice of the press regulator (see Chapter 22, section 22.2.1) or, for broadcasting, Codes supervised by Ofcom and the BBC).

Section 12(4) may be of symbolic rather than real effect. As Sedley LJ noted in *Douglas* v *Hello!* [2001] 2 All ER 289 (paras 131–137), giving particular regard to Article 10 must include considering Article 10(2). This necessarily means seeking a fair balance with competing rights, such as private life in Article 8. It follows that section 12(4) does not give the right of free expression 'a presumptive priority' over other rights (para 137). This view has been accepted by the House of Lords in *Campbell* v *MGN Ltd* [2004] UKHL 22, para 111.

17.4 The scope of Article 10(1)

Article 10 protects 'freedom of expression', not just freedom of speech. Expressive activity is not confined to speech. It can, for example, extend to expressive acts that do not involve words at all, such as the playing of music, dancing, or the wearing of particular clothes. Of particular importance, frequently reiterated by the ECtHR, is that Article 10(1) protects speech which 'offends, shocks or disturbs'. The mere fact that an expression is offensive, etc. does not, of itself, justify it being banned. Any restrictions on such speech need to be justified under the terms of Article 10(2), discussed at section 17.6.

Political expression is given particular protection under Article 10. 'Political' has a wide definition and includes, for instance, participating in political demonstrations. Article 10 also extends to artistic and commercial expression, although restrictions may be easier to justify in these areas than in respect of political speech.

An expressive act can, of course, give rise to issues within the ambit of more than one Article. Restrictions on dress, for example, could give rise to issues under Article 8, the right to private life, or under Article 9, the right to freedom of thought, conscience, and religion. The tendency of the Court is to decide that one Article is the one predominantly in issue and that all substantive issues can be dealt with under its terms.

Article 10 protects not just the substance of the ideas and information but also the chosen form of expression (*News Verlags GmbH* v *Austria* (2001) 31 EHRR 8, para 39). In *R (BBC)* v *Secretary of State for Justice* [2012] EWHC 13, for instance, the Justice Secretary allowed journalists to interview a prisoner and discuss the contents of the interview on air, but not to broadcast the interview itself. The High Court held the ban on broadcasting was disproportionate and incompatible with Article 10.

17.4.1 Freedom to receive information

Access to information held by government and other public bodies is essential for an effective political democracy. The judgments and choices of a political kind that citizens make depend on the information that is available and that depends, largely, on the ability of individuals and organisations and, most importantly, the media to obtain information. In a way, receiving information is the most important aspect to freedom of expression since the overwhelming majority of people have no realistic access to the media in order to express their views and opinions.

The ECtHR has consistently held that the right to receive information prevents the government from restricting the flow of information that others are prepared to give. It cannot be used to compel the government or others to disclose information they wish to keep secret.

In *Leander* v *Sweden* (1987) 9 EHRR 433, the applicant claimed that he was entitled to see his security vetting, which had found that he was a security risk. He had been unable to challenge this and, as a result, he had lost his job. The ECtHR held that there had been no violation of Article 10. The right to receive information does not impose an obligation on the government to impart such information.

This view was confirmed by the Grand Chamber in *Roche* v *United Kingdom* (2006) 42 EHRR 30, para 172.

The ECtHR has, however, recognised that a right to receive information, even from an unwilling government, may arise not under Article 10 but, rather, where it is necessary in order to uphold other Convention rights and freedoms such as the right to private and family life under Article 8. Information that has a particular significance for an individual's private life, for his or her sense of identity, for example, may need to be disclosed (see *Gaskin* v *United Kingdom* (1990) 12 EHRR 36). Similarly, information necessary to enable an individual to assess environmental or other dangers to health (see, for example, *Guerra* v *Italy* (1998) 26 EHRR 357) may need to be disclosed.

The general position under the Convention has been followed by courts in England and Wales. In *R (Persey)* v *Secretary of State for the Environment, Food and Rural Affairs* [2002] EWHC 371, for instance, the Administrative Court followed *Leander* and refused to hold that Article 10 was engaged when the government refused to hold an inquiry into the foot and mouth outbreak of 2001 in public. This can be compared with *London Regional Transport* v *Mayor of London* [2001] EWCA Civ 1491, where the Court of Appeal ordered the publication of a commercially sensitive report, partly on the basis of a right to receive information in Article 10.

There is some indication that the ECtHR is, slightly, shifting its position. In *Tarsasag a Szabadsagjogkert* v *Hungary* (2011) 53 EHRR 3 (paras 35–38), the Court held that Article 10 was violated when the Hungarian Civil Liberties Union was denied access to details of a complaint made to the Hungarian Constitutional Court by an MP about the constitutionality of new drug laws. The ECtHR did not establish a general right to public information (so that all interferences would need to be justified by reference to Article 10(2)). But it may have moved in that direction in order to prevent the *Leander* principle being used to allow interferences by an 'information monopoly' with the ability of a 'watchdog', such as the media, to scrutinise public affairs. However, the extent of the shift in *Tarsasag* remains unclear. Under the HRA the UKSC in *BBC* v *Sugar (No 2)* [2012] UKSC 4 refused to read the case as indicating a general shift towards a general right to receive information from an unwilling provider (paras 85–94). *Kennedy* v *Charity Commissioners* (2014) UKSC 20 involved an attempt by K to compel the Charity Commission to disclose information about the Miriam Fund, a controversial charity focused on Iraq. The UKSC considered relevant cases decided since *Tarsasag* (see paras 73–88). However, the majority could not find a clear direction of travel away from the principle in *Leander* towards a right to receive from an unwilling provider. Article 10 was not becoming a freedom of information provision. At most the cases suggested there might be a duty to disclose where a body was resisting disclosure ordered by a domestic court (see *Youth Initiative for Human Rights* v *Serbia* App 48135/06, judgment of 25 September 2013). Indeed, for the majority, the common law principle of access to justice might offer more by way of requiring disclosure than Article 10. Significantly, the two Justices in the minority did accept that *Tarsasag* and subsequent cases disclosed a reasonably coherent direction of travel which, in the case, the applicant could have relied upon.

17.5 Freedom of the media

Time and again the ECtHR has emphasised the importance of a free media. It is essential for democracy, and democracy is the system which best upholds human rights. The press and audio-visual media are the main mechanisms for imparting ideas on public matters which the public have a right to receive. The media is vital as a 'watchdog' against oppression. Similarly, though states are allowed to regulate the media, they must also ensure that there is a pluralism, a reasonably wide range of knowledge and ideas available to the public; and so it must protect against too much concentration of media power in too few hands. At the same time the ECtHR has stressed the 'duties and responsibilities' of the media—there are rights of others and public interests which may need to be protected by limits on media freedom. These important matters are pursued further in Chapter 22.

17.6 Restrictions under Article 10(2)

Any restrictions on speech or expressive acts that are within the scope of Article 10(1) will be violations unless the state can prove that the restriction is justified in terms of Article 10(2). The general principles governing the proper judicial scrutiny of the justification for any interference with the right to freedom of expression in Article 10(1) have been laid down by the ECtHR in numerous cases; see, for example, *Pentikäinen* v *Finland* App 11882/10, judgment of 20 October 2015, paras 82–91. These principles are discussed in sections 17.6.1 to 17.6.4.

These principles have been adopted into UK law under the HRA in cases such as *R* v *Shayler* [2002] UKHL 11 (see Lord Hope's summary in paras 54–61).

17.6.1 **There must be an interference**

There needs to have been some interference for which the authorities were directly or indirectly responsible. Usually this is obvious but can occasionally be challenged by the authorities (e.g. because the applicant was not charged with an offence relating to expression).

17.6.2 **The interference is prescribed by law**

Restrictions on freedom of expression must meet the standard of 'legality' which pervades the Convention. Specifically:

- there must be a basis in law for the restriction;
- the law must be accessible to the individual likely to be affected by it;
- the terms of the law must be sufficiently precise for the individual to be able to regulate his or her conduct without breaking the law;
- the 'law' must not be arbitrary and incompatible with the 'rule of law'.

> **CROSS REFERENCE**
>
> The Convention concept of 'law' is discussed in Chapter 6, section 6.2.

In the context of freedom of expression, the standards of 'prescribed by law' can be quite undemanding. In *Chorherr* v *Austria* (1994) 17 EHRR 358, an offence of 'causing a breach of the peace by conduct likely to cause annoyance' was felt to be sufficiently precise for a person to regulate his or her conduct: the issue had to be approached in context (see para 25). Nevertheless, the concept has not lost all its significance.

> ### 🔍 CASE CLOSE-UP
>
> **R (Miranda) v Secretary of State for the Home Department** [2016] EWCA Civ 6.
>
> A journalist's spouse, M, was detained at Heathrow by the Metropolitan Police under Schedule 7, the Terrorism Act 2000. This allows the questioning of a person at a port or airport about being connected in some way with terrorism.
>
> M was carrying stolen security data supplied to his husband by Edward Snowden (a US security analyst who had disclosed the massive scale of US surveillance of its own citizens and the UK's use of data obtained).
>
> The Court of Appeal held that the questioning of M was lawful under UK domestic law. It was a lawful and proportionate exercise of the power in Schedule 7.
>
> However, the Court of Appeal also held that Schedule 7 itself did not meet the 'prescribed by law' requirement of Article 10(2), specifically in relation to claims by journalists that their rights to freedom of expression had been interfered with. In the context of protecting journalistic material, the Court of Appeal held that Schedule 7 had insufficient safeguards.
>
> This is, in effect, a declaration of incompatibility. As the Court said, the remedy lies with Parliament. What was necessary, the court suggested, was for Schedule 7 to be made to require some form of judicial or independent scrutiny to ensure that proper journalistic confidentiality was respected.
>
> The point is that, as with surveillance and data retention cases under Article 8, safeguards are necessary for an interference with rights to be 'prescribed by law'. This is a matter for the courts. Safeguards are not a matter just of the proportionality where greater deference to the authorities may be appropriate (see Chapter 15, section 15.10.2).

Media Codes of Practice have also been considered for compatibility with Article 10 under the HRA. These are the rules followed by media regulators aimed at protecting, for example, people's privacy. In *R v Advertising Standards Authority ex parte Matthias Rath BV* [2001] EMLR 22, the High Court accepted that the ASA's Code of Practice was sufficiently clear to meet the prescribed by law standards for the purposes of advertising.

17.6.3 The interference serves a legitimate purposes

Restrictions are only legitimate if for one of the purposes listed in Article 10(2). Article 18 ECHR makes it clear that restrictions for other purposes are not permissible. These purposes are described in loose and open-textured phrases, such as 'national security' or 'protection of morals', and it is usually relatively easy for states to show that their reason for restricting expression can be brought within one or more of them.

'the interests of national security'

The 'interests of national security' has been accepted as a legitimate purpose in situations such as the following:

- Maintaining the secrecy of the secret services (see *Observer and the Guardian* v *United Kingdom* (1992) 14 EHRR 153, discussed at section 17.7.3.
- Preserving order in the armed forces by suppressing unofficial magazines distributed amongst soldiers (*Vereinigung Demokratischer Soldaten Österreichs and Gubi* v *Austria*

(1995) 20 EHRR 56, where the Court held that, though for a legitimate purpose, there was a violation of Article 10).

National security is likely to be relevant in respect of areas of UK law such as:

- Official secrets. In *R* v *Shayler* [2002] UKHL 11, S was prosecuted under the Official Secrets Act 1989. He argued that compatibility with Article 10 requires a public interest defence. This was rejected by the House of Lords—in particular because of the availability of internal complaint mechanisms available to civil servants.

- The civil remedy of an injunction to prevent a breach of confidence can be sought by the government to try and prevent publication in the media of secret government information (e.g. *Ministry of Defence* v *Griffin* [2008] EWHC 1542, where the court enforced the terms of a confidentiality agreement signed by a member of UK Special Forces). The compatibility of such 'prior restraint' injunctions with Article 10 was at the heart of *Observer and Guardian Newspapers* v *United Kingdom* (1992) 14 EHRR 153, an important case discussed at section 17.7.3.

'territorial integrity and public safety'

The 'interests of . . . territorial integrity' has been accepted as a legitimate purpose in situations such as the following:

- Expelling a member of the European Parliament who had taken part in a banned anti-nuclear march in French Polynesia (*Piermont* v *France* (1995) 20 EHRR 301).

- Anti-terrorism laws, such as those restricting freedom of expression in the context of armed struggle aimed at constitutional change including separatism. The armed struggle between Turkey and the PKK over 'Kurdistan' in 1990 has provided many examples, such as *Sürek* v *Turkey (No 4)* App 24762/94, Grand Chamber judgment of 8 July 1999, paras 46–49.

'the prevention of disorder or crime'

This is widely used as part of the claim of justification for restrictions on, for example:

- political meetings, marches, and demonstrations, such as in *Steel* v *United Kingdom* (1999) 28 EHRR 603;

- provisions in anti-terrorism legislation which restrict speech and other forms of expression. In a number of cases involving Turkey, the ECtHR accepted that anti-terrorism measures, including prohibiting 'separatist propaganda' or the publication of material from banned organisations, were, at least in the context of violent struggle between the PKK and the Turkish state, for 'the protection of national security and territorial integrity and the prevention of disorder and crime' (e.g. *Baskaya and Okçuoglu* v *Turkey* (2001) 31 EHRR 10, para 56).

CROSS REFERENCE

See also Chapter 18, section 18.1; Article 10 and political speech generally is discussed at section 17.7.

Under the HRA, the courts of England and Wales have to deal with restrictions on freedom of expression imposed, for example, under public order legislation such as the Public Order Act 1986, the common law power to arrest for 'breach of the peace' or offences of incitement, including to racial or religious hatred. The main issue, usually, is whether some restraint on free expression is necessary and proportionate.

Some early cases gave a wide view to 'disorder' (e.g. including matters which need regulation, see *Groppera Radio AG* v *Switzerland* (1990) 12 EHRR 321, paras 69–70 and *Autronic AG* v *Switzerland* (1990) 12 EHRR 485, para 59). However, in *Perincek* v *Switzerland* App 27510/08, Grand Chamber judgment of 15 October 2015, a Grand Chamber confined the term to situations involving disorder in the sense of public disturbance (paras 146–154).

'the protection of health'

This purpose has been accepted, under the HRA, as part of the justification for restrictions imposed on advertising and publicity promoting health products (as in *R* v *Advertising Standards Authority ex parte Matthias Rath BV* [2001] EMLR 22).

'the protection of . . . morals'

This purpose is used as part of the justification for legal measures taken against speech and other forms of expression on the grounds of obscenity and indecency (e.g. *Müller* v *Switzerland* (1991) 13 EHRR 212). It can also be relevant to laws which aim at upholding deeply held moral values in a society.

 CASE CLOSE-UP

Open Door Counselling and Dublin Well Woman v Ireland (1993) 15 EHRR 244

Irish law imposed a legal ban on giving advice and counselling to Irish women seeking abortions in the United Kingdom. It was challenged on Article 10 grounds. The ECtHR held that the ban embodied 'the profound moral values concerning the nature of life', which the Irish people had, in those days, endorsed in a referendum (paras 61–63). However, in all the circumstances, the Court went on to find that the ban was disproportionate.

Article 10 and laws against obscenity are discussed in section 17.12.

'protection of the reputation . . . of others'

This provision is part of the justification for:

CROSS REFERENCE

The issue of the media and qualified privilege is discussed in Chapter 22, section 22.3.

- Actions for defamation. 'Libel' and 'slander' (in English law terms) involve a claim for damages against a person who has expressed him or herself in ways that undermine the reputation of the person seeking damages. Convention cases have involved actions brought to defend the reputation of public officials (see section 17.8.4). Since the courts are public authorities (and also because of section 12 HRA, discussed in section 17.3), Article 10 is relevant to defamation proceedings brought between private persons, including the media. The law is developed in ways that are compatible with Convention rights.

- Hate speech. Laws that criminalise various forms of hate speech, such as incitements to violence on racial or religious grounds, can be justified by reference to protecting the reputation of others. This issue is discussed later in the chapter (section 17.9).

'protection of the . . . rights of others'

This provision can be part of a state's justification for a restriction on freedom of expression designed to protect some legal right that others enjoy. This includes the protection of other Convention rights, such as the right to respect for private life under Article 8. Balancing Article 10 and Article 8 is central to breach of confidence cases brought, for example, by celebrities against what they see as intrusive newspaper reporting (see Chapter 22, section 22.5).

The protection of ordinary property rights can also be a legitimate purpose which might justify an interference with freedom of expression. Examples include:

- the protection of intellectual property rights through, for example, laws of copyright, trade marks, and patents (*Ashdown* v *Telegraph Group Ltd* [2001] EWCA Civ 1142). In

Twentieth Century Fox v *British Telecommunications* [2011] EWHC 1981, an injunction was issued requiring BT to block access by its ISP subscribers to Newzbin2, a website which facilitated film downloads in breach of the claimants' copyrights. The injunction was compatible with Article 10;

- the protection of other forms of property such as the rights of shopping mall owners to restrict political demonstrations (*Appleby* v *United Kingdom* (2003) 37 EHRR 38).

Protecting the 'rights of others' has been used by the Court to protect certain background rights that have not been clearly established in law. In *Chassagnou* v *France* (2000) 29 EHRR 615, this was recognised but confined, by the ECtHR, to important rights embodying an 'indisputable imperative', para 113. However, the concept of rights of others is applied quite generously. Examples include rights of:

- people not to be offended or insulted in their religious beliefs (*Otto-Preminger Institute* v *Austria* (1995) 19 EHRR 34);
- people not to suffer gratuitously offensive material broadcast into their own home *(Pro-Life Alliance)* v *BBC* [2003] UKHL 23);
- victims of racial abuse (*Jersild* v *Denmark* (1995) 19 EHRR 1);
- candidates and electors to a fair election which is not distorted by the power of money (*Bowman* v *United Kingdom* (1998) 26 EHRR 1, para 38).

 BIGGER PICTURE

For discussion of the rights of others in a freedom of expression context see *Connolly* v *DPP* [2007] EWHC 237, paras 23–27.

'for preventing the disclosure of information received in confidence'

This provision can be part of the justification by states in situations such as the following:

- legal actions requiring the disclosure by journalists of their sources;
- prosecutions of journalists for disclosing parts of confidential diplomatic reports (see *Stoll* v *Switzerland* (2008) 47 EHRR 59.

> **CROSS REFERENCE**
> Disclosure of journalists' sources is discussed in Chapter 22, section 22.4.

'for maintaining the authority and impartiality of the judiciary'

Laws and measures which may restrict media reporting of trials in order to protect the rights of others, such as children, or the overall fairness of trials, may have this purpose as their justification. It is clearly linked to Article 6 (see *A* v *BBC* [2014] UKHL 25, para 50).

> **CROSS REFERENCE**
> Contempt of court is discussed in Chapter 12, section 12.8.2, Contempt of court.

17.6.4 'Necessary in a democratic society'

Not only must the authorities prove that the restriction on freedom of expression is 'by law' and is aimed at one or more of the purposes listed in the second paragraph of Article 10, but also they must show that the restriction is 'necessary in a democratic society'. Most Article 10 cases turn on this issue, the issue of proportionality.

The general Strasbourg principles have been summarised, in the context of Article 10, by Lord Hope in *Shayler* (section 17.6), paras 54–61:

- Restrictions must be based on relevant and sufficient reasons.

> **CROSS REFERENCE**
> These general principles have been discussed in Chapter 6, section 6.5 and Chapter 14, section 14.4.3.

- Restrictions must aim to meet a pressing social need.
- The pressing social need must be met in a 'proportionate' way.
- Proportionality involves a balancing of interests, but the starting point is freedom of expression, with the burden of proof on the authorities to justify the need for the restrictions and that the restrictions are no more than are necessary.
- The authority's reasons must be subject to close scrutiny by a court.

17.6.5   Duties and responsibilities

The text of Article 10 recognises that freedom of expression carries with it 'duties and responsibilities' and it is on this basis that speech can reasonably be restricted. Whilst the duties and responsibilities clause can influence the way a court views various issues, it does not relieve a court of the need for close scrutiny of the reasons adduced by states for restricting expression.

Duties and responsibilities have been emphasised by the ECtHR and UK courts in the following situations:

- The duties of publishers of books aimed at children which had allegedly obscene content (*Handyside* v *United Kingdom* (1979–80) 1 EHRR 737, para 49).

❯ CROSS REFERENCE

'Responsible journalism' is discussed in Chapter 22, section 22.3.

- The duties of the media, owners, editors, and journalists, in the context of reporting terrorism and armed struggle, to ensure that their reports do not 'become a vehicle for the dissemination of hate speech and the promotion of violence' (*Sürek* v *Turkey (No 4)* (1999) App 24762/94, Grand Chamber judgment of 8 July 1999, para 60).
- The duties and responsibilities of former members of the security services, as in *Shayler*, section 17.6.

17.7   Expression on political and public issues

In assessing the democratic 'necessity' of any restriction on speech, the ECtHR has emphasised, again and again, the importance of protecting political speech. Restraints on speech which, for example, involve criticism of government policy will be hard to justify. Nevertheless this is not a distinction of category. Even expression dealing with political matters and clearly in the public interest may be legitimately restrained if there are very strong counterbalancing reasons such as ones relating to national security (*Stoll* v *Switzerland* (2008) 47 EHRR 59).

❯ CROSS REFERENCE

Stoll is further discussed in Chapter 22, 22.1.

17.7.1   Broad definition of 'political' speech

Political speech is given a very broad definition. It is not confined to party political matters but includes information about, and comment on, matters of general public interest. The political or public dimension to speech can trigger Article 10 protection even if there may be other aspects to it (such as commercial self-interest) which, without the political aspect, might make restriction easier to justify.

In *Barthold* v *Germany* (1985) 7 EHRR 383, a private veterinary surgeon gave an interview in which he was critical of the lack of emergency vet services at night in Hamburg. His practice provided such services. Proceedings were successfully brought against the vet for breaching professional rules relating to advertising and publicity. The ECtHR held that there had been a violation of Article 10. By focusing on the fact that the applicant vet gained publicity for his practice, the German court had not recognised that the primary purpose of the interview was to address an important issue of concern. The ban was disproportionate.

Political marches, meetings, demonstrations, and other types of political activity can be forms of 'expression' and so within the scope of Article 10; if 'peaceful' they may also be within the scope of Article 11.

❯ CROSS REFERENCE

Convention law relating to political meetings, marches, and demonstrations is discussed in fuller detail in Chapter 18.

🔍 CASE CLOSE-UP

***Steel* v *United Kingdom* (1999) 28 EHRR 603**

Demonstrators were detained for breach of the peace. The first and second applicants had attempted to disrupt, in the first case a grouse shoot, and in the second case the construction of a motorway. The third, fourth, and fifth applicants had handed out leaflets and held up banners at an arms fair.

The ECtHR held that Article 10 applied to the situation of all five applicants; although it found that there had been a breach of the Article only in respect of the third, fourth, and fifth defendants.

Likewise Article 10 gives protection to activists.

🔍 CASE CLOSE-UP

***Steel and Morris* v *United Kingdom* (2005) 41 EHRR 22**

S and M published leaflets which made serious allegations against McDonalds who sued them for libel. The main point of the case deals with whether they had a fair trial given the absence of legal aid (see Chapter 12, section 12.6.2, Legal aid in civil cases). The ECtHR held that states had a margin of appreciation over whether or not massive commercial companies could sue individual campaigners for libel. However, the importance of freedom of expression meant that if companies did have this right, the law needed to ensure that the defendants were properly represented so that all the issues could be raised and freedom of speech not unreasonably 'chilled'. The failure to provide legal aid, therefore, was also a breach of Article 10.

The ECtHR said, at para 89:

> in a democratic society even small and informal campaign groups . . . must be able to carry on their activities effectively and that there exists a strong public interest in enabling such groups and individuals outside the mainstream to contribute to the public debate by disseminating information and ideas on matters of general public interests such as health and the environment.

17.7.2 **General principles**

General principles that the Court follows in assessing the need for restrictions of political speech include the following:

> **CROSS REFERENCE**

The Court's understanding of 'democracy' is discussed in Chapter 6, section 6.4.

- Freedom of expression is recognised as an essential condition of a 'democratic' society, as that term is understood by the Court.

- The courts, not the authorities, have the last word on whether or not a restriction on political speech is 'necessary'; such restrictions must be subject to the closest scrutiny by the Court.

- Pluralism, the recognition that different people have different standards, means that Article 10 must protect ideas and expressions even if they 'offend, shock or disturb' the majority of respectable citizens.

- The protection offered by Article 10 extends to groups or individuals who are seeking constitutional change, such as the abolition of the monarchy (or even the possible break-up of the state or at least considerable autonomy for certain regions); such expression may be protected even when it takes place against a background of violent disorder (there are a number of cases involving Turkey which relate to this).

However:

- Article 10 permits states to adopt appropriate measures to guarantee public order and, in particular, to use the criminal law to suppress incitement to violence.

17.7.3 **Restrictions on political speech**

Despite the importance of speech and expressive acts that deal with public and social affairs, the ECtHR does recognise the right of states to suppress such speech in certain circumstances. Proportionate restrictions aimed at protecting national security, for example, are permitted. An important example arose out of the long-running *Spycatcher* saga of the late 1980s.

Q | CASE CLOSE-UP

Observer and The Guardian v United Kingdom (1992) 14 EHRR 153

Peter Wright, a retired member of the security services, published his memoirs. These contained serious allegations about illegal or at least improper activity by the security service (they 'bugged and burgled their way around London' and their targets included the homes of members of the then Labour government). Peter Wright was liable to prosecution under the Official Secrets Act (which he avoided by living in Australia). More importantly, Mrs Thatcher's government sought to prevent the press from discussing the book or publishing excerpts from it. This they did by seeking a civil injunction on the grounds, recognised by English courts, of protecting confidential information. The House of Lords upheld an 'interlocutory', or holding, injunction that had been issued by the courts to maintain confidentiality until the issue could be finally decided. This injunction was maintained even after *Spycatcher* was published in the United States and copies were widely available throughout the world.

When the injunction was tested before the ECtHR, it was upheld on the grounds of being a lawful, proportionate restriction on freedom of expression, done in the interests of national security. However, maintaining the injunction after publication in the United States was disproportionate and a breach of Article 10. Like it or not, confidentiality was lost and so the injunction could not be 'necessary'. The government's argument that continuing the injunction was necessary in order to protect the general integrity of the security services was rejected.

17.8 Political expression and the political process

17.8.1 Politicians and the political process

It is particularly important that the laws must protect the freedom of speech of political actors, particularly elected representatives and those putting themselves forward for election.

In *Jerusalem v Austria* (2003) 37 EHRR 25, a member of the Vienna Municipal Council was subject to an injunction prohibiting her from repeating remarks she had made about religious sects in the Council chamber. The ECtHR found a violation of Article 10 and upheld the importance of free speech for elected representatives (para 36).

17.8.2 Parliamentary privilege

This is the freedom of Parliament to organise itself and conduct its own affairs free from any legal control enforced by the courts or from other forms of improper influence (see, for the UK, *R v Chaytor* [2010] UKSC 52). The law recognises, in particular, that MPs enjoy freedom of speech (see Article 9 of the Bill of Rights 1688) and so it is not possible to seek either criminal or civil remedies against an MP for things said in Parliament. Fair and accurate media reports of things said in Parliament, including additional explanatory material which does not take the matter beyond what was said under privilege, are protected by 'qualified privilege': see *Curistan v Times Newspapers Ltd* [2008] EWCA Civ 432.

In *A v United Kingdom* (2003) 36 EHRR 51, an MP, speaking in a parliamentary debate, had connected the applicant to anti-social behaviour. A claimed that the absolute nature of parliamentary privilege prevented her from suing for defamation (in violation of her right to a fair trial). The ECtHR held that parliamentary privilege performed a necessary function in a democratic society of allowing Parliament to work effectively, and protecting it by limiting the right to sue for defamation did not violate Article 6.

17.8.3 Election restrictions

Freedom of expression can be restricted in the context of elections. The aim is to achieve a 'level playing field' on which political parties can set the political agenda at election time, present their policies, and compete for votes. The law can be used to try to ensure that, at election time, the political agenda is not hijacked by wealthy and powerful pressure groups. This is a complex matter. In the United Kingdom:

- there is a complete ban on the broadcasting (TV and radio) of paid-for political advertisements but no restrictions on press and poster political advertising (indeed, such advertising receives less regulation than ordinary commercial advertising);

- registered political parties have the right to make party political and party election broadcasts;

- at election times there are strict limits on expenditure at the constituency level—the amounts are quite small and, generally, only the candidates and their agents can spend money. Third parties who wish to spend money to influence an election in a particular constituency are limited to £500. National expenditures (e.g. on poster campaigns) are restricted but the limits are quite high (both political parties and third parties could spend up to about £20m if they campaigned throughout the United Kingdom).

Political advertising

The complete ban on broadcast political advertising was upheld by the English courts in *R v Radio Authority ex parte Bull* [1997] 2 All ER 561. This involved advertising by Amnesty International aimed at promoting human rights, specifically in the context of Rwanda. However, in *VgT Verein gegen Tierfabriken v Switzerland* (2002) 34 EHRR 4, a similar ban was held to violate Article 10: a complete ban prevented political speech by an animal charity, by no means powerful, that was seeking to counter claims made in commercial advertising by the meat industry.

Despite this case, UK law has retained (in sections 319 and 321(2) Communications Act 2003) the outright ban on broadcast political advertising. The minister introducing the bill acknowledged, under section 19 HRA, that it might, on this point, not be compatible with Convention rights (see Chapter 4, section 4.9.2).

 CASE CLOSE-UP

R (Animal Defenders International) v _Secretary of State for Culture, Media and Sport_ [2008] UKHL 15

ADI, an animal charity, campaigning to change animal welfare law, was prevented, under the Communications Act 2003, from using broadcast adverts to promote its 'My Mate's a Primate' campaign aimed at raising public awareness of the treatment of primates. Despite the similarities with the *VgT* case, the House of Lords refused a declaration of incompatibility and upheld the ban. The sole issue was whether the clear and complete statutory ban was proportionate. It was held that:

- the ban went no further than was necessary to achieve the important purpose in a democracy of fair elections that are not determined by money;

- there was no practical way of achieving this purpose by a more flexible rule which would, for example, allow advocacy on social issues by pressure groups (the policy could be hijacked by powerful interests);

- a high level of deference was owed to Parliament on such an issue which affects the processes of British democracy.

In *Animal Defenders v UK* (2013) 57 EHRR 21, a Grand Chamber held that the legislation did not violate Article 10. The legislation was within the UK's margin of appreciation. Of particular significance was the care with which Parliament had considered the issue and balanced the various interests.

DISCUSSION TOPIC

The *Animal Defenders* case confirms that pressure groups representing the poor, the marginal, and the dispossessed are unable to pursue political campaigns aimed at changes in the law or government policy through TV advertising (probably the most effective form of advertising). Is this a necessary consequence of maintaining a fair democracy in which all voices are equal or is it an undesirable constraint on political life?

CASE CLOSE-UP

Core Issues Trust v Transport for London [2014] EWCA Civ 34.

TfL had rules allowing it to refuse bus adverts which could cause widespread or serious offence or which concerned matters of political controversy or sensitivity. They accepted an advert from Stonewall, a gay rights group, ('Some People Are Gay – Get Over It') but rejected a counter-advert from Core Issues, an evangelical group concerned with sexuality ('Not Gay! Ex Gay, Post Gay and proud – get over it'). On the issue of the ban's compatibility with Article 10 the Court of Appeal accepted that, despite the protection of Article 10(1) for expression which 'offends, shocks and disturbs', the interference was for a legitimate purpose (including protecting the Article 8 rights of gay people) and proportionate—given the prominence of the advert, its capacity to stimulate homophobic views and the fact that the Trust had other ways to promote its views.

Speaking *obiter* the judges disagreed on whether it was right to have accepted the original Stonewall advert.

Party political broadcasts

Who has the last word on the content of party political broadcasts in the UK? Is it the political parties or the broadcaster? The issue arose, under the HRA, in *Pro-Life Alliance* v *BBC*.

CASE CLOSE-UP

Pro-Life Alliance v BBC [2003] UKHL 23

The Pro-Life Alliance was entitled to a Party Election Broadcast and proposed to use the opportunity to broadcast graphic and disturbing images of abortions. The BBC, which has a legal responsibility not to broadcast matter which offends 'taste and decency', prohibited the broadcast of the images even though, normally, political parties control the content of election broadcasts. The courts were divided. The Court of Appeal held that the BBC had indulged in unlawful censorship; the House of Lords, by a majority, found for the BBC and decided that the broadcaster had simply exercised the discretion it was allowed over these matters by the law.

- The general rule (here in the BBC's Licence and Agreement with the government) that matters offensive to taste and decency should not be broadcast, was not itself tested against Article 10 (it might well have proved justifiable under Article 10(2)).

- In issue, rather, was the way the BBC had put the rule into effect. A majority of the House of Lords deferred to the broadcaster's decision on this matter. The court's job was just to ensure that the broadcasters had thought about freedom of expression and not behaved eccentrically. This was in stark contrast to the Court of Appeal, which imposed its own view of what freedom of speech required.

- Critics of the case suggest the House of Lords did not do enough to uphold freedom of speech. This was political speech at election time and it was also speech that was restricted just because it was thought shocking and disturbing. Article 10 is supposed to give a high priority to protecting such speech. Supporters of the decision argue that Parliament had approved the principle that decisions on taste and decency should be taken by the broadcasters and not the courts. The House of Lords had merely upheld this principle.

- The BBC did not object to the message but to the particular way in which the Pro-Life Alliance chose to express itself. Critics of the decision argue that not enough weight was given to the principle, found in the Strasbourg case law, that Article 10 protects not just what a person wants to say but must also allow people to express themselves in the way they think appropriate.

▣ BIGGER PICTURE

Critical articles on this important case include Barendt, E. 'Free Speech and Abortion' [2003] *Public Law* (Winter) 580–591. Supportive articles include Geddes, A. 'What Future for Political Advertising on the United Kingdom's Television Screens?' [2002] *Public Law* (Winter) 615–625—commenting on the Court of Appeal's decision.

The importance at election times of allowing free speech about candidates by other candidates has been recognised by the High Court in *Culnane* v *Morris* [2005] EWHC 2438 (QB). However, UK election law (in the Representation of the People Act 1983) creates certain offences dealing with conduct of elections and these can include 'free speech' offences such as undue influence (e.g. of a spiritual kind, see *Erlam* v *Rehman* M/350/14 QBD) and impugning the personal character, as distinct from the political views, of the opponent. These cases are dealt with by an Election Court whose judgments can be reviewed by the High Court. In *Watkins* v *Woolas* [2010] EWHC 3169, for example, the candidate linked his opponent with terrorist groups. This was taken to be an unjustified impugning of his personal character (suggesting he was a man who condoned violence) and the election offence was made out. The High Court, in *Woolas*, reviewing the election court's judgment, found the procedure to be compatible with Article 10.

17.8.4 **Criticising politicians and defamation**

The importance of political speech means that the law may restrict the right of a public body to protect its reputation by an action for defamation (libel or slander). To succeed in such an action, a public body may have to prove that the speaker who made the defamatory statement (e.g. a newspaper) was motivated by malice. This is because the public body may be met by a rule of law that denies it the right to bring an action to protect its reputation in the absence of malice (the principle was adopted in England and Wales in *Derbyshire County Council* v *Times Newspapers* [1993] AC 534, and extended to political parties in *Goldsmith* v *Bhoyrul* [1998] QB 459). Or it may be that individuals (elected officials, for example, who are not covered by the rule in *Derbyshire* and may seek to protect their reputations) who sue newspapers are met with the defence of qualified privilege, which, again, requires proof of malice (see *Reynolds* v *Times Newspapers*, discussed in Chapter 22, section 22.3).

THINKING POINT

Are the courts right to reject the view that this qualified privilege should also apply to criticism of major commercial corporations—see *Jameel* v *Wall Street Journal* [2006] UKHL 44, para 27 and *Steel and Morris* v *United Kingdom*, section 17.7.1, para 94.

The justification for restricting the legal rights of politicians or public bodies to sue for defamation lies in the protection of freedom of speech. It is too easy for those in power to inhibit or 'chill' freedom of speech by using the law against their critics.

Under the Convention the issue is not clear cut. The Convention upholds the need to ensure that politicians and political bodies can be effectively and robustly criticised (e.g. *Lingens* v *Austria* (1986) 8 EHRR 407). Nevertheless, it is also an accepted principle that politicians and public figures do not lose their other Convention rights, such as their right to respect for private life, under Article 8, and their right to protect their reputation. Cases often involve a court seeking a fair balance between the Article 8 rights of a public figure and the rights of the media to freedom of expression (see, for example, *von Hannover* v *Germany* (2005) 40 EHRR 1).

For the Court, the proportionality of defamation proceedings brought by politicians may depend on whether it is a statement of 'fact' or 'opinion' that is objected to. Statements of opinion about politicians are much more strongly protected by Article 10.

In *Lindon* v *France* (2008) 46 EHRR 35, for instance, Jean-Marie Le Pen (the leader of a nationalist, some say neo-fascist, political party in France) had successfully sued the writers of a novel in which he was a named character to whom violently racist sentiments were attributed. The ECtHR (by a majority with strong dissents) held there was no violation of Article 10. An important part of its reasoning was that the novel had gone far beyond opinion and fiction and was, in effect, making unproven factual statements about the real politician.

DISCUSSION TOPIC

Politicians and the media

Is the cause of democracy advanced or retarded by legal rules that give politicians and public officials lesser protection from the unfair, untrue, or unreasonable criticism of others?

The cause of democracy is advanced because:

- Politicians exercise power and they often have considerable resources at their disposal. They should not be able to use the law to prevent criticisms of their actions.
- They accept and enjoy the rewards of power and public life and as such they should be prepared to accept public criticism.
- Unlike most people, politicians are likely to be part of a representative assembly and have access to the media. They are therefore able to answer their critics. Political argument should take place in such places rather than in the courts.

The cause of democracy is retarded because:

- Politicians are normally trying to serve the public as best they can and should not be subject to damaging accusations of fact or slurs on their reputations which they are unable to refute.
- In a democracy we should encourage people to enter public life and serve their country or community; the threat of unfounded criticism and attack is likely to be a deterrent.

17.8.5 **Immigration control**

Article 10 is relevant where the authorities (the Home Secretary in the UK) refuse entry to a foreign politician or activist (under immigration or anti-terrorism law). This clearly involves an interference not just with the freedom of expression of the person involved but also with the right of the inviters, and other members of the public, whose right to receive the ideas and also to experience the political presence of the person involved is limited.

Usually this is done in relation to persons holding violent or extreme views. In *R (Farrakhan)* v *Secretary of State for the Home Department* [2002] EWCA Civ 606, the exclusion of the leader of the Nation of Islam was held to be compatible with Article 10. Wide deference was shown to the Home Secretary on the issue of the need for the ban to prevent disorder and to maintain peaceful relations between the Jewish and Muslim citizens in the UK (rightly or wrongly Farrakhan was associated with anti-Semitic views.)

However in *R (Lord Carlile)* v *Secretary of State for the Home Department* [2014] UKSC 60, the UKSC accepted that, in the context of the case, it was a proportionate restriction of the rights of MPs to receive information to prevent a peaceful and democratic Iranian dissident politician from entering the country. The reason was the need to protect the UK's fragile diplomatic relationship with Iran.

At the heart of both these judgments is the 'deference' to be shown to the executive in this context. This matter is discussed in Chapter 4.

 THINKING POINT

Consider both *Farrakhan* and *Carlile* and compare with *Pro-Life Alliance* (section 17.8.3). Do these cases suggest the courts are properly protecting freedom of expression?

17.9 The limits to political speech: hate speech, racism, and incitement

The extent of tolerance of intolerant political speech is one of the ongoing dilemmas of a liberal society. Article 10(1) covers political speech which disturbs, shocks, or offends. Therefore, if it is legitimate under the Convention to restrict political speech, something more than the speech being merely offensive etc. must be at stake. Restrictions must, of course, meet the tests of Article 10(2). The test for being 'prescribed by law' is normally satisfied if the suppressing laws are formulated by statute. Often, the suppression of such speech can have the aim of preventing 'disorder or crime' or protecting 'the rights of others'. Compatibility with Article 10 then depends on the proportionality of any ban in the circumstances of the case.

17.9.1 Political outcomes which would violate human rights

One issue is the extent to which political parties and others are free to advocate the passing of laws which, if they were brought into effect, would create a society in which important human rights would be violated. The ECtHR has shown itself willing to uphold bans on, for example, Islamist political parties in Turkey, which, if they came to power, might bring about such a state of affairs.

> **CROSS REFERENCE**
> This topic is discussed in more detail in Chapter 18, section 18.7.2.

17.9.2 Advocacy of political violence

Article 10 does not protect speech which aims at inciting violence or hatred. The reaction of the Turkish government to the insurrection against it by part of its Kurdish population has given rise to a large case law on the issue. Whether speech or other expression is an incitement depends not just on the dictionary meaning of the words but also on the context. Issues such as:

- who is speaking (whether in an official capacity or not),
- the nature of the medium (suppression of the mass media may be easier to justify than of a small circulation magazine),
- the area in which the words will be read or listened to,

are the kinds of issues that are relevant to a context-dependent judgment.

17.9.3 Hate speech

Article 10 ECHR does not expressly require the suppression of hate speech, such as racist speech (unlike Article 20 ICCPR, which requires the prohibition by law of 'advocacy of national, racial or religious hatred that constitutes incitement to discrimination, hostility or violence'). Nevertheless, in *Jersild* v *Denmark* (1995) 19 EHRR 1, the ECtHR held that the expression of vicious racist sentiments would not be protected by Article 10. They were likely to go beyond being merely disturbing, shocking, or offensive.

> There can be no doubt that the remarks [made by racists during a television programme] were more than insulting to members of the targeted group and did not enjoy the protection of Article 10.
>
> (para 35)

Jersild was about the prosecution of journalists who had allowed a racist group to broadcast their views as part of a programme on Danish television dealing with the rise of racism in that country.

HRA

In England and Wales, Part III of the Public Order Act 1986 (POA 1986) creates a range of offences dealing with incitements to racial hatred in various contexts. Legislation dealing with football hooliganism criminalises racist chanting. Under the Crime and Disorder Act 1998, some offences can be more severely punished if there is evidence of a racial motive and, since 2001, an anti-religious motive. All these Acts criminalise expression and must be interpreted consistently with Article 10.

Parts 3 and 3A of the POA 1986 make the 'stirring up' of religious hatred and hatred on grounds of sexual orientation by threatening words, behaviour, or displays, a crime. The links between religion and ethical and moral issues mean that criticism of religion is not necessarily unreasonable. Section 29J POA 1986 therefore makes the protection of freedom of expression a statutory principle: the offence of stirring up religious hatred is not committed by those who express 'antipathy, dislike, ridicule, insult or abuse' of religions and their adherents. There is no similar defence in respect of race or sexual orientation.

Section 5 POA 1986 allows, amongst other things, for the prosecution of a person who causes 'harassment, alarm or distress' by using 'insulting words or behaviour'. This crime, therefore, can be committed without there being any threat of violence and on the basis of words or other expressions alone. The provision has been widely used in the context of aggressive but non-violent demonstrations and racist or other offensive forms of speech and signs made for political purposes. There is a defence under section 5(3) for the defendant to show that his or her conduct was reasonable, and at this point the fact that they were otherwise lawfully exercising their rights to freedom of expression under Article 10 can be relevant.

- In *Percy* v *DPP* [2001] EWHC 1125, P burnt the US flag, seen by some Americans as a desecration, as part of a protest against US defence policy: her conviction was quashed as being a disproportionate interference with freedom of expression.

- In *Norwood* v *DPP* [2003] EWHC 1564 (Admin), the defendant was convicted under section 5 POA 1986 for an ordinary public order offence aggravated by an anti-religious motive. He had displayed posters advocating 'Islam out of Britain' and associating Islam with the attacks on the World Trade Center. The Administrative Court held that the prosecutions were compatible with Article 10. Norwood's application to the ECtHR was rejected by applying Article 17 (see Chapter 7, section 7.3)—his expression was aimed at undermining the rights of others. The posters involved a 'general, vehement attack against a religious group, linking the group as a whole with terrorism'. It was 'incompatible with basic Convention values of tolerance, social peace and non-discrimination' (*Norwood* v *United Kingdom* (2005) 40 EHRR SE 11).

- In *Hammond* v *DPP* [2004] EWHC 69, the conviction, also under section 5 POA 1986, of a religious campaigner who had preached against gay rights, thereby stirring up a hostile reaction, was also held to be compatible with Article 10.

Norwood and *Hammond* raise the issue of the value of Article 10. The expressions in issue did not incite violence. They were, no doubt, offensive, but offensive words about public affairs are supposed to enjoy protection under Article 10(1). The High Court held both convictions were justified in terms of Article 10(2) as proportionate ways of protecting the rights of others. The danger is that English courts may be creating a right not to be offended, which renders the protection of offensive speech under Article 10(1) of little worth. On the other hand, supporters of the judgments could say that the morality behind human rights law clearly stands against forms of discrimination that are based on assumptions that other people, their identity, or their beliefs are in one sense or another inferior. The recognition of the dignity of others, on which human rights is based, involves respect for others as equals, and applying section 5 in this way puts that important moral principle into effect. A decent society requires laws such as this: there is no right to offend.

17.9.4 **Morally worthless speech**

Convention case law on Article 10 suggests that some expression is outside the protection of Article 10 (and therefore can be subject to criminal penalties) because it is morally worthless. It is worthless in the sense that it is expression which contradicts the basic values on which the Convention is based and may involve the denial of clearly established facts. Article 17 can be invoked against such speech. Under Article 17 a person cannot claim Convention rights in order to suppress the rights of others. In *Lehideux and Isomi* v *France* (2000) 30 EHRR 665, for example, the ECtHR accepted that there is a 'category of clearly established historical facts— such as the Holocaust—whose negation or revision would be removed from the protection of Article 10 by Article 17' (para 47).

▶ **CROSS REFERENCE**
Article 17 is discussed in Chapter 7, section 7.3.

Holocaust denial is an offence is some countries. In numerous cases (see *Perincek* v *Switzerland* (below), paras 209 and 210 for examples) the Strasbourg authorities (Commission and from 1998 the Court) have found applications from those prosecuted for Holocaust denial to be inadmissible. This is particularly so in relation to countries in which the Holocaust remains an important cultural memory. An example is *Remer* v *Germany* App 25096/94, admissibility decision of 6 September 1995, where the Commission found there could be no breach of Article 10 in respect of Holocaust denial; the speech was unprotected because of Article 17.

Legitimate debate about controversial and sensitive matters is protected by Article 10 so long as the debate does not involve attitudes, assumptions, and the assertion of falsehoods which are incompatible with the basic values underlying the Convention. (The reassessment of the reputation of Marshall Pétain, the leader of the Vichy government in France, which, during the Second World War collaborated with the Nazis, was legitimate, see *Lehideux and Isomi* v *France*, discussed earlier.)

The distinction between morally worthless speech and legitimate debate on controversial matters can be hard to draw.

 CASE CLOSE-UP

Perincek v *Switzerland* **App 27510/08, Grand Chamber judgment of 15 October 2015**

P was prosecuted in Switzerland for denying that the killings of Armenians by Turks in the late nineteenth and early twentieth centuries was 'genocide'. He was convicted for 'seeking to justify genocide', an offence under Swiss law.

A Grand Chamber held, 10–7, that there had been a violation of Article 10. The Court:

- Declined to rule on whether there had been genocide—such a ruling was not within its jurisdiction.

- Held that the prosecution was lawful and that it pursued a legitimate purpose—this was protecting the rights of others, namely the right to dignity of Armenians and their forefathers.

- On whether the conviction was necessary in a democratic society, the Court saw itself as balancing the right to expression of the applicant with the Article 8 right to 'private life' of Armenians (private life including ideas of identity, self-worth, and self-confidence as well as the reputation of ancestors).

- The balancing came down in favour of the applicant. Though denying genocide, his statements were not incitements to violence nor expressions of contempt nor indirectly these things by innuendo. Furthermore, Switzerland's interest in the case was not based on its own history and culture; it was under no international obligation to prosecute. Finally the impact of P's statements on the Article 8 rights of the Armenian community was slight.

Strong dissents included the view that it was within the jurisdiction of the Court to declare these killings to have been genocide.

▶ CROSS REFERENCE

Perincek also refers to Articles 16 and 17—see Chapter 7.

17.10 Freedom of expression and Article 8

The right to freedom of expression, especially freedom of the media, can often lead to challenges brought by those who feel that their privacy, protected by Article 8, has been violated. These issues are explored in Chapter 22, section 22.5.

17.11 Freedom of expression and contempt of court

Legal limits on the way in which trials and matters before the courts are reported involve one of the most significant interferences with freedom of expression, especially media freedom. The issue is considered in Chapter 12, section 12.8.2, Contempt of court.

17.12 Artistic expression

There is no expressed protection for 'artistic' speech in Article 10 (unlike Article 19(2) ICCPR, which protects a person's freedom of expression 'orally, in writing or in print, in the form of art, or through any other media of his choice'). Nevertheless, the ECtHR has made it clear that the protection of Article 10(1) extends to artistic works: both the freedom to create artistic works and the freedom to disseminate them through exhibitions and other methods. In *Müller v Switzerland* (1998) 13 EHRR 212, the ECtHR understood artistic expression as affording 'the opportunity to take part in the public exchange of cultural, political and social information and ideas of all kinds'.

Works of art that have overt political and social themes can enjoy the high degree of protection given to political speech. However, Article 10 also protects works that have no social or political purpose and which aim, for example, simply to be beautiful. However, works without an overt social and political purpose may have a lower degree of protection. In other words, absent a clear political purpose, it is easier for the state to show that an act of censorship or restriction is justified in terms of Article 10(2).

Work which is merely pornographic and makes no claim to be otherwise enjoys little protection under the Convention. The problem here is that the right to freedom of artistic expression under Article 10 may give little assistance to artists whose work is vulnerable to state claims that it is indecent or pornographic but who are seeking, through artistic production, to challenge conventional conceptions of 'art' or conventional moralities (for a statement of the issue see *Belfast City Council* v *Miss Behavin' Ltd* [2007] UKHL 19, para 38, Baroness Hale).

Any such bans on artistic work must meet the tests in Article 10(2). First, a ban must be 'prescribed by law'. The vagueness of terms like 'obscenity' or 'indecency' might, in principle, create a problem, though this has not generally occurred.

 CASE CLOSE-UP

S and G v United Kingdom **App 17634/91, Commission admissibility decision of 2 September 1991**

An artist and gallery owner had displayed sculptures in an art gallery that included modelled heads to which earrings made from freeze-dried human foetuses had been attached. They were prosecuted for the common law offence of outraging public decency. The Commission of Human Rights found that the application was manifestly unfounded and inadmissible.

The offence of outraging public decency, although a common law offence and vague when considered in abstract terms, had been defined by the UK courts with sufficient clarity for it to meet the Convention standards for 'law' of 'foreseeability' and 'accessibility'.

The prosecution was a proportionate way of achieving the purpose of protection of morals.

Second, any ban must be to further one of the purposes listed in Article 10(2). In the context of art works and alleged obscenity or indecency, the ECtHR has accepted that bans and prosecutions, etc. can be for 'the protection of . . . morals'.

Third, therefore, any such ban or prosecution must be 'necessary in a democratic society'. In the context of expression that is banned or prosecuted in order to protect morals, the ECtHR has allowed a wide margin of appreciation (at least since *Handyside* v *United Kingdom* (1979–80) 1 EHRR 737, one of its earliest cases). The ECtHR does not accept that there is a tension between its insistence that expression is protected by Article 10, even if (in the often repeated formula) it 'offends, shocks or disturbs', and giving states a wide margin of appreciation over the banning of works on the grounds that they are seriously offensive though not otherwise harmful. Nevertheless, context and changing social standards are very important.

In *Müller* v *Switzerland* (1988) 13 EHRR 212, a group of artists and others were prosecuted for obscenity offences. Some of the pictures depicted, in large and graphic scale, acts of sodomy, fellatio, bestiality, and also erect penises. The ECtHR held that, in the circumstances (the pictures were displayed in a free and public exhibition) the prosecutions were within the state's margin of appreciation.

In *Vereinigung Bildender Kunstler* v *Austria* (2008) 47 EHRR 5, an injunction preventing the public display of a picture containing sexually explicit caricatures of well-known people, including a prominent politician, was a violation of Article 10.

Prosecutions in England and Wales under, for example, the Obscene Publications Act 1959, are likely to be compatible with Article 10 given the wide margin of appreciation and the lack of any public interest served by publication (see, for example *R* v *Perrin* [2002] EWCA Crim 747).

17.13 Commercial expression

Commercial speech, such as that found in catalogues or advertising, is capable of protection under Article 10(1). However, the ECtHR accepts that states have a very wide margin of appreciation over the need for restrictions. Speech which is entirely or predominantly commercial enjoys only a low level of protection: it is relatively easy for the authorities to show that the public good requires restriction on speech (see *Markt Intern Verlag* v *Germany* (1990) 12 EHRR 161, para 33). If commercial speech also has political overtones, then it will enjoy greater protection, as in *Barthold* v *Germany* (1985) 7 EHRR 383, see section 17.7.1.

Restrictions on commercial advertising are also, usually, compatible with Article 10 so long as the public interest served by the ban outweighs the interest of the public in hearing about the products in issue.

In *R (British American Tobacco)* v *Secretary of State for Health* [2004] EWHC 2493 (Admin), the ban on tobacco advertising in the United Kingdom was upheld by the Administrative Court. It satisfied the need for proportionality where restrictions on human rights are concerned. Proportionality was measured against the wider margin of appreciation left to the national authorities by the ECtHR.

 Summary

- Freedom of speech is protected in both common law and as a Convention right.

- Article 10 of the Convention involves asking, first, whether some form of expression is protected by Article 10(1) and then whether any restriction on expression can be justified in terms of Article 10(2).

- Under the Convention, the highest degree of protection is accorded to speech and other expressions which concern political and public affairs. Media freedom is protected.

- Nevertheless, Article 10(2) permits restriction to freedom of expression on various grounds, such as national security and protecting the authority of the judiciary; also racists and others may be denied protection for their speech under Article 17.

- Artistic and other forms of expression, including commercial expression, are protected, although on moral issues, such as laws on obscenity, states enjoy a wide margin of appreciation.

? Self-test questions

1. What is included in the idea of expression that goes beyond speech?

2. What is meant by 'prior restraint' and what significance does it have in respect of protecting freedom of expression under Article 10?

3. What rights are protected by Article 10(1)?

4. Give examples of the 'rights of others' in the context of reasons for restricting freedom of expression which may be compatible with Article 10.

5. Identify a case in which the importance of the media is recognised and give the reasons for that importance.

6. What is the general approach of the ECtHR to domestic bans on films etc. on the grounds that they are obscene?

7. In *Observer and Guardian v UK* (the *Spycatcher* case, discussed earlier) which part of the injunctions in issue were upheld as being compatible with Article 10?

8. What approach is taken by the ECtHR regarding restrictions, in domestic law, on expenditure on advertisements, pamphlets, etc. during elections?

9. On what grounds might speech be considered so worthless that it is outside the protection of Article 10?

10. Give two cases involving the cases where journalists and others have been punished or sued for criticising politicians—consider the approach taken by the ECtHR.

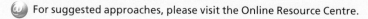 For suggested approaches, please visit the Online Resource Centre.

? Exam questions

1. Suppose that a local government department bans all officials from wearing any badge or insignia with racist overtones, and does so, as required under the Race Relations Act 1976 (amended in 2000), to 'promote good race relations'. If the ban is challenged, how would the issue be approached by an English court in respect of considering its compatibility with Article 10?

2. Discuss the approach taken by the ECtHR and the courts in the United Kingdom to the borderline between restraints on political speech, protected by Article 10, which cannot be justified under Article 10(2), and restraints on such speech which can be justified. Consider, giving reasons, whether the courts have got the balance right.

For suggested approaches, please visit the Online Resource Centre.

Further reading

Barendt, E. *Freedom of Speech* (2001) Oxford: OUP

Davis, H. 'The Rights Approach to the Right to a Public Hearing' [2012] (Jan) *Public Law* 11–18

Khan, A. 'A "Right Not to be Offended" under Article 10(2) ECHR' [2012] 2 *EHRLR* 191–204

Lester, A, Pannick, D. and Herberg, J. (see Preface) Chapter 4, Article 10

Scott, A. 'A Monstrous and Unjustifiable Infringement? Political Expression and the Broadcasting Ban of Advocacy Advertising' (2003) 66 *MLR* 224–244

Schauer, F. *Freedom of Speech: A Philosophical Inquiry* (1982) Cambridge: CUP

18 Article 11: freedom of assembly and association

☐ LEARNING OBJECTIVES

● The right to peaceful assembly, including political meetings, marches and protests (Article 11(1)).

● The grounds on which the right to peaceful assembly can be legitimately interfered with, considered with reference to the law of public order in England and Wales.

● The right to freedom of association.

● The grounds on which the right to association can be legitimately interfered with.

● Trade unions.

● Restrictions on the political activity of public officials.

Article 11 Freedom of assembly and association

(1) Everyone has the right to freedom of peaceful assembly and to freedom of association with others, including the right to form and to join trade unions for the protection of his interests.

(2) No restrictions shall be placed on the exercise of these rights other than such as are prescribed by law and are necessary in a democratic society in the interests of national security or public safety, for the prevention of disorder or crime, for the protection of health or morals, for the protection of the reputation or rights of others. This article shall not prevent the imposition of lawful restrictions on the exercise of these rights by members of the armed forces, of the police or of the administration of the state.

Introduction

The burdens of austerity, the impact of the 'global economy' and free trade, the threats to the climate from global warming, the threat to the environment from 'fracking' and other industrial processes, opposition to war and military solutions in the Middle East—these are among the issues that many people feel are too important to be left to representative democracy. They are the subject of public protest, action, and organisation. Article 11 (along with Article 10) guarantees the right to do this so long as it is non-violent. But even non-violent demonstrations can have significant impact on the interests and rights of others, and so (like Articles 8, 9, and 10) it is a qualified right. The restriction or suppression of a demonstration is permitted so long as justified under the terms of Article 11(2).

18.1 Political rights and the Convention

CROSS REFERENCE

On democracy see Chapter 1, section 1.1.1 and Chapter 6, section 6.4.

Article 11 is one of the rights by which political freedom (the right to political action or to participate in public affairs) is secured under the Convention (see *R (Countryside Alliance) v AG* [2007] UKHL 52, paras 117–118, Baroness Hale). As such, it needs to be read and understood in the light of the Convention concept of democracy. The promotion of democracy is one of the aims of the Council of Europe and is central to the general philosophical justification of human rights. A 'democratic' political system is the only one acceptable under the Convention.

CROSS REFERENCE

Article 3 is discussed in Chapter 25.

The right to vote, and the right to stand for election and, if elected, to take one's seat is guaranteed in terms of Article 3 of the First Protocol.

But it would be a narrow conception of democracy (as merely a four- or five-yearly competition for votes by political elites) that was sufficiently encapsulated by those three rights. People need to pursue their political aims through extra-parliamentary means such as joining political parties and pressure groups, promoting their aims through various media, and by holding meetings and marches and taking part in demonstrations. This broader political freedom is protected in the Convention, in particular, by Article 10 (freedom of expression: see Chapter 17) and by Article 11. Like Article 10, Article 11 is understood to be fundamental to a democracy. The right to peaceful assembly and association can only be interfered with by laws or actions which aim to protect democracy. As with Article 10, assembly or association can involve promoting ideas and policies that 'disturb, shock and offend'. Both rights can be interfered with by state action which is lawful (in the Convention meaning of the term), for one of the legitimate purposes listed in Article 10(2) or 11(2), and proportionate.

It is not unusual that a case could be decided by both Article 10 or Article 11. Political marches, meetings, and demonstrations are protected under the Convention, and Article 11 has an important role to play in this. However, such activity can also be a type of expression and so within the scope of Article 10. It is not unusual that cases dealing with political demonstration are dealt with using Article 10. Any Article 11 claim is dismissed by the European Court of Human Rights (ECtHR) on the grounds that no new issues are raised which have not already been raised under Article 10 (see, for example, *Steel v United Kingdom* (1999) 28 EHRR 603, discussed in Chapter 17, section 17.7.1).

In such a case the courts will normally apply one Article only. This is the '*lex specialis*' and whether it is Article 10 or 11 will depend on the facts. Only passing reference is made to the other Article unless separate issues arise.

18.2 The structure of Article 11

Like Articles 8–10, Article 11 has a two-paragraph structure. A court (including the ECtHR) dealing with a case in which it is claimed that Article 11 is involved, must first decide whether the facts disclose an issue covered by the terms 'peaceful assembly' or 'association'. Then a court must decide whether the assembly or association has been interfered with. If so, finally, a court must decide whether the state has shown the interference to be justified in terms of Article 11(2).

- Any interference must be 'prescribed by law'.
- Any interference must be for one of the purposes listed in paragraph 2, and not for any others.
- Any interference must be 'necessary' in the sense of being a proportionate exercise of power.

> **CROSS REFERENCE**
> This basic structure is common with Articles 8, 9, 10 and is discussed in Chapter 14.

18.3 Peaceful assembly: meetings, marches, and demonstrations

18.3.1 **A fundamental democratic right**

Article 11 protects only the right to peaceful assembly. This right is recognised by the ECtHR as a 'fundamental right in a democratic society … one of the foundations of such a society' (*Adali v Turkey* App 38187/97, judgment of 31 March 2005, confirmed in *Kudrevicius*, discussed later in this chapter). As such it must not be applied narrowly or restrictively. It applies to both meetings and marches whether they take place on private land or in public places including highways.

18.3.2 **Peaceful assembly**

It applies only to 'peaceful assembly'. This excludes demonstrations where the organisers have violent intentions. However, a person does not lose the protection of Article 11 just because of the violent actions of others. The exercise of a right to, specifically, peaceful assembly must be judged by the conduct of the applicant. In *Ezelin v France* (1991) 14 EHRR 362, for example, there was a breach of Article 11 when a French lawyer was disciplined by his professional body for not disassociating himself from a demonstration when it began to turn disorderly. The Commission, whose view was accepted by the Court, held that:

> generally speaking, an individual does not cease to enjoy the right to freedom of peaceful assembly simply because sporadic violence or other punishable acts take place in the course of the assembly, if he himself remains peaceful in his intentions and behaviour.

> (confirmed by the Court in R *Ziliberberg* App 61821/00, admissibility decision of 4 May 2004)

The boundary between peaceful and non-peaceful protest is hard to draw. A peaceful protest is where organisers and participants do not have 'violent intentions' (*Stankov* v *Bulgaria* App 29221/95, judgment of 2 October 2001, para 77). The Convention does not confine 'peaceful' to meetings etc. which are entirely based on rational persuasion conducted by words alone. Non-violent but obstructive behaviour can be peaceful. The distinction is hard to draw and is likely to depend on the facts.

Q | CASE CLOSE-UP

Kudrevicius v Lithuania App 37553/05, Grand Chamber judgment of 15 October 2015

Farmers took part in a demonstration to protest against the fall of prices and the lack of state subsidies for agriculture. They were permitted to hold a demonstration in various places but, in breach of these permits they blocked major highways, in some cases for two days. This caused significant disruption to others but the demonstration was non-violent.

A Grand Chamber held that there had been no breach of Article 11. The applicants Article 11 rights had been interfered with but the interference was justified under Article 11(2).

The Grand Chamber, confirming earlier cases, made it clear that merely because there is interference with the ordinary life of others (by obstructing traffic, as in the case), a demonstrator does not lose his or her Article 11 rights. The authorities must balance this interference against preserving the effectiveness of the right to peaceful assembly, and in doing so the authorities must show 'a certain degree of tolerance towards peaceful gatherings if the freedom of assembly guaranteed by Article 11 of the Convention is not to be deprived of all substance' (para 154). The 'degree' of tolerance depends on the circumstances. In this respect the authorities are entitled to lay down reasonable conditions which the demonstrators should obey. If the demonstrators intentionally refuse to obey these conditions then the authorities have a wide margin of appreciation over what steps to take (para 156).

These principles concern the issue of whether Article 11 is engaged at all (i.e. that the assembly is 'peaceful'). If it is engaged, the attention then shifts to whether there was a justified interference with the applicant's freedom of assembly under the terms of Article 11(2).

Of course, whether peaceful or not, demonstrators continue to enjoy other Convention rights such as Article 5 (liberty), Article 2 (the right to life—which is not violated if lawful, potentially lethal, force is used to quell a 'riot or insurrection') and Article 3 (the right not to suffer inhuman or degrading treatment, for example at the hands of the police or others). Article 17, however, prevents demonstrators from using their Convention rights to undermine the rights of others.

18.4 Positive duties

Given the fundamental nature of the right of assembly in a democracy, the question has arisen whether states have positive duties to promote democratic politics (e.g. by making facilities available for meetings etc.) and to protect those taking part in demonstrations. There is little case law on the former. However, states do have positive duties to protect those taking part in meetings from the violence and intimidation of those opposed to them. In *Plattform Ärzte für das Leben v Austria* (1988) 13 EHRR 204, a group of 'pro-life' doctors alleged that there was insufficient police protection of their march from a 'pro-choice' counter-demonstration. On the facts there was no violation of the Convention, but the ECtHR did say that:

> Genuine, effective freedom of peaceful assembly cannot … be reduced to a mere duty on the part of the state not to interfere: a purely negative conception would not be compatible with the object and purposes of Article 11. Like Article 8, Article 11 sometimes requires positive measures to be taken even in the sphere of relations between individuals, if need be. (para 31)

However, the duty is not absolute—there is no duty to ensure that the peaceful assembly can take place. Rather, it is to take 'reasonable and appropriate' measures, over which the states have a wide margin of appreciation. Positive duties include, for instance, the duty to ensure the safety of citizens and the 'smooth conduct of the event' (*Kudrevicius*, section 18.3.2, paras 158–160).

The duty to take positive measures requires states to try to inhibit the 'opposition veto' by which those making a lawful protest might be stopped by a threat of violence coming from those who oppose the demonstration. In order to keep the peace it might be easier to detain a person lawfully making a speech rather than confront a violent mob. Under Article 11 any such decision by the police has to give proper weight to the Article 11 rights of the individuals involved. The English law on 'breach of the peace' used to focus on maintaining order. Under the influence of Article 11 (and Article 10) the law has begun to shift.

 CASE CLOSE-UP

Redmond-Bate v DPP [2000] HRLR 249

A group of female Christians were preaching on the steps of Wakefield Cathedral. They began to irritate tourists and passers by. The police, fearing a breach of the peace, took action against the women. The High Court held that the arrest of the women for breach of the peace was unlawful under common law, partly as measured against the women's Convention rights.

The importance of this case is:

- Its stress on the need for the police to consider the reasonableness of the actions of the claimant.

- The police must do more than take the easiest way of preserving the peace. It is necessary to consider, for example, the source of the threat of violence and whether the claimant's actions are really provocative.

- If people are exercising their Convention rights, of free expression or peaceful assembly, then there is likely to be a presumption that their actions are reasonable and it is unreasonable for a person to respond violently.

- If, on the other hand, demonstrators are preventing others from lawful activities, the possibility of violence is likely to be more reasonable and Convention rights less likely to offer a defence to the demonstrators (see, for example, *Nicol and Selvanayagam v DPP* [1996] Crim LR 318, which, though decided before the Human Rights Act 1998 (HRA), nevertheless refers to Convention rights).

BIGGER PICTURE

Local authorities in England and Wales have a statutory duty to make school and other premises available for election meetings, but whether there are broader positive duties is unclear. Over-broad refusals to allow political activity of any kind, at a local festival, for example, can already be unlawful exercises of power under common law, a point reinforced by Article 11 (see *R* v *Barnet LBC ex parte Johnson* (1990) 89 LGR 581 (QB)).

Positive duties are not absolute. Rights to demonstrate peacefully may, for example, be restricted in order to give recognition to the rights of others, such as property owners. This can be so even if the property owner controls a large shopping area which has, as it were, taken over the centre of a city (see *Appleby* v *United Kingdom* (2003) 37 EHRR 38).

DISCUSSION TOPIC

Should political activists have the right to protest and demonstrate if, in so doing, they interfere with the freedom of others and, perhaps, break laws or prevent activities which have been endorsed by the majority of the population through the process of electoral politics and representative government?

- Consider the concept of 'peaceful' in the idea of a peaceful assembly.
- Consider the 'rights of others' provision in Articles 10(2) and 11(2).
- Is there a difference between, on the one hand, interfering with people going about their ordinary daily tasks and, on the other hand, trying to prevent a lawful activity which the protestors oppose?
- Is there a difference (as some political theorists contend) between a range of issues which are appropriate for decision on the basis of majority votes (and so we should all accept the majority view as embodied in the law), and other more fundamental issues which are more like moral absolutes. If the law allows actions which are inconsistent with these 'moral absolutes' then, perhaps, law breaking by demonstrators or interfering with the freedom of others might be justified? If this distinction can be made, what examples might be given?

The legal (and also moral) limits to the rights of demonstrators are discussed by Lord Hoffmann in *R* v *Jones* [2006] UKHL 16, see paras 74–89.

18.5 Interference with rights

Any restrictions, by the police and other authorities, on the right to peaceful assembly and association, including the right to demonstrate, must be justified in terms of Articles 10(2) and 11(2).

> **CROSS REFERENCE**
>
> For 'law' see Chapter 6, section 6.2; for a summary in a political context see *Rekvényi v Hungary* (2000) 30 EHRR 519, para 34.

18.5.1 Is the restriction 'prescribed by law'?

Public order law often gives the police and magistrates wide discretionary powers. Such powers must be prescribed by law and not only be lawful under national law, but the national law must also fulfil the Convention requirements of being 'accessible' and 'foreseeable'.

In the context of meetings, marches, and demonstrations, the ECtHR takes a tolerant view of open-textured powers granting wide discretion.

In *Chorherr* v *Austria* (1994) 17 EHRR 358, the ECtHR accepted that a legal power to arrest for an offence of 'conduct likely to cause annoyance' was, in the circumstances, sufficiently precise.

By contrast, in *Hashman and Harrup* v *United Kingdom* (2000) 30 EHRR 241, the ECtHR held that the power of magistrates in the United Kingdom to bind over for 'good behaviour' failed the 'foreseeablity' test. (A person could agree to restrictions on their behaviour, not to take part in future demonstrations, for example, often as an alternative to a criminal conviction.) What good behaviour might require could not, in the view of the Court, be predicted by the person bound over. The distinction with other cases is that they refer, no matter how vaguely, to the effects of actions; good behaviour limits only conduct, irrespective of results.

18.5.2 Is the interference for a legitimate purpose

Police action against demonstrators must also be justified, under Article 11(2), as being for one of the purposes listed in Article 11(2). The 'prevention of disorder or crime' will normally be sufficient and easy to establish. In *Kudrevicius* (section 18.3.2), the ECtHR accepted that seeking to maintain an orderly flow of traffic was protecting 'the rights of others' (para 157).

18.5.3 Is the restriction 'necessary in a democratic society'

Such action must also be 'necessary in a democratic society'. This requires a judgment of proportionality. The issue will depend very much on the specific facts. The case law suggests that the Strasbourg authorities tend to give a wide margin of appreciation to states on whether there is a real threat of disorder.

In *Christians against Racism and Fascism* v *United Kingdom* App 8440/78 (1980) 21 DR 138, the applicants were unable to hold a non-controversial march because of a general ban on all marches imposed, under public order legislation, in order to stop a controversial racist march. UK law only permitted general bans in order to protect the political impartiality of the police and authorities. The Commission took the view that a general ban was only justified if necessary to prevent disorder, not just to protect official impartiality. On the facts, however, they held that the ban was proportionate.

18.6 English law and the Human Rights Act

18.6.1 Introduction

There is in the United Kingdom a long tradition of political dissent and protest which has, sometimes, been violent. The law needs to find an appropriate balance between allowing people to express their rights (political protest can involve both Article 11 (assembly) and Article 10 (expression)) and keeping the peace and protecting the rights of others which a demonstration may interfere with. In this the focus is largely on the police and their powers under both common law and statute (in particular the Public Order Act 1986 (POA 1986)). The police are a public authority under section 6 HRA and so can be proceeded against in court, under section 7 HRA, if they fail to act compatibly with Convention rights; alternatively a breach of Convention rights can be part of a defence or of some other cause of action.

18.6.2 Use of land

Any meeting, march, or process must, obviously, take place on land, which will be in the possession of someone: an individual, a corporate body, or a public authority. Likewise, if a person uses a highway for an obstructive or otherwise improper purpose, they lose their right to be there and the owner of the underlying land can seek a remedy, usually for trespass.

The courts are public authorities under section 6 HRA, and so an injunction must be compatible with Convention rights. Likewise, if the possessor of the land is a public authority (e.g. a local council) then its action in seeking a remedy must be compatible with the Convention. Clearly any injunction will interfere with peaceful assembly, so the issue of justification under Article 11(2) will be central. Injunctions and other judicial remedies have a well-established legal basis in English law, so the issue of legality is unlikely to be decisive. Likewise, one of the purposes for which interference with freedom of assembly is legitimate is to 'protect the rights … of others' and property rights come within this concept. It follows that the main focus of justification will be on the proportionality of any interference and this may involve some balancing of property rights with Convention rights.

In *Appleby* v *United* Kingdom (2003) 37 EHRR 38, an environmental pressure group sought to obtain signatures for a petition by setting up a stall in a shopping mall in the centre of Washington, in Tyne and Wear. The owners refused permission on the grounds of maintaining political neutrality. The ECtHR held that the property rights of the owners (Article 1 of the First Protocol) had to be taken into account. The political rights of the applicants had not been fully extinguished since there were other places where they could go to seek signatures. The Court did suggest that if there were no effective alternatives then, perhaps, the state would have positive duties to allow political activity.

In *City of London* v *Samede* [2012] EWCA Civ 160, the City of London successfully sought possession orders and injunctions in respect of land occupied (as part of the Occupy Movement) by S and others. The court agreed that S was exercising her rights under Articles 10 and 11; however, these Articles could not justify requiring a court to allow a permanent occupation. The importance of the issues behind the protest are relevant matters but not decisive. The court also agreed that case management powers could be used by a judge in future cases to limit the exposition of political views in the court.

18.6.3 Police powers: common law

In policing demonstrations, the police may exercise their power to take necessary steps in order to prevent an imminent 'breach of the peace'. These powers can include 'arrest or other action short of arrest' and extend to where the breach is 'about to occur'—*R (Laporte)* v *Chief Constable of Gloucester Constabulary* [2006] UKHL 55, para 29.

CROSS REFERENCE

Steel is discussed in Chapter 11, section 11.4.3; see also Chapter 20, section 20.1.2.

The general principle that a person may be detained for an apprehended or anticipated breach of the peace has been accepted as being compatible with Convention rights in *Steel* v *United Kingdom* (1999) 28 EHRR 603. In the court's view any concern that the power could be used arbitrarily (and therefore not lawfully in the Convention sense) had been met by a body of

English case law (such as *Redmond-Bate* v *DPP* [2000] HRLR 249 and *Nicol and Selvanayagam* v *DPP* [1996] Crim LR 318), which had clarified the way the power can be exercised in ways that gave proper recognition to Convention rights and made the exercise of the power, in the context of a political demonstration, sufficiently 'foreseeable' to satisfy the legality requirement on Article 11(2).

Of particular, more recent, importance is *R (Laporte)* v *Chief Constable of Gloucestershire* [2006] UKHL 55, which contains a full discussion of the history and development of the law on breach of the peace and which takes into account the requirements of Article 11. It makes it clear that it is not enough for the police to have reasonable grounds to apprehend a breach of the peace in the future; the threat to the peace must be also 'imminent', in the context of the demonstration. A court must consider the reasonableness of the police view of whether a threat is imminent (i.e. was there evidence upon which the police could reasonably form the view that a threat was imminent) and not substitute its own view on the matter (*R (McClure and Moos)* v *CPM* [2012] EWCA Civ 12).

18.6.4 Control of meetings, marches, and demonstrations: statutory powers

Police powers and the HRA

In addition to their common law powers, police officers have a range of statutory powers dealing with the control of meetings, marches, and demonstrations. These powers, of course, should be interpreted (under section 3 HRA) so that (unless impossible) they can only authorise (and make lawful) police actions which are compatible with Article 11 and other Convention rights. Declarations of incompatibility (under section 4 HRA) have not been necessary in the public order context and so it can be presumed that the legislation (e.g. POA 1986) is capable of being exercised in Convention compliant ways and that police officers will not have the defence under section 6(2) HRA that they are putting into effect an incompatible but still valid statute.

CROSS REFERENCE

Sections 3, 4, and 6 HRA are discussed in Chapter 4.

Prior notification, section 11 POA 1986

Section 11 POA 1986 requires prior notice of political or commemorative processions to be given, by organisers, to the police (there are exceptions on practicality grounds).

In *Kudrevicius* (section 18.3.2) the Grand Chamber confirmed that prior notification, even prior authorisation (i.e. requiring consent by the authorities), can be compatible with Article 11 so long as the real purpose is to enable the police to impose conditions aimed at ensuring that the demonstration can take place in a way that properly and proportionately balances the demonstrators' rights with the rights and interests of others affected. Importantly, sanctions for breaking the conditions can be imposed but only on organisers. Peaceful participation even in an unauthorised demonstration is still protected by Article 11. In dealing with an unauthorised demonstration, the police have a wide margin of appreciation but, in the end, must behave in a proportionate way in terms of why and how they respond (i.e. their response should reflect the reasons behind the conditions that the demonstrators have breached). There need to be lawful opportunities to hold spontaneous (and hence unauthorised) demonstrations if an immediate response by demonstrators to an event is justified.

This approach, reflecting earlier cases, was adopted by the UK House of Lords in respect of prior authorisation in the POA 1986 in *Laporte* (section 18.6.3), para 82.

Imposing conditions on marches, section 12 POA 1986

If voluntary negotiations with marchers fail, the police may seek to impose conditions on marchers as to, for example, route or timing. The general compatibility of imposing conditions on demonstrations (moving and static) has been confirmed by a Grand Chamber in *Kudrevicius* (section 18.3.2). Section 12 POA 1986 permits the police to impose conditions on marches, and the compatibility with Article 11 was confirmed by the House of Lords in *Laporte* (section 18.6.3), para 130. Any challenge based on the HRA, therefore, is likely to focus on the necessity and proportionality of the individual interference.

Imposing conditions on meetings, section 14 POA 1986

There are similar powers to impose conditions on 'public assemblies'. The exercise of these powers by the police can be challenged by judicial review or using the HRA directly but, again, a lawful and proportionate exercise of the power is likely to be compatible with Article 11.

In *R (Brehony)* v *Chief Constable of Greater Manchester Police* [2005] EWHC 640, a police use of section 14 POA 1986, based on the disruption trigger, was held compatible with Article 11 as well as Article 10. The case involved a demonstration against Marks and Spencer because of that company's alleged support for Israel. For the Christmas period there was a counter-demonstration and protestors were required to move away from outside the store to a park. Of particular importance was:

> **CROSS REFERENCE**
>
> Counter-demonstrations and an 'opposition veto' is discussed in section 18.4.

- the duty on the police to give reasons for the section 14 order; and
- the recognition that there is a right to counter-demonstrate but not for the counter-demonstrators to seek to create conditions in which all demonstrations would need to be banned.

> **CROSS REFERENCE**
>
> For breach of the peace see section 18.6.3.

The power in section 14 can be used during a meeting, though this requires the police to be lawfully present. Section 17(6) Police and Criminal Evidence Act 1984 gives statutory footing for the police to enter private premises to deal with breaches of the peace. In *Thomas* v *Sawkins* [1935] 2 KB 249, these powers were said to include political meetings where the breach of the peace is anticipated. In *McCleod* v *United Kingdom* (1999) 27 EHRR 493, the general power of entry for breach of the peace was upheld and this suggests that the power in *Thomas* can, if exercised proportionately, be exercised compatibly with Convention rights. The obvious 'chilling' effect on freedom of assembly and also expression suggests that justification in any particular case needs to be strong.

Banning marches, section 13 POA 1986

Where the police believe that the section 12 power to impose conditions on a march is not sufficient to prevent serious disorder, they may apply, under section 13, to the local council for a banning order. The council can then make an order, but only with the consent of the Secretary of State. In London, the order is made by the police directly with the consent of the Secretary of State. This is a draconian power, which must be exercised compatibly with Article 11. There are various safeguards (see section 13), especially the requirement that a ban must encompass all public processions or at least a class of public procession: there is no power to ban a single march. The point of this blanket ban is to enable the police to appear neutral as between competing political ideologies. It means, however, that entirely peaceful marches can be caught up in the ban.

The issuing of the banning order can be challenged in the courts of England and Wales by way of judicial review. Cases based on the law prior to POA 1986 suggested that the legal test both in the UK courts and by the ECtHR, applying Article 11 directly, would be unlikely to challenge the view of the authorities as to the need for the ban (see, for example, *Kent* v *Metropolitan Police Commissioner* The Times, 15 May 1981 and *Christians against Racism and Fascism* v *United Kingdom* (1978) 21 DR 138). In *Laporte* (section 18.6.3), para 130, a post-HRA case, Lord Brown took the view that the banning power in section 13 POA 1986 could, if the conditions were properly followed, be exercised in a manner compatible with Article 11—as interpreted in *Ziliberg* (section 18.3.2). This might be optimistic. It has been suggested (Helen Fenwick, *Civil Liberties*) that the blanket ban approach might be hard to make compatible with Article 11. It can lead to the ban of a peaceful march solely to enhance police neutrality—which is not expressly a legitimate purpose in Article 11(2).

Banning meetings, section 14A POA 1986

Section 14A POA 1986 gives the police a limited power to apply for an order from the appropriate local authority and, with the consent of the Secretary of State, to prohibit the holding of trespassory open air meetings.

The power must be exercised lawfully. In *DPP* v *Jones* [1999] 2 AC 240, the House of Lords held (by a majority) that a non-obstructive, static, political meeting held on a highway could be by right (and so not trespassory). A highway can be used by right in order to pass and repass, and also for incidental uses. The court accepted that holding a political meeting could be an incidental or a reasonable use of the highway. Though this was a pre-HRA case, two Law Lords based their reasoning on the influence of Article 11 ECHR.

As indicated earlier, a ban on a political meeting or demonstration is not in itself incompatible with Article 11. Prior authorisation is not, if for the right reasons, incompatible with Article 11 and a refusal to authorise a meeting could, if for a legitimate purpose, be a proportionate response. Clearly the reasons triggering the ban will need to be strong, though it should be remembered that nothing in Article 11 protects the rights of people to organise demonstrations they intend to be violent. Article 11 may still protect the right of an individual to participate in a banned meeting peacefully—the ban does not give carte blanche to the police simply to suppress the meeting by whatever means. The authorities have a wide margin of appreciation but, in the end, must behave proportionately (see, for example, *Primov* v *Russia* App 17391/06, judgment of 12 June 2014).

18.7 Freedom of association

18.7.1 **Association**

The right of individuals to join, and take part in the activities of, associations is recognised by the ECtHR as being fundamental to the concept of a democratic society if it is to be pluralist and tolerant. Article 11 protects association in the sense of a relatively organised group with a common aim, rather than association in the sense of being in the company of others (see *Anderson* v *United Kingdom* (1998) 25 EHRR CD172).

Political parties and associations, religious organisations, pressure groups, professional bodies, etc. are the typical forms of association protected by Article 11. They are non-governmental. Professional bodies which also have a statutory, regulatory function (such as the Law Society for England and Wales) may be outside the scope of Article 11—*Le Compte* v *Belgium* (1982) 4 EHRR 1, paras 64–65. Associations within the scope of Article 11 should be properly recognised by the laws of the signatory states. The laws of a state should enable people to form, join, and participate in the activities of such organisations. Any restrictions are interferences which need to be justified under the terms of Article 11(2). The fact that a group is not recognised as an association under the laws of a state is not sufficient. States should not be able to close down opposition groups, for example, by simply declaring them not to be an association. The concept of association under Article 11 is, therefore, another autonomous Convention concept.

The extent that the right of association includes the right of the association to exclude people from membership is controversial. Associations are private bodies with their own rules and should be able to accept and reject members as they see fit. On the other hand, some associations have a form of monopoly power (the major political parties, for example, control access to the legislature and, thereby, to representative public service) and should not be allowed to exclude people on arbitrary grounds.

In *RSPCA* v *Attorney-General* [2001] 3 All ER 530, the High Court held that attempts by the Royal Society for the Prevention of Cruelty to Animals to exclude fox hunting supporters from membership did not breach Article 11. Article 11 includes the right to exclude from membership those it honestly believes are damaging the interests of the society.

18.7.2 **Proscription of political organisations**

Some of the most difficult and controversial decisions of the ECtHR involve cases brought by political parties or associations that have been banned ('proscribed').

🔍 CASE CLOSE-UP

United Communist Party of Turkey v *Turkey* (1998) 26 EHRR 121

The Turkish Constitutional Court upheld the dissolution of the Communist Party of Turkey before it was able to start acting as an association. The reasons for the ban were connected with the alleged support of the party for constitutional change in Turkey, including support for separatism and other values held to be inconsistent with the Turkish constitution.

The ECtHR held that there was a violation of Article 11. The Communist Party had been banned because of its name and programme, not its actions. The ban, though prescribed by law and for a legitimate purpose, was not proportionate to the aim pursued and hence not necessary in a democratic society.

- States can take actions to protect their major institutions and, as in the case of Turkey, their national unity.

- Nevertheless, both Article 11 and Article 10 require that the laws permit the advocacy and promotion of constitutional change.

- This advocacy and promotion of constitutional change needs the protection of the laws even if it takes place against a background of political violence (as in Turkey at the time, with the ongoing insurrection of the Turkish Kurd population).

Freedom of political association has its limits under the Convention. This is illustrated by one of the most significant decisions the ECtHR has ever made.

CASE CLOSE-UP

***Refah Partisi (the Welfare Party) v Turkey* (2003) 37 EHRR 1**

Refah Partisi, the Welfare Party, was the largest single party in the Turkish Parliament and, in 1996, in coalition with another party, it was part of the government. Opinion polls suggested that at the next general election, in 2000, it could obtain an overall majority of seats with as much as 67% of the vote. In 1998 the party was banned by the Turkish Constitutional Court on the grounds that the party intended to introduce Islamic law (Sharia), which was incompatible with the secular nature of the Turkish state. A Grand Chamber of the ECtHR held that there had been no violation of Article 11. There had been an interference with the party's right of association under Article 11(1), but it was justified under Article 11(2). The ban was legally based, it was for a number of the purposes listed in Article 11(2), and, in all the circumstances, it was necessary in a democratic society for the protection of Turkish democracy.

This case involves no less than the banning of a party that had non-violent aims and methods, which participated in the democratic political process, and had won a general election for the legislature. Nevertheless, the ECtHR upheld the ban and, in doing so, asserted the strong commitment of the Convention to the principles of maintaining democracy and the egalitarian approach to human rights.

- Following *United Communist Party*, the Court accepted that states can take reasonable steps to preserve their institutions. Here the main reason for the ban was the struggle by Turkish state institutions to protect the secular character of the state (as distinct from the predominantly Muslim character of society).

- States can ban political parties and groups which incite or promote violence. They can also act against groups which advocate unlawful action. This is a more complex issue: incitement depends upon context. The Refah Partisi did not advocate violence.

- States may ban (they may even have a duty to ban) groups and organisations that promote a state of affairs which is undemocratic or which would be likely to undermine the human rights of others. This was the position accepted by the ECtHR in *Refah Partisi*.

- Pre-emption. As part of the protection of democracy, states can use the law to pre-empt (prevent) an anti-democratic outcome. The Welfare Party sought the introduction of Islamic law (Sharia). In the Court's analysis, such a legal system, if introduced in the Turkish context, would create a legal and constitutional system which would, in important ways, be incompatible with the Convention. The Muslim population of Turkey would be governed by a law whose ultimate authority was divine revelation rather than the consent of the people and, in particular, the evidence was that this would have significantly detrimental effects on the rights of women. The need to defend democracy extends, in the view of the Court, even to restricting the outcomes that the people can vote for.

 THINKING POINT

Consider the arguments justifying the decision in Refah Partisi—do they give adequate protection to the rights of a people, by majority rule, to choose their own government?

18.8 Trade unions

Article 11 expressly includes a person's 'right to form and to join trade unions for the protection of his interests'. This right is widely accepted by Council of Europe states. It is also enshrined in other instruments of international law, such as the statutes of the International Labour Organization (ILO). This is the United Nations' specialist agency to promote the rights of workers. Its Convention 87 requires states to guarantee the rights of workers to organise.

Article 11 does not require any specific system of trade union regulation, and states have a wide margin of appreciation on how trade unions are controlled and what powers they may have (see *Swedish Engine Drivers' Union* v *Sweden* (1979–80) 1 EHRR 617).

The issue in modern capitalist societies is the extent to which laws must ensure that workers have the effective freedom to join a trade union when their employers put economic or other pressures on them not to join. In the past, the issue has been whether workers have a right not to belong to a trade union. This has been particularly important where the trade union negotiates the workers' terms and conditions and gives them some power in the workplace.

Non-membership, in such circumstances, can seem like a form of free riding in which non-members avoid the costs of membership but benefit from the willingness of members to contribute to and support the union. In *Young, James and Webster* v *United Kingdom* (1982) 4 EHRR 38, the ECtHR declined to rule that a 'closed shop' in itself violated Article 11. Since this case, however, the ECtHR has moved further towards accepting that Article 11 includes both the positive right to join and the negative right not to join associations including trade unions. In *Sorensen* v *Denmark* (2008) 46 EHRR 29, a Grand Chamber ruled that though compulsory membership may not always be contrary to the Convention, it will be if compulsion strikes at the heart of freedom of association by, in effect, forcing trade union membership on reluctant workers (see para 54).

Where there is no closed shop, trade unions have greater freedom to reject members who also support racist or other political causes the union opposes: *ASLEF* v *United Kingdom* (2007) 45 EHRR 34.

18.9 Political restriction

The last sentence of Article 11 expressly allows national laws to restrict the rights of assembly and association of 'members of the armed forces, of the police or of the administration of the State'. In the United Kingdom, for example, there are severe restrictions on the freedom of the police, the military, senior civil servants, and some local government officers to do things like stand for Parliament or take part in the activities of political parties. The House of Commons Disqualification Act 1975 lists a large number of posts and offices, the occupiers of which are unable to sit in the House of Commons. The reasons for these restrictions are to ensure that the public services maintain the appearance of political impartiality and that elected representatives do not have divided loyalties.

The scope of the restrictions and the need for them in respect of thousands of workers who neither deal directly with the public nor have a major impact on policy has been questioned. However, the ECtHR has not found such restrictions to be incompatible with Article 11.

In *Ahmed v United Kingdom* (2000) 29 EHRR 1, the ECtHR held that political restrictions on certain local government workers were compatible with Articles 10 and 11, and Article 3 of the First Protocol (there were strong dissenting judgments).

In 1983 the government banned the workers at the General Communications Headquarters in Cheltenham (a centre for electronic intelligence-gathering) from being members of an independent trade union. The taking of industrial action by such workers endangered national security, according to the government. The Commission held that the ban was justified in terms of the second sentence of Article 11(2), as it was a restriction on the rights of association of members of the 'administration on the State': *Council of Civil Service Unions v United Kingdom* (1988) 10 EHRR CD 269.

Summary

- Article 11 represents one of the important political rights guaranteed by the Convention, under which people have rights of 'assembly' (which includes the right to take part in political demonstrations), and rights of 'association' (which includes the right to form, join, and take part in the activities of a political party).

- These rights are subject to restriction under the terms of Article 11(2). The importance of Article 11 rights for democracy is fully recognised and any restrictions will need to be consistent with the principles of tolerance and pluralism.

- The promotion of constitutional change is a protected purpose under Article 11, but assemblies or associations which incite violence or promote anti-democratic outcomes may be restricted by states acting lawfully and proportionately.

- Article 11 protects trade union activity.

- Article 11 permits significant restrictions on the political freedom of police, civil servants, and other public officials.

? Self-test questions

1. Apart from Article 11, how else are the rights to political action outside Parliament guaranteed?

2. Article 11 protects 'peaceful' assembly—what does the word 'peaceful' mean in this context?

3. What does 'prescribed by law' mean in the context of Article 11? Give two cases in which it has been discussed.

4. Identify the main common law powers of the police in the context of UK demonstrations.

5. Identify the main statutory powers of the police in the context of UK demonstrations.

6. What was the reasoning in *Ahmed* v *United Kingdom* (section 18.9) and do you think it failed to give proper protection to ordinary local government workers wishing to take part in political activities?

 For suggested approaches, please visit the Online Resource Centre.

 ## ? Exam questions

1. The government is concerned that a radical religious organisation is planning to campaign in one of the major cities of the UK in order to control its local government and, thereby, seek to impose a strict religious discipline in some of the schools. The organisation is popular and may well win the election. The minister is pursuing various options. One possibility being considered is to propose legislation which would enable her to ban the organisation were it to win the local election.

   As a government lawyer, advise the minister on whether such a step could be compatible with Article 11.

2. Do you agree with the proposition that Article 11 provides states with ample scope for a reasonable and effective law on public order which balances rights to demonstrate with the rights of others to live their own lives? Exemplify your answer from the law of the United Kingdom.

 For suggested approaches, please visit the Online Resource Centre.

☰ Further reading

Fenwick, H. *Civil Liberties and Human Rights* 4th edn (2007) Abingdon: Routledge-Cavendish, Chapter 9

Fenwick, H. 'Marginalising Human Rights: Breach of the Peace, "Kettling", the Human Rights Act and Public Protest' [2009] (Oct) *Public Law* 737–765

Lester, A., *Pannick*, D. and Herberg, J. (see Preface) Chapter 4, Article 11

D. Mead 'A Chill Through the Back Door? The Privatised Regulation of Peaceful Protest' [2013] (Jan) *Public Law* 100–118

19 Article 12: right to marry

> ☐ **LEARNING OBJECTIVES**
>
> ● The right to marry and the kinds of relationships that are included in the concept of 'marriage'.
>
> ● The states' rights to regulate marriage and the kinds of purposes such regulations can promote.
>
> ● The right to found a family.
>
> ● The rights of non-married couples.

Article 12 Right to Marry

Men and women of marriageable age have the right to marry and to found a family, according to the national laws governing the exercise of this right.

Introduction

Over the last decades the social practices of marriage and family life have changed considerably. A high proportion of family relationships do not involve marriage. Conversely, European societies have had to adjust or react to different culturally informed conceptions of purpose and obligations of marriage. At the same time, the desire of homosexual couples to establish their relationships on a legal basis has led, first, to civil partnerships and, secondly, a redefinition of civil marriage to include couples of the same sex. Likewise, transgendered persons have sought and obtained legal recognition of their acquired gender which, amongst other things, has enabled them to marry. All these developments point to the on-going significance of marriage as the 'natural and fundamental group of society' (Article 23 ICCPR, see Chapter 1, section 1.4.4) and as being important for giving social status. The family, if not marriage, remains the primary unit through which children are conceived and brought up, and is also a source of human happiness (though Lord Millett's view, in *Ghaidan v Godin Mendoza* [2004] UKHL 30, is also correct and avoids sentimentality: marriage gives 'legal status to a relationship between men and women (which need not be loving, sexual, stable, faithful, long standing or contented)' (para 78)). It is this deep seated but changeable nature of marriage and family life that explains why it needs protection as a human right.

19.1 Article 12 and Article 8

CROSS REFERENCE

Article 8 is discussed in Chapter 15 and Article 14 in Chapter 7.

Article 12 creates a right to marry and found a family. The right is qualified by reference to 'national laws'. This permits states to regulate and restrict marriage so long as the 'essence' of the right is not compromised. It complements Article 8, the right to respect for private and family life. The issues mentioned in the Introduction, dealing with the changing nature of family relations in the modern world, may also involve Article 8, the right to respect for private and family life. The focus on marriage in Article 12 means that different legal issues can arise under the two different Articles, and this is reflected in the case law. Likewise, issues of discrimination on the grounds of marriage can engage Article 14 when linked to Article 12.

19.2 Marriage

Marriage, in the context of Article 12, is defined as the 'formation of a legally binding association between a man and a woman', which thereby involves the acquisition of legally recognised social status (see *Hamer* v *United Kingdom* (1982) 4 EHRR 139). Marriage has a particular status in Article 12 and is not to be equated with other forms of relationship or simple cohabitation (*Burden* v *United Kingdom* (2008) 47 EHRR 38, Grand Chamber, para 63).

Article 23 ICCPR expressly requires marriage to be based on the full and free consent of spouses, asserts the need for equality between spouses regarding the rights and responsibilities of marriage, and accepts the fact of divorce and the need for adequate protection for children if that happens. Such matters as consent and equality are not expressly mentioned in Article 12 of the European Convention on Human Rights (ECHR) but may be implied from its text.

19.2.1 **Homosexual marriage and civil partnership**

Article 12 refers to 'men and women'. The European Court of Human Rights (ECtHR) takes the view that marriage is, by definition, a relationship between men and women. In *Rees* v *United Kingdom* (1987) 9 EHRR 56, the Court said:

> In the Court's opinion, the right to marry guaranteed by Article 12 (art. 12) refers to the traditional marriage between persons of opposite biological sex.

(para 49)

CROSS REFERENCE

See Chapter 15, section 15.5.3 on same-sex relationships and Article 8.

It follows that there is no positive duty on states to recognise marriages between homosexuals or civil partnerships. These principles have been confirmed by a Grand Chamber in *Hämäläinen* v *Finland* App 37359/09, Grand Chamber judgment of 16 July 2014, and accepted by English courts, see *Wilkinson* v *Kitzinger* (2006) EWHC 2022, paras 44–48. As a positive duty, there remains a wide margin of appreciation on the matter. There is no prin-cipled move towards requiring recognition of same-sex marriage. The Convention, it seems, will evolve only through recognition of changes in domestic law and, in 2014, the ECtHR's examination of the practice of European states found no consensus on same-sex marriage (*Hämäläinen*, paras 73–74).

The right to marry and found a family in Article 9 of the European Union's Charter of Fundamental Rights is expressed without reference to gender. However, the associated Commentary makes clear that this does not involve a positive duty on member states to recognise civil partnerships or homosexual marriage.

THINKING POINT

Should there be a human right to same-sex marriage? Consider, for example, Johnson (Further reading).

19.2.2 Divorce

Neither Article 12 nor Article 8 require states to allow divorce, see *Johnston v Ireland* (1987) 9 EHRR 203 (see paras 51–58). Since Article 15 of the UN Declaration of Human Rights refers to the dissolution of marriage but this reference is not repeated in Article 12 ECHR, the ECtHR was convinced that the absence of a right to divorce in the Convention was therefore deliberate.

19.2.3 Right not to marry and forced marriage

Marriage would not be a 'right' if there were not an equal and opposite right not to marry. The voluntary, consensual nature of the relationship would be lost. Nevertheless, the issue has not been authoritatively decided by the ECtHR, though Lord Bingham, in *R (Pretty) v DPP* [2001] UKHL 61, was 'inclined' to support it (para 6). A non-consensual marriage that is valid under foreign law may not be recognised in the United Kingdom: *City of Westminster v C* [2008] EWCA Civ 198. In *XCC v AA* [2012] EWHC 2183, the Court of Protection (which deals with the interests of those with limited mental capacity) refused, despite arguments about cultural issues, to recognise the 'marriage' of a woman, with significant learning difficulties, which lacked consent and was probably done to enable the husband to obtain a visa.

A marriage that is forced or coerced will be incompatible with Article 12. International law (e.g. Article 23 ICCPR) requires voluntary marriage and it must be assumed that, even though express words on this point are absent from Article 12, states have a duty to ensure that their marriage laws require freely given consent. The extent to which the duty goes further and re-quires, for example, state support for those threatened with, or embroiled in, a non-voluntary marriage is unclear and the lack of clear words is to be regretted. In the United Kingdom, for example, there is an acknowledged problem of 'forced marriage'. Administrative action (e.g. by consular offices abroad) and legal remedies (orders and directions issued by a court) are available. This is done under statute and common law, but may also be a duty required under Article 12 and Article 8.

BIGGER PICTURE

On legal action see *Re SK* [2004] EWHC 3202. On administrative action see the website of the Forced Marriage Unit (see: https://www.gov.uk/guidance/forced-marriage#forced-marriage-unit). A criminal offence is created by Part 10 of the Anti-Social Behaviour, Crime and Policing Act 2014, which also strengthens civil remedies available through the Forced Marriage (Civil Protection) Act 2007.

Attempts at regulation which interfere with the right to marry and with private life must be proportionate. In *R (Aguilar Quila)* v *Secretary of State for the Home Department* [2011] UKSC 45, regulations meant that marriage visas would only be granted to spouses aged over 19. The regulations were designed to help prevent forced marriage. However, they had a severe impact on couples whose marriages were entirely voluntary. The Supreme Court subjected the regulations to careful analysis and held, by a majority, that the Secretary of State had failed to demonstrate that they were proportionate to the aim.

19.3 Founding a family

19.3.1 **Married couples**

Article 12 also gives men and women a right to 'marry and to found a family'. The right to marry applies even in the absence of an intention or ability to have children at the time of marriage (so the transgendered may have rights under Article 12 even though the couple have no physical ability to have children—see *Goodwin* v *United Kingdom* (2002) 35 EHRR 18, para 98).

The main effect of the right to found a family is to bring within the scope of Article 12 national laws and regulations on the means by which married couples can have children. Adoption and artificial insemination are the main examples. On such issues states have a wide margin of appreciation on the kinds of regulations they impose.

There is a presumption in favour of married couples having a right to live together (see *Abdulaziz* v *United Kingdom* (1985) 7 EHRR 471, para 62). In that case the ECtHR said that Article 8(1) did not impose a positive duty on states to admit non-national spouses to residence. Different views have been taken in later cases (e.g. *Tuquabo-Tekle* v *Netherlands* [2006] 1 FLR 798) and, in *Aguilar* (section 19.2.3), the Supreme Court held that Article 8(1) was engaged in respect of entry decisions affecting private life, which, therefore, needed justification under Article 8(2).

19.3.2 **Unmarried persons**

However, the human right to found a family under Article 12 probably does not apply to unmarried persons. Therefore their position and status on this issue can be more freely regulated (or ignored) by the state. In a case dealing with the rights of illegitimate children, the ECtHR denied that Article 12 rights should apply equally in other marriage-like situations (*Marckx* v *Belgium* (1979–80) 2 EHRR 330, para 67).

- Cohabiting unmarried couples. The Court has not extended the full range of Article 12 rights in this context. For example, an unmarried father's claim to the custody of his children cannot be based on Article 12 rights (*B, R and J v Germany* (1984) 36 DR 130).

- Homosexual relationships. As stated previously, there is no positive duty on states to recognise homosexual relationships as being capable of acquiring legal status.

- Legitimacy. From some of its earliest case law, the Court has required states to recognise equality in their laws between legitimate and illegitimate children. However, this is based on developing Article 8 rights rather than the right to found a family in Article 12 (see *Marckx*).

These are all matters of social change and development in Europe. As the position of transgendered men and women discloses (discussed in section 19.5) the ECtHR is capable of changing its case law, within the terms of Article 12, to reflect a changing consensus. As large proportions of children are brought up in unmarried families, and as homosexual couples are increasingly given legal status and allowed to adopt children, etc., it may be that the case law of Article 12 will need to develop. But, it seems, it will develop by keeping pace with general developments in Europe (which do not always go in a liberal direction) rather than as abstract arguments of right based upon the principle of autonomy.

19.4 Regulating marriage

19.4.1 General principles

The right to marriage is 'according to the national laws governing the exercise of this right'. The meaning of the terms 'marriage' and 'founding a family' are governed by the laws of the signatory states. States have their own rules, policies and practices on the matter and the ECtHR accepts that a wide margin of appreciation must exist in this context. The familiar language of proportionality and the 'fair balance' between individual freedoms and social benefits is found in respect of the Court's evaluation of these laws. Nevertheless, the Court retains the final word on what is required by Article 12 and, as illustrated from the transgendered persons' cases discussed in section 19.5, is prepared to limit the margin of appreciation if the circumstances so warrant.

General principles were stated in *F v Switzerland* (1988) 10 EHRR 411 (involving Swiss laws which imposed a temporary ban of up to three years on a person remarrying after divorce). The ECtHR said (in para 32):

- The institution of marriage 'gives rise to personal, social and legal consequences'. Therefore it is necessary for it to be regulated and limited by law.

- The normal regulations are those that apply 'procedural' limits (such as requiring marriage to be a public matter or stipulating some minimal ceremonial requirements) and 'substantive' limits such as those relating to capacity (e.g. age, gender, or not being already married), consent, and other impediments to marriage such as those describing the 'degrees' of marriage by which marriage to relatives is barred.

- Any such limitations must not impair the 'very essence' of the right. It is the Court's job to ensure that this has not happened in the particular cases that are brought before it. Thus in *F* the majority felt that the fact of a ban on marriage impaired the essence of the right, whilst the minority, by focusing on its temporary nature, disagreed (see also *B and L v United Kingdom* App 36536/02, judgment of 13 September 2005).

19.4.2 **The purposes of regulation**

For what purposes can marriage be regulated? Can these go beyond factors about marriage itself and extend to other legitimate state purposes such as immigration control and the good order of prisons? The issue has arisen under the Human Rights Act 1998 (HRA).

Immigration

> **CASE CLOSE-UP**
>
> ***R (Baiai)* v *Secretary of State for the Home Department* [2008] UKHL 53**
>
> Section 19 of the Asylum and Immigration (Treatment of Claimants) Act 2004, in essence, allowed the Secretary of State to refuse permission to marry (other than under the rites of the Church of England) to a person subject to immigration control (a person who requires leave to enter the UK). In many situations the policy adopted under the Act was to refuse permission on the assumption that the proposed marriage was a 'sham'.
>
> The House of Lords held that the Secretary of State was pursuing an inflexible policy that caught genuine as well as 'sham' marriages. But (save for the provision discriminating in favour of Anglican marriage) section 19 could and should be read down (under section 3 HRA) to mean that permission to marry could not be refused except where there was a marriage of convenience. Nor could section 19 authorise other conditions that were incompatible with Article 12 (regulations that imposed a high, deterrent, fee on applicants were to that extent unlawful). The instructions on which civil servants worked were incompatible with the proper reading of section 19.
>
> The Law Lords adopted a narrow and focused approach to the subject matter of legal restrictions on marriage. These must relate to the terms of lawful marriage. Restricting marriage for social purposes, such as immigration control, is unlawful. Article 12 allows no balancing of individual rights and social interests as is possible under Article 8(2). However, only real marriages are protected by Article 12 and so a state is permitted to regulate against accepting marriages of convenience and this is what section 19, properly interpreted, does.

Prisoners

The regulation of the rights of prisoners to marry is discussed in Chapter 21, section 21.9.2.

19.5 Transgendered persons

The position of transgendered persons has always been difficult. In the past, states have refused to give full legal recognition to the acquired gender. In particular they refused to allow a change of birth certificate, thus making marriage (if legally defined as being between a man and a woman) impossible, and with this comes a range of other legal obstacles, difficulties, and unfairness.

The original position of the ECtHR was that the failure by states to give full legal recognition to transgendered men and women did not involve a violation of either Article 8 or Article 12, because states enjoyed a wide margin of appreciation over the issue. However, from as early as *Rees v United Kingdom* (1987) 9 EHRR 56, the Court was aware of medical, social, and attitudinal developments in European society and culture, and suggested that states keep the issue under review. The Court fully revised its view in *Goodwin v United Kingdom*.

CASE CLOSE-UP

Goodwin v United Kingdom (2002) 35 EHRR 18

Christine Goodwin was a post-operative male-to-female transsexual. She complained of a range of legal disadvantages stemming from the fact that UK law did not allow her to change her birth certificate. These included not being able to bring a sexual harassment case, having to pay higher car insurance premiums, and not being able to marry. The ECtHR held that there had been a violation of Articles 8 and 12.

The Court's underlying view was that there was now a clear European consensus emerging which required legal recognition for transsexuals in their acquired gender. The margin of appreciation on the matter was withdrawn. States can no longer base their legal definitions of gender solely on 'biological criteria' determined at the time of birth. Given present-day attitudes and conditions, and given the seriousness of the problems faced by transsexuals, there was an overriding need for the Court to depart from its earlier case law.

In *Bellinger v Bellinger* [2003] UKHL 21, under the HRA, the House of Lords issued a declaration of incompatibility in relation to the Matrimonial Causes Act 1973 under which marriages were void unless between a man and a woman (see Chapter 4, sections 4.4.3 and 4.4.7). The government responded with the Gender Recognition Act 2004. This establishes a Gender Recognition Panel to which people with gender dysphoria and intending to live the rest of their lives in their acquired gender can apply for legal recognition in the form of a gender recognition certificate.

Summary

- Article 12 establishes both a right to marry and to found a family. The right is often asserted in tandem with Article 8.

- This right can be regulated by states according to their laws. Restrictions and regulations on issues such as age, capacity, and ceremony are acceptable, but any limits which undermine the essence of the right will be a violation.

- Though marriage does not imply an intention to found a family, specific rights related to founding a family are not available to unmarried persons.

? Self-test questions

1. How is the idea of a 'family' defined in Article 12; is it confined to married relationships?

2. Does Article 12 require the legal recognition in domestic law of homosexual relationships?

3. Does Article 12 place a positive duty on states to admit into the country the foreign spouses of residents?

 For suggested approaches, please visit the Online Resource Centre.

? Exam questions

1. On what principles and for what purposes is a state entitled to regulate and restrict a person's freedom to marry and to found a family compatibly with Article 12?

2. John and Joan have been living together for a number of years in a close, stable, and (they both think) permanent relationship. They have philosophical and religious objections to the idea of marriage and think they are entitled to enjoy social and legal recognition of their relationship through a Civil Partnership. Currently the law only allows Civil Partnerships for same-sex couples.

   Advise John and Joan on whether Article 12 might provide a basis for advancing their claim.

 For suggested approaches, please visit the Online Resource Centre.

≡ Further reading

Johnson, P. ' "The choice of wording must be regarded as deliberate': same-sex marriage and Article 12 of the European Convention on Human Rights' *EL Rev* 2015, 40(2), 207–224

Lester, A., Pannick, D., and Herberg, J. (see Preface) Chapter 4, Article 12

Tew, Y. 'And They Call It Puppy Love: Young Love, Forced Marriage and Immigration Rules' (2012) 71(1) *CLJ* 18–19

20 Applications: police powers

LEARNING OBJECTIVES

The impact of Convention rights on the law of England and Wales respecting the general powers of the police at common law and in statute, in particular the Police and Criminal Evidence Act 1984.

Introduction

In *Aston Cantlow* v *Wallbank* [2003] UKHL 37, the police were 'instinctively' listed as a 'core' public authority (para 7): policing is self-evidently a public function (they exercise directly the coercive authority of the state). This means police are required, by section 6 of the Human Rights Act 1998 (HRA), to act compatibly in all they do with Convention rights. Failure to do so means they can be acted against under section 7 HRA.

> **CROSS REFERENCE**
> For the definition of a core public authority see Chapter 4, section 4.5.5.

Equally, as discussed in this chapter, the authority of the police (their legal right to do the things they do) is largely (though not exclusively) based on legislation which, under section 3 HRA, must be interpreted, so far as possible, for compatibility with Convention rights.

> **CROSS REFERENCE**
> For the interpretation of legislation under the HRA see Chapter 4, section 4.4.

20.1 Police powers in general

20.1.1 **Outline**

Statute

The Police and Criminal Evidence Act 1984 (PACE) provides the principal statutory basis for police actions. The powers of the police lawfully to stop and search, arrest, detain suspects, take fingerprints and samples, search property and seize items, etc. are found in this Act. In the Act these powers are specified, the circumstances in which they can be exercised detailed, and the safeguards enjoyed by those affected identified. Failure to act according to the statutory provisions can be unlawful and can be the basis of an action against the police or can give rise to other consequences, such as the possibility of evidence being inadmissible at a trial. Many other Acts of Parliament also give police powers to search and arrest, etc. Examples are the Public Order Act 1986, the Firearms Act 1968, and the Misuse of Drugs Act 1971. Significant increases in police powers are found in anti-terrorism legislation, in particular the Terrorism Act 2000 (discussed in Chapter 26).

Police powers in PACE and other statutes have to be exercised in the light of guidance in Codes of Practice (with attached 'Notes for Guidance') produced under the Act by the Home Secretary (section 66 PACE). Failure to comply with a Code is not in itself unlawful, but police compliance can be taken into account in determining the outcome of criminal and civil trials (section 67 PACE).

BIGGER PICTURE

The Codes are regularly updated. There are eight Codes (A–H) (as updated between 2011 and 2016), available on the Home Office Police website: https://www.gov.uk/guidance/police-and-criminal-evidence-act-1984-pace-codes-of-practice

Common law

> **CROSS REFERENCE**
>
> For breach of the peace see Chapter 18, section 18.6.3.

As well as statutory powers, the police have common law powers. These are the ordinary powers that all persons in England and Wales enjoy: to walk the streets, enter premises such as shops that are open to the public, etc. An important power (which private persons also have) is to take reasonable steps to deal with a breach of the peace, including one that has not occurred but is anticipated. A great deal of ordinary public order policing is done on this basis.

20.1.2 The Human Rights Act: legality

> **CROSS REFERENCE**
>
> For the Convention concept of legality see Chapter 6, section 6.2.

The compatibility of these provisions with the substantive Convention rights in Schedule 1 HRA will be considered in the rest of this chapter. The general point is that, in so far as the police take action that interferes with an individual's rights (as arrest interferes with the right to liberty in Article 5 or a search may interfere with the right to private and family life, home, and correspondence in Article 8), they must act in accordance with the law. This means that compliance with the Convention requires not only that the police act lawfully in terms of domestic (national) law, but that the domestic law itself meets the standards of accessibility, foreseeability, and non-arbitrariness that are at the heart of the autonomous Convention concept of law and the rule of law.

The European Court of Human Rights (ECtHR) accepts a wide definition of law. The rules that must be accessible and foreseeable need not only be in legislation but can also be in non-statutory written sources (such as Codes of Practice) and in 'unwritten' sources such as common law. The ECtHR has held that the legal basis on which the common law power to detain for breach of the peace is exercised with sufficient clarity to be consistent with the Convention concept of law (*Steel v United Kingdom* (1999) 28 EHRR 603, paras 54–55).

20.1.3 **The use of force by the police**

The police can use force in the exercise of their powers. There is a general provision, that applies to all, including the police: section 3 of the Criminal Law Act 1967 allows a person to use 'such force as is reasonable in the circumstances in the prevention of crime, or in effecting or assisting in the lawful arrest of offenders or suspected offenders or persons unlawfully at large'. Under section 117 PACE, a constable may use 'reasonable force, if necessary' when exercising a power conferred on the police by PACE.

Under the HRA, of course, this use of force must be exercised in ways that are compatible, in particular, with Article 2 (the right to life: see Chapter 8, section 8.2.1), Article 3 (the prohibition on torture etc.: see Chapter 9, sections 9.4 and 9.5) and Article 8 (the qualified right to private life etc.: see Chapter 15).

> **CROSS REFERENCE**
> On the lethal use of force, including that based on an honest mistake, see Chapter 8, sections 8.2.1 and 8.2.5.

20.1.4 **Assaulting and obstructing the police**

It is an offence under section 89 of the Police Act 1996 to assault or obstruct a constable 'in the execution of his duty'. People are, however, allowed to use force that is reasonable in the circumstances to resist a police officer who is not executing his duty. The importance of section 89 is that it can be the judicial vehicle through which the precise scope of police powers under the law are determined.

20.1.5 **Remedies against the police**

In respect of unlawful or improper actions by the police, a range of remedies are available. These include:

- a civil action for damages;
- an action under section 7 HRA;
- judicial review (e.g. where the challenge is to a policy the police are pursuing);
- a judge's exercise of his or her discretion, in section 78 PACE, not to admit evidence obtained unlawfully (breach of PACE, for example) or in breach of one of the PACE Codes (though neither common law nor Article 6 of the Convention requires unlawfully obtained evidence to be inadmissible);
- a complaint to the Independent Police Complaints Commission (IPCC).

The Convention point is that, under Article 13 ECHR, these remedies must provide adequate protection for those who allege that the police behaviour they complain of is a breach of their Convention rights. The courts and the IPCC have to be able to provide a forum in which all the issues relating to the alleged violation can be properly and fairly determined.

> **CROSS REFERENCE**
> For Article 13 see Chapter 5, section 5.1.

Many serious issues start out as a complaint to the IPCC. This body was created, in part, because its predecessor, the Police Complaints Authority, was held, in *Khan* v *United Kingdom* (2001) 31 EHRR 45, not to be sufficiently independent of government and the police to meet the standards of Article 13. Article 13 is not one of the scheduled Convention rights in the HRA so, if domestic remedies cannot be given effect to give proper consideration of alleged Convention violations, a complaint to Strasbourg will be necessary.

20.2 Stop and search

20.2.1 General

The police have powers to compel people to stop and be searched whilst they are in public places; people can be detained by the police for that purpose. The main power, which is in Part 1 PACE, is to stop, detain, and search for stolen or prohibited articles including articles with blades and prohibited fireworks. A number of other statutes also have stop and search powers, such as in relation to firearms (Firearms Act 1968, section 47(3)) or drugs (Misuse of Drugs Act 1971, section 23(2)). Stops and searches under all these Acts are subject to the guidance in PACE Code A.

20.2.2 Restrictions and safeguards

The stop and search power, in PACE and other statutes, involves a significant interference with people's basic liberty to be in public places.

There are important safeguards:

- A stop and search under PACE can only be conducted on the basis of 'reasonable suspicion' that the person is carrying stolen or prohibited articles. Code A (paras 2.2–2.11) gives extensive guidance on this. Other powers allow stop and search without the need for specific suspicion against the individual searched (a random search). Examples are under the Terrorism Act 2000 (discussed in Chapter 26, section 26.8.1) and under section 60 Criminal Justice and Public Order Act 1994. This allows the police to designate an area (such as one where serious crime is anticipated) as one in which random stops and searches may take place for a limited period and under certain conditions.

- A search is limited in its nature: the person cannot, in public, be required to remove any clothing other than coats, jackets, or gloves. A more intensive search can only be done out of the public view, and searches involving the exposure of intimate bodily parts must be done at a police station (Code A, para 3.7).

- A search is unlawful unless certain information about the officer conducting the search and the reason for it is given before the search commences (section 2 PACE) and a full record is made afterwards (section 3 PACE). Code A gives additional detail.

20.2.3 Convention compliance: Articles 8–11

A person's physical integrity, correspondence, etc. is protected by Article 8(1) and may be interfered with by a personal search.

The *Gillan* case (which is discussed in Chapter 26, section 26.8.1) involved the compatibility with Convention rights of a random stop and search conducted under section 44 Terrorism Act 2000. In *R (Gillan)* v *Metropolitan Police Commissioner* [2006] UKHL 12, the House of Lords found that the lawful and proper conduct of a stop and search will normally be superficial and not a sufficiently serious interference with these rights to require justification. If there are circumstances where a stop and search does involve an interference, then, assuming it is lawfully and properly conducted, it is likely to be capable of justification under the second paragraphs of Article 8, 10, or 11. The ECtHR (*Gillan* v *UK)* (2010) 50 EHRR 45) took a dramatically different view and found that the random basis of selection for search and the lack of adequate controls meant that the powers could not be exercised lawfully, in the Convention sense of the term. As discussed in Chapter 26, section 26.8.1, the power was revised and replaced in 2012. Post-*Gillan*, the Court of Appeal has held that the power to conduct random stops and searches under section 60 Criminal Justice and Public Order Act 1994 (see above, section 20.2.2) is sufficiently focused and controlled to be a 'lawful' interference with private life and so compatible with Article 8—*R (Roberts)* v *Commisioner of Police for the Metropolis* [2014] EWCA Civ 69.

A search conducted in an inhuman and degrading way would be incompatible with Article 3, but it would also be inconsistent with Code A. This requires the powers to be used 'fairly, responsibly, with respect for people being searched and without unlawful discrimination' (para 1.1).

Depending on context, articles with religious significance can be seized, raising issues under Article 9. Part 1 PACE makes no particular reference to religion; however, in the Notes for Guidance attached to Code A, it is made clear that religious headdress cannot be removed unless the police officer believes it is being worn for the purpose of disguise (other than the simple fact that it has the effect of disguise) and removals may have to take place away from public view.

BIGGER PICTURE

Other police powers to seize items, such as knives, give a statutory defence that the item was for a religious purpose: see Criminal Justice Act 1988, section 139(5)(b).

20.2.4 Convention compliance and Article 5

Stop and search powers, including under Part 1 PACE, authorise the police to 'detain' the suspect for the purposes of the search. If such a detention were to involve a 'deprivation of liberty' then a stop and search would engage Article 5 of HRA Schedule 1. This would mean it could only be done for the purposes listed in Article 5(1). The point of stop and search is to allow officers to 'allay or confirm suspicions' without needing to arrest on reasonable suspicion of an offence, and so Article 5(1)(c) would normally be breached.

> **CROSS REFERENCE**
> For Article 5(1) see Chapter 11, section 11.4.

In *Gillan* (the UK case), the House of Lords held that:

- An ordinary stop and search, lawfully and properly conducted, is unlikely to involve a deprivation of liberty (para 25).

- If there are additional factors (the person stopped and searched is detained for more than a brief period, is taken to a police station for a more intimate search, or hand-cuffed, for example) there may have been a deprivation of liberty. In that case the stop and search is likely to fall within Article 5(1)(b) as being necessary to fulfil 'an obligation prescribed by law'; namely the obligation of submitting to a stop and search where the grounds (reasonable suspicion, for example, of carrying stolen or prohibited articles) exist (para 26).

In *Gillan* v *UK*, the ECtHR found it unnecessary to rule on this specific issue and so the House of Lords' position remains authoritative in the UK. In *Roberts* (section 20.2.3) the Court of

Appeal suggested that deprivation of liberty in this context would depend on the time necessary to conduct the search.

Stop and search under PACE remains controversial. In 2014, the Home Secretary accepted the findings of a report which suggested a disproportionate use against ethnic minorities, a low success rate in the sense of few consequential arrests, and, most disturbingly, that over a quarter of PACE stop/searches were, on the face of the record, not based on reasonable suspicion (and so may have been illegal). Code A is to be revised to clarify 'reasonable suspicion' and, in February 2015, the Home Secretary threatened a change in the law unless police forces used stop and search in more focused and intelligence-led ways.

20.3 Arrest

20.3.1 **The concept of arrest**

An arrest means that the arrested person loses his or her physical liberty and is brought under the compulsory control of the police. Both police and private persons can (on significantly different grounds) effect an arrest. Reasonable force can be used for a lawful arrest, though, equally, a person can use reasonable force to resist an unlawful arrest. Under the law of England and Wales, an arrest requires an act of physical restraint by the arrester or clear words indicating to the person, and understood by him or her, that he or she is now under compulsion (*Alderson* v *Booth* [1969] 2 QB 216).

20.3.2 **Arrest under the law of England and Wales**

Warrant

Arrest on the basis of a warrant means there has been at least some degree of judicial supervision of the decision to arrest. The main general power is in section 1(1)(b) of the Magistrates' Courts Act 1980, under which a magistrate can issue an arrest warrant on the basis of information laid before them that a person is suspected of an indictable (usually the more serious) criminal offence.

Summary arrest

Summary arrest is done by the police (or a private person) without any form of prior judicial supervision. Police have the power of summary arrest under a large number of statutes. The general power for a police officer is contained in section 24 PACE, with guidance in Code G. A person can be arrested for any offence so long as certain conditions apply. For the police these are (in summary) that:

- the person is about to commit, is committing, or has committed a criminal offence; *and*
- to arrest the person is necessary (compared with the alternatives of obtaining a summons to appear in court or a warrant for an arrest from a magistrate, for example); *but*
- the officer must have reasonable grounds for believing the arrest is necessary in order to identify the suspect, to prevent injury to the suspect or others, to prevent loss or damage to property, to prevent the suspect committing offences against public decency, to prevent the suspect causing an obstruction of the highway, to protect a child or vulnerable person, to allow the prompt and effective investigation of the

offence, or to prevent any prosecution being hindered by the disappearance of the suspect.

Summary detention is also permitted in respect of apprehended breaches of the peace. This is discussed in Chapter 11, section 11.4.3.

20.3.3 Convention compliance: reasonable suspicion

Arrest, by definition, involves a deprivation of liberty and so the laws allowing the issuing of warrants and summary arrest must be applied in ways that are compatible with Article 5(1)(c). This requires that any arrest must be lawful, effected for the purpose of bringing the arrested person before the competent legal authority and based on 'reasonable suspicion' of the offence or 'when it is reasonably considered necessary to prevent his committing an offence or fleeing after having done so'. Lawfulness includes the requirement that the decision to arrest needs to be a proportionate exercise of power.

CROSS REFERENCE
For Article 5(1)(c) see Chapter 11, section 11.4.3.

Section 24 PACE is generally compatible with Article 5. In particular, the terms of section 24 mean either that the arrest is based, as a matter of law and fact, on an offence being committed or on the arresting officer having reasonable suspicion. An arrest on a lesser standard, such as mere suspicion based on a hunch, would not be lawful under either the Act or the Convention. Under Article 5 the suspicion must be honestly held and based on 'facts or information which would satisfy an objective observer that the person concerned may have committed the offence in question' (see *Fox, Campbell and Hartley* v *United Kingdom* (1991) 13 EHRR 157, para 32).

CROSS REFERENCE
For reasonable suspicion, see Chapter 11, section 11.4.3.

The application of Article 5 ECHR to English law in this context was considered in *Cumming* v *Chief Constable of the Northumbria Police.*

> **CASE CLOSE-UP**
>
> ***Cumming*** v ***Chief Constable of Northumbria* Police [2003] EWCA Civ 1844**
>
> CCTV footage that contained evidence of a crime appeared to have been tampered with. All the local authority employees controlling the CCTV were arrested on suspicion of perverting the course of justice. They were all innocent. They sought damages from the police for wrongful arrest and false imprisonment. The Court of Appeal agreed with the trial judge that their arrests had been lawful.

The pre-HRA law was found in *Castorina* v *Chief Constable of Surrey* (1988) 138 *NLJ* 180. The test was:

- did the police suspect the arrested persons had committed the offence,
- were there reasonable grounds for that belief, and
- in all the circumstances was it reasonable to arrest?

Under the HRA, these basic principles are retained but revised to ensure Article 5 is taken into account. The Court of Appeal in *Cumming* said:

> The court must consider with care whether or not the decision to arrest was one which no police officer, applying his mind to the matter could reasonably take bearing in mind the effect on the appellants' right to liberty.
>
> (para 43)

CROSS REFERENCE
'Proportionality' and 'reasonableness' in administrative law are discussed in Chapter 4, section 4.6.1.

In *Shields* v *Chief Constable of Merseyside* [2010] EWCA Civ 1281, the Court of Appeal said that the law on arrest, which was given its present form in 2006, 'takes into account the principles of Article 5, which therefore do not require separate consideration'. So a lawful arrest under section 24 PACE will be compatible with Article 5.

20.3.4 Lawfulness and breach of the peace

Although the power to 'detain' for 'breach of the peace' is common law, the ECtHR has found that, given the way this power has been defined by the English courts, it can only be lawfully exercised in a way that is compatible with the Convention conception of law and legality. This is discussed in Chapter 18, section 18.6.3.

20.3.5 Information on arrest

Article 5(2) requires that everyone 'arrested' 'shall be informed promptly, in a language which he understands, of the reasons for his arrest and of any charge against him'. Such a requirement has long been part of common law (see *Christie* v *Leachinsky* [1947] 1 All ER 567) and is confirmed by section 28(3) PACE. Section 28 requires that arrested persons be informed both of the fact that they are under arrest and also of the reasons for their arrest. This information must be given 'as soon as is practicable'. In *Taylor* v *Chief Constable of Thames Valley Police* [2004] EWCA Civ 858, the formula adopted by the ECtHR in *Fox, Campbell and Hartley* (1991) 13 EHRR 157, para 40 (see Chapter 11, section 11.5) was accepted as part of English law:

> having regard to all the circumstances of the particular case [the accused] was told in simple, non-technical language that he could understand, the essential legal and factual grounds for his arrest.

The point is to allow the arrested person to instigate a legal challenge and so the information given must be sufficient for that purpose (*Clarke* v *Chief Constable of North Wales Police* The Independent, 22 May 2000).

20.4 The treatment of an arrested person

20.4.1 General

Part V PACE deals with the treatment of arrested persons being held in custody in a police station. Code C on Detention, Treatment and Questioning applies.

Under the Convention and the HRA, there is the need to treat arrested persons in a manner that does not involve inhuman or degrading treatment in violation of Article 3; also to ensure that the interferences with private life that are likely can be justified under the terms of Article 8(2). Questioning must not be oppressive (Code C, para 11.5). A confession obtained by oppression is not admissible as evidence (section 76 PACE) and other kinds of improperly or unfairly obtained evidence can be excluded at the discretion of the judge (section 78 PACE).

20.4.2 Article 6 and access to a lawyer

As said many times, the rule of law pervades the Convention (including Article 5) and so police behaviour in respect of an arrested person must adhere strictly to the law and the Convention conception of the rule of law. Given that arrest may lead to charge and then to prosecution, the lawfulness of what happens to an arrested person under the control of the police can affect their right to a fair trial under Article 6. Article 6 'has some application at the pre-trial stage' (*Reinprecht* v *Austria* (2007) 44 EHRR 39, para 37). The significance of Article 6 over pre-trial events depends upon the circumstances, specifically whether what happens could prejudice the likely outcome of the trial.

Access to legal advice during police questioning is likely to be necessary in this context. Legal advice is particularly important since, under English law, a jury at the trial can draw a presumption of guilt from the accused person's silence or failure to mention certain matters whilst under police questioning (sections 34, 36, and 37 Criminal Justice and Public Order Act 1994). In *Murray* v *United Kingdom* (1996) 22 EHRR 29, the ECtHR held that in circumstances where what the accused does or says under police interrogation can have decisive consequences at the resulting trial, Article 6 normally requires that the accused have legal assistance; though this right, since it is only implied from Article 6, may be 'subject to restrictions for good cause'.

Section 58 PACE gives a suspect held in custody in a police station the right to consult a solicitor privately. A senior police officer can authorise a delay of up to 36 hours under certain circumstances, such as a belief that exercising the right will lead to interference with evidence. Most importantly, regarding Convention rights, under the Criminal Justice and Public Order Act 1994, presumptions tending to guilt cannot be drawn if, whilst in custody, the suspect did not have access to legal advice.

20.5 Detention

20.5.1 The power to detain

An arrested person should be charged or released. Detention is possible under certain circumstances.

- **Detention after charge.** Section 37 PACE requires the 'custody officer' to decide whether there is sufficient evidence to charge the arrested person. If there is and the person is charged, he or she will then be released, either with or without bail, unless the custody officer thinks it is necessary to detain the person, under section 38 PACE. There are various grounds for this, such as a fear that the person will not voluntarily attend court. A person so detained must then, under section 46, be brought before a magistrate on the same day or the day following.

- **Pre-charge detention.** If there is insufficient evidence for an immediate charge, section 37 requires that the arrested person should be released (with or without bail). However, PACE permits the police to detain an arrested person against whom, at the time of arrest, there is insufficient evidence to charge. This is where detention is considered 'necessary to secure or preserve evidence relating to an offence for which he is under arrest or to obtain such evidence by questioning him' (section 37).

- Pre-charge detention is for a maximum of 96 hours but after 36 hours judicial authority from a magistrate is required: see sections 41–44 PACE:

  - The initial police detention can be for up to 24 hours.
  - That can be extended by another 12 hours, to a maximum of 36, but only with the authority of a senior police officer and only in respect of **indictable** offences—these are the most serious offences The indictment is the document that specifies the alleged offence, the trial will be with a jury in the Crown Court. 'Summary' offences are the less serious offences which are dealt with by magistrates. Accused people receive a 'summons' to the court. Many offences can be tried 'either way' giving the defendant an option to choose jury trial.
  - Detention beyond 36 hours requires a warrant from a magistrate.
  - A warrant from a magistrate can be for no more than 36 hours, although it can be renewed for a second time so long as the overall period in detention without trial does not exceed 96 hours.

20.5.2 **Article 5(3) and detention.**

Pre-charge detention is a deprivation of liberty and thus must be done compatibly with Article 5. Assuming detainees have been arrested on reasonable suspicion of an offence, their detention is in principle permitted under Article 5(1)(c). The important provision is Article 5(3). This embodies the idea of the rule of law and the need that the police's power to detain should be in accordance with law and properly supervised by an independent judiciary.

In *McKay* v *United Kingdom* (2007) 44 EHRR 41, a Grand Chamber distinguished the 'arrest period' part of Article 5(3) from the 'pre-trial or remand' part.

Arrest period

This requires a detained person to be brought 'promptly' before a judicial body who can exercise judicial power by, for example, ordering the release of a person unlawfully detained.

As discussed in Chapter 11, section 11.7.1, the ECtHR has been reluctant to lay down definite periods to correspond with the word 'promptly'. *Brogan* v *United Kingdom* ((1989) 11 EHRR 117) was an anti-terrorism case and even here a delay of more than four days was held to be a breach. The PACE provisions, given earlier, seem to meet Article 5(3) requirements. They require judicial involvement after 36 hours (in the case of pre-charge detention) and within a day or at the first possible moment regarding detainees who have been charged.

The job of the magistrates dealing with the arrest period aspect of Article 5(3) is to give a proper examination of the grounds for detention. In *Re McAuley's Application* [2004] NIQB 5, para 24 (a Northern Ireland terrorism case concerned with the effect of Article 5(3)), this was said to include examining the basis for reasonable suspicion, the basis for the charge, and whether there have been any procedural defects. At this stage it is not necessary for the magistrate to consider the issue of bail: *McKay* v *United Kingdom* (paras 35–40).

Under the Convention, detainees also have a right that the investigation will be reviewed and conducted with due diligence. PACE meets this requirement by the requirement of a review, conducted by a review officer independent of the investigation, after six hours and then at nine-hourly intervals (section 40 PACE and Code C, Notes for Guidance, note 15A).

Pre-trial or remand period

Article 5(3) requires 'trial within a reasonable time or release pending trial'. Section 37 PACE gives the police the power to release where there is insufficient evidence to charge (section 37(2)) or, where there is sufficient evidence to charge, either with or without bail (section 37(7)). These provisions must be exercised compatibly with Article 5(3), which creates a presumption in favour of release (see Chapter 11, section 11.7.2). Issues of bail or remand then fall to the courts to determine under the Bail Act 1976.

Different provisions apply under anti-terrorism legislation and these are discussed in Chapter 26, section 26.8.2.

20.6 Fingerprints, samples, and other data

Normally fingerprints and bodily samples cannot be taken from a person without their consent (sections 61, 61A, 62, and 63 PACE). However, the requirement for consent can be dispensed with where a person who is detained in a police station has been arrested or charged for a recordable offence. In those circumstances the police can, without consent, take:

- fingerprints (section 61(3) and (4) PACE);
- an impression of the person's footwear (section 61A(3) PACE);
- non-intimate samples, such as head hair, saliva and mouth swabs, or a skin impression (section 63 PACE).

Intimate samples (defined as blood, semen, other tissue fluid, urine, pubic hair, a dental impression, or a swab from an orifice other than the mouth) can only be taken with written consent (section 62 PACE). However, under section 62(10) inferences can be drawn (e.g. by a jury in a subsequent trial) if a police request for an intimate sample is unreasonably refused. It is, of course, from these samples that DNA information can be obtained. Code D applies to the exercise of these powers.

The fingerprints and samples taken can then be checked against others, such as those found at the scene of a crime (section 63A PACE).

20.6.1 Taking and Convention rights

PACE confines the non-consensual taking of fingerprints and samples to persons under reasonable suspicion of an offence (for which they have been arrested or charged) and it limits the use of such material to, broadly speaking, the investigation of crimes. The taking of samples and fingerprints clearly involves a person's physical integrity and so is an interference with private life under Article 8(1); therefore, in principle, it requires justification under Article 8(2). Normal applications of the power in PACE are likely to be easily justified under Article 8(2). This was the view of the House of Lords in *R (Marper)* v *Chief Constable of South Yorkshire Police* [2004]

UKHL 39 (para 21), following the view of the Commission of Human Rights in *McVeigh* v *United Kingdom* (1983) 5 EHRR 71, para 224:

- the PACE provisions are clearly accessible and the circumstances in which they will be invoked reasonably foreseeable;
- the taking of samples etc. is done for the 'prevention of crime'; and
- is necessary for that purpose.

20.6.2 Retention and Convention rights

Attention and concern is focused less on taking and more on the power and the policy of retaining samples or, more importantly, the DNA information that can be obtained from them.

Authority to retain samples (from which the DNA profiles are obtained and which can then be stored on a database) is found in section 64 PACE. It permits the retention of samples etc. after they have fulfilled the purpose for which they are taken, but only for purposes related to the prevention, detection, investigation, and prosecution of crime or to assist with the identification of a dead person or a body part (section 64(1A) PACE).

🔍 CASE CLOSE-UP

Marper v UK (2009) 48 EHRR 50

This was a challenge to the wide-ranging and indiscriminate policy in the UK by which the police retained samples and DNA profiles. Such samples and profiles could be retained indefinitely from juveniles and also from people arrested and charged but who had been acquitted or whose case did not come to trial. The profiles were researched using a massive database.

A Grand Chamber held that:

- The 'mere storing' of personal data (such as cellular samples, DNA profiles, and fingerprints) interferes with a person's private life.
- Therefore the issues is justification under Article 8(2).
- The interference was not justified under Article 8(2). The Court accepted the utility of retention in fighting crime. However, this would have to be compatible with human rights. The Article 8(2) requirements that interferences be in accordance with law and proportionate were merged. In these and other matters (such as secret surveillance), there need to be detailed rules and proper safeguards, dealing with issues like storage, accessibility, and destruction. These were needed in order to minimise the risk of arbitrariness. In the Court's view, the legal provisions failed to offer these safeguards. There was a breach of Article 8 because the 'blanket and indiscriminate' policy of retaining the samples and fingerprints of all suspected but unconvicted persons (persons presumed innocent) was disproportionate and not justifiable under Article 8(2).

CROSS REFERENCE

For discussion of the direct consequences of *Marper v UK* see Chapter 4, section 4.4.7.

Following *Marper* the Protection of Freedoms Act 2012 (PFA 2012) amended PACE with a detailed scheme for the retention and destruction of DNA profiles.

THINKING POINT

Consider whether it is still necessary to store DNA profiles on a national database and whether the PFA 2012 reforms are adequate.

20.6.3 Retention and disclosure of other information

Police can take, retain, use, and, sometimes, disclose all sorts other information. For example, they have direct access to criminal records and may take and store visual images of people.

In so far as this involves information that 'relates to an individual's private life' it is likely to engage Article 8. The ECtHR has developed a wide understanding of private life in this context; it can include 'public information' such as political activities and prior convictions (see *Rotaru v Romania* App 28341/95, Grand Chamber judgment of 4 May 2000, paras 43–44). Article 8 is engaged when such information is collected, stored, and released.

For the UK courts the general test (reflecting ECtHR jurisprudence) which triggers the guarantees of Article 8 is information over which there is a 'reasonable expectation of privacy' (confirmed in *R (Catt) v CPM* [2015] UKSC 9). This term must accommodate the wide, inclusive, view of 'private' information developed in *Rotaru*, above. In *Catt*, for example, police retained photographic and other data about C as he attended public demonstrations and meetings. The UKSC held that, though these were all public meetings, C's Article 8(1) rights were interfered with. On the facts, the interference was justified under Article 8(2).

However, there are limits to a reasonable expectation of privacy. In *In re JR38* [2015] UKSC 42, the UKSC held that the publication of photographs of young persons engaged in rioting did not engage their Article 8 rights—they had no reasonable expectation of privacy in the context.

Generally, therefore, the focus of the human rights scrutiny of retention and disclosure is on justification under Article 8(2). It is usually easy enough to show that the police have acted for the prevention of crime or for one of the other purposes listed in Article 8(2). More problematic is whether the retention or disclosure is in accordance with the law and proportionate.

CASE CLOSE-UP

***R (T) v Chief Constable of Greater Manchester* [2014] UKSC 35**

In the context of child protection, police were allowed to disclose, to relevant employers and some regulatory bodies, information about a person's previous convictions. These included convictions which, under the Rehabilitation of Offenders Act, were 'spent' and did not need, normally, to be disclosed (thus ex-offenders had a reasonable expectation of privacy).

The UKSC held that there was a violation of Article 8. In particular, the legal rules permitting these disclosures were indiscriminatory and failed to require the police to consider the proportionality of particular disclosures (T's caution for stealing a cycle when he was 11 was disclosed and prevented him getting a job when he was 17). The failure (for the

> **CROSS REFERENCE**
>
> T raises significant questions about remedies, discussed in Chapter 5, sections 5.3 and 5.4.

> majority) was that the interference was not 'in accordance with the law'. Proper safe-guards were a matter of 'law' and hence their adequacy was for the courts to determine, there was little margin of appreciation.

20.7 Entry, search, and seizure

The police have extensive powers to enter and search premises and seize matters found there. As we shall see, these can raise issues involving Convention rights, such as under Article 8 (respect for private and family life, home, and correspondence) and Article 1 of the First Protocol (peaceful enjoyment of possessions).

20.7.1 Consent to enter, search, and seizure

No particular authority is needed for a police officer to enter homes, offices, shops, factories, etc. with the consent, express or implied, of the owners or occupiers. In that sense the police are in the same position as everybody else. If the occupier withdraws consent then the police (assuming they have no other legal basis for being there) should leave and, if they do not, reasonable force can be used.

Consent to enter is not the same thing as consent to a search. PACE Code B (para 5.4) makes it clear, for example, that the occupier should be reminded of their right to refuse if the police seek consent to search.

There is, of course, no freedom to seize goods and items from places just because there was an express or implied right to enter. Goods could be taken with consent, of course. However, if the police are in premises lawfully (e.g. with the occupier's consent), they have a broad statutory power to seize anything believed to be there as a consequence of a criminal act, so long as seizure is believed to be necessary to prevent the thing being 'concealed, lost, altered or destroyed' (section 19 PACE).

20.7.2 Statutory power to enter without consent

Section 17 PACE abolished most of the pre-existing common law powers police had to enter premises without consent. A few remain, such as the power to abate a nuisance. Section 17 PACE gives the police statutory authority to enter premises in order to arrest persons, under various circumstances, or to save life and limb. This is a power the police exercise without the need for judicial authority from a warrant. Section 17(6) expressly reserves the common law power to enter premises to deal with a breach of the peace.

 CASE CLOSE-UP

McCleod v United Kingdom (1999) 27 EHRR 493

Police, advised by Mrs McCleod's ex-husband's solicitors that there might be a breach of the peace, assisted the ex-husband whilst he removed property from Mrs McCleod's house. The husband was trespassing since, under a legal settlement between them, ownership of the property, at that time, had not yet transferred to him. The police refused Mrs McCleod's request to restore the property. The courts held that the police had acted lawfully under section 17(6) PACE. The ECtHR held that there had been a violation of Article 8.

The Court held that:

- the entry under section 17 was an interference with the rights protected by Article 8(1) and so the interference must be justified under Article 8(2);

- breach of the peace was defined with sufficient clarity to be 'in accordance with the law';

- the power was used for a legitimate purpose, the 'prevention of disorder or crime';

- however, the exercise of power, especially because not enough attention was paid to Mrs McCleod's legal rights under the court order, was disproportionate and so there was a breach.

Given the narrow, proportionality, ground on which this case was decided, it is likely that, in general terms, the powers in section 17 (not just subsection (6)) will be, if properly exercised, compatible with Article 8.

Of course section 17 does not give a power of search for goods or seizure. Section 19 (mentioned at section 20.7.1), however, applies since the arresting officers will have entered the premises lawfully.

20.7.3 Statutory power to search premises

Section 32 PACE gives the police power to search the premises where an arrested person was immediately before being arrested. There must be a reasonable belief that there is evidence relating to the offence on the premises. Under section 18 PACE, a constable may search premises 'occupied or controlled' by an arrested person. The power is to search for evidence connected to the arrest. In a Convention-related case, the Court of Appeal has adopted an objective test on whether the property is occupied or controlled.

 CASE CLOSE-UP

Khan v Commissioner of Police for the Metropolis [2008] EWCA Civ 723

M was arrested by the police. He gave a false address—the claimant's home. The police searched the claimant's home and found nothing. The claimant sued the police for trespass. The police defence was that they had acted under section 18 and so were on the property lawfully. The judge awarded damages against the police and the police appeal was rejected by the Court of Appeal.

The Court of Appeal held that:

- Section 18 should be given its ordinary meaning—it referred to an arrested person's actual address. There was nothing in the section that referred to the police needing only reasonable grounds for believing it was the arrested person's address.

- The police could have used section 32 or obtained a warrant under section 8.
- This approach flowed from a section 3 HRA reading of section 18 PACE and, with regard to Article 8, gave proper respect to a person's home.

The police have powers of entry and search under other statutes. In addition there are some circumstances where the police are able to rely on traditional common law powers which have not been superseded by PACE. Search of premises after the arrest of a person in pursuit of an extradition warrant is outside PACE, because the offence in question is under the law of a foreign country. Nevertheless, the House of Lords, in *R (Rottman)* v *Commissioner of Police for the Metropolis* [2002] UKHL 20, held that the police retained a common law power of entry and search.

20.7.4 Power of entry, search, and seizure on the basis of a warrant

Section 8 PACE allows a constable to apply to a magistrate for a search warrant. An indictable offence must have been committed, the officer must have reasonable grounds for believing that a search will give rise to material of 'substantial value' to an investigation, and the warrant must be necessary for various reasons such as that entry would otherwise be refused. There are many other statutes that also authorise the issuing of warrants to the police. Section 8(2) allows a police officer to seize any matter for which the search was warranted.

A warrant means that there is some element of judicial supervision of this power of significant interference with premises, including a person's 'home'. It helps to establish that searches are, for the purposes of Article 8, in accordance with the law. The courts have stressed the seriousness of a warrant and the need that it is issued with proper care. ('The obtaining of a search warrant is never to be treated as a formality. It authorises the invasion of a person's home': *Redknapp* v *City of London Police* [2008] EWHC 1177, para 13.)

The malicious procurement of a warrant (when the police do not act in good faith) is a tort and can give rise to an action for damages. Mere negligence (not checking an address for instance) is not enough.

> ### Q CASE CLOSE-UP
>
> **Keegan v United Kingdom** (2007) 44 EHRR 33
>
> Acting on the basis of a warrant, police forced an entry to the home of Mr and Mrs Keegan. The address had been used by the mother of a suspected armed robber, but she had left six months previously when the Keegans moved in. The Court of Appeal found that the police had been negligent (they had not made elementary checks) but had acted in good faith. Therefore the tort of malicious procurement of a warrant was not made out (*Keegan* v *Chief Constable of the Merseyside Police* [2003] EWCA Civ 936). The Keegans, therefore, had no remedy under English law. The ECtHR held that the failure to check meant that the interference with the Keegans' right to a home was disproportionate and so a breach of Article 8. Furthermore, the insistence on their having to prove malice meant they had no effective remedy and so there was also a breach of Article 13.

Sections 15 and 16 of PACE introduce a range of procedural protections and these are emphasised in Code B. Section 15 deals with issuing, e.g. the warrant must specify who it relates to, the date issued, and the premises to be entered and searched. Section 16 deals with execution, e.g. the execution should normally be at a reasonable hour unless this would frustrate the purpose of the search. A warrant undertaken in breach of these provisions may be unlawful, but it needs to be remembered that there is no absolute bar in the law of England and Wales, nor under Article 6, to unlawfully obtained evidence being admitted as evidence.

CROSS REFERENCE

For Article 13 see Chapter 5, section 5.1.

The normal and lawful exercise of these powers (both statutory and common law) is likely to be compatible with Article 8 as being in accordance with law (even the common law power is sufficiently well defined), for a legitimate purpose (the prevention of crime), and, because of the safeguards, proportionate (see *R (Rottman)* v *Commissioner of Police for the Metropolis* [2002] UKHL 20, para 80, a decision on the common law power).

20.7.5 **Protected material**

Section 8 cannot be used to search for certain kinds of material. These are:

- Material subject to legal privilege, such as communications between the person searched and his or her legal advisor. The principle of upholding legal privilege is firmly entrenched in common law and is also fully recognised as necessary to a person's right to a fair trial under Article 6 and private life under Article 8 (see, for example, *Niemietz* v *Germany* (1993) 16 EHRR 97 and *Campbell* v *United Kingdom* (1993) 15 EHRR 137). Nothing in section 8 or other provisions of PACE authorise a search for privileged material and section 9 repeals any earlier Acts under which this might have been possible. In *R (Daly)* v *Secretary of State for the Home Department* [2001] UKHL 26, the House of Lords, referring to Article 6, upheld the importance of legal privilege in relation to the powers of a prison governor to search prisoners' correspondence in their absence. There are serious problems about searching a body of correspondence some of which may be privileged: Part 2 of the Criminal Justice and Police Act 2001 provides a scheme for this.

- 'Excluded' or 'Special Procedure' material cannot be searched for under section 8. Excluded material describes professionally held confidential records relating to physical or spiritual health or welfare; or human tissue taken for medical purposes and held in confidence. Special procedure material describes other types of confidential records (see PACE, sections 10–14). This is confidential and personal material that is given extra protection under the law; a protection that Article 8 may also require.

Under section 9(1) and Schedule 1 PACE, the police may seek a court order from a circuit judge requiring the handing over of such material. The main procedural protection for this kind of confidential and private material lies in the fact that the police must apply to a circuit judge rather than just a magistrate and that there is the opportunity for a proper hearing to oppose the application (ordinary warrants under section 8 PACE are obtained *ex parte* without the person involved knowing).

Journalistic material can be either excluded or special procedure material depending on whether it is personal records held in confidence or other material held in confidence. Therefore it can only be obtained under Schedule 1.

A judge can order journalistic material, which is special procedure material, to be disclosed if the material would be of substantial value to an investigation and disclosure would be in the public interest having regard to that value. However, even if these 'access conditions' are made out, the judge still has a residual discretion to decide whether to make a disclosure order. It is at this point, in particular, that freedom of the press must be considered (in addition, section 12 HRA requires the courts to have particular regard to the importance of freedom of expression in this context—see Chapter 17, section 17.3). In *R* v *Central Criminal Court ex parte Bright* [2001] 2 All ER 244, the police sought the disclosure of files held by a journalist which might disclose that an offence under the Official Secrets Act 1989 had been committed. The judgment in this pre-HRA case contains strong words in favour of media freedom (see especially the opinion of Judge J) and a concern that 'investigative journalism will be discouraged, perhaps stifled'.

Applications by the police for journalistic material are obviously of great sensitivity and involve balancing the needs of criminal justice with media freedom. In this respect it is not allowable under common law for all or part of the police's reasons for seeking the material not to be disclosed to the broadcaster (*R (BSkyB)* v *Central Criminal Court* [2014] UKSC 17).

These general principles are reflected in post-HRA cases.

 CASE CLOSE-UP

R (BSkyB) v Chelmsford Crown Court [2012] EWHC 1295

Essex Police sought the disclosure of footage recorded by broadcasters of the controversial and violent eviction of travellers from Dale Farm. On appeal by the broadcasters, the Divisional Court stressed the need for the judge to make a careful, evidence-based analysis of whether the access conditions (such as the 'substantial value' test, section 20.7.4 and above, this section) are made out. Furthermore, assuming they are made out, Article 10 then requires a careful balancing exercise between the public interest in the suppression of crime and the public interest in media freedom (para 24). Eady J stressed the relevance of the issue that effective reporting of controversial issues might be discouraged if judges, by issuing disclosure orders too easily, compromise the impartiality and independence of broadcasters and put cameramen at risk (para 25).

The broadcaster's appeal succeeded because the police had not given sufficient evidence of the need for disclosure.

⟩ **CROSS REFERENCE**

On protection of sources see also Chapter 22, section 22.4.

 BIGGER PICTURE

For discussion of a similar power under the Terrorism Act 2000, see *Shiv Malik* v *Manchester Crown Court* [2008] EWHC 1362.

Summary

- Police have extensive powers under common law and PACE. As public authorities these need to be exercised compatibly with Convention rights, especially Article 5 (regarding arrest and detention) and Article 8 (regarding searches and seizure).
- English and Welsh courts adjudicating on these powers have generally found them to be compatible with Convention rights at the general level. Attention is focused on particular applications in individual cases.

? **Self-test questions**

1. Why does the HRA mean that the police must act compatibly with Convention rights?

2. Does stop and search always engage Convention rights or only sometimes—what Convention rights are involved?

3. What are the main Convention rights that apply to the power of arrest?

4. In respect of Convention rights, how does a court in the UK approach an application by the police for access to journalistic material held by a media organisation?

 For suggested approaches, please visit the Online Resource Centre.

? **Exam questions**

1. Critically evaluate the extent to which Articles 5 and 8 have an impact on the exercise of their powers by the police.

2. As a lawyer for the police you are tasked with writing a briefing paper which discusses the restraints on their powers, sourced in Convention rights:

   (a) to retain data, including DNA profiles and also records of criminal convictions and all recorded encounters with the police. The aim is that this data would be available to any police force to help it solve any crime and also to other public authorities which might find the information useful;

   (b) to make public any criminal convictions of any person if the police think this will assist in the investigation of any crime.

   Provide the basic outline on which the briefing paper will be written.

 For suggested approaches, please visit the Online Resource Centre.

Further reading

Austin, R. 'The New Powers of Arrest: Plus ça Change: More of the Same or Major Change?' [2007] *Crim LR* 459–471

Fenwick, H. *Civil Liberties and Human Rights* 4th edn (2007) Abingdon: Routledge-Cavendish, Part IV

HM Inspector of Constabulary *Stop and Search Powers: Are the police using them effectively and fairly?* https://www.justiceinspectorates.gov.uk/hmic/media/stop-and-search-powers-20130709.pdf

Stone, R. *Textbook on Civil Liberties and Human Rights* 9th edn (2012) Oxford: OUP, Chapters 3–5

21 Applications: prisoners rights

LEARNING OBJECTIVES

The impact of Convention rights on the law of England and Wales respecting prisoners' rights.

Introduction

There are approximately 85,000 prisoners in the United Kingdom. Like all prisoners, they are under the complete control of the state as regards their everyday life. Whilst some are violent and repellent, the majority are also psychologically vulnerable, often suffering from alcoholism and drug dependency. They may be ill, mothers with dependent children, or foreigners imprisoned far from home. They may be in need of protection from fellow prisoners or they may be those doing the threatening and so subject to punishment and segregation. Overall the prison system is experiencing severe financial restraints which make it hard to keep the prisons in decent condition and to enable enlightened and rehabilitative policies to be pursued. In contexts such as these, the Convention rights of prisoners can be important and decisive of the duties of the authorities.

21.1 Prisons and the Human Rights Act

Within its territory the state exercises a 'monopoly of legitimate force'. Given the abolition of capital punishment, the ultimate expression of that force is imprisonment—depriving individuals of their liberty. Not surprisingly, therefore, it is a public function for which the state is responsible under the Convention.

21.1.1 Legislation

The Prisons Act 1952 provides the basic authority for prisons in England and Wales. The Act authorises the making of subordinate legislation, in particular section 47 authorises the Secretary of State to make rules for the regulation, management, discipline, etc. of prisons and prisoners. The Prison Rules, thus made, deal with the general regulation and management of prisons and are regularly updated. The Prison Service Orders and Prison Service Instructions, authorised by the Rules, deal in detail with long-term and short-term matters.

The Act, the Rules, the Orders and the Instructions all come within the definitions (in section 21 HRA) of primary and subordinate legislation that (under section 3 HRA) must be interpreted, if possible, for compatibility with Convention rights. Some Prison Rules have been redrafted to build in Convention compliance.

21.1.2 Public authorities

Prisons legislation authorises the actions of a range of officials and authorities. In England and Wales it is the Secretary of State for Justice (prior to 2007 it was the Home Secretary) who has ultimate responsibility for prisons and prisoners. Direct, day-to-day, responsibility lies with the Prison Service, an executive agency that has a degree of independence from ministers. Individual prisons are under the direct control of a prison governor, who is a civil servant. Some prisons are privately owned and operate on the basis of a contract with the Prison Service.

CROSS REFERENCE

See Chapter 4, sections 4.4 and 4.5 for sections 3 and 6 HRA.

These officials and agencies are 'public authorities' under section 6 HRA and so must act compatibly with Convention rights (private prisons are performing a public function and so, also, are public authorities under section 6(3)(b) HRA).

Regarding Scotland and Northern Ireland (not Wales), matters concerning prisons are the responsibilities of the devolved institutions. If a human rights point is raised, however, it is the UK Supreme Court which has the final judgment.

21.2 The rights of prisoners in general

Prisoners in England and Wales are not outlaws. In *Raymond* v *Honey* the House of Lords confirmed that:

> a convicted prisoner, in spite of his imprisonment, retains all civil rights which are not taken away expressly or by necessary implication.

> (Lord Wilberforce [1983] 1 AC 1, at p 10)

A general power to make rules, such as section 47 of the Prisons Act, does not allow the making of rules that deny prisoners their fundamental rights. Only express and clear statutory words can do this. This common law recognition that prisoners retain those rights that are not necessarily incompatible with imprisonment is also found in the ECHR. In *Hirst* v *United Kingdom (2)* (2006) 42 EHRR 41, for example, a Grand Chamber made it clear that:

prisoners in general continue to enjoy all the fundamental rights and freedoms guaranteed under the Convention save for the right to liberty.

(para 69)

Of particular importance is the recognition that both remand and convicted prisoners are under the more or less total control of the state and so are particularly vulnerable to abuse. The state has a clear duty to provide a proper and safe regime in which prisoners can enjoy the Convention rights and freedoms they retain.

21.2.1 Access to court

Of the rights retained by prisoners, in a way the most fundamental is the right of access to a court to vindicate civil rights. It means that prisoners' retained rights are not illusory and they can obtain genuine remedies from the courts. Access to a court for prisoners has long been recognised both at common law (e.g. *R (Daly)* v *Secretary of State for the Home Department* [2001] UKHL 26, para 5) and under the Convention (*Golder* v *United Kingdom* (1979–80) 1 EHRR 524).

> **CROSS REFERENCE**
> The Convention right of access to court is discussed in Chapter 12, section 12.6.

In England and Wales this means that prisoners can pursue:

- Private law rights such as actions for negligence, trespass, breach of statutory duty, and misfeasance in public office. These include actions against the authorities based on either the behaviour of, for example, police or the Prison Service or the behaviour of fellow inmates, against whom the authorities should provide proper protection.

- Public law rights. These include the right that the prison authorities should only act within their powers, should exercise their discretion over policies and individual decisions in reasonable ways, and, importantly, ensure that in disciplinary and other proceedings prisoners are given a fair hearing before an unbiased tribunal. These public law rights are obtained through the process of 'judicial review'.

- Convention rights. Where a prisoner alleges he or she has been directly affected by a violation of a Convention right they can use section 7 HRA. This can be by way of a direct challenge to the authorities or by using their Convention rights in other civil or criminal proceedings in which they are involved.

> **CROSS REFERENCE**
> Section 7 HRA is discussed in Chapter 5, section 5.4.

21.2.2 The substance of prisoners' rights: general

But what are the substantive rights that prisoner's enjoy? In England and Wales this is a matter of the judges interpreting and applying the relevant statutory and common law provisions. Of course, as public authorities themselves, the judges must do this in ways that are compatible with Convention rights—indeed sometimes they will be directly applying a Convention right. What must be stressed is that, mostly, prisoners' rights are not absolute but are flexible and context dependent, and this is true under both the common law and the Convention. The courts recognise the necessity for restrictions and qualifications on the application of rights to prisoners where such restrictions would not be acceptable in the situation of free persons. For instance, in *R (Cannan)* v *Governor of Full Sutton Prison* [2003] EWCA Civ 1480, the Court of Appeal held that a prisoner's right of access to the courts under Article 6 was violated in respect of conditions imposed on the transmission of documents between a prisoner and his legal advisor. However, restrictions on other types of communication with legal advisors served a legitimate purpose and did not violate Article 6.

21.3 The basis of imprisonment: Article 5

21.3.1 Article 5(1)(a)

Prisoners lose their liberty but not their rights under Article 5. Lawful imprisonment, however, is compatible with Article 5. Any deprivation of liberty (which includes imprisonment) must be on the basis of a 'procedure prescribed by law' and, exclusively, for one of the purposes in Article 5(1). Article 5(1)(a) allows 'the lawful detention of a person after conviction by a competent court'.

Thus prisoners in England and Wales must have been convicted:

- for offences that are properly defined in law (otherwise there could also be a violation of Article 7: see Chapter 13, section 13.3);
- through a fair criminal procedure. Defendants have the right to a fair trial under Article 6(1)–(3): see Chapter 12.

A prisoner's detention will not be 'lawful', even if it complies with domestic law, if it is 'arbitrary' as the European Court of Human Rights (ECtHR) understands that term. In *James* v *United Kingdom* (2013) 56 EHRR 12, the ECtHR identified four requirements relevant to that understanding (paras 192–195):

- the authorities act with good faith;
- there is a clear link between the facts and circumstances of imprisonment with the purposes of permitted detention in Article 5(1)(a)–(f);
- likewise there must be a relationship between the permitted ground in Article 5(1)(a)–(e) relied on and the place and conditions of detention;

> **CROSS REFERENCE**
> For Article 5(1)(a) see Chapter 11, section 11.4.1.

- the decision to detain on one of the permitted grounds must be proportionate to that ground. The scope of proportionality depends on the context—the length of lawful imprisonment after conviction will normally be accepted, but decisions not to release for reasons that are not related to the original conviction might violate Article 5(1).

21.3.2 Article 5(4) and indeterminate sentences

Under Article 5(4) there must be legal procedures by which prisoners can make an effective challenge to the lawfulness of their detention.

In England and Wales there are 'determinate' sentences (where the number of years is given at the time of conviction—e.g. five years' imprisonment) and 'indeterminate' sentences (e.g. a life sentence, where the prisoner may only be released if it is safe to do so and he or she can be recalled to prison).

Determinate sentences

The prisoner should have been sentenced according to law by a properly constituted criminal court that is independent, impartial, and follows fair procedures. The trial, including any subsequent appeals, are taken to satisfy the requirements of Article 5(4): a position confirmed by the House of Lords in *R (Giles)* v *Parole Board* [2003] UKHL 42, para 25.

Indeterminate sentences

The passing of an indeterminate sentence is compatible with Article 5(1). However, the decisions on release and recall must be taken in a manner consistent with Article 5(4) (see *R (Smith)* v *Parole Board* [2005] UKHL 1, para 36).

There are three main forms of indeterminate sentence:

- A 'mandatory' life sentence must be imposed by a court on a person convicted of murder.
- A 'discretionary' life sentence can be imposed as the maximum punishment for particularly grave offences.
- A life sentence must normally be imposed for a second, particularly grave offence (section 122 Legal Aid, Sentencing and Punishment of Offenders Act 2012). Indeterminate sentences for 'public protection' were abolished by this Act (section 123) and replaced by a power to impose a sentence extended by a maximum of 5 to 8 years (sections 123 and 125) allowing for release on licence during the extended period.

The basic structure of these sentences is that the prisoner serves a minimum term (the custodial period) for the purpose of punishment and can then be released on licence but only if the requirement of public safety is satisfied (the risk period). Under a life sentence the licence remains in place for life. The released person can be returned to prison for breaching the terms of the licence.

Under Article 5(1)(a) the minimum term should be determined judicially and, likewise, under Article 5(4) it should be possible to challenge the 'risk period' before a judicial body. In the past, under the law of England and Wales, the Home Secretary, a member of the executive, had a decisive role in both matters. A series of adverse decisions from the ECtHR led to changes in the law. Under the Criminal Justice Act 2003 the minimum custodial period, for all indeterminate sentences, is determined by the trial judge (see, regarding mandatory life sentences, section 269).

A 'whole life' tariff is allowed under English law. Compatibility with Article 5 was accepted by a majority in *Bamber* v *UK* App 33742/96, Commission admissibility decision of 11 September 1997. Regarding Article 3, *Vinter* v *UK* App 66069/09, Grand Chamber judgment of 9 July 2013 held that holding a prisoner for the rest of his or her life was not in itself incompatible with Article 3. However, human dignity, inherent in Article 3, required at least the possibility of atonement and rehabilitation. This was recognised in European penology. Therefore there had to be the possibility that a whole life term could be reduced in exceptional circumstances and a prisoner released. Following this judgment, the Court of Appeal in *R* v *McLochlin* [2014] EWCA Crim 188 confirmed that the Home Secretary's powers in section 30 Crime (Sentences) Act 1997, to release in 'exceptional circumstances' on 'compassionate grounds', were, as a matter of law, to be exercised compatibly with Article 3.

To satisfy Article 5(4), the Parole Board has to meet the requirements of independence, impartiality, and fair procedures required by Article 5(4). In *Osborn* v *Parole Board* [2013] UKSC 61, for example, the Supreme Court laid down the conditions, under domestic law on procedural fairness, by which the Parole Board was required to hold an oral hearing and held these to be compatible with Article 5(4).

The Parole Board requires that some prisoners must have attended anger management or other courses before their case can be considered. The Prison Service has been unable to provide these courses. In *James* (section 21.3.1), the ECtHR held the failure to provide the courses violated Article 5(1). The principle of non-arbitrariness in Article 5 required there to be a 'real opportunity' for rehabilitation and this was missing. In *R (Kaiyam)* v *Secretary of State for Justice* [2014] UKSC 66, the UKSC accepted that there was a duty to promote rehabilitation in Article 5. But it refused to follow the ECtHR in finding this in the express wording of Article 5(1) or 5(4). Rather it is a duty 'ancillary' to Article 5 but, crucially, not affecting the lawfulness of any imprisonment. The remedy lay in low damages.

21.4 General conditions

The ECHR has no provision equivalent to Article 10 of the International Covenant on Civil and Political Rights (ICCPR), which says:

> (1)   All persons deprived of their liberty shall be treated with humanity and with respect for the inherent dignity of the human person . . .

> (2)   The penitentiary system shall comprise treatment of prisoners the essential aim of which shall be their reformation and social rehabilitation.

▶ CROSS REFERENCE

The ICCPR is discussed in Chapter 1, section 1.4.4.

Article 3, since it embodies a general requirement that everyone, including prisoners, should be treated with humanity and dignity, is being increasingly used in respect of prison conditions—for example, the rather shocking conditions that can be found in Russian prisons (e.g. *Kolunov* v *Russia* App 26436/05, judgment of 9 October 2012). Given the vulnerability and powerlessness of prisoners, Article 3 imposes a positive duty on states to ensure that the punitive regime provides proper protection compatible with a prisoner's dignity.

The general principles concerning the application of Article 3 to prison are stated in, for example, *Kehayov* v *Bulgaria* App 41035/98, judgment of 18 January 2005, paras 62–65:

- There will only be a violation of Article 3 if the treatment is above a minimum level of severity required. This minimum level cannot be stated in general or abstract terms but depends upon a range of contextual factors.

- Article 3 can be violated even if there was no intention by the authorities to cause suffering or to humiliate and degrade.

- A violation of Article 3 only occurs in respect of prison conditions that go beyond conditions that are necessary for imprisonment: 'the suffering and humiliation involved must in any event go beyond that inevitable element of suffering or humiliation connected with a given form of legitimate treatment or punishment' (*Kalashnikov* v *Russia* (2003) 36 EHRR 34, para 95).

- It follows that the mere fact of, for example, imprisonment on remand, or imprisonment in a special prison regime does not, of itself, give rise to a violation of Article 3.

- In assessing the conditions for compatibility with Article 3, it is necessary to take into account not only the physical conditions (overcrowding, ventilation, food, etc.) but also the nature of the regime under which the prisoner is being held.

- In any event the general, positive duty of the state is to ensure that a person is detained in conditions that are compatible with respect for his human dignity, that the manner and method of the execution of any measures do not subject him to distress or hardship of an intensity exceeding the unavoidable level of suffering inherent in detention, and that, given the practical demands of imprisonment, his health and well-being are adequately secured. When assessing conditions of detention, account has to be taken of the cumulative effects of those conditions and the duration of the detention (para 64).

The application of Article 3 to prison conditions is fully accepted under English and UK law (see, for example, *R (Spinks)* v *Secretary of State for the Home Department* [2005] EWCA Civ 275, para 35). Article 3 is only violated if the conditions are sufficiently serious to cross the threshold of severity. Where that threshold is situated depends on context and circumstances. In *Napier* v *Scottish Ministers* 2005 1 SC 229, the Scottish courts held that the sanitary provisions (where prisoners, confined to shared cells, had to urinate into bottles and defecate into chamber pots), combined with other factors, crossed that threshold. But in *Grant* v *The Ministry of Justice* [2011] EWHC 3379, the case was distinguished in respect of prisoners in single cells: the threshold for a violation of Article 3 had not been passed, nor had there been a violation of Article 8.

Article 3 has significance not just in respect of the physical conditions under which prisoners are kept but also to other aspects of their treatment. A strip search is not itself a breach but must be conducted in a way that minimises degradation.

- In *Valasinas* v *Lithuania* App 44558/98, judgment of 24 July 2001, the ECtHR held that a strip search of a male prisoner in front of a woman was such a violation.
- In *R (Carroll)* v *Secretary of State for the Home Department* [2005] UKHL 13, intimate searches properly conducted under Prison Rules did not directly raise an Article 3 issue.

> **CROSS REFERENCE**
> On handcuffs, see also Chapter 9, section 9.5.

The use of handcuffs and other restraints does not normally give rise to a breach of Article 3, but may do if it is unnecessary or particularly humiliating. Where they are used on, for example, very ill prisoners who are incapable of escape, there may be a violation of Article 3 (*R (Graham)* v *Secretary of State for Justice* [2007] EWHC 2940).

21.5 Seclusion

Prison Rules (Rule 45) allow a prisoner to be placed in seclusion if this 'appears desirable, for the maintenance of good order or discipline or his own interests'. In extreme situations this could violate Article 3—sensory deprivation and total social isolation and the lack of any procedural safeguards, for instance (*Ahmad* v *United Kingdom* (2013) 56 EHRR 1 paras 205–212). Seclusion also engages Article 8(1) since the concept of 'private life' includes self-development, including through association with others. The issue then becomes justification under Article 8(2). In *Shahid* v *Scottish Ministers* [2015] UKSC 58, the UKSC found a breach of Article 8 based on (from time to time) lack of proper legal authority for seclusion and also the absence of other factors such as any serious efforts to bring about re-integration; this was in respect of a prisoner held in seclusion for 56 months.

21.6 Physically and mentally ill or disabled prisoners

States have positive duties in respect of prisoners who are particularly vulnerable on account of illness or disabilities.

> **CASE CLOSE-UP**
>
> ### *Keenan* v *United Kingdom* (2001) 33 EHRR 38
>
> A seriously disturbed and sometimes violent young man committed suicide in prison. It was held by the ECtHR that there had been a violation of Article 3 based on inadequacies of the medical treatment that he received and the fact that, shortly before he died, a serious disciplinary punishment, segregation, had been imposed. (There was not, however, a violation of Article 2—see section 21.7.1.)

General principles relating to physically and mentally ill patients are discussed by the Court in paras 90–112:

- Nothing in Article 3 requires the state to refrain from imprisoning the ill, the old, the frail, or those with mental or physical disabilities.

- However, Article 3 does require that the nature of the regime to which such persons are subjected is properly adapted to their needs. Given their greater needs, such people would otherwise suffer disproportionately; it will not do for the state to claim that such a person has been treated the same as an able-bodied person.

- A failure to give appropriate treatment, including proper medical treatment, to an ill, disabled, or otherwise incapacitated prisoner is likely to be a violation of Article 3.

Examples of breaches of Article 3 include *Price* v *United Kingdom* (2002) 34 EHRR 53 (the failure to provide appropriately for a woman with severe physical disabilities) and *McGlinchey* v *United Kingdom* (2003) 37 EHRR 41 (the failure to give adequate medical treatment to a prisoner who was both asthmatic and a heroin addict).

These principles can apply to prisoners with serious illnesses requiring intensive treatment.

In *R (Spinks)* v *Secretary of State for the Home Department* [2005] EWCA Civ 275, the Court of Appeal found there was no violation of Article 3 in the case of a prisoner with terminal cancer. On the facts, a full risk assessment had been made and the difficulties he experienced were, in the circumstances, below the threshold of severity. The case was compared with *Mouisel* v *France* (2004) 38 EHRR 34, where a prisoner with leukaemia received treatment but no other special measures were taken. The ECtHR held that there had been a breach of Article 3.

21.7 Deaths in custody

Deaths in custody engage Article 2. State responsibility for those it has taken into custody is clearly established.

21.7.1 The substantive duty

The 'substantive' duty under Article 2 means that the Prison Service must take adequate steps to ensure the safety of prisoners. In *Edwards* v *United Kingdom* (2002) 35 EHRR 19, the ECtHR found a violation of Article 2 ECHR in respect of a remand prisoner killed by his cell mate. The cell mate had a known history of violence linked to mental illness.

The *Osman* duty (that states must take positive measures to protect a person for whom they are responsible from a real and immediate threat to life) applies not only where there is a real risk of attack from other prisoners that was understood at the time by the prison authorities: it also applies to prisoners at risk of suicide.

CROSS REFERENCE

The Osman duty is discussed in Chapter 8, section 8.3.2.

In *Keenan v United Kingdom* (section 21.6), the ECtHR stressed that the positive duties under Article 2 ECHR are not absolute and that, in all the circumstances, the authorities had done what could be reasonably expected of them (there was, however, a breach of Article 3 ECHR).

🔍 CASE CLOSE-UP

R (Bloggs 61) v Secretary of State for the Home Department [2003] EWCA Civ 686

The Prison Service removed Bloggs 61, a prisoner, from a protected witness unit back to the mainstream prison. The prisoner argued that he was at risk from his former associates (drug traffickers) against whom he was to give evidence.

It was held by the Court of Appeal that returning Bloggs 61 to mainstream prison would not violate the Prison Service's positive duty under Article 2 to protect the prisoner's life (nor were other principles of administrative law breached).

Although in *Bloggs 61* the Court of Appeal stressed the need for anxious scrutiny in such cases, they also held that the duty is not absolute and that a court must give a measure of deference to the authorities over the assessment of the risk and its nature.

In non-prison cases, UK courts have stressed that the *Osman* duty arises when a proposed action will increase the risk faced by the person at risk (*Re Officer L* [2007] UKHL 36) and that the assessment of the duty must be based on the facts as they were understood at the time (*Van Colle* [2008] UKHL 50).

In *R (MJ) v Secretary of State for the Home Department* [2004] EWHC 2069, the prisoner feared that, because he had given evidence against fellow prisoners, he would be attacked if moved to a different prison. The court held that there was no evidence that the transfer would result in a real and immediate threat to the prisoner. Much of the reasoning is based on the risk assessment carried out by the Prison Service.

21.7.2 The procedural duty

The 'procedural' duty under Article 2 is for the state to provide a proper investigation into deaths of people for which it is responsible.

CROSS REFERENCE

For the procedural duty see Chapter 8, section 8.5.

The duty arises in respect of violent deaths of prisoners. The leading case in England and Wales, *R (Amin) v Secretary of State for the Home Department* [2003] UKHL 51, involves the failure of the authorities to hold a full and independent investigation, with proper family involvement, in the case of a prisoner who was the victim of a racist killing by his cell mate. Where a prisoner commits or attempts to commit suicide the English courts also accept that an investigation under Article 2 is necessary.

CASE CLOSE-UP

***R (JL) v Secretary of State for Justice* [2006] UKHL 68**

JL, a remand prisoner, was known by the prison authorities to be a real and immediate suicide risk. He attempted suicide but was revived, though he sustained irreversible brain damage. The House of Lords held that Article 2 required an enhanced (more than in-house) investigation. Whether it required a fuller, public, investigation (which would be very expensive) would depend on the facts and the results of an independent preliminary investigation.

21.8 Discipline and security

21.8.1 Offences against discipline

Prisoners in England and Wales can be prosecuted in the ordinary courts for criminal offences they commit in prison. More usually, however, they will be punished for 'offences against discipline' as these are defined in Rule 51 of the Prison Rules (for example, disobeying a lawful order: Rule 51(22)). There are a range of punishments available to a governor (Rule 55). Under the HRA, these powers need to be exercised compatibly with Convention rights. There are other provisions in the Rules that, for reasons of good order and security, allow removal from association, close supervision, and other forms of control and restraint.

21.8.2 The Convention

Nothing in Article 3 prevents the prison authorities from imposing disciplinary punishments on prisoners or from having special regimes for difficult or dangerous prisoners based on high levels of security. Such punishments or regimes must, albeit in context, not involve treatment that humiliates and degrades more than is necessary for the purposes of punishment or security.

In *Lorse v The Netherlands* (2003) 37 EHRR 3, the applicant had been convicted of drugs and firearms offences. He was kept in a special unit, which involved, amongst other matters, regular weekly strip searches, including anal inspections, and these were imposed automatically whether or not the prisoners had been out of their cells or the unit. The ECtHR could see no need for these humiliating practices and found that there was a violation of Article 3.

Strip searches, particularly involving intimate search, are likely to violate Article 3 unless they are clearly necessary and a proportionate way of achieving prison security. It is easy for such searches to be used by guards as a form of humiliation of prisoners.

21.8.3 England and Wales

Punishment

The imposition of a punishment and security measures must be compatible with the law, as expressed in the Prison Rules. For example, a governor has some discretion over the way food and clothing is provided. However, to withdraw food and clothing from a prisoner as a punishment would be unlawful and also likely to be a violation of Article 3 (reduced diet was one of the techniques used in *Ireland* v *United Kingdom*: see Chapter 9, section 9.2; see *R (Russell)* v *Governor of Frankland Prison* [2000] 1 WLR 2027).

Force-feeding

Prisoners may refuse food. The force-feeding of a prisoner on hunger strike can involve Article 3. The general position under the Convention is that where there is a genuine medical necessity (to save the life of the person, for example) then there is no objection in principle to force-feeding subject to procedural guarantees being complied with and that the method does not go above a minimum level of severity. Where these conditions do not apply, particularly if force-feeding is part of a disciplinary response or punishment, then Article 3 is likely to be breached and could, given the method, even amount to 'torture' (see, for instance, *Nevmerzhitsky* v *Ukraine* (2006) 43 EHRR 32, especially paras 93–99).

Under the HRA, in England and Wales, these are matters for the courts to decide (*R (Wilkinson)* v *Responsible Medical Officer, Broadmoor Hospital* [2001] EWCA Civ 1545). Where a prisoner of sound mind chooses to maintain a hunger strike, then his or her right to autonomy (recognised by the common law and reinforced under Article 8) is likely to outweigh any argument of medical necessity (*R (Robb)* v *Secretary of State for the Home Department* [1995] 2 WLR 722).

21.8.4 Punishment and fair trials

The right to a fair hearing before an unbiased tribunal has been extended to prisoners in England and Wales under the common law and this is reinforced, perhaps in a more hard-edged way, by the Convention, which recognises that prisoners have rights to a fair trial under Article 6.

In *Leech* v *Deputy Governor of Parkhurst Prison* [1988] 2 WLR 290, the House of Lords held (building on an earlier case involving the Board of Prison Visitors, who no longer have a disciplinary role) that governors' disciplinary procedures were subject to judicial review and needed to meet proper fair trial standards. The basic principles are that the prisoner should know precisely what is alleged against him or her and have the opportunity to answer the charge.

The common law rights are context dependent and flexible. In *R* v *Home Secretary ex parte Tarrant* [1985] 1 QB 251, for example, it was held that the rules of natural justice did not mean that a prisoner was in all circumstances entitled to be represented when subject to a governor's discipline. A similar situation was challenged before the ECtHR.

 CASE CLOSE-UP

Ezeh v United Kingdom (2004) 39 EHRR 1

Prisoners had been awarded 'additional days' (meaning they would stay in prison for longer than they would otherwise anticipate) in disciplinary hearings before their prison governor. Their claim, under the common law, to be represented had been denied. A Grand Chamber held that given the severity of the punishment, the governor had been determining a 'criminal charge', thus invoking Article 6(1)–(3). Article 6(3)(c) in particular gave an entitlement to representation that the English courts had denied.

CROSS REFERENCE
For Article 6 and 'criminal charge' see Chapter 12, section 12.4.

As a result of the case the Prison Rules were changed. A disciplinary charge that might result in an additional days' punishment must now be heard not by the governor but by an independent adjudicator before whom there is a right of representation.

21.9 Prisoners and Convention freedoms: private life

Prisoners are subject to the continuous day-to-day control of the authorities over all aspects of their lives. At the same time they retain their Convention rights and their freedom under the common law to the extent that it is not necessarily restricted by imprisonment. A number of issues have arisen in which the policies of the authorities have been tested against Convention rights.

 BIGGER PICTURE

For a listing of these rights by a Grand Chamber see *Hirst* v *United Kingdom (2)* (2006) 42 EHRR 41, para 69.

> **CROSS REFERENCE**
>
> For Article 8 see Chapter 15.

Of particular importance are prisoners' rights under Article 8, the right to private life and correspondence. Prisoners retain these rights, but the question is the extent to which, in the context of imprisonment, the authorities can show that some restriction they have imposed can be justified under the second paragraph of the Article: the restrictions must be imposed on the basis of law, be for a legitimate purpose, and be proportionate. Proportionality often involves a requirement that the authorities are sensitive to individual circumstances and do not apply blanket rules.

21.9.1 Search

The prison authorities have powers, based in the Prison Rules, to search prisoners and their cells. This power clearly engages prisoners' rights to private life and correspondence under Article 8(1); it also engages Article 6, the right to a fair trial (especially the implied right of access to the courts) in so far as searches may involve a prisoner's correspondence with legal advisors.

In *R* v *Secretary of State for the Home Department ex parte Daly* [2001] UKHL 26, the House of Lords accepted that a policy of always removing prisoners during cell searches that could include searches of legal correspondence was disproportionate and hence not justified under Article 8(2).

21.9.2 Article 8, family life: artificial insemination

> **CROSS REFERENCE**
>
> For Article 12 see Chapter 19.

Separation means that long-term prisoners may not have the opportunity to conceive children. They retain the simple right to marry under Article 12 (*Hamer* v *United Kingdom* (1982) 4 EHRR 139) but the more extensive right to found a family in that Article requires balancing individual interests with the need for prison order and security that Article 8 explicitly allows. There is no Convention right to 'conjugal visits' (e.g. *X* v *United Kingdom* (1975) 2 DR 105) and nothing in the Prison Rules permits these. The Home Office and Prison Service did not normally allow prisoners access to artificial insemination facilities and in *R (Mellor)* v *Secretary of State for the Home Department* [2001] EWCA Civ 472, the Court of Appeal had denied this policy was a breach of either Article 8 or Article 12.

In *Dickson* v *United Kingdom* (2008) 46 EHRR 41, however, a Grand Chamber, held that there had been a violation of Article 8 in respect of a long-term prisoner denied by the Prison Service the opportunity of artificial insemination. Article 8 was engaged and, in relation to justification and proportionality, the evidence did not suggest that proper consideration was given to individual cases.

21.9.3 Mothers and babies

The issue of the treatment of prisoner mothers and their children engages Article 8(1).

Q CASE CLOSE-UP

R (P and Q) v Secretary of State for the Home Department [2001] EWCA Civ 1151

Prison policy meant that babies were separated from their prisoner mothers after 18 months. The Court of Appeal held that the policy was only justified under Article 8(2) if applied flexibly and in a way that centred on the consequences for the children. P was serving a long sentence and would probably be deported; Q was serving a short sentence and there were no suitable arrangements for her child outside the prison. In Q's case Article 8 had been violated. The case was followed in respect of the policy of prison leave to facilitate rebuilding relations with children in *R (MP)* v *Secretary of State for Justice* [2012] EWHC 214.

21.10 Prisoners and Convention freedoms: freedom of expression

Prisoners retain their Convention rights, including freedom of expression in Article 10, and under the common law they retain those rights that are not necessarily incompatible with imprisonment. Restrictions on prisoners' rights to freedom of expression may be seen by the authorities as necessary incidents to imprisonment. In which case they still have to be compatible with Article 10 but it may be relatively easy for the authorities to show that a restriction is justified. Alternatively they will be an interference with the Article 10 rights that is not strictly an incident of imprisonment, in which case it will need compelling justification under Article 10(2).

▶ CROSS REFERENCE

For Article 10 see Chapter 17.

Article 10(1) includes the right to receive information. Some restrictions on the availability of reading and writing materials for prisoners may be a necessary incident of imprisonment; others may need justification under Article 10(2).

As regards prisoners' communications with the outside world, Rule 34 of the Prison Rules allows restrictions to be imposed by the authorities but only those that are compatible with Convention rights such as Article 10 (i.e. necessary incidents to imprisonment or justifiable under Article 10(2)). There are likely to be ample justifications for the Prison Service to retain powers to scrutinise writings by prisoners, though punishment of a prisoner for writing critically about prisons is likely to be a breach, as it was in *Yankov* v *Bulgaria* (2005) 40 EHRR 36. A ban on a prisoner seeking to publish his autobiography, which might contain discussion of his crimes, was upheld by the Court of Appeal in (*R (Nilsen)* v *Governor of Full Sutton Prison* [2004] EWCA Civ 1540).

Total bans on prisoners' contacts with the media may be disproportionate and violate Article 10 (*Bamber* v *United Kingdom* App 33742/96, admissibility decision of 11 September 1997).

 CASE CLOSE-UP

R (Hirst) v Secretary of State for the Home Department [2002] EWHC 602 (Admin)

A Prison Service Order banned, other than in exceptional circumstances, prisoners from telephoning to the media with material that might be broadcast. The Order was applied to Hirst, a serving prisoner who campaigned on prisoners' rights issues and wanted to be able to comment in broadcast media on such matters. The court held that the total ban involved a disproportionate impact on the defendant and was an unlawful policy.

Other violations include the complete ban on links with journalists, even when this prevented prisoners pursuing claims to have been wrongly convicted (*R* v *Secretary of State for the Home Department, ex parte Simms* [2000] AC 115.

21.11 The right to vote

The right of prisoners to vote, based on Article 3 of the First Protocol, became, in 2011, a major matter of political controversy in the United Kingdom. It is discussed in Chapter 25, section 25.3.2.

 Summary

Prisoners retain their Convention rights. These are consistent with normal, lawful, imprisonment. These include not only rights to the non-arbitrary loss of liberty and rights to fair procedures, but also not to be disproportionately denied the rights and freedoms in Articles 8 to 11. These rights are applied in context and a wide margin of appreciation is allowed to the states.

? Self-test questions

1. Do prisoners keep all their Convention rights, some or none?

2. What are the duties, based on the ECHR, on the Prison Service, the government, and the courts in respect of murders and suicides in prisons?

3. How do Article 3 and Article 8 relate to the application of any policy allowing seclusion of prisoners?

4. What impact does Article 6 have on the procedures for disciplining prisoners?

5. Many prisoners are ill—what duties based on Convention rights does the Prison Service have towards them?

 For suggested approaches, please visit the Online Resource Centre.

? Exam questions

1. A significant number of prisoners are 'transgender' in the sense of their going through or having gone through a process of living in the gender different from that in which they were born.

   The Ministry of Justice and Prison Service are perplexed at the correct policy to pursue in relation to many issues, including whether to send these prisoners to male or female prisons and whether special facilities are necessary.

   Advise on what, if anything, is required to ensure compatibility with Convention rights (reference to Chapter 19, section 19.5, will be helpful).

2. Discuss, with reference to Convention and UK case law, whether the imposition of a 'whole life tariff' on a prisoner convicted of murder can be compatible with the Convention. Give, with reasons, your opinion on whether the law on this provides proper protection for human rights.

 For suggested approaches, please visit the Online Resource Centre.

≡ Further reading

Easton, S. *Prisoner's Rights* (2011) London: Routledge

Livingstone, S., Owen, T., and Macdonald, A. *Prison Law* 4th edn (2008) Oxford: OUP

22

Applications: media law and privacy

□ **LEARNING OBJECTIVES**

- The importance of media freedom under the Convention.
- Media regulation in the United Kingdom.
- Journalism and Convention rights (qualified privilege and the protection of sources).
- Balancing Article 8 and Article 10—celebrity cases.

Introduction

▶ **CROSS REFERENCE**

Article 10, including political speech, is considered in Chapter 17; Article 8 is considered in Chapter 15.

The media is a two-edged sword. For most of us our information about the world and our entertainment comes from the media—online, broadcast, and print. At the same time the media can pander to our baser instincts for sensation and vicarious engagements with violence and sex. Both these aspects become all the more significant as the media is privatised in the sense that the role of private individuals in getting their voice 'out there' begins, slowly, to overcome the role of the organised and regulated professional broadcaster. Two fundamental human rights are involved in the encounters that result: freedom of expression and privacy. How the law can properly balance these with each other in the context of the modern media is discussed in this chapter.

22.1 The importance of the media

The importance of the audio-visual media has been emphasised time and again by the ECtHR. Freedom of the press, broadcasting, and other forms of media are clearly protected under Article 10(1).

The principles derived from leading Convention cases on media freedom such as *Lingens* v *Austria* (1986) 8 EHRR 407, paras 41–42 and *Fressoz and Roire* v *France* (2001) 31 EHRR 2, para 45 include:

- Safeguarding the freedom of the media is of particular importance for the maintenance of freedom of expression.

- The media has the 'task' or 'duty' of imparting information and ideas of public interest.

- The public has a 'right' to receive such information and ideas.

- The media has a vital 'watchdog' role to play in a democracy.

- It is incumbent on the media to 'impart information and ideas on political issues', defined broadly and including controversial ones. In particular the 'audio-visual' media, as a whole, needs to be independent of government and be able to uphold pluralism and diversity of ideas in society.

- In performing this duty a certain leeway (journalistic exaggeration and provocation, for instance) is allowed. Nevertheless, given, in particular, the 'duties and responsibilities' clause in Article 10, 'the press must not overstep the bounds set, *inter alia*, for protection of vital State interests, such as national security or territorial integrity, against the threat of violence or the prevention of disorder or crime', or to protect the reputation of others. This is particularly true in the context of reporting political violence (e.g. *Sürek and Özdemir* v *Turkey* (1999) App 23927/94, Grand Chamber judgment of 8 July 1999, para 58).

Q | CASE CLOSE-UP

Stoll v *Switzerland* (2008) 47 EHRR 59

A journalist published extracts from a confidential strategy document which was extremely critical of the Swiss ambassador to the United States over his approach to negotiating compensation for Holocaust victims. The journalist was prosecuted, convicted, and fined by the Swiss courts.

A Grand Chamber, reversing the Chamber judgment, found there had been no violation of Article 10. The Court emphasised that, Article 10 notwithstanding, journalists are bound by the criminal law. They must act in good faith and on an accurate factual basis and provide accurate and precise information in accordance with the 'ethics of journalism'. These considerations are particularly relevant to the modern world because, in it, the media do not just inform they also suggest how information is to be assessed. In this world 'monitoring compliance with journalistic ethics takes on added importance' (see paras 102–104).

Similar principles on the importance of a free media can be found in the law of England and Wales. For example:

> The proper functioning of a modern participatory democracy requires the media be free, active, professional and enquiring. For this reason the courts, here and elsewhere, have recognised the cardinal importance of Press freedom and the need for any restriction on that freedom to be proportionate and no more than is necessary to promote the legitimate object of the restriction.

> (*McCartan Turkington Breen* v *Times Newspapers* [2000] 4 All ER 913, 922, Lord Bingham)

22.2 The Human Rights Act and the regulation of the media

These principles are given effect through the application not only of the general law as it applies to the media but also through the regulation of both the press and broadcasting.

22.2.1 The press

The press is commercially owned, typically by major corporations with a wide range of media interests. There are provisions under competition law (which includes European law) that, in the name of a free media, are designed to prevent market dominance. In the past individual owners have had a significant influence on the broad editorial stance. This continues today, although, for a corporation, profitability is central.

Regarding content, there are no special laws that apply to the press. There is no formal censorship. However, newspapers are subject to the ordinary law on matters such as obscenity, defamation, and breach of confidence. Some statutory provisions, though applying generally, have a particular relevance for the press and media. Section 5 of the Official Secrets Act 1989 is an example: a person (such as a newspaper editor) commits an offence if he or she makes a damaging disclosure of information known to have itself been obtained in breach of the Act. Other statutory provisions apply expressly to journalists, such as the protection given to 'journalistic material' in the context of police powers of entry, search, and seizure.

CROSS REFERENCE

For indirect horizontal effect see Chapter 4, section 4.7.1.

Being privately owned, newspapers are unlikely to be 'public authorities' for the purpose of section 6 HRA (though, given the public importance of a free press, they might be thought to be performing a public function and thus covered by the Act under section 6(3)(b)). This does not matter much because newspapers tend to be subject to the 'indirect horizontal effect' of the Act.

The courts, as public authorities, must act compatibly with Convention rights and, depending on context, may develop the common law that relates to important issues involving the press in ways that reflect Convention rights. *Campbell* v *MGN* [2004] UKHL 22 involved a conflict between media freedom and the right to private life—it was expressly decided by the House of Lords by balancing the terms and values found in Articles 8 and 10 (paras 17–18; 132).

Press behaviour has often not been unlawful but, rather, been harassing or intrusive into people's private lives. A simple, cheap, and accessible form of regulation has been sought. But it has always been difficult to balance regulation with the independence and also the commercial power of the press.

In 2011–2012 a major press scandal dominated British public life (the 'phone-hacking' scandal). At its heart were allegations of unlawful or unethical intrusions by journalists (and private investigators they employed) into the private lives not just of celebrities but of others, including the victims of crime. The 'Leveson Inquiry' reported on the scandal in 2012 and some editors and journalists have been convicted of phone hacking crimes (the criminal process was wound up in 2015).

An important aspect of the scandal was the inability of the Press Complaints Commission (the regulator at the time) adequately to investigate and deal with the allegations made, and its general lack of knowledge and of power to keep the press within the law and subject to decent ethical standards. It closed in 2014.

The choice of replacement is controversial. The Leveson Report, victims' groups such as 'Hacked Off', and the government wanted a body which, though fully independent of both government and the industry, nevertheless has a proper basis in law and whose authority over the press is not merely voluntary. Dominant elements of the press, on the other hand, have fully accepted the idea of independence but strongly resist the idea of compulsion—of a legal as distinct from voluntary requirement to accept regulation.

As a result the majority of the press (most national and local newspapers and numerous magazines) have established and agreed to be bound by their own regulator which they believe to be sufficiently powerful and independent to provide proper regulation. This is the Independent Press Standards Organisation (IPSO). It decides complaints that its 'Editors' Code' has been broken. This Code has provisions including ones relating to accuracy (with an opportunity to reply), privacy, harassment, children, and payments to criminals. Importantly, some provisions (e.g. on privacy) are subject to a public interest exception, though the burden is on the editor to prove a reasonable belief that the public interest outweighs what would otherwise be prohibited by the Code. The public interest includes, but is not confined to:

- detecting or exposing crime or a serious misdemeanour;
- protection of public health and safety;
- preventing the public from being misled by some statement or action of an individual or organisation;
- disclosing individual or organisational failure to fulfil obligations;
- disclosing miscarriages of justice;
- contributing to public debate on alleged serious impropriety, unethical conduct, or incompetence which concerns the public;
- disclosing concealment of the above.

The Code also recognised that '[t]here is a public interest in freedom of expression itself'.

THINKING POINT

Does the IPSO Editor's Code, http://www.editorscode.org.uk/the_code.php, provide the basis for a proper balance between freedom of the press and the rights and freedoms of others?

Significant elements of the press, in particular the Guardian, the Independent, and the Observer, have rejected the ethos of absolute self-regulation and chosen not to be regulated by IPSO. There is an alternative possibility. The coalition government accepted the Leveson steer towards a legal foundation for regulation but were fearful of too much political involvement in setting up a regulator. The Press Recognition Panel (PRP) was established in 2014. Its authority comes not from statute but from a Royal Charter. Unlike IPSO, the PRP is not itself a regulator. Its principal task is to choose and supervise a regulator which will be independent, properly funded, and able to protect the public. Its chosen regulator will have some statutory support: sections 34–42 Crime and Courts Act 2013 will protect newspapers from aggravated damages but only if regulated by a PRP-chosen regulator, and section 96 Enterprise and Regulatory Reform Act 2013 protects the Charter from change. Whether there ever is a PRP-chosen regulator and how it relates to IPSO, is, after the Conservative victory in the 2015 election, a sensitive political question.

The principal remedy of IPSO (and, by presumption, any alternative) is to require editors to publish an adjudication with proper prominence and, perhaps, a retraction. It does not have power to stop a story from being published in the first place, nor can it require the payment of compensation. By itself it is unlikely to be a fully sufficient remedy for breaches of human rights such as Article 8 (see *Peck* v *United Kingdom* (2003) 36 EHRR 41). Therefore, access to the courts for damages (breach of confidence, defamation etc.) are still a necessary part of control. In *Venables* v *News Group Newspapers* [2001] EMLR 10, for example, the High Court accepted that the remedies available from the then regulator were insufficient to prevent the press identifying the homes of notorious child murderers after their release (para 97). This situation the court remedied by issuing a protective injunction. Under section 12 HRA, courts considering remedies involving freedom of the press must take into account any 'relevant privacy code'.

22.2.2 **Broadcasting**

Broadcasting companies are corporately owned, like the press, but, unlike the press, are subject to external, statute-based regulation. This is performed partly by Ofcom itself and partly by the broadcasters under the auspices of Ofcom. Ofcom's authority comes from the Communications Act 2003 and, as such, it will be a public authority under section 6 HRA or subject to Article 10 through judicial review (*Gaunt* v *Ofcom* [2011] EWCA Civ 692). Furthermore, it has statutory duties that must be applied in ways that are compatible with Convention rights. Much of the Communications Act is to do with technical matters but, under section 319, Ofcom produces a Broadcasting Code (covering standards, sponsorship, fairness, and privacy), which licensed broadcasters must obey. Complaints can be made to Ofcom for breach of the Code, after a programme has been broadcast. The Code deals (in much more detail than the Editors' Code) with a range of issues, such as offensiveness, due impartiality in political matters, fairness, and privacy. Ofcom, therefore, is a central part of the system for providing remedies for breaches of (in particular) Article 8 and to do so in ways that enable a fair balance to be achieved with freedom of expression in Article 10.

Any inadequacy in the Ofcom process for respecting private life and protecting media freedom can be brought before the High Court under section 7 HRA or 'ordinary' judicial review. *Pro-Life Alliance* v *BBC* [2003] UKHL 23 (where the House of Lords upheld the broadcaster's refusal to show an anti-abortion party election broadcast: see Chapter 17, section 17.8.3) suggests that the courts may show significant 'deference' to the regulators who have been specifically empowered with the task.

The BBC is different: it is established by Royal Charter. Nevertheless, the courts treat it as they would a statute-based organisation. Control over programme standards is, ultimately, the responsibility of the BBC Trust (who replaced the governors in 2007) and is derived from provisions in the Charter and the Agreement. Standards are based partly on the Trust's own codes (such as on due impartiality) whilst others are standardised with commercial broadcasting—this includes the provisions on fairness and privacy. Complaints can be made initially to BBC management with the Trust acting as a 'final court of appeal'. As with Ofcom, any inadequacies in human rights protection should (for compliance with Article 13) be dealt with in the courts.

Internet content is not regulated by Ofcom. It is, however, subject to ordinary law (defamation, for example), so long as there is someone responsible and within the jurisdiction of the law. English courts can, for example, force disclosure from a website owner (not an ISP) who hosts defamatory material (see, for example, *Sheffield Wednesday FC* v *Hargreaves* [2007] EWHC 2375). The website owner can then be proceeded against.

22.3 Legal control: defamation and responsible journalism

As well as through regulation, content-related control of the media to protect people's rights to privacy can be based on the ordinary law. An important instance is an action for defamation. This provides a remedy to a claimant who can prove that a publication lowers his or her reputation in the view of reasonable people. If the claimant can satisfy the court that the publication does this, damages will be awarded unless the defendant can establish that what was published was true or that what was published was not a simple statement of fact but a value judgment that amounted to fair comment on a matter of public interest.

Defamation is a restriction on freedom of expression that is likely to be justifiable under Article 10(2) as a legal and proportionate restriction aimed at protecting 'the reputation or rights of others'. Reputation is an aspect of private life respect for which must be secured under Article 8. But in practice this has a potentially 'chilling' effect on media freedom. This potential has been recognised by the courts in the way they attempt to balance Article 10 and Article 8 rights. Thus in *Cumpana* v *Romania* (2005) 41 EHRR 14, for example, a Grand Chamber accepted that journalists had defamed an official and had been properly convicted; however, there was a breach of Article 10 because the severity of the punishment did not take the protection of media freedom into account.

> **CROSS REFERENCE**
> The impact of defamation laws on political speech is also explored in Chapter 17, section 17.8.4.

The need to counteract the chilling effect on freedom of expression that defamation proceedings may cause has led the UK courts to grant a qualified privilege to the press. Qualified privilege means that statements can be made without the threat of defamation unless the claimant can prove that the publication was made maliciously (intending harm to the claimant) or in bad faith. Qualified privilege applies to reports of various official matters including parliamentary proceedings (see the Defamation Act 1996, section 15 and Schedule 1). Absolute privilege applies to fair and accurate contemporaneous reports of court proceedings (section 14).

There is also qualified privilege available in some situations under common law and it is this that the courts have extended to general media stories that would otherwise be defamatory and that are either in fact untrue or whose truth the defendant is unable to prove. The principles were established in *Reynolds* v *Times Newspapers* [2001] 2 AC 127 (see later in this section) and the law was confirmed and clarified by the House of Lords in *Jameel*.

CASE CLOSE-UP

Jameel v *Wall Street Journal Europe Sprl* [2006] UKHL 44

A Saudi company alleged that an article in the *Wall Street Journal* had linked them to terrorist funding. The House of Lords allowed the newspaper's appeal from a finding that they had libelled the claimants. The newspapers had media privilege ('*Reynolds* privilege').

The central points of media privilege are:

- The publication, taken as a whole, must be in the public interest. This is a development of the law and means that media privilege is a distinct form of qualified privilege. In many earlier cases, qualified privilege required a duty to publish and a reciprocal duty or interest to receive the information. This duty/interest approach does not adequately encompass the situation of the media, who publish to the public in general, and so it has been adapted.

- The court determines whether the story is in the public interest. An important difference is recognised between stories that the public might like to know about (celebrity gossip, for instance) and stories of sufficient importance for their publication to be in the public interest. However, it is not necessary to go so far as proving that the public have a 'need to know'.

- Responsible journalism. Publication can only be in the public interest (and therefore privileged) if the journalists have behaved (considered in the context) properly and responsibly in the way they have obtained and checked the story.

Responsible journalism and factors that go to establishing the public interest in a story were considered in *Reynolds*.

 CASE CLOSE-UP

Reynolds v *Times Newspapers* [2001] 2 AC 127

R, the former Taoiseach (Prime Minister) of Ireland, alleged that Times Newspapers had defamed him by suggesting he had deliberately misled the Irish Parliament during a political crisis. In its defence the newspaper argued that, because of the importance of media freedom, it should enjoy 'qualified privilege' over political reporting. The House of Lords rejected the idea that there should be a blanket privilege for the media on political stories. Their Lordships developed the general principles confirmed in *Jameel* (above). On the facts of the case there was no public interest requiring publication.

In *Reynolds* Lord Nicholls (p 205) suggested that, in determining public interest, a range of factors need to be taken into account. These include (but are not confined to) the seriousness of the allegation, the nature of the information in issue, the source of the information, the steps taken to verify it, the status of the information, the urgency of the matter, whether comment was sought from the claimant, whether the 'gist' of the claimant's side of the story was published, the tone of the story (particularly if the newspaper adopts the allegation as fact), and the circumstances, including timing, of the publication.

> **CASE CLOSE-UP**
>
> ***Flood v Times Newspapers*** [2012] UKSC 11
>
> A national newspaper reported allegations of bribery and corruption against a serving, named police officer. The officer was exonerated; however, the allegations remained, unamended, on the newspaper's website. The officer brought defamation proceedings. The newspaper successfully argued that the original story and its continued presence on the website was protected by media (*Reynolds*) privilege. The Supreme Court, applying *Reynolds* and *Jameel*, agreed.

Part of the argument was to recognise that qualified privilege was necessary to ensure compatibility of common law defamation with Article 10 (paras 44–47). It was held that it could be in the public interest to publish mere allegations, despite the fear of 'trial by media'. The Supreme Court (unlike the Court of Appeal) accepted that the journalism had been 'responsible' because the journalists had done enough to justify their belief that there was a serious case against the officer.

Media (*Reynolds*) privilege aims at reducing the chilling effect of defamation proceedings on freedom of speech where there is a clear public interest in the publication. Its impact is not confined to the media (e.g. *Charman* v *Orion Publishing Group Ltd* [2007] EWCA Civ 972, where it is applied to book publishers, and *Seaga* v *Harper* [2008] UKPC 9, where it is applied to statements made at a public meeting).

22.4 Protection of sources

The need for journalists to protect the identity of their sources is an axiom of journalist ethics. It is reflected in the IPSO Editors' Code, 'Journalists have a moral obligation to protect confidential sources of information', para 14); under section 12 HRA this Code may need to be taken into account in freedom of expression cases.

The ECtHR has frequently recognised that 'the protection of journalists' sources is one of the cornerstones of freedom of the Press' (*Cumpana* v *Romania* (2005) 41 EHRR 14, para 106). In *Goodwin* v *United Kingdom* (1996) 2 EHRR 123, the ECtHR held that a court order requiring a journalist to disclose his sources, done in order to enable a company to identify a disloyal employee, was disproportionate. The Court said:

> Without such protection [the confidentiality of sources], sources may be deterred from assisting the Press in informing the public on matters of public interest. As a result the vital watchdog role of the Press may be undermined and the ability of the Press to provide accurate and reliable information may be adversely affected . . . such a measure [a court order requiring disclosure] cannot be compatible with Article 10 of the Convention unless it is justified by an overriding requirement in the public interest. (para 39)

Under English law, section 10 of the Contempt of Court Act 1981 (CCA 1981) establishes the general rule that journalists may not be compelled to disclose their sources but allows for disclosure to be ordered in certain circumstances.

10 Sources of information

No court may require a person to disclose, nor is any person guilty of contempt of court for refusing to disclose, the source of information contained in a publication for which he is responsible, unless it be established to the satisfaction of the court that disclosure is necessary in the interests of justice or national security or for the prevention of disorder or crime.

First, a court must decide whether one of the three grounds of exception in section 10 CCA 1981 are engaged:

- Interests of justice. This has been said to mean: 'to exercise important legal rights and to protect themselves from serious legal wrongs'. This is a narrower meaning than 'justice as the opposite of injustice' but broader than justice as requiring a resort to the courts. The term encompasses the right of an employer to seek the name of a disloyal employee so that he or she might be dismissed (e.g. *X* v *Morgan Grampian Ltd* [1991] 1 AC 1; quotation is at p 43).

- National security. This has been used to identify a civil servant responsible for a leak to the media (*Secretary of State for Defence* v *Guardian Newspapers Ltd* [1984] 2 WLR 268).

- Prevention of disorder or crime. This has been used to require disclosure of evidence that might be used in a fraud prosecution: *Re an Inquiry under the Company Securities (Insider Dealing) Act 1985* [1988] AC 660.

Second, a court must decide whether disclosure is necessary in the public interest. Here the point is whether the public interest in, for example, preventing crime, could be secured other than by ordering disclosure. In *Interbrew SA* v *Financial Times Ltd* [2002] EWCA Civ 274, for example, disclosure was ordered as necessary to permit a company to take court action to seek to protect confidential commercial information.

Third, a court must decide whether the public interest in disclosure outweighs the public interest in media freedom and the protection of sources. On this point there was some evidence that greater weight was given to protection of sources in Strasbourg than in the United Kingdom, at least in some of the pre-HRA cases mentioned earlier.

When the *Interbrew* case was considered by the ECtHR, it found a violation of Article 10. The company had other means available to it by which it might seek damages and minimise harm from future disclosures. Therefore there was no overriding requirement of the public interest that required an interference with freedom of expression by forcing the journalist to disclose his source (*Financial Times Ltd* v *United Kingdom* (2010) 50 EHRR 46).

Following the coming into force of the HRA, English courts unambiguously bring together section 10 and Article 10 on the issue of when the assumption in favour of protecting sources can be overridden.

 CASE CLOSE-UP

Ashworth Hospital Authority v *MGN* [2002] UKHL 29

MGN published in the *Daily Mirror* excerpts of the medical records of Ian Brady, a notorious child killer detained at a security hospital. The source was probably an employee of the hospital who disclosed them (via an intermediary) in breach of his contract of employment. The hospital obtained a court order requiring the newspaper to disclose the original source so that he could be dismissed (a matter 'in the interests of justice'). One of the issues was whether the journalist could be compelled to disclose his source. The House of Lords confirmed the order. (The matter was returned to the lower courts, which, in the end, did not order disclosure: *Mersey Care NHS Trust* v *Ackroyd* [2007] EWCA Civ 101.)

The House of Lords held that:

- Section 10 and Article 10 have the same purpose: to protect journalist freedom.

- Following *Goodwin*, any overriding of the right to protect sources requires an overriding public interest that must be 'convincingly established' and given, by the court, the most 'careful scrutiny' (paras 49 and 61).

- On the facts of the case great weight was given to the need to protect medical records, particularly in the context of psychiatry and the need, found in Article 8, that the law provide appropriate safeguards to protect medical records.

> **CROSS REFERENCE**
>
> Ashworth is also discussed in Chapter 15, section 15.10.6.

22.5 Celebrity cases

22.5.1 Introduction

The courts in England and Wales have had to deal with cases brought by public figures and celebrities who allege the media have interfered with their privacy. At the heart of the cases is the question of what weight to give to the competing interests of the media's freedom to publish (which may be commercially motivated and the story may have little public significance), contrasted with a celebrity's privacy (perhaps already compromised by those who use the media to create and advance their financially valuable images).

22.5.2 The Convention position

The Grand Chamber has laid down the basic principles dealing with these cases.

Q | CASE CLOSE-UP

von Hannover* v *Germany (No 2) (2012) 55 EHRR 15/***Axel Springer AG* v *Germany*** (2012) 55 EHRR 6

In *von Hannover*, Princess Caroline of Monaco (a celebrity in Germany) claimed that her right to private life under Article 8 was infringed when German courts failed to prevent by injunction a German magazine publishing stories and photographs of her on a skiing holiday. In *Axel Springer*, a newspaper publisher argued that their right to impart information, under Article 10, was infringed when the German courts prevented them publishing articles concerning the arrest and conviction of a well-known TV actor on drugs offences.

In both cases there were interferences with the rights. The issue was justification and, in particular, proportionality. This involves the balancing of the interests protected by Article 8 and Article 10 in the detail of the cases.

Despite the Article 8 focus in *Von Hannover* and the Article 10 focus in *Axel Springer*, the Grand Chamber identified the general criteria which need to be balanced

- The contribution of the publication to debate of general interest; mere celebrity gossip has a low weighting. This can include exposure of criminal activity, as in *Axel Springer*.

- How well known is the person concerned. Public figures are not denied protection of their private life but must expect a greater degree of public examination. Article 10 could protect stories about the private life of public figures but not if there was little contribution to public debate, rather just a desire to satisfy public curiosity.

- Prior conduct of the person. E.g. earlier cooperation with the press, though this is not enough to remove all their right to private life.

- Method of obtaining the information and its veracity. For example—whether the journalism has been responsible and done in good faith; whether there had been consent or subterfuge, etc.

- Content, form, and consequences of the publications. Photographs, for instance, can contribute to debate but also be particularly intrusive (as in *von Hannover*).

- Severity of the legal sanction.

Applying these principles, the Grand Chamber found (in *von Hannover*) that German courts had not breached Princess Caroline's right to private life but (in *Axel Springer*) that they had breached the publisher's right to freedom of expression.

At the heart of these decisions is an attempt to find a way of accepting that public figures retain some rights of privacy but not ones that can interfere with the proper interest of the people in public matters.

22.5.3 HRA: protecting a reasonable expectation of privacy

The common law of England and Wales has not developed an abstract, background right to privacy. Most of the concrete incidents of privacy are covered by existing law, such as laws of property and the torts of trespass to the person (see *Wainwright* v *Home Office* [2003] UKHL 53, paras 15–35).

▶ CROSS REFERENCE

The 'indirect horizontal effect' of Convention rights is discussed in Chapter 4, section 4.7.

But the HRA means that UK law needs to provide adequate remedies for breaches of Article 8, even in the private sphere (e.g. regarding newspapers and broadcasters). The UK courts, being public authorities, have duties to develop the common law in ways that secure these rights.

▶ CROSS REFERENCE

For confidentiality in a political context see Chapter 17, section 17.7.3.

Under the influence of Article 8, the courts have developed the traditional protection of confidential relationships (e.g. as between doctor and patient) into a wider remedy available where a person has 'in respect of the disclosed facts…a reasonable expectation of privacy': *Campbell* v *MGN* [2004] UKHL 22, para 21.

🔍 CASE CLOSE-UP

Campbell v _MGN_ [2004] UKHL 22

Naomi Campbell, a celebrity supermodel, claimed that the publication in the *Daily Mirror* (owned by the defendant) of information about her receiving treatment for drug addiction and a photograph of her leaving a meeting of Narcotics Anonymous violated her privacy, and was arguably incompatible with her rights under Article 8. On the facts it was held (3–2) that the claimant's rights had been violated.

Important points in the judgment are:

- The House of Lords accepted that an action for breach of confidence was now to be understood as an action to uphold a person's 'reasonable expectation of privacy'.

- If a person has such an expectation, the issue for a court is to balance rights to respect for private life under Article 8 with the media's freedom under Article 10.

- On the facts of the case the House of Lords departed from the Court of Appeal's assessment and, by a majority, found that Campbell's Article 8 rights outweighed the right of the press to freedom of expression. The fact that it was evidence of medical treatment that was disclosed had, in the context of a person's struggles with addiction, particular weight.

Whether a person has a reasonable expectation of privacy depends upon the facts. In *JR 38's Application* [2015] UKSC 42, the UKSC endorsed *Murray* v *MGN* [2008] EWCA Civ 446—the court should consider the attributes of the claimant (e.g. whether children), the nature of the claimant's activity (e.g. domestic or professional), the venue, the nature and purpose of the media's intrusion, the factor of consent, the effect on the claimant, and role of the publisher.

There have been many cases following *Campbell*. For example, in *Weller* v *Associated Newspapers Ltd* [2015] EWCA Civ 1176, children of Paul Weller, a famous musician, alleged that the publication, in Mail Online, of photographs of them shopping with their father breached their Article 8 rights. Following the *Murray* criteria (discussed earlier), the court accepted that the children had a reasonable expectation of privacy and that, applying the *von Hannover* criteria, discussed earlier, their rights to private life clearly outweighed the Article 10 rights of the media.

Injunctions

Given that any confidentiality or reasonable expectation of privacy is necessarily destroyed by publication, the courts can issue an interim injunction to prevent publication in the first place. An interim injunction prevents publication pending the full hearing. An injunction has a major impact on media freedom and, in respect of Article 10, is not easily obtained (for example Catherine Zeta-Jones and Michael Douglas were unable to prevent unauthorised photographs of their wedding being published: *Douglas* v *Hello!* [2001] 2 All ER 289). Section 12 HRA means that interim injunctions should only be awarded if the applicant would be likely to win at a full hearing, and this applies as much to fully confidential information as it does to claims of simple privacy (*Cream Holdings Ltd* v *Banerjee Ltd* [2004] UKHL 44).

A major issue for UK courts has been the extent to which Article 8 (and common law protection of privacy) might require not only the injunction but also further restraints, such as anonymity or withholding even general facts about the case. In *JIH* v *News Group Newspapers* [2011] EWCA Civ 42, the Court of Appeal laid down general guidance (in para 21). The principle of open justice (Article 6 and common law) is important, but there may be overwhelming reasons for it to be restricted (see Chapter 12, section 12.8.2). Judges should impose no more than the minimum restraints on publication necessary to protect Article 8. The question is whether the public interest in publishing names and normally reported subject matter outweighs the need to protect the person's privacy. These are fact-sensitive issues and an appeal court should not normally interfere with the way the judge at first instance has balanced the issues.

BIGGER PICTURE

The report of Lord Neuberger MR, *Super-Injunctions, Anonymised Injunctions and Open Justice*, contains a full discussion of these issues. True 'super-injunctions' (where the very existence of an injunction cannot be published) are shown to be very rare. Anonymity, discussed earlier, is a much bigger issue.

Summary

Convention rights have had a significant impact, both directly and indirectly, on media law. However, often the issue involves balancing the clear commitment to media freedom derived from Article 10 with other rights such as in Article 8. Here the issue is less one of legal principle and more of application on the particular facts of cases.

? Self-test questions

1. How does the 'duties and responsibilities' clause in Article 10 affect the media?

2. Explain the principles, inherent in Article 10, which allow journalists to protect their sources.

3. What impact do Convention rights have on the regulation of broadcasting?

4. Does regulation (of press and broadcasting) by itself provide effective remedies for persons aggrieved by what they see as a breach of their privacy?

 For suggested approaches, please visit the Online Resource Centre.

? Exam question

1. Evaluate, with reference to European and UK cases, the way the balance of media freedom with the rights of individuals, including prominent ones, to protect their privacy is undertaken.

2. A group of newspaper editors and broadcasters are perplexed by the concept of 'responsible journalism'.

Prepare a lecture in which you explain the concept, put it in context, and relate it to the rights and obligations of the media in respect of, in particular, Article 8 and Article 10.

 For suggested approaches, please visit the Online Resource Centre.

 Further reading

Kenyon, A. and Richardson, M. (eds) *New Dimensions in Privacy Law: International and Comparative Perspectives* (2006) Cambridge: CUP

Price, D. *Defamation: Law, Procedure and Practice* 4th edn (2009) London: Sweet & Maxwell

Smartt, U. *Media and Entertainment Law* (2014) London: Routledge

23 Article 1 of the First Protocol: protection of property

The First Protocol

Article 1 Protection of Property

Every natural or legal person is entitled to the peaceful enjoyment of his possessions. No one shall be deprived of his possessions except in the public interest and subject to the conditions provided for by law and by the general principles of international law.

The preceding provisions shall not, however, in any way impair the right of a state to enforce such laws as it deems necessary to control the use of property in accordance with the general interest or to secure the payment of taxes or other contributions or penalties.

Introduction

A right to protect possessions (property) is controversial. On the one hand, it can be seen as essential to human flourishing. Without legal support for property there would be little security for individuals choosing the lives they wish to lead (albeit in conditions not of their own choosing) and taking rational steps to achieve it. On the other hand, property represents social and political power. It is distributed unequally and the minorities who own and control the land and the wealth of the country are able to exercise indirect control over the political, economic, and social system. In the twenty-first century, economic power and dominance is in corporate, non-personal, hands. The self-interested decisions of huge corporations have enormous social, economic, and political impact, and this is a power that depends upon the possession and exercise of property rights. Given the relationship between property and power, it is not surprising that governments have often sought the constitutional freedom to control the production and distribution of wealth in society and this may require limiting the right to property.

These kinds of arguments were very real at the end of the Second World War. They explain why the issue of the protection of property was not settled until after the European Convention on Human Rights (ECHR), in its original form, came into effect. In particular, Britain had an 'old' Labour government that, in the late 1940s, was pursuing a vigorous programme of nationalisation (public ownership). As Lord Hoffmann said in *R (Alconbury)* v *Secretary of State for the Environment, Transport and the Regions* [2001] UKHL 23, para 71:

> All democratic societies recognise that while there are certain basic rights which attach to the ownership of property, they are heavily qualified by considerations of the public interest. This is reflected in the terms of art 1 of Protocol 1 to the Convention.

23.1 Article 1 of the First Protocol–general features

Article 1 of the First Protocol (Article 1) is couched in terms which seem to accept wide powers of states to control property in the 'public' or 'general' interest. As we shall see, the European Court of Human Rights (ECtHR) has narrowed this power considerably in the way the Article has been interpreted.

23.1.1 Companies

It should be noted that Article 1 expressly gives rights to any 'legal person'. This means that companies, in themselves, may seek the protection of the Article. Although companies have rights under other Articles (e.g. Article 6, the right to a fair trial), Article 1 contains the only express reference to companies in the whole Convention. Thus companies, which are artificial legal persons, enjoy 'human' rights irrespective of the social power they can exercise on the basis of their economic strength. Shareholders, however, may not have a claim if the interference is really with the company's rights and the company chooses not to act.

> **CROSS REFERENCE**
> The position of companies and shareholders under the Convention is discussed in Chapter 2, section 2.7.1 Corporations (companies).

23.1.2 Human Rights Act 1998

Property rights are firmly established in English law. They can be inherent in Acts of Parliament, such as those dealing with estates in land, credit controls, or intellectual property. They are also inherent in common law principles relating, for example, to contract, estates in land, and to torts such as trespass to land or to property. Under the Human Rights Act 1998 (HRA) these statutory and common law provisions must be interpreted and developed for compatibility with Convention rights, especially Article 1.

Q   CASE CLOSE-UP

Wilson v *First County Trust Ltd* [2003] UKHL 40

FCT, a credit company, lent W money to buy a car. The credit agreement was regulated by the Consumer Credit Act 1974. The Act prevented the enforcement of an agreement by creditor against debtor unless, amongst other matters, the exact amount of the loan was expressed in the paperwork. In this case the expressed amount of the loan did not include a £250 administration fee. It was held that the agreement could not be enforced against W. The House of Lords held that FCT's right to possessions under Article 1 had not been violated.

In *Wilson*:

- A majority of Law Lords held that Article 1 applied, either because the credit company had been deprived of their possessions or because it had been restricted in its enjoyment of its possessions.

- However, there was a 'fair balance' between the public interest in controlling credit and the fundamental rights of the creditors.

- Considerable deference was shown to Parliament's view on the proper balance the public interest required between debtors' and creditors' interests.

23.2 The definition of 'possessions'

The concept of a possession is an autonomous Convention concept (a concept developed by the ECtHR and not dependant on the way the matter is defined in national law). Possessions are defined in a broad and inclusive way which focuses on a person's entitlement to valuable assets of a tangible or intangible kind.

It includes the obvious such as vested legal rights to land, to personal property (things), and to money. It also includes 'intangible' property, a right to something of value to the holder, for example, a licence to engage in economic activity (as in *Tre Traktörer Aktiebolag v Sweden* (1991) 13 EHRR 309). It includes contractual rights over personal property (as in *Wilson*, section 23.1.2) and intellectual property rights such as copyright, registered trademark, and patents (*Anheuser-Busch v Portugal* (2007) 45 EHRR 36 and, for English law, *Ashdown v Telegraph Group Plc* [2001] EWCA Civ 1142). It includes a legally recognised right to compensation consequent to a court judgment. A person may have a possession, under Article 1, even if their legal title is uncertain or irregular. In *Öneryildiz v Turkey* (2005) 41 EHRR 20, a Grand Chamber held that the slum dwelling in which the applicant lived was a possession for the purposes of Article 1 as distinct from the land on which he lived illegally (paras 124–129).

23.2.1 The acquisition of possessions

No right to acquire possessions

From its earliest cases the Court has denied that Article 1 guarantees a right to acquire possessions not currently enjoyed. (In *Marckx* v *Belgium* (1979–80) 2 EHRR 330, the ECtHR held that Article 1 does not guarantee children's rights to acquire property by inheritance from their parents, see para 50.)

Legitimate expectations as 'possessions'

However, there are ways in which anticipated property can be protected by Article 1.

The 'goodwill' in a business, on which future profits may be anticipated, can count as a possession, though this has to be distinguished from profits that might accrue from hoped-for contracts (as in *Breyer Group* v *Department of Energy and Climate Change* [2015] EWCA Civ 408).

Article 1 can protect certain 'legitimate expectations'—property interests which are in the 'nature of a claim' which have a clear and uncontested basis in domestic law. Article 1 does not guarantee that the applicant will have the asset but, by treating it as a 'possession', requires that any refusal or withdrawal should be justified in terms of Article 1. An example is the right to bring a tort action, as in *Pressos Compania Naviera SA* v *Belgium* (1996) 21 EHRR 301, discussed at section 23.7.4.

In *Centro Europa 7 SRL* v *Italy* App 38433/09, Grand Chamber judgment of 7 June 2012, the applicant TV company had a licence for national terrestrial broadcasting in Italy. But it could only begin broadcasting once the Italian authorities had allocated frequencies; and over this there were considerable delays. A significant portion of the judgment concerns Article 10 (see Chapter 17)—the failure to allocate frequencies was, in the circumstances, an unjustified interference with the applicant's right to 'impart information and ideas'. However, there was also a violation of Article 1 of the First Protocol. The allocation of the licence created a legitimate expectation of being able to broadcast, which was a 'possession'. Given that the interference with this 'possession' was unlawful (because in breach of Article 10), it was also a breach of Article 1.

Under the HRA, in *R (PCSU)* v *Minister for the Civil Service* [2011] EWHC 2041, the High Court accepted that the expectation to benefits under the civil service pension were possessions for the purpose of Article 1 (though government interference with these benefits was justified).

23.2.2 The right to practise a profession

A licence or other permission necessary to practise a profession may involve a possession but only if the applicant already enjoys a valuable asset in his or her practice, such as business goodwill.

In *Van Marle* v *Belgium* (1986) 8 EHRR 483, Belgium law was changed to require existing accountants to register with a professional body. The ECtHR held that a refusal by the professional body to register the applicants (experienced accountants with an existing clientele) would be detrimental to their existing business with its valuable goodwill and was an interference with their possessions.

Van Marle can be compared with *R (Malik)* v *Waltham Forest NHS PCT* [2007] EWCA Civ 265, where the Court of Appeal denied that a doctor's inclusion on the medical performers list (entitling the doctor to provide NHS services) was a possession. Inclusion had no marketable value and amounted, in effect, to no more than an expectation of future earnings. The doctor's unlawful suspension from the list did not, therefore, engage Article 1.

23.2.3 **Welfare payments**

Nothing in the Convention imposes a duty on a state to provide welfare benefits. Disputes frequently arise over entitlements to the complex range of benefits that modern European states do provide their citizens in the context of the 'welfare state'. The question can arise whether rights to such benefits are possessions and so engage Article 1. Originally the case law, from both the Commission and the Court, suggested (though not consistently) that only contributory benefits (such as under a national insurance scheme to which individuals have made identifiable contributions and which are, in that sense, like private insurance schemes) were possessions. Non-contributory benefits (like the basic state old age pension, for example), which were funded from general taxation, were not possessions and so not protected by Article 1. The Court changed this in *Stec* v *United Kingdom*.

🔍 CASE CLOSE-UP

Stec v United Kingdom (2005) 41 EHRR SE18, Grand Chamber admissibility decision

S alleged that a non-contributory benefit was distributed in a way that involved sex discrimination, contrary to Article 14. Article 14 would only apply if she could also show that she had a right to the benefit under Article 1 of the First Protocol (Article 14 is confined to discrimination in the way other Convention rights are secured). Although the ECtHR held that there had not been a violation of the Convention, it did accept that S's entitlement to the benefit was a possession and so Article 1 of the First Protocol was engaged.

In *Stec* the Court made it clear that Article 1 applied to all benefits whether contributory or non- contributory (see paras 38–53).

- The Court adopted an 'evolutive' approach to the Convention (one which recognises social and legal changes in Europe) which took into account the reality of the complex way in which states organise and fund their benefits systems. Many benefits are interlocking and it is artificial to distinguish contributory from non-contributory benefits.

- The Convention needs to be read as a whole and to be internally consistent. Article 6 (the right to a fair trial) no longer distinguishes between contributory and non-contributory benefits as regards the right to a fair trial and so the interpretation of Article 1 should be consistent with this.

- Nevertheless, the Court reiterated the point that nothing in Article 1 of the First Protocol gives an individual a right to a benefit which the state has not chosen to provide (para 53).

The merging in *Stec* of contributory and non-contributory benefits has been followed by the House of Lords in *R (RJM)* v *Secretary of State for Work and Pensions* [2008] UKHL 63, holding that disability benefit was a possession, thus engaging Article 1. Likewise the UKSC accepted that the benefits subject to the 'benefits cap' were possessions for the purposes of Article 1 (*R (SG) v Secretary of State for Work and Pensions* [2015] UKSC 16). These cases may cast doubt on the correctness of the Court of Appeal's refusal to treat jobseeker's allowance as a possession in *R (Couronne) v Crawley* [2007] EWCA Civ 1086.

23.3 General approach: three rules or one?

The approach of the ECtHR is to break Article 1 down into three separate but interrelated rules (see *Sporrong and Lönnroth v Sweden* (1982) 5 EHRR 35, para 61).

- Rule 1 (the first sentence of the first paragraph) invokes a general principle of peaceful enjoyment of possessions.
- Rule 2 (second sentence of the first paragraph) deals with the state depriving an owner of property.
- Rule 3 (second paragraph) deals with the state exercising control over the uses of property, short of deprivation.

In the text the rules appear to have different significance. Rule 2 seems to inhibit deprivation of property unless done 'in the public interest and subject to the conditions provided for by law and by the general principles of international law'. Rule 3, by contrast, does no more than require states to act in the 'general interest'. It could easily be read as imposing few if any justiciable restrictions on the freedom of the state to control the uses of property.

The ECtHR has not accepted this. Rules 2 and 3 are to be interpreted in the light of Rule 1, an unqualified right to the 'peaceful enjoyment of possessions'. Being unqualified, Rule 1 is interpreted by the Court in terms of general Convention principles. In particular, interferences with property must be considered in respect of the general Convention concepts of 'lawfulness' and, above all, 'proportionality'. They must serve a 'legitimate purpose' and represent a fair balance between the achievement of the purpose and the burdens imposed upon the individual (see *James v United Kingdom* (1986) 8 EHRR 123, para 37).

> The court must decide whether a fair balance was struck between the demands of the general interest of the community and the requirements of the protection of the individual's fundamental rights.
>
> (*Sporrong and Lönnroth v Sweden* (1982) 5 EHRR 35 (a case decided under Rule 1))

The ECtHR has made it clear that this applies to Rules 2 and 3 as well. These rules are to be understood as:

> particular instances of interference with the right to peaceful enjoyment of property [i.e. Rule 1] and should therefore be construed in the light of the general principle enunciated in the first rule.
>
> (*Broniowski v Poland* (2005) 40 EHRR 21, para 134)

Thus proportionality applies to Rule 2 and also, despite its wording, Rule 3. However, these rules refer to the 'public' and the 'general' interests, respectively. Proportionality in this context does not, therefore, mean that a court can substitute its own view for that of the authorities.

Rather it is to ensure that, in determining the public or general interests, the authorities have not simply ignored the property owners but sought a fair balance with their interests.

23.4 Has there been an interference and, if so, of what type?

Article 1 is relevant where a possession has been interfered with. Usually the matter is clear: a decision or act by a public authority directly affects the applicant's enjoyment of his or her possessions (though in *Breyer*, see section 23.7, mere proposals made in a consultation document sufficed).

CROSS REFERENCE
Positive duties generally are discussed in Chapter 6, section 6.6.

The state may have 'positive duties' to act, or to ensure that a certain state of affairs exists, rather than a mere obligation not to do certain things.

Interferences can include a failure to pay compensation or a refusal to take effective measures (as where environmental hazards have an impact on property rights, as in *Oneryildiz* v *Turkey* (2004) 41 EHRR 20, see Chapter 8, section 8.3.5). Positive duties to maintain a system of law protecting property rights between private parties are illustrated by *James* v *United Kingdom* (discussed at section 23.6.1). Where, however, the interference with possessions is entirely a private contractual matter, and not a consequence of government action or inaction, then it may hold that Article 1 is not involved (see *Gustafsson* v *Sweden* (1996) 22 EHRR 409, involving a dispute between a restaurant owner and a trade union over which the government had no legal powers).

As the ECtHR has often said, the distinction between negative and positive duties can seem arbitrary. The overriding question is not the type of duty but whether there has been an interference with property which involves state responsibility.

23.4.1 The basic approach

Where there is an interference for which the state is responsible, the general method of the Court is to consider, first, whether there has been a deprivation of property or a control of use and, if possible, to deal with the matter under either Rule 2 or Rule 3. If the interference cannot be classified by either of those two terms, the Court will deal with the matter as an interference with peaceful enjoyment, under Rule 1. These classifications are not 'watertight' and little now seems to turn on them since the same basic issue, the existence of a fair balance between the individual and the collective interest, applies whichever of the three rules is in issue. In both Convention cases and cases under the HRA it is not necessarily made clear which rule is being followed.

23.4.2 Deprivation (Rule 2)

A 'deprivation' of property involves the idea that the reality of the interference suffered by the applicant is a compelled, full transfer of ownership rights. Examples from the case law include:

- Nationalisation, as in *Lithgow* v *United Kingdom* (1986) 8 EHRR 329, where aircraft and shipbuilding companies objected to the compensation terms of their nationalisation.

- Forced sale of land, as in *Hentrich* v *France* (1994) 18 EHRR 440 (see section 23.5.1).
- Expropriation of land, as in *Scordino* v *Italy (No 1)* (2007) 45 EHRR 7, where the authorities expropriated the applicant's land under a general development plan; the case focused on compensation.

23.4.3 **Control of use (Rule 3)**

Where there has been no total loss of ownership rights, the Court will consider whether the interference complained of involves a control of use rather than the elimination of the rights of ownership.

- Development control (town and country planning) can give rise to issues under Rule 3. For example, in *Pine Valley Developments Ltd* v *Ireland* (1992) 14 EHRR 319, the ECtHR held that Rule 3 applied to a dispute over whether the Irish authorities could grant the applicant permission to build on 'green belt' land. Rule 3 is not always seen as applying to development control, which is sometimes treated by the ECtHR as involving an interference with the peaceful enjoyment of possessions under Rule 1.
- The loss of effective ownership may be the consequence of laws that control the use of property. These are dealt with under Rule 3. Confiscation and forfeiture of property, in the context of the suppression of crimes, is an example (see *Air Canada* v *United Kingdom* (1995) 20 EHRR 150 (forfeiture of an aircraft on which smuggled drugs had been discovered) and *Allgemeine Gold- und Silberscheideanstalt AG* v *UK* (1987) 9 EHRR 1 (seizure and forfeiture of smuggled Krugerrands (gold coinage))). Adverse possession (the legal rule by which a landowner's title is extinguished if they have not objected, for at least 12 years, to another person's trespassory use of the land) was held by a Grand Chamber to be a restriction on use and not, as the Chamber had held, a deprivation of property: *Pye (Oxford) Ltd* v *United Kingdom* (2008) 46 EHRR 45, para 66.
- Rent control schemes that limit the economic freedom of landlords, such as in *Hutten-Czapska* v *Poland* (2007) 45 EHRR 4, engage Rule 3.

23.4.4 **Peaceful enjoyment (Rule 1)**

There can be interferences with property which, in the Court's view, do not cause a total loss of ownership rights nor are they conveniently understood as controls over use. In these circumstances, the ECtHR will deal with the issue under Rule 1, as interferences with the peaceful enjoyment of possessions. Examples include:

- Planning blight: planning issues are sometimes dealt with under Rule 3. Where government plans for redevelopment or other schemes diminish the value of property or involve other constraints, an issue under Rule 1 may arise (as in *Sporrong and Lönnroth* v *Sweden* (1983) 5 EHRR 35—various restrictions on property in Stockholm were imposed for up to 23 years to enable city council redevelopment plans that did not materialise).
- Restitution. Alleged failure of governments to provide effective compensation for losses of property can be considered in terms of Rule 1. This can include, for instance, failure to make proper restitution for the behaviour of previous regimes (see, for instance, *Papamichalopoulos* v *Greece* (1993) 16 EHRR 440 or *Broniowski* v *Poland* (2005) 40 EHRR 21).
- Pre-emption rights to prevent the sale abroad of an old master (in *Beyeler* v *Italy* (2001) 33 EHRR 52) were dealt with under Rule 3.

- In *Thomas* v *Bridgend CBC* [2011] EWCA Civ 862, section 3 HRA was used to read into section 19 Land Compensation Act 1973 a right to compensation in respect of noise nuisance from an unadopted road in order to make it compatible with Article 1.

23.5 Is the interference lawful?

An 'interference' with possessions is not itself a violation. The issue for the court is whether the interference can be justified. The interference must be lawful, for a legitimate purpose, and proportionate.

23.5.1 Legality and the Convention

▶ CROSS REFERENCE

Convention concept of 'law' is discussed in Chapter 6, section 6.2.

Article 1 will be breached if the state's interference with possessions is not lawful. It must be in accordance with national law (as determined by national courts) and also meet the Convention requirement of accessibility and foreseeability. In *Scordino* v *Italy (No 3)* (2009) 48 EHRR 9, the Italian courts had condoned an unlawful expropriation of land. The ECtHR awarded €3,300,000 for pecuniary damage and €40,000 for non-pecuniary damage.

A law that gives officials a wide discretion to interfere with property where it is very hard to determine in advance the circumstances in which that discretion is likely to be exercised may fall foul of the legality principle.

In *Hentrich* v *France* (1994) 18 EHRR 440, the ECtHR held that the power of 'pre-emption' exercised by the French tax authorities (by which they could force an individual to sell land if it had been bought at a price so low it implied tax evasion) was highly discretionary and exercised in unpredictable ways. Therefore it failed the 'legality' test.

As well as acting on the basis of law, the legality principle requires that the state and its agencies themselves comply with judicial orders made against them (see, for example, *Amat-G Ltd* v *Georgia* (2007) 45 EHRR 35).

23.5.2 International law

Rule 2 requires any deprivation of property to be compatible with 'international law'. The main impact of this provision is on the principles dealing with compensation, and is considered at section 23.8.

23.6 Justification: legitimate purpose

There will be a violation of Article 1 unless the state can prove that the interference was for a legitimate purpose and, as regards the imposition on the individual claimant, was not an unreasonable burden on the applicant. Although the language of the three rules is different, the concept of seeking a fair balance between the common good aimed at by an interference and the individual burden imposed, applies to all. The Court has consistently made it clear that the second and third rules should 'be construed in the light of the general principle enunciated in the first rule' and that this compatibility with the first rule requires, in relation to the second and third rules, a ' "fair balance" between the demands of the general interest of the community and the requirements of the protection of the individual's fundamental rights' (from *Pye (Oxford) Ltd v United Kingdom* (2006) 43 EHRR 3, paras 52–53).

However, the permissive language of Article 1 and its references to justifying interferences in the public or general interest, means that states have a wide margin of appreciation over the identification of what purposes and policies are in their public or general interest (see *Broniowski v Poland* (2005) 40 EHRR 21, para 149).

This margin of appreciation raises the issue of the degree of appropriate deference to be shown by the courts to government and Parliament on the issue of where the public or general interest lies. In *Alconbury* (Introduction), Lord Hoffmann, at para 72, argued that on the public interest a high degree of deference was owed on the issue of the purpose to be pursued—this was a matter for 'elected local or central bodies or by ministers accountable to them' and not for judicial bodies such as courts or tribunals. But the same degree of deference may not apply to the question of proportionality (see section 23.7).

THINKING POINT

What degree of deference should be shown in possessions cases? Compare Lord Hoffmann, above, with some of the cases under 'proportionality', section 23.7.

23.6.1 Social policy and the redistribution of wealth

Governments (often those of the 'old' left or associated with the 'social market') might want to distribute property in the name of social justice in order to improve the lives of the least well off in society or some other disadvantaged group. Article 1 does not seem a barrier to effective schemes of this kind. For example, in *James v United Kingdom* (1986) 8 EHRR 123, a statutory scheme by which tenants holding very long leases had the right to purchase the freehold of their dwellings from their landlords was held to be compatible with Article 1. This was so even though the landlords stood to make considerable losses and received no compensation beyond the sale price. The Act pursued a legitimate purpose (preventing the unjust enrichment of landlords) and the burden on the applicants was proportionate, including the level of compensation. The Court implicitly rejects, therefore, any view that the Convention somehow protects and insists upon freedom of contract and the values of the free market. Nationalisation (the taking of individual businesses or whole industries into public ownership) has also been accepted as a legitimate aim in cases such as *Lithgow v United Kingdom* (1986) 8 EHRR 329.

The views of the elected legislature on important social objectives will also weigh heavily against Article 1 claims by landowners. This is demonstrated by *R (Countryside Alliance v Attorney General* [2007] UKHL 52. The House of Lords held that the Hunting Act 2004, which banned hunting with dogs, interfered with landowner's use of their own land and lowered the value of the hounds and related equipment. But the interference was justified—a proper deference by the court to Parliament's assessment of the rights and wrongs of hunting was necessary.

23.6.2 Development control and town and country planning

Most states adopt policies to protect the environment by placing restrictions on building and development, such as producing plans to organise land use and requiring planning permission before developments can go ahead. Cases objecting to planning decisions are dealt with under Article 1 either as an example of Rule 3 (control of use) or Rule 1 (interference with peaceful enjoyment). The ECtHR is reluctant to interfere with good faith decisions taken in this regard (see, for example, *Katte Klitsche de la Grange* v *Italy* (1995) 19 EHRR 368). However, as in *Sporrong and Lönnroth* v *Sweden*, discussed in section 23.7.1, procedural problems, like serious delay, may mean that the authorities have acted disproportionately.

Similar deference to the planning authorities is illustrated in HRA cases.

- In *Davies* v *Crawley* [2001] EWHC 854, the council adopted a street trading scheme which had a highly detrimental impact on D's mobile catering business. Nevertheless, there was a fair balance of competing interests and Article 1 did not require compensation to be paid.
- In *Belfast City Council* v *Miss Behavin' Ltd* [2007] UKHL 19, there was a challenge, partly on Article 1 grounds, to the refusal of Belfast Council to license a sex shop. It was held that, at best, the impact of Article 1 would be very weak with interferences easily justified; indeed Lord Neuberger referred to case law suggesting that a refusal of planning permission could, of itself, never give rise to a violation of Article 1.

23.6.3 Prevention of crime

Measures that have an impact on people's property may be taken in order to promote the prevention or punishment of crime.

In *Raimondo* v *Italy* (1994) 18 EHRR 237, the ECtHR held that there was no violation of Article 1 when a mafia suspect was arrested and his property confiscated whilst the criminal issues were decided. There was a breach, however, caused by the delay in returning the property after the applicant had been acquitted.

In this and other forfeiture cases (such as *Air Canada* v *United Kingdom* (1995) 20 EHRR 150, see section 23.4.3), the matter is treated as a temporary transfer of property and is dealt with under Rule 3. Where full ownership transfers entirely to the state, then there is likely to be a deprivation of property to be dealt with under Rule 2.

In the United Kingdom there are increasingly tough laws by which the state can impose what is, in effect, a levy aimed at denying a convicted person the proceeds of crime.

In *R* v *Rezvi* [2002] UKHL 1 and *R* v *Benjafield* [2002] UKHL 2, the House of Lords held that the procedures for dealing with confiscation orders under the Criminal Justice Act 1988 and the Drug Trafficking Act 1994 respectively, were compatible with Article 1. Confiscation had a legitimate aim of denying criminals the profits of crime; the measures in the Acts were rationally related to these aims and represented a fair balance of interests.

23.6.4 The seizure of goods to guarantee the payment of taxes

▶ CROSS REFERENCE

See *Lindsay*, in section 23.7.2, for an example of a disproportionate exercise of this power.

Since this is expressly mentioned in the third sentence of Article 1, seizure of goods to enforce taxes is accepted as a legitimate activity by the state over which it is given a wide margin of appreciation (see, for example, *Gasus Dosier- und Fördertechnik GmbH* v *Netherlands* (1995) 20 EHRR 403).

23.7 Justification: proportionality

The bite of Article 1 lies in the proportionality test. Demonstrating a legitimate purpose is not enough. The means chosen must be 'proportionate' and this applies whether the issue is dealt with under Rule 1, 2, or 3. There must be a fair balance or 'reasonable relationship of proportionality' between the demands on the individual and the public interest. If there is an 'individual and excessive burden' on the individual, the Court may find a violation of Article 1. However, in *James* v *United Kingdom* (discussed earlier, at section 23.6.1), the ECtHR rejected an approach to proportionality which required proof that a burden was strictly necessary and no less onerous alternatives were available (para 51). Thus states have room to pursue legitimate objectives in their own way appropriate to the circumstances.

On the issue of proportionality, the courts do not necessarily show a high level of deference. In *International Transport Roth GmbH* v *Secretary of State for the Home Department* [2002] EWCA Civ 158, a majority of the Court of Appeal held that the statutory scheme by which lorry companies were fined for every illegal entrant found in their lorries (liability was more or less strict, defences hard to establish) was disproportionate. The scheme went beyond what was necessary and imposed too severe a burden on the companies (Laws LJ dissented on the grounds that greater deference should have been shown to Parliament).

Similar apparently low deference has been shown to the executive.

> **CROSS REFERENCE**
> Proportionality under HRA is discussed in Chapter 4, section 4.6.

Q CASE CLOSE-UP

Breyer Group v *Department of Energy and Climate Change* [2015] EWCA Civ 408

The government, in a consultation document, proposed an earlier than expected lowering of the rate paid for electricity from small-scale low carbon producers. Although the proposal was eventually held to be unlawful, the making of it had an immediate and damaging effect on the producers. They sought damages based on breach of their Article 1 rights. The Court of Appeal, agreeing with the High Court on most points, held:

- The proposal in the consultation document was an 'interference' with producers' peaceful enjoyment of their possessions, which included profits anticipated from business goodwill (this is a 'Rule 1' case).

- The interference was lawful (consulting on an unlawful proposal is lawful)—Article 1 would have been breached had it not been.

- The interference was disproportionate. The High Court's assessment was accepted. There was a legitimate purpose (reduction in costs falling on electricity consumers in a time of austerity) but the Secretary of State had not properly taken into account the size of the investments undertaken given the producers' reasonable reliance on the time structure in the original scheme. The detriment to the environment of the change could also be taken into account.

It is clear that the Court of Appeal accepts the close proportionality assessment by the High Court. This does not seem to be a case in which a high level of deference is shown to the government.

23.7.1 Delay, procedure, and remedies

The fact that a person's rights over their property are suspended for long periods of time without a final resolution of the matter can be an important feature indicating a disproportionate burden on the applicant. This is often linked to the failure of the state to provide an adequate legal mechanism and set of remedies by which the tardiness of public bodies and officials can be challenged. Although Article 1 says nothing about procedural rights (i.e. rights to go to court and challenge the lawfulness of the actions of the authorities), their absence is taken seriously by the Court. In this context, Article 1 claims often include an Article 6 claim.

 CASE CLOSE-UP

Sporrong and Lönnroth v Sweden (1983) 5 EHRR 35

S and L owned property in central Stockholm which was scheduled for redevelopment. The city obtained legal permits enabling it to compulsorily purchase the land and to prohibit building. These permits were eventually cancelled but only after various periods between 12 and 25 years. Swedish law did not provide a legal process by which the city's need for the permits could be reconsidered, nor was there an effective system for compensation. The ECtHR held that there had been a violation of Article 1. The permits were for a legitimate purpose (development control) but the system was inflexible and so, in this case, imposed disproportionate burdens. The lack of a fair procedure also violated Article 6.

23.7.2 An indiscriminate, blanket policy

State action which is based on applying a policy in a way that treats people the same who ought to be treated differently can be challenged on proportionality grounds. An HRA case illustrates the point.

 CASE CLOSE-UP

Lindsay v Customs and Excise Commissioners [2002] EWCA Civ 267

L purchased a new car for £12,000, which he later used to transport large amounts of cigarettes and tobacco from Calais to the UK. He was stopped by Customs and Excise who, alleging he was avoiding paying duty of about £3,500, confiscated not only the cigarettes and tobacco but also the car. A tribunal accepted, as fact, that the goods were for personal and family use (the Court of Appeal was sceptical). The Court of Appeal held that the policy of confiscating both goods and vehicle served a legitimate purpose. However, as a policy, it was potentially disproportionate and so violated Article 1. It did not distinguish between private smugglers and smugglers intending to make a profit. Regarding the former, the need for a fair balance required greater sensitivity to individual factors like the value of the confiscated goods, whether it was a first offence, potential hardship, etc. The decision had to be retaken in this light.

23.7.3 The conduct of the parties

The conduct of the parties is another feature that can determine whether an interference is proportionate.

CASE CLOSE-UP

Beyeler v Italy (2001) 33 EHRR 52

B was a Swiss national who purchased a Van Gogh from a Rome art dealer. He did not disclose his identity but used an intermediary. B wished to sell his painting. The Italian state had legal powers of pre-emption by which, in order to preserve the Italian heritage, they could insist on buying a picture from its owner, thus preventing it from being sold abroad. The Italian government eventually exercised this power and obtained the painting for a sum below the market price. The ECtHR held that there had been a violation of Article 1. The burden on B was disproportionate.

The Court's reasons stress the conduct of both parties: some of B's actions were not as open and honest as they might be, whilst the authorities had delayed for five years in exercising its powers and had treated B in an ambivalent way, which left him uncertain of his situation. The extent of the discretion enjoyed by the authorities under the law also contributed to the finding that the burden on B was disproportionate.

23.7.4 Compatibility with the rule of law

State actions that are incompatible with the rule of law may also indicate that a disproportionate burden is involved.

 CASE CLOSE-UP

Pressos Compania Naviera SA v Belgium (1996) 21 EHRR 301

The Belgium legislature enacted retrospective legislation which removed from the applicant shipping companies a right, affirmed by a decision of the highest court in Belgium, to sue for negligence pilots working in Belgium waters. The ECtHR held there was a violation of Article 1. Although for a legitimate purpose, the burden on the applicant was disproportionate. One objection the Court had was to the retrospective nature of the legislation: had the legislation been prospective there would have been no Convention difficulty.

23.8 Compensation

23.8.1 Rule 2, deprivation of possessions

Convention principles

Where a person is lawfully deprived of their property under Rule 2, it will normally be a breach of Article 1 not to provide reasonable compensation. This is partly because compensation is normally a requirement of international law, which is expressly mentioned in Rule 2. More importantly, the payment of compensation is a crucial factor for determining whether or not a fair balance has been achieved between the public interest that justifies the deprivation and the burden placed upon the individual or company who loses a possession. However, compensation is not an absolute necessity: see, for example, *Jahn* v *Germany* (2006) 42 EHRR 49. Nor is the payment of full compensation always necessary since there may be significant social and economic reasons that justify a lesser amount (as in a nationalisation case, *Lithgow* v *United Kingdom* (1986) 8 EHRR 329). The Grand Chamber summed up the position in *Pye (Oxford) Ltd* v *United Kingdom* (2008) 46 EHRR 45, para 54:

> A taking of property under the second sentence of the first paragraph of Article 1 without payment of an amount reasonably related to its value will normally constitute a disproportionate interference that cannot be justified under Article 1. But full compensation is not guaranteed since legitimate objectives of 'public interest' may call for less than reimbursement of the full market value.

In *Scordino* v *Italy* (2007) 45 EHRR 7, building land was lawfully expropriated by the authorities, but the Court found the compensation paid under Italian law to be inadequate and awarded €580,000 and €12,400 to the applicants in two separate cases. In *Yukos* v *Russia* App 14902/04, judgment of 31 July 2014, pecuniary losses for a forced bankruptcy of a major oil company, in breach of Article 1, were assessed at €1,866,104,634, a massive sum—see Chapter 5, section 5.5.2.

Human Rights Act 1998

These principles have been adopted under the HRA. In *Beaulane Properties* v *Palmer* [2005] EWHC 817, the High Court ruled that the application of 'adverse possession' laws was a deprivation of property engaging Rule 2, and so the total absence of compensation for the original owner was disproportionate and a violation of Article 1. (By conceptualising adverse possession as not a deprivation but an interference engaging Rule 3, the Grand Chamber, in *Pye (Oxford) Ltd* v *United Kingdom* has undermined the basis of this case: see section 23.4.4.)

R (SRM Global Master Fund) v *Treasury Commissioners* [2009] EWCA Civ 788 involved a dispute over the way shares in the bank Northern Rock were valued when it was nationalised. The effect of the method of valuation was that compensation paid to shareholders was minimal. The Court of Appeal found that Article 1 was not violated. The government had a wide margin of appreciation and had acted on the basis of coherent policy objectives.

23.8.2 Rule 1 and Rule 3

There is no general principle requiring compensation to be paid to a person whose use or peaceful enjoyment of their possessions has been restricted or interfered with.

In *R (Trailer Marina (Leven) Ltd)* v *Secretary of State for the Environment, Food and Rural Affairs* [2004] EWCA Civ 1580, the applicants had been prevented from the commercial exploitation of their canal for the purposes of nature conservation. Statutory changes meant that compensation could no longer be paid. The Court of Appeal held that there was no breach of Article 1.

In contrast, in *Dennis* v *Ministry of Defence* [2003] EWHC 793, serious noise nuisance was caused by RAF planes. This, the High Court held, was an interference with W's Article 1 rights, which, as a matter of a fair balance of interests, required compensation (£950,000) to be paid.

DISCUSSION TOPIC

Should property and possessions be the subject of human rights or should the state have a free hand in the distribution of wealth? Would it make any difference to your answer if 'human rights' were confined to human beings and companies were excluded?

 ## Summary

- Article 1 is analysed by the Court in terms of three rules (peaceful enjoyment, deprivation and control of use).

- Whatever rule is in issue, the same general concepts seem to apply: interferences by the state must be lawful, for a legitimate purpose, and proportionate in the sense of there being a fair balance between the interests of the community and the restrictions imposed on individuals.

? Self-test questions

1. How are 'possessions' defined for the purposes of Article 1?

2. In what circumstances, if any, is there a right to possession of a right or interest in the future?

3. Distinguish 'Rule 1', 'Rule 2' and 'Rule 3'.

4. How was the issue of proportionality of justification approach by the UK court in *Breyer Group* (section 23.7)?

5. Why was there a breach of Article 1 in *Sporrong and Lönnroth* v *Sweden* (section 23.7.1)?

6. Why was there a breach of Article 1 in *Pressos Compania Naviera* v *Belgium* (section 23.7.4)?

 For suggested approaches, please visit the Online Resource Centre.

? Exam questions

1. In the context of a global economic recession affecting the housing market, the Treasury is considering the taking into public ownership of a major bank that will otherwise go bankrupt. The intended compensation is to be based on the bank's very low share price at the time of this nationalisation and most shareholders will receive little if any return.

Advise the Chancellor of the Exchequer on the main issues that a court in the United Kingdom would have to consider if shareholders or the bank bring actions on the basis that their rights under Article 1 of the First Protocol have been violated?

2. There should not be a human right to property—it only serves the interests of well-off people and great corporate power.

Discuss this statement in respect of both general principle and also the case law and jurisprudence of the ECtHR in relation to Article 1.

 For suggested approaches, please visit the Online Resource Centre.

Further reading

Allen, T. *Property and the Human Rights Act* (2005) Oxford: Hart Publishing

Lester, A., Pannick, D. and Herberg, J. (see Preface) Article 1 of the First Protocol

Waldron, J. *The Rule of Law and the Measure of Property* (2012) Cambridge: CUP

24 Article 2 of the First Protocol: right to education

LEARNING OBJECTIVES

- The right to education: a right of access to the education system that is provided.
- The nature, scope, and limits to the right of parents that their children's education should accord with their beliefs.

The First Protocol

Article 2 Right to education

No person shall be denied the right to education. In the exercise of any functions which it assumes in relation to education and to teaching, the State shall respect the right of parents to ensure such education and teaching in conformity with their own religious and philosophical convictions.

Introduction

One of the recognised features of a totalitarian society is that it seeks to indoctrinate children, through the education system, into conformity with the ideology of the state. Fear of this was one of the main motivations behind Article 2 of the First Protocol. As we shall see, it has been interpreted so that it guarantees a reasonable level of diversity in education and it also places an obligation on the state to ensure that the religious and philosophical convictions of parents over the education of their children are respected. But in the twenty-first century there is perhaps a different concern—that parental control of the values underlying their children's education may be limiting and restricting their children's intellectual development. The report into some Birmingham schools following allegations of an attempt to establish a radical Muslim ethos in some schools, may be an example of this (see Peter Clark *Report into allegations concerning Birmingham schools arising from the 'Trojan Horse' letter* 2014 HC 576).

Article 2 is one of the few provisions of the Convention directly involving 'social rights' (there are no express rights to health or welfare, for example). Legally enforceable social rights are problematic because they can compel states to large expenditures and can distort democratically chosen priorities for expenditure (these matters have been discussed in Chapter 1, section 1.3.2).

24.1 General principles and the basic right

Q   CASE CLOSE-UP

Belgian Linguistics Case (No 2) (1979–80) 1 EHRR 252

Belgium is a linguistically divided country. In the Walloon region French is the predominant language, Dutch is the predominant language in the Flemish region, and there are other areas in which no language predominates. French-speaking parents in the Flemish region complained to the European Court of Human Rights (ECtHR) that Article 2 of the First Protocol had been violated because the Belgian education system was organised on language grounds and they were effectively required to send their children to Dutch-speaking schools. The ECtHR held that, apart from the impact of laws on children living in the areas in which no language predominates, the Belgian education system did not violate Article 2.

From the case some important general principles regarding the 'right to education' can be identified:

- Although Article 2 is expressed in negative terms ('no person shall be denied') it does, nevertheless, create rights for individuals. However, these rights are limited.

- The basic right is the right of a child to access to the education system that exists; there is no right to a particular form or type of education.

- States are entitled to regulate and control the education system and the nature of the education that is available but in doing so must ensure that the education system:

  - is compatible with the basic right of access;

  - does not discriminate in a way that is prohibited by Article 14;

  - is compatible with the other provisions of the Convention (an educational system that did not protect freedom of thought, conscience, or religion, as recognised in the terms of Article 9, for example, would not be compatible with Article 2); and

  - respects the religious and philosophical convictions of parents, as required by the second sentence of Article 2.

- There is a right to the recognition of qualifications obtained: without this the right of access to education would lose much of its point and would not be effective.

- There is a right to be educated in one of the official languages of the state. This is implied from the principle that the education must be effective. As *Belgian Linguistics* generally showed, it cannot be inferred from Article 2 that there is a right to be educated in a language of choice.

24.2 The education system

24.2.1 The provision of education

States have a wide discretion over the education system. The negative formulation of the right has been taken to mean that the 'Parties do not recognise such a right to education as would require them to establish at their own expense, or to subsidise, education of any particular type or at any particular level' (see *Belgian Linguistics*, para 3). It is possible that the complete absence of state-funded provision of specifically elementary education might violate Article 2 since such education was recognised by all states at the time of signature.

24.2.2 The scope of the right of access to the education provided

The right of access to whatever education provision is provided applies to all levels of education, including university education (*Leyla Sahin* v *Turkey* (2007) 44 EHRR 5 (see Chapter 16, section 16.4.8)). In *R (Hurley)* v *Secretary of State for Business, Innovation and Skills* [2012] EWHC 2012, the High Court held that Article 2 required effective, and (in respect of Article 14) non-discriminatory, access to whatever university education was provided. Tuition fees (here the £9,000 maximum charged in England) were, in the context of the scheme as a whole, a proportionate restriction on access and did not violate Article 2. In *R (Tigere)* v *Secretary of State for Business, Innovation and Skills* [2015] UKSC 57, the Supreme Court found that basing the provision of undergraduate student loans on a strictly applied, rule-based, definition of being 'settled' in the UK (which failed to allow exceptions in respect of applicants brought up and educated in the UK) violated Article 14 in the context of Article 2.

24.2.3 The system

Regulation

There is no right to any particular form of educational provision. States have wide discretion over the type of education they provide and the right of access to this system is subject to the legitimate power of the state to regulate the education service. For example:

- There is no obligation on the state to provide education in a particular language (*Belgian Linguistics*, see section 24.1).

- There is no obligation on the state to fund schools for religious or ethnic groups, although discriminating in favour of some groups and not others could raise an issue under Article 14.

- Article 2 cannot be used to compel the provision of a particular type of education for children with special needs (see *SP* v *United Kingdom* (1997) 23 EHRR CD 139). It is not clear what the position would be if there was a complete absence of provision for children with special needs.

- Separate education for children belonging to linguistic and cultural minorities is not necessarily a breach of Article 2 so long as there is a proper justification and sufficient safeguards (*DH* v *Czech Republic* (2008) 47 EHRR 3). If, however, the context and inadequacy of provision suggests discrimination, there may be a breach (*Orsus* v *Croatia* (2011) 52 EHRR 7).

Private education

Article 2 guarantees the existence of private or independent education. In *Kjeldsen v Denmark* (1979–80) 1 EHRR 711, at para 50, the ECtHR treats the legal possibility of private education as a necessary though not sufficient condition of freedom from indoctrination and also as giving a proper respect to parental convictions, as required by the second sentence of Article 2. Based on this the Commission has expressly stated that Article 2 'guarantees the right to start and run a private school' (*Verein Gemeinsam Lernen v Austria* (1995) 20 EHRR CD 78). Nothing in Article 2 prevents states from regulating private schools on matters such as curriculum and standards and ensuring general compatibility with the wider system of public education. Nor do states have a duty to fund or to give indirect financial support to such schools.

24.2.4 Pupil exclusions

The basic right is for persons to 'avail themselves of the means of instruction existing at a given time' (*Belgian Linguistics*, section 24.1, para 3). Excluding a child from one part of the education system, if done lawfully, is not necessarily a breach of Article 2. The issue has come up under the Human Rights Act 1998 (HRA).

In *Ali v Head Teacher and Governors of Lord Grey School* [2006] UKHL 14, the House of Lords held that Article 2 had not been violated in the case of an excluded pupil. The House of Lords stressed:

- Article 2 created a right to be educated to a minimum standard; there was no right to a particular type of education within the system.
- At all times the system had provided some form of education, or at least the opportunity of it.

If an exclusion results entirely from the difficulties of a child's circumstances and the authorities have behaved reasonably, there will be no violation of Article 2: see, for example, *A v Essex CC* [2008] EWCA Civ 364.

If exclusions result from children properly exercising their right to freedom of thought, conscience, and religion (e.g. in a dispute over religious dress), then there is the potential for a breach of Article 2 (see *R (Begum) v Denbigh High School* [2006] UKHL 15, a case decided predominantly in respect of Article 9 and discussed in Chapter 16, section 16.4.8).

24.3 The curriculum: pluralism and diversity

The education provided must meet reasonable standards of pluralism and diversity. Pluralism assumes there is no ultimate truth on religious, moral, and political issues (or at least no agreement on this), and so the social and political system must be open to a range of different ideas and principles.

The need for pluralism relates to the 'parental convictions' provision of the second sentence of Article 2 but also reflects that diversity is inherent in the idea of education appropriate to a democratic society and which avoids mere 'indoctrination'. Pluralism and diversity must be provided by the state through the policies and curriculum adopted in maintained schools and also in the way private schools are regulated. In *Kjeldsen* (see section 24.4.2) the ECtHR said that:

> the state, in fulfilling the functions assumed by it in regard to education and teaching, must take care that information or knowledge included in the curriculum is conveyed in an objective, critical and pluralistic manner.

(para 53)

As well as placing a duty on the state not to restrict educational diversity, pluralism and diversity also restrict the freedom that parents and others may have to object to the kind of education their children are getting in terms of standards and curriculum.

24.4 Parental convictions

The second sentence of Article 2 requires the state to 'respect' the religious and philosophical convictions of parents in the way it fulfils its educational functions. The second sentence reflects the fear of state indoctrination through education and embodies what is seen as the 'natural' parental functions of enlightening and guiding their children in terms of the convictions that they, the parents, consider valuable and important.

Respect means more than merely being acknowledged or taken into account: it imposes obligations on the state which limit the way in which its educational policy is performed. For instance, English courts, under the HRA, have said that parents' religious convictions need to be sought and taken into account when allocating children to schools (see *R (K)* v *Newham LBC* [2002] EWHC 405, paras 29, 38).

'Convictions' implies something more than just 'opinions' and 'ideas' referred to in Article 10. States must respect only those religious and philosophical convictions which are reasonable in the sense of being 'worthy of respect in a "democratic society" and [which] are not incompatible with human dignity'. Furthermore, 'they must not conflict with the fundamental right of the child to education, the whole of Article 2 being dominated by its first sentence'—*Campbell and Cosans*, para 36: see section 24.4.1.

In other words, the state has no duty to respect religious or philosophical beliefs which are unreasonable, particularly those which would have a significantly restrictive impact on a child's education. Parents who seek to withdraw their children from science classes that presuppose evolution, might not, on these grounds, be able to claim the support of Article 2. In *Williamson* (see section 24.4.1), Lord Walker found this judgmental approach to other people's convictions 'alarming' (para 60). On the other hand, he agreed that allowing parents too much influence on the basis of the second sentence of Article 2 could have the effect of damaging a child's education.

24.4.1 **Punishment**

The duty to respect parental convictions applies not just to the classroom curriculum but to the full range of education regulation that the state legitimately performs, including school discipline and punishment.

Convention law

 CASE CLOSE-UP

Campbell and Cosans v United Kingdom (1982) 4 EHRR 293

Parents objected to the potential use of corporal punishment (being hit on the hand with a 'tawse') in the Scottish state schools which their children attended. The local authority refused to assure Mrs Campbell that the tawse would not be used on her son, and Mrs Cosans' son was suspended from school for refusing the punishment. The ECtHR held that parental convictions about punishment involved a 'weighty and substantial aspect of human life, namely the integrity of the person' and that there had been a breach of Article 2.

HRA

The converse to *Campbell* failed under the HRA.

 CASE CLOSE-UP

R (Williamson) v Secretary of State for Education and Employment
[2005] UKHL 15

A group of parents, through the teachers and governors of a group of private Christian schools, objected to the statutory ban, applicable to all schools in England and Wales, on corporal punishment. They argued, following *Campbell and Cosans*, that views about school discipline could be expressions of philosophical and religious convictions. The House of Lords accepted that both Article 2 of the First Protocol and Article 9 were engaged but that Parliament had adopted a reasonable and proportionate policy in banning corporal punishment even though it limited parental choice. Neither Article, therefore, had been violated.

24.4.2 **The curriculum**

In *Valsamis v Greece* (1997) 24 EHRR 294, the ECtHR said, in respect of the curriculum:

> democracy does not simply mean that the views of a majority must always prevail: a balance must be achieved which ensures the fair and proper treatment of minorities and avoids any abuse of a dominant position.

(para 27)

If the curriculum adopts a pluralistic but balanced approach to ethical and political matters, for example, and is informative rather than aiming at indoctrination, it is likely that parental objections to the curriculum and other school activities will fail.

In *Kjeldsen v Denmark* (1979–80) 1 EHRR 711, parents objected to compulsory sex education lessons for their children in state schools. Given the ethically neutral and information-based way in which the sex education was delivered, the ECtHR held that the policy 'in no way offends the applicant's religious and philosophical convictions to the extent forbidden by the second sentence of Article 2'.

In *Folgero* v *Norway* (2008) 46 EHRR 47, on the other hand, a Grand Chamber found (by a narrow majority) that Article 2 was violated in respect of a compulsory course on Christianity, religion, and philosophy. Christianity was given a particular emphasis and seeking exemption involved parents in having to disclose matters of personal belief.

In contrast: in *Lautsi* v *Italy* (2012) 54 EHRR 3, a Grand Chamber held that the Italian tradition of displaying a crucifix in classrooms did not amount to indoctrination nor did it influence the content of educational provision. Given this, it was a matter over which the state enjoyed a wide margin of appreciation.

24.5 The UK's reservation

When the United Kingdom signed the First Protocol, in 1952, it reserved its position regarding parental convictions:

> the principle affirmed in the second sentence of Article 2 is accepted by the United Kingdom only so far as it is compatible with the provision of efficient instruction and training, and the avoidance of unreasonable public expenditure.

This reservation is maintained under section 15 HRA, but, under section 17, is due for review. The impact of the reservation is unclear and, if it were asserted by the government in any proceedings, it is likely it would be challenged on the grounds that it lacks the precision and clarity as to its scope that is required under Article 57 (this was suggested in *SP* v *UK* (1997) 23 EHRR CD 139).

▶ CROSS REFERENCE

For 'reservations' in general, see Chapter 2, section 2.4.4.

 DISCUSSION TOPIC

Values and parental choice

The second sentence of Article 2 embodies, in a qualified way, the principle that parents be allowed to control the values and beliefs their children come into contact with through education. Is this a good principle?

In favour:

- The danger of state indoctrination of children.
- Individual flourishing depends upon the transmission of religious and moral traditions. Without these we are all empty shells with no basic values and no language or symbols by which such values might be expressed.

Against:

- It is also true that human flourishing requires a degree of openness and curiosity, otherwise traditions and beliefs may become mere orthodoxies.
- Traditions and systems of belief very often hide the exercise of social and political power.
- It is enough that the state is under an obligation to educate the children in a manner that is non-doctrinaire and is liberal, pluralist, and diverse.

Summary

- Article 2 of the First Protocol contains the basic right of a child not to education in itself but of equal access to the educational provision that is available and to establishing the effectiveness of such education through the recognition of educational qualifications.

- What else Article 2 provides in terms of a child's rights to education is unclear; states have a wide margin of appreciation over issues such as the education system, the types of schools, and the content of the curriculum. Nevertheless, there is a duty to maintain diversity and pluralism in education.

- The second sentence of Article 2 gives parents rights to have their religious and philosophical convictions respected in the way their children are educated. States must take this duty into account in the way they discharge their educational function, but it is not a right which will always restrict states in their reasonable attempts to regulate education in the public interest.

Self-test questions

1. How does the *Belgian Linguistics* case (section 24.1) guide our understanding of the scope and application of Article 2?

2. Would it be possible, consistently with Article 2, to abolish private education in the United Kingdom?

3. Describe the duty that states have, under Article 2, in respect of providing an education to children and young persons.

4. What is meant by a curriculum under which information is conveyed in an 'objective, critical and pluralistic' manner (*Kjelsden*, section 24.4.2)?

 For suggested approaches, please visit the Online Resource Centre.

Exam questions

1. Able has been involved in vandalism against his school. His parents think this is because the school is not demanding enough of their child, who they consider to be very bright. The school intends to exclude him and, if they do, the local authority will be able to provide ten hours per week special tuition in a centre for troubled and troublesome children.

   (a) Comment on whether the actions of the school and the special tuition is sufficient to meet the requirements of Article 2.

   (b) Advise Able's parents on whether they can, under Article 2, insist that their child receive a 'more demanding' education in a different school.

2. Discuss the second sentence of Article 2. How extensive is this right and does it, in your judgment, get the balance correct of, on the one hand, parental control over children and, on the other, the interests children have in an open, broad, and inquiring education?

 For suggested approaches, please visit the Online Resource Centre.

 Further reading

Kearns, P. 'Religion and the Human Rights Act 1998' (2001) 151 *NLJ* 498

Lester, A., Pannick, D., and Herberg, J. (see Preface) Article 2 of the First Protocol

Mountfield, H. 'The Implications of the Human Rights Act 1998 for the Law of Education' (2000) 1(3) *Education Law* 146–158

25

Article 3 of the First Protocol: right to free elections

☐ LEARNING OBJECTIVES

● The obligation on states to hold elections.

● Implied individual rights to vote, stand, and take a seat if elected.

● Wide but not unlimited scope over the electoral system.

● Wide but not unlimited scope for reasonable limits and restrictions on individuals' rights to vote etc.

The First Protocol

Article 3 Right to free elections

The High Contracting Parties undertake to hold free elections at reasonable intervals by secret ballot, under conditions which will ensure the free expression of the opinion of the people in the choice of the legislature.

Introduction

The Preamble of the Convention suggests that the best way of maintaining 'justice and peace' is not only through the recognition of fundamental freedoms and the human rights by which those freedoms are protected, but also by upholding 'an effective political democracy'. At the heart of democracy is the idea of self-government by the people and there are many different theories of how that is to be achieved. For example, some theories focus on the people's choice of representatives; other theories find that too limiting and argue the need for a full range of rights and opportunities for people to participate in the collective decisions of the society. There is no human right to democracy. That would not mean much. Human rights require states to respect various rights and freedoms which are necessary for any system if it is to be democratic. Pre-eminently these include rights to freedom of expression (Article 10), freedom of association and assembly (Article 11), and freedom from state oppression such as torture or inhuman treatment or arbitrary detention, etc. imposed by the state on its political opponents (Articles 2, 3, and 5).

There also need to be rights to vote for the government and to participate in the political process and public life of the nation. It was these last rights that proved difficult to agree upon and which were left out of the original Convention, to be added two years later in the First Protocol. At the heart of the disagreement was the fear of states that the Convention would require a particular form of political system. In fact, the final agreed text, on its face, merely obliges states to hold free elections for the legislature. As is clear from what follows, this obligation has been worked up by the European Court of Human Rights (ECtHR) into a set of (highly qualifiable) rights.

25.1 General principles

The general principles dealing with Article 3 were first laid down, authoritatively, by the ECtHR in *Mathieu-Mohin and Clerfayt* v *Belgium* (1988) 10 EHRR 1; they have been recently restated by a Grand Chamber in *Yumak and Sadak* v *Turkey* (2009) 48 EHRR 4, paras 105–108 and 109(i)–(vi).

 CASE CLOSE-UP

***Mathieu-Mohin and Clerfayt* v *Belgium* (1988) 10 EHRR 1**

The case involved the complex constitutional arrangements in Belgium for establishing a system of government acceptable to the two principal language groups in the country. The applicants were French-speaking 'Walloons', who lived in a Dutch-speaking ('Flemish') area of Brussels. Like all people in the area, they were subject not only to the laws passed by the Belgian national parliament but also, on matters like education and the environment, to those passed by the Flemish Council. Membership of the Flemish Council was confined to Dutch-speaking members of the national parliament and it was not open to French speakers. As French-speaking members of the national parliament, the applicants could not be members of the Flemish Council; furthermore French speakers living in a Dutch-speaking area could only be represented by Dutch-speaking representatives.

The ECtHR departed from the view of the Commission and held that this system did not involve a violation of Article 3 of the First Protocol. The Court considered the place of the Flemish Council in the constitutional system as a whole, particularly the Belgian approach to dealing with the rights of and relations between the two principal language communities in the country. It decided that the restriction complained of was reasonable and proportionate to these legitimate aims.

The Court took the opportunity to lay down some general principles (in paras 46–54).

25.1.1 **The importance of democracy**

The right to fair elections in Article 3 'enshrines a characteristic of democracy'.

An effective political democracy is one of the principal means of protecting human rights, peace and democracy.

▶ CROSS REFERENCE

'Democracy', as a Convention concept, is discussed in Chapter 6, section 6.4.

25.1.2 Individual rights

Article 3 appears to do no more than impose a general duty on states to hold effective elections. In *Mathieu-Mohin* the Court implied individual rights into Article 3. These are:

- a right to vote in elections,
- a right to stand for election,

and, from later cases:

- a right to sit as a member of the legislature if elected (see *Sadak* v *Turkey* (2003) 36 EHRR 23, para 33).

The significance of implying individual rights from Article 3 is that individuals can assert these rights in the courts without having to prove that the will of the people has been thwarted because there would have been a difference to the outcome of the election.

25.1.3 The Convention does not require any particular electoral system

The Court recognised that there are many different political and electoral systems in Europe which can all claim to be reasonably effective democracies. The countries of Europe are different from each other in terms of history, culture and social make-up, and internal tensions. These will determine the political and election system. It is not for the Court to insist that all states adopt a particular electoral or legislative system—such as proportional representation.

25.1.4 Article 3 rights may be subject to reasonable conditions; these conditions must not deprive these rights of their essence and effectiveness

The ECtHR recognises that the individual rights to vote, to stand, and, if elected, to sit, are implied rights and, as such, may be subject to a range of restrictions and conditions. States have a wide margin of appreciation over the electoral system and individual rights. However, it is the Court's job to ensure that the essence of the rights in Article 3 is maintained.

 CASE CLOSE-UP

***Sitaropoulos* v *Greece* (2013) 56 EHRR 9**

S and others complained that they were denied the right to vote in the Greek general election of 2007 because they were resident in France. The Grand Chamber held that there had been no violation of Article 3. The restriction was reasonable and within the margin of appreciation enjoyed by states.

The Grand Chamber confirmed the basic principles applying to Article 3 (see paras 63–68).

- Article 3, interpreted in respect of the travaux préparatoires and the Convention as a whole, guarantees individual rights to vote and to stand.
- These rights are subject to implied limitations over which states have a wide margin of appreciation.
- The role of the Court is a reviewing one: to satisfy itself that any restrictions do not impair the very essence of the right and deprive it of effectiveness in the particular

situation. Any restrictions must meet the Convention test of 'lawfulness', be imposed for a legitimate aim, and not involve disproportionate means.

- Since the rights to vote etc. are implied, restrictions do not need to be considered with the same degree of rigour as applies to Articles 8–11 (i.e. there is no need for the state to prove a pressing social need).

- The Grand Chamber confirmed that no particular type of election system was required.

BIGGER PICTURE

In *Sitaropoulos* the Grand Chamber confirmed that voting is a fundamental right and not a privilege. In the UK the right to vote is statutory—subject to the intention of Parliament. Nevertheless, in *Moohan*, see section 25.4.2, the UKSC suggested that voting could be a fundamental right at common law and that any serious abuse by Parliament of its primary right to determine the franchise could be invalidated by the courts—an ultimate limit to parliamentary supremacy.

25.1.5 Equality of treatment is the essential requirement

The essence of the rights in Article 3 is that each person enjoys equal treatment under the electoral system, whatever it is. There is no requirement, for example, that every vote should have the same impact on determining the outcome of an election or that all candidates should have equal chances of winning, since these would require particular electoral systems and are not required by Article 3.

25.1.6 The electoral system must be judged in terms of its specific social and cultural evolution

It follows from the emphasis on the margin of appreciation and the refusal of the Court to interpret Article 3 as requiring any particular electoral system that:

> For the purposes of Article 3 of the First Protocol, any electoral system must be assessed in the light of the political evolution of the country concerned; features which would be unacceptable in the context of one system may accordingly be justified in another.

In deciding whether some restriction on a person's Article 3 rights is allowable, the ECtHR has to be fully aware of the particular constitutional context within which the restriction has been imposed.

25.2 The electoral system

States have a wide margin of appreciation over their political and electoral system.

25.2.1 **Pluralism**

▶ **CROSS REFERENCE**

Pluralism is discussed in Chapter 6, section 6.4.2, and Chapter 18, section 18.7.1.

The right to fair elections is part of the Convention's commitment to democracy. Part of this is the upholding of 'pluralism'. This involves states acknowledging the existence of different social groups in society and accepting that these may wish or need to protect their interests politically, through standing in elections, for instance. Article 3 (as well as Article 11 (freedom of assembly and association)) has an important function here (see, for instance, *Sadak* v *Turkey* (2003) 36 EHRR 23).

25.2.2 **The voting system**

A range of different voting systems is compatible with ensuring the 'free expression of the opinion of the people in the choice of the legislature'. Different systems can derive from the different aims of an election and reflect the historical and cultural evolution of societies. In particular, the court recognises that an electoral system can have the primary purpose of creating a legislature which can express a clear electoral will rather than one which represents the full range of political views.

Proportional representation is not a requirement, nor is there a need for each vote cast to have the same weight, or the same ability to determine the outcome of the election, as every other vote.

In *Liberal Party* v *United Kingdom* (1982) 4 EHRR 106, the Commission held that the first-past-the-post system in the United Kingdom satisfies Article 3 despite evidence that it systematically disadvantages third parties.

Similarly, election systems that require evidence of support before a party can put up candidates in an election, or take seats under a system of proportional representation, are normally acceptable. A demonstration of a minimum level of support is reasonable in order to maintain the public nature of the right to stand. Many cases, mainly decided by the Commission of Human Rights, demonstrate the point. For example:

In *Tete* v *France* (1989) 11 EHRR CD91, the requirements that parties had to pay FF100,000, with limited rights of refund, was held to be compatible with the Article 3 right to stand.

25.2.3 **Maintaining the essence of the right to free elections within the political system**

▶ **CROSS REFERENCE**

Article 14, prohibition of discrimination, is discussed in Chapter 7, section 7.1.

Article 3 of the First Protocol is not without teeth. There can be violations of the right to free elections if restrictions allowed by the electoral system violate the 'essence' of the Article; specifically, if they mean that the opinion of a significant section of the people cannot be freely expressed, or that individuals or groups are not treated equally under the rules of the system. Above all, any disputed features of an electoral system must not be such as to 'thwart the free expression of the opinion of the people over the choice of the legislature'.

There is no requirement under Article 3 that ethnic, national, or other minorities should have special standing or protection in the election system. However, an electoral system that systematically discriminates against a national or ethnic minority or which treats members less favourably under the system, is likely to fall foul of both Article 3 and Article 14 in respect of Article 3.

In *Aziz* v *Cyprus* (2005) 41 EHRR 11, for example, Article 3 was violated when Turkish Cypriots living in the Republic of Cyprus (effectively the southern, Greek Cypriot part of Cyprus) were unable to vote for the Cypriot House of Representatives. This can be contrasted with *Yamuk and Sadak* v *Turkey* (2009) 48 EHRR 4. The Grand Chamber found no violation in respect of an electoral system that resulted in a Parliament in which approximately 45% of the population was not represented by the party of their choice. In the context of Turkish history and politics, a system that inhibited the progress of parties representing narrow regional interests was legitimate.

A system that puts disproportionate burdens on political parties might be a violation of Article 3. An example is where disproportionately large monetary deposits by candidates are required (as in *Sukhovetskyy* v *Ukraine* App 13716/02, judgment of 28 March 2006). Similarly, violations of Article 3 are possible if there are long gaps between elections (see *Timke* v *Germany* (1995) 20 EHRR CD 133), or where there is widespread evidence of fraud but no action being taken by the authorities.

If the system imposes burdens on individuals which deter voting, then there may be a violation of Article 3. This issue has arisen under the Human Rights Act 1998 (HRA). In *R (Robertson)* v *Wakefield MDC* [2001] EWHC 915 (Admin), it was held that the sale of the electoral register to commercial organisations without the applicant's consent violated W's Article 3 rights (as well as Article 8 and EU law).

25.3 Individual restrictions

25.3.1 Acceptable and unacceptable restrictions

Individual rights to vote, to stand as a candidate, and to sit as a member of the legislature if elected, are subject to reasonable restrictions over which the states have a wide margin of appreciation. These restrictions are subject to review by the Court. The Court must ensure that the 'essence' of the rights is not impaired and that restrictions are a proportionate means to a legitimate end and, above all, that the free expression of the will of the people is not thwarted (see, also, section 25.1.4).

A wide range of restrictions have been accepted by the Strasbourg authorities.

Acceptable restrictions on the right to vote include that:

- voters be resident in the country (see, for example, *Hilbe* v *Liechenstein* App 31981/96, admissibility decision of 7 September 1999).

Acceptable restrictions on the right to stand in elections include:

- a ban on members of foreign legislatures (*M* v *United Kingdom* App 10316/83 (1984) 37 DR 129);
- political restrictions on police, civil servants, and other officials are also, in principle, compatible with Article 3. This issue has been discussed in the context of Article 11: see Chapter 18, section 18.9.

Acceptable restrictions on the right to sit once elected include:

- the denial of parliamentary services to an MP who refused to take the oath of allegiance to the Crown and hence could not take his seat (*McGuiness* v *United Kingdom* App 39511/98, admissibility decision of 8 June 1999).

But not all restrictions on individual rights are non-arbitrary and acceptable. It is the Court which has the final word. For example, in *Podkolzina v Lativia* App 46726/99, judgment of 9 April 2002, the applicant, who was from the minority Russian community in Latvia, was removed from the list of candidates because of insufficient knowledge of Latvian, the official language. The ECtHR held that there had been a violation of Article 3 not because the principle of a language requirement was wrong but because of the arbitrary and politically partial way in which the language test had been applied.

25.3.2 Prisoners' right to vote

A number of countries, including the United Kingdom, ban all or some convicted prisoners from voting in elections. Whether it is right for the ECtHR to hold such bans incompatible with Article 3 has been and remains highly controversial in the United Kingdom. As noted in Chapter 21, prisoners retain their human rights though their application will be limited as a consequence of imprisonment; however, as noted in section 25.3.1, the right to vote in Article 3 is subject to reasonable restrictions over which states have a wide margin of appreciation.

Q CASE CLOSE-UP

Hirst v *United Kingdom* (2006) 42 EHRR 41

Section 3 of the Representation of the People Act 1983 (ROPA 1983) (as amended in 2000) excludes serving prisoners from the right to vote. In *R (Pearson)* v *Secretary of State for the Home Department* [2001] EWHC 239 (Admin), a challenge to this ban was brought in the English courts under the HRA. It failed on the grounds that the interference with rights was within the state's margin of appreciation. However, when the case was taken to Strasbourg, a Grand Chamber of the ECtHR held that there was a violation of Article 3. The Grand Chamber in *Hirst* ruled (see paras 76–85):

(1) Imprisonment should mean that prisoners lose only the right to liberty, not all other Convention rights.

(2) Disenfranchisement plays no overt role in sentencing in the UK; there is no evidence that it deters crime. Furthermore, the penalty is arbitrary: the vote is lost only if a prisoner is in prison at the time of an election.

(3) People convicted of crimes with a strong anti-social element but not put in prison do not lose the vote; some convicted prisoners, on the other hand, may have committed offences which may have some moral excuse or public support (e.g. the murder of a violent husband) but will nevertheless lose the vote.

(4) Parliament had not, seriously and deliberately, considered the competing arguments for and against the ban; this affected the operation of the margin of appreciation.

At the heart of the Grand Chamber's position, therefore, is an objection to the 'blanket' nature of the ban: that it is 'automatic' (i.e. applied with no thought as to its appropriateness to the individual concerned), 'general' (i.e. applied to all convicted prisoners), and 'indiscriminate' (i.e. applied without reference to relevant criteria such as seriousness of offence or length of sentence).

The UK, therefore, was under an obligation, in Articles 1 and 46 ECHR, to give effect to this judgment.

CROSS REFERENCE
On implementation of judgments, see Chapter 2, section 2.5.3.

The issue was highly controversial, government consultations were inconclusive, and there was no political will to change the law.

Judicial enforcement in domestic courts has only had limited success. A declaration of incompatibility was made in Scotland regarding section 3 ROPA 1983 (*Scott* v *Smith* [2007] SC 345). In *R (Chester)* v *Secretary of State for Justice* [2013] UKSC 63, the UKSC accepted that the blanket ban on prisoners voting was incompatible with the Convention (following *Scoppola*, discussed later in this section). However, it found that the will of Parliament was clear and so the legislation could not be 'read down' (under section 3 HRA) to make it compatible. The UKSC also refused a declaration of incompatibility (under section 4 HRA) because (some justices argued) the applicants' individual rights had not been violated. As prisoners serving long sentences, they would be likely to be barred from voting even by a Convention-compliant law. In a related case, the UKSC also held that there was no free-standing right to vote to be found in the EU Charter of Fundamental Rights (but see *Delvigne*, in 'Bigger picture'). It also held that there was no case, based on Convention law (see *Greens*, later in this section) to award damages. Domestic law, therefore, is unable to compel the executive in Parliament to bring forward proposals to change the law. The solution is political.

BIGGER PICTURE

The UKSC's position on EU law may now need to be qualified. In *Delvigne* v *Commune de Lesparre-Medoc* Case C-650/13, the Court of Justice of the European Union applied the EU's Charter of Fundamental Rights (see Chapter 3, section 3.4) to French domestic law on voting for the EU Parliament. It held that the Charter did not prevent a ban on a prisoner convicted of a 'serious offence' from voting. This is not inconsistent with Strasbourg, since it is to the blanket nature of the ban (all prisoners, however serious) that the ECtHR objects.

Meanwhile, at the Convention level, the Committee of Ministers (which has responsibility for supervising the enforcement of ECtHR judgments), expressed, in various documents, its concern at the UK's lack of action. At the judicial level, the ECtHR took further steps. In *Greens* v *UK* (2011) 53 EHRR 21, it confirmed its opposition to a blanket ban in *Hirst* and then used the 'pilot judgment' procedure to impose a six-month time limit on the UK (after years of inaction) to remove the blanket ban and come up with a Convention-compliant solution.

▶ CROSS REFERENCE

Greens and the pilot judgment procedure is discussed further in Chapter 2, section 2.5.3.

The ECtHR did, though, confirm that damages were not appropriate at this stage and that its general policy of not awarding exemplary damages applied.

The UK then obtained a further stay to await a further Grand Chamber decision.

CASE CLOSE-UP

Scoppola v Italy (No 3) (2013) 56 EHRR 19

The case involved a challenge to the Italian law under which certain categories of prisoners are denied the vote. The Grand Chamber:

- confirmed, with its final authority, the position in *Hirst*: that bans which are 'automatic, general and indiscriminate' are arbitrary and disproportionate denials of the right to vote and violate Article 3;

- refused to confirm an earlier Chamber judgment (*Frodl* v *Austria* (2011) 52 EHRR 5) that removal of the right to vote had to be a judicial act linked to sentencing: Parliament, by statute, could establish non-arbitrary criteria on this matter;

- found that the Italian law was not arbitrary—loss of the vote depended on proportionate criteria, such as the type of offence and the length of sentence: it was within the margin of appreciation.

The Grand Chamber makes clear, therefore, that so long as there is no automatically imposed ban on all convicted prisoners, states have a wide margin of appreciation over the criteria (e.g. of type of offence or length of sentence) that can be used to determine whether prisoners may vote or not. The applicants in *Hirst* and *Chester* were all serving significant prison terms and, as mentioned earlier, could be legitimately excluded from the vote even in a Convention-compliant scheme.

Following *Scoppola* and *Greens*, the United Kingdom is required to come up with a system which allows some prisoners to vote. Its continual failure to do so is, in itself, a violation (*McHugh* v *UK* App 51987/08, judgment of 10 February 2015). In 2012, the government produced a draft bill giving options. These were considered by a Joint Committee of both Houses which reported in December 2013 and recommended that prisoners serving less than a year or who were nearing the end of their sentence should have the vote. In December 2014, the government announced it was still considering the Joint Committee report and that prisoners would remain disenfranchised for the General Election of May 2015. The Conservative victory in that election means that the issue is subsumed by the general policy of repealing the HRA and replacing it with a 'British Bill of Rights'.

 DISCUSSION TOPIC

Should disenfranchisement be used as a punishment?

The moral arguments for and against prisoner voting are well covered in the *Hirst* decision. Where do you stand on the issue? Remember the argument has two basic strands:

(a) whether, as a matter of principle, all or some prisoners should be denied the vote;

(b) whether this is an issue that ought, properly, to be decided by an international court applying an agreed text or whether it is a matter for national courts, Parliaments, or executives.

 BIGGER PICTURE

For recent developments see Horne, A. and White, I. *Prisoners' voting rights* House of Commons Library Standard Note: SN/PC/01764 Last updated: 11 February 2015.

25.4 'The legislature' and wider rights of political action

25.4.1 **The legislature**

The major point is that Article 3 of the First Protocol only applies to elections for the 'legislature'. The meaning of 'legislature' was discussed in *Matthews* v *United Kingdom*.

CASE CLOSE-UP

Matthews v United Kingdom (1999) 28 EHRR 361

Residents of Gibraltar were subject to European Community law. They were unable to vote for the European Parliament. The UK's Convention obligations extended to Gibraltar, and the question for the ECtHR was whether the inability of Gibraltarians to vote in European elections was a violation of the UK's obligations under Article 3. The issue turned on whether the European Parliament was a legislature for the purposes of Article 3.

The ECtHR held that there had been a violation of Article 3.

The Court held that:

- The legislature involves those institutions with decisive roles in the enacting of primary legislation in the country.
- The legislature can only be identified in terms of the constitutional structure of the state. In a federal or devolved constitution there is likely to be more than one body with primary legislative responsibilities.
- The legislature can, therefore, be made up of more than one body. It can include, but is not necessarily confined to, the national parliament. Other bodies such as regional parliaments in a federal structure and, as in the case of the European Parliament, an international body with a role which affects national laws, can also be part of the legislature.
- Where a body is part of the legislature there must be evidence in the constitution of power to initiate and adopt primary legislation or at least (as in the case of the European Parliament) to have a decisive role in the legislative process. This role must be more than merely 'advisory and supervisory' or 'purely consultative'.
- A body which has only subordinate legislative powers, which makes rules only in so far as it is authorised to do so by primary legislation, is not part of the legislature.

On this definition, the legislature includes federal and regional assemblies (like the German Lander, the Belgium regional councils, and the assemblies of Spain's Autonomous Communities).

The United Kingdom legislature includes the Scottish Parliament and the Northern Ireland legislative assembly (both of which have primary legislative responsibility for matters such as health and education). The application of Article 3 to elections for the Northern Ireland Parliament is confirmed by the High Court in Northern Ireland in *Re McKinney's Application* [2004] NIQB 73, para 33. The Welsh Assembly (which originally had a more subordinate legislative role) has had its powers increased and may now, also, be part of the UK's legislature. As *Matthews v United Kingdom* demonstrates, the European Parliament is part of the legislature of the member states. The European Parliament is treated as a unique institution whose democratic role within the European Union should be recognised.

25.4.2 **Public participation**

As a consequence of this narrow definition of legislature, wider rights of participation in the political and public affairs of the country are not protected by Article 3 (though will be by other Convention rights). There is no equivalent in the Convention to, for example, Article 25 of the International Covenant on Civil and Political Rights, which refers to the rights of citizens to 'take part in the conduct of public affairs, directly or through freely chosen representatives'. In particular, Article 3 does not apply to:

- Local government elections. The powers of local councils, including making 'byelaws', are entirely dependent on primary legislation from the national parliament.

- Referendums. Article 3 does not give a right to vote in referendums even if, like the Scottish Independence Referendum 2014, they concern a choice of which legislature to be governed by (*Moohan v Lord Advocate* [2014] UKSC 67). If there is a direct link between the outcome of a referendum and particular legislation it is arguable that the referendum is part of the legislative process.

- Consultative assemblies. There are no Article 3 rights in respect of a body, such as the Northern Ireland Political Forum, which was established as a consultative link between the people and government (*Lindsay v United Kingdom* (1997) 23 EHRR CD 199).

- Public regulatory bodies. There are no Article 3 rights in respect of various 'quangos', which may have regulatory as well as adjudicative powers over individuals, usually in a commercial or business context (*X v Netherlands* App 9926/82 (1983) 32 DR 278).

Article 3 does not apply to election for a largely ceremonial head of state (such as the Federal President of Austria, see *Habsburg-Lothringen v Austria* App 15344/89, admissibility decision of 14 December 1989). Executive presidents, however, will normally have significant legislative powers such as to 'initiate and adopt legislation' and enjoy wide powers 'to control the passage of legislation or the power to censure the principal legislation-setting authorities'. In such circumstances the application of Article 3 can be presumed (*Boskoski v Former Republic of Macedonia* App 11676/04, admissibility decision of 2 September 2004).

Nevertheless, by not applying to referendums and to local government elections, the reach of Article 3 is surprisingly narrow. In *Moohan* (mentioned earlier), Lord Kerr and Lord Wilson dissented strongly and thought that not applying the right to vote to, at least, independence referendums (which involve the right of self-determination) was, broadly speaking, inconsistent with democracy and a 'bizarre anomaly'.

Summary

- Article 3 has been interpreted to provide for individual rights to vote, to stand, and to sit, if elected.
- States are given a very wide margin of appreciation over, first, the kind of electoral and voting system they have and, second, the kinds of restrictions and limits they can impose on the individual rights.
- The ECtHR has the last word on whether the 'essence' of the collective and individual rights in Article 3 has been adhered to. Restrictions will violate the Article if held to be for an improper purpose, imposed unlawfully, disproportionately, or likely to 'thwart' the free expression of the people.
- Article 3 does not provide wide rights to participate in the political processes (the main political rights are in Articles 10 and 11). Its scope is confined to elections for 'the legislature', a complex, multi-institutional term, which does not include local elections or referendums.

? Self-test questions

1. What rights for individuals are implied into Article 3; what character (absolute or qualified) do these rights have?

2. What is the proper role of the ECtHR in considering exceptions to the individual rights in Article 3?

3. What kind of voting system does Article 3 require?

4. Does Article 3 require a fully democratic political system with all parts elected?

 For suggested approaches, please visit the Online Resource Centre.

? Exam questions

1. Should the Convention support a wider range of rights to public participation in the public and political life of the nation than it does? Explain the range of rights as currently understood and discuss, in particular, whether they ought to apply to voting in referendums.

2. Advise the Ministry of Justice on an appropriate scheme, appropriate to all but the most die-hard opponents in the House of Commons, for giving at least some prisoners a vote.

   Explain your scheme by reference to a state's obligations under Article 3.

 For suggested approaches, please visit the Online Resource Centre.

Further reading

Lester, A. and Pannick, D. (see Preface) Article 3 of the First Protocol

Briant, S. 'Dialogue, diplomacy and defiance: prisoners' voting rights at home and in Strasbourg' EHRLR 2011, 3, 243–252

26 Anti-terrorism law and human rights

LEARNING OBJECTIVES

- Special powers in an anti-terrorism context and human rights law.
- United Kingdom's anti-terrorism laws: proscription, controls on terrorist suspects, and increases in police powers.
- Fair trials and anti-terrorism law.

Introduction

Terrorism is notoriously difficult to define. Broadly speaking, it is the unlawful use of violence for political, religious, or social ends, particularly where the violence aims at change through terrorising the civilian population. Responses by states to the threat of 'terrorism' is a major theme of global politics. Specifically, the dominant risk in the early twenty-first century is said to be from groups, such as the Al-Qaida network and ISIS/Daesh, who are promoting a political programme aimed, at least, at the removal of Western capitalist influence from the Islamic world. Methods used by states (such as special powers, alleged torture, and internment beyond the reach of the normal law) raise significant human rights dilemmas.

States, of course, may commit acts of aggression against other states or attack elements of their populations with great brutality. This is outside the scope of this chapter.

26.1 Special powers

Terrorist actions, such as bombing a civilian building, are likely to involve the commission of crimes such as murder and firearms and explosives offences. But states may feel these are insufficient to deal with the threat. Therefore state responses have included the use of special powers: laws which give extra powers to the executive, the police, the security services, or courts and tribunals which only apply in a 'terrorist' context. Such special powers can raise significant problems for human rights law. Many countries do not see the need for such powers. In the United Kingdom, by contrast, they have been extensively adopted. They were introduced in respect of the 'troubles' in Northern Ireland and have been reinvigorated to deal with international terrorism. Special powers can include:

- banning ('proscribing') political or religious organisations or political parties (which can raise issues under Article 11, freedom of assembly and association—see Chapter 18, section 18.7.2);

- extended periods of arrest and detention for questioning (which can raise issues under Article 5, the right to liberty and security—see Chapter 11);

- detention or other forms of deprivation of liberty without conviction (also likely to involve Article 5);

- increased powers for the police and security services to conduct searches and undertake secret surveillance (which can raise issues under Article 8, the right to respect for private and family life—see Chapter 15);

- new offences specific to the promotion and organisation of terrorism; and

- restrictions on various forms of speech and expression which might involve the advocacy or encouragement of terrorism (such restrictions might be incompatible with Article 10, freedom of expression—see Chapter 17).

26.2 The underlying principles

The issue of terrorism and how to deal with it is, and has been, a major concern of the Council of Europe. Under the Council of Europe's Convention on the Prevention of Terrorism 2005, which came into force in June 2007:

- states have an obligation to protect the human rights of their populations (in particular, the right to life in Article 2), and to agree to take a range of measures. An additional Protocol of 2015 requires states to take measures against people who participate in terrorist groups, terrorist training, and travelling abroad for terrorist purposes.

However, central to the Council of Europe's approach is that:

- any measures taken must be in conformity with human rights (see Article 12).

The general position of the European Court of Human Rights (ECtHR), interpreting the European Convention on Human rights (ECHR), reflects these basics (see, for example, *Klass* v *Germany* (1979–80) 2 EHRR 214, paras 49–50).

26.2.1 **Special measures may be necessary in a democracy**

From early cases, the Court has accepted that special measures may be necessary if a democracy is to defend itself from terrorism.

- The need for secret surveillance to meet a terrorist threat was accepted in *Klass* v *Germany* (1979–80) 2 EHRR 214 (para 48).

- The need for longer periods of detention for terrorist suspects (in the Northern Ireland context) was accepted in *Brogan* v *United Kingdom* (1989) 11 EHRR 117 (para 61).

In *Fox, Campbell and Hartley* v *United Kingdom* (1991) 13 EHRR 157, the Court said (in relation to Article 5 (1)(c)):

> the Convention should not be applied in such a manner as to put disproportionate difficulties in the way of the police authorities of the Contracting States in taking effective measures to counter organized terrorism.
>
> (para 34)

And in *Othman* v *United Kingdom* (2012) 55 EHRR 1 the Court emphasised that:

> throughout its history it has been acutely conscious of the difficulties faced by States in protecting their populations from terrorist violence, which constitutes, in itself, a grave threat to human rights.
>
> (para 183)

26.2.2 **Safeguards and the avoidance of abuse**

The ECtHR is insistent that special measures must be exercised in a manner that is compatible with the Convention. Special measures are open to abuse and a democracy is in danger of destroying its democratic quality unless the essential protections of the different Convention rights are maintained. In particular, the application of special powers must be:

- proportionate to the threat they deal with; and
- embody adequate safeguards for those affected.

States are given a wide margin of appreciation over issues such as the need for special measures. The proportionality of the application and the adequacy of the safeguards, however, remain a matter for proper judicial supervision.

Of course a great deal depends on which Convention right is in issue.

Article 3 (the prohibition on torture and inhuman treatment, the topic of Chapter 9) applies 'absolutely'. Torturing a terrorist suspect (or subjecting him or her to inhuman treatment) in order to get information is prohibited even if that information might directly save lives (see Chapter 9, section 9.1). CIA methods used against detainees in the 'war on terror' have been found to violate the Convention in a number of cases (e.g. *Husayn* v *Poland* (2015) 60 EHRR 16).

Other Convention rights are more flexible and context-dependent in their application. Questions such as whether a deprivation of liberty is 'arbitrary' (see Article 5) or whether restrictions on freedom of expression or association (see Articles 10 and 11) are 'necessary in a democratic society' are context-dependent. What is required (say, of police exercising their powers) may be different, the controls less exacting, regarding special powers when compared to 'ordinary' crime. Likewise, some of the specific components of a 'fair trial' in Article 6 can be applied, in a terrorist context, in a way that would not be tolerated in respect of 'ordinary' trials.

The focus is, therefore, on the safeguards and the need to ensure the 'essence', the basic requirements of a right, is secured. Terrorist suspects cannot be simply denied their rights. The language of 'balance' is, as so often, appropriate. Necessary limitations on application of rights for terrorist suspects need to be counterbalanced by special safeguards if the requirement of proportionality is to be satisfied. In particular, proper procedural safeguards, usually involving some form of effective judicial scrutiny, may be necessary in order to achieve Convention compatibility.

26.3 Anti-terrorism legislation in the United Kingdom

The legal basis of United Kingdom anti-terrorism law is found in:

- the ordinary law (such as criminal offences which apply to terrorist offences as much as to 'ordinary' crime) and general police powers under the Police and Criminal Evidence Act 1984 (PACE); and

- a body of specific anti-terrorism laws, which has been developed in response to the threat as understood by the government.

The coalition government, 2010–2015, had an independent review conducted of the legislation and made a number of consequential reforms.

 BIGGER PICTURE

The pre-2010 strategy is described in *Countering International Terrorism: The UK's Strategy* Cm 6888, 2006. The independent review is *Review of Counter-Terrorism and Security Powers Review Findings and Recommendations* Cm 8004.

The major pieces of special powers legislation are now outlined.

26.3.1 Terrorism Act 2000

The basic legislation is the Terrorism Act 2000. It was enacted before the '9/11' attacks in Washington and New York but after there had been a significant reduction in political violence associated with Northern Ireland. The central point about the Terrorism Act 2000 is that it enacts, as general law, a range of special powers which, previously, had been confined to the particular problem of Northern Ireland (though this was beginning to change). The Terrorism Act 2000 is general, in the sense that it applies to terrorism in all contexts and in respect of any political goal, and permanent, in that it does not require regular renewal by Parliament (although there is a requirement for reports by the Home Secretary to Parliament).

The Terrorism Act 2000 is a long and complex piece of legislation, which has been subject to amendment. It is outside the scope of this book to give it full examination. Its principal parts deal with:

- proscription: to allow the Home Secretary to ban ('proscribe') political parties and other organisations on the grounds that they are terrorist; and the Act creates a number of offences for activities connected with banned organisations;

- requiring disclosure of information about terrorism to the police;

- terrorist property: the Act creates a range of offences and powers linked to the use of money and other property for terrorist purposes;

- police powers: the Act increases police powers over terrorist investigations, including powers to arrest and detain for questioning, stop and search, and search of property;

- offences: the Act creates a number of terrorism offences such as inciting terrorism overseas.

Although the Terrorism Act purported to be general and permanent, and followed a thorough investigation by Lord Lloyd into the nature of the threat to the United Kingdom, it seems, for the government, not to have been adequate. It has been added to by other Acts, which have been the legislative responses to particular terrorist outrages. These other Acts depend upon the Terrorism Act 2000 at least insofar as they are all based on the definition of terrorism found in the 2000 Act (see section 26.4).

26.3.2 **Anti-Terrorism, Crime and Security Act 2001– detention without trial**

This was enacted after the 9/11 attacks. It creates a wide range of powers over terrorist property, strengthens duties to disclose information to the police, and contains a range of other powers over various matters which steadily increase the powers of government. It has been widely criticised because some of the powers within it are of general application and not confined to terrorism, and yet it was pushed through as an emergency response to a terrorist outrage.

Its most notorious power authorised the Home Secretary to imprison indefinitely, without charge, trial, or conviction, foreigners who were suspected of 'international terrorism'. In *A* v *Secretary of State for the Home Department* [2004] UKHL 56, a nine-judge House of Lords held that the derogation from Article 5, which was necessary for the power to be compatible with the Convention, was unlawful because it did not meet the requirements of Article 15 of the Convention; consequently a declaration of incompatibility in respect of the relevant sections of the 2001 Act was made.

This power was then repealed in 2005.

26.3.3 **Prevention of Terrorism Act 2005–control orders**

The government's response was to introduce 'control orders' in the Prevention of Terrorism Act 2005. These allowed a variety of restrictive measures (short of imprisonment) to be imposed on terrorist suspects, including British nationals. The Act was repealed by the Terrorism Prevention and Investigation Measures Act 2011.

26.3.4 **Terrorism Act 2006–control on speech and other measures**

This Act introduces a number of measures creating criminal offences regarding acts which are preliminary to terrorism. Thus the encouragement of terrorism (through its 'glorification') or doing acts preparatory to terrorism are made offences. The Act also has a range of miscellaneous provisions which amend proscription and increase the powers of the police and others in respect of terrorist investigations. The offence of encouraging terrorism is considered further in section 26.10.

26.3.5 **The Counter-terrorism Act 2008**

The Act increases police powers in various matters, such as seizure of documents, the sharing of information with the security services, and powers to act against terrorist financing. Since

July 2012, as part of the reform programme, it has allowed post-charge questioning of terrorist suspects to be authorised.

26.3.6 Terrorism Prevention and Investigation Measures Act 2011

This Act, as part of the reform programme, abolishes control orders by repealing the Prevention of Terrorism Act 2005. Control orders are replaced by TPIMs, which moderate the most onerous effects of control orders. TPIMs, in respect of human rights issues, are discussed in more detail in section 26.7.2.

A draft bill, which, if enacted, would give the government more draconian powers in a significant emergency, has been published (see section 26.7.2, Draft Enhanced Terrorism and Investigation Measures Bill).

26.3.7 Counter-terrorism and Security Act 2015

The Act focuses on restricting travel abroad to support terrorism and preventing radicalisation. It allows the seizure of passports and travel documents and also permits the Home Secretary to refuse to allow a person to return to the United Kingdom. It puts the strategy of preventing radicalisation amongst young Muslims on to a statutory basis.

26.3.8 The need for special powers

Commentators have challenged the need for such special powers. Arguments include:

- The 'ordinary law' is sufficient to meet the challenges of terrorism. Terrorism involves ordinary crimes such as murder, and there is no reason why these should be treated differently just because the crimes are done with a political or religious motive. The police and other agencies already have considerable powers and do not need any more (this is especially challenging to the legislation passed after the 2000 Act). Part of the argument is that special measures may not work, may be counter-productive (they may alienate parts of society), and seem to be motivated by a desire of government to placate public opinion by being seen to be responding.

- Special measures involve the restriction of the traditional civil liberties enjoyed by British people. The real threat to our institutions and way of life comes from government overreaction rather than from terrorism itself. Insofar as this argument seeks support from British traditions, it is worth reminding ourselves that at times of national crisis (e.g. the French Revolutionary and Napoleonic Wars of the late eighteenth and early nineteenth centuries, and the First and Second World Wars in the first half of the twentieth century), special powers and invasion of civil liberties have been regularly used by the British government.

- The acceptability of special powers depends on their being proportional to the threat. The problem here is one of trust. Special powers are justified, if at all, by the need to protect the population from a credible threat. The existence of the threat is based on intelligence. There is some scepticism about the effectiveness of intelligence. The intelligence failure over the invasion of Iraq and over particular issues, such as the intelligence-led police raids in Forest Gate, London, in June 2006, caused great concern.

26.3.9 **Constitutional processes**

The way in which special powers are introduced can be constitutionally controversial. Special powers legislation, though controversial and invasive of fundamental rights and liberties, tends to get less scrutiny by Parliament than ordinary legislation. There may be pre-legislative discussion (such as, for the Terrorism Act 2000, the Lloyd Report, mentioned previously, and numerous papers produced by the Home Office).

Nevertheless, parliamentary procedures are often curtailed. The House of Commons is more likely to accept government pressure and pass the measure quickly. Fuller scrutiny may be undertaken by the House of Lords but, given their constitutional position, in the end they may have to give way if the government, through the Commons, refuses to accept their amendments.

The Anti-Terrorism, Crime and Security Act 2001 is a good example. Though introducing detention without trial and many other severe powers, it went through all its Commons stages in three days, but it was considered for eight days by the House of Lords. The Terrorism Act 2006 was enacted only after six rounds of 'parliamentary ping pong' (the process by which amendments made in the House of Lords are considered by the House of Commons and, if rejected, returned to the House of Lords); in the end the House of Lords gave way to the Commons. The Counter-terrorism and Security Act 2015 was 'fast-tracked' through Parliament. This did not restrict opportunities for debate but it did limit the ability of the Joint Committee on Human Rights to provide detailed consideration of its compatibility with the Convention.

The situation should not be exaggerated, however. Important concessions, bearing on human rights and civil liberties, can be extracted from government. Originally, for instance, the 2006 Act would have extended the period for which a terrorist suspect can be detained for questioning from 14 to 90 days. This was defeated in Parliament and a compromise of 28 days agreed.

26.4 The definition of terrorism

The Terrorism Act 2000 defines terrorism. This definition applies to that Act and also to the other anti-terrorism Acts mentioned in section 26.3. The new offences created by all these anti-terrorism statutes and the numerous special powers for the Home Secretary, the police, and other agencies that they authorise, all depend upon this definition.

Section 1 of the Terrorism Act 2000 defines terrorism in terms of a person or persons using or threatening action which has certain characteristics.

26.4.1 **The action is designed to force a political change directly or by intimidating the public**

The action must be 'designed to influence the government or an international governmental organisation, or to intimidate the public or a section of the public' (this does not need to be proved if explosives or firearms are used).

26.4.2 The action must have a political, religious, racial, or ideological purpose

The action must be 'made for the purpose of advancing a political, religious, racial or ideological cause' ('racial' was introduced by the Counter-Terrorism Act 2008).

26.4.3 The action must involve serious violence or damage to others

It must be action which:

- involves serious violence against a person;
- involves serious damage to property;
- endangers a person's life, other than that of the person committing the action;
- creates a serious risk to the health or safety of the public or a section of the public; or
- is designed seriously to interfere with or seriously to disrupt an electronic system.

 BIGGER PICTURE

There is no internationally accepted definition of terrorism. The European Union's definition, for example, includes the words: 'seriously destabilising or destroying the fundamental, constitutional, economic or social structures of a country or an international organisation' (Council Framework Decision of 13 June 2002 on Combating Terrorism).

See generally Lord Carlile, *The Definition of Terrorism* Cm 7052 (Lord Carlile was the independent reviewer of terrorist legislation).

26.4.4 Analysis

The definition given in section 1 of the Terrorism Act is controversial.

- It makes no distinction between 'armed struggle' aimed at an undemocratic tyranny and violence used against civilians in a democracy, albeit an imperfect one. The presumption is that violence and serious damage to property can never be legitimate, even for a proper cause. Critics are unconvinced by the government's view that, in the early twenty-first century, no population group anywhere in the world has a just cause of war against its own state or against some other state that is in occupation of what it takes to be its land. In *R v Gul* [2013] UKSC 64, the defendant had been accused of the offence of encouraging terrorism (section 2 Terrorism Act 2006) by uploading videos onto the internet showing attacks on coalition forces in Afghanistan and Iraq. His defence was that these attacks were legitimate acts of resistance against a foreign invader, not terrorism. However, the UKSC held that attacks by insurgents on the armed forces of a state were clearly within the definition of terrorism, and there was nothing in the Convention or international law to suggest otherwise.
- The definition appears to exclude terror used by states against their populations or a section of their populations. From the point of view of the victims, actions by state agents can be indistinguishable from other forms of terror (actions by the Turkish state against the Kurds or by the Israelis against the Palestinians are examples).

- The definition could involve the suppression of radical politics such as those practised by environmental and animal rights groups. Actions such as destroying crops or animal laboratories might become subject to special powers rather than the normal criminal law. For some people there are important moral differences between violence against people and damage to property, which the definition does not acknowledge.

26.5 Convention compatibility

The definition of terrorism triggers a range of offences and powers. In the next sections of this chapter some of the special powers introduced by the UK's anti-terrorism legislation are considered from the point of view of their compatibility with Convention rights. The law is very complex and there is no attempt here to explore its details. The aim is to point out the main areas in which the policies of the law raise questions of compatibility with human rights.

The HRA needs to be recalled:

- Anti-terrorist legislation must be read and given effect 'so far as it is possible to do so' in a manner that is compatible with Convention rights. If this is not possible the legislation remains valid and effective, although the courts may issue a declaration of incompatibility.

- Ministers, the police, the security services, etc. are 'public authorities'. They act illegally if they act incompatibly with the Convention unless such actions are required by valid legislation (i.e. legislation that cannot be read for compatibility).

26.6 Proscription

26.6.1 **Proscription and deproscription**

The Terrorism Act 2000, Part 2, gives a power to the Secretary of State to ban or proscribe organisations. The test is that the Secretary of State believes the organisation is 'concerned in terrorism'. A proscribed organisation can apply to the Secretary of State to be 'deproscribed' and any refusal to deproscribe can be appealed to a special tribunal, the Proscribed Organisations Appeals Commission, which has the power to require the Secretary of State to lift the ban. It is the Commission (rather than the High Court) which has the principal jurisdiction to determine HRA challenges to proscription and provide remedies as required by Article 13 (see *R (Kurdistan Workers Party)* v *Secretary of State for the Home Department* [2002] EWHC 644).

26.6.2 **Article 11**

Proscription must be compatible with the Convention, in particular Article 11, freedom of assembly and association.

> **CROSS REFERENCE**
> Proscription in general is discussed in Chapter 18, section 18.7.2.

Major issues under Article 11 include:

CROSS REFERENCE

'Prescribed by law' in respect of Article 11 is discussed in Chapter 18, section 18.5.1 (for the Convention's conception of law—see Chapter 6, section 6.2).

- Whether the ban is 'prescribed by law'. Being 'concerned in terrorism' is a vague expression. It says little about the degree of involvement in or knowledge of political violence by an organisation and its supporters that is required to justify proscription. In *Lord Alton v Secretary of State for the Home Department* PC/02/2006 (the only case it has, so far, decided), the Commission held that the overall procedure established by the Act met the requirements of being 'prescribed by law'; and this view was upheld by the Court of Appeal in *Secretary of State for the Home Department v Lord Alton* [2008] EWCA Civ 443.

- Whether the ban is for one of the legitimate purposes listed in Article 11(2) (see Chapter 18, section 18.5.2). This is likely to be easy for the government to satisfy since the protection of national security and public safety are two of the purposes.

- Whether the ban is 'necessary in a democratic society'. The state must be able to show that the ban has been imposed to prevent a political organisation pursuing its aims by violent means. It is the actions of the organisation and not just the rhetoric associated with it that is decisive. A political organisation should not be proscribed just because it is pursuing radical, constitutional change against a background of political violence.

CROSS REFERENCE

Article 17 is discussed in Chapter 7, section 7.3.

- Article 17. The Convention cannot be used by organisations wishing to avoid a ban in order to pursue a political programme that is likely to lead to violations of the rights of others.

The Court's support for pluralism, and its recognition that 'democracy' is the only political system compatible with the Convention, means that a political organisation whose aim is a non-democratic society, or a society in which important human rights would not be respected, will find it difficult to show that its Convention rights have been violated (and this may apply even if it uses non-violent means).

26.6.3 **Fair trials**

Appearing before the Proscribed Organisations Appeal Commission can place a proscribed organisation under considerable procedural disadvantages. It may not know the full extent of the evidence against it or be able to challenge that evidence. This is a general problem found in relation to the exercise of special powers and is discussed below in section 26.9.

In *Lord Alton* (see section 26.6.2), the Commission, agreed with by the Court of Appeal, held that the procedure was fair and Convention compliant because of its duty (flowing from principles of administrative law) to subject the decision to proscribe to 'intensive scrutiny' (para 113) with only limited deference to the Secretary of State on issues such as national security. The Commission's order that the organisation be deproscribed was upheld by the Court of Appeal.

26.7 Treatment of terrorist suspects

The most controversial aspects of the special powers introduced in UK law involve the treatment of terrorist suspects. These are individual men and women who have not been convicted of any offence (whether under the general laws or anti-terrorism legislation) but whose personal liberty is severely restricted because they are suspected of being terrorists or supporting terrorism.

From the government's point of view, the issue is its duty, under general principles of good government but also under Article 2 of the Convention, to take appropriate measures to try to ensure the safety of the population. The typical situation is said to be one in which the suspect is probably involved in terrorism but the evidence does not demonstrate this beyond a reasonable doubt (i.e. to the criminal standard which would justify a prosecution); or the evidence suggests terrorist involvement without doubt, but the evidence is inadmissible (e.g. because it would disclose the workings of the intelligence services); or, most likely, a combination of these two situations. At the heart of the matter is the intelligence on which the suspicions are based and whether it is reliable and the way it has been interpreted. Of particular concern, therefore, about the treatment of such suspects is their inability to know of, and challenge, the evidence against them.

26.7.1 **2001 to 2011**

The official response to this problem, at the height of the terrorist fears was, first, to use powers in Part IV of the Anti-terrorism, Crime and Security Act 2001 and detain in prison a small number of foreign terrorist suspects who could not be deported (usually because they might be tortured in the receiving country). Following *A* (section 26.3.2) this power was repealed and replaced by control orders which were themselves replaced by Terrorism Prevention and Investigation Measures (TPIMs).

26.7.2 **Terrorism prevention and investigation measures**

The Terrorism Prevention and Investigation Measures Act 2011 (TPIMA 2011) allows the Secretary of State (Home Secretary) to impose a TPIM if he or she:

- 'is satisfied, on the balance of probabilities' that the individual is or has been 'involved in terrorism-related activity' (some of which must be 'new');
- 'reasonably considers it necessary' for protecting the public to impose the measures;
- has obtained prior permission by application to the High Court.

There is an urgent cases procedure by which the Secretary of State can impose the TPIM, subject to consideration by the High Court, within seven days.

Involvement in terrorism is defined widely in section 4 to include not just commissioning, preparing, or instigating terrorist acts, but also encouraging, supporting, or assisting such acts by others.

Schedule 1 specifies the restraints that can be imposed by a TPIM. These include 'requirements, restrictions and other provisions' relating to residence (if he or she agrees a person may be required to live up to 200 miles from their current residence), travel, places where the person may be and where they may go, finance and property, computer use, association with others, and work and study. Individuals may be required to report to the police and be subjected to monitoring devices. It is a criminal offence to break the terms of a TPIM.

In a number of ways TPIMs are less severe than control orders, and this makes it more likely that, even though they remain a departure from the norms of ordinary criminal justice, they will be compatible with human rights.

- Following amendment by the Criminal Justice and Security Act 2015, the Home Secretary must be satisfied to the civil standard (balance of probabilities) of the person's terrorist involvement.

- TPIMs do not, generally, last beyond two years (one year which can be extended for another year by Home Secretary so long as the conditions still apply).

- There is a greater emphasis on using the criminal justice system against terrorist suspects—the police must be consulted on whether there is a realistic possibility of prosecution as an alternative (section 10).

- Individual TPIMs must be kept under review.

The Act is not permanent. The powers to make TPIMs will lapse after five years unless the Home Secretary revives them with the approval of Parliament (section 21).

For compatibility with human rights, judicial supervision of TPIMs is important. First, the role of the court (in non-urgent cases) is to consider whether the Home Secretary's application is 'obviously flawed' and, if not, whether to give permission for the measures. Second, there must be a 'review hearing' at which the court must consider whether the relevant conditions authorising a TPIM have been met. The standard of review is that of judicial review – which is a highly variable standard of review but one which can be compatible with intense scrutiny by the court; though this is not stipulated in the Act.

TPIMs and Article 5

▶ CROSS REFERENCE

JJ and deprivation of liberty is discussed in Chapter 11, section 11.2.1

The compatibility of a TPIM with Convention rights has been tested in the courts. Control Order cases, such as *Secretary of State for the Home Department* v *JJ* [2007] UKHL 45, make it clear that a long period of 'house arrest' (in that case 16 hours) coupled with other factors can be a deprivation of liberty and so engage Article 5. TPIMA does not expressly authorise anything like this and its provisions can be read down, under section 3 HRA, to exclude them. Relocation provisions in the Act may restrict a person's movements, but the UK is not bound by Protocol 4 ECHR and anyway they require agreement.

TPIMs and other rights

The restrictions that can be imposed under Schedule 1 can engage other Convention rights such as the right to respect for private life (Article 8), the right to manifest religious beliefs (Article 9), and freedom of expression (Article 10). Of course such interferences can be justified under the terms of the second paragraph to each Article, and in the counter-terrorism context this may be relatively easy for the government to do. In *R (AP)* v *Secretary of State for the Home Department* [2010] UKSC 24, for instance, the judge had found that a control order requiring the controllee to live 150 miles from family and friends was a proportionate and justified interference with his Article 8 rights (though the interference could be a factor in deciding whether there had been, also, a deprivation of liberty). In *DD* v *Secretary of State for the Home Department* [2015] EWHC 1681, the terms of a TPIM were required to be modified because the intensity of the suffering caused to the appellant violated his Article 3 rights. The applicant was mentally ill and suffered, in particular, extreme anguish from the need to wear a tag. His children's Article 8 rights were violated by the disproportionate extent of restrictions on computer use. The court accepted that the threshold for the application of Article 3 was not just a matter of the intensity of suffering—'purpose, legitimacy, intent, alternatives and care provided' should also be taken into account (para 74).

Fair trials

Although TPIMs are subject to judicial approval, there are significant procedural barriers that a person may face when seeking to challenge the measure before the High Court. The Act itself and procedural rules made under it allow for the exclusion of the person and his or her representatives from proceedings, possible determination without a hearing, and the non-disclosure of information relating to the reasons for the order (Schedule 4). Since similar restraints are found in respect of other counter-terrorist measures, their compatibility with Convention rights is discussed in section 26.9.

Draft Enhanced Terrorism and Investigation Measures Bill

The review of counter-terrorism powers (Review 2010) recognised that tougher control might be necessary if terrorist threats became more pressing. The government has produced a draft bill which, if enacted, would authorise somewhat more stringent restrictions than can be imposed under the TPIMA 2011 (Cm 8166). For example, it would allow the Home Secretary to require the person to remain at a specified residence within defined hours (i.e. more than just overnight), or to exclude the person from a defined area of the United Kingdom. As a draft bill it is not law, but is available for pre-legislative scrutiny. The idea is that it should be available for swift enactment by Parliament if circumstances so require. The draft bill is closely linked to TPIMA 2011 and adopts its provisions on most issues, including the process of application, the nature of judicial supervision, and the procedures before the court. There will be a similar need to ensure that the application of the measures do not (in the absence of any derogation) violate Article 5 and are consistent with other Convention rights, including Article 8 and, in particular, the fair hearing provisions in Article 6.

26.7.3 Deportation of terrorist suspects

The nature of the alleged threat from international terrorism means that a number of terrorist suspects are likely to be foreigners and so are liable to exclusion from the country. This might be because:

- they can be removed if they came to, or remain in, the United Kingdom illegally;
- they may be deported following conviction and punishment for a crime.

In particular, in this context:

- they may be deported because the Home Secretary believes their staying in the United Kingdom is not in the public interest;
- they may be 'extradited' (returned to another country to stand trial).

Under the Convention (and international law generally) a person cannot be excluded if they face a 'real risk' of torture, ill-treatment, or the gross violation of other Convention rights in the receiving country.

Reassessing *Chahal*?

The leading authority, *Chahal* v *United Kingdom* (1997) 23 EHRR 413, prevents any weighing of the danger a terrorist suspect may pose to national security against the degree of real risk of torture etc. in the receiving country. In the case, dissenting judges argued that, in such circumstances, a weighing exercise was reasonable, so that a suspect might be deported if, for instance, the threat he or she posed was considerable and the likelihood of being tortured not very great or very difficult to assess in advance. The UK government intervened in a terrorist deportation case to argue that weighing the risk of torture etc. to the individual against the threat he or she poses in the expelling country, was reasonable in a national security context and where the risk of torture did not come from the expelling state. A Grand Chamber, specifically addressing these points, rejected them and confirmed the established position in *Chahal*: *Saadi* v *Italy* (2009) 49 EHRR 30, paras 137–142.

> **CROSS REFERENCE**
> This issue is discussed in general terms in Chapter 9, section 9.8.2.

Diplomatic agreements

The UK government has also entered into diplomatic agreements with countries against which torture allegations are made, so that suspects can be deported without a danger of torture. Whether such agreements will pass muster with judges authorising deportation will depend upon the circumstances.

🔍 CASE CLOSE-UP

Othman v United Kingdom (2012) 55 EHRR 1

O, born in Jordan, had leave to live in the UK. He was suspected of involvement in terrorism. He was detained (under the Anti-terrorism, Crime and Security Act 2001: see section 26.3.2) and, on the Act's repeal, made subject to a control order (under the Prevention of Terrorism Act 2005: see section 26.3.3). The Home Secretary sought to deport him to Jordan on public interest grounds. Convincing allegations are made that, in Jordan, torture of prisoners is widespread (para 191). The UK government had obtained specific assurances from the Jordanian authorities that O would not be tortured.

The ECtHR held that deporting O to Jordan would not violate Article 3 because the assurances were, on the facts, likely to be effective. However, deportation would violate his right to a fair trial (Article 6) since there was a real risk of his being tried on the basis of evidence obtained by torture (see Chapter 12, section 12.16).

The Court, in _Othman,_ noticed that, in general terms, the use of diplomatic assurances in this context was controversial and assurances in themselves, though relevant, are not sufficient to protect a person's Convention rights (para 186). The Court has to concern itself with the practical effect of the assurances in the particular circumstances of the case (the Court referred to the Grand Chamber in _Saadi_ v _Italy_ (2009) 49 EHRR 30 on this point).

In assessing the practical worth of assurances, the Court will consider the general human rights position in the receiving country (though it would be unusual for this to be such that assurances could never be valid). More importantly, it identified a range of factors (para 189) that need to be considered. These include: the degree to which the assurances are specific, whether assurances given at a national level are likely to filter through to local authorities who will have specific responsibility for the person, and the receiving state's record in abiding by its assurances (there are eleven criteria altogether).

The Court then applied these factors, carefully and in detail, to the instant case and held that the assurances had, indeed, removed the real risk of torture if the applicant was returned to Jordan (paras 190–205).

Regarding Article 6, the United Kingdom, in July 2013, entered into a Mutual Legal Assistance Treaty with Jordan to the effect that O would not be tried there on the basis of certain evidence believed to have been obtained by torture. On the strength of that Treaty, O voluntarily returned to Jordan. The Committee of Ministers, somewhat reluctantly, accepted that there had been no breach of Article 6.

The position of UK courts is generally in line with the sceptical but fact-centred approach of the ECtHR. In the domestic hearing of Othman's case, _RB (Algeria)_ v _Secretary of State for the Home Department_ [2009] UKHL 10, the UKHL had decided, following earlier Strasbourg cases, that the issue of the credibility of diplomatic assurances was not a matter of law but of fact. The Special Immigration Appeals Commission (see section 26.9.2) deals with appeals involving public interest deportations and, unless wholly unreasonable, its factual judgments would be accepted. In *Rahmatullah v Secretary of State for the Foreign and Commonwealth Office* [2012] UKSC 48, a Memorandum of Understanding between the US and UK concerning the transfer of 'terrorist' prisoners was ignored by both sides. The Supreme Court accepted that the Memorandum was not directly legally binding but was legally important as the 'means by which the courts have been invited to accept that the assurances they contain will be honoured'.

26.7.4 Torture

The fear that terrorist suspects may be subjected to torture, if not in the United Kingdom, then in other countries, is a real one. The issue for the United Kingdom is whether government powers, such as making someone subject to a TPIM, might be based on intelligence gained from people under torture. The general principle is that, although it is unlawful for a court knowingly to admit evidence based on torture, it is not illegal for the executive, the minister, the police, etc. to act on the basis of such evidence: they do not need to enquire into its origins.

> **CROSS REFERENCE**
> The admissibility of torture evidence has been considered in Chapter 9, section 9.4.3.

DISCUSSION TOPIC

What should be done with terrorist suspects?

Is there any appropriate policy that (a) is compatible with Convention rights; and (b) can be applied to persons who, on the basis of intelligence, are 'probably' terrorists but who cannot be prosecuted for a number of reasons to do with the degree of proof the evidence discloses or the secret nature of the intelligence? Can the circle of security and human rights be squared?

26.8 Police powers

The Terrorism Act 2000 authorises a number of increased powers for the police. These include powers to create a 'cordon' around an area and require people to leave; to stop and search a person reasonably suspected of being a terrorist; and increased powers to obtain search warrants, remove documents, take fingerprints and samples, share information with other agencies, etc. All these powers are predicated on the wide definition of terrorism found in the Act.

26.8.1 Stop and search

A major objection to the special powers in the Terrorism Act and other legislation is that there is little to prevent their use in the context of 'ordinary' politics, including meetings, marches, and demonstrations. In Britain there is a long history of disorder breaking out in a political context. It is suggested that this is perfectly well dealt with under general public order legislation. Counter-terrorism powers should be more carefully defined to maintain the distinction between demonstrations (which might be disorderly and even violent) and the deliberate, deadly attacks on civilians which are at the core of the moral case against terrorism.

CROSS REFERENCE

The Convention concept of 'law' is discussed in Chapter 6, section 6.2.

Section 44 of the Terrorism Act 2000 was particularly controversial. It allowed an 'authorisation' to be made by a senior officer which then permitted police to make random stops and searches (for articles that could be used for terrorism) in the area and for the duration of the authorisation. Under regular police powers (such as in Part 1 PACE), stop and search powers require 'reasonable suspicion', relating to the individual being searched, that some prohibited article will be found.

No such person-specific suspicion was required under section 44. The grounds for making the authorisation was merely that the police believed it 'expedient' to prevent terrorism.

> ### CASE CLOSE-UP
>
> ### *Gillan v Commissioner of Police of the Metropolis* [2006] UKHL 12
>
> G, a student, and Q, a journalist, attended a demonstration in London against the arms trade. They were stopped and searched by police exercising section 44 powers. Nothing was found. An authorisation under section 44, covering the whole of London, had been made and continually renewed since February 2001. It had not been publicised. The House of Lords found that the police had acted lawfully.

On compatibility with Convention rights the House of Lords held that:

- stop and search (in a terrorist or non-terrorist context) would not normally be a 'deprivation of liberty' engaging Article 5;

- nor, in the context of political demonstrations, would a stop and search be a sufficiently serious 'interference' with private life, freedom of expression, or the right of assembly to bring it within the ambit of Articles 8(1), 10(1), and 11(1). In any event, non-trivial interferences would normally be justified under the terms of these Articles;

- despite the lack of publicity, the authorisation was, in the context, sufficiently 'accessible and foreseeable' to be compatible with the Convention.

> ### CASE CLOSE-UP
>
> ### *Gillan v United Kingdom* (2010) 50 EHRR 45
>
> At the ECtHR, however, an entirely different view of Convention compatibility was taken. It was held that section 44, which the police had lawfully put into effect, involved an interference with private life which was unjustified under Article 8(2). At the heart of this judgment was the view that the police's discretion was not properly controlled by 'law'.

CROSS REFERENCE

'Ordinary' stop and search is discussed in Chapter 20, section 20.2.

The ECtHR's point was that the effect of the statute was not foreseeable in respect of the purposes; likewise there was insufficient control and safeguards over the operation of the section through, for example, the process of authorisation by senior officers. As well as Article 8 there could also be a violation of Articles 10 or 11 based on the same lack of legal control under which the exercise of the powers could be foreseeable. Because of the Article 8 finding, the ECtHR did not consider whether there was a deprivation of liberty which engaged and perhaps breached Article 5.

Following *Gillan* v *UK* the power was suspended using a remedial order under section 10 HRA; further criticism was expressed in the Review 2010. Section 44 was repealed by the Protection of Freedoms Act 2012. A new power, inserted as section 47A Terrorism Act 2000, still allows individuals to be stopped and searched without reasonable suspicion. However, the trigger for the necessary authorisation is raised from a belief that stop and search is 'expedient' to a reasonable belief that an act of terrorism will take place, that the power is necessary, and the area and time for the authorisation is no greater than necessary. Other measures, including the introduction of a Code of Practice, are designed to ensure that the new power, when lawfully exercised, is foreseeable in its effects and subject to sufficient controls. The House of Lord's position, that a stop and search will not normally be a deprivation of liberty, or if there is one it will be allowed under Article 5(1)(b), still stands. This is strengthened, domestically, by the position articulated in *Austin* v *Commissioner of Police for the Metropolis* [2009] UKHL 5 (see Chapter 11) that proportionate actions by the police in a public order context are unlikely to involve deprivations of liberty.

26.8.2 Arrest and detention for questioning

Terrorism as an offence

Under the Terrorism Act 2000, someone who is suspected of an offence under that Act can be detained for questioning (and to preserve evidence) for up to 48 hours by the police. The same applies to someone suspected of being involved in terrorism. The problem is that, in this context, Article 5 only permits detention on reasonable suspicion that an 'offence' has been committed (Article 5(1)(c)). Terrorism is not an offence. However, terrorism implies actions which are likely to be offences, and it is likely to satisfy the Convention so long as the questioning relates to specific events.

CROSS REFERENCE
See also the discussion of 'an offence' in Chapter 11, section 11.4.3.

Judicial authorisation of detention

Article 5(3) requires that a person, deprived of his or her liberty by being arrested for a criminal offence, be brought before a judge 'promptly' in order that the legality of the detention can be tested before an independent and impartial judicial body. In *Brogan* v *United Kingdom* (1989) 11 EHRR 117 (relating to Northern Ireland under the old Prevention of Terrorism Acts), the ECtHR held that holding a suspect for four days without access to a judge was not 'prompt' and so violated Article 5(3): see Chapter 11, section 11.7.1.

The principle of judicial supervision has been adopted into the Terrorism Act. After an initial 48 hours of detention by the police, a person can be detained for a further 12 days (14 days in total). The detention beyond 48 hours requires judicial authority and a court hearing. A long period of detention will, roughly speaking, require weekly judicial authority. Given that the extended detention must be authorised by a court with opportunities for a hearing, the provisions of Article 5(3) are likely to be met by these provisions. So long as there is judicial supervision, review, and the active pursuit of the case by the authorities, the absolute length of detention is unlikely to violate Article 5(1).

The Protection of Freedoms Act 2012 reduced the detention period from 28 days to 14. However, a draft bill which would allow 28 days to be restored in time of emergency was published in 2012.

A power under Schedule 7 Terrorism Act 2000 to detain and question travellers at ports or airports suspected of involvement in terrorism, was declared to be incompatible with Article 10, at least in respect of journalists. In that context the safeguards were insufficient (*R (Miranda)* v *Secretary of State for the Home Department* [2016] EWCA Civ 6).

CROSS REFERENCE
See Chapter 17, section 17.6.2.

26.9 Fair trials

26.9.1 Equality of arms

Although the reforms to counter-terrorism laws since 2010 have reduced their severity, they still sit uncomfortably with the rule of law and British traditions of political and civil freedom under the law. A crucial aspect of the proportionality of these powers and their ability to offer those affected sufficient safeguards to protect their rights, is the requirement that such powers are exercised under judicial supervision. The quality and effectiveness of this supervision depends greatly on the ability of the person affected knowing the evidence against him or her. They can then understand, challenge, answer, and explain the facts on which the suspicions of the Secretary of State are based. The problem is that, from the police and government viewpoint, disclosing the evidence may compromise national security—it may, for instance, show that a political group has been infiltrated by informants, or it may involve evidence obtained from a foreign country on condition that it is kept confidential. Therefore the law on, for instance, proscription, TPIMs, and detention without charge for questioning, can require judicial supervision to be conducted on the basis of 'closed evidence', which is not known to the person or his or her legal representative and so cannot be directly challenged.

> **CROSS REFERENCE**
>
> Fair trial rights in Article 5(4) are discussed in Chapter 11, section 11.8; equality of arms in Chapter 12, section 12.11.3.

Where there is a deprivation of liberty (e.g. detention for questioning: see section 26.8.2), a fair trial procedure is required by Article 5(4). Likewise, Article 6 (right to a fair trial) is likely to be engaged because TPIMs are likely, like control orders before them, to involve the determination of a 'civil right'.

On the face of it, the use of closed evidence would seem to violate the Article 6 principle of 'equality of arms' (that the defence has equal access to the information on which the court decides the case). However, requirements of a fair trial can depend upon the context. The ECtHR (e.g. in *Chahal v United Kingdom* (1997) 23 EHRR 413, para 131) recognises that there can be legitimate reasons, relating to counter-terrorism or national security situations, for a court to determine an issue on the basis of confidential evidence kept from the parties. What is required are effective counterbalancing safeguards. The Court appeared to approve, at para 144, the use of 'security-cleared counsel' who would act on behalf of the detained or controlled person.

> **CROSS-REFERENCE**
>
> Special counsel are discussed in Chapter 12, section 12.11.3, Disclosure and public interest immunity.

In the United Kingdom, 'special counsel' are available for use in the counter-terrorism context (e.g. before special courts, discussed later in this section, and in the procedures discussed here). The interests of the person are represented by an advocate who has access to the closed material. The system is controversial because the special counsel, after seeing the closed material, cannot contact the person involved to take instructions in respect of the particular allegations.

'Solely or to a decisive degree'?

The position of the ECtHR has been that the use of closed procedures is acceptable providing, first, that there are adequate counterbalancing provisions and, second, that a decision 'based solely or to a decisive degree' on closed material would not satisfy the Convention. In the terrorism context, these principles were adopted in *A v UK* (2009) 49 EHRR 29. This was the case brought by foreign terrorist suspects who had been detained without trial under the Anti-terrorism, Crime and Security Act 2001 (discussed earlier, section 26.3.2). The detention could be challenged before the Special Immigration Appeals Commission (section 26.9.2), but on the basis of closed material procedures, including the use of special counsel. The Grand Chamber held there had been a breach of Article 5(4).

A v *UK* concerned persons who were deprived of their liberty—a deprivation of liberty cannot be compatible with Article 5(4) of the Convention if it is based solely or decisively on closed evidence. However, the Strasbourg Court was clear that it was equating the fair procedures required by Article 5(4) with the standards of a fair trial under Article 6 (para 217). As a result, in *Secretary of State for the Home Department* v *AF (3)* [2009] UKHL 28, the House of Lords applied the sole or decisive test to a non-derogating control order—one which by definition did not involve a deprivation of liberty but which needed a procedure that satisfied Article 6. Lord Phillips said that the Strasbourg ruling established that the person:

> must be given sufficient information about the allegations against him to enable him to give effective instructions [to special counsel] in relation to those allegations.

The control order legislation could be read down, under section 3 HRA, to require this. It meant that judicial supervision of control orders could continue only if the authorities are prepared to disclose at least the essential core of the case against the applicant.

Since then the Convention law relating to Article 6 has changed. In *Al-Khawaja* v *UK* (2012) 54 EHRR 23 (a non-terrorist criminal case), the Grand Chamber, whilst upholding the sole or decisive rule, accepted that it was not absolute and, if there are sufficient counterbalancing measures, a decision based solely on closed evidence is not necessarily a breach of Article 6.

The extent to which this change in the Convention law (which, given it merely gives a degree of ultimate flexibility to the ban on decisions based solely or decisively on closed procedures, is a modest change) will apply in the counter-terrorism context is unclear. The sole or decisive rule has been applied in other contexts such as in special courts (discussed later in this section). It has been applied to TPIMs in *Mohammed and CF* v *Secretary of State for the Home Department* [2014] EWCA Civ 559. Here, although *Al-Khawaja* was not cited, the seriousness of the TPIM context meant that at least the gist of the case had to be disclosed and there was no principle that the Secretary of State should not be required to choose between pursuing the case by disclosing the information or withdrawing the case and leaving an arguable dangerous terrorist suspect at large. Where the liberty of the subject is not involved, the courts may be more prepared to accept that there is no rule requiring, at the least, a gist of the case (*Home Office* v *Tariq* [2011] UKSC 35, upholding the use of closed materials in an employment law context). However, it was held that there is no power to hold closed procedure hearings in the context of extradition proceedings: *VB* v *Westminster Magistrates' Court* [2014] UKSC 59.

 THINKING POINT

Compare the 'sole or decisive' rule in the context of terrorist and non-terrorist criminal trials—see Chapter 12 section 12.15.4.

26.9.2 **Special courts**

The use of special courts and tribunals in an anti-terrorist context is not necessarily inconsistent with the Convention. In the United Kingdom, the Special Immigration Appeals Commission (SIAC) has been created to hear appeals against deportations which have been ordered because the Home Secretary believes the deportee's presence is not in the public interest, because they threaten national security, perhaps on suspicion of terrorism. The court can see secret intelligence that the Home Secretary has relied upon but which would not be admissible in an ordinary court. The Proscribed Organisations Appeal Commission, mentioned earlier, at sections 26.6.1 and 26.6.2, is another example.

Such courts, because they enable at least some judicial supervision of intelligence, can be important in balancing individual rights against national security and so achieving proportionality in the way special powers are applied. However, such tribunals cannot fulfil this role if, given their purpose and given the context, they are unable to provide a fair trial. If they lack independence and impartiality, for example, or if their procedures involve a disproportionate restriction on 'equality of arms' between state and suspect, then there will still be a violation of Article 6 or 5(4). SIAC, for example, uses special counsel whose compatibility with the Convention is uncertain. In *R (U)* v *Special Immigration Appeals Commission* [2009] EWHC 3052, the principle in *AF*, discussed earlier, that the applicant was entitled to know of the case against him to give effective instruction to special counsel, was applied to SIAC.

The Justice and Security Act 2013 introduces closed material procedures into ordinary civil actions where rules preventing the disclosure of sensitive material might otherwise prevent the trial from proceeding. A court can grant a government application, in civil actions, to use closed material proceedings—including the use of special counsel. The court must be satisfied that the case requires the disclosure of sensitive material and that closed procedures would be in the interest of the fair and effective administration of justice.

26.10 Glorification of terrorism

The European Convention on the Prevention of Terrorism places a duty on states to make 'public provocation to commit a terrorist offence' an offence. The response of the United Kingdom is in the Terrorism Act 2006. This makes the direct or indirect encouragement of terrorism an offence, and a statement which 'glorifies' past or future terrorism is deemed to be such a direct or indirect encouragement (see section 1). Disseminating information with the purpose of directly or indirectly encouraging terrorism is also an offence.

The argument in favour of such restrictions is partly a practical one: speech may encourage terrorists and, indirectly, cause more attacks. It is also an argument about civility: expressions of support for political violence are improper ways of conducting the public life of a democratic society, whether or not such expressions actually cause others to commit violent acts.

The following statement, taken from trial evidence against Sheik Abdullah el Faisal, illustrates why the offence may be necessary.

> The way forward can never be the ballot. The way forward is the bullet . . . We spread Islam by the Sword and so what, and today we are going to spread by the Kalashnikov and there is nothing you can do about it . . . if you see a Hindu walking down the road you are allowed to kill him and take his money.

(R v Faisal [2004] EWCA Crim 456, para 15)

The European Convention on the Prevention of Terrorism clearly states that the offences must be compatible with the ECHR, most obviously with Article 10, freedom of expression. The offences in the 2006 Act have been strongly criticised on the grounds that they fail this test of compatibility.

Glorification is an uncertain term. It seems to go further than incitement to violence (which can be prohibited under Article 10), but it is not clear how much further. When this uncertainty is linked to the wide meaning given to terrorism (see section 26.4), there are doubts whether the Article 10 requirement that an offence be defined in ways that make its application foreseeable (and hence 'prescribed by law') will be met. These concerns are partly answered by the fact that prosecutions require the consent of the Director of Public Prosecutions, and that the most serious prosecutions will be before a jury. Supporters of the jury system are likely to argue that jurors will only convict if their common sense tells them that the prosecution was properly made and non-oppressive.

There is doubt whether the interference is 'necessary' given that there already exist offences that cover much of the ground of the glorification offence. An example is 'solicitation to murder' (section 4 of the Offences against the Person Act 1867), which makes it an offence to 'solicit, encourage, persuade or endeavour to persuade' a person to commit murder. Sheik Abdullah el Faisal, referred to earlier, was convicted under section 4 (February 2003).

The offence has been used against persons responsible for uploading videos onto the internet (see *R* v *Gul*, section 26.4.4).

26.11 Conclusion

There are many other counter-terrorism powers that have not been mentioned, such as powers over surveillance, disclosure of information, property, finance, and so on. Because these powers are special they are controversial. They are hard to make compatible with the rule of law because they involve serious restraints on individual freedoms whilst, at the same time, often denying the normal rights to a fair trial which are associated with a society committed to the rule of law. At the heart of the reason for these powers is that the UK government, along with other countries, believes it is facing a threat equivalent to war, which cannot be met by the ordinary criminal law. The problem is that the degree of threat cannot be publicly tested. The government's understanding of the threat is based on intelligence which is not available either to the public or to the individuals directly affected. There is, therefore, a problem of trust. Reforms, following Review 2010, have moderated the most severe effects but, significantly, the government has published draft bills which would allow tough measures to be restored (see section 26.7.2). Restoration will require parliamentary scrutiny and, perhaps, a derogation from the Convention under Article 15. The scale of any new threat justifying such restored powers would, therefore, need some degree of public assessment.

The ongoing question is whether the special powers can be applied in ways that are compatible with human rights. In the context of counter-terrorism, Convention rights seem to be at their most open-textured and amenable to adjustment to the circumstances. Nevertheless, there is evidence that the courts are taking a more demanding line in which the essence of rights, to a fair trial in particular, will not be compromised in the name of the alleged emergency.

Summary

- The fight against terrorism is conducted in the United Kingdom partially on the basis of special powers. These include, for example, TPIMs, powers of extended detention for questioning, and random stop and search.

- Special powers are not necessarily inconsistent with the Convention. Many (but not all) Convention rights are open-textured and their application can be context-dependent and involve 'weighing' individual rights with important public interests, such as the safety of the population and the protection of democratic institutions.

- Nevertheless, special powers which are applied disproportionately and which totally undermine an individual's Convention rights will violate the Convention.

? **Self-test questions**

1. Outline the arguments in favour and against giving state agents special powers in the context of counter-terrorism.

2. What are the main special powers in the Terrorism Act 2000?

3. What are the main factors to be considered in ensuring that TPIMs are only imposed in ways that are compatible with the subject's Convention rights?

4. What Convention rights can inhibit the capacity of the Home Secretary to order the deportation of a foreign terrorist suspect?

5. What position did the ECtHR adopt in *Gillan* v *United Kingdom* and what were its consequences for UK law?

6. What are 'special counsel' and in what situations are they significant in the counter-terrorism procedures?

7. How has the 'sole or decisive' rule affected the application of counter-terrorism measures in the UK?

8. What does Part 2 of the Justice and Security Act 2013 permit; how does it compare with the common law position (see Chapter 12, section 12.11.3, Disclosure and national security cases)?

 For suggested approaches, please visit the Online Resource Centre.

? **Exam questions**

1. You are asked to advise the Home Secretary on any changes that may be necessary to ensure that counter-terrorism law is compatible with Article 10 (the right to freedom of expression, see Chapter 17). In your report:

(a) identify and describe the legal provisions, civil or criminal, which have the capacity to interfere with freedom of expression;

(b) consider whether they can be applied in ways that are compatible with Article 10; and

(c) make any recommendations for reform that you consider necessary (or explain why, in your view, no such changes are necessary).

2. Describe the post-2010 reforms of counter-terrorism law and the reasons for the reform. Consider whether the law following those reforms is reasonable in the circumstances and not oppressive.

 For suggested approaches, please visit the Online Resource Centre.

 ## Further reading

The Reports of the House of Lords, House of Commons Joint Committee on Human Rights are an important source. All counter-terrorism bills are closely and critically scrutinised.

General texts on counter-terrorism laws

Council of Europe, *The Fight against Terrorism Council of Europe Standards* 3rd edn (2005)

Fiss, O. 'The War against Terrorism and the Rule of Law' (2006) 26(2) *OJLS* 235–256

Walker, C. *Terrorism and the Law* (2011) Oxford: OUP

Walker, C. 'The Terrorism and Investigation Measures Act 2011: One Thing but Not Much the Other? [2012] *Crim LR* 6, 421–438

Wilson, R. *Human Rights in the 'War on Terror'* (2005) Cambridge: CUP

Index